DISCARDED

NEW FRONTIERS IN HISPANIC AND LUSO-BRAZILIAN SCHOLARSHIP

Como se fue el maestro

Derek W. Lomax

NEW FRONTIERS IN HISPANIC AND LUSO-BRAZILIAN SCHOLARSHIP

Como se fue el maestro

for Derek W. Lomax in Memoriam

Edited by
Trevor J. Dadson
R.J. Oakley
P.A. Odber de Baubeta

The Edwin Mellen Press
Lewiston/Queenston/Lampeter

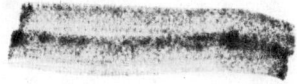

Library of Congress Cataloging-in-Publication Data

New frontiers in Hispanic and Luso-Brazilian scholarship : "como se fue el maestro"--for Derek W. Lomax, in memoriam / edited by Trevor J. Dadson, R.J. Oakley, P.A. Odber de Baubeta.
    p.   cm.
English and Spanish.
Includes bibliographical references.
ISBN 0-7734-9117-1
  1. Spanish literature--History and criticism. 2. Spain--Literatures--History and criticism. 3. Spanish American literature--History and criticism. 4. Civilization, Hispanic. 5. Portugal--Civilization. I. Lomax, Derek W. II. Dadson, Trevor J. III. Oakley, R. J. IV. Baubeta, Patricia Anne Odber de, 1953-

PQ6004.L65N4 1995
860.9--dc20
                                            94-37934
                                               CIP

A CIP catalog record for this book is available from the British Library.

Copyright © 1994 The Edwin Mellen Press

All rights reserved. For information contact

The Edwin Mellen Press
Box 450
Lewiston, New York
USA 14092-0450

The Edwin Mellen Press
Box 67
Queenston, Ontario
CANADA L0S 1L0

The Edwin Mellen Press, Ltd.
Lampeter, Dyfed, Wales
UNITED KINGDOM SA48 7DY

Printed in the United States of America

'Como se fue el maestro':
For Derek W. Lomax *in Memoriam*

CONTENTS

Preface
R. J. OAKLEY   1

Derek W. Lomax: A Bibliography of his Publications
PATRICK QUINN   7

MEDIEVAL AND GOLDEN AGE

La reconquista gallega del norte de Portugal: una reaproximación
CARLOS BALIÑAS PÉREZ   17

A *Crónica Galega dos Reinos de León e Castela* na Historia e na Historiografía Galegas
HENRIQUE MONTEAGUDO ROMERO   33

Marcas de oralidad en la sintaxis narrativa del *Poema de Mio Cid*
GERMÁN ORDUNA   57

The Popes, the Inquisition and Jewish Converts in Spain, 1440-1515
JOHN EDWARDS   71

Spaniards, 'Germans' and the Invention of Printing: Diego de Valera's Eulogy in the *Crónica abreviada*
DAVID MACKENZIE   87

Conflicting Views towards the Mozarabs after 1492
RICHARD HITCHCOCK   105

Un caso de intervención del narratario: *Amadís de Gaula*, I, 41
LILIA E. F. DE ORDUNA   117

The Road to Villarrubia: The Journey into Exile of the Duke of Híjar, March 1644
TREVOR J. DADSON   123

'Scheming Idolaters' or 'Tender Plants': Alternative Interpretations of Native Religious Beliefs and Rites in Seventeenth-Century Peru
NICHOLAS GRIFFITHS   155

NINETEENTH CENTURY

Canon and Prejudice
ANA DE BRITO — 173

Pereda's *Pedro Sánchez*: the Dickens Connection
ANTHONY H. CLARKE — 187

Womanpower in Galdós's *Voluntad* (1895)
LISA CONDÉ — 209

The Novelist interprets History: Galdós's *La de los tristes destinos*
GEOFFREY RIBBANS — 225

Mirror of Change: The Black in the Nineteenth-Century Cuban Novel
SHARON ROMEO-FIVEL-DÉMORET — 241

Triste Fim de Policarpo Quaresma and the Shadow of Spencerism
R. J. OAKLEY — 255

Business and Politics in Late Porfirian Mexico: The Reconstruction of the Tehuantepec Railway 1896-1907
PAUL GARNER — 275

TWENTIETH CENTURY

Forms of Spirituality in the Early Poems of Juan Ramón Jiménez
DEREK FLITTER — 293

'Como se fue el maestro...'
PATRICIA MCDERMOTT — 311

De Unamuno, submarinos y condenas. Unos apuntes sobre discrepancias de Unamuno y su *lesa majestad*
DAVID ROBERTSON — 327

Confessional Increment or Credibility Gap? The Rhetoric of Exculpation in *La familia de Pascual Duarte*
C. A. LONGHURST — 341

'No pas el dol: el desencís'. Mourning and Exile in Josep Carner's *Absència*
JOSEP-ANTON FERNÁNDEZ — 361

Lectura de 'Llàtzer el ressuscitat', de Carles Riba
ENRIC SULLÀ   385

'Salus Ecclesiae Suprema Lex': Monarchists, Catholics and the
First Portuguese Republic, 1910-1926
RICHARD A. H. ROBINSON   411

Iberianism Revisited: José Saramago's *A Jangada de Pedra*
MIGUEL ALARCÃO   443

Public Service Broadcasting in the United Kingdom and Spain
BARRY JORDAN   457

Aspects of the Neo-Picaresque in Twentieth-Century German
Literature
WILFRIED VAN DER WILL   481

Un ejemplo de la presencia inglesa en Buenos Aires: la
construcción del túnel de cargas
MARTÍN BLAS ORDUNA   501

Borges Transluz Chesterton
WALTER CARLOS COSTA   509

Family History and Social Change in Two Short Stories of Julio
Ramón Ribeyro
JAMES HIGGINS   517

Uruguay: The Burden of the Past
HENRY FINCH   531

The Deceptive Simplicity of Mario Benedetti: Narrative
Technique in 'El presupuesto'
P. A. ODBER DE BAUBETA   547

Between History and Literature: A Dialogue by Juan José
Arreola
MAURICE BIRIOTTI DEL BURGO   563

Preface

On a chill February morning in the University of Ulster, I heard the best lecture on the Spanish Civil War I have ever attended. It was given by Derek Lomax whose memory we celebrate today with the publishing of the present volume. Derek, David Mackenzie, Salut Llonch, and I had travelled from Birmingham to Coleraine in order to participate in a Spanish Studies VIth Form Day. Medieval Spanish history was clearly not going to be on the agenda, but we all had to make a contribution; and, historiographically speaking, the Civil War was uppermost in the minds of Ulster's youthful Hispanists preparing for their Spanish A level that summer of 1987.

It is doubtful that at that time Derek realized he was just two and a half years away from retirement. He had been running his department with relentless energy and boundless enthusiasm since inheriting Joe Manson's gentlemanly mantle in the palmier days of the early seventies, and on through the Thatcherite squeeze of the mid eighties when, at one time, he saw Hispanic Studies at Birmingham, along with three other departments in the Faculty of Arts, threatened with closure. He weathered this crisis; but the managerial ethos that overtook the university world in the eighties ultimately wore him down; and in July 1989, suddenly, shockingly, he announced to me his decision to retire with the words: 'I still love my subject, but I no longer enjoy my job'. These were strange words from a man whose watchword was precisely enjoyment -- a man with an enormous appetite for life, and especially, for the study of history. From the time he announced in 1954 to his teacher at Oxford, Professor Roger Highfield, his intention of learning Spanish with a view to doing postgraduate research on Iberian history, Derek was a man who lived and breathed Hispanism. As he beat his breast and spoke of failure in the summer of 1989, it seemed, superficially at least, as though he had given up on life -- the life of the crusader for Hispanism, that is. He may have felt, fleetingly, that his career had ended with defeat.

He was, of course, mistaken. In reality, his whole life was nothing but a long, majestic series of successes: a scholarship to Merton College, Oxford in 1951; a First in Modern History three years later; fruitful research back in Merton after National Service in the Army; thirteen very happy years in the

Department of Hispanic Studies at the University of Liverpool; and his crowning achievement, certainly as teacher and administrator, seventeen years as professor in the Department of Hispanic Studies at the University of Birmingham.

These activities apart, there was always the thinking and the writing. His greatest accomplishment as a historian of medieval Spain will always be, of course, his opening up of the vast and exciting field of the Military Orders. The fruits of his doctoral research were a magisterial thesis on the Order of Santiago. His account of the development and fortunes of the Order of Santiago in the twelfth and thirteenth centuries not only brought him his doctorate but became the standard work in this important field. A logical follow-up to *La Orden de Santiago, 1170-1275*, was a short, accessible account of the entire Reconquest of Spain. When Derek wrote this in the early seventies, he cannot have dreamed that the book, entitled *La reconquista* in its Spanish version, would in the eighties become required reading and the standard account in Spain as it already was in England.

Derek's last years as a full-time teacher and academic may have been clouded by what he saw as the persecution of his subject and of the humanities in general, yet readers of this volume interested in following in detail the trajectory of his published research will seek in vain any drying up of ideas or inspiration, any sign of creeping disenchantment. The bulk of his contribution to the book *The English in Portugal* was written in 1987, and the following year found him absorbed in co-editing *God and Man in Medieval Spain*, the *festschrift* in honour of Roger Highfield. His works-in-progress and other projects at his death were various and daunting. These included an edition of medieval charters of the Convent of San Marcos de León, and a substantial contribution to a new history of the Spanish Church.

His entire corpus of books, pamphlets and articles runs to over a hundred publications, a number of which have still to appear. Eight of the first nine contributions to this volume reflect Derek Lomax the historian, as do three of the nineteenth-century essays and most of the twentieth-century ones. The very title of the final essay, *Between History and Literature: A Dialogue by Juan José Arreola*, provides one of the keynotes of this book. It also reminds us of the breadth of Derek's interests. Although he was a deeply conservative man, he needed no lessons from marxist cultural historians and littérateurs concerning the interaction of literature and society. Obliged at Liverpool to teach Spanish Literature from Berceo to the present day (surely the acid test of the good Hispanist!) he came to focus his historian's eye on a classic of the canon, *Lazarillo de Tormes*. The fruits of his meditations on this much studied book was an article that turned upside down the persistent theory concerning the supposed link between poverty and the genesis of the Picaresque -- a theory brilliantly refuted by Derek's 1973 article which in time helped fuel the ideas of our colleague in the Department of German Studies at Birmingham, Wilfried van der Will, whose essay printed below provides startling glimpses of the fortunes of the Picaresque in mid-twentieth-century Germany.

Historians of Iberia, Richard Hitchcock from the University of Exeter, David Robertson of the University of Stirling, and his colleagues in the School of History at Birmingham, Richard Robinson and John Edwards, have experienced Derek's enthusiastic encouragement and the excitement of crossing historiographical swords with him -- especially in the bar! His junior colleagues during the hey-day of his years as full-time professor and departmental head at Birmingham, Anthony Clarke, Barry Jordan, Pat Odber de Baubeta, David Mackenzie, and myself, all benefitted from having known him and worked closely with him; but also, like the historians, from encouragement, guidance, and advice on numerous and bewilderingly disparate topics. I can think of no colleague of my close acquaintance in the Faculty of Arts at Birmingham who has enjoyed such a degree of unqualified admiration and respect as an academic and as an intellect. Above all, he made this impression on younger minds. It became a challenge to win an argument over Derek. Few, if any, did so. He seemed a man of inexhaustible intellectual capacity. This is what attracted to him people whose research interests were not in the least germane to his own. Even in the case of research areas one was positive that Derek could have no knowledge of, colleagues and students would find it worthwhile consulting him. A striking example of this phenomenon as well of the brutal suddenness of Derek's death is the poignant case of the Catalan scholar Josep-Anton Fernández, who worked under Derek as Spanish language assistant for a year before the latter's retirement. Josep-Anton, now lecturing in London, had not spoken

4   Preface

with Derek for some six months; but was planning to travel to Birmingham on the very day Derek died in order to seek advice on matters relating to his research on the twentieth-century Catalan poet Carner.

Josep is one of those much appreciated 'birds of passage' who make such a contribution to departments of modern languages -- the colloquial assistants; and some of the best at Birmingham over the years have, along with Josep, written essays for this volume: Enric Sullà from Barcelona and Quique Monteagudo from Santiago de Compostela; and the Portuguese assistants of former years, Miguel Alarcão from Lisbon and Ana de Brito from the Minho. The foreign contributions as a whole are a most gratifying feature: Germán, Lilia and Martín Orduna in Argentina; Walter Costa in Brazil; and Carlos Baliñas in Galicia.   Readers will observe that the sequence of essays is chronological. Therefore, Carlos's piece on early Galician-Portuguese history heads the list. This is particularly appropriate in view of the fact that Carlos suffered the trauma of being a guest in Derek's house at the very moment of his death.

Derek's entire career as teacher and researcher is, in a sense, laid before us in this book's contents: from Geoffrey Ribbans, the man who had the discernment to appoint him assistant lecturer in Liverpool in 1959, to Trevor Dadson, his successor in the Birmingham Chair; from his old comrades-in-arms of Liverpudlian days, Henry Finch, Alex Longhurst, and Jim Higgins, to four young scholars whose academic careers and intellectual sensibilities were all too briefly touched by him -- Sharon Romeo, Maurice Biriotti Del Burgo, Derek Flitter, and Nick Griffiths. Perhaps most important of all, there are his students past and present.   Lisa Condé and Paul Garner were taught at Birmingham by Derek and went on to make their mark elsewhere. Our list is completed by the alpha and omega of Derek's teaching career: Pat McDermott, who is currently rounding off a distinguished career in the Department of Spanish and Portuguese at the University of Leeds and was a member of the very first Spanish language and philology classes Derek taught at Liverpool in 1959; and Patrick Quinn, Derek's last postgraduate student, who began his doctoral thesis on Don Juan Manuel under Derek's supervision only six months before his death, and who has gladly undertaken the task of being our academic sleuth, painstakingly unearthing and documenting, in so far as this will ever be possible, every last publication Derek wrote.

This introduction to our homage volume in memory of 'DWL' could have been a lengthy panegyric. Derek would have hated that. He would also have preferred a roistering wake to a somber mourning. Like Antonio Machado in his elegy on the death of Giner de los Ríos, he would not have had us dwell on the past but look to the future: *¡Yunques, sonad; enmudeced, campanas!* The last time I saw him alive, less than forty-eight hours before his death, he stood in my room and talked of nothing but the future: trips to Spain, correspondence with foreign scholars, research projects... I have said that a striking feature of Derek's daily life on divesting himself of the responsibilities of the Birmingham Chair which had weighed so heavily upon him at the end, was the constant society of his younger colleagues. A lifelong bachelor, who devoted so much time and energy in later years to the loving care of his mother and father in their extreme old age, he nevertheless empathized with the young. It is the young who have provided the backbone of this volume. He would have liked that too.

Like Machado's Giner, the inspiration and example he left behind him shall be sufficient for us: and so I remember again that February day in Ulster. Derek spoke for exactly sixty minutes with a few notes and an apparently encyclopaedic knowledge of a topic on which so many claim to be authorities, but the complexities and ambiguities of which have defied all but the very greatest historians of modern Spain. He solved no problems; he broke no new ground; but he laid before us the causes and the course of the Civil War with that deceptive simplicity and extraordinary clarity which were the singular hallmark of both his teaching and his writing; and so the bones of the perfect book on the Spanish Civil War, that still has to be written, emerged quite distinctly. 'Bones' is perhaps not quite the word; 'banquet' is better -- a banquet austere but nourishing, and above all, accessible to all who were there that day. ...*Así se fue el maestro*...

R. J. Oakley
University of Birmingham

Derek W. Lomax:
A Bibliography of his Publications

Books

La Orden de Santiago, 1170-1275 (Madrid: C.S.I.C., 1965). xxxvi+307 pp.

Another Sword for Saint James. Inaugural Lecture delivered at the University of Birmingham, 19 February 1974 (Birmingham: University of Birmingham, 1974). 19pp.

Las órdenes militares en la Península Ibérica durante la Edad Media (Salamanca: Instituto de Historia de la Teología Española, 1976). 111pp; tirada aparte del *Repertorio de Historia de las Ciencias Esclesiásticas en España*, 6 (Salamanca, 1976), 9-110.

The Reconquest of Spain (London: Longman, 1978). xii+212pp; translated as *Die Reconquista. Die Wiedereroberung Spaniens durch das Christentum* (Munich: Wilhelm Heyne Verlag, 1980), and as *La reconquista* (Barcelona: Editorial Crítica, 1984).

[with R.J. Oakley] *Fernão Lopes: The English in Portugal, 1367-87. Extracts from the Chronicles of Dom Fernando and Dom João*, with an introduction, translation and notes by Derek W. Lomax & R.J. Oakley (Warminster: Aris and Phillips, 1988). xxxiv+369pp. 2nd edition, 1989.

[Ed. with D. Mackenzie] *God and Man in Medieval Spain. Essays in honour of J.R.L. Highfield* (Warminster: Aris and Phillips, 1989). xxiv+168pp.

The Order of Santiago (The Confraternity of Saint James. Occasional Paper No 2, 1990). 13pp.

Articles

'A Note on *Gilibertus poeta*', *Estudis Romànics*, 6 (1957-58), 169.

'The Order of Santiago and the Kings of León', *Hispania*, 70 (1958), 3-37.

'El arzobispo don Rodrigo Jiménez de Rada y la Orden de Santiago', *Hispania*, 76 (1959), 323-65.

'Algunos estatutos primitivos de la Orden de Calatrava', *Hispania*, 84 (1961), 483-94.

'España en el siglo XIX', *El Clarín*, 33 (1961), 4-5.

'A Lost Medieval Biography: the *Corónica del Maestre Pelayo Pérez*', *Bulletin of Hispanic Studies*, 38 (1961), 153-54.

'Report on the Liverpool Conference of Teachers of Spanish', *El Clarín*, 34 (1962), 9-10.

'The Date of Don Juan Manuel's Death', *Bulletin of Hispanic Studies*, 40 (1963), 174.

'The Authorship of the *Chronique latine des rois de Castille*', *Bulletin of Hispanic Studies*, 40 (1963), 205-11.

'Las milicias cistercienses en el reino de León', *Hispania*, 89 (1963), 29-42.

'Report on the Liverpool Conference of Teachers of Spanish', *El Clarín*, 37 (1963), 7-8.

'Los «Magni Rotuli Pipae» y el medievo hispánico', *Anuario de Estudios Medievales*, 1 (1964), 543-48.

'Spanish Studies: Medieval Literature', in *The Year's Work in Modern Language Studies (1963)* (Cambridge: MHRA, 1964), pp.155-61.

'Don Ramón, Bishop of Palencia (1148-84)', in *Homenaje a Jaime Vicens Vives* (Barcelona: University of Barcelona, 1965), I, 279-91.

'Report on the Liverpool Conference of Teachers of Spanish', *El Clarín*, 43 (1965), 9-10.

'Spanish Studies: Medieval Literature', in *The Year's Work in Modern Language Studies (1964)* (Cambridge: MHRA, 1965), pp.194-205.

'A mais antigua biografia de El-Rei D. Afonso III de Portugal', *Ocidente*, 71 (1966), 71-75.

'Spanish Studies: Medieval Literature', in *The Year's Work in Modern Language Studies (1965)* (Cambridge: MHRA, 1966), pp.169-78.

'Recusants in the Spanish Inquisition', *Recusant History*, 9 (1967), No. 1, 53-59.

'Los estudios medievales en Inglaterra', *Anuario de Estudios Medievales*, 4 (1967), 519-35.

'Spanish Studies: Medieval Literature', in *The Year's Work in Modern Language Studies (1966)* (Cambridge: MHRA, 1967), pp.182-93.

'Spanish Studies: Medieval Literature', in *The Year's Work in Modern Language Studies (1967)* (Cambridge: MHRA, 1968), pp.172-85.

'Spanish Studies: Medieval Literature', in *The Year's Work in Modern Language Studies (1968)* (Cambridge: MHRA, 1969), pp.194-200.

'Una visita a San Marcos de León en 1442', *Archivos Leoneses*, 23 (1969), 317-49.

'The Lateran Reforms and Spanish Literature', *Iberoromania*, 1 (1969), 299-313.

'Algunos peregrinos ingleses a Santiago en la Edad Media', *Príncipe de Viana*, 118-19 (1970), 159-69.

'Spanish Studies: Medieval Literature', in *The Year's Work in Modern Language Studies (1969)* (Cambridge: MHRA, 1970), pp.190-98.

'Fuentes para la historia hispánica del siglo XIV en los archivos ingleses', *Anuario de Estudios Medievales*, 7 (1970-71), 103-13.

'La lengua oficial de Castilla', in *Actele celui de-al XII-lea Congres International de Lingvistica çi Filologie Romanica*, ? vols (Bucharest: Editions de l'Académie de la République Socialiste de Roumanie, 1971), II, 411-17.

'Spanish Studies: Medieval Literature', in *The Year's Work in Modern Language Studies (1970)* (Cambridge: MHRA, 1971), pp.210-19.

'Pedro López de Baeza, «Dichos de los santos padres» (siglo XIV)', in *Miscelánea de Textos Medievales*, 2 vols (Barcelona: Universidad de Barcelona, Instituto de Historia Medieval, 1972-74), I, 147-78.

'El catecismo de Albornoz', in *El Cardenal Albornoz y el Colegio de España*, *Studia Albornotiana*, 11 (Publicaciones del Real Colegio de España, 1972), 215-33, 725-26.

'¿Cuándo murió Don Jorge Manrique?', *Revista de Filología Española*, 55 (1972), 61-62.

'Spanish Studies: Medieval Literature', in *The Year's Work in Modern Language Studies (1971)* (Cambridge: MHRA, 1972), pp.239-52.

'On Re-reading the *Lazarillo de Tormes*', in *Studia Iberica. Festschrift für Hans Flasche* (Berne-Munich: Francke Verlag, 1973), 371-81.

'The Peers Collection in Liverpool University Library', *Iberian Studies*, 2 (1973), 40-51.

[with D.M. Atkinson] 'Les enquêtes internationales, Portugal d'aujourd'hui. "Les échanges commerciaux et culturels"', *L'Européen*, 133-34 (juin-juillet 1973), 16-17.

[under pseudonym 'Lusophile'] 'The Oldest Alliance', *Vida Hispánica*, 21 (1973), No. 3, 2-3.

'La historiografía de las órdenes militares en la Península Ibérica (1100-1550)', *Hidalguía*, 23 (1975), 711-24.

'Spanish Studies: Medieval Literature', in *The Year's Work in Modern Language Studies (1975)* (Cambridge: MHRA, 1976), pp.238-46.

'Los documentos primitivos del archivo municipal de Ciudad Rodrigo', *Archivos Leoneses*, 59-60 (1976), 185-203.

'Datos biográficos sobre el Arcipreste de Talavera', *Filología*, 17-18 (1976-77), 442-47; and in *Actas del Cuarto Congreso Internacional de Hispanistas (1971)*, ed. by Eugenio de Bustos Tovar, 2 vols (Salamanca: Consejo General de Castilla y León/Universidad de Salamanca, 1982), II, 141-46.

'Una crónica inédita de Silos', in *Homenaje a Fray Justo Pérez de Urbel, OSB*, 2 vols (Silos: Abadía de Silos, 1976), I, 323-37.

'The Date of the *Poema de Mio Cid*', in *'Mio Cid' Studies*, ed. by A.D. Deyermond (London: Tamesis, 1977), pp.73-81.

'Rodrigo Jiménez de Rada como historiador', in *Actas del Quinto Congreso Internacional de Hispanistas (1974)*, ed. by M. Chevalier and others, 2 vols (Bordeaux: Université de Bordeaux III, 1977), II, 587-92.

'Algunos autores religiosos, 1295-1350', *Journal of Hispanic Philology*, 2 (1977), 81-90.

'Una nueva obra andaluza: la Crónica de Fernando de Salmerón', in *Actas del I Congreso de Historia de Andalucía (1976). Andalucía medieval*, 2 vols (Córdoba: Monte de Piedad y Caja de Ahorros de Córdoba, 1978), I, 271-73.

'Las órdenes militares en León durante la Edad Media', in *León medieval: doce estudios* (León: Colegio Universitario de León, 1978), pp.85-93.

'¿Cuándo ocurrió la reconquista de Cáceres?', *Alcántara*, 194 (1979), 26-28.

'La fecha de la reconquista de Cáceres', *Archivos Leoneses*, 66 (1979), 309-19.

'The "*Istoria del Sanct Ladre*" attributed to St. Pere Pasqual', in *Miscel.lania Aramon i Serra. Estudis de llengua i literatura catalanes oferts a R. Aramon i Serra en el seu setantè aniversari* (Barcelona, 1979), I, 389-94.

'La fecha de la Crónica Najerense', *Anuario de Estudios Medievales*, 9 (1974-79), 405-06.

[with J.H. Edwards] *Spain in the Middle Ages* (Audio Learning: tape and text, London, 1979).

'Reforma de la Iglesia y literatura didáctica: sermones, ejemplos y sentencias', in *Historia y Crítica de la Literatura Española. I. Edad media*, ed. by A. Deyermond (Barcelona: Editorial Crítica, 1980), pp.182-86.

'A Medieval Recruiting Poster', *Estudis històrics i documents dels arxius de protocols*, 8 (1980), 353-63.

'La obra histórica de Rades y Andrada', introductory study to facsimile reprint of Francisco de Rades y Andrada, *Crónica de las tres órdenes de Santiago, Calatrava y Alcántara*, Toledo, 1572 (Barcelona: El Albir, 1980), pp.v-xi.

'Calatrava y su bulario', introductory study to facsimile reprint of *Bullarium Ordinis Militiae de Calatrava*, ed. by I.J. de Ortega y Cotes, J.F. Álvarez de Baquedano and P. de Ortega Zúñiga y Aranda, Madrid, 1761 (Barcelona: El Albir, 1981), pp.v-vii.

'La reforma de la Orden de Alcántara durante el maestrazgo del infante don Sancho, 1411-1413', *Anuario de Estudios Medievales*, 11 (1981), 759-73.

'Catalans in the Leonese Empire', *Bulletin of Hispanic Studies*, 59 (1982), 191-97; translated as 'Catalanes en el imperio leonés', *Toletum*, 17 (1985), 201-13.

'El padre de Juan Manuel', in *Don Juan Manuel. VII Centenario* (Murcia: Universidad de Murcia/Academia Alfonso X el Sabio, 1982), 163-76.

'El *Cronicón Cordubense* de Fernando de Salmerón', in *Estudios en memoria del Profesor D. Salvador de Moxó, 1* (Madrid: Universidad Complutense, 1982), pp.595-641.

'El rey D. Diniz de Portugal y la Orden de Santiago', *Hidalguía*, 30 (1982), 477-87.

'Notes sur un métier: los jongleurs castillans en 1316', in *Les Espagnes médiévales. Aspects économiques et sociaux. Mélanges offerts à Jean Gautier-Dalché*. Extraît des *Annales de la Faculté des Lettres et Sciences Humaines de Nice*, 46 (Nice: Université de Nice, 1983), 229-36.

'La Orden de Santiago y el obispado de Cuenca en la Edad Media', *Anuario de Estudios Medievales*, 12 (1982), 303-10.

'Apostillas a la repoblación de Alcaraz', in *Congreso de Historia de Albacete. II. Edad Media* (Albacete: Instituto de Estudios Albacetenses, 1984), pp.19-30.

'The First English Pilgrims to Santiago de Compostela', in *Studies in Medieval History Presented to R.H.C. Davis* (London: Hambledon Press, 1985), pp.165-75.

'The Medieval Predecessors of Rades y Andrada', *Iberoromania*, 23 (1986), 81-90.

'Una biografía inédita del Cid', in *Estudios en Homenaje a Don Claudio Sánchez Albornoz en sus noventa años* (Buenos Aires: Universidad de Buenos Aires, 1985), III, 225-39.

'Las dependencias hispánicas de Santa María de la Selva Mayor', in *Homenaje a José María Lacarra, Príncipe de Viana*, Año 47, Anejo 3 (1986), 491-506.

'Un poema político de 1462', in *Homenaje al profesor Juan Torres Fontes* (Murcia: Universidad de Murcia/Academia de Alfonso X el Sabio, 1987), II, 891-99.

'St. James's Friars and Pilgrims', *Bulletin of the Confraternity of Saint James*, 25 (1988), 8-11.

'La conquista de Andalucía a través de la historiografía europea de la época', in *Andalucía entre Oriente y Occidente (1236-1492). Actas del V Coloquio Internacional de Historia Medieval de Andalucía* (Córdoba: Diputación de Córdoba, Area de Cultura, 1988), 37-49.

'Aspectos de la vida castellana en la época de Alfonso VI reflejados en la "Vita Dominici Siliensis"', in *Estudios sobre Alfonso VI y la Reconquista de Toledo. Actas del II Congreso de Estudios Mozárabes* (Toledo: Instituto de Estudios Visigótico-Mozárabes, 1988), II, 291-304.

'La fecha de *Castigos e Documentos*', *Anuario de Estudios Medievales*, 18 (1988), 395-97.

'Un nuevo significado del topónimo España', *Espacio, Tiempo y Forma. Revista de la Facultad de Geografía e Historia, UNED, Madrid. Serie III. Historia Medieval. Homenaje al Profesor Eloy Benito Ruano*, 4 (1989), 309-15.

'Heresy and Orthodoxy in the Fall of Almohad Spain', in *God and Man in Medieval Spain. Essays in Honour of J.R.L. Highfield*, ed. by D. Lomax and D. Mackenzie (Warminster: Aris and Phillips, 1989), pp.37-48.

'La Orden de Santiago y la Peregrinación', *Peregrino*, 12 (1990), Servicio de Documentación, 1-3.

'Los peregrinos ingleses a Santiago', *Peregrino*, 14 (1990), Servicio de Documentación, 1-4.

'«El Conde Lucanor» como fuente de comedias', in *Teatro del Siglo de Oro: Homenaje a Alberto Navarro González* (Kassel: Edition Reichenberger, 1990), pp.367-77.

'English Pilgrims to Santiago', in *Pilgrims from the British Isles to Santiago de Compostela in the Middle Ages* (London: Confraternity of Saint James, 1991), pp.10-18.

'Un historiador de la Edad Media', *La Voz de Asturias*, 3 October 1991, p.40.

'Medieval Spain: Some Evidence on Oath', in *Hispanic Studies in Honour of Geoffrey Ribbans*, edited, with an introduction, by Ann L. Mackenzie and Dorothy S. Severin (Liverpool: University Press, 1992), pp.25-35.

'La última colonia africana en Europa', in *Actas del I Congreso Anglo-Hispano, celebrado en Huelva, marzo de 1992*, 3 vols (Madrid: Editorial Castalia), III (in press).

Derek W. Lomax: A Bibliography 13

Dictionaries and Encyclopaedias

Forty entries on Spanish and British history in *Diccionario Enciclopédico Salvat*, 13th edn (Barcelona: Salvat Editores, 1968-).

Three entries on the military orders of Alcántara, Calatrava and Santiago in *Diccionario de Historia Eclesiastica de España*, III (Madrid: C.S.I.C., 1973).

'Santiago, Ordine militare di', entry in *Dizionario degli Istituti de Perfezione* (Rome: Edizioni Paoline, 1974).

'Alcántara, Orden v.', entry in *Lexikon des Mittelalters* (Munich: Artemis Verlag, 1977), I.

Twelve entries on medieval Spanish history, in *The New Catholic Encyclopaedia*, 15 vols (Washington: The Catholic University of America, 1967-81).

Various entries on the military orders in Portugal in *Dicionário de História da Igreja em Portugal* (Lisbon: Editorial Resistência, 1981-).

Three entries in *The Blackwell Dictionary of Historians* (Oxford: Blackwell, 1988), pp.243-44, 276-77, 431-32.

Two entries in *The Dictionary of the Middle Ages* (New York: Scribner's, 1982-89).

Map spreads in *The Atlas of the Crusades*, ed. by Jonathan Riley-Smith (London: Guild Publishing/Swanston Publishing and Times Books, 1991), pp.32-33, 54-55, 72-73, 124, 126-27, 162-63.

Twelve entries on medieval English history in *Enciclopedia Pro-Liber Navarra* (Madrid: Rialp).

'Benavente', 'Echegaray', two entries in *The International Dictionary of Theatre* (London: St James Press)

Patrick Quinn
University of Birmingham

MEDIEVAL AND GOLDEN AGE

LA RECONQUISTA GALLEGA DEL NORTE DE PORTUGAL: UNA REAPROXIMACIÓN

CARLOS BALIÑAS PÉREZ
Universidad de Santiago de Compostela

To Derek W. Lomax: Non Angli, sed Angeli

El proceso de la reocupación por los cristianos del Norte peninsular de las tierras del Occidente peninsular ubicadas entre los cursos de los ríos Miño y Mondego, que tiene lugar en la segunda mitad del siglo IX y comienzos del X, parece a primera vista un fenómeno histórico digno del mayor interés. Es un proceso rápido --apenas unas decenas de años-- y a través del cual el reino astur-galaico-leonés alcanza su expansión máxima en dirección sur, en contraste con la expansión paralela por la Meseta Norte, más lenta y de alcances más limitados. De él surgen un país --Portugal-- y una cultura --la galaico-portuguesa-- con proyecciones hasta la actualidad y sus consecuencias en lo social y lo económico influirán decisivamente en la evolución del N.O. peninsular hacia una estructuración feudal de la sociedad. Y sin embargo, historiográficamente, ha sido en general un tema marginal. No queremos decir con ello que no haya sido objeto de profundos y serios estudios. Ahí están para demostrarlo las obras de un Sánchez-Albornoz, un Merêa o un Sousa Soares. Pero para el común de los historiadores españoles la 'verdadera' Reconquista ha sido casi siempre la del valle del Duero, crisol de la formación de Castilla, origen a su vez de ese concepto de España al que su obra rinde tributo.[1] En justa reciprocidad, la historiografía tradicional portuguesa ha tendido a minimizar el influjo colonizador astur-galaico y a poner el acento en el presunto desarrollo autóctono de las bases fundacionales de la nacionalidad portuguesa.[2] Afortunadamente, a uno y otro lado de la frontera luso-española se han ido desarrollando nuevos criterios de racionalidad y cientificidad con el resultado lógico de una aproximación mucho más esclarecedora a este período histórico.[3]

Nuestra modesta intención es retomar estas nuevas perspectivas y, sobre todo, efectuar una reaproximación al estudio de la ocupación de las tierras entre Miño y Mondego desde la documentación coetánea y, singularmente, desde el auténtico punto de partida del fenómeno: la Galicia altomedieval desde donde parte el proceso de reconquista y a cuyo destino se vincularán durante cerca de dos siglos las tierras de tal modo reocupadas. Más que aportar nuevos datos --no hay muchos más de los ya conocidos--, pretendemos sistematizar nuestras informaciones en un marco explicativo surgido de esas mismas realidades objeto de análisis. Y, por encima de todo, rendir con ello homenaje a uno de los autores británicos que más ha hecho por dar a conocer la Reconquista peninsular entre el hispanismo de las Islas Británicas y cuyas aportaciones, en muchos casos, nos han hecho a los propios historiadores hispanos entender mucho mejor nuestro sujeto de estudio: el llorado maestro y amigo Derek W. Lomax.

El contexto y las motivaciones

A la altura del año 850, el espacio político que conocemos convencionalmente como el reino de Asturias ha dejado de ser meramente el marco político de la resistencia de un pequeño grupo de cristianos del Norte ante la invasión islámica para convertirse en un pequeño estado con peso específico en el concierto peninsular. A ello ha contribuido esencialmente su propia evolución interna: la habilidad de su clase dirigente en combinar felizmente tanto la herencia hispano-goda y sus modelos culturales y sociales como las tradiciones autóctonas y la belicosidad de la poblacón indígena cántabro-astur, la firme interrelación entre Iglesia y poder civil que da sustento y cohesión a las estructuras de gobierno de tierras y hombres y, como consecuencia de todo ello, la facilidad que demuestra esta nueva formación política para acoger e integrar en su seno a las poblaciones de las regiones vecinas --Galicia y Alava-- y servir de referente para buena parte de los cristianos bajo poder musulmán. Pero no es menos cierto que también ha jugado su papel la difícil situación por la que su principal rival --el Al-Andalus de los conquistadores árabes-- está pasando en esos mismos momentos. La dinastía emiral de los Omeya ve discutida su preeminencia en la España islámica por continuos estallidos de rebeldía que motivan que importantes áreas de la España musulmana rechacen su soberanía: Toledo, el valle del

La reconquista gallega del norte de Portugal: una reaproximación   19

Ebro, Extremadura, entre otras. La propia crisis por la que el Al-andalus está atravesando tiene su reflejo en conflictos internos apenas disfrazados de motivos religiosos y étnicos: el fundamentalismo islámico atizado por los mullahs entre las capas sociales inferiores de las ciudades, los continuos choques entre árabes, berberiscos y muladíes, la 'epidemia de mártires' y la inmigración en masa al norte de la población cristiana mozárabe. La ocasión era inmejorable y el reino asturiano supo aprovecharla, duplicando su extensión y población en apenas medio siglo: el primer gran avance de la Reconquista cristiana de la Península --pues ahora sí se arrebatan realmente tierras al control musulmán-- estaba teniendo lugar.

Un primer grupo de motivaciones de este avance expansivo, causa y consecuencia a la vez de su desarrollo, son las ideológicas. En efecto, un esfuerzo colectivo y que, como veremos, moviliza a amplios estratos de la población, tal como la reocupación del cuadrante nor-occidental de la Península, era imposible si no se convertía en mayor o menor medida en una causa común de toda la sociedad. Mucho, quizás demasiado, se ha escrito sobre el sustento ideológico de estas primeras etapas de la Reconquista. Para el caso que nos ocupa, tanto por huir de la excesiva ideologización como para acercarnos mejor al verdadero sentimiento del momento, es mejor que cedamos la palabra al gran protagonista de esta 'marcha hacia el sur', el rey Alfonso III (866-910):

> Extremi fines prouincie Gallecie ab antiquis pre impulsione sarracenorum in occidentali plaga deserti iacerent, et per longa tempora ipsa pars predicte prouincie herema maneret. Postea quidem presenti tempore Deo fauente, nosque illius gratia in regni culmine consistente, dum per Domini pietatem nostra fuisset ordinatio ut de Tudense urbe usque Mineo ciuitatem omnis ipsa extrema a Christi plebe popularetur.[4]

Parece pues innegable --como confirman otras expresiones de la cronística y la diplomática astur-galaica de la época-- la vivencia de este proceso recolonizador como un conflicto religioso entre cristianos y musulmanes, encaminado a la reocupación y reconstrucción del antiguo marco socio-político del reino hispano-godo de Toledo. A esta labor de creación de una mentalidad propicia debemos atribuir asimismo fenómenos propagandísticos coetáneos, tales como la redacción de la *Crónica Profética* inserta en el corpus literario de las crónicas regias asturianas --que, basándose en la exégesis de textos tomados del Apocalipsis y de los Apócrifos neotestamentarios, presagia el pronto levantamiento del castigo divino impuesto a los cristianos hispanos y, en consecuencia, el definitivo final de la dominación musulmana para el futuro inmediato-- o el supuesto hallazgo de los restos mortales de Don Rodrigo, el último rey godo, en la recién reconquistada ciudad de Viseo.[5]

Un segundo elemento a tener en cuenta es la directa impulsión por la monarquía asturiana del proceso reconquistador y la utilización de éste y de sus resultados para la reafirmación del papel dirigente de la realeza astur al frente del conjunto de la sociedad. De hecho, contra lo que se afirma normalmente, la incontestabilidad de la autoridad monárquica en el reino de Asturias sólo existió de hecho en la mente de los propagandistas regios: de los doce monarcas que rigieron Asturias entre los años 718 y 910, seis (exactamente la mitad) encontraron gravísimos problemas para el ejercicio de su autoridad, siendo bien asesinados, depuestos, considerados como usurpadores por buena parte de sus súbditos o habiendo de recobrar o defender su trono frente a rivales con amplio respaldo popular por la fuerza de las armas. Las razones para ello son múltiples y complejas, y no es éste el lugar para detenerse en su estudio, pero podemos cuanto menos indicar el difícil equilibrio entre la tradición de una monarquía fuerte y de raíces teocráticas de los inmigrantes hispano-godos y el concepto mucho más sencillo de la realeza como una suerte de caudillaje tribal propio de los pueblos del Norte entre los que estos inmigrantes se asientan, la inexistencia de unas claras reglas de sucesión al trono, la necesidad de que el rey sea un afortunado caudillo militar y un gobernante lleno de tacto en el contexto de un reino sometido a contínuas presiones externas y estructurado alrededor de una amalgama de territorios y pueblos aún deficientemente integrados entre sí o, por último, la difícil interdependencia de monarquía y nobleza, necesitadas cada una de la otra para fundamentar su poder social y a la vez con objetivos contrapuestos.

La dirección de una empresa reconquistadora, como la que nos ocupa, proporciona a la realeza asturiana un refuerzo de su papel dirigente al frente del reino obtenido en base al prestigio ganado con los éxitos militares y propagandísticos de dicha empresa y la capacidad de atraerse y recompensar

La reconquista gallega del norte de Portugal: una reaproximación   21

la fidelidad de los más poderosos de sus súbditos en base al reparte o concesión de las tierras y riquezas ganadas en dicha expansión. En una situación como la del reino de Asturias en las décadas finales del siglo IX, un rey victorioso y en condiciones de recompensar generosamente a sus partidarios era un rey seguro en el trono y que podía contar con la obediencia y asentimiento de sus gobernados. Y así lo expresa el mismo Alfonso III cuando, enfrentado a una insurrección de parte de la nobleza gallega proclama los méritos de su reinado y las razones por las que su voluntad ha de ser obedecida: 'cum obtinuisse provincias de inimicis victoria potitus, et aliis inimicis resisterem, et christicolas que de manu sarracenorum eriperem, Deo adjuvante'.[6]

Pero, evidentemente, ni una coyuntura favorable ni la existencia de un poder director explican por sí solos un movimiento de masas como el que comporta la reocupación y, en determinados casos, repoblación de las tierras entre Miño y Mondego: es precisa una fuerza motriz a gran escala y que afecte a todos los niveles a la sociedad galaica que protagoniza la ocupación y colonización de dicho territorio. Una tradución historiográfica aún muy asentada atribuye el avance reconquistador a la presión demográfica que supuestamente se estaría experimentando en las tierras del Norte peninsular: sería el exceso populacional resultante el que proporcionaría la base humana de la expansión galaico-astur en dirección Sur, cubriendo el vacío humano dejado por la invasión islámica. Esta teoría se ha desarrollado a partir del análisis --un tanto sesgado-- del proceso de ocupación del valle del Duero. Desgraciadamente, no parece corresponderse con la realidad que dejan translucir nuestras escasas informaciones sobre la situación poblacional del área que estudiamos. Si bien es innegable que la dinámica demográfica de la Galicia nuclear tiene un ritmo positivo --se incrementa el número de los hombres--, no lo es menos que es incorrecta la idea de una Galicia superpoblada en estos momentos: de hecho, extensas zonas del territorio gallego permanecerán desocupadas hasta bien entrado el siglo XII o aún más tarde. Por otra parte, las tierras portuguesas objeto de reocupación en esta época, aunque han sufrido una palpable pérdida de población en el período posterior a la conquista musulmana, están lejos de estar vacías.[7]

Creemos más acertado --como hemos defendido en otros trabajos--

desechar esa falsa idea de un boom demográfico y hablar en cambio de una superpoblación de carácter *funcional*. En un nivel social y tecnológico como el existente en la Galicia de la segunda mitad del siglo IX la capacidad humana para cultivar y poner en explotación tierras de cultivo es limitada: el desbroce y roturación de tierras vírgenes requiere a partir de determinados niveles de dificultad unos recursos técnicos y un nivel de organización socioeconómica que no se dan en la relativamente infradesarrollada Galicia e incluso menos en el conjunto del reino de Asturias. A la altura del año 850 las mejores tierras de cultivo en territorio gallego ya tienen dueño y la legislación y la autoridad regia protegen a los propietarios --en buena medida instituciones eclesiásticas y aristócratas locales--. Ello tiene consecuencias no sólo económicas, sino sociales: la base de la condición libre en esta época es la propiedad alodial. Y dentro del conjunto de los hombres libres, el fundamento social de la clase aristocrática es la riqueza en tierras. Pero en un mercado fundiario por así decirlo 'congelado', las expectativas que pequeños propietarios libres e incluso familias aristocráticas en ascenso tienen de mantener o incrementar su status se ven drásticamente reducidas y de hecho constatamos en la documentación gallega de mediados del IX un notable incremento de los conflictos por la propiedad de la tierra y un paralelo malestar social generalizado ante la falta de espacios cultivables.[8] En la Galicia de la primera Edad Media hay por tanto 'hambre de tierras' y frente a las dificultades que la roturación de espacios improductivos presenta, las ricas tierras agrícolas del Sur aparecen como una palpable tentación.

En cierto sentido, y salvando las diferencias cronológicas y sociales, la expansión de Galicia por la orla atlántica se asemeja a la ocupación del *Far West* por la socieded norteamericana --en gran medida compuesta por inmigrantes-- del siglo pasado. Serán pues los pequeños propietarios libres amenazados por la presión social y económica de Iglesia y nobleza, la nobleza gallega naciente que necesita afirmar o ampliar su base eocnómica frente a la competencia de sus propios compañeros de clase y, en general, todos aquellos miembros de la población galaica que no encuentran un lugar apropiado dentro de la sociedad o que ambicionan uno mejor que el que tienen --y ello incluye a una amplia gama de personas, desde el pobre segundón de una familia de campesinos libres empobrecidos al ambicioso aristócrata deseoso

La reconquista gallega del norte de Portugal: una reaproximación   23

de incrementar su riqueza y su poder-- los verdaderos motores de la conquista y colonización del Norte de Portugal.

Procedimientos y ritmos de la reocupación

Las tierras al Sur del Miño que van a ser el sujeto de la colonización, aún formando parte en líneas generales del mismo paisaje histórico que aquellas de donde proceden sus nuevos ocupantes --la Galicia nuclear--, presentan características propias que determinan ciertos aspectos de su conquista y ocupación. En su mayor parte se trata de una serie de valles fluviales paralelos entre sí, que dividen en segmentos longitudinales un territorio de orografía generalmente más suave que la presente en las regiones septentrionales peninsulares. Igualmente, la climatología y el influjo marítimo posibilitan una agricultura de tipo más mediterráneo y de mejores resultados productivos. Pero las diferencias no son sólo o principalmente físicas. Estas regiones habrían constituido el tercio meridional de la antigua provincia romana de *Gallaecia* y, más precisamente aún su corazón y centro neurálgico: el grado de penetración de la romanización había sido mucho mayor que en las áreas al norte del Miño --para no hablar ya de Asturias o Cantabria--, la estructuración de la población alrededor de centros urbanos era un factor habitacional consolidado y el desarrollo socio-político, económico y cultural de sus habitantes contrastaba favorablemente con el del común de los pobladores del Norte peninsular en el tránsito de la Antigüedad a la Edad Media. La capital política, económica y cultural de la vieja provincia romana, así como posteriormente la sede metropolitana de la Iglesia católica --la ciudad de Braga-- estaba ubicada en esta zona, como también la virtual totalidad de los centros urbanos de importancia --con la excepción de Lugo-- o los centros culturales y espirituales del país galaico se hallaban eclavados en las tierras entre Miño y Mondego.[9] En resumen, hablar de *Gallaecia* en los primeros siete siglos de la Era Cristiana era casi exlusivamente hablar de esta región, la cuna de Hidacio y Paulo Orosio, el lugar donde vivieron y trabajaron los santos evangelizadores Martín de Dumio y Fructuoso, el centro neurálgico del primer estado germánico en el occidente europeo, el reino suevo de Braga.

Precisamente, por este mayor desarrollo social, esta zona sufrió más severamente las consecuencias de la crisis del mundo urbano y del caos social, económico y demográfico subsiguiente al derrumbe del reino hispano-godo de Toledo y la invasión musulmana que sus vecinas septentrionales. Parte de ella fue efectivamente ocupada por los conquistadores árabes --Coimbra era una fortaleza musulmana a mediados del siglo IX-- y en el resto de la región es innegable el abandono de las ciudades y una reducción, que no es fácil cuantificar, en el numero de los habitantes. Es por ello que la historiografía tiende a calificar el proceso de reocupación y recolonización de este territorio como un episodio más de la llamada Repoblación del Norte peninsular. Es una denominación comunmente aceptada y que podemos hacer nuestra, siempre y cuando entendamos por 'repoblación' el proceso de inducción exterior mediante el cual se reconstruyen las estructuras productivas y la organización social --estructuras políticas, jurídicas, eclesiásticas, las redes de articulación del poblamiento, la estructuración clasista del tejido social-- en los territorios del futuro sur de Galicia y norte de Portugal. Un proceso que conlleva en sí mismo la inmigración de masas de población provenientes del territorio del espacio político astur-galaico que protagoniza dicha ocupación y reconstrucción como necesario refuerzo demográfico, suplementando las carencias de la población local. Pero siempre teniendo en cuenta que el hecho fundamental no es esta inmigración en sí, sino la estructuración y repolitización del espacio reocupado conforme a las pautas sociales e ideológicas de los ocupantes. Repoblar es reorganizar, reconstruir una organización social y del poblamiento deteriorada. Pero, como ya hemos dicho y como creemos haber probado para el caso de la Galicia al sur del Miño,[10] es inconcebible una auténtica repoblación *ex nihilo* sobre unos espacios desiertos y abandonados en estos parámetros espaciales y temporales.

Un rasgo fundamental en el desarrollo de la ocupación de la región cismiñota por los gallegos del norte es su carácter de repoblación oficial, reglamentada, bajo dirección del poder público. En efecto, la iniciativa primera de proceder a la ocupación de una comarca, la asignación de las responsabilidades concretas de los dirigentes de la ocupación y de las condiciones generales en que ésta tiene lugar, y la supervisión final de sus logros y resultados, así como el arbitraje y resolución de los conflictos planteados son --cuanto menos teóricamente-- prerrogativa de la monarquía astur-galaica. Ya hemos citado las palabras de Alfonso III en las que reclamaba su papel rector de la ocupación del territorio entre Tuy y Coimbra. Que no se trata de una mera declaración formal, lo testimonian las noticias de los reyes de Oviedo convocando *concilia* para planificar la reconquista de áreas determinadas o la atribución de competencias en su colonización, dando órdenes e instrucciones a los magnates repobladores sobre aspectos concretos de su tarea e, incluso, dirigiendo bien personalmente --caso del valle del Duero-- o mediante personas de su confianza --caso de las comarcas galaico-portuguesas-- momentos concretos de la reconquista.[11] Cuanto menos formalmente, la autoridad real dirige y preside todo el esfuerzo expansivo de parte de la sociedad gallega en dirección sur. Ciertos testimonios documentales documentan como la ocupación de áreas específicas del futuro Portugal se realizó *cum cornu et albende regis* -- 'por convocatoria y bajo bandera del rey'.[12] Cuando no se especifica tan claramente, de la propia documentación se deriva que para legitimar la posesión de tierras de repoblación, tanto al nivel del pequeño propietario libre como del gran latifundista laico o eclesiástico, es precisa la autorización real --*iussio regis*--, bien sea previamente o, lo que es más común, con posterioridad, tanto directamente como, nuevamente lo más usual, por mediación de sus representantes legitimados. Y esto marca una sustantiva diferencia con el caso de la reocupación de espacios abandonados o sin propietario en el primer siglo de existencia del reino de Asturias, efectuada en base a la presura, un modelo de ocupación del espacio virtualmente independiente del poder público y basado en la libre iniciativa de los repobladores.[13]

Pero, por supuesto y salvo casos excepcionales por motivos políticos o estratégicos, el monarca en la práctica delega en oficiales a su servicio o en artistócratas que disfrutan de su confianza y favor el ejercicio de la dirección efectiva de la reocupación. Las responsabilidades y poderes de estos caudillos de la reconquista galaico-portuguesa son tremendamente amplias y, de hecho, la lejanía cada vez mayor de la realeza del centro de las operaciones, absorbida como está por la progresiva complejidad de un reino engrandecido vertiginosamente, y el grado de iniciativa cada vez mayor que ostentan estos delegados regios motiva que casi se pueda hablar de ellos como de auténticos 'virreyes' con amplio margen de autonomía. Veamos en el caso concreto de uno de los más connotados --Odoario, el repoblador de A Limia, Chaves y Viseo-- los marcos concretos de su actuación:

> data est terra ae populandum illustrissimo uiro domno Odoario... a principe serenissimo domno Adefonso [*Alfonso III; año 872*]. Qui uenit in ciuitate Fauias [*hoy la ciudad portuguesa de Chaves, en Tras-os-Montes*] secus fluuium Tamice, uicos et castella erexit, et ciuitates muniuit et uillas populauit atque eas certis limitibus firmauit, et terminis certis locauit, et inter utrosque abitantes diuisit et omnia ordinate atque firmate bene cuncta disposuit.[14]

En líneas generales, se ocupa primeramente una ciudad, una localidad importante o un centro eclesiástico significativo que ejerce el papel de centro rector de la reocupación y capital comarcal. Normalmente se trata de recobrar centros territoriales ya existentes y de infundirles nueva vida dentro de la nueva situación derivada de la Reconquista y, aunque puede haber cambios en la estructuración del núcleo urbano o en su ubicación --caso de Eminium/Coimbra, por ejemplo--, es inusual que se funden nuevos emplazamientos -- una excepción podría ser Guimarães. Desde este centro directriz la reocupación del territorio circundante se produce en ondas concéntricas por la comarca desde él regida, si bien determinados espacios especiales --enclaves estratégicos, centros eclesiásticos-- pueden ser sujeto de procesos recolonizadores propios bajo responsables específicos y con fines especiales: en especial, asegurar la defensa del territorio o reconstruir las estructuras eclesiásticas anteriores. Por supuesto también, como veremos, los intereses personales de los magnates repobladores o circunstancias coyunturales pueden alterar aspectos concretos de esta reocupación-modelo aunque raras veces dando lugar a mutaciones significativas.

Las etapas y los protagonistas

Aunque, como casi siempre en la Historia, cualquier periodización que establezcamos no podrá reflejar enteramente el ritmo real del acontecimiento histórico, atendiendo a las coordenadas espaciales y temporales del proceso de reocupación de las tierras entre Miño y Mondego creemos posible distinguir tres etapas en él consecutivas geográfica y cronológicamente.

La primera de ellas tendría lugar entre los años 850 y 868 y en su transcurso se reocuparían las tierras de la Galicia meridional hasta la desembocadura del Miño y el curso medio del río Limia. Estrictamente hablando, no se trata de tierras pertenecientes al futuro Portugal, pero el proceso de su integración al espacio político astur-galaico será el prólogo y el crisol de pruebas del movimiento expansivo exterior en dirección sur. Por otra parte, tampoco es un fenómeno específicamente galaico y se enmarca dentro del movimiento general de ocupación de las tierras entre la Cordillera Cantábrica y el río Duero protagonizada por los cristianos del Norte peninsular. Un rasgo común a toda esta etapa es la directa impulsión regia de la reconquista y el estricto control que el monarca --en este caso concreto, Ordoño I (850-866), cuyo reinado cubre la casi totalidad del período-- ejerce sobre su desarrollo. El rey en persona dirige *in situ* la reocupación de las nuevas comarcas de su reino, como fue el caso de León, y solo delega dichas funciones en personas estrechamente vinculadas al trono y objeto de su total confianza. Un ejemplo prototípico podría ser el conde galaico Gatón, señor de Triacastela --en la parte oriental de la actual provincia de Lugo--, cuñado del propio rey y *dux* del ejército real, quien con un contingente de gallegos del oriente lucense y de inmigrantes mozárabes ocupó hacia 850/54 el Bierzo y Astorga; aún en el caso de un servidor de confianza y familiar próximo, como era el caso de Gatón, se constata la continua supervisión de la monarquiá y la vigilancia que ejerce sobre la actuación del oficial reconquistador.[15] Volviendo al área objeto de nuestro interés, hacia el año 860 es retomada Tuy y reocupado el Val Miñor circundante bajo la dirección de los condes Hermenegildo Gutiérrez, yerno de Gatón y pariente del rey, y Alfonso Betote. En los primeros años de la década del 860 se ocupa y repuebla Orense bajo la dirección titular del príncipe Alfonso --el futuro Alfonso III-- y se restaura su sede episcopal, instalando como primer obispo al mozárabe Sebastián, antiguo prelado de *Arcabrica* en territorio musulmán.[16] Por esos mismos años, Odoario, conde de Castela --valle del Avia--, organiza el poblamiento y colonización de Bande, la futura comarca de Celanova y la Limia.[17] También este personaje, al que la documentación califica de *digno bellatori*, debía de ser miembro del círculo dirigente del reino.

La segunda etapa transcurre entre los años 868 y 880, período en el que la expansión colonizadora extiende los dominios cristianos hasta el curso bajo y la desembocadura del río Duero. Como ya hemos visto, aunque del rey emanan la autoridad para ocupar estas nuevas tierras y determinadas estrategias para su conquista y reorganización, serán los magnates gallegos quienes protagonicen y lleven a cabo dicha ocupación con amplia autonomía, afrontando los riesgos posibles pero capitalizando en su beneficio los resultados materiales de sus esfuerzos. Se constata asimismo la existencia de dos grandes vectores geográficos del avance repoblador, sucesores en buena medida del período anterior: un primero a través del litoral costero desde Tuy en dirección Oporto y un segundo por las tierras altas interiores con meta en Lamego. Así, Alfonso Betote ocupa las tierras de la ribera meridional del Miño, donde también vemos intervenir a Nepociano, un pariente de Hermenegildo Gutiérrez. El año 868 queda señalado por la reocupación de la ciudad de Oporto obra del conde Vimara Pérez, al que la tradición asigna también la fundación de Guimarães. Tras la temprana muerte de Vimara su hijo Lucido completará la repoblación de las comarcas aledañas. Más al interior y también por esta época se retoma la semi-abandonada ciudad de Braga, labor en la que destaca la actuación del conde Pelayo Pérez --muy posiblemente el homónimo conde de Bergantiños, en el noroeste de Galicia--, complementada por Vimara Pérez. De todas maneras, el caso de la ciudad de Braga es especial en tanto en cuanto la dirección e interés regios son evidentes en todas las fases de la conquista y porque los magnates laicos han de ceder por mandato real la propiedad de la ciudad y buena parte de las tierras vecinas a la Iglesia de Lugo, heredera de los derechos de la extinta metrópolis bracarense. Un caso semejante, aunque desconocemos el nombre del magnate reconquistador, es el de la vecina villa episcopal de Dumio, en este caso y por razones semejantes en beneficio del obispado de Mondoñedo. Mientras tanto, el ya mencionado conde Odoario toma el año 872 la ciudad de Chaves, desde donde organiza la recolonización de la región de Tras-os-Montes.[18] Al lado de estos grandes hitos y personajes por supuesto están actuando otros pequeños nobles o campesinos libres, tanto en el entorno de sus más poderosos contemporáneos como por cuenta propia. Pero, evidentemente, el peso y las posibilidades de unos y otros son muy distintos.

La tercera y última etapa se extiende entre los años 880 y 920, período en el que se integran en el reino de Asturias los territorios entre el Duero y el Mondego. Los primeros pasos serán obra de los dirigentes de la etapa anterior: así en el año 878 Hermenegildo Gutiérrez toma por la fuerza Coimbra, resiste un posterior contraataque musulmán hasta ser socorrido por Alfonso III y repuebla y guarniciona la ciudad con pobladores venidos de Galicia.[19] De igual manera, en un período anterior al año 899 pasan a manos cristianas las ciudades de Lamego y Viseo, esta última gracias a los esfuerzos del omnipresente Odoario.[20] Apropiados los grandes centros de la región, el desarrollo ulterior de la ocupación y defensa del espacio conquistado recaerá en la segunda generación de magnates repobladores, tales como Arias Menéndez, hijo de Hermenegildo Gutiérrez, o Lucido Vimáraz, hijo de Vimara Pérez. Pero el esfuerzo demográfico que supuso la ocupación en apenas unas decenas de años de tal cantidad de territorios agotó las reservas galaicas y aunque a comienzos del siglo X vemos actuar en este área a magnates foráneos, como el castellano Diego Jiménez --gente que, por otra parte, se integran rápidamente en las filas de la nobleza galaica--, esta región estará débilmente poblada, albergando un importante contingente de habitantes mozárabes y aún musulmanes, y siempre insegura ante la amenaza de un contraataque andalusí. Ello explica la rápidez con la que la región caerá en el último cuarto del siglo X ante la ofensiva de Almanzor, mientras las tierras al norte del bajo Duero consiguieron resistir en manos cristianas.[21]

NOTAS

1. Sirva como ejemplo la clásica obra de Claudio Sánchez-Albornoz, *Despoblación y repoblación del valle del Duero* (Buenos Aires: Instituto de Historia de España, 1966). Las orientaciones y resultados de esta obra de investigación son inseparables de las líneas maestras de la ideología 'españolista' del autor tal como aparecen plasmadas en *España, un enigma histórico* (Barcelona: Edhasa, 1991 [reed.]). Una orientación más ponderada puede encontrarse en Salvador de Moxó, *Repoblación y sociedad en la España cristiana medieval* (Madrid: Rialp, 1979.)

2. Cfr. por ejemplo trabajos como los de Paulo Merêa, 'Ainda sobre "Portugal" no século X. (Pro domo mea)', *Revista Portuguesa de História*, 11 (1964), 144-50; y Torquato de Sousa Soares, 'Reflexões sobre a origem e a formação de Portugal', *Revista Portuguesa de História*, 7 (1957), 193-342.

3. Son de destacar entre otras, obras como la de José Mattoso, *O essencial sobre a formação da nacionalidade* (Lisboa: Imprensa Nacional, 1985); o José Ángel García de Cortázar y Otros, *Organización social del espacio en la España medieval. La Corona de Castilla en los siglos VIII a XV* (Barcelona: Ariel, 1985). Conviene tener en cuenta, sin embargo, que la primera es una obra de divulgación mientras la segunda apenas se ocupa del caso del Portugal septentrional.

4. Documento de 883-08-17, reproducido en Antonio López Ferreiro, *Historia de la Santa A.M. Iglesia de Santiago de Compostela* (Santiago: Imprenta del Seminario Conciliar, 1898-1910), II (1899), apéndice documental nº XV. Por *Mineo ciuitatem* el documento quiere referirse a la antigua Aeminium romana, que substituyó en época altomedieval a la antigua Conimbriga, distante pocos kilómetros de ella y cuyo nombre acabaría por asumir.

5. Cfr. Eloy Benito Ruano, 'La historiografía en la Alta Edad Media. Ideología y estructura', *Cuadernos de Historia de España*, 17 (1952), 50-104; y Manuel C. Díaz y Díaz, *De Isidoro al siglo XI. Ocho estudios sobre la vida literaria peninsular* (Barcelona: El Albir, 1976).

6. 875-03-1, reproducido en Antonio García Conde, 'Diploma de D. Alfonso III a Florenzo y Aldoreto Tritóniz', *Boletín de la Comisión Provincial de Monumentos de Lugo*, 6 (1954-55), 3-8. Floriana y García fechan el documento en el año 900.

7. Cfr. Carlos Baliñas Pérez, 'Do mito á realidade: a definición social e territorial de Galicia na Alta Idade Media (séculos VIII e IX)', Santiago, tesis doctoral inédita, 1990, pp.127-64 (actualmente a punto de aparecer publicada por Editorial Coordenadas).

8. Dos claros ejemplos en 867-01-20, López Ferreiro, *Historia de la Santa Iglesia de Santiago*, ap. doc. nº VI; y 878-04-22, Tumbo de Samos, Arquivo Universidade de Santiago, fol. 59v.

9. En realidad las tierras al sur del bajo Duero --y, por ende, ciudades y sedes episcopales como Coimbra, Lamego o Viseo-- pertenecían en época romana a la provincia de *Lusitania* y no a *Gallaecia*. Pero desde el siglo V, con el reino suevo, su destino en lo político y lo eclesiástico se vinculó al de la Galicia germánica y altomedieval.

10. Cfr. Baliñas, 'Do mito á realidade', pp.245-49 y, en general, *passim*.

11. 'Ambiguum quidem esse non potest, quod omnibus notum est, eo quod prehendiderunt

uillas sub nomine regis comites uel forciores de stirpe antico' (951-03-5, López Ferreiro, *Historia de la Santa Iglesia de Santiago*, ap. doc. nº LXI, se refiere específicamente al área de la desembocadura del Miño y a esta época). Otro ejemplo, entre muchos posibles, *infra* nota 14 y texto correspondiente.

12. *Portugalia Monumenta Historica. Diplomata et Chartae* (Liechtenstein: Kraus Reprints, 1967), I, doc. nº V (870-02-11) y nº VI (870-04-30), y 1025-08-30, Arquivo Distrital de Braga, reproducido en Torquato de Sousa Soares, 'Um testemunho sobre a presuria do bispo Odoário de Lugo no território Bracarense', *Revista Portuguesa de História*, 1 (1941), 151-60. Un análisis terminológico en Joseph M. Piel, 'Duas notas etimológicas: "presuria/presura" e "albende/alvende"', *Anuario de Estudios Medievales*, 6 (1969), 435-39.

13. Baliñas, 'Do mito á realidade', pp.233-58.

14. 982-10-01, Tumbo de Celanova, fols 97v-100v.

15. Cfr. 854-05-6, en Claudio Sánchez-Albornoz, 'Serie de documentos inéditos del reino de Asturias', *Cuadernos de Historia de España*, 1-2 (1944), 327-28.

16. (900)-08-28, Archivo del Reino de Galicia, Reales, I, 2 -- hay varias ediciones impresas del documento y una copiosa bibliografía sobre su autenticidad.

17. Cfr. 909-05-9, Tumbo de Celanova, fols 103v-104r y 1054-03-23, Tumbo de Celanova, fol. 101v.

18. Un estudio más pormenorizado y con aparato crítico de esta etapa en Carlos Baliñas Pérez, *Defensores e traditores: un modelo de relación entre poder monárquico, e oligarquía na Galicia altomedieval (718-1037)* (Santiago: Ediciones Xunta de Galicia, 1988), pp.40-41 y 48-51.

19. 'Era DCCCCXVIª prendita est Conimbria ad Ermegildo comite (*Chronicon Laurbanense*). (Alfonso III). Coinbriam quoque ab inimicis obsessam defendit suoque imperio subiugavit' (*Sampiro y la monarquía leonesa en el siglo X*, edición y comentario de Fr. Justo Pérez de Urbel (Madrid: Escuela de Estudios Medievales, 1952), pp.280-81). Cfr. nota siguiente.

20. (Alfonso III). 'Conimbriam ab inimicis possesam eremavit et gallecis postea populavit... Urbes quoque... Eminensis, Vesensis atque Lamezensis a christianis populantur' (*Crónica Albeldense*, ed. de Gómez Moreno, p.604). Hacia 899: 'Hodarius Castelle et Veseo comes' (Pérez de Urbel, *Sampiro*, p.291).

21. Y así fue sobre esa zona que los habitantes cristianos de la frontera transduriense se replegaron: 'Avitabit Egas Erotez in terram Portugalensis cum gens sua in logo predicto inter Doiro et Vauga per plures annos, et consurrexerunt filii ismaelitarum super christianos, et exivit ipse domno Egas de sua terra ante ipsius gens ismaelitarum et pervenit in terram inter urbium Durio et Limie, et ganavit ereditates in ipsa terra' (*PMH-DC*, nº CCCLXXXIV; el documento hace referencia al reinado de Vermudo II, entre 982 y 999).

A *CRÓNICA GALEGA DOS REINOS DE LEÓN E CASTELA* NA HISTORIA E NA HISTORIOGRAFÍA GALEGAS

HENRIQUE MONTEAGUDO ROMERO
Universidade de Santiago de Compostela

*Para Derek W. Lomax,
manantío de sabedoría,
lareira de humanidade;
coa saudade sen fondo do amigo
e a sinxela admiración do discípulo.*

A *Crónica Galega dos reinos de León e Castela*[1] é dos textos máis importantes da prosa literaria escrita en lingua galega na Idade Media. Polo seu volume (a edición moderna enche 900 páxinas de texto), constitúe unha achega da maior importancia para o coñecemento do galego medieval. Polo seu contido, constitúe unha peza notable do complexísimo crebacabezas no que se perde a tradición da *Crónica General de España* afonsina. A primeira sección da obra, que corresponde coa *Crónica de León*, non parece presentar un interese especial, pois é simple versión dun orixinal castelán coñecido; pero a sección que corresponde coa *Crónica de Castela* resulta ser o máis antigo especime coñecido do texto na historiografía peninsular. O texto, como toda a tradición á que pertence, presenta numerosos problemas: moitos, especialmente os referentes á datación do texto e os lingüísticos, foron resoltos polo seu editor moderno, Ramón Lorenzo; outros permanecen mesmo sen abordar. En concreto, nós ímonos deter en dous asuntos que reclamaron a nosa atención despois de entrarmos en contacto coa *Crónica Galega dos reinos de León e Castela*: primeiro, o da 'oportunidade histórica' deste texto (¿por que ou para que se dispuxo a composición en galego dunha *Crónica Galega dos reinos de León e Castela*?); segundo, e intimamente vencellado co anterior, o da 'responsabilidade editorial' da obra (¿quen dispuxo a redacción galega da obra?).

Coidamos que unha exploración das posibles respostas a estas preguntas pode botar luz sobre o propio texto, e axudar tamén a unha valoración crítica do mesmo. Para responder á primeira pregunta, imos partir dun dato que nos parece sumamente elocuente: a *Crónica do Reino de León* comeza no reinado de Ramiro I (842-850), isto é, xustamente despois do reinado de Afonso II, durante o que se produciu a invención da tumba apostólica en Compostela. Descartando que nos atopemos ante un texto fragmentario, é forzoso preguntarse polas razóns que puideron ter os responsables da versión *galega* do texto para ignorar precisamente a sección da obra castelá que corresponde ó período de fundación de Compostela e cimentación da súa gloria. Para entender isto, é preciso referirse á tradición historiográfica medieval sobre o descubrimento da tumba de Santiago e o desenvolvemento do Camiño xacobeo. A miña hipótese é que a tradición compostelá daba por boa a versión que ofrece o *Pseudo-Turpín*, que lle concedía a Carlos Magno un papel protagonista no asunto. Esta tradición chocaba coa da historiografía castelá, que impugnaba a veracidade do *Pseudo-Turpín*. A *Crónica General de España* afonsina inscríbese de cheo na tradición historiográfica castelá, e por iso a sección da obra a que nos referimos debeu parecer inadmisible ós ollos dos clérigos galegos que andaban por detrás da versión á nosa lingua.

Para responder á segunda pregunta, exploraremos o marco histórico en que se produciu a versión, na procura dun persoeiro galego ó que se poida atribuír a responsabilidade na decisión de constituír estes textos, que contase cos medios para levar adiante o labor e que se sentise suficientemente motivado a realizalo. Como se mostrará, as nosas pesquisas apuntan a Rodrigo de Padrón, arcebispo de Compostela de 1307 a 1316, e que durante os mesmos anos foi sobranceiro personaxe nos reinos de Castela-León.

A *Crónica de León* e a *Crónica de Castela* na tradición da *Crónica General de España*

O século XIII foi decisivo para o cultivo literario das *linguas vulgares* ou romances, que entran en compentencia aberta co latín. Neste senso, o labor de Afonso X como mecenas literario foi decisivo para o castelán. Centrándonos no terreo da prosa, notaremos que despois dunha primeira etapa, aproximadamente entre 1250 e 1260, durante a que realizara os primeiros ensaios de emprego prosístico do castelán coa traducción de varias obras árabes de carácter científico literario, o rei Afonso embarcouse na década de 1270 na compilación de magnas crónicas históricas que esixían a creación e dirección de varios grupos de traballo especializado. Primeiro proxectou escribir unha *General Estoria* ou Historia Universal, e despois abandonou o proxecto para centrarse na elaboración dunha *Estoria de España* ou *Crónica General de España* que abranguese desde a prehistoria e as máis antigas noticias sobre a península de que dispuña ata o seu propio reinado.

Afonso X utilizou o *vulgar* castelán e non o latín para redacta-la súa *Crónica General* ou *Estoria de España*, aínda que se baseou fundamentalmente en dúas obras producidas en medio clerical e escritas en latín: o *Cronicon Mundi* do bispo Lucas de Tui (rematada en 1236) e a *Historia rebus Hispaniae* do arcebispo Rodrigo de Toledo (rematada en 1243). Como xa se dixo, de primeira intención, parece que Afonso X pretendía reunir na *Estoria de España* tódalas noticias históricas que tivesen relación coa Península Ibérica e os feitos producidos nela. Pero a obra demorouse nos antecedentes (as fábulas sobre os seus primeiros moradores, a historia novelada do imperio romano e as orixes dos pobos godos) que estaban destinados a formar a primeira parte da obra, de xeito que a segunda parte quedou incompleta, con lagoas e incoherencias. Polo de agora, non está resolto o debatido problema da data de composición das distintas partes da obra. En resume, só se pode asegurar que a 1ª parte da *Estoria de España*, que vai ata a conquista musulmana, foi compilada e completada durante o reinado de Afonso X. A 2ª parte da obra, que comeza coa conquista musulmana, debeu ser no fundamental arranxada no reinado de Afonso X, pero a irresolta redacción última é dos tempos de Sancho IV.

Esta actitude favorable ó cultivo dos *romances* sería precisamente a que conduciría á versión de varios textos producidos nos obradoiros rexios de Toledo á lingua galega. O pulo que o rei sabio lle imprimira á prosa cronística en castelán comunicouselles ós seus súbditos e veciños occidentais: durante o reinado de Fernando IV (1295-1312) compilouse en galego unha *Crónica de Castela* específica que comeza co reinado de Fernando I (1035-65), o instaurador da dinastía navarro-castelán, e que se pecha coa reunificación definitiva dos reinos cristiáns centro-occidentais na persoa de Fernando III (1232). Pouco despois de constituída esta *Crónica de Castela* en galego, en data indeterminada, decidiuse completala coa versión dunha parte da *Crónica General* ou *Estoria de España*, a que se ocupaba da dinastía leonesa, desde

Ramiro I (842-850) ata Vermudo III (que comezou a reinar en 1028 e foi deposto por Fernando I de Castela en 1032). Aínda que o contido desta sección da *Estoria de España* presta unha grande atención a Castela e non esquece a historia de Navarra, Aragón e Al-Andalus, ben puidera considerarse unha auténtica *Crónica de León*. Esta parte da obra foi traducida ó galego directamente da *Estoria de España*, e procede con toda probabilidade da sección compilada en tempos de Sancho IV. A *Crónica de León* traducida ó galego responde máis fielmente cá *Cronica de Castela* ós obxectivos e métodos de traballo de Afonso X, tanto no emprego e trabazón das fontes da historia peninsular coma no seu enmarque cronolóxico, polo que pode considerarse 'estructuralmente acabada', aínda que non totalmente rematada. Os relatos de Lucas Tudense e Rodrigo Toledano complétanse con sustanciosas achegas da tradición épica e lendaria, da que se toman, entre outros, os relatos de Maynet e Bernardo del Carpio. O resultado é un texto moi rico e abundante, bastante completo e regularmente compacto e conxuntado.

Cando se decidiu amplia-la *Crónica de Castela* polo seu inicio coa *Crónica de León*, tamén se procedeu á súa continuación, para o que se lle engadiu a *Crónica de San Fernando*, que narra en 96 capítulos os feitos de Fernando III --coroado rei de Castela en 1217-- desde a súa asunción do reino de León á morte de Afonso IX (1032) ata a súa morte (1252). A obra constituída pola ensamblaxe das versións galegas da *Crónica de León*, da *Crónica de Castela* e da *Crónica de San Fernando* consérvasenos en un só manuscrito pergamenáceo, o 8817 da Biblioteca Nacional de Madrid, no que a primeira sección ocupa os folios 1-88 (*Cronica de León*), e a última (*Crónica de San Fernando*) os fols. 230-265. Da que conviñemos en chamar *Crónica de León* (isto é, a parte que trata da dinastía galego-leonesa na *Estoria de España*) consérvase outra copia manuscrita en 137 folios de papel, probablemente da segunda metade do s. XIV, custodiada actualmente na Biblioteca Universitaria de Salamanca (nº 2497). Esta versión non presenta variantes significativas con respecto á conservada polo ms. 8817 da Biblioteca Nacional de Madrid, polo que se supón que existe unha estreita relación entre ámbolos dous.

Visión da historia hispánica na *Estoria de España*

Cando Afonso decidiu a elaboración da *Estoria de España*, o ideal que viñera xustificando a Reconquista peninsular desde os fins do s. XII, a Cruzada, despois da conquista de boa parte de Al-Andalus durante o reinado de Fernando III, e logo das tremendas derrotas dos cruzados de Ultramar (que tocarían fondo coa caída de Xerusalén e a fin dos reinos cristiáns de Terra Santa), estaba en franca decadencia. A ideoloxía lexitimadora da política da coroa de Castela na segunda metade do s. XIII e primeiros anos do s. XIV era o neogoticismo, no nome da cal se pretendía que a guerra de Reconquista estaba en realidade destinada a consegui-la reunificación política de toda a Península baixo o trono castelán,[2] segundo o punto de vista que actualizara e impuxera o arcebispo toledano e historiador Rodrigo Ximenez de Rada. Este estaba interesado especificamente polo aspecto eclesiástico da cuestión: a afirmación da súa autoridade como titular da Sede Primada de Toledo sobre toda a península. Efectivamente, nunha certa tradición historiográfica clerical, na que se alían os intereses da monarquía castelá cos da mitra toledana, ofrécese unha interpretación do decorrer histórico en clave ideolóxica goticizante. Con ela aválanse as aspiracións hexemonistas do reino castelán, presentado como principal protagonista da guerra da reconquista, e ó que se lle asigna como misión a restauración da monarquía dos visigodos, baixo a cal a península unificada se configurara como nación, e coñecera unha gloriosa época de esplendor. En nome desa visión da historia peninsular, o destino e os intereses dos pobos hispánicos aparecen subordinados ós do reino castelán, que adquire unha posición absolutamente central e un protagonismo indisimulado. Pero ó mesmo tempo, no terreo eclesiástico Toledo recupera e afirma a súa posición de sede primacial de España, que perdera durante a dominación islámica.

Simplificando, pódese afirmar que as intencións que moveron a Afonso X a realizar a súa *Estoria de España* están relacionadas coa situación que se estaba debuxando na Península naquel momento. Dunha banda, tratábase de afirmar e asegurar no plano ideolóxico a hexemonía política adquirida polo reino de Castela na Península. Esta hexemonía política castelá conseguirase en primeiro lugar en competencia cos veciños cristiáns, algúns dos cales xa estaban integrados e pretendíase asimilalos (León e Galicia), mentres que no caso de outros tencionábase subordinalos (Portugal e o reino de Aragón); en segundo lugar a hexemonía castelá atinguírase en aberta confrontación cos árabes do sur, confinados despois dos importantísimos avances de Fernando III no reducido reino de Granada, pero aínda presentes en grande número e importantes pola súa influencia na vida económica, social e cultural, xunto ós xudeus, en boa parte dos reinos sometidos á coroa castelá. Neste senso, non semella esaxerado afirmar que a *Estoria de España* anuncia, e ó mesmo tempo prepara desde o punto de vista da propaganda, a política imperialista de Castela.

Carlos Magno e Santiago, Toledo e Afonso Contra Compostela

No século XIII, a extraordinaria voga das peregrinacións comezaba a perder forza en Europa, en parte debido ós problemas que presentaba a viaxe a Ultramar, e en parte a que novos desenvolvementos da espiritualidade e o culto viñeran competir coa veneración das reliquias dos santos. Entre eles, convén salientar moi especialmente o fervor crecente da devoción pola Virxe María, do que san Bernaldo e a Orde de Cister foron importantes impulsores desde os mediados do s. XII. Non por causalidade, o monumento lírico-musical máis importante do s. XIII nos romances peninsulares foron as *Cantigas de Santa María*, compiladas en lingua galega por un rei, Afonso X, que, como se sabe, contribuíu á decandencia da peregrinaxe xacobea. De feito, está admitido pola crítica que as *Cantigas de Santa María* foron concebidas en parte como obra de propaganda da competencia anti-xacobea. Ademais, durante o reinado de Afonso, como veremos, a sede xacobea viuse paralisada pola política de Afonso X, que, entre outras consecuencias, obrigou a exiliarse ó arcebispo e a boa parte do clero capitular.

Pero, fixándonos no terreo estrictamente historiográfico, é moi relevador observar como recolle Afonso a tradición castelá contraria a unha obra de propaganda xacobea, *Historia de Carlos Magno e de Roldán* ou *Pseudo-Turpín*,[3] composta nunha data indeterminada, probablemente situada no primeiro tercio do s. XII. Esta é unha obra en prosa latina que se presenta como testemuña contemporánea ó protagonista, escrita da man do arcebispo

Turpín, famoso personaxe do ámbito carolinxio, na que se narran uns acontecementos ofrecidos como absolutamente históricos e que sen embargo son case totalmente ficticios. A *Historia de Carlos Magno e de Roldán*, peza principal e epítome das lendas de ampla circulación na Europa do tempo que vencellaban a Carlos Margno co Camiño de Santiago, aparece moi frecuentemente formando parte do *Liber Sancti Jacobi*, considerado na catedral de Santiago obra de carácter litúrxico, e como tal empregada nos ritos xacobeos.[4] Dos máis de 250 manuscritos medievais que nos conservan a *Historia de Carlos Magno e de Roldán*, o conxunto máis abundante está representado polos especimes en que esta se acompaña doutros textos procedentes do *Liber Sancti Jacobi*, pero nun importante grupo deles asóciase a un corpus de textos especiais sobre Carlos Magno, probablemente reunidos en 1165 co gallo da canonización do emperador. Noutros manuscritos aparece en serie con diversas narracións haxiográficas. Finalmente, tamén se relaciona con outras obras de carácter histórico, pois a partir do s. XII comeza a ser utilizado como fonte de primeira man para as crónicas da monarquía francesa.

A estructura básica da *Historia de Carlos Magno e de Roldán* pode considerarse constituída por tres tramas diferentes, se cadra na súa orixe independentes: 1) Carlos Magno, inducido polo Apóstolo Santiago, entra en Hispania, conquístaa, expulsando os mouros, e libera Compostela (capítulos 1-5); 2) O tema épico de Aigolando (caps. 6-18); 3) O relato épico da morte de Roldán e Oliveros na ciada de Roncesvales, que semella basearse nunha narración antiga, quizais anterior á versión da *Chanson de Roland* (caps. 19-33). O capítulo 19, que describe os privilexios supostamente recoñecidos e outorgados por Carlos Magno á igrexa de Santiago, serve de vencello ó conxunto da obra. O tema desenvolvido na primeira sección é o que máis interesa ó noso obxecto.

¿Como explicarnos que se pretendan presentar como feitos históricos fantasías como que Carlos Magno participou no descubrimento da tumba do apóstolo e na propagación do seu culto, e que Carlos Magno reconquistou a península enteira de mans ismaelitas? A intervención da nobreza franca na guerra da Reconquista a fins do s. XI significou unha notable mutación na natureza desta guerra: por unha banda, a Reconquista deixou de ser unha cuestión de correlación de forzas e reaxuste de fronteiras entre reinos peninsulares (mouros e cristiáns) e pasou a converterse en conflagración internacional, cargada dun intenso contido relixioso. Ámbalas tendencias se viron reforzadas por parte musulmana coa intervención almorávide que seguíu á conquista de Toledo (1085) por Afonso VI. Por outra banda, a conquista de Toledo polos cristiáns levantou un problema para a igrexa hispánica: como Toledo fora a sede primacial da Hispania visigótica, o seu recén instalado arcebispo e os sucesores deste reclamaban que a cadeira de Toledo volvese ter un lugar de privilexio fronte ás demais da península. Pero esta pretensión chocaba coas doutras sedes da Hispania, e moi en concreto coa ascendente Compostela.

Efectivamente, Compostela, aproveitando a voga cada vez maior da peregrinaxe a Santiago e o espacio vougo que deixara na xerarquía da Igrexa hispánica a ocupación polos musulmáns de boa parte das sedes bispais da península, e concretamente Toledo, viña reclamando unha posición cada vez máis importante no cadro eclesiástico peninsular. Primeiro, a mediados do s. XI conseguiu que se trasladase a sede do bispado da antiga capital, Iria, á propia Compostela. Pouco despois (c. 1070) restaurábase a sede bispal de Braga, que estivera vacante á causa da súa posición próxima á fronteira de guerra. Braga fora a sede arcebispal da que nos tempos anteriores á invasión musulmana dependía a diócese de Iria, polo que a restauración de Braga representaba unha seria ameaza para o clero xacobeo. Na procura dun título arcebispal, o clero compostelán conseguira no Concilio de Clermont-Ferrand (o mesmo no que Urbano II proclamou a Primeira Cruzada) a exención da sede compostelana de toda dependencia peninsular, colocándoa baixo o padroado directo de Roma. Conforme Toledo, sempre baixo a éxida do clero francés, reafirmaba o seu importante papel no reino de Castela, Diego Xelmírez manobraba ata conseguir que Compostela fose declarada por Calixto II sede arcebispal. Aínda así, os conflictos entre Compostela, Toledo e Braga (nesta ocasión interésanos salienta-la rivalidade entre as dúas primeiras sedes) prolongáronse, nalgún caso ata case o final da Idade Media, de xeito que estiveron presentes permanente no ánimo dos cleros respectivos.

Por outra banda, os anos finais do s. XI e os primeiros do s. XII estiveron dominados nos reinos cristiáns da península pola problemática sucesión de

Afonso VI, que desembocaría na suba ó trono dunha nova dinastía, personificada en Afonso VII, o Emperador de Hispania. O conquistador de Toledo, Afonso VI, casara dúas das súas fillas, as destinadas a herdar as súas mellores posesións, con nobres de alén-Pirineos: a maior, Urraca, co Raimundo de Borgoña, outra, Tareixa, con Henrique de Borgoña. Dada a inexistencia de descendentes masculinos do monarca, Raimundo estaba destinado a ser o herdeiro de Afonso ou a repartir os seus dominios con Henrique de Borgoña, e no entanto, o primeiro foi nomeado Conde de Galicia, e o segundo Conde de Portugal. Pero o camiño de ascenso ó trono de dinastía borgoñona foi moi esgrevio, e só o fillo de Raimundo e Urraca, Afonso Raimúndez, conseguiría completalo moito máis tarde, en 1126. Afonso VI presentou serias resistencias á entronización dos borgoñóns, mostrando claramente a súa preferencia por candidatos hispanos.[5] Se cadra, Afonso VI tentou resucitar un proxecto político pan-hispánico e añoraba os seus vellos tempos, anteriores á conquista de Toledo, de 'Emperador das tres relixións'. Isto estaría en aberta contradicción co proxecto de 'occidentalizar' os cristiáns da península, do que a Igrexa romana e o clero franco eran principais inspiradoras e os franceses vindos á península instrumentos máis eficaces. En todo caso, parece que este proxecto de 'occidentalización' chocou con certa resistencia en España, seguramente procedente dos sectores máis tradicionalistas da nobreza e o clero. No s. XIII as reticencias destes sectores puideron ser interpretadas como manifestación dunha conciencia neogótica. Así o vía o bispo Lucas de Tui no *Libro dos miragres de san Isidoro*: 'O rei Afonso designou a Urraca para a sucesión ata que Deus lle dese un fillo da liñaxe dos godos',[6] Pero probablemente o neogoticismo responde máis ben ós intereses da coroa castelá no s. XIII do que á mentalidade hispana do s. XII.

Despois de reviradas peripecias, Afonso Raimúndez acabou ascendendo ó trono como Afonso VII e esforzouse en ser recoñecido como emperador de toda Hispania por parte de tódolos príncipes cristiáns da península e mesmo de varios importantes magnates occitanos e gascóns, o cal conseguiu simbolicamente cando a súa coroación en León (1135). Consecuente co seu título de emperador, Afonso VII repartiu á súa morte os seus reinos entre os fillos Fernando e Sancho: o primeiro quedou como rei de Galicia e León, e o segundo como rei de Castela. Unha crónica anónima da época, de ámbito anglos-normando, aínda lle atribúe o título de emperador galego a Fernando II.

Podemos agora volver preguntarnos. ¿Cales eran os obxectivos da serie de autores e compiladores do enigmático *Pseudo-Turpín*? Entre estas finalidades debe contarse sen dúbida a exaltación xacobea, que aparece na obra na forma de teoría das tres meirandes sedes da cristiandade (Xerusalén, Roma e Santiago), o cal implica a preeminencia da sede arcebispal de Santiago sobre toda a península e avala a reivindicación do Primado de España, en pugna con Toledo.[7] Pero é no marco político na primeira metade do s. XII onde hai que situar afirmacións da *Historia de Carlos Magno e de Roldán* como a do capítulo III 'Carlos Magno conquereu no seu tempo toda España'[8] que xustificarían desde o punto dinástico as aspiracións dos borgoñóns, pois os duques de Borgoña considerábanse descendentes de Carlos Magno, xa que estaban emparentados coa casa real de Francia. Deste xeito, a obra respaldaría as aspiracións de Raimundo e de seu fillo en tanto descendentes de Carlos Magno, ou así o entenderían os lectores daquel tempo.[9] É indubitable que a *Historia Caroli Magni et Rotholandi* ofrecía unha fundamentación ideolóxica á intervención dos francos na península, moi concretamente á ascensión do borgoñón Afonso Raimúndez a un trono hispánico, e especialmente á súa proclamación como Emperador.

A partir do éxito esmagador da *Historia de Carlos Magno e de Roldán*, na literatura de tema carolinxio o emperador Carlos Magno aparece xa estreitamente ligado ó camiño de Santiago. O *Pseudo-Turpín* serve para aguilloa-lo maxín dos xograis, que poñen en xogo elementos que o texto e as lendas do camiño lles ofrecían. Por exemplo, o *roman* titulado *Anseïs de Cartage* (composto c. 1200, refeito sobre un poema máis antigo) baséase na *Historia*; nel o personaxe principal xa non é Carlos Magno, senón o camiño de Santiago.[10] No *Gui de Bourgogne*, poema en versos alexandrinos do s. XIII, dise de Carlos Magno 'Chegou a Santiago, el e os seus baróns / a súa ofrenda presenta, feita alí súa oración'.[11] Nos dous poemas, especialmente o primeiro, Carlos Magno e os combatentes de Roncesvales aparecen, pois, como cabaleiros de Santiago. Así figuran tamén nos poemas da *Entrée en Espagne*, composto por un rimador de Padua na variedade lingüística franco-italiana na primeira metade do s. XIV,[12] e da *Prise de Pampelune* ou *Tomada de Pamplona*, de Nicolau de Verona, c. 1350, que se ofrecen como prólogo á *Chanson de Roland*, xa que esta comeza cando Carlos ten a península conquistada, despois de sete anos de loitas.[13]

Esta tradición de Carlos Magno cruzado do apóstolo e libertador do camiño 'do bo santo de Galicia' debeu ser admitida tamén de boa gana na tradición literaria hispánica máis antiga, a xulgar pola afirmación que se pón en beizos de Carlos Magno no pequeno fragmento que se salvou do poema épico *Roncesvalles* (¿navarro, do primeiro tercio do s. XIII?) 'adobé los caminos del apóstol Santiague' (verso 75 do fragmento conservado).[14] Pero a reacción na literatura castelá propiamente dita non se fixo esperar. Nun poema de inspiración épica, pero de feitura e ámbito clerical, a mediados do s. XIII, xa se alza a protesta castelanista:

> Dixo que más quería commo estava estar
> que el reygno de Espanna a França sojuzgar,
> que non se podrían deso los françeses alabar.
> ¡Que más querían ellos en çinco annos ganar![15]

Polo tanto, no século XIII, a *Historia de Carlos Magno e de Roldán* constituía un atranco ideolóxico para o movemento centrípeto que procedía da coroa de Castela. Nun momento en que importaba sobre todo destaca-lo poder do monarca e a tradición unitarista da coroa castelá e mais de ensalza-la capital político-relixiosa do reino, Toledo, dificilmente se poderían atura-las fachendosas afirmacións compostelanistas da *Historia de Carlos Magno e de Roldán*, case aldraxantes para Toledo, e que para colmo viñan respaldadas por un poder estranxeiro ó que se lle atribuían importantes méritos na Reconquista, sendo que esta era unha guerra na que a monarquía castelá se gababa de ser principal protagonista. Así, se ben aínda Lucas de Tui acepta que 'o moi cristián rei Carlos viñera visita-la casa do benaventurado Apóstolo Santiago',[16] o campeón do neogoticismo, Rodrigo Ximénez de Rada, arcebispo de Toledo, exclama alporizado 'algúns crédulos que se fían das fábulas dos comediantes, din que Carlos Magno tomou moitas cidades, castelos e prazas fortes, que emprendeu con enerxía moitos combates cos sarracenos e que dirixiu unha estrada dereitiña desde as Galias e Xermania ata Santiago... [en realidade] ...non pasou dos Pirineos'.[17] Está claro que aquí o Toledano non está desmentindo soa nin principalmente a *Chanson de Roland*, nin textos como o 'Roncesvalles', pois a referencia ó camiño de Santiago é demasiado directa. Semella máis ben que é unha impugnación plena da *Historia de Carlos Magno e de Roldán*, que quizais se alude de xeito disimulado e indirecto, pois a fin de contas tratábase dun texto moi autorizado, mesmo de carácter sacro, e Santiago seguía exercendo un poderoso influxo, sobre todo ideolóxico, sobre tódolos cristiáns da península.

Afonso X faría súas as afirmacións de Rodrigo de Toledo. No capítulo 623 da súa *Estoria de España* afirma:

> algunos dizen en sus cantares et en sus fablas de gesta que conquirio Carlos en Espanna muchas cipdades et muchos castiellos, et que ovo y muchas lides con moros, et que desembargo et abrio el camino desde Alemannia fasta Sanctiago. Mas en verdat esto non podria ser... Pues non veemos nin fallamos que Carlos ganase ninguna cosa en Espanna... onde mas deve omne creer a lo que semeja con guisa et con razon de que falla escriptos et recabdos, que non a las fablas de los que cuentan lo que non saben. Ca cierta cosa es que si quier de moros, si quier de cristianos, Carlos con su hueste fue vencido en Ronçasvalles, et luego se torno dende con gran danno et grant perdida de su hueste. Pues non es con guisa que el abriese el camino de Sanctiago quando non paso del puerto de Ronçasvalles; ca luengo tiempo despues del, por muchas lides et muchas faziendas et por grant trabajo, fue abierto et poblado el camino de Sanctiago; et los que dantes yvan por sendas encobiertas, pasaron despues por carrera poblada por o vienen et pasan fascas todas las tierras del mundo o cristianos a.[18]

Isto merece dúas observacións: 1ª) Afonso X ten, obviamente, razón en afirmar que Carlos Magno non fixo grandes conquistas na península; pero non é a procura da verdade histórica o que o move, vista a facilidade con que acepta e mesmo glorifica outras moitas patrañas, e concretamente a de *Mainete*, que se basea na fábula de que Carlos Magno pasou a súa mocidade en Toledo (caps. 597-99 da *Primera Crónica General*), e a de *Bernardo del Carpio*, heroe anti-francés a quen se atribúe un papel destacado, xunta a Afonso II o Casto na batalla de Roncesvales (véase cap. 619); 2ª) Aínda que admitamos que el só coñecía, como afirma, as lendas carolinxias en forma de cantares de xesta, debemos ter en conta que esta non era, con toda seguridade, a situación en Galicia, onde se debía coñecer e, probablemente asumir, a versión dos feitos que ofrecía, coa enorme autoridade dun libro litúrxico, o *Liber Sancti Jacobi*.

A oportunidade política da compilación galega das *Crónicas dos reinos de León e Castela* e a figura de don Rodrigo do Padrón

Durante a minoridade do neto de Afonso X e sucesor de Sancho IV, Fernando IV (rei 1295-1312), que durou ata 1301, viviuse unha situación política extraordinariamente confusa.[19] A lexitimidade da posición do herdeiro do trono víase contestada en varias frontes, ó mesmo tempo que só a custa de penosos esforzos e continuas concesións se mantiña a autoridade da coroa. En primeiro lugar, o neno Fernando herdou o conflicto dinástico que enfrontara ó seu pai Sancho IV cos infantes de la Cerda, fillos do primoxénito de Afonso X, Fernando, ó que unha morte prematura cortara ó acceso ó trono. A anciá viúva de Afonso X, dona Violante, apoiaba a causa do seu neto maior Alfonso de la Cerda contra o cativo Fernando. En segundo lugar, a legalidade do matrimonio dos pais de Fernando, Sancho IV e María de Molina, era contestada pola Igrexa. Para máis, os infantes Enrique e Xoán tamén presionaban para tirar proveito da coxuntura: Xoán, tío de Fernando IV, chegou mesmo a reclama-la coroa para si, aspiración na que contou co apoio do rei portugués don Denís. Despois apareceu como rexente o vello infante Enrique el Senador, irmán de Afonso X, que levara unha vida de trafego internacional, implicado na política imperial, e regresara a Castela como rexente. En vista da parálise dos poderes centrais, nos que o único apoio sólido para Fernando IV proviña da súa nai, María de Molina, poderosas casas da aristocracia castelá e a nobreza galega, ós que se aliaban circunstancialmente os reis Denís de Portugal e Xaime II de Aragón, tentaron tirar proveito da situación. Nun momento dado, chegou a establecerse un pacto que abranguía a ampla nómina de inimigos do monarca e a rexente casteláns e que preía a división dos reinos: o Reino de León, con Galicia, León, Asturias, Extremadura e Sevilla, adxudicábanse ó infante Xoán (coroado en León, 1296); Castela, Toledo e Andalucía tocáballe ó infante Alfonso de la Cerda, proclamado rei o mesmo ano en Sahagún; e Murcia a Xaime II Aragón. O infante don Xoán só renunciou á coroa de León en 1300, pero isto non significou a fin dos problemas para Fernando IV.

En Galicia, o descontentamento e as tentativas separatistas provocaron continuos abrollos de rebeldía, que despois de seren infructuosamente capitalizados polo infante Xoán, víronse capitaneados por Fernán Ruíz de Castro, Adiantado Maior de Galicia, Pertigueiro Maior da Terra de Santiago e Comendeiro de Lugo. Fernán de Castro viña sendo o sucesor, como líder político e militar da nobreza galega, dos antigos titulares do Condado de Trastámara, a extinguida familia de Traba. A tal punto subiu a contestación galega, que a raíña viúva María de Molina se viu mesmo obrigada a enviar a Galicia o seu fillo Filipe, neno de sete anos (1299). Despois de varios episodios de loita, Fernán Ruíz de Castro acabaría morrendo fronte ás tropas do infante Filipe en Monforte en 1307. Deste xeito, a maioría dos títulos do finado e os seus dominios patrimoniais ían pasar a mans do infante don Filipe, que acabou convertido nunha especie de vice-rei de Galicia.[20]

No clima de desafección da nobreza galega fronte á coroa castelá e de grave crise da sede xacobea, en contraste con Fernán de Castro, apareceu na época un personaxe clave na defensa dos intereses do contestado Fernando IV na Galicia da época: o arcebispo don Rodrigo do Padrón. Imonos deter neste persoeiro, que, como se verá, nos interesa moi especificamente.[21] Este arcebispo sentouse na cadeira de Compostela despois dunha longa crise, que arrincaba dos tempos de Afonso X, cando á morte do arcebispo Xoán Arias (1266) o Cabido de Santiago se dividira en dous bandos irreconciliables: un deles apoiaba ó candidato favorito do monarca, Fernando Afonso, e o outro ó arcediago Bernaldo, capelán do Papa. Ningún dos dous foi confirmado canonicamente en Roma, de xeito que se produciu unha situación de vacancia que durou ata 1272, situación que foi aproveitada por Afonso X para impoñe-la súa autoridade, e polo Concello da cidade para arreporse na súa vella retesía coa mitra compostelá. Nestas circunstancias, c. 1273, Roma decidiuse a nomear arcebispo de Santiago ó cóengo Gonzalo Gómez, pero os burgueses composteláns, alentados por un Afonso X doente contra o papa (lembremos que nesta época o Papa rexeitara a súa candidatura ó Imperio), negáronse a recoñecelo por señor. Afonso X humillouno, quixo privalo de diversas facultades e dereitos, e apoiou as reivindicacións dos burgueses. O papa Nicolau III dirixiulle unha severa censura desde Roma (1278), pero Afonso despoxou o arcebispo do señorío, apropiouse dos cargos e castelos da mitra e non cesou nas súas tentativas de destituílo da sede arcebispal, solicitando a súa deposición ó papa Martiño IV e colocando como administrador da diócese o abade de Valladolid. No entanto, Gonzalo Gómez tiña que refuxiarse en Francia ou quizabes en Roma.

Cando Sancho IV se rebelou contra o seu pai (1282), o abade de Valladolid fuxiu para Sevilla, onda Afonso. Sancho IV mandou restituírlle á Igrexa de Santiago tódolos señoríos, castelos e lugares, e revocou as cartas que o seu pai promulgara en favor dos cidadáns de Santiago a custa da igrexa. Pero Gómez González continuou ausente da cidade de Compostela (na que a maioría do Cabido, favorable a Afonso X, se exiliara a Portugal ou se refuxiara en Sevilla), á que nunca voltaría. A situación en Compostela era moi grave, como mostran os acordos secretos do cabido de 1285, nos que se garantía esteo e mantenza para os cóengos que se visen forzados a abandonar o reino. Cando Sancho IV visitou Galicia en peregrinación a Santiago (1286), había cincuenta anos que ningún monarca viñera ó país (xa que Afonso X non trepara a cidade xacobea). Por fin aparece como arcebispo electo de Santiago o Provincial dos Dominicos en España, Frei Rodrigo González de León (1286-1304), designado polo Papa e persoa do agrado de Sancho IV, que o favoreceu moderadamente, aínda sen lle devolver o señorío da cidade. O novo arcebispo tentou coutar a dexeneración de costumes en que caera o xa de seu relaxado clero compostelán durante o longo e turbulento período que a igrexa compostelana acababa de atravesar, pero despois da morte de Sancho IV (1295), estala a tormenta da sucesión. Parece que o arcebispo apoiou a María de Molina e Fernando IV, o cal lle debeu de custar graves disgustos, dado que o Fernán Ruíz de Castro encabezaba a rebeldía en Galicia contra eles. As loitas que sen dúbida se produciron arredor da catedral provocaron que esta fora declarada en interdicto (1303).

É lóxico supoñer que o arcebispo que se fixo cargo da cadeira xacobea neste momento crítico, Rodrigo do Padrón, fose galego. Semella probable que fixera carreira en Boloña, de onde volvería para formar parte do cabido compostelán como arcediago do Salnés. En Roma, participou nas negociacións destinadas a lexitima-los matrimonios de María de Molina co finado Sancho IV e de Fernando IV con Constanza de Portugal. En 1307, aparece xa consagrado como arcebispo de Santiago, onde permaneceu ata o outono de 1309.²² En xullo do mesmo ano de 1309, Rodrigo acudiulle ó rei ó sitio de Algeciras, onde debeu de permanecer ata primeiros de 1310, nunha campaña combinada con Xaime II de Aragón, que no entanto sitiaba Almería. A asistencia do arcebispo compostelán foi un importante alivio para o monarca, e en premio por isto, Fernando IV restituíulle a Chancelería do Reino de León e a Capelanía da súa casa. En 1310, Rodrigo de Padrón presidiu a xuntanza da liga do clero do reino de León en Toro, á que se sumaron aínda máis prelados noutra reunión celebrada o mesmo ano en Salamanca, e presidida tamén por el. En xullo de 1311, presidiu unha xunta dos prelados de León, Castela e Galicia (na que estaba presente o arcebispo de Braga), na que se decidiu reforza-la liga para defendérense contra as presións dos nobres laicos e os burgueses. Finalmente, empregando a fondo o seu ascendente na corte, o arcebispo recuperaría o señorío da cidade e Terra de Santiago en 1311.

En 1311, Rodrigo participou con María de Molina nunha delicada misión de mediación entre o monarca e un grupo de nobres rebeldes liderados polo infante don Juan Manuel, pai do célebre prócer e escritor castelán don Juan Manuel. Resulta que este último consignou unha anécdota das conversas daquel encontro, presentándoa como recollida dos beizos do seu pai. Hai un anaco deste relato que nos interesa especialmente por razóns que logo se exporán, así que o imos reproducir:

> Acaeció que un día [mi padre] ... díxome que avía un arçobispo en Santiago quel dixieran don Roy Padrón, que era mucho su amigo ... [e] porque el arçobispo avía ante conbidado a don Johan ... fue comer con él. Et desque ovieron comido fincaron amos en la cámara apartados, departiendo muchas cosas; ca el arçobispo era muy buen omne et de muy buen entendimiento et de buena palabra. Et en manera de departimiento et de plazer, assí como amigos que ellos eran, començógelo dezir en su lenguage gallego por esta manera:
>
> --Don Johan, mío sennor e mío amigo, vien vos dezimos en verdat que nós beyemos muchas estorias et muchas corónicas, et sienpre fallamos en ellas que los fijos de los infantes fuera muy bien si fueran mejores. Et nunca fallamos que fueron muy buenos. Et aun los fijos de los infantes que agora son en Castiella, parésçenos que si maravilla non fuere non querrán fazer mintrosas las scripturas. Et plazernos ía mucho que vós,

que sodes mucho nuestro amigo, que vos trabajedes que non
fuessen en vos verdaderas...[23]

Don Rodrigo tiña tal intimidade na corte real que, cando en agosto de
1311 se produciu o nacemento do infante Afonso (o futuro Afonso XI), foi o
encargado de bautizar o neno, como Capelán maior da casa real. Pouco
despois da morte de Fernando IV, que soprendeu o noso prelado no concilio
xeral de Viena (1312), xa estaba outra vez mergullado na axitada política dos
reinos, e no mes de decembro, atopámolo enviando unha carta desde Toro ó
arcebispo de Toledo don Gutierre, da que conservamos copia, e que,
sorprendentemente, está escrita en galego.[24] En xullo de 1314, achámolo en
Valladolid, presidindo unha xunta do clero de tódolos reinos: nas actas desta
xunta figura antes cós arcebispos de Toledo e Sevilla. Pouco despois asistiu ás
cortes de Palazuelos e actuou como voceiro nas cortes de Burgos (1315). A
morte chegáballe en 1316, despois de que conseguira remonta-la terrible crise
en que a súa diócese estivera mergullada por máis de corenta anos. O Cabido
catedralicio gardou lembranza do ilustre finado, como mostra un documento,
de xaneiro de 1316, no que se establecen festas na súa honra, 'para que os
seus vindeiros sucesores alcancen os seus méritos seguindo o seu exemplo
erudito', como se di na súa gabanza.[25]

Un conflicto de lealdades: a versión galega da *Crónica General de España*

Demoramos un treito un pouco longo na traxectoria de Rodrigo de Padrón
fundamentalmente por mor de mostrar ata que punto é verosímil a atribución
a el da responsabilidade da compilación da *Crónica Galega de León e Castela*.
Que a traducción da *Crónica de León* se realizou para completar unha
Crónica de Castela compilada anteriormente, parece deducción lóxica do
estado actual do texto. Que a compilación galega da *Crónica de Castela* non é
moi anterior á traducción da de León parece evidente, pois sabemos que a
serie das Crónicas de Castela comezou a elaborarse despois do reinado de
Afonso X. O grao de elaboración da compilación galega mostra o proceso
nun estadio medio de desenvolvemento. Descartando o reinado de
Sancho IV como momento axeitado para que a realización desta compilación
galega, pois parece momento lixeiramente temperá, ademais de

culturalmente pouco propicio, volvemos a situarnos no reinado de Fernando IV (1295-1312). Esta é, de feito, a datación que adianta con bos argumentos Ramón Lorenzo, o editor mais recente da obra. Recoñecendo de plano a carencia de datos positivos que permitan adxudicarlle indubitablemente a responsabilidade da compilación a Rodrigo de Padrón, semella difícil negarlle ó arcebispo compostelán e chanceler real as cualidades necesarias e os medios imprescindibles para levar adiante unha tarefa tan laboriosa e custosa para a época. A oportunidade para emprender tal empresa non faltaba: despois dunha época crítica en que Galicia mostrara fortes veleidades separatistas fronte un rei castelán que a duras penas conseguira a lexitimación interior e exterior, era ben preciso realizar unha obra de propaganda unitarista e monárquica, como efectivamente pode ser lida a *Crónica Galega de León e Castela*. Á vista disto, e tamén coas reservas que quedan explicitadas, atrevémonos a propór a Rodrigo de Padrón, como arcebispo de Compostela e Chanceler do Reino de León, como patrocinador e editor desta obra, que, polo tanto, se debeu de realizar aproximadamente entre 1308 e 1312.

Quizais isto nos axude a comprender por que os traductores galegos da 'Crónica de León' contida na *Crónica General de España* preferiron comeza-lo seu labor polo capítulo 628, nos comezos do reinado de Ramiro I, ignorando toda a sección adicada a Afonso II, onde entre outras cousas figuraban as tremendas palabras de Afonso X no cap. 623 que reproducimos anteriormente. Se non se acepta esta explicación, débese buscar outra alternativa para aclarar convincentemente un feito tan rechamante como o de que a traducción galega da *Crónica General de España* comece xustamente despois do reinado de Afonso II. Dous datos máis avalan a nosa teoría: a portuguesa *Crónica Geral de Espanha* de 1344 tampouco recolle as graves afirmacións de Afonso X e, o que é aínda máis abraiante e coido que definitivo, a Crónica galega de 1404, que comeza polo principio da *Crónica General de España*, ó chegar ó reinado de Afonso II interpola unha curiosa xeografía universal e salta os capítulos referentes a este importantísimo rei, pasando ó seu inmediato sucesor, Ramiro I, xustamente por onde comeza a traducción galega que mencionamos máis arriba. Polo tanto, dixese o que dixese a historiografía oficial castelá, que en xeral se aceptaba con poucos matices na Galicia dos séculos XIV e XV, a *Historia de Carlos Magno e de*

Roldán debía ser admitida en Compostela (o que vale dicir por parte da intelectualidade galega do momento) como a versión verdadeira de historia da invención da tumba apóstólica.

A tradición que relaciona Carlos Magno con Santiago, que debeu de ser moi cara a Compostela e ó seu clero, seguiu escocendo durante algún tempo ós historiadores da monarquía castelá. Aínda no século XVI, o coñecido Ambrosio de Morales, cronista de Filipe II, na relación que depuxo da súa inspección polas igrexas do noroeste peninsular realizada en 1572, escribe, referíndose á minguada biblioteca da catedral compostelá: 'El otro libro que tienen está entero, y fuera harto mejor que no lo estuviera: es el libro de los Milagros del Apóstol Santiago, que dicen escribió el Papa Calisto II ... Quien quiera que fue el Autor, puso alli cosas tan deshonestas y feas, que valiera harto mas no haberlo escrito. Ya lo dige alli al Arzobispo Valdotano, que haya gloria, y à los canonigos, para que no tuviesen alli aquello'.[26] Efectivamente, seica a mutilación do *Códice Calixtino* da catedral de Compostela (do que se arrincou a *Historia de Carlos Magno e de Roldán*), se debe ás recomendacións do cronista español. Por fortuna, os clérigos compostelás non mostraron moito celo en seguir as recomendacións de Ambrosio de Morales, e conservaron á parte o texto do *Pseudo-Turpín*. Agora sabemos que se trataba de cercernar unha parte importante e interesantísima da nosa tradición cultural.

NOTAS

1. La *traducción gallega de la Crónica General y de la Crónica de Castilla*, ed. de Ramón Lorenzo, 2 vols (Ourense: Instituto 'Padre Feijoo', 1975). Dado que o texto medieval non está titulado, decidinme a denominar o texto *Crónica Galega dos Reinos de León e Castela*, que coido que reflexa ben o seu contido.

2. No prólogo da *Crónica General de España* afírmase explicitamente: 'Et esto fiziemos por que fuesse sabudo el comienço de los espannoles, et de quales yentes fue Espanna maltrecha ... et por mostrar la nobleza de los godos et como fueron viviendo de tierra en tierra, venciendo muchas batallas et conquiriendo muchas tierras, fasta que llegaron a Espanna, et echaron ende a todas las otras yentes, et fueron ellos sennores della; et como por el desacuerdo que ovieron los godos con so sennor el rey Rodrigo et por la traycíon que urdio el conde don Yllan et el arçobispo Oppa, passaron los dAffrica et ganaron todo lo mas dEspanna; et como fueron los cristianos despues cobrando la tierra; et del danno que vino en ella por partir los regnos, por que se non pudo cobrar tan ayna: et, despues como la ayunto Dios, et por quales maneras et en qual tiempo, et quales reyes ganaron la tierra fasta en el mar Mediterraneo' (véase *Primera Crónica General de España*, ed. de Ramón Menéndez Pidal, 2 vols (Madrid, 1977), I, 4).

3. A edición máis citada do texto latino desta obra é a de Meredith Jones, *Historia Caroli Magni et Rotholandi ou Chronique du Pseudo-Turpin* (Paris, 1936; reimpr. 1972).

4. O *Liber Sancti Jacobi*, que foi coleccionándose probablemente no segundo tercio do século XII (quizabes a súa redacción final date de c. 1160) e recibiu ampla difusión a través do Camiño de Santiago, contén nas súas versións completas, coma a que conservamos no *Codex Calixtinus* que se custodia na Catedral de Santiago, cinco libros: o Iº está adicado á liturxia e ó culto específicos do apóstolo Santiago Zebedeu ou o Maior (lecturas, homilias, misal das festas xacobeas); o IIº, denominado 'Liber Miraculis' ('Libro dos Miragres'), narra vintedous milagres atribuídos á intercesión do devandito apóstolo; o IIIº, a paixón deste e a traslación do seu corpo a Compostela; o IVº recolle a 'Historia de Carlos Magno e de Roldán', atribuída á pluma do bispo franco Turpín (por iso é coñecido como 'Pseudo-Turpín'); finalmente, o Vº libro coñécese como 'Guía de peregrinos', é unha especie de itinerario turístico-relixioso que ensinaba os principais atractivos do camiño de Santiago ou Camiño Francés e da propia cidade de Santiago de Compostela. Véase sobre o *Liber Sancti Jacobi* e o *Códice Calixtino* a recente obra de M. Díaz y Díaz, *El Códice Calixtino de la Catedral de Santiago. Estudio codicológico y de contenido* (Santiago de Compostela, 1988).

5. Primeiro, Afonso VI quixo deixar como herdeiro o seu fillo Sancho, habido da moura toledana Zaida c. 1090, máis tarde do probable pacto sucesorio con Raimundo de Borgoña. O Conde de Galicia Raimundo morreu en 1107, pero en 1105 tivera un fillo de Urraca, o infante Afonso Raimúndez, que representaba un serio contrincante para Sancho. Aínda que o príncipe Sancho faleceu a mans almorávides moi pouco despois da morte de Raimundo, isto non aliviou os temores do partido pro-borgoñón, capitaneado polo arcebispo compostelán Diego Xelmírez (que apoiaba ó neno Afonso Raimúndez). O colmo da impaciencia para este partido viuse rebordado cando o vello Afonso VI, antes de morrer (1109), arranxou a voda da súa filla viúva Urraca co rei de Aragón, Afonso o Batallador, coa evidente intención de deixar a este como herdeiro de todos ou o mellor do seus dominios. Felizmente para Afonso Raimúndez e os seus partidarios, o matrimonio entre a nai daquel e o rei aragonés foi un fracaso, e non produciu ningún fillo.

6. Citado por M. Defourneaux, *Les françaises en Espagne aux XIe et XIIe siècles* (Paris, 1949), p.203.

7. Explicitado con meridiana claridade na *Historia de Carlos Magno e de Roldán*, cap. XIX, que afirma (seguimos o texto galego do s. XV): 'Carlos ... por consello dos bispos d'España e dos princepes que i eran, por amor de Santiago, estabeleceu que tódolos rex e príncipes d'España e de Galiza, atán ben os que entón eran como os que havían de viîr, obedecesen ao bispo de Santiago. E en Padrón non quis fazer bispo, que a non contavan por vila, e mandou que fose sojeita aa igleja de Santiago... E sujugou o emperador aa igleja de Santiago toda a terra d'España e de Galiza, e mandou que lle desen cada âno de quantos i houvese para sempre quatro diñeiros e que fosen por ende quitos de toda serviduê. E estabelesceu en aquel día que d'aí en deante a igleja de Santiago fose chamada apostolical porque *i* jaz o corpo do Apóstolo, e tódolos bispos d'España fezesen i concello moito ameúde, e que tódolos reis d'España recebesen as coroas dos reinos da mâo do bispo d'i, e tódolos bispos d'España trouxesen os bágoos... Tres iglejas apostolicaes e principaes ontre tódalas outras son êno mundo que os cristiaâos acustuman a honrar, porlos merecementos dos santos que en elas son, mais que tódalas outras: a igleja de Roma e a de Santiago e a de San Johán en Efeso' (*Miragres de Santiago*, ed. de J. L. Pensado Tomé (Madrid, 1958), pp.128 e ss).

8. No texto latino reza 'sed hic Karolus magnus totam Yspaniam sui temporibus sibi subiugavit' (a cita está tirada do texto do *Historia Caroli Magni et Rotholandi* tal como está editado por Meredith Jones, p.101).

9. A relación xenealóxica está suxerida explicitamente pola *Chronica Adefonsis Imperatoris* (*Crónica do Emperador Afonso [VII]*, c. 1150), ó calificar a Afonso VII como 'facta sequens Caroli' ('digno sucesor de Carlos Magno'). A tese do carácter pro-borgoñón da obra está amplamente defendida por M. de Menaca, *Histoire de Saint Jacques et des ses miracles au moyen-âge* (Nantes, 1987), esp. pp.191-99. Con todo, non parece sostible unha interpretación tan estrictamente unilateral como a proposta por esta autora.

10. Isto é o que afirma J. Bédier, *Les légendes épiques*, 4 vols (Paris, 1929^3), III, 140-52; 'le personnage principal n'est ni Charlemagne, ni Anseïs, ni la belle Gaudisse, c'est le chemin de Saint Jacques' (p.145). No poema lemos: '...Nostre emperere s'est a la voie mis, / cevaucant va li rois par le païs / el fait refaire mostiers et edefis... / Droit a Saint Jaque est Karles revertis, / l'offrande fait, au saint congié a pris' (Bédier, p.150).

11. 'Venus est a Saint Jake, il et sa baronie; / faite i a s' orison, s'offrande a establie...' (Bédier, p.140).

12. Esta epopea é, na opinión de J. Bédier, 'un poema en honor de Carlos Magno, pero tamén de Santiago. Se o emperador tenta conquerer España, é porque lle prometeu ó apóstolo liberta-la súa tumba e franquea-lo camiño que conduce a ela, 'la stree / qui as bons peregrins stoit tolue et vehee'. E os baróns franceses lembran a feito esta promesa, en todo momento e á menor oportunidade: 'venus somes conquerre Aragon et Castelle / et dou baron saint Jacques eslargis la sentelle'. O rimador explota a *Historia de Carlos Magno e de Roldán*, como el mesmo afirma moitas veces. O arcebispo 'Trepin, nostre doctor', como lle chama el, é a súa principal autoridade' (*Les légendes épiques*, pp.117-18).

13. É ben coñecido o comezo da *Chanson de Roland*: 'Carles li reis, nostre empereire magnes / Set ans tuz pleins ad estet en Espaigne / Tresqu'en la mer cunquist la tere altaigne' (vv. 1-3). Na *Prise de Pampelune*, traducindo as palabras de J. Bédier, 'como na *Entree en Espagne*, Carlos Magno combate para maior gloria de Santiago... trátase de 'conquir le zamin dou saint

galicien' --así se expresan os nosos cabaleiros na súa xerga italiana-- queren 'franchir le seint apostre, recobrer sa glise,..'. queren 'tournier en franchise / le zamin et la voie dou buen saint de Galise' (*Les légendes épiques*, p.122).

14. Editado por R. Menéndez Pidal, *Textos medievales españoles. Ediciones críticas y estudios* (Madrid, 1976), p.19. Máis adiante 'nuestro juglar, que acepta sin el menor reparo las conquistas de Carlos en España, contadas por la epopeya francesa ... es, con toda probabilidad uno de los juglares contradichos por el Toledano en 1243, y por la *Primera Crónica General* en 1289' (Menéndez Pidal, pp.55-56). Nótese ben que segundo o autor, 'en suma, el *Roncesvalles* español no debió tener presente el *Turpín*, sino todo lo más las mismas leyendas que inspiraron al *Turpín*, o bien otras análogas' (Menéndez Pidal, p.87).

15. Do poema de *Fernán González*, c. 1250, citado por R. Menéndez Pidal, *Textos medievales españoles. Ediciones críticas y estudios* (Madrid, 1976), p.53. Os cinco anos fan referencia ó tempo que lle levaría a Carlos Magno conquistar España, segundo unha versión descoñecida da lenda.

16. Véase Lucas de Tui, *Crónica de España*, ed. de Julio Púyol (Madrid, 1926), p.288.

17. De Menaca, *Histoire de Saint Jacques*, pp.85 e 86.

18. *Primera Crónica General de España*, ed. de R. Menéndez Pidal (Madrid, 1977), II, 356.

19. Unha narración destes acontecementos pode atoparse en Luis Suárez Fernández, *Historia de España. Edad Media* (Madrid, 1970), pp.319-56.

20. Estes títulos disputaríanllos Alfonso de la Cerda (que recibiu as terras de Lemos) e sobre todo o seu tío o infante don Xoán. Don Filipe, a fin de contas, quedou como Comendeiro de Lugo e cos señoríos de Cabrera y Ribera en León e mais cun fiel partidario seu, Afonso Suárez de Deza, como Adiantado Maior do Reino. A loita entre os dous infantes en Galicia aínda se prolongaría uns anos máis, e no transcurso dela Filipe recobraría o cargo de Pertigueiro de Santiago, situándose como magnate principal de Galicia. Para 1320, o infante era o vice-rei *de facto* de Galicia.

21. O traballo máis importante sobre Rodrigo de Padrón segue a ser o de Antonio López Ferreiro, *Historia de la S. A. M. Iglesia de Santiago* (Santiago de Compostela, 1902), V, cap. IX, 279-346.

22. Este ano presidiu o sínodo compostelán na mesma cidade, no que se tomaron acordos para a reforma do clero. Das actas deste sínodo interésanos desataca-la constitución xlvii: 'establecemos que tódolos arciprestes teñan copia destas constitucións en romance...' ('statuimus quod omnes archipresbiteri habeant copiam istarum constitutionum in romancio et publicent clericis in calendariis suis', *Synodicum Hispanum*, I, p.290). Isto expresa unha preocupación enteiramente nova, que ben pode considerarse un signo dos tempos: as constitucións debían traducirse ó romance para que as entendesen os interesados.

23. Don Juan Manuel, *Libro de los Estados*, ed. de R. B. Tate and I. R. Macpherson (Oxford, 1974), cap. lxxxv, pp.170-71.

24. A carta é moi notable, dunha banda pola elegancia do seu estilo e doutra banda, porque mostra patentemente a inclinación do arcebispo polo cultivo da lingua galega. Véase A. López Ferreiro, *Historia de la S.A.M.I. de Santiago*, V, 302-03.

25. Iterum etiam ab Iltmo. bone memorie dno. Fernando rege Legionis et Castelle cuius anima requiestcat in pace officium cancelarie regni legionensis, in cuius possesione raro eius antecessore extiterat, et quod officium idem dns. Archiepiscopus nunc tenet et possidet et per officiales suos exercet prospere extitit assecutus, a quo etiam dno. Rege suis meritis exigentibus in maiorem capellanum cum honore nimio est assumptus... et ut eius futuri successores simili exemplo eruditi ad simila perducantur... (A. López Ferreiro, *Historia de la S.A.M.I. de Santiago*, apéndices, núm. LIX, pp.167-71 (pp.168, 169)).

26. *Viage de Ambrosio de Morales por orden del Rey D. Phelipe II a los Reinos de León, y Galicia, y Principado de Asturias*, ed. de Antonio Marín (Madrid, 1765), pp.130-31. Cito pola edición facsímil da Biblioteca Popular Asturiana (Oviedo, 1977).

MARCAS DE ORALIDAD EN LA SINTAXIS NARRATIVA DEL *POEMA DE MIO CID*

GERMÁN ORDUNA
Universidad de Buenos Aires

A Derek, en Birmingham, en enero de 1980

El estudio de la épica primitiva desde la perspectiva de la oralidad[1] ha constituido, desde mediados del s. XX,[2] una renovación en la metodología aplicada al campo tan vasto y todavía enigmático de un género narrativo nacido en épocas anteriores al registro de la escritura.[3]

La épica románica y particularmente la castellana tienen ya una amplia bibliografía crítica que indaga las marcas de oralidad en los testimonios de cantares puestos por escrito durante los siglos XI y XII, y conservados en códices uno o dos siglos posteriores a su primer registro.[4]

La distancia temporal que media entre los testimonios hoy conservados de la épica primitiva y la fecha posible de su primera puesta por escrito implica una tradición manuscrita que puede haber afectado diversamente el texto primero. Pero esas variantes posibles, que pueden llegar a la refundición o reelaboración no son, a nuestro propósito, tan importantes como las que puedan haberse dado en el proceso de la 'puesta por escrito' de un poema oral.[5]

El paso de la historia cantada al texto escrito implica un cambio en el código de comunicación que afecta esencialmente su entidad o factura artística.

Hoy no podemos conocer cabalmente los cambios producidos en casos concretos como es el del *Poema de Mio Cid* (versión del códice de Vivar). Tenemos evidencias de la existencia de una tradición manuscrita del texto (siglos XIII-XIV) así como de la existencia de una versión cantada sobre las hazañas del héroe (s. XII). Puede postularse con fuertes posibilidades de certeza que hubo una versión puramente oral de la historia narrada en nuestro *Poema de Mio Cid*, de la que probablemente perduren versos o recursos propios de su forma oral;[6] con más seguridad podemos aseverar que la versión escrita hoy conocida utiliza conscientemente recursos mnemotécnicos de la repetición oral como fórmulas eficaces en la organización de la sintaxis narrativa. Estos procedimientos estaban además afianzados por la etapa cultural en que vivía el anónimo autor que dio al *PMCid* la forma hoy conocida: él mismo vivía en un lapso en que coexistían grupos de cultura totalmente oral con individuos y grupos iniciados en la cultura escrita y literaria.[7] Los recursos de elaboración del discurso épico propios de la oralidad pura eran un hecho vivo en un medio histórico-cultural en el que el anónimo autor de la 'puesta por escrito' estaba inmerso. Las psicodinámicas de la oralidad no eran, como para nosotros, elementos de análisis crítico o meros recursos de composición, sino hábitos normales de la creación y emisión de un discurso narrativo destinado a un público no letrado.

La crítica ha estudiado y catalogado estos recursos mnemotécnicos en los poemas hoy conocidos, con el título general de 'fórmulas épicas' o 'fórmulas orales', lo que a veces ha llevado a la deformación de su verdadera funcionalidad al tratarlos como elementos de un análisis químico o matemático, a lo que contribuyó el uso de porcentajes. Esas estadísticas son útiles y contribuyen a dar apariencia de objetividad 'científica' a nuestros estudios; pero pueden llevarnos a despojar al estudio de la épica de su dimensión esencial de acto de comunicación participativa, que se concreta en un signo lingüístico que es el poema. A través del poema nosotros tenemos hoy una vía de acceso para actualizarlo en su vital relación intersubjetiva. Ya Lord señaló en su momento que la fórmula en sí no es lo que importa sino su interacción dinámica en los esquemas repetidos: la fórmula en su función constructora del acto de comunicación.[8]

Con estas líneas básicas de pensamiento queremos ahora mostrar cómo el encadenamiento y la repetición variada son procedimientos utilizados para la estructuración narrativa del *PMCid*. Esos recursos están vinculados al nivel semántico del relato, es decir a la constitución del tema como fórmula dotada de su propio dinamismo vital en la narración. Nuestro análisis mostrará esas fórmulas-tema como entidades no estáticas, sino vitales, cambiantes, adaptables a la creación artística del discurso narrativo.[9]

Menéndez Pidal y Edmund de Chasca han estudiado la función de las series gemelas y encadenadas en el episodio de la Afrenta de Corpes (tir. 128-

129-130), donde la situación dramática que viven las hijas del Cid y su desvalimiento ante la crueldad de los infantes de Carrión contribuyen a teñir de lirismo la iteración y encadenamiento de hemistiquios.[10]

También Menéndez Pidal anota la serie gemela en las tiradas 50-51, en las que se presenta el regocijo con que reciben a Minaya Alvar Fañez.[11] El tópico se anuncia al terminar la tir. 49 y se desarrolla en tir. 50 y 51. Son series gemelas que reiteran el mismo tópico, primero en la campaña del Cid y luego en el Cid mismo. La situación narrativa se manifiesta organizada por la repetición de la misma estructura exclamativa:

>¡Dios commo fue alegre...! (v. 926)[12]
>¡Dios commo es alegre...! (v. 930)
>¡Dios commo fue el Çid pagado! (v. 933)

Las dos primeras fórmulas inician tirada; la tercera es hemistiquio inicial del penúltimo verso de la tirada 51, que se cierra con la reiteración conceptual en estilo directo del v. 925, que termina la tirada 49:

>mientra uos visquieredes, bien me yra a mi, Minaya (v. 925)
>¡Ya Alvar Fañez, biuades muchos dias! (v. 934)

Los versos 925 y 934 enmarcan iterativamente el tópico narrativo y, aunque no podrían clasificarse como 'formulísticos', lo son en su funcionalidad textual de estructuración de la sintaxis narrativa de este tópico. Notemos que el encadenamiento se muestra aquí con una estructura más rica y trabada que la de una mera repetición formulística.

Hemos relevado este procedimiento en otros lugares del *PMCid* y comprobamos su variedad y la complejidad de estructuras logradas.

A. *Encadenamiento por repetición o variación por paralelismo sintáctico o semántico*

1. *Entre verso final e inicial de la tirada siguiente*
1.1. El encadenamiento entre tir. 19 y 20:

>[...] *la cara se santigo/Sinaua la cara* [...] (vv. 410-11)

1.2. El encadenamiento entre tir. 22 y 23:

mio Çid *se echo en çelada* [...] / Toda la noche *yaze en çelada* [...] (vv. 436-37)

1.3. Un nuevo caso de encadenamiento conceptual por paralelismo aparece entre el hemistiquio final de tir. 33 y el inicial de la tir. 34:

[...] complidas tres semanas

[34]

Acabo de tres sedmanas [...] (vv. 664-65)

1.4. Encadenamiento entre primer hemistiquio del verso final de tirada y el segundo hemistiquio del verso inicial de la tirada siguiente:

çercar quiere a Valençia pora christianos la dar.

[73]

quien quiere yr comigo *çercar a Valençia* (vv. 1191-92)

Menéndez Pidal señala a 72-73 como series gemelas; es de notar que v. 1191 pertenece a la transposición en estilo directo de la exhortación, convocatoria del Cid y v. 1192 integra el discurso directo del Cid.

2. *Encadenamiento entre verso interior e inicial de la tirada siguiente.*
2.1. Penúltimo verso e inicial de la tirada siguiente:

Fueron los mandados a todas partes
que el salido de Castiella asi los trae tan mal.

[55]

Los mandados son ydos a todas partes (vv. 954-56)

2.2. Antepenúltimo verso e inicial de la tirada siguiente:

Vençido a esta batalla el que en buen [ora] nasco;
al conde don Remont a preson le an tomado;

La sintaxis narrativa del *Poema de Mio Cid* 61

hy *gaño a Colada* que mas vale de mill marcos [de plata].

[59]

Y bençio esta batalla por o ondro su barba (vv. 1008-11)

Excurso: El logro de Colada nos recuerda el hecho similar ocurrido posteriormente con la ganancia de Tizón:

Mato a Bucar, al rrey de alen mar,
e *gano a Tizon* que *mill marcos doro val,*
vençio la batalla maravillosa e grant
aquis *ondro myo Çid* e quantos con el son (vv. 2425-28)

El poeta repite los tópicos formulísticos de la 'ganancia', pero no los incluye en una fórmula estructuradora de la sintaxis del relato como ocurre en 2.2.
2.3. Encadenamiento de hemistiquio final con segundo hemistiquio del segundo verso de la tirada siguiente:

A myo Çid, el que en buen ora nasco,
dentro a Valençia *lieuan le el mandado*

[85]

Alegre fue myo Çid que nunqua mas nin tanto,
ca de lo que mas amaua *yal viene el mandado* (vv. 1560-63)

2.4. Encadenamiento del verso ante-antepenúltimo de una tirada con el inicial de la siguiente.

El encadenamiento se logra con la repetición de una fórmula inicial de discurso, que encabeza las dos partes de una misma arenga cuando cambia el tema a tratar:

sobresto todo a uos quito Minaya (v. 886)

Sobre aquesto todo, dezir uos quiero Minaya (v. 890)

B. *Encadenamiento múltiple como estructura formulística*

3.1. La estructura de iteración lograda en tir. 26-27 y 28-29 es más compleja porque se extiende y profundiza a nivel semántico con la repetición del nombre de Alcocer, al que acompañan otras marcas de repetición:

> e *sobre Alcoçer* myo Çid *yva posar,*
> en vn *otero* redondo, fuerte e grand
> açerca corre Salon, *agua* nol puedent vedar
> mio Çid don Rodrigo *Alcoçer* cueda ganar.

[27]

> Bien puebla el *otero,* firme *prende las posadas,*
> los vnos contra la sierra e los otros contra la *agua;*
> el buen Campeador, que en buen ora nasco,
> derredor del *otero,* bien çerca del *agua* (vv. 553-61)

> el *castiello de Alcoçer en paria ua entrando* (v. 569)

[29]

> *Los de Alcoçer a myo Çid yal dan parias* de grado (v. 570)

> quando vio *myo Çid que Alcoçer non se le daua* (v. 574)

> *myo Çid gaño a Alcoçer,* sabent por esta maña (v. 610)

Vemos como el nombre de *Alcoçer,* que encadena (junto con *posar, otero, agua*) las tir. 26-27-28-29, se reitera dentro de la tir. 29: en el primer verso (570), en el quinto (574) y en el último de la extensa tirada (610), para reaparecer en el primer verso de la tir. 32 (623) y en el último (655):

> myo Çid con esta ganançia *en Alcoçer esta* (v. 623)

> el bueno de myo Çid *en Alcoçer le uan çercar* (v. 655)

El procedimiento estructurador implica una repetición acumulativa y progresiva que está al servicio de la sintaxis narrativa de la secuencia del relato de la toma de Alcocer.

3.2. El encadenamiento por paralelismo semántico entre versos de distintas asonancias es, a veces, una de las marcas de una estructura de encadenamiento más compleja y trabada que se extiende por varias tiradas y es portadora del mensaje propio del episodio que se relata. Precisamente la repetición de tópicos y el paralelismo semántico actúan como ecos del concepto central. Los versos que integran las asonancias 65 a 75 (vv. 1094-1221) relatan los avances de la conquista que terminará con la toma de Valencia:

dentro en Valençia non es poco el miedo.

[66]

Pesa *a los de Valençia*, sabet, non les plaze (vv. 1097-98)

fata Valençia duro el segudar (v. 1148)

non es con rrecabdo *el dolor de Valençia* (v. 1166)

mal se aquexan *los de Valençia* que non sabent ques far (v. 1174)

çercar quiere a Valençia pora christianos la dar

[73]

quien *quiere* yr comigo *çercar a Valençia* (vv. 1191-92)

adeliño pora Valençia e sobrellos' va echar (v. 1203)

quando *myo Çid gaño a Valençia* e entro en la çibdad (v. 1212)

El eco del nombre de *Valençia* perdura hasta que el Cid entre en ella (tir. 74) y la larga secuencia narrativa se cierra con el tópico del gozo por las ganancias y el botín (vv. 1211-21) y el encadenamiento del final de tir. 74 con el primer verso de tir. 75 sobre el tópico del 'gozo' y la distensión por la victoria:

Alegre era el Campeador con todos los que ha
quando su seña cabdal sedie en somo del alcaçar

[75]

Ya *folgaua myo Çid con todas* sus compañas (vv. 1219-21)

El verso siguiente (v. 1222) ya introduce el episodio del rey de Sevilla; la secuencia narrativa que llevó a la toma de Valencia ha concluido; no obstante, tiene interés a nuestro propósito, volver sobre ella para buscar las marcas mnemotécnicas que estructuran la secuencia.

Hemos señalado las apoyaturas temáticamente básicas sobre el nombre de *Valencia* reiterado en sintagmas con verbos o preposiciones que indican la distancia o la aproximación paulatina hasta llegar a la posesión. Pero la estructura de la secuencia 'conquista de Valencia' está integrada por submotivos secuenciales que contribuyen al avance del relato:

a. 'Dios guia y ayuda el obrar de Mio Cid':

Myo Çid *gaño* a Xerica e a Onda el Almenar (v. 1092)
tierras de Borriana *todas conquistas las ha*.

[65]

Aiudol el Criador, el Señor que es en çielo:
el con todo esto, *priso a* Muruiedro.
*Ya vie myo Çid que Dios le yua valiendo,
dentro en Valençia non es poco el miedo.*

[66]

Pesa a los de Valençia, sabet, non les plaze (v. 1098)

Violo myo Çid, tomos a marauillar: '*grado a ti, Padre spirital*' (v.1102)

yo fio por Dios que en nuestro pro enadran (v. 1112)

La sintaxis narrativa del *Poema de Mio Cid* 65

grado a Dios, lo nuestro fue adelant (v. 1118)

b. 'Conquistas de Mio Cid y crecimiento de su fama':

Prisieron Çebola e quanto que es y *adelant* (v. 1150)

entrauan a Muruiedro con estas *ganançias* que traen grandes.
Las nueuas de myo Çid, sabet, sonando van.
Miedo an en Valençia, que non saben que se far,
Sonando van sus nueuas alent parte del mar.
Alegre era el Çid e todas sus compañas,
que Dios le aiudara e fiziera esta arrancada (vv. 1153-58)

Ganaron Peña Cadiella, las exidas e las entradas.
[70]
Quando el Çid Campeador *ouo Peña Cadiella* (vv. 1163-64)

Çercar quiere a Valençia pora christianos la dar
[73]
quien quiere yr comigo *çercar a Valençia* (vv. 1190-91)

Andidieron los pregones, sabet, a todas partes,
el sabor de *la ganançia* non lo quiere detardar (vv. 1197-98)

Sonando van sus nueuas todas a todas partes (v. 1206)

c. 'Toma de Valencia, ganancia y gozo':

Versos 1211-21 [presentados más arriba].

La lectura de la larga secuencia de la conquista de Valencia nos permite algunas observaciones, que entendemos se confirmarían si tratáramos desde esta perspectiva el episodio de la Afrenta de Corpes (precedido por el motivo de los augurios y presagios siniestros y destacado sintácticamente por el juego de las series gemelas y encadenadas) o el del viaje de Ximena y sus hijas a Valencia[13] o el de las Cortes de Toledo.

El poeta trabaja el discurso por secuencias temáticas. Cada una de ellas tiene su tema básico --sustentado en la reiteración variada y progresiva de un motivo elegido-- y sub-temas o sub-secuencias que suelen armarse sobre estructuras sintácticas basadas tanto en el paralelismo y encadenamiento como en la iteración conceptual. Esta armazón de apoyatura tópico-semántica y de enlace conceptual facilita la memorización del recitante y la memoria auditivo-conceptual del auditorio. Si a esto sumamos la capacidad actualizadora de las imágenes descriptas o sugeridas tendríamos las claves de la factura del poema épico, nacido en una etapa de oralidad plena y destinado a un público predominantemente inmerso en la oralidad.

El *Poema de Mio Cid* ha conservado marcas relevantes de esta factura oral. Podemos preguntarnos enseguida 1) si en el *PMCid* éstas son recursos mnemotécnicos de la tradición oral o 2) si se conservan en él constituidos ya en recursos estructuradores del discurso narrativo, con prescindencia de su eficacia como fórmula mnemotécnica del relato destinado a un auditorio; es decir, si de fórmulas activas en la progresión del relato han pasado a ser retórica caracterizante del estilo épico.[14] Nos inclinamos a sostener la primera propuesta.

Las marcas mnemónicas son válidas tanto para la memoria del juglar como para la del auditorio que está dispuesto y habituado a usar de esas apoyaturas para constituir el texto oral audio-comprensible. Sólo en esta consideración de las marcas orales como elementos claves del hecho de comunicación participativa --válidas para el recitador (memoria repetitiva) como para el auditor-espectador (memoria oral receptiva y reconstructiva)-- puede encontrarse, a nuestro juicio, un método para relevar las marcas de oralidad en la épica románica que tardíamente fue registrada por la escritura. Al crearse el *PMCid* estaban aún vivas y vigentes los procedimientos orales de elaboración del discurso narrativo que habían sido patrimonio de la épica primitiva.

NOTAS

1. Por 'perspectiva de la oralidad' entendemos tanto los estudios sobre los juglares y su público como las investigaciones sobre la psicodinámica de la memoria oral en el emisor y en el receptor y las técnicas de elaboración del discurso narrativo para un público iletrado.

2. Con el romanticismo comienza el estudio de los transmisores orales de la poesía narrativa de la Edad Media: los juglares. Recordamos la obra de E. Faral (1910) precedida por las observaciones de Leon Gautier (1892), así como *Poesía juglaresca y juglares* (1924) de R. Menéndez Pidal tiene el antecedente de M. Milá y Fontanals (*De los trovadores de España*, 1861). Será R. Menéndez Pidal el defensor tenaz de la tradición oral de la épica medieval en pleno auge del positivismo, lo que culminó a mediados del s. XX con la formulación de la teoría neotradicionalista en el Prólogo a *Reliquias de la poesía épica española* (1951), donde expone su 'teoría del estado latente', y en la forma ampliada de *Poesía juglaresca y orígenes de las literaturas románicas* (1957), especialmente la Parte Cuarta. La tradición oral será concepto básico de sus estudios sobre el romancero antiguo, confirmado con sus investigaciones sobre el romancero tradicional en versiones modernas (*Romancero Hispánico*, 1953 y ¿*Cómo vive un romance?*, 1954, en colaboración con A. Galmés y Diego Catalán, éste último, continuador de los trabajos sobre el romancero oral moderno).

3. La tesis de Milman Parry sobre el epíteto tradicional en Homero (París, 1928) abrió modernamente las posibilidades del estudio científico de la elaboración artística de un poema épico; pero es después de 1929 cuando se publica el libro de Mathías Murko sobre los cantos populares yugoslavos, cuando Parry lanzó su teoría de 'estilo formulario -- estilo oral improvisado'. En unión con Albert B. Lord continuó las investigaciones que se publicaron más tarde en los *Serbocroatian Heroic Songs* (1954). A la muerte de Parry, en 1935, Lord tomó la tarea de dar forma final a las ideas de Parry, lo que se concretó en *The Singer of Tales* (Cambridge, Mass.: Harvard University Press, 1960; reimpr. N. York, 1965); antes, Cecil Bowra, *Heroic Poetry* (London, 1952), difundió en la crítica literaria la línea de trabajo de Parry-Lord. Desde ese momento los estudios de aplicación crecen, empezando por Jean Rychner, *La Chanson de Geste. Essai sur l'art épique des jongleurs* (Genève, 1955). R. Menéndez Pidal revisa sus estudios a la luz de estos aportes en 'Los cantores épicos yugoeslavos y los occidentales. El *Mio Cid* y dos refundidores primitivos', *Boletín de la Real Academia de Bellas Letras* (Barcelona), 31 (1965-66), 195-225; allí manifiesta su coincidencia en general, pero su divergencia esencial: 'La memoria del juglar que dictó la copia del *Mio Cid* a fines del siglo XII era de las que abundaban entonces, una memoria vasta y firme, algo casi como una escritura analfabética de deseada fijeza. La poesía oral que nos trasmite es una épica que vive de modo muy distinto al en que vive la moderna épica yugoslava, improvisadora y refundidora de la totalidad. La antigua épica románica, aunque anónima, merecía del juglar repetidor una fidelidad conservatriz --si bien no tanta como exigía el autor trovadoresco--, y merecía del juglar o poeta refundidor gran respeto' (pp.222-23). Menéndez Pidal y Parry-Lord se oponen por sus puntos de mira: Menéndez Pidal ubicado en el campo de la épica medieval, que nos conservó la escritura, y Parry-Lord, en la realidad viva de los cantores ambulantes. Para los estudios derivados de la obra de Parry-Lord, véanse Edward R. Haymes, *A Bibliography of Studies Relating to Parry's and Lord's Oral Theory* (Cambridge, Mass.: Harvard University Press, 1973); PMPC, Docum. and Planning Series, I; *Oral Traditional Literature. A Festschrift for Albert Bates Lord* (Columbus, Ohio: Slavica Publishers, 1981). Para la aplicación a la épica francesa y castellana pueden verse John S. Miletich, 'Medieval Spanish Epic and European Narrative Traditions', *La Corónica*, 6:2 (1977), 90-96, y Margaret Chaplin, 'Oral-Formulaic Style in the Epic: A Progress Report', en *Medieval Hispanic Studies presented to Rita Hamilton* (London: Tamesis, 1976), pp.11-20. El impacto

en los estudios de épica francesa puede verse en la polémica entre Joseph J. Duggan y William Calin, *Olifant*, 8:3 (1981), 226-316. Profundización y amplia perspectiva en esta línea de trabajo aportan los estudios recientes sobre la oralidad y los que derivan de la consideración del lenguaje como acto de comunicación: Walter J. Ong, *Orality and Literacy. The Technologizing of the Word* (London: Methuen and Co., 1982; trad. esp.: México: FCE, 1987); Maria Corti, 'Oralità bifronte', *Strumenti critici*, II (1987), 1-16; Valeria Bertolucci Pizzorusso, 'Présence des instances du locuteur et de l'énonciateur dans les textes médiévaux' y Donald Maddox, 'Vers un modèle de la communauté textuelle au Moyen Age: les rapports entre auteur et texte, entre texte et lecteur', ambos en *Actes du XVIIIe. Congrès International de Linguistique et de Philologie Romanes. Université de Trèves (Trier) 1986*, VI (Tübingen: Max Niemeyer Verlag, 1988), 470-79 y 480-90 respectivamente.

4. Remitimos en parte a las referencias de la nota 2, a las que pueden agregarse los trabajos de Ruth H. Webber, 'Narrative Organization of the Cantar de Mio Cid', *Olifant*, 1:2 (1973), 21-34 y 'The *Cantar de Mio Cid*: Problems and Interpretations', en *Oral Tradition in Literature: Interpretation and Context*, ed. de John M. Foley (Columbia: University of Missouri Press, 1986); Joseph J. Duggan, 'Formulaic Diction in the *Cantar de Mio Cid* and Old French Epic', *Forum for Modern Language Studies*, 10 (1974) (reimpr. en *Oral Literature* (Edinburgh: Scottish Acad. Press, 1975)); Edmund de Chasca, 'Composición escrita y oral en el *Poema del Cid*', *Filología*, 12 (1966-67), 77-94 y *El arte juglaresco en el 'Cantar de Mio Cid'* (Madrid: Gredos, 1967); Thomas Montgomery, 'The "*Poema de Mio Cid*": Oral Art in Transition', en *'Mio Cid' Studies* (London: Tamesis, 1977), pp.91-112; Diego Catalán, 'Análisis semiótico de estructuras abiertas: el modelo "Romancero"', en *El Romancero hoy: Poética* (Madrid: Seminario Menéndez Pidal, 1979), pp.231-49 y 'El proceso de transmisión oral y el estudio de modelos literarios abiertos', *Ethnica* (Barcelona), 18 (1982), Parte II, pp.53-66.

5. El problema fue planteado ya en el Coloquio de Lieja (1957) por Martín de Riquer, 'Epopée jongleresque à écouter, épopée romanesque à lire', en *La technique littéraire des Chansons de geste* (Paris, 1959), pp.75-84, y se ha actualizado en la última década ante los estudios especiales sobre oralidad y escritura (véase nota 2 al final).

6. En el enfoque de nuestro análisis tiene valor secundario el debate sobre la procedencia de estas técnicas, a las que algunos creen de origen francés y otros, originadas en la retórica latina (véase, por ejemplo, el planteamiento de esta problemática en Colin Smith, 'Some Thoughts on the Application of Oralist Principles to Medieval Spanish Epic', en *'A Face not turned to the Wall': Essays on Hispanic Themes for Gareth Alban Davies* (Leeds, 1987), pp.9-26); creo más fecunda la consideración de una épica europea en vulgar para la que no había fronteras nacionales sino públicos de lenguas distintas.

7. Desechamos la acepción posible de 'oralidad' o 'versión oral' en el sentido de 'performance' o recitado por un juglar que memoriza un texto puesto por escrito.

8. Lord destaca reiteradamente la función vital, dinámica de las fórmulas y los temas en el proceso de creación y en el de comunicación del poema: 'Lo importante no es el recitado oral, sino la composición durante el recitado oral' (*The Singer of Tales*, p.5). 'Dicho brevemente, el canto épico-oral es poesía narrativa compuesta en un proceso desarrollado a través de muchas generaciones por cantores de historias, que no conocían la escritura; consiste en la construcción de versos y medios versos mediante el uso de fórmulas y giros formulísticos, y en la construcción de cantares mediante el uso de temas' (*The Singer of Tales*, p.4).

9. Una contribución importante de Lord a la teoría oralista es su detallado análisis de los

procedimientos mediante los cuales un poeta oral compone y memoriza un relato sin recurrir a la escritura; uno de esos recursos es el uso de los temas épicos. En el tratamiento del tema, Lord ha organizado ideas dispersas de Parry a las que sumó observaciones propias (*The Singer of Tales*, pp.68-98). Finalmente parece resumir su definición como incidentes y pasajes descriptivos que se repiten en la canción o grupos de ideas usadas regularmente en el relato de un cuento en el estilo formulístico de la canción tradicional. La presencia y recurrencia de temas tradicionales, en una canción heroica, como la de las fórmulas, es una indicación de que al menos tales procedimientos son de naturaleza oral. El tema como la fórmula posee su propio dinamismo: 'No es una entidad estática, sino vital, cambiante, adaptable a la creación artística' (*The Singer of Tales*, p.94).

10. Menéndez Pidal, *Cantar de Mio Cid. Texto, gramática y vocabulario. Pt 1. Crítica del texto-gramática* (Madrid: Espasa-Calpe, 1944), pp.110-11; E. de Chasca, *El arte juglaresco en el 'Cantar de Mio Cid'*, pp.198-200.

11. *Poema de Mio Cid.* Cuarta edición (Madrid: Espasa-Calpe, 1944), p.157.

12. Nuestras citas se basan en el texto paleográfico editado por R. Menéndez Pidal en *Cantar de Mio Cid*, III, 909-1016. Destacamos con itálicas los fragmentos de verso a que hacemos referencia.

13. Germán Orduna, 'El Cantar de las Bodas. Las técnicas de estructura y la intervención de los dos juglares en el Poema de Mio Cid', en *Studia Hispanica in honorem Rafael Lapesa*, 3 vols (Madrid: Gredos, 1972-75), II (1974), 411-31.

14. Llamamos 'retórica' a la utilización mecánica de un molde como procedimiento de 'escuela', recurso 'de receta' con el que se caracterizaría al discurso como discurso épico. Es posible que esto hubiera llegado a darse en el s. XII-XIII, pero aún puede rescatarse el hecho de que estos recursos convencionales del género son caracterizantes del mismo para un público muy amplio, que espera su aplicación y conoce por hábito los elementos propios de cada estructura temático-formulística. El autor del *PMCid* lo que ha hecho es darles relieve -- por los medios que hemos descripto-- a los signos lingüísticos que son requeridos por la memoria cultural.

THE POPES, THE INQUISITION AND JEWISH CONVERTS IN SPAIN, 1440-1515

JOHN EDWARDS
University of Birmingham

As many of you as were baptized in Christ have put on Christ. There is neither slave nor free, there is neither male nor female; for you are all one in Christ Jesus [Galatians 3: 27-29].

The history of Spain between 1440 and the eve of the Reformation seems to demonstrate that little practical attention was paid to Paul's words to the Church in Galatia, when it came to converts from Judaism and their descendants. Historical studies have customarily concentrated on issues and documentary sources within the Iberian peninsula itself; and the story has thus become all too familiar. Attacks were made on Jews in the spring and early summer of 1391, spreading from Seville in the south-west to Barcelona in the north-east.[1] As a result of this violence, and of earlier and subsequent pressures, hundreds of Jews were baptized, and those who remained faithful to the old religion were subjected to increasingly irksome legal measures, as well as the missionary activities of Christian preachers, in particular those of the Catalan Dominican friar Vincent Ferrer. After these conversions, or at least baptisms, had taken place, it took a further generation or more before doubts and suspicions concerning the Christian orthodoxy of the converts began to emerge as a political and social issue. In the traditional narrative, the revolt in Toledo against the government of John II, and his constable of Castile, Don Álvaro de Luna, produced, in 1449, the first expression of what would today be described as 'racist' feeling against the 'New Christian' converts from Judaism. In that year, a dialogue began between the then pope, Nicholas V, and the Castilian government.

The occasion for this debate, which was to have drastic consequences for Jewish converts in Spain, and for Spanish Jews who later chose to leave the country rather than be baptized, was the 'Sentence-Statute' devised by Bachelor Marcos García de Mora (nicknamed 'Marquillos'). This 'rebel' document stipulated, 'that all the aforesaid *conversos*, descendants of the perverse lineage of the Jews, in whatever guise this may be ... should be had and held, as the law has and holds them, as infamous, unable, incapable and unworthy to have any public and private office in the aforesaid city of Toledo and its land, territory and jurisdiction.[2] In the context of Spanish studies, papal interest in the fate of converts from Judaism is normally held to have begun with Nicholas V's bulls, which were issued in response to Castilian requests for support in the quelling of the Toledan rebellion. The best known of these is *Humani generis inimicus*, which was issued on 24 September 1449, and in which the pope condemned the segregation of Jewish converts, which had been carried out by the Toledan rebels, using not only Scripture and other religious arguments, but also Castilian legislation, which probably included a privilege for *conversos* which had been granted by Henry III and confirmed by John II.[3] In a famous passage, Nicholas affirmed that, 'between those newly converted to the [Catholic] faith, above all from the Israelite people, and old Christians, no distinction should be made in the honours, dignities and offices, both ecclesiastical and secular, which they may receive and hold'.[4] In this way, the pope seemed to rule out any possibility of subsequent 'purity of blood' (*limpieza de sangre*) statutes in Spain, and, in the immediate Toledan situation, this bull was accompanied by another, excommunicating the author of the *Sentencia-Estatuto*.[5]

However, a fuller examination than has previously been undertaken of papal legislation concerning Spanish Jews and *conversos* in this period reveals that the 1449 Toledo case was not the first to cause Nicholas to interest himself in the fate of the Spanish New Christians. In addition, it appears that, like his successors up to the very eve of the Reformation, Nicholas by no means followed a consistent line in such matters. Indeed, in October 1450, this same pope suspended the application of his own bull, *Humani generis inimicus*, though in the following year, on 20 November, he once again affirmed the equality, before God and society, of 'Old' and 'New' Christians in Spain.[6] In subsequent years, two interrelated questions were to preoccupy popes concerning the Spanish *conversos*. The first of these was New Christians' rights to equal treatment with the existing membership of the Catholic Church, which inevitably involved consideration of the validity, and hence the efficacy, of their baptism, while the second was the issue of the subsequent orthodoxy or otherwise of their Christian faith and practice. To begin with, though, it is worth examining Nicholas V's first intervention in the affairs of Spain's unconverted Jews, which took place earlier, in 1447.

In this first year of his pontificate, on All Souls' Day, 2 November, and possibly hoping to avoid the spread to Spain of the conversionist efforts then being made in Italy, mainly by Dominican and Franciscan friars, Nicholas forbade active missionary campaigns directed at the Jews of the Spanish kingdoms.[7] By this action he was doing no more than follow his predecessor Eugenius IV (1431-47), who had, on 8 August 1442, addressed to John II of Castile the bull *Super gregem dominicam*, which reaffirmed the policy of the Fourth Lateran Council (1215) on the restriction, but also the protection, of Jews. Of course, the canons of Lateran IV in themselves reflected much earlier legislation, which originated in the late Roman empire.[8] Nicholas was to take a rather more original stance, in response to a specific situation, when, on 1 May 1449, he issued a bull which guaranteed the right of the Jews of Seville to hold their own rogation procession, alongside that of their Christian neighbours, to ask God for an end to famine and plague.[9] Here too, the pope seems to have been attempting to secure the ecclesiastical and secular *status quo*, in the face of growing tension on the ground. The incidents in Seville to which he was reacting indicate both that Jewish-Christian coexistence in the city was still normal, and that this coexistence was under strain. The role of the *conversos* in this situation was soon to become clearer, both in Seville and elsewhere in Castile.

Over all, then, Nicholas V, who issued no further rulings and prescriptions concerning Spain's Jews and *conversos* between November 1451 and his death in 1455, did not depart in any significant way from traditional papal theology. This aimed firstly to protect the Jewish 'remnant' as an underprivileged minority, until its eventual conversion, which would precede the 'end of days', and secondly to prevent danger and loss to those individual Jews who became Christians in the meantime. Particularly since the thirteenth century, with the growth of the papal 'monarchy' in western Europe and the friars' efforts to bolster Catholic devotion and orthodoxy, this protection of the Jews had sometimes suffered lapses, just as individual converts often had a hard time, finding themselves in a kind of limbo between the actual community of

Judaism and what was generally, for them, the merely theoretical and abstract community of the Church.[10] The Spanish case was to test traditional papal theology and social attitudes almost to destruction, between 1450 and Luther's first act of defiance in 1517.

Initially, though, there is little sign, in the surviving records, that the popes were aware of the problems that were arising, in Spain in general and in Castile in particular, as a result of the 'mass' conversion of Jews to Christianity, in the period 1390-1420. Nicholas V's successor, Calixtus III (1455-58), took no initiative in this matter, except to start canonization procedures in the case of Vincent Ferrer, and while such an action may with hindsight seem provocative, in that it appears to condone and reward a major attack on the integrity of Spanish Jewry, it is unlikely that it was thus seen at the time, even by most *conversos*. However ghastly his views and methods may seem to many today, Ferrer was apparently a holy man, and there was nothing in his teaching and activity which fell outside the parameters of papal teaching on the Jews and conversion. In the event, this canonization went through on 1 October 1458, in the succeeding reign of the distinguished humanist Pius II (1458-64), who otherwise seems to have paid little attention to Spain. Nevertheless, it is worth noting that the rapidity of this 'sainting' fits in all too well with the onslaught on the religious and social integrity of Jews which was being undertaken at the time in Italy. This was initiated and mainly carried out by friars, especially Franciscans and those of Ferrer's own Dominican order, and took such forms as an attack on Jewish banking, through the cheap pawn-bank, or *monti di pietà*, movement, and the encouragement of a special devotion to the 'Name of Jesus', which spread to Spain in the mid-fifteenth century, in a form particularly dangerous to 'New Christians'.[11]

All was not well, then, when, after a period of papal inactivity concerning Spain's Jews and *conversos*, Sixtus IV ascended the papal throne in 1471. At this stage, though, it is necessary to return, in due order, to the two main subjects of papal concern in subsequent years, which were the ability of Jewish converts to become fully accepted as Catholic Christians -- the question of 'purity of blood' (*limpieza de sangre*) and the related question of the foundation and operation of the 'Spanish' Inquisition. In each of these cases, the role of Sixtus IV (1471-84) was to be crucial. On the question of the 'limpieza' of Castilian *conversos*, the new pope's initial reaction was to stand by the rulings of his predecessors and, in particular, the 'Toledan' bulls of Nicholas V. On 1 July 1477, in his first action in the matter, Sixtus instructed Pedro González de Mendoza, archbishop of Seville, Alfonso de Burgos, bishop of Cordoba, and the dean of Segovia, after due investigation, to excommunicate any municipal officials in Ciudad Real who had attempted to impose a *limpieza* statute on candidates for public office in the town. The analogy with Toledo in 1449 was obvious, and it was made explicit by Sixtus's direct reference to Nicholas's *Humani generis inimicus*.[12]

As late as 1479, this pope adopted a similar attitude, when, on 27 April of that year, he ordered the abbot of St Mary of Mount Zion, outside the walls of Toledo, together with a canon of Toledo Cathedral, and the prior of San Bartolomé de Lupiana, to allow Diego de la Caballería, a citizen of the town, to become a knight of Calatrava, despite a ban on certain converts 'in those parts', 'descendants of the Jewish race' [*de genere Iudaeorum descendentes*].[13] By 1483, though, Sixtus seems to have changed his attitude. On 8 June of that year, he appears to have accepted a similar *limpieza* statute for another military order, that of Alcántara, which declared that no-one might be admitted as a brother or a knight [*in fratrem, vel militarem*], unless he were an 'old Christian' on both sides [*nisi de antiquo Christianorum genere ex utraque parente procreatus*]. It should be noted, though, that this particular bull was not registered with the others in the Vatican, and may not be authentic.[14] At this point, it is necessary to turn to the subject of the Inquisition, its refoundation, and subsequent papal attempts to restrain it.

Little needs to be said here about Sixtus IV's bull, *Exigit sincere devotionis*, issued on All Saints' Day (1 November) 1478, in which he authorized the Catholic Monarchs (as they were later to be entitled) to appoint inquisitors to investigate alleged 'heretical depravity' in the archdiocese of Seville, on the lines set down for earlier tribunals in western Europe, including the Crown of Aragon.[15] It is worth noting, though, that this action was not as innovative as it might appear. The possibility of employing an Inquisition to test the religious orthodoxy of *conversos* had already been proposed at the time of the Toledan rebellion, and the controversy surrounding the *Sentencia-Estatuto*, and Nicholas V had indeed responded favourably to such a request from John

II of Castile, in one of a group of bulls issued on 20 November 1451.[16] Although, in the political and social chaos which followed in Castile, no further action had been taken, when a firm request eventually came from Isabella and her consort Ferdinand, Sixtus and his advisers may well have felt that their hands were tied by precedent.

As is well known, it was a couple of years before the new inquisitors, in their headquarters in the castle of Triana, reached the stage of parading penitents in *autos de fe*, and handing 'judaizers' over to the 'secular arm' for burning. Thus the first sign of papal concern at possible abuses in Seville appears in a letter from Sixtus to Ferdinand and Isabella [*Numquam dubitavimus*], dated in Rome on 29 January 1482.[17] In it, the pope states that he had 'never doubted' that the king and queen had asked for an Inquisition 'out of zeal for the Catholic faith' [*zelo fidei catholice*], and with 'an upright and sincere heart' [*recto et sincero corde*]. His meaning, though, was of course precisely the opposite of that which appeared on the surface. Ominously for Ferdinand and Isabella, he not only stated that the new Inquisition was explicitly set up to deal with the 'Jewish superstition', but adds the remarkable admission that his own 1478 bull, and possibly other documents, had been issued in terms which went against 'the decrees and common observance of the Holy Fathers [of the Church] and our [papal] predecessors', though he blamed this error on a confused presentation of the aims of the proposed tribunal by the representatives of the Castilian Crown. The implication was that Ferdinand and Isabella's new tribunal did not conform to papal guidelines, established in the thirteenth century, because it was too 'specialized' and did not aim to tackle general 'heresy' in Christendom. In any case, the result had been 'many quarrels and lamentations', against Sixtus and against the king and queen, as well as the inquisitors, Fray Miguel de Morillo and Fray Juan de San Martín. The pope continued with a devastating indictment of the manner in which the two Dominicans had proceeded, supposedly with his approval. Without consulting any authority other than themselves, they were illegally and unjustly imprisoning large numbers of people, falsely declaring them to be heretics, despoiling them of their goods and sending them to the stake [*ultime supplicio*].

As was normal in such cases, many *conversos* had brought their complaints to Rome, the Holy City here being modestly described as 'the safest refuge of the oppressed'. Having heard the appeals of the 'New Christians', Sixtus had called the cardinals together in conclave, and in this document gives some account of the deliberations which took place, as well as their results. Firstly, although some of those present had expressed the view, given what they had been told, that Morillo and San Martín should be 'deputari' [a charming equivalent of that other euphemism, 'early retirement'], the final decision had been to leave them in post. Sixtus states that he would not wish the friars' future careers to be damaged by the fact of their having been nominated by the Crown. In the previous lines he had, of course, made it clear that he had only agreed to let them stay because of Castilian royal representations. Having thus firmly put the blame for the troubles in Seville on the rulers themselves, Sixtus proceeded to his second main point, which was that any future teams of inquisitors in Castile who behaved in a similar manner would indeed be removed from office, and appeals against their verdicts would be heard by the 'commissioner of causes' in Rome. Thirdly, if further Dominicans were to be appointed as inquisitors in Castile, this should be done by the prelates of the Dominican order, which was, of course, ultimately under papal control. Fourthly and lastly, in future, Morillo and San Martín were to act, in Seville, in conjunction with the normal 'secular' ecclesiastical authorities [*una cum ordinariis*]. Sixtus concluded this somewhat barbed communication with the expectation that 'your serenities' would support the future decisions, both of the inquisitors and of the ordinaries.

At this point, in order to assess the significance of Sixtus's 1482 letter, it may be advisable to refer back to the 1478 bull, in what concerns the appointment of Morillo and San Martín. The document states that the new inquisitors were to be over forty years old, of good knowledge and life, bachelors or masters of theology or doctors of canon law, or, failing that, licentiates by 'rigorous examination', and 'God-fearing'.[18] What appears to have happened in 1482 is that the pope, having seen Ferdinand and Isabella go to the absolute limit of what was permitted by the 1478 bull, took the opportunity afforded by the Seville controversy to attempt to regain some lost ground. He repented of concessions previously made, such as the admission that inquisitors in Spain should give priority to their tribunals' work, even when other papal bulls were in force, which had not been intended for exploitation by two friars who were under heavy pressure from their royal masters, in a highly-charged political atmosphere, such as that of Andalusia at that time.

It was in May of the following year that Pope Sixtus made an intervention in the affairs of the Seville Inquisition which was to have considerable implications for the future of the tribunal and of Spain's *conversos*. On 23 May 1488, he sent a letter to Íñigo Manrique, archbishop of Seville, which, after flattering him in a somewhat ominous fashion, appointed him as papal judge-delegate for all appeals against the sentences of the Seville inquisitors.[19] In the process, he regularized the legal position by withdrawing previous privileges, granted to 'reconciled' *conversos*, whether as individuals or groups, which had been made in a form which was not in accordance with canon law. The editor of the papal documents concerning the Jews, Shlomo Simonsohn, takes this to be a measure aimed against Jewish converts to Christianity, but this seems unlikely. In view of what had gone before, it seems more probable that the papal letter was part of the continuing campaign to reduce royal influence over the Seville tribunal. Sixtus concluded by stating that all appeals in inquisitorial cases would henceforth go to the archbishop, who was guaranteed full papal support against local resistance. Sixtus's letter to the monarchs, confirming Manrique's appointment, revealed that his action resulted from the report of an investigatory commission, consisting of Cardinal Rodrigo Borja (later Pope Alexander VI), three other cardinals, and the Catalan humanist Joan Margarit, bishop of Gerona, who was Ferdinand and Isabella's ambassador in Rome at the time.[20]

While Archbishop Manrique was taking up his new job, on 2 August, Sixtus appointed judges in the Roman Curia to hear appeals which had previously been lodged against the actions and sentences of the Seville inquisitors.[21] The document in question refers to burnings in effigy and accusations and convictions of 'judaizing', which had taken place in the city, and declares that all wrongful convictions would be annulled, whatever the court in which they had originated. Later that month, the pope appeared to withdraw from this militant posture, telling the king and queen that the earlier document had been issued on the basis of information which was now being subjected to 'more accurate examination'. The appointment of Archbishop Manrique was being revoked, so that 'more mature consultation' could take place.[22] No doubt the Spanish lobbyists (*oratores*, in the language of the Curia) had been at work, but it soon appeared that the papacy of Sixtus was not going to abandon its efforts to undo the damage done by the All Saints' bull of 1478. On 25 November 1483, the pope commissioned inquisitors Morillo and San Martín to 'rehabilitate' Juan Fernández de Sevilla, and his wife, Leonor Fernández, both citizens of Seville.[23] As this document proved to be the precursor of important future developments, it is worthy of closer examination.

Surely with tongue firmly placed in cheek, Sixtus first declares that the Roman pontiff, in true scriptural fashion, desired 'not the death but the conversion and penitence of sinners'. The meaning was plain: the inquisitors' verdict was not to be overturned, because that would reflect on the Papacy, as well as the Crown and the Inquisition, but, nevertheless, Juan Fernández and his wife were not to suffer for what they may or may not have done. They were, of course, no ordinary *conversos*. Juan was the *contador* (accountant, in Latin, *computator*) of the leading magnate of the region, Enrique, duke of Medina Sidonia. The story of the trial, as outlined in the papal document, is that Juan and his wife had been summoned by the inquisitors' 'associate', Juan de Medina, doctor of [canon law] decrees, to appear in Triana castle within thirty days. The tribunal's procurator fiscal, Juan López del Barco, had carried out the summons. However, the couple did not respond, fearing that, if they appeared, they would be proceeded against with excessive rigour and might be imprisoned. After a year of non-appearance, Juan and Leonor were sentenced to be burnt in effigy. However, they declared themselves to be contrite and penitent because of their 'judaizing', and appealed to the pope. Although Sixtus remitted the case to the Seville inquisitors, he clearly expected the friars concerned to 'break and annul' [*cassari et annullari*] their earlier sentence. This, however, was to be only the beginning of the popes' efforts to ensure that 'repentant' converts might be reintegrated into Spanish society, despite any previous involvement with Jewish faith and practice.

Indeed, by June of the following year, Sixtus was quashing inquisitorial convictions and annulling sentences without any pretence of referring to the

Seville inquisitors. Behind a smokescreen of pious language concerning 'apostolic clemency', 'peace, tranquillity and safety', the pope intervened in the case of Pedro Fernández, a parish councillor [*jurado*] of Seville, and his wife, Francisca de Herrera.[24] The couple had been summoned to appear before the Inquisition, and their property had been confiscated. However, they had appealed to Rome, where their case had been heard in the Curia by Antonio de Grasso. In the meantime, they had been sentenced in Seville to be 'relaxed' to the secular arm, or else burnt in effigy. The papal auditor 'annulled and revoked' this sentence, and Sixtus, confirming his judges' action, absolved the couple of all their offences, ordering that all those who went against the papal sentence should themselves be handed over to be burnt. Thus Sixtus IV went out on a strong note, apparently regretting the 1478 bull to the end and trying to keep to the guidelines of his predecessors in general and Nicholas V in particular. Sixtus died on 12 August 1484, and on the 29th of that month he was succeeded by Innocent VIII (1484-92), who was to continue the battle.

The new pope wasted little time in beginning to tackle the question of the Spanish *conversos* and the Inquisition. On 15 July 1485, he sent an encyclical to all the Spanish inquisitors, who were by then active in Aragon and Catalonia, as well as in large parts of Castile. Innocent was now proposing that the reconciliation of repentant 'judaizers' should henceforth take place, not only in individual cases in public, but also in secret [*in occultam*], and in batches. Delightfully, in view of Papal-Spanish exchanges in Sixtus's reign, the new pope expressed the wish that the king and queen themselves should be present on such occasions.[25] Innocent was clearly determined, like his predecessors, to implicate Ferdinand and Isabella in his policies, thus undermining theirs and re-affirming papal power. Later, the Crown itself was to adopt a similar policy, but at this stage conflict between the monarchy and the Papacy was bound to arise.[26] On several occasions during the rest of his reign, Innocent made efforts to ensure that 'rehabilitations' of convicted 'New Christians' took place. On 11 February 1486, he granted a faculty to inquisitors in Castile to carry out fifty such 'rehabilitations', 'in the presence of the king and queen'.[27] On 31 May of that year, he authorized fifty more of these 'secret reconciliations', this time, with royal permission but not

The Popes, the Inquisition and Jewish Converts in Spain 81

necessarily in the presence of the monarchs themselves.[28] Thereafter, Innocent seems to have moved on to other matters, but, in 1489, by which time Ferdinand and Isabella had effectively won the battle for 'their' Inquisition, the pope intervened once again in the question of reconciliation and 'rehabilitation'. On 18 August of that year, he issued a 'reconciliation' absolution to another 'judaizing' Sevillian couple, Alfonso Alemán and Isabel de Jerez.[29] More interesting, however, is a subsequent document, dated 14 October 1489, which explicitly links the restoration of Jewish converts to the Church with the question of 'purity of blood'.

Once again, by the terms of this instruction, the Spanish inquisitors, in this case those of the whole of Ferdinand and Isabella's kingdoms and not just those of Castile, were authorized to carry out a further fifty reconciliations of 'judaizers'. They were to be secretly reconciled and readmitted to the church, 'even if statements had been received against them'. They would then be able to 'receive and similarly retain' 'benefices and offices both ecclesiastical and secular'. However, Innocent added to this reaffirmation of Nicholas V's Toledan bulls by further specifying that the same would apply to the sons and other relatives of those who were reconciled under these provisions, provided that they, personally, were not found guilty of a similar heresy.[30] It is worth noting that Innocent had previously, in 1486, hedged his bets by appointing a committee of Castilian bishops to investigate, when the Jeronymite friars of Guadalupe had attempted to use Nicholas V's bull to protect a Jew who had lived in that house for about forty years, but who had never been baptized.[31] By the end of his reign, however, this pope had adopted a clear stance against inquisitorial abuses and against the 'purity of blood' principle.

Things were to change markedly when the Borja pope, Alexander VI, came to occupy the see of St. Peter, in the year of the conquest of Granada, the expulsion of Spanish Jews, and Columbus's first voyage. It was not long before the new pope began to undermine the policy of his two immediate predecessors. On 12 August 1493, he wrote to the Spanish inquisitors to overrule a secret reconciliation and rehabilitation which had been granted by Sixtus ten years earlier, to Pedro Fernández and his wife Francisca. When they were originally charged, they had appealed to Rome, but now they came up against a new and harsher regime. Alexander rejected their appeal and, while not, of course, directly criticizing Sixtus, he none the less suggested that his predecessors had been misled by the appellants. More significantly, he indicated that the other 'reconciliations' granted by Sixtus and Innocent should be condemned because they brought the Inquisition into disrepute.[32] A year later, Alexander returned to the case. According to the details here supplied, Pedro and Francisca had been reconciled, under the terms of Sixtus's bull, by the bishop of Evora, but the Seville inquisitors had continued to assert that the couple's flight indicated guilt, whatever the pope of the time may have said. A trial was conducted, and the couple were burnt in effigy, their goods having already been confiscated, as was normal in such cases. The couple's continuing protests and appeals were meanwhile bringing the Inquisition itself into disrepute.[33] There had been some wavering in Sixtus's policy, particularly during the summer of 1483, when Pedro and Francisca's case first got under way. Now, with a new Spanish pope in occupation, and a mood of Spanish triumphalism in the air, those of Sixtus's documents which were more favourable to Ferdinand and Isabella's policy were stressed. The earlier documents, in favour of 'New Christians', issued by Sixtus and Innocent, were not, of course, repealed. Rather, the earlier hard line was reaffirmed, so that Alexander might appear, at least to the superficial onlooker, to be continuing the policies of his predecessors. Such caution was soon to be thrown to the winds.

On 19 December 1496, Alexander VI conferred on Ferdinand and Isabella the title by which they are known to history, 'the Catholic Monarchs'.[34] Thus emboldened, he proceeded, on 29 August 1497, to revoke all papal dispensations, rehabilitations and exemptions from the intervention of the Spanish Inquisition. He was, of course, thus responding to the petition of 'the Catholic kings of the Spains'.[35] Apparently, Alexander did not write to inform the inquisitors themselves of this until 17 September 1498. Significantly, the latter document gave the Spanish tribunals free rein to pursue suspects to the best of their abilities and confirmed that the guilty were to lose their absolutions, reconciliations, privileges, grants, dignities and honours.[36] It seems clear that the way was being paved here, at the very least for a weakening of the previously firm Papal stance against 'purity of blood' statutes. However, no doubt because of his many other preoccupations,

Alexander did not return to this subject until just before his death, in 1503, when he issued a document, on 26 May, which allowed the then inquisitor-general, the Dominican bishop Diego Deza, then of Palencia and later of Seville, again at the Catholic Monarchs' request, to authorize tribunals in Spain and Sicily to sentence those convicted of heresy to serve on the royal galleys, or else to be banished, so as to alleviate prison overcrowding.[37] On this characteristic note, the infamous Borja pope departed this life and was replaced by the equally notorious Julius II (1503-13).

For Spain's Jewish Christians, however, the new pope should not, to judge from his documentary rulings, be seen as the failure that he appeared to be in the eyes of 'reformers' such as Erasmus. Julius turned to Inquisition matters in 1506. On 10 January of that year, he granted absolution to another couple from Seville, Álvaro López and María Díaz, who had been convicted of 'judaizing'. The language of the text, stressing the desirability of repentance, returns to the style of Sixtus and Innocent.[38] Thus it seemed characteristic that the last document issued concerning this subject, before the fiery Julius departed this life, leaving his successor, Leo X, to cope with Brother Martin Luther, was a full absolution, granted on 4 October 1510, to Diego de Cuéllar, in the diocese of Segovia.[39] Diego's case related to the issue of *limpieza de sangre*, as the problem with the Inquisition had arisen in the case of his grandfather. Diego was hereby absolved of all blame that might attach to his family, so that he and his descendants could enjoy any offices and benefices which might come to them. Not only did this ruling contradict the whole principle of *limpieza* statutes, but the document also explicitly claimed the pope's right to go against the rulings of his predecessors (he names Sixtus, Innocent and Alexander) and also those of Ferdinand and his now deceased queen, Isabella. The vocabulary used to describe these earlier papal documents is significant, as it employs the word *innovatis* ('innovation' being tantamount to heresy in papal legislation), and refers to 'unaccustomed and irritating decrees' [*insolitis, irritantibusque decretis*].

Inevitably, this examination of papal rulings concerning the 'new' Spanish Inquisition and the 'rehabilitation' of 'judaizing' *conversos* has remained close to the texts of the papal documents. None the less, Julius II's reaction to Diego de Cuéllar's case clearly shows how politics influenced successive popes' actions in relation to Spain's problems, which, in the period 1440-1515 and beyond, were so often focused on Jews and 'judaizers'. Julius's ruling in the Segovia case was clearly intended to set a seal on far more than this one specific affair. With Isabella safely in heaven (or wherever),[40] popes no longer had to collude with Spanish monarchs in this matter -- or indeed in others, as events during what remained of the sixteenth century were to show. Political turmoil in Castile, following Isabella's death, provided an opportunity for the Papacy to reassert its historic control over the repression of heresy, though, in the long run, the ambition of Spanish rulers to control 'their' Inquisition was to be very largely achieved, however dire the consequences. Derek Lomax would no doubt have enjoyed debating this view of papal policy in Spain. Whether or not he would have agreed with all or any of it cannot be known, but he would probably have acknowledged that the subject of Jews, *conversos* and the Inquisition, which loomed so large in late medieval and early modern Spain, was comparatively small beer to Nicholas V and his successors. For them, it was a matter of defending rights and prerogatives which had been painfully won since the days of Gregory VII and Innocent III. In this centuries-long process, the Borja Alexander was a glaring anomaly.

NOTES

1. J. N Hillgarth, *The Spanish Kingdoms. 1250-1516. 2. 1410-1516. Castilian Hegemony* (Oxford, 1978), p.149; John Edwards, 'Why the Spanish Inquisition?', in *Christianity and Judaism. Studies in Church History*, 29, ed. by Diana Wood (Oxford, 1992), pp.222-23.

2. Eloy Benito Ruano, *Toledo en el siglo XV. Vida política* (Madrid, 1961), p.194; Edwards, 'The beginnings of a scientific theory of race? Spain, 1450-1600', *Proceedings of the Seventeenth International Congress of Historical Sciences*, 2, *Chronological Section* (Madrid, 1992), p.626.

3. Text in Benito Ruano, *Toledo*, pp.198-201 and Shlomo Simonsohn, *The Papacy and the Jews. Documents: 1394-1464* (Toronto, 1990), pp.935-37; Benito Ruano, *Los orígenes del problema converso* (Barcelona, 1976), pp.51-52.

4. Simonsohn, *1394-1464*, p.936.

5. Benito Ruano, *Toledo*, pp.201-03.

6. Simonsohn, *1394-1464*, pp.779, 979-80.

7. Simonsohn, *1394-1464*, pp.919-21; Edwards, *The Jews in Christian Europe, 1400-1700* (revised edition, London, 1991), pp.80-81.

8. Simonsohn, *1394-1464*, pp.767, 738-41; Edwards, *The Jews*, pp.15-16.

9. Simonsohn, *1394-1464*, pp.930-32.

10. Edwards, *The Jews*, p.19.

11. Simonsohn, *1394-1464*, p.844.

12. Simonsohn, *Documents: 1464-1521* (Toronto, 1990), pp.1237-40.

13. Simonsohn, *1464-1521*, pp.1254-56.

14. Simonsohn, *1464-1521*, pp.1310-11.

15. Simonsohn, *1464-1521*, pp.1247-49; Edwards, *The Jews*, pp.21-22.

16. Edwards, 'Why the Spanish Inquisition?', pp.222-23; Simonsohn, *1394-1464*, pp.974-75.

17. Simonsohn, *1464-1521*, pp.1280-82.

18. Simonsohn, *1464-1521*, pp.1247-49.

19. Simonsohn, *1464-1521*, pp.1301-05.

20. Simonsohn, *1464-1521*, pp.1305-07 (25 May 1483).

21. Simonsohn, *1464-1521*, pp.1311-17.

22. Simonsohn, *1464-1521*, pp.1317-18 (13 August 1483).

23. Simonsohn, *1464-1521*, pp.1319-21.

24. Simonsohn, *1464-1521*, pp.1330-34 (17 June 1484).

25. Simonsohn, *1464-1521*, p.1341.

26. Edwards, 'Why the Spanish Inquisition?', p.234.

27. Simonsohn, *1464-1521*, pp.1345-46.

28. Simonsohn, *1464-1521*, pp.1355-56.

29. Simonsohn, *1464-1521*, pp.1396-97.

30. Simonsohn, *1464-1521*, pp.1398-1400.

31. Simonsohn, *1464-1521*, pp.1361-63.

32. Simonsohn, *1464-1521*, pp.1437-38.

33. Simonsohn, *1464-1521*, pp.1439-41.

34. Simonsohn, *1464-1521*, pp.1446-48.

35. Simonsohn, *1464-1521*, pp.1449-50.

36. Simonsohn, *1464-1521*, pp.1454-55.

37. Simonsohn, *1464-1521*, pp.1465-66.

38. Simonsohn, *1464-1521*, pp.1486-88.

39. Simonsohn, *1464-1521*, pp.1510-12.

40. Edwards, 'Jews and Christians in 1492 and 1992' [= The Cardinal Bea memorial lecture, given at Heythrop College, London], *The Month*, 253, no. 1499 (November 1992), 421-27.

SPANIARDS, 'GERMANS', AND THE INVENTION OF PRINTING: DIEGO DE VALERA'S EULOGY IN THE *CRÓNICA ABREVIADA*

DAVID MACKENZIE
University of Birmingham

It is not uncommon in the early period for manuscript copies to be made of printed books,[1] and a previously unknown example of this is British Library MS Egerton 286, which copies the 1482 *princeps* of Diego de Valera's *Crónica abreviada de España*, printed by Alonso del Puerto at Seville.[2]

The MS is in a nineteenth-century dark green leather binding, and is written on paper in a fifteenth-century Gothic book-hand; the text is in two columns apart from the contents-list, with red paragraphs at the beginning of chapter-rubrics, and simple painted capitals throughout, in blue, green, and red. The paper measures 274 x 195 mm., and the script covers approximately 195 x 150 mm. There are 162 folios (excluding a guard-sheet at the beginning); an earlier foliation from 1-183 shows that the MS lacks 23 leaves between fols 13 and 37 in the old foliation.

The MS omits the following passage at the beginning of the text, containing the statement of authorship:

> Comiença la coronica de españa dirigida a la muy alta & muy excelente princesa Serenissima Reyna & Sennora nuestra sennora donna ysabel Reyna de espanna de sevilla & de cerdenna Duquesa de athenas Condessa de barcelona. abreuiada por su mandado por mosen diego de ualera su maestresala & del su conseio. [A₁]

The reason for this omission is not clear: it is, for example, most unlikely that there was any restriction on the reproduction of a printed book at this early period in the history of printing. It is perhaps more than coincidence that this passage is printed in red; could the scribe have copied from a proof copy for which it was not thought worth the trouble inking the section to be rubricated?

At the head of the introduction on fol. 10r there is the following note in a seventeenth-century hand:

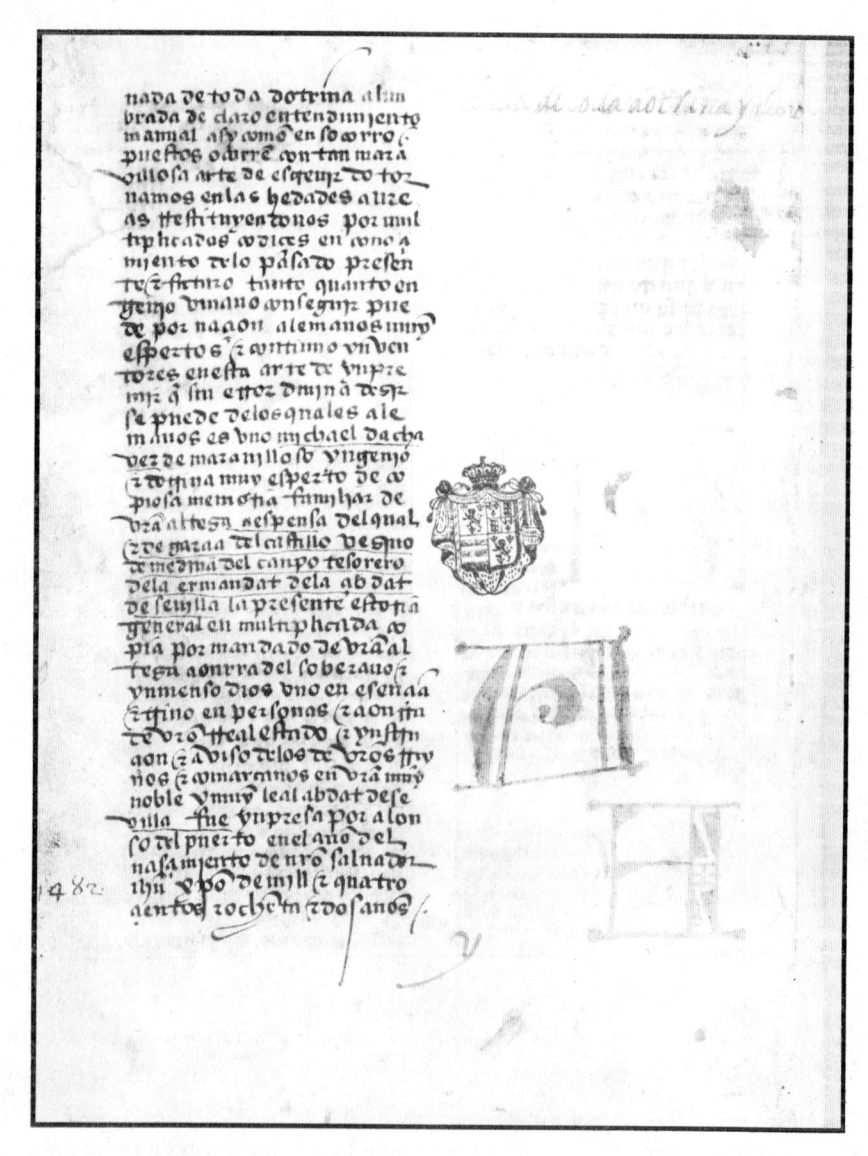

Plate 1: MS Egerton 286, fol. 163v. By permission of the British Library.

> uchas cosas son illustrissima princesa queme persuaden asi
> alguna cosa por ingenio o trabajo de estudio fallar se pue
> da a nuestros cōtenporaneos ↄ aun alos que venirse espe
> ran por modo de breuedad. la qual es amiga de todo sa
> no entendimiento la comuniquemos. por que nuestra bedad o tiempo
> que alos ante pasados varones en parte paresce auer enbidia no sea
> engañada. ¶la qual bedad a pena cede ni lugar dar quiere a algun si
> glo delos que fueron antes del nuestro presente. ↄ por que las istorias
> cronicas que por luengos interualos de tiempo por guerras ↄ otras
> varias dissensiones parescen ser sepultas ↄ enmudecidas sin fruto. a
> cabsa dela penuria de originales ↄ trasuntos. que por peresa o flaca
> liberalidad es interuenido. ¶ agora de nueuo serenissima princesa
> de singular ingenio adornada de toda dotrina alūbrada de claro en
> tendimiento manual. asi como en socorro puestos ocurren con tan ma
> rauillosa arte de escreuir do tornamos enlas bedades aureas restitu
> yendonos por multiplicados codices en conoscimiento delo pasado
> presente ↄ futuro tanto quāto ingenio bumano conseguir puede. por
> nascion alemanos muy espertos ↄ continuo inuentores enesta arte de
> inprimir que sin error. diuina desir se puede. delos quales alemanos
> es vno michael dachauer de marauilloso igenio ↄ dotrina. muy esper
> to de copiosa memoria familiar de vuestra altesa a espensa del qual
> ↄ de garcia del castillo vesino de medina del canpo tesorero dela ber
> mandad dela cibdad de seuilla la presente istoria general en multipli
> cada copia por mandado de vuestra altesa. a honrra del soberano ↄ
> inmenso dios vno en esencia ↄ trino en personas. ↄ a hōrra de vuestro
> real estado ↄ instrucion ↄ auiso delos de vuestros reynos ↄ comarca
> nos en vuestra muy noble ↄ muy leal cibdad de seuilla. fue inpresa por
> alonso del puerto. enel año del nascimiento de nuestro saluador ibū
> xpo de mill ↄ quatrocientos ↄ ochenta ↄ dos años.

PLATE 2: IB 52308 Y$_6$. By permission of The British Library.

Dia de santa sabina. que fue. a ttreinta / Dias del mes de dicienbre -- 1604. me naçio. sa/bina. bautiçose enla puerta. fueron padrinos bartolome / duran. y su muger. / murio esta nina -- domingo. 22 / de otubre -- 1606 años Alonso de mesa.

Alonso de Mesa was an officer in the Spanish army, and a native of Puerto de Santa María. The Puerto de Santa María connection is suggestive: Alonso del Puerto lived in this busy port, and Diego de Valera had two periods of residence there (he was in the service of the Duke of Medinaceli), from 1470 until 1478, when he left to take up his position as Corregidor of Segovia, and after retiring from that position in the early 1480s until his death. His son was alcaide and corregidor of Puerto de Santa María in 1478, and Diego joined him in command of a fleet or squadron patrolling the Straits of Gibraltar after 1482.[3]

The incunable collates as follows: Folio. $+^{10}$; A-Y^8 . 186 leaves, 11 blank, and presumably also 186. 36 lines. 168 x 109 mm. Gathering A is incorrectly signed [A$_1$], Aiij, aiiij, av, followed by four unsigned leaves. The British Library copy is imperfect, wanting A$_8$.[4]

It seems clear beyond any reasonable doubt that the MS copies the incunable, not merely because it reproduces the 1482 colophon (see Plate 1), and follows the lay-out of material in the table of contents, but also because there are in the MS no printer's marks of the kind one would have expected if it had been used as copy-text.[5] It is therefore ironic that the scribe should have transcribed the well-known statement on printing on Y$_6$, which is reproduced --from the incunable-- in Plate 2. I give a translation:

> Most noble princess: many things there are that persuade me that as soon as some thing by ingenuity or studious work should be found for our contemporaries, and even for those who come after us, in the way of saving time, which is the friend of every healthy understanding, we should make it known, in order that our age, or time, which seems in part to envy the ancients, might not be disappointed. Which age only with difficulty gives way to any century preceding our own, since the histories and chronicles --because of the passage of long periods of time, and because of wars and other disturbances-- seem buried and silenced, without fruit, as a result of the lack of originals and copies caused by sloth or want of patronage. Now, most serene princess of singular mind illuminated by great learning and of clear practical vision, these men of the German nation, continual innovators in this art of printing which, as it is without

error, may be called divine, come as though rushing to our aid with such a marvellous art of writing by means of which we may return to the Golden Age, bringing us back with multiple copies to a knowledge of the past, present and future, insofar as human ingenuity is able. One of these Germans is Michael Dachauer, of marvellous wit and very expert learning, with a prodigious memory, a member of your majesty's household, at whose expense, and that of García del Castillo, native of Medina del Campo and treasurer of the Brotherhood of the city of Seville, the present General History --at the commandment of your majesty and to the honour of Almighty and Omnipotent God, one in essence, threefold in persons, and to the honour of your Royal Estate and for the instruction and guidance of your subjects in the whole kingdom and in your most noble and loyal city of Seville-- was printed by Alonso del Puerto in the year of the Nativity of our Saviour Jesus Christ of one thousand and four hundred and eighty-two.

It is clear then that the German, Dachauer, was the backer of this edition, in association with the Spaniard García del Castillo, and it is implied that the German has some expertise in the craft of printing. This seems to be confirmed by two entries in the Registro General del Sello (RGS) in 1477 and 1478, in which he is called 'impresor alemán'; the documents to which these entries refer are exemptions from taxes.[6] García del Castillo is also mentioned: he is appointed jeweller to their majesties in 1477, so that his connection with early printing is not remarkable.[7]

However, the first book printed at Seville, so far as we know, came from the press of three native Spaniards --Antonio Martínez, Bartolomé Segura and Alonso del Puerto-- who on 1 August 1477 sign Sánchez de Vercial's *Sacramental*; del Puerto and Segura sign the first illustrated book produced in Spain, Rolewink's *Fasciculus temporum*, in 1480.[8] It is curious, and yet typical of early printers, that these first efforts seem to display none of the hesitation associated with apprenticeship. Another book was produced in Seville in 1477 by the original trio (this time they provide neither day nor month): Díaz de Montalvo's *Repertorium*. This book and the *Sacramental* both contain a verse colophon exhibiting none of the reverence for German expertise apparent in the statement on printing in the Valera:

Si petis artifices primos quos Ispalis olim
vidit et ingenio proprio monstrante peritos

Tres fuerunt homines martini Antonius atque
de portu Alphonsus segura et Bartolomeus.[9]

We may therefore assume that Dachauer, already engaged in the book trade at Seville,[10] was keen to have the talents of his compatriots emphasized in this statement addressed to the Queen, and that, as financial backer of the edition, he was able to stifle the patriotic sentiments of his Spanish printers. Present evidence allows us to do no more than speculate as to his involvement in the bringing of German printers to Seville in subsequent years. The Spanish volume of the British Museum catalogue of incunabula[11] charts the vicissitudes of early printing in Seville: the Spaniards --Alonso del Puerto, Bartolomé Segura, Alonso Martínez, in various combinations-- worked from 1477-87, followed, after a three-year hiatus, by the waves of Germans and other foreigners -- Compañeros Alemanes, then Ungut and Polonus, Brun and Gentil. It is tempting, in the light of entries in the RGS, to posit a key role in the arrival of German printers for Michael of Dachau, if indeed he may be identified as the Michael in question:

> II 2504, 10 Feb 1480, Toledo. [Provisión] a petición de 'Maestre Miguell, librero', en amparo de ciertas cartas de seguro y licencia que tienen él y sus factores para entrar en el Reino libres de derechos los libros que para la venta trajeren.

> III 829, 28 Nov 1480, Medina del Campo. Para que conforme al tenor de la ley de las Cortes de Toledo de 1480 que se inserta, no se le exija a maestre Miguel Alemán, alcabala ni otro derecho alguno sobre los 'libros de molde' que trajere al reino...

It may be of course that this Maestre Miguel (Alemán) has no connection with Michael of Dachau, but it could also be that Dachauer was not in fact a printer (no work signed by him survives, though this is not proof positive, as the case of Francisco de Torres, mentioned by Norton[12] illustrates) despite the epithet in the entries unquestionably relating to Dachauer in RGS (cited above, page 91), but an entrepreneur of the sort described by Norton: a 'group of...nebulous figures who styled themselves merchants, for whom there is no evidence that they engaged in the retail trade, and who may have been wholesale dealers in books, or even general merchants with an eye for a profitable investment'.[13] It is a pity that we do not know from where he imported his books: Italy would be a possibility, and would provide the sort of link we need, because we know that the *Cuatro Compañeros* and Ungut and Polono came to Spain via Italy;[14] Pedro Brun of Geneva had printed in Catalonia before coming to Seville, and he may have reached there by way of Italy -- his partner, Juan Gentil, was certainly Italian.[15] This would allow us to picture the merchant/entrepreneur Dachauer, either sensing himself that there was a gap in the market for printed material that his imports could not satisfy and suggesting to the Monarchs that they should contact his acquaintances in Italy, or responding to a royal request for information that led to the royal commands summoning the Cuatro Compañeros and Ungut and Polono from Venice and Naples respectively.[16] In this connection, it is interesting to note that in 1485 three Italians --Antón Cortés, Francesco de Bolonia, Gaudencio de la Marca-- calling themselves 'impresores' and also 'mercaderes italianos' petition to avail themselves of the tax-exemption on the import of books. They do not hesitate, in a phrase reminiscent of Dachauer's own, to link themselves with the new invention, saying that they are 'principales inventores e fatores de la arte de faser libros de molde'.[17]

Dachauer perhaps did not sense the irony in the fact that Alonso del Puerto, no German, should have printed the statement on printing. But most of the printers who put out later editions of this popular work clearly saw the propaganda value of it, and included it, inserting their own names and deleting those of Dachauer, García del Castillo and Alonso del Puerto.

The first of these was Fadrique de Basilea, who in 1487 produced a second edition of Valera's *Crónica* at Burgos, a virtual reprint of Alonso del Puerto's 1482 *princeps*.[18] The statement on printing is substantially identical, until we come to the mention of Dachauer:

> Delos quales alemanos es vno frederico de basilea de marauilloso ingenio & doctrina. muy esperto de copiosa memoria familiar de v*ues*tra alteza. a honrra del soberano & inme*n*so dios vno en esencia & trino en personas. E a honrra de vuestro rreal estado & instruçion & auiso delos de vuestros rreynos y comarcanos e*n* vuestra muy noble & muy leal çibdad de burgos. Fue impresa por el dicho frederico. Enel año del nasçimiento de nuestro saluador ihesu christo De mill & quatroçientos & ochenta E siete años.

94   David Mackenzie

The 'noble and loyal city' is now Burgos; we may ask ourselves in what sense Fadrique de Basilea is Her Majesty's *familiar*. Palau's claim --presumably based on Haebler 656-- that there is a 1491 printing by Fadrique in the Biblioteca Estense at Modena, has recently been confirmed by Soave.[19] It is clear from his description that this printing (presumably a simple reprinting of that of 1487) also contains the statement.

The next printer to produce an edition of our chronicle is Heinrich Mayer of Toulouse, whose proximity to the Spanish frontier led him to print a number of works in Spanish.[20] Whereas Fadrique de Basilea had chosen the folio format, Mayer put the work out in quarto, two columns, 35 lines to the column: his use of the so-called 'r perruna'[21] doubtless reflects the lack of sufficient type in a set not designed for Spanish.[22] Mayer reproduced the statement on printing much as Fadrique de Basilea had done, changing the names to protect the innocent:

>Delos quales alemanos es vno Henrico mayer de marauilloso ingenio & doctrina. muy esperto de copiosa memoria familiar de vuestra alteza. a honrra del soberano & immenso dios vno en essençia & trino en personas E a honrra de vuestro rreal estado & instruçion & auiso delos de vuestros rreynos & comarcanos enla muy noble çibdad de Tholosa.
>Fue impresa por el dicho Henrico Enel ano del nasçimiento de nuestro saluador ihesu christo De mill & quatroçientos y ochenta & nueue años.
>Deo graçias.[23]

Mayer, following his model, claims, even more improbably, to be the Queen's *familiar*; he does not appear to have any difficulty either in changing the name of the city to Toulouse, even though there can have been few of Her Majesty's *comarcanos* there.

The work was now becoming popular, and the next edition appeared at Zaragoza in 1493, from the press of another German, Paulo Hurus from Constance. Again, the statement on printing is substantially identical, until we come to the mention of Dachauer:

>Delos quales Alemanos es vno Paulo hurus de Constancia de marauilloso ingenio y doctrina muy esperto de copiosa memoria familiar de vuestra alteza: a honrra del soberano & immenso dios vno en essencia & trino en personas. Y a honrra de

vuestro real estado: & instrucion y auiso delos de vuestros reynos: y comarcanos. En vuestra muy noble & insigne cibdad de çaragoça: fue impresa a costa y espensas del dicho Paulo hurus. Enel año del nascimiento de nuestro saluador Jesu christo de mill y quatrocientos y nouenta y tres anos. A veynte y quatro dias de setiembre. Laus deo.[24]

There are some noteworthy alterations here: although Hurus still claims to be the Queen's *familiar*, he seems to have difficulty with *comarcanos*, separating them from the city (which is now *insigne* rather than *leal*), and using that mention of Zaragoza to begin the colophon. He also says that he paid for the edition.

In the same year, the anonymous printer of Nebrija's *Gramática* also put out an edition of the *Crónica*, and here there are some quite interesting variations. So keen does this man appear to have been to maintain his anonymity that he ignored this opportunity for easy publicity; we may also deduce from his suppression of any reference to the Germans that he was not of that nation.[25] The statement is more or less faithfully reproduced, but only until the mention of the Queen:

...agora de nueuo serenissima princesa de singular ingenio adornada: de toda dotrina alumbrada: & de claro entendimiento Assi como en socorro puestos ocurren con tan marauillosa arte de escriuir: do tornamos en las hedades aureas: rrestituyendo nos por multiplicados codices en conocimiento delo pasado presente & futuro: tanto quanto ingenio humano conseguir puede: alumbrado por spiritu santo & inuentor continuo enesta arte de impremir que sin herror diuina dezir se puede: a onra del soberano & inmenso dios vno en esencia & trino en personas Fue impresso en la noble ciudad de Salamanca: enel año del nacimiento del señor de mill & cccc & xciij años.[26]

This printer is sensitive enough to the Spanish language to remove the somewhat unregal adjective *manual* from *entendimiento*. Anonymous folk rush in to help with the marvellous invention of printing, and the *inventor continuo* can only be the Holy Spirit, which links quite neatly with the statement that printing is error-free and therefore divine. It is clear that these modifications are not the result of inertia: the printer took the positive step of removing references to the Germans and the previous printer's name, made the conscious decision not to insert his own, and then attempted to make sense of what was becoming increasingly incomprehensible.

The same printer, or at least a man using the same types, produced three more editions of the work, all anonymously and all at Salamanca. They seem to be virtually page-for-page reprints of the 1493 version, but a more detailed examination than has proved possible would be necessary to establish this with complete certainty. The details are as follows:

Salamanca: [Printer, Nebrija's *Gramática*], 1495 8th May
Salamanca: [Printer, Nebrija's *Gramática*], 1499 20th January
Salamanca: [Printer, Nebrija's *Gramática*], 1500 17th June[27]

For our purposes here, it is sufficient to note that each subsequent Salamanca printing includes the statement on printing in the same form as it appeared in 1493. The desire for anonymity thus remains strong in the face of temptation, which may support F. J. Norton's theory that the same printer was responsible for the entire output of what have been regarded as two distinct Salamanca presses (that of the printer of Nebrija's *Introductiones Latinae* being the other).[28]

The next printing known to us is yet more revealing of printers' attitudes, and comes from the press of Jorge Coci in Zaragoza with the date of 20th April 1513. As Norton has remarked, Coci inherited the business and the types of Hurus;[29] here he uses the same woodcut on his title page as his predecessor, and the book as a whole looks remarkably like the 1493 printing. At the end, however, where Hurus allows the statement on printing to run on normally after the concluding statement by Valera, Coci leaves a blank half-column on 107r (the text in both printings is in two columns) and prints the statement over the whole page on 107v. The text is substantially the same as that in Hurus's version, save that 'Jorge Coci Theutonico' is substituted for 'Paulo Hurus de Constancia' in the first mention, and 'Jorge Coci' for 'Paulo Hurus' in the colophon. If it is remarkable that the Salamanca printers should have neglected this opportunity for publicity, it is surely no less noteworthy that Coci should have taken the trouble to give prominence to a statement of printing's virtues addressed to a monarch who had died nine years previously, in 1504. The repetition of the dedication to Isabella on 2r would pass unnoticed as the reproduction of the author's prefatory remarks to the first edition; but the cavalier adaptation by Coci of the statement on printing demonstrates either carelessness --because the Queen is not mentioned by name as she is in the dedication-- or a great desire for publicity.

The next printer to undertake an edition of this popular work was another German, Jacobo Cromberger, who was more careful than Coci, and excised the statement. It was perhaps unusual for Cromberger to have overlooked an opportunity to proclaim his expertise, but he may have considered it not worth the effort of recasting a somewhat stilted eulogy in 1517, when the novelty was wearing off. Nevertheless, it is interesting to note that Cromberger resorts to a similar, if more detailed, encomium in his 1527 edition of Alfonso de la Torre's *Visión delectable*, which he printed with his son, Juan:

fol. 80r

> En donde y por quien fue inventada la arte de imprimir libros: y en que año se diuulgo.
>
> Entre las artes & inuenciones subtiles que por los hombres han sido inuentadas se deue tener por muy señalada inuencion la arte de imprimir libros por dos principales razones. La primera porque concurren enella muchos medios para peruenir a su fin que es sacar impresso vn pligo de escriptura o cient mill pligos: y cada vno de aquellos medios es de muy subtil inuencion & cas i admirable. La segunda razon es por la grande vtilidad que della se sigue. Notorio es que antes de su inuencion eran muy raros los que alcançauan los secretos assi de la sagrada scriptura como de las otras artes o sciencias: porque todos no tenian possibilidad de comprar los libros por el mucho precio que valian: y pocos bastauan a sortir librerias. Empero despues dela inuencion desta diuina arte a causa dela mucha copia de libros: manifiesta es la multiplicacion y gran fertilidad que ay en toda la christiandad de grandes hombres en todas las sciencias: y quan en la cumbre estan oy todas las artes & sciencias. Pues vn arte tan subtilissima y de tanta vtilidad: razon es que se sepa la prouincia en do fue inuentada: y en que ciudad: y mas con razon la persona por quien fue inuentada. Y tambien el año: porque sabida la tierra & ciudad & persona a quien todos somos tan deudores lo tengamos en la veneracion que por ello merece. Assi que fue inuentada en Alemania: en vna ciudad que se dize Maguncia: la qual es situada sobre vn grande rio que se dize Rin: la qual ciudad es cabeça de arçobispado. Inuentola vn noble ciudadano muy rico desta ciudad que se llamaua Pedro fuest. Diuulgo se la dicha arte enel año del señor de mil y quatro cientos & veynte y cinco años. Y despues enel año de mill y quatro cientos y .xxxi. ouo diferencia entre dos

arçobispos: y el que no posseya touo cierta forma con ciertos ciudadanos dela dicha ciudad que le abriessen la puerta la noche de sant Simon & Judas: y entro con su gente: y mato quasi todos los hombres de la dicha ciudad: fue tanta la matança que corrian las calles sangre como de agua quando llueue: entonces mataron a este memorable varon Pedro fuest: cuya anima aya gloria con todos los passados. Amen.[30]

Cromberger seems to have had commercial reasons for inserting such a passage: he and his colleague, Juan Varela de Salamanca, had been chosen by the printers and booksellers of Seville to persuade the Emperor Charles V to ratify a privilege granting tax exemption on the export of books from the city, in the face of an attempt by the local municipal authorities to impose such a tax.[31] This takes us back to Michael of Dachau and the earlier statement on printing: whereas the other printers were content to reproduce almost mechanically what they found in the popular text they were reprinting, Cromberger, combining the practical skill of the printer, the sensitivity of the publisher and --like Dachauer-- good business sense, excised the dated passage from a work in which it had appeared every time it had been reissued over a period of thirty-one years, and wrote his own version when circumstances once again made it necessary to fend off the tax-collector.

APPENDIX

List of all known printings of Diego de Valera's *Crónica abreviada de España*

1	1482	Seville: Alonso del Puerto
2	1487	Burgos: Fadrique de Basilea
3	1489	Toulouse: Heinrich Mayer
4	1491	Burgos: Fadrique de Basilea
5	1493 [24 September]	Zaragoza: Pablo Hurus
6	1493	Salamanca: [Printer, Nebrija's *Gramática*]
7	1495 [8 May]	Salamanca: [Printer, Nebrija's *Gramática*]
8	1499 [20 January]	Salamanca: [Printer, Nebrija's *Gramática*]
9	1500 [17 June]	Salamanca: [Printer, Nebrija's *Gramática*]
10	1513 [20 April]	Zaragoza: Jorge Coci
11	1517 [2 October]	Seville: Jacobo Cromberger
12	1527 [2 February]	Seville: Juan Varela
13	1534 [31 August]	Seville: Juan Cromberger
14	1538 [?12 July]	Seville: Juan Cromberger
15	'1542'/1543 [9 April]	Seville: heirs of Juan Cromberger
16	1553 [10 March]	Seville: Jácome Cromberger
17	1562 [4 December]	Seville: Sebastián Trujillo
18	1567 [8 January]	Seville: Sebastián Trujillo

If each edition consisted of 500 copies, this would mean that a total of 9000 were printed.

No other edition is noted by Palau until that published in vol. 70 of the *Biblioteca de Autores Españoles* in 1878, which has been successively reprinted in the same collection. So far as I am aware, there has been no attempt at a modern, critical edition.

NOTES

1. See, for example, C. F. Bühler, *The Fifteenth-Century Book* (Philadelphia, 1960), especially p.33: 'A calligraphic text was, of course, the prerogative of the wealthy, but the routine, prosaic copy of a classic can only be accounted for on the basis that, as the fifteenth century was dying, it was still more economical to write out your own manuscript than to buy a printed version, even a second-hand one'; and p.39 where he reports a similar case: Theodoricus Nycolaus Werken de Abbenbroek, in his copy done in 1477 of the Sweynheym and Pannartz printing [Rome 1468] of St Jerome's *Epistolae*, 'solemnly transcribed' the statement in the editor's preface 'that the most desirable books could henceforth be purchased for what blank paper and unused vellum formerly fetched -- and that books were now priced for what one had been wont to pay for a binding. Furthermore, these volumes were correctly "written", not most erroneously made, as the work of the scribes is characterized'.

2. This is the title by which the work has become known among historians. It is indeed an abridged history, for not only does it cover the whole of Spanish history to the middle of the fifteenth century, but it deals also with geography and world history -- all in under 200 folios. It was compiled from the national chronicles of Castile and Aragon, in the same fashion as the contemporary, but longer, *Compendio historial* of Diego Rodríguez de Almela. Men like Valera and Almela put themselves at the service of the Catholic Monarchs as propagandists of their political programmes in the newly-unified country; see, for example, the tracts published in Diego Rodríguez de Almela, *Cartas*, ed. by D. Mackenzie (Exeter: Hispanic Texts, 1980).

3. *Enciclopedia universal ilustrada europeo-americana*, 70 vols (Bilbao, [n.d.]), art. Mesa. 'Alonso de Mesa: Militar español del siglo XVI n. en Cádiz. Pertenecía a los tercios de Flandes como alférez'. For Valera, see J. de Mata Carriazo's introduction to his edition of Diego de Valera's *Crónica de los Reyes Católicos* (Madrid, 1927), *passim*, especially p.lxii.

4. The description of this book in the *Catalogue of Books printed in the XVth century now in the British Museum, part X. Spain and Portugal* (London, 1971) [= *BMC X*] suggests (p.32) that *av* is a half-sheet inserted into the centre of quire A. This is, of course, possible as an alternative collation, but it has the difficulty of positing a blank first leaf for the quire, and the insertion of a half-sheet containing the same amount of text as would have fitted on to that leaf. Irregular signing is not an uncommon feature of early printing, and seems the more likely explanation, especially in view of the upper- and lower-case used for the letter A, which seems to indicate some confusion.

5. See P. Gaskell, *A New Introduction to Bibliography* (Oxford, 1972), p.50. The MS does have rather a grubby look, but there are no marks corresponding to the lines or pages of the incunable: even if set in pages, the printer would have marked the end of the page on his copy. The MS was clearly read frequently, as the many marginalia testify, and this would account for its worn appearance.

6. *Registro General del Sello* [= *RGS*] (Valladolid, 1950-), I: 3264, 18 December 1477, Sevilla. 'Exención de alcabala, almojarifazgo y de otro cualquier derecho, hecha (en virtud de cierta ley, que se inserta) en favor de Miguel da Chanty, "impresor alemán"'; II: 736, 24 June 1478. 'Sobrecarta a petición del maestre Miguel de Chauro, impresor alemán, de una de Sus Altezas que se inserta --su fecha 18 dic 1477--...' [This is a cover letter including the previous]. The 'ley' in question was probably the decree exempting him from taxes on imported books

Spaniards, 'Germans', and the Invention of Printing 101

issued in favour of the Belgian printer Thierry Martins in Seville in 1477, published by W. J. Knapp, *The Earliest Royal Decree on Printing, or, Thierry Martins in Spain* (New Haven, 1881). In it the Catholic Monarchs explain that Martins 'nos fiço rrelaçion por su petiçion disiendo que el a seydo vno de los prinçipales inbentores y factores que han seido desta arte de faser libros de molde'. It is a particular pleasure to acknowledge that it was at Derek Lomax's suggestion that I consulted the *RGS*.

7. *RGS* I: 2291, 7 May 1477, Medina del Campo. 'Nombramiento de joyero de Sus Altezas hecho en favor de García del Castillo, vecino de la villa de Medina del Campo'. It will be recalled that Gutenberg was himself a silversmith. Such skills were of course necessary for the cutting of the punches from which the matrices to cast type were made.

8. J. P. R. Lyell, *Early Book Illustration in Spain* (London, 1926), pp.3-5. I owe this reference to Dr Clive Griffin.

9. See *BMC X*, lii, liii. The editors seem to imply that only the *Repertorium* contains the verses, but it is clear from Haebler [I: 220, 597] that they are present in the *Sacramental* also. (I am grateful to Professor Dadson for bringing this to my notice). Haebler argues for the priority of the *Repertorium* on the grounds that the verses 'se ponen en vez del colofón con solo el anuario, en tanto que el Vercial tiene un colofón explícito que sigue a los versos ... y casi los hace supérfluos', and he is probably correct.

10. J. Hazañas y la Rua, *La imprenta en Sevilla*, 2 vols (Seville, 1945), I, 13. Hazañas publishes a letter to the Cathedral Chapter at Seville from the King and Queen confirming Dachauer's exemptions; he spells the name *Deschaner*, and says: 'Debió ser impresor, residía en Sevilla en 1480, pero no creo que en España fuese más que mercader de libros'. The document refers to him as 'Maestre miguel desachaner [*sic*], maestro de los libros de molde'. I assume that these variations in the spelling of the surname merely evidence lack of palaeographic expertise and/or transcription or printing error.

11. *BMC X*, lii, liii.

12. F. J. Norton, *Printing in Spain, 1501-1520* (Cambridge, 1966), p.15.

13. *Printing*, pp.131-33.

14. *Printing*, pp.8-9.

15. *BMC X*, lvi.

16. *BMC X*, liv-lv; Norton, *Printing*, p.8.

17. *RGS* IV: 774. 16 April 1485, Córdoba.

18. There is a copy in the British Library, pressmark G. 6394. The statement on printing appears on fol. 205v.

19. A. Palau y Dulcet, *Manual del librero hispanoamericano*, 28 vols (Barcelona, 1948-77), XXV, 68; V. Soave, *Il fondo antico Spanuolo della Biblioteca Estense di Modena* (Kassel, 1985), p.8.

20. He was not, of course, the only Toulouse printer to exploit the Spanish market; Johannes

Parix of Heidelberg printed an Aesop in Spanish in 1488, and two further books in 1489. Parix had business dealings with his fellow Heidelbergan, Juan Rosenbach, printer at Valencia (*BMC VIII*, lxxi-lxxii), and printed five books at Segovia, including the first book printed in Spain, the *Sinodal de Aguilafuente* (*BMC X*, xxxvi).

21. I can find no reference in Norton or *BMC* to this term, nor does it appear in the Dictionary of the Royal Spanish Academy. Haebler uses it, but adding --surely incorrectly-- a til: *perruña*. The letter reproduces a variety of the double r used in Spanish book-hands of the period, but none of the manuals of Spanish palaeography I have consulted uses the term to describe it.

22. It is surely significant that Mayer only uses the character in the books he produced in Spanish (*BMC* VIII, 357 and plate LIX). Fadrique de Basilea had the same problem (and the same solution), but Alonso del Puerto, a native Spaniard, did not. Spanish, because of the relative frequency of *rr*, needs sorts produced with a higher quantity of this letter, and it may be that printers in the early period, perhaps not having the punches or the matrices to make more letters in a particular fount, resorted to this home-made solution in imitation of the scribal version, whereby the double r is formed by two vertical bars transversed by a horizontal one; none of these bars has any serif in the printed forms I have examined, giving the letter a rather rough and ready appearance. This surely implies that the printers of foreign origins brought founts with them and had insufficient skill to cut new matching punches. Someone who did produced this new character for the Spanish market, and the rest acquired it; they were insufficiently preoccupied with aesthetics to care about harmonizing its appearance with the Gothic founts in which it was inserted, and in which it sticks out like a sore thumb. Weight is perhaps given to this theory by the fact that the letter disappears in the early sixteenth century, as printing becomes more common. Does this mean that Alonso del Puerto and his companions had a fount cast with Spanish in mind?

23. I am grateful to the photographic service of the Bibliothèque Nationale, Paris, for providing me with photographs of their copy, which has the pressmark Rés. Fol. Oa 3.

24. I am grateful to the Library of Congress for supplying me with photocopies of their copy, which has the number 155770 in the Vollbehr collection.

25. He does, however, use an 'r perruna' (see above, n. 21) of the same sans serif kind as the printers of German origin. The use of this letter clearly merits further investigation.

26. The librarian at the University of British Columbia kindly sent me a photocopy of the colophon of this printing taken from microfilm.

27. The printings of 1495 and 1500 are in the British Library (pressmarks C. 8. i. 6. and IB. 52851), and the latter is indeed a page-for-page reprint of the former, though with slight orthographic variations. I am once again grateful to the Librarian of the University of British Columbia for sending me a photocopy of the colophon of the 1499 printing.

28. See Norton, *Printing*, p.27, and *BMC* X, lvii-lvix.

29. Norton, *Printing*, pp.69-70; the book is described in F. J. Norton, *A descriptive catalogue of printing in Spain and Portugal, 1501-1520* (Cambridge, 1978), no. 657.

30. The attribution of the invention of printing to Peter Schöffer or to his father-in-law Johann Fust ('Pedro Fuest' presumably being a composite of the two) derives from the early

fifteenth century, in a widely-diffused account circulated by Schöffer's son Johann. Fust was Gutenberg's financial backer in the early 1450s, who foreclosed on him, seizing his press and materials and setting up as a printer himself in partnership with his future son-in-law. See *Encyclopaedia Britannica*, 15th edn (Chicago, 1974), XIV, 1054.

31. I am grateful to Dr Clive Griffin, of Trinity College, Oxford, for having drawn my attention to the statement on printing in the *Visión delectable*; and for having read an earlier version of this article. Griffin's book, *The Crombergers of Seville* (Oxford, 1988), is the latest and most complete account of this important family of printers, and he deals with the Cromberger/Varela approach to Charles V on p.66. It is a pleasure also to acknowledge the help of Professor Jeremy Lawrence and Dr Nigel Griffin, both of whom kindly read the typescript and made suggestions for improvement. I have modified my original in places in the light of their comments, but none of course bears responsibility for any interpretation I may have placed on them.

CONFLICTING VIEWS TOWARDS THE MOZARABS AFTER 1492

RICHARD HITCHCOCK
University of Exeter

Interest in the Mozarabs after 1492 is generally though not exclusively focused on the city of Toledo. Here, in the sixteenth century, there were a number of families who were descendants of Christians who, it was believed, had maintained their Christianity throughout nearly four centuries of Muslim power over them, and who, during this period, had six (or seven) parish churches in the city in which they were free to celebrate Mass and to receive the Holy Sacraments. According to the authoritative lexicographer, Sebastián de Cobarruvias, in 1611, following the thirteenth-century definition of Archbishop Rodrigo Jiménez de Rada, because such Christians mingled with Muslims, they were known as 'mixtiarabes', 'eo quod cum arabibus viverent', -- because they lived amongst Arabs. After Toledo was captured from the Muslims in 1085, the memory of these 'mixtiarabes' was perpetuated and preserved, and the form of the word developed into 'mozárabes'.[1]

The Mozarabic families continued to enjoy the benefits of the privileges and exemptions that had been granted them by Alfonso VI, and which were subsequently confirmed and endorsed by successive Kings of Castile.[2] The fact that these royal Charters went on being ratified right up until the sixteenth century and indeed until as late as the eighteenth, was one source of dissension. In the same way, the provision in perpetuity of the Mozarabic liturgy in Toledo for the parishioners of the six Mozarabic parish churches was both a distinguishing and potentially alienating factor. Between 1085 and 1492, as the reasons for the political distinctiveness of the Mozarabic community decreased, so it gradually blended into the Christian community wherein the reformed liturgy was used. There were many fewer Mozarabic families where the traditions were retained; the number of priests had dwindled, and some of the churches were in a state of disuse. It was the well-known reforming vigour of Cardinal Cisneros which resuscitated the Mozarabic community in the city of Toledo. In 1504, he founded the Chapel of Corpus Christi in Toledo Cathedral and in 1508 provided a lavish endowment of thirteen chaplaincies so that priests could recite the Mozarabic rite daily. This higher profile which was accorded to the Mozarabic rite, would have enhanced the status of those Mozarabic families still clinging to their ancient privileges. It is easy to see in this action of Cisneros a desire to exalt the descendants of those Christians who had stood fast against Muslims at an earlier period in Spain's history. He had, after all, had his resolve strengthened by a visit to the Cid's tomb near Burgos when about to impose sanctions on the Muslims of Granada in the late 1490s,[3] but one must not forget also the prestige enjoyed by the city of Toledo itself, capital city and seat of the Primate of the Church in the Peninsula in Visigothic times, and now dignified by a Cathedral where the head of the Church in Spain could again preside with honour.

Gómez de Castro, Cisneros's biographer, thought that it was necessary to explain Cisneros' attitude, and hence attempted an explanation of the meaning of the word used to describe this favoured sector of the Toledan community. These Mozarabs had, he said, lived cheek by jowl among Arabs and were thereby called Mistarabes, but time had taken its toll and the form of the word was corrupted to Mozarabs. However distasteful this explanation may have been to Gómez de Castro, he went on to name those churches in which the Muslims allowed the Christians to practise their divine service.[4] There is just the suspicion of his sensitivity towards using a word that might conceivably suggest collaboration with, or contamination by the Arabs. As the century progresses, we find the Mozarabic community in Toledo more sensitive about their past, more conscious of their present status, and we see a surprising hardening of attitudes by sundry commentators.

In Bernard of Luxembourg's *Catalogus Haereticorum*, first published in Cologne in 1522, there is an evident awareness that adherents to Islam, or the 'secta Mahomet', as it is termed, constitute the enemy. Muhammad, the Arabs, the Mamluks, Ghazali, Averroes and Avicenna all figure.[5] Similarly, those related in some way to Judaism are also proscribed, Iudei, Reiudeizantes and Marrani. The compiler of the catalogue shows himself to have been aware of the Spanish context, not only because of the inclusion of the Marrani, but also because there are named heretics including Ramón Llull. One would not expect to find the Mozarabs listed, and indeed there is no entry for them, nor in the subsequent editions of this catalogue that I have been able to consult.[6] Curiously, however, Alonso de Castro in his *De Iusta haereticorum punitione*, first published in Salamanca in 1547, brackets the Marrani and Mozarabs together, and defends both of them against the charge of heresy.[7] He defines a heretic as someone who, after having received true baptism and after having been sufficiently prepared in the Catholic religion, persistently errs against it. This is true, he says, neither of the Marrani, nor of the Mozarabs. Speaking specifically of the Mozarabs he says 'nec haeritici, nec de haeresi suspecti sunt'. 'They have never gone astray from the Catholic religion', he says 'and they even have an *opulenta capella* in the famous Cathedral of Toledo where services according to their rites are celebrated daily'. Castro disclosed all this information about the Mozarabs to demonstrate that Bernard of Luxembourg had no justification whatsoever in placing them amongst his list of heretics. The prime suspect has thus been convincingly exonerated, but there has been no crime, because Bernard of Luxembourg had not in fact impugned the faith of the Mozarabs. Alonso de Castro (1495-1558) is not a negligible authority and it is significant that someone writing in Salamanca in the 1540s should consider it necessary to speak out so forcefully in favour of the Mozarabs. He was a Franciscan theologian who achieved fame with his *Adversus Haereses* (1534), who went to Bruges to combat the influence of Lutheranism, who is credited as being the founder of penal law in Spain, who became a chaplain of Charles V, and even travelled to England on the occasion of Philip's marriage to Queen Mary, as his spiritual mentor.[8] He was not therefore someone to make elementary blunders. The mystery, however, remains as to why he should have laboured under the mistaken impression that the Mozarabs were believed to have been amongst the ranks of the heretics. Alonso de Castro was not a Toledan, so was not *parti pris*, but he was familiar with the status of the Mozarabs in that city. A clue might be provided in the bizarre form of the word, which he uses frequently. The form of the word which he uses is 'mopsarabes' which is, to my knowledge, registered nowhere else.[9] It might conceivably represent his, albeit defective attempt, as a scholar, to reproduce the form of the Arab word *musta^caraba* from which 'mozárabe' is derived. Was Castro perhaps endeavouring to indicate, from a position of neutrality, that those possessed of the knowledge of the true definition of the word would not persist in their mistaken belief that 'mozárabe' implied contamination with Arabs and Islam? From the histories and chronicles written in the sixteenth and seventeenth centuries, it becomes apparent that the Mozarabs are brought into the discussion at four principal points: firstly, when the country was conquered by the Muslims at the beginning of the eighth century; secondly, when Alfonso VI captured the city of Toledo in 1085; thirdly, when the Mozarabic liturgy achieved a privileged status; and fourthly, in matters of lineage, either relating to nobility or to purity of blood. Seldom does any one source deal with all of these factors, but most authors seem to be anxious to justify the posture that they, as individuals, adopt towards the Mozarabs.

The first witness is Pedro de Alcocer (1554), author of one of the earliest, if not the earliest, histories of the city of Toledo. He describes himself as a citizen of the city. Indeed his name figures as an inhabitant in the census of 1561, and his work was held in high regard by his successors.[10] He is knowledgeable about the Mozarabs, and favourably disposed towards them, but not an impassioned partisan, and not apparently of a Mozarabic family himself. He applauded the decision made by Alfonso VI to grant greater privileges to the Christians he found living in Toledo when he conquered it than to those he brought with him to settle there, 'porque como buenos avian perseverado siempre, ellos y sus predecessores en nuestra sancta fee catholica, sin aver sido corrompidos de la secta y desonesto bivir de los Moros' -- 'because they and their ancestors had courageously persevered in our Holy Catholic Faith, refusing to be corrupted by Islam and the knavish behaviour of the Muslims.'[11] He was not unaware of the subsequent history of the Mozarab community, because he mentions that descendants of those originally favoured by Alfonso VI 'still live in this city'; 'aunque por las mudanças que las cosas en ella han hecho, se han mezclado unos con otros, de manera que este nombre de Muçarabes esta ya casi del todo desecho', -- 'although through changes that affairs in the city have brought about they have merged with others with the result that the name Mozarabs is now almost entirely set aside'. It is a pity for those of us looking back to this era that Alcocer is not more explicit here, and that he does not amplify 'las cosas'. He is saying, I think, that Mozarabic families were not blazoning the fact from the roof-tops, not that they do not exist. After all, the Mozarabic chapel in the Cathedral still flourished.[12] It is worthy of note that in the census of the city in 1561, it seems as though the inhabitants had to declare their status, as the word 'moçarabe' is appended to a number of the names in the register, as 'lorenzo de sebilla moçarabe', 'sebastian de guerta moçarabe', and 'baltasar de eredia moçarabe', for example.[13] There are some dozen named Mozarabs in the small parish of San Pedro adjacent to the cathedral, three very close to where the old Mosque used to be situated.[14] It is not difficult, perhaps, to imagine the germ of suspicion developing when it was common knowledge that people known as Mozarabs were seen to occupy a little square adjacent to the site where the old Mosque stood.

The historian Garibay, Philip II's Librarian and Chronicler whose work was completed by 1567, was one of the first apologists of the Mozarabs, although 'de nacion Cantabro, vezino de la villa de Mondragon, de la provincia de Guipuzcoa'. He drew on Alcocer but dwelt more on the origin of the word. He discussed the two possibilities 'mixti arabes' and 'Muza arabes', before opting for the latter as a more plausible explanation. If this seems strange to us now, we are perhaps inclined to forget the power of the argument.[15] If Musa b. Nusayr, who occupied the city after Tarif (this person was, in fact, Tariq b. Ziyad and not Tarif), permitted the Christians there to worship in seven named parishes, and if he wished to outdo Tariq in the amount of privileges and tax exemptions lavished upon them, what more natural way for the Christians to respond than perpetuating his name in honour of his memory? Such considerations would have been dismissed out of hand by Blas Ortiz, Canon of Toledo Cathedral who, in his description of it in 1549, had scathingly dismissed the idea of Muzarabe being a hybrid Muza Arabe, with the withering comment on Musa: 'nescio quo Arabum duce'.[16] Garibay goes into some detail about the Mozarabic liturgy which Alonso Ortiz had prepared at the instigation of Cisneros at the beginning of the century, providing unequivocal testimony that the liturgy sanctioned by the Pope and going back to pre-Islamic times, was practised both in the Cathedral and in some of the designated Mozarabic parish churches.

It comes as something of a shock after these generally sympathetic references to the Mozarabic community in Toledo to encounter the vitriolic condemnation of Mozarabs by a well-known Dominican preacher from Andalucía, Agustín Salucio. Not for him the genteel comments of the Toledan lobby. His remarkable treatise *Del Origen de los Villanos que llaman Christianos Viejos* was first published by López Estrada in 1951.[17] Salucio (1523-1601) was born in Jérez, of a family that originally came from Genoa. As a Dominican, he became widely known and respected as a preacher, even attracting the praise of Santa Teresa (1598). He was a frequent preacher in Seville Cathedral, and when Philip II died, in 1598, was accorded the honour of preaching the funeral oration in Cordoba. He was the author of a number of works, including a controversial study, written late in his life (1600), but not sanctioned for publication during his life-time, on the *Limpieza de sangre* statutes.[18] His *Tratado de los villanos* merits critical study. It is couched in the form of an epistle in response to a request to explain the origin of the 'villanos que llaman christianos viejos'. The people of Spain, in Salucio's view, could be divided into four categories: firstly, those who descended from the conquerors; secondly, from the conquered; thirdly, from neither the conquerors nor the conquered; and fourthly, from a mixture of the two.[19] The conquerors were the remnants of the Visigothic nobility who took refuge in the fastnesses of Asturias, Galicia and Navarre when Roderic lost Spain in 711, and from there gradually launched a campaign of reconquest. The conquered fell into two groups, Muslims and Jews who remained in their homes after the Christian recaptured Muslim territory. The Muslims in this category would have been called Mudejars, although Salucio does not use this word. Over the centuries they converted to Christianity, received holy baptism and were known as New Christians, 'christianos nuevos'. These were mainly people of modest aspiration whose origins in the late sixteenth century were now obscured in the mists of time. The second group of 'conquered' people were converts to Christianity during the reign of the Reyes Católicos, 'moriscos' and 'conversos', but Salucio uses neither of these words in his treatise. The description of new Christians should only be applied to these comparatively recent converts.

Salucio reserves most of his attention and his venom for those who fall into the third category -- those who were descendants from neither conquerors nor conquered, those who made terms with the invading Muslims so that they could keep their lands and possessions, eschewing the discomfort of exile in the mountainous regions of Spain, preferring instead a life of compromise under Muslim domination. These were the Mozarabs, known pejoratively as 'Mistos o Metis' who, although calling themselves Christians, owed all their loyalty and obedience to the Muslims. The word 'Metis' is an unusual one which I have not been able to locate elsewhere, but which must surely be associated with 'mestizo', and so signify 'of mixed race'. Salucio calls them 'falsos y fríos christianos sin zelo ni amor de religión', who had been compromisers ('contemporizadores') since the eighth century. He claims that King Pelayo called them 'Metrárabes o Muzárabes, que es decir Metis'. The significance of the two words 'metrárabe' and 'muzárabe' is that they both evidently derive from the same Arabic triliteral, ⁽araba, the former from the fifth form of the verb with the meaning of 'assimilating Arabic behaviour', and the latter from the tenth form, with the similar sense of 'having absorbed Arabic customs and language, wishing to pass for an Arab'. In other words they are Arabs made and not born. They were despised by the Muslims as apostates 'malditos de Dios y de los hombres'. The Mozarabs suffered persecution nonetheless, and their numbers were drastically reduced over the centuries until only a few remained: in the city of Toledo 'en cuya memoria quedó su Missa y capilla muzárabe' --'in whose memory the Mozarabic Mass and Chapel remained'--, and a handful more in Cordoba. Salucio argues that when Muslim lands were reconquered, the noble Christians --his category of 'conquistadores' or 'conquerors'-- liberated these 'míseros e infames muzárabes', who were essentially 'villanos' and lacking all entitlement to noble status. However, Alfonso X el Sabio called all the Christians in his kingdom apart from the 'hidalgos cavalleros conquistadores' 'old Christians', irrespective of their origin, and these included Mozarabs. So other people in Salucio's time who call themselves Old Christians either descended from Muslims and Jews or from Mozarabs and marranos (apostates) 'gente tan vil e infame y soez que introduxo a los moros en España, 'a people so rustic, so lacking in honour, and so worthless that they were responsible for bringing the Muslims into Spain.'[20]

This diatribe should properly be considered as falling within the *limpieza de sangre* debates, but there is no doubt that Salucio, widely regarded as one of the most academic apologists of his generation, was enunciating a historical argument with scholarly apparatus. He is the only person, to my knowledge, who used the word 'metrárabe' in the debates, not to mention the enigmatic 'metis'. Perhaps he was aware that the Arabs maintained a distinction between the ^c*arabun muta*^c *arribun* or ^c*arabun musta*^c *ribun*, naturalized Arabs, those who are not pure or genuine Arabs but who have borrowed Arabic customs and adopted the Arabic way of life.[21] Leo Africanus knew this in the 1520s, as did Luis del Mármol Carvajal, but it was articulated with greater clarity by the Cordoban Canon Bernardo de Aldrete in 1614, citing the earlier two as his sources.[22] The parallel with his own argument is striking. One cannot argue that Salucio's treatise achieved any propagandist impact and there is no evidence that his views were ever known by the Toledan lobby, but there is one curious point of contact between his views and those expressed by the Castilian historians. I refer to the acceptance that the word Mozarab implied being amongst the Arabs and not apart from them, 'mixtiarabes'. Writers continued to air Archbishop Rodrigo's definition, including such influential figures as Ambrosio de Morales, Juan de Mariana and Covarrubias. The area was still a sensitive one, and unresolved.

If the arguments respecting the *limpieza de sangre* debates had been one complicating factor, the emergence of the false chronicles towards the end of the reign of Philip II proved to be another. These chronicles purported to fill out Spain's past history, to dignify former achievements, to provide a past glorious enough to compare the greatness of the imperial age. Lost chronicles of Dexter, Liutprand and Julián Pérez of Toledo amongst others were discovered at the monastery of Fulda in Germany, and brought back to Spain. An attempt was made in the 1590s to get episcopal approval to publish one by a fifth-century historian, but the necessary sanction was not forthcoming as the Bishop of Segorbe was suspicious.[23] However the chronicles were soon known and their contents incorporated in future histories of Toledo including Francisco Pisa's, which was published posthumously in 1617.[24] The source of these new discoveries was a Jesuit Professor of Latin in the Jesuit College of Toledo, Dr Jerónimo Román de la Higuera (1538-1611), generally but not unkindly regarded as the author of these apocryphal works. Suffice it to say that the evidence of Julián Pérez's chronicle, in particular, provided much fuel to the debate concerning the noble origin of the Mozarabs.[25] Their steadfastness throughout the centuries of Muslim occupation of the city is amply testified and the names of major families are given, Portocarrero, Barroso, Godiel, Toledo, and Ficulneo from which Higuera derived his own name, thus introducing the ingredient of personal involvement.[26] What Julián Pérez, who purported to be the Archpresbyter of the Mozarabic parish of Santa Justa, at the time of Alfonso VI's conquest of the city, is appearing to argue, is that the Mozarabs were known as such since the Muslim conquest. They did make treaties with the Muslims, but these were an honourable price to pay for the survival of the Catholic faith in Toledo. Román de la Higuera is also credited with the authorship of many other works, including an Ecclesiastical History of Toledo, and more significantly a *Libro de los Linages de la Nobleza de Toledo*. Although these works are not now known, a common theme is quite apparent. The Mozarabic families of which both he and his literary creation Julián Pérez were members owed their nobility of status which had been ratified by numerous royal charters to their Christianity maintained throughout nearly four centuries of Muslim 'occupation' of Toledo.[27]

The strands that may be drawn together are, I think, these. The Toledan historians gradually recognized the increasing significance of evaluating the Mozarabs' past history. Historicizing thus became less objective, as the status of the Mozarabs within the city at the time of writing became more and more of an issue. The three distinct groups of etymologies reflected contemporary opinions in unexpected ways; Muza Arabe, the more far-fetched of the three, is very much a pro-Mozarab explanation, despite the fact that it involves the collaboration of the chief Arab conqueror of the Peninsula. The Arab etymon *musta^criba*, ideologically neutral, was known throughout the century, but was neglected in favour of the historically plausible 'mixtiarabes', which, however, could attract pejorative implications. Rogue variants are 'mopsarabes' and 'metrarabes'. There were two complicating factors, the *limpieza de sangre* question which led to claims that the Mozarabs were of suspect lineage, and the false hares started by the False Chronicles, which were used as a means to enhance the external perception of the Mozarabs' claim to nobility of lineage. Both these factors were to bring much more heat to the debates in the seventeenth and eighteenth centuries, when the literary knives were to be drawn with vengeance. As yet the contenders were merely sparring.[28]

NOTES

1. S. de Covarrubias (sic), *Tesoro de la lengua castellana*, ed. M. de Riquer (Barcelona, 1943), p.817a.

2. There exists a copious bibliography on the privileges granted to the Mozarabs. F. J. Simonet, *Historia de los mozárabes de España* (Madrid: Real Academia de la Historia (Memorias XIII), 1897-1903), assembled much of the data; Tomas Muñoz y Romero, *Colección de Fueros Municipales y Cartas: Pueblos de los reinos de Castilla, León y Corona de Aragón y Navarra II*, supplies many of the texts; J. A. Dávila y García-Miranda, *La nobleza e hidalguía de las familias mozárabes de Toledo* (Madrid, 1966), discusses the nobility of Mozarabic families.

3. Basil Hall, *Humanists and Protestants 1500-1900* (Edinburgh: Clark, 1990), pp.1-51.

4. Alvaro Gómez de Castro, *De Rebus Gestis a Francisco Ximenio Cisnerio* (Compluti: Andreas de Angulo, 1569), fol. 41.

5. Bernardo Lutzenburgo, *Catalogus Haereticorum* (Cologne: 1522), fols 17-77.

6. Lutzenburgo, *Catalogus Haereticorum*, Editio quinta (Colonia: Johannes Kempensis, 1537). See also Francisco López Estrada, 'Dos tratados de los siglos XVI y XVII sobre los mozárabes', *Al-Andalus*, 16 (1951), 331-61; López Estrada checked the second edition of Bernard's *Catalogus Haereticorum* (Paris, 1524), but he could not trace the entry either: 'sólo hallé la referencia a Marranus en la lista alfabética de herejías' (p.361).

7. Alfonso de Castro Zamorensis, *De Iusta haereticorum punitione* (Lugduni: Iacobus Faure, 1556), pp.76-79. The preface is dated 1547, the year of the first Salamanca edition.

8. Marcelino Rodríguez Molinero, *Origen español de la ciencia del derecho penal. Alfonso de Castro y su sistema penal* (Madrid: Cisneros, 1959). For a discussion of Castro's views on heresy, see pp.323-33.

9. Rodríguez Molinero, p.77.

10. Linda Martz and Julio Porres, *Toledo y los toledanos en 1561* (Toledo: Patronato 'José María Cuadrado', 1974), p.171: 'pedro de alcoçer' inhabiting the *Adarbe de la macerilla* in the parish of Santo Tomé.

11. Pedro de Alcocer, *Historia o Descripcion de la Imperial Cibdad de Toledo*, agora nuevamente impresa (Toledo: Juan Ferrer, 1554), fols 54r and 54v.

12. The churches however had fallen on hard times, two probably having disappeared by 1570. See Linda Martz, *Poverty and Welfare in Hapsburg Spain. The Example of Toledo* (Cambridge: University Press, 1983), p.164.

13. Martz and Porres, pp.192-93, from where these particular examples are taken.

14. Martz and Porres, pp.188-93, and p.123. Note also 'morales moçarabe', one of four inhabitants of the Puerta Nueva de la Iglesia, alongside 'El capellan mayor de toledo' (p.193).

15. Esteban de Garibay y Çamalloa, *Los XL libros del Compendio Historial De las Chronicas y Universal Historia de todos los reynos de España* (Antwerp: Christophoro Plantino, 1571). The 'aprobación' is dated 1567; p.381.

16. Blas Ortiz, *Summi Templi Toletani et graphica descriptio* (Toledo, 1549), fol. 96v. A Dr Ortiz figures in the 1561 census, as one of the chaplains of the Cathedral: Martz and Porres, p.283.

17. See n. 6.

18. Agustín Salucio, *Avisos para los predicadores del Santo Evangelio*, ed. by Alvaro Huerga (Barcelona: Juan Flors, 1959), especially pp.17-22. Huerga's study is thorough but he was not aware of López Estrada's publication in 1951 of the text under discussion here.

19. López Estrada, 'Dos tratados', p.337.

20. López Estrada, 'Dos tratados', p.344. The translation here, as elsewhere in this article, is mine.

21. E. W. Lane, *An Arabic-English Lexicon* (London: Williams and Norgate, 1874), Book I, Part 5, pp.1991-93, quoting various Arabic sources.

22. Leo Africanus, *De totius Africae descriptione, Libri IX* (Antwerp: Joan Latium, 1556). My reference is to fol. 16 of this later edition; Luis del Mármol Carvajal, *Primera Parte de la Descripcion general de Africa* (Granada: Rene Rabut, 1573), Part II, fol. 53; Bernardo Aldrete, *Varias Antiguedades de España, Africa y otras provincias* (Amberes: Juan Hasrey, 1614), pp.433-34.

23. The two principal sources for the false chronicles are José Godoy Alcántara, *Historia crítica de los falsos cronicones* (Madrid: Rivadeneyra, 1863), and T. D. Kendrick, *Saint James in Spain* (London: Methuen, 1960).

24. Francisco de Pisa, *Descripcion de la Imperial Ciudad de Toledo*, publicada ... por Don Thomas Tamaio de Vargas (Toledo: Diego Rodriguez, 1617).

25. Julián Pérez's chronicle was published by Lorenzo Ramírez de Prado in 1628: *Iuliani Petri Archipresbyteri S. Iustae Chronicon cumeiusdem adversariis* (Luatetiae Parisionum: Laurentium Sonnium, 1628), 158 + 149 pp. + unnumbered indices.

26. The best source here is Gregorio Mayans i Siscar, *Censura de historias fabulosas, obra posthuma de Don Nicolas Antonio* (Valencia: Antonio de Bordazar de Artazu, 1742), pp.623-24.

27. One of the most persuasive apostles of Román de la Higuera was Pedro de Rojas, Conde de Mora, whose *Historia de la Imperial nobilissima, inclita, y esclarecida ciudad de Toledo* (Madrid: Diego Díaz de la Carrera, Parte Primera 1654, Parte Segunda 1663), is an impassioned and convincing defence both of Higuera and of Julián Pérez.

28. This paper is offered in affectionate memory of Derek W. Lomax, with whom many happy and fruitful hours were spent discussing issues and interpretations of early Spanish history.

UN CASO DE INTERVENCIÓN DEL NARRATARIO: *AMADÍS DE GAULA*, I, 41

LILIA E. F. DE ORDUNA
Universidad de Buenos Aires.

En estos últimos años de nuestro siglo, proliferan --como bien se sabe-- las más diversas líneas críticas, aunque (¿quizá por avizorarse un nuevo milenio en el que tal vez se aspire a menos análisis agresivos, en procura de una auténtica serenidad, en muchos casos, perdida?) pareciera que las actuales investigaciones en torno a la obra de arte quisiesen retomar o adquirir la objetividad en el juicio, abandonando ciertas actitudes inútilmente polémicas o artificiosamente contestatarias. Cada tendencia que iniciaba su abordaje de un texto específico, indudablemente quería, o necesitaba, coherente consigo misma, recorrer el 'camino' --fiel a su 'método'-- que a priori se había demarcado. Así, sin enumerar ejemplos impertinentes, recordamos haber asistido desconcertados a interpretaciones que nunca los autores, aunque modélicos, o lectores anteriores, aunque privilegiados, hubieran podido lejanamente sospechar. De ahí que la crítica fuera generando, a su vez, duras críticas y, sabido es también que se multiplican las revisiones de teorías que, en su momento --'tempus fugit...'-- sedujeron acaso en demasía.[1]

No obstante, todo deseo de esclarecer, de buena fe, un texto, ha sido y será siempre enriquecimiento verdadero ya que contribuye a hacerlo accesible, aun cuando el autor mismo haya intentado (¿recurso o auténtica voluntad?) su indescifrabilidad: si bien producto de su imaginación, dejó de pertenecerle y está ahora librado al mecanismo de comprensión --acorde o no con lo que su creador pretendió lograr-- del lector ingenuo y del lector crítico. A esta zona, justamente, la del público oyente, espectador, lector..., receptor, en suma, sea cual fuere el vehículo expresivo del mensaje a transmitir, se ha prestado particular atención en estos tiempos finales de nuestra centuria. El análisis, en la mayoría de los estudios, se centra en obras recientes cuya complejidad estructural hace más apasionante la búsqueda de hilos conductores que permiten relevar las sutiles relaciones AUTOR-NARRADOR-NARRATARIO, unidas a infinitas posibilidades de desdoblamientos en casi infinito abanico de comportamientos. Por ejemplo, la noción de 'intertextualidad' necesitó ampliarse y Genette mismo justificó el concepto de 'transtextualidad', de límites y diferenciaciones no siempre nítidos pero siempre incitadores a exégesis nuevas.[2] Precisamente, es la literatura actual la que ofrece mayor cantidad de elementos aptos para la aplicación de técnicas novedosas: en ocasiones, una obra determinada semeja haber sido escrita como ejemplo exacto de la teoría correspondiente. Pero, la obra de arte de siglos atrás, cuando era regida por códigos actualmente perimidos, también hoy puede ser escudriñada a la luz de otros sistemas de abordaje.

Hemos creído oportuno comentar unos segmentos significativos de *Amadís de Gaula*, al terminar el capítulo XL del Libro Primero,[3] en los que la estética de la recepción tiene un excelente ejemplo mediante el cual se comprueba la incidencia de la actitud del receptor en la decisión del emisor y, como consecuencia, en la virtual configuración de la obra literaria, y no es casual que se ubique en uno de los pasajes más cercados de misterio que ofrece aquel lejano libro de caballerías castellano. Fue muy discutido por varias razones: muestra el desarrollo de un personaje que había surgido sólo con un modo apelativo reiterado, 'la fermosa niña' (capítulo XXI), al prestar ayuda a Amadís como 'la donzella que los leones soltara', y que en este momento se alza como una futura rival de Oriana al enamorarse perdidamente del 'más fermoso cavallero que nunca viera', 'y por cierto tal era en aquel tiempo' (agregará el narrador, con distinto tono de voz según cree el lector percibir). Además, la irrupción de 'Briolanja',[4] cuyo nombre sólo ahora se da a conocer, provoca la alteración de la armonía de la relación Amadís-Oriana pues, por malentendidos, recelos e indiscreciones, 'la sin par' enviará la famosa carta de cólera y despecho a su enamorado que motivará la penitencia de la Peña Pobre. Por otra parte, y de este modo nos aproximamos al aspecto que queremos destacar, en este punto ha de aparecer mencionado 'el señor infante don Alfonso de Portugal', cuya inclusión origina observaciones conjeturales acerca de su identidad. Sería hermano del rey don Dionís de Portugal (¿?) y habría vivido entre 1263 y 1312, determinación cronológica que permite ubicar esta refundición de *Amadís de Gaula*, que el mismo infante habría ordenado elaborar,[5] en un lapso exacto: dos últimas décadas del siglo XIII y primera década del XIV.

Un caso de intervención del narratario: *Amadís de Gaula* 119

Dejando de lado el presunto acervo documental que pudiera testimoniar tal hipótesis, lo que aquí nos importa es la función que tiene en *Amadís de Gaula*. Briolanja, como se dijo, ama al doncel, quien no puede retribuir su pasión pues sólo Oriana es y será la señora de sus sentimientos; en el momento en que se describe la desesperación de la joven no correspondida, leemos en el texto conservado:

> ahunque el señor infante don Alfonso de Portugal, aviendo piedad desta fermosa doncella, de otra guisa lo mandase poner. En esto hizo lo que su merced fue, mas no aquello que en efecto de sus amores se escrivió. (612)

Ya Cacho Blecua, agudo anotador de la obra, indicaba: 'la intervención del infante don Alfonso de Portugal implica que un lector participa en el desarrollo de un episodio al mostrarse en desacuerdo con los resultados narrativos'.[6] Y, evidentemente, la voluntad manifestada por el infante no queda en mero 'desacuerdo' sino que se impone y logra reconstituir la peripecia para que con los cambios que seguramente sugirió u obligó, Briolanja no resultara tan desdichada.

Este trozo que comentamos, pese a su brevedad, descubre un aspecto en el que deseo detenerme. Por una parte, los interrogantes que plantea la inclusión del infante Don Alfonso de Portugal tienen que ver con la naturaleza del pasaje en totalidad. Recordemos que para Avalle Arce es 'muy probable que el capítulo XXI sí perteneció a la versión primitiva del *Amadís*, y que la niña hermosa que no tiene nombre, fue un personaje episódico más, sin mayor trascendencia', en cambio 'la Briolanja, que aparece en el capítulo XXI, y todo este episodio, fueron producto de un refundidor [...] ajeno por completo a la versión original primitiva del *Amadís*'.[7]

Si continuamos la lectura del texto, advertimos que las opciones narrativas que siguen son varias:

> De otra guisa se cuentan estos amores que con más razón a ello dar fe se deve. (612)

Así el lector es enterado del nacimiento de mellizos, hijos de Amadís y Briolanja; no obstante, cuando empieza a salir de su estupefacción, la adversativa inmediata vuelve a sorprenderlo:

Pero ni lo uno ni lo otro no fue assí (613)

con lo que recibe un mensaje de cordura, a través de la aceptación de su destino asumida por Briolanja, merecedor, ciertamente, de la aprobación del narrador:

Esto leva más razón de ser creído. (613-14)

Varias versiones, pues, de un mismo hecho, preanuncio de la permanente estrategia cervantina --'unos dicen', 'otros creyeron'-- que, aunque no original en la segunda mitad del XVI, en la mayoría de los ejemplos del *Quijote* y de las *Novelas Ejemplares*, constituye el aporte imprescindible de voluntaria ambigüedad que posee toda su obra. Sin embargo, la existencia de distintas versiones de este episodio de *Amadís de Gaula* es importante ya que Montalvo parece (¿simula?) querer decirnos que pertenecen a sucesivas etapas de elaboración de la materia narrativa: 'mas no aquello que en efecto de sus amores se escrivió', 'de otra guisa se cuentan'. ¿Cuándo, quiénes? El problema que subyace, entonces, en torno al episodio de la 'niña fermosa' que se convirtió en 'dama enamorada', es el de las varias refundiciones de los diversos episodios de *Amadís*. Avalle Arce supone que 'los evidentes intereses literarios de don Alfonso de Portugal le llevaron a ordenar una temprana refundición del *Amadís*. El único testimonio de esta refundición que ha mantenido Montalvo se refiere al episodio de Briolanja'.[8]

Podemos añadir que aun cuando se demostrara con certeza esta hipótesis, el comportamiento de este narratario privilegiado no quedaría demasiado en claro y en este caso la dificultad es la misma que recorre irremediablemente los cuatro extensos libros de *Amadís* y que los fragmentos estudiados minuciosamente por Rodríguez-Moñino, Lapesa y Millares Carlo vinieron a corroborar:[9] no sabremos nunca cuál fue la verdadera labor de Rodríguez de Montalvo, el único que declaró su actividad de 'refundidor'; sólo un inesperado hallazgo de algún manuscrito que atesorara lo que se da en llamar 'el *Amadís* primitivo' podría echar alguna luz en este panorama inextricable.[10] ¿Cuál es la verdadera voz de Montalvo, narrador? La del Prólogo, sin duda, y

Un caso de intervención del narratario: *Amadís de Gaula*

la de los incisos didácticos. Pero, en el pasaje en cuestión, ¿quién se apiadó de la 'niña fermosa'?, ¿el narrador, acaso? ¿Pudo ser el mismo Montalvo que fingió atribuir la modificación de la historia a la compasión del infante, en afán --tal vez-- de dar verosimilitud a una incipiente peripecia, los amores de Briolanja y Amadís? O quizá la influencia auténtica de este lector privilegiado obtuvo del narrador la posibilidad del cambio... Sea como fuere, lo que creo destacable es que en el ocaso de la Edad Media, el autor haya aceptado que el narrador diera papel preponderante a un receptor (por importante que fuese en la realidad) hasta el punto de permitirle cambiar su mensaje.

Todo propósito de iluminar una obra de arte, de un allá y un entonces, contribuye a hacerla, para nosotros, más próxima. Desde nuestro *hic et nunc*, una relectura del *Amadís de Gaula* nos enfrenta a problemas que pudieron parecer propios de una narrativa posterior.

El narratario, ya visible en obras anteriores, en *El Conde Lucanor*, por cierto, que escucha y aprueba el mensaje, se ha convertido en manos de Montalvo, siglo y medio después, en un receptor activo y modificador. Podríamos preguntarnos qué actualizó aquel destinatario, cuál era su competencia, pero ignoramos su circunstancia. Si también *Amadís de Gaula*, como cualquier texto, involucra dos componentes inevitables, parafraseando a Eco[11] podríamos concluir que en este libro de caballerías se ha producido algo desacostumbrado con 'la información que proporciona el autor y la que añade el lector modelo', en tanto la primera no determina y orienta a la segunda. Dicho de otro modo, *Amadís* ofrece, en este pequeño sector que hemos indagado, la presencia de un 'lector modelo' apócrifo, el infante, que en su doble papel --o actitud-- de oidor y lector no acepta la 'determinación y orientación' que le brinda la información del autor. Por el contrario, él mismo habrá de hacer torcer el rumbo, obligando así al narrador a cooperar con este lector que --histórico o no-- se ha convertido por su actuar, en un personaje más de la ficción.

NOTAS

1. 'En una época como la nuestra en la que se vive la fascinación de la teoría literaria', afirmaba Mary Gaylord (véase 'Los espacios de la poética cervantina', en *Actas del Primer Coloquio Internacional de la Asociación de Cervantistas* (Madrid: Anthropos, 1990), I, 357).

2. Véase Gérard Genette, *Palimpsestes. La littérature au second degré* (Paris: Seuil, 1982).

3. Todas las citas corresponden a la magnífica edición de Juan Manuel Cacho Blecua (Madrid: Cátedra, 1987).

4. El estado de la cuestión en torno al nombre queda expuesto por Juan Bautista Avalle Arce en su *Amadís de Gaula: el primitivo y el de Montalvo* (México: Fondo de Cultura Económica, 1990). Resume así las interpretaciones divergentes: 'Briolanja deriva de Briolande, castillo que tiene cierta prominencia en L'estoire de Merlin (Sommer, II, 168-169), y no como quisieron Menéndez Pelayo (*Orígenes*, NBAE, I, CCXV) y Williams (art. cit., 53), de *Brion*, nombre que no aparece en las fuentes favoritas de los primeros autores y refundidores, como el *Merlin*, el *Lancelot*, y el *Tristan en prose*' (p.401).

5. Compareuna síntesis del problema hecha por Avalle Arce, con la sugerente reflexión final: 'todo esto me invita a la irónica consideración de que el asesino de su mujer histórica tuvo piedad de Briolanja criatura literaria' (*Amadís de Gaula*, p.163, n. 25).

6. *Amadís de Gaula*, p.612, n. 30.

7. Avalle Arce, *Amadís de Gaula*, pp.161-62. El subrayado es nuestro.

8. Avalle Arce, p.240.

9. Véanse Antonio Rodríguez-Moñino, 'El primer manuscrito del *Amadís de Gaula*'; Agustín Millares Carlo, 'Nota paleográfica sobre el manuscrito del *Amadís*'; Rafael Lapesa, 'El lenguaje del *Amadís* manuscrito', en *Boletín de la Real Academia Española*, 36 (1956), 199-225.

10. Quizá las permanentes búsquedas o la gravitación del azar logren alcanzar el objetivo, si se encuentran las teselas de este enorme mosaico. Véase, por ejemplo, José Luis Pérez López, 'Otra noticia del *Amadís de Gaula* anterior a Montalvo: una referencia a Beltenebros', en *Dicenda*, 9 (1990), 207-08, encontrada en copias de un cancionero del Marqués de Santillana, una de ellas fechada en 1470.

11. Umberto Eco, *Lector in fabula. La cooperación interpretativa en el texto narrativo* (Barcelona: Lumen, 1987).

THE ROAD TO VILLARRUBIA: THE JOURNEY INTO EXILE OF THE DUKE OF HÍJAR, MARCH 1644

TREVOR J. DADSON
University of Birmingham

The life of Rodrigo de Silva y Sarmiento, Duke of Híjar, Count of Salinas and Ribadeo, began in misfortune and tragedy and ended in much the same way.[1] He was born prematurely in March 1600, the only son of Diego de Silva y Mendoza and his third wife, Marina Sarmiento y Ulloa, seventh Countess of Salinas, but he never knew his mother since she died shortly afterwards.[2] Rodrigo himself was not expected to live long, if we are to judge from the observations of the court chronicler Luis Cabrera de Córdoba: 'murió la semana pasada la Condesa de Salinas de sobreparto, de la qual quedó un hijo, que se cree no vivirá, en lo qual ha sido muy desgraciado el Conde, por haber casado con dos hermanas condesas y no quedarle sucesión de ellas'.[3] But live he did, achieving the not inconsiderable age of sixty-three, dying 2 January 1664. However, his death was not that of a man of advanced years dying peacefully at home and in his bed. Rodrigo de Silva y Sarmiento died as a prisoner of state in the Castle of León where he had been held since 1648, for his part in a conspiracy to overthrow the King, Philip IV, and place himself, the Duke of Híjar, on the throne of Aragon.

This tragic frame that surrounds his life acts a recurring leitmotiv throughout it as well. This is not the place to go into Rodrigo de Silva's life in any detail, but in order to place the circumstances of his exile and banishment of 1644 (the subject of this paper) into some sort of context, it is necessary to run through the salient points of his life up until that date.

After the death of Marina Sarmiento in 1600, Diego de Silva y Mendoza decided not to marry again. Thus Rodrigo, left motherless at birth, grew up without that stable family and emotional support. However, this not uncommon occurrence in the Golden Age where death from parturition was a frequent cause of female mortality, was palliated to some extent by the existence of a network of family relationships. Rodrigo was almost certainly left in the care of his maternal grandmother doña Antonia de Ulloa until her death in 1605, and then in that of his aunt Magdalena Sarmiento.[4] By the time Magdalena came to marry the Count of Villalonso in 1608, Rodrigo was of an age to be left in the care of tutors. Presumably by then he lived with his father and accompanied him on his numerous journeys around the kingdom, visiting his extensive estates situated in Galicia (Ribadeo), Burgos, Valladolid, the border lands between Alava and Castile (Miranda del Ebro, Pancorbo, Salinas de Añana, and many other small towns), the Campo de Calatrava (Villarrubia de los Ojos de Guadiana), and, later, Portugal.

During the period Diego de Silva y Mendoza was Viceroy in Portugal (1617-22), Rodrigo was often in his company, and was given important tasks to carry out in the administration and in the preparation of the fleets for the Indies.[5] And it was while they were in Portugal that the negotiations for Rodrigo's future marriage to Isabel Margarita Fernández, heiress of the dukedom of Híjar in Aragón, took place, with Rodrigo's uncle Pedro González de Mendoza, Archbishop of Zaragoza (and younger brother of Diego de Silva y Mendoza) acting as intermediary with the bride's family.

This marriage, celebrated in October 1622, a few months after Salinas's abrupt recall to Madrid on the orders of the new administration of the Count-Duke of Olivares, gave the family a moment of joy and hope in the midst of the bitterness felt at Salinas's political fall from favour.[6] Through his marriage to one of the wealthiest heiresses of Spain and his acquisition of the title of Grandee of Spain, Rodrigo, only twenty-two years of age, must have felt that the future could only hold for him the brightest of political prospects. Under the benign (and, it must be said, corrupt) regime of Lerma, many nobles had flourished and occupied important court posts, none more so than Rodrigo's own father who had risen through the Council of State for Portugal to become its President and finally Viceroy and Captain General of Portugal. Unfortunately for Híjar and other aspiring nobles of the younger generation, the new order instituted by Olivares seemed to be based on two fundamental premises: 1) to distance itself as far and as fast as possible from its predecessor; 2) to return in so far as was possible to the austere times of Philip II where the nobles were kept at arm's length from the seat of power. To prosecute the first of these premises, Olivares, working through the *Junta de Reformación*, carried out a campaign of systematic harassment against former office-holders under Lerma. Thus the Viceroyalty of Salinas was subjected to unprecedented scrutiny, in particular his handling of the Portuguese kingdom's finances.[7] Olivares's agents in Portugal, supported by his henchmen in Madrid, initiated a number of lawsuits against Salinas during the 1620s, most of which concerned his financial (mis)management but some of which were more personally directed against his holding of lands and titles in Portugal: the Marquesate of Alenquer, for example.[8] It should be noted, however, that Salinas survived all these spiteful attacks on his name and reputation and eventually his title and right to Alenquer were confirmed by Philip IV himself.

The campaign against Salinas during these years and Olivares's aim of keeping the nobles away from real power (unless, of course, they were members of his own, recently elevated, family) meant that Híjar's chances of advancement were slim in the extreme. As premier nobleman of Aragon and heir to the title and estates of Salinas and Ribadeo, Rodrigo de Silva y Sarmiento cannot but have felt that these were wasted years. Furthermore, there is evidence that he had inherited his grandmother, the Princess of Éboli's overweening ambition, and he would almost certainly have remembered his grandfather Éboli's key role as premier councillor to Philip II. To men like Híjar, Olivares was little more than a minor Andalusian upstart who had usurped their true role and position.[9]

During the 1620s Híjar's life seems to have been dedicated to the incessant round of court festivities, attendance at which was the only way to maintain the fiction of being in attendance on the king. At most of these Salinas and his son were to be seen together. Salinas, whilst fighting to defend himself against the attacks instigated by Olivares's creatures in Portugal, tried to help his son as best he could, and in the spring of 1625 he drew up a comprehensive plan for the defence of Aragon in the hypothetical case that the French should decide to initiate an attack there.[10] This was a rather timely initiative as it happened, for on 15 October 1625 Olivares launched his ambitious plan for the Union of Arms, which required each province to prepare defence plans and outline the contribution it could make in human and economic resources.[11] Presumably the idea behind Salinas's document was that Híjar, as premier nobleman of Aragon, would present it to the King as his own piece of work and thus gain favour. Although nothing came of it then --no French attack was forthcoming--, it is interesting to note that Olivares's plans for the defence of Catalonia in the late 1630s owe much to the spirit of this Salinas-inspired document.

By the late 1620s it is clear that Olivares's opponents were running out of patience. Taking advantage of the King's sudden illness in 1627, they launched a rapid strike against the Count's hold on power. A number of leading nobles were involved in the virulent pasquinade that circulated at court condemning the favourite's handling of affairs, and although it is difficult to assign any particular authorship to the piece (the Duke of Sessa is often cited as its author), one copy in Portugal is clearly attributed to the hand of Salinas.[12] Híjar is usually associated with this group of conspirators.

The death of Salinas in June 1630 did not greatly improve Híjar's prospects at Court. Throughout the 1630s he was kept on the margins and seems to have spent most of his time trying to improve the economic health of his estates. Rapid inflation had dealt a harsh blow to many nobles whose estates were mortgaged to the hilt but who could not sell off any parts of them to pay their creditors due to the laws of entailment ('mayorazgo'). One example will suffice to show the effects of this on Híjar's own holdings: when Philip II incorporated into the Crown in 1564 all the salt mines still in private hands, their owners were compensated with state bonds or 'juros'.[13] But as Híjar spelt out to the King in a *memorial* of 1638, 'los quales [*es decir, los juros*] an baxado en valor y estimacion quando en vno y otro an crecido mucho las salinas y alfoli'.[14] He is referring to the Salinas de Añana and the Alfoli de Ribadeo which had previously belonged to the Counts of Salinas. Whilst the state bonds have depreciated considerably, the value of his former salt mines has increased. And now that the state has decided to suspend payment of the interest on the bonds, Híjar's position has become unsustainable. The only thing stopping him taking up litigation is, he says, that it would 'manifestar a todos la estrecheza en que se alla'.[15]

By the late 1630s and early 1640s Híjar was closely associated with the noble opposition to Olivares, which was doing its best to undermine his position of confidence with the King. The fall of the favourite in January 1643 opened up new and enticing possibilities for those nobles like Híjar who had

The Road to Villarubia: The Journey into Exile of the Duke of Híjar   127

waited for this opportunity so long, but the expected call from the King did not come, and after a short period where Philip IV tried to govern alone, the consternation of the nobles can be imagined when the former favourite's nephew, D. Luis Méndez de Haro, became the new 'valido'. Híjar's own unlimited ambition for political power had been augmented and encouraged by a letter written by Sor María de Agreda to the King on 14 April 1643 in which, displaying an unfortunate lack of prescience, she had personally recommended him with these words: 'Parece ministro de buen celo y fiel a V.M. A Dios pido lo sean todos los que van en compañia de V.M.'.[16]

Híjar, who quite obviously aspired to be Philip's new favourite (although ardently opposed in public to the whole notion of kings having favourites!), took an instant dislike to Haro, a situation which was not ameliorated when Haro offered him the Viceroyalty of Aragon (to get him out of the way), under the pretext that he had his mother-in-law there. A good enough reason, argued Híjar, for staying in Madrid! For the next twelve months Híjar conspired actively with other discontented nobles (among them the Dukes of the Infantado, Osuna, Montalto, and the Count of Lemos) to topple Haro. They came up with a bizarre plan to substitute Haro with the fallen Olivares, arguing that 'dado que Su Majestad hubiese de tener Privado, volviese al Conde, que estaba dueño de las materias del Gobierno, diestro y ejercitado, y que repudiase a D. Luis de Haro'.[17] Their first choice for the post, the Count of Oñate, who had had the good sense to turn them down, seems to have acted as a double agent, punctually informing Haro of everything the group discussed. When the Duke of the Infantado sought an audience with the King in Zaragoza in the spring of 1644 to obtain the resignation of Haro, the King had been previously warned and the whole group was put under house arrest. The King wanted an exemplary punishment for them all, but Haro convinced him that the ringleader was the Duke of Híjar and that the rigour of the law should fall on him alone as 'instrumento principal y cabeza de la Junta y de otros cuentecillos insulsos de que el Rey se había cansado'.[18] On 15 March he was ordered to leave the court within the space of twenty-four hours and go into exile to his village of Villarrubia de los Ojos de Guadiana, where he was to reside until further notice, 'hasta tanto que se le enviase otra orden, porque en aquel retiro se enseñase a callar y aprendiese la cordura y la buena prudencia', in the caustic words of the court chronicler Matías de Novoa.[19] In the distant and somewhat remote Villarrubia he was to while away his time for the next two years.

Híjar's last act before leaving Madrid was to dictate a *memorial* to the King asking for clemency. The *memorial* ends with the words 'Mañana, que es el plazo, ha parecido que me baya; y así lo haré'.[20] In other words, he left Madrid on 16 March 1644. Somewhat unfortunately, a recent writer on this episode in Híjar's life forgot that he was dealing with the seventeenth century and all its problems of communication and transportation, and fondly supposed that Híjar left Madrid on 16 March and arrived in Villarrubia the same day.[21] Even with a car in the twentieth century this would be no small journey to undertake; with, in this case, a caravan of seventeen mules, and at least fifteen servants and attendants, such journeys in the seventeenth century tended to last a number of days.[22] And anyway, in Híjar's case there was no reason on earth why he should want to hurry into exile. In fact, his journey took just over five days, from 16 to 21 March.

Whilst searching for biographical material on Diego de Silva y Mendoza, Count of Salinas and Híjar's father, I recently came across a fascinating document entitled 'Cuaderno de lo que se gasta en las comidas del duque mi s[eño]r y el marques mi s[eño]r, en la jornada que sus ex[celenci]as acen de madrid a billarubia y de lo que montan las raciones de los criados y comidas de diecisiete mulas y demas gastos echos en la jornada'.[23] Biographical information concerning noblemen and their involvement in court life and politics is not usually difficult to come by. Far rarer and harder to find is the detail behind their everyday lives, their likes and dislikes, their taste in food, how they spent their time. The importance of the aforementioned document cannot therefore be underestimated. Here we have punctually recorded by the Duke's accountant every detail of Híjar's journey into exile: where they stopped and spent the night; what they ate; how much they paid for food, lodging, and forage for the mules; who accompanied the Duke and their wages and rations. This *Cuaderno de gastos* therefore allows us to reconstruct in considerable detail the Duke's journey from Madrid to Villarrubia during the third week of March 1644.

Don Rodrigo was accompanied by his eldest son Jaime Francisco (who

The Road to Villarubia: The Journey into Exile of the Duke of Híjar 129

held at that time the title of Marquis of Alenquer).[24] Also in his party were don Lesmes de Valdés, his gentleman-in-waiting; his pages Antonio Garcés and Domingo de Barrios; his barber Pedro; Juan González the cook; Marcos, steward and pastrycook ('repostero y despensero'); Beltrán the chief coachman, and Domingo Soto and Juan, under-coachmen; three lackeys (Francisco, Pedro and Alonso); and two muleteers (Pedro and Marcos). Each was assigned a daily wage, which varied from the 9 reales for the chief coachman Beltrán and the 8 reales for don Lesmes de Valdés to the 4 reales for the page Antonio Garcés. The total daily outgoings in *raciones* were 88 reales, which were just under double what they normally received, for once they had arrived in Villarrubia the rations were reduced to a daily total of 50 reales 14 maravedises.

The Duke's party left Madrid during the afternoon of Wednesday 16 March (after lunch) and reached Getafe on the outskirts of the capital, a distance of about 13 kilometres, where they had supper and spent the night. A local canon gave them as a gift most of their food (oysters, sweetmeats, stuffed eggs, eggs in sugar, and cakes), which was probably just as well since they invited the priest to sup with them. The rest of the food they paid for: bread, ½lb. figs, half a dozen eggs 'en paguela',[25] olives, wine. Coal for the fire cost 3 reales and forage for the mules (barley) came to 72 reales 12 maravedises, an average price. Finally, they paid 4 reales for their lodgings and bought 1½ lbs. of candles (costing 10½ reales).[26] Expenses for the day thus came to 6182 maravedises (238 for food, and 5944 for other expenses -- rations, forage, lodgings).

Obviously in no hurry to reach Villarrubia and almost certainly waiting to see if there was any response from the King to his *memorial* of 15 March begging clemency, Híjar stayed in Getafe through the following day Thursday, only leaving after lunch on Friday afternoon when they continued on their way to Illescas. Lunch in Getafe on Thursday 17 March consisted of cauliflower (the most expensive item at 2 reales each cauliflower), limes, eggs (fried and 'en paguela'), salmon, sardines, and bread. Rather than supper they had a light collation ('colación') of cauliflower (again!), olives, cakes and fried breadcrumbs (*migas*). To while away his time in Getafe the Duke attended mass, where he gave 4 reales as alms plus another 16 reales to the

Confraternity of the Santísimo Sacramento. Don Jaime, for some reason, gave 2 reales to an 'hortelana' --an act of pure charity or had she brought them all the cauliflowers they ate that day?-- and the Duke ordered his accountant to pay 10 reales to the 'mozos de caballos del Andalucía': to carry a message perhaps to his administrator in Villarrubia warning him of their imminent arrival. It is also possible that some of the party went on ahead to Illescas, since that night the cost of beds was only 3 reales rather than the usual 4. Expenses for Thursday 17 March came to 7668 maravedises, 856 for food and 6812 for forage, rations and lodgings.

After a midday meal of limes, eggs (fried and 'en paguela'), salmon, dried salted cod (*pescado abadejo*), *migas*, the party travelled the 28 kilometres or so to Illescas, where they had a light collation of olives, cauliflower, pastry and more *migas*. Four friars were invited to sup with them, and it is interesting to note that one of the items on the bill was one litre ('medio azumbre') of wine costing 1 real. 10 reales of alms were given to the Confraternity of the Santísimo of Illescas, plus another 2 reales of unspecified donations. 20 reales went to the owner of the inn or 'posada' in Illescas where they stayed. The Duke was joined in Illescas by the Count of Lemos, one of his fellow conspirators (his horses received one peck [*dos celemines*] of barley), who perhaps came with news of events in Madrid. Up until then Híjar had taken his time in journeying into exile: from Wednesday 16 March (when he left Madrid) until Saturday 19 March (when he finally left Illescas) he had travelled a mere forty kilometres, which is slow even by seventeenth-century standards. His dilatoriness obviously corresponds to his hopes for a reprieve, for a change of heart on the part of the King. It is possible that he had prearranged with Lemos to meet up somewhere between Getafe and Illescas so that this nobleman could bring him definitive news. The news Lemos had to tell him was certainly not good or what Híjar wanted to hear, and so, with little or no hope left of a quick return to court, Híjar pushed on more quickly to Villarrubia.

Before leaving Illescas in the afternoon of Saturday 19 March, the Duke, perhaps to restore his flagging spirits a little, sat down to a substantial meal: pomegranates in sugar, salmon, sardines, cured fish (*pescado cecial*),[27] omelettes, cheese, olives, pastry, melon, stuffed eggs, milk and biscuits, honey

The Road to Villarubia: The Journey into Exile of the Duke of Híjar 131

and sugar. The journey from Illescas took them to Mascaraque, their next stop, to the south-east of Toledo. The decision not to go via Toledo (a surprising one that is unexplained in the document) caused Híjar and his party no few problems, in particular the crossing of the River Tagus. The lack of bridges over the major rivers was a notorious fact of life in seventeenth-century Spain, and in many parts of the country the only way to cross rivers was by finding the appropriate ford, a dangerous expedient in the rainy season.[28] The exact route our party followed is not specified, but given their general direction, they must have crossed the Tagus somewhere between Mocejón and Añover de Tajo (most likely at or near this latter village). Surprisingly, no-one in the party seemed to know the way, for they had to hire a guide in Illescas to take them to the boat to cross the Tagus (6 reales), and another guide from the river crossing to Mascaraque (16 reales).[29] A further 20 reales was spent on the crossing itself. Not unexpectedly, Saturday 19 March was the most expensive day of the journey: 9504 maravedises (610 on food and 8894 on the rest). And to add to the overall cost, one of the mules, 'la pelada', got injured (7 reales the cost of treatment) and they had also to buy twelve horseshoes (14 reales 20 maravedises). Supper, however, was a frugal affair: the ubiquitous cauliflower, cakes, 1lb. of figs, and *migas*.

As was their custom, the following morning was spent in their place of lodging, the journey only recommencing after lunch. Since, in this instance, the morning was that of Sunday 20 March, the party attended mass in the local church, where 4 reales were given as alms for the mass and another four for general alms for the church. Lunch, as perhaps befitted a holy day, was reasonably light: 6 fried eggs, 6 eggs in omelettes, sardines, two lemons, and bread.

The journey from Mascaraque took them to nearby Mora (about 7 kilometres away) where the Duke had to pay a porter two reales to find a guide to take them to La Venta (location unspecified and impossible to determine). Another guide then took them from La Venta to Fuente el Fresno, total distance from Mascaraque 68 kilometres. Each guide cost 6 reales to hire. It would appear that they knew the way from Fuente el Fresno to Villarrubia (16 kilometres), for no more guides are mentioned. Although the *Cuaderno de gastos* is not clear on this point, it seems certain that the party spent the Sunday night somewhere en route (for 14 reales were spent on 'posada y camas') and that they arrived in Villarrubia the following morning. Perhaps they stayed at La Venta (given the name, the most likely), or indeed at Fuente el Fresno which was under the jurisdiction of the Duke of Híjar as lord of Villarrubia. There is no mention of any evening meal that day, but this could be explained if they arrived late. The cost of whatever they ate was no doubt included in the 14 reales they paid for 'posada y camas': beds alone normally cost them 4 reales.

To summarize Híjar's journey:[30] during this period the principal route south from Madrid to Ciudad Real ran through Getafe, Illescas, Toledo, Orgaz, Yébenes, Fernán Caballero, Ciudad Real.[31] The Duke of Híjar's route, as we have seen, left the main road at or just south of Illescas, crossed the Tagus to the east of Toledo and picked up another road system to the south east of the city, probably near Nambroca (on the present-day N400). At Almonacid the road branched, one fork going south to Villaminaya and Manzaneque, the other eastwards to Tembleque via Mascaraque and Mora. This latter is the one taken by Híjar, perhaps because he had business to transact in Mascaraque (where he spent the night of Saturday 19 March). From Mora his route must have led him to Manzaneque, Los Yébenes and Fuente el Fresno, on the main road south (the present-day N401).[32] It was because Híjar, for whatever reason, did not follow the main route south (which would have taken him through Toledo) but had to criss-cross, to an extent, two or three different systems, that he needed to hire guides in Illescas and Mora.

Once the party reached Villarrubia on the morning of Monday 21 March, there was an immediate change in the arrangements: all the servants saw their daily rations reduced by between one half and one third, and costs were otherwise reduced by eating in the Duke's palace and by being invited by diverse local worthies.[33] Although the principal aim of this study was to reveal the details of Híjar's journey into exile in March 1644, which ended when he arrived in his town of Villarrubia de los Ojos de Guadiana on Monday 21 March, the *Cuaderno de gastos* which I have been using continues through to the end of the month, Thursday 31 March being the last entry. A glance at

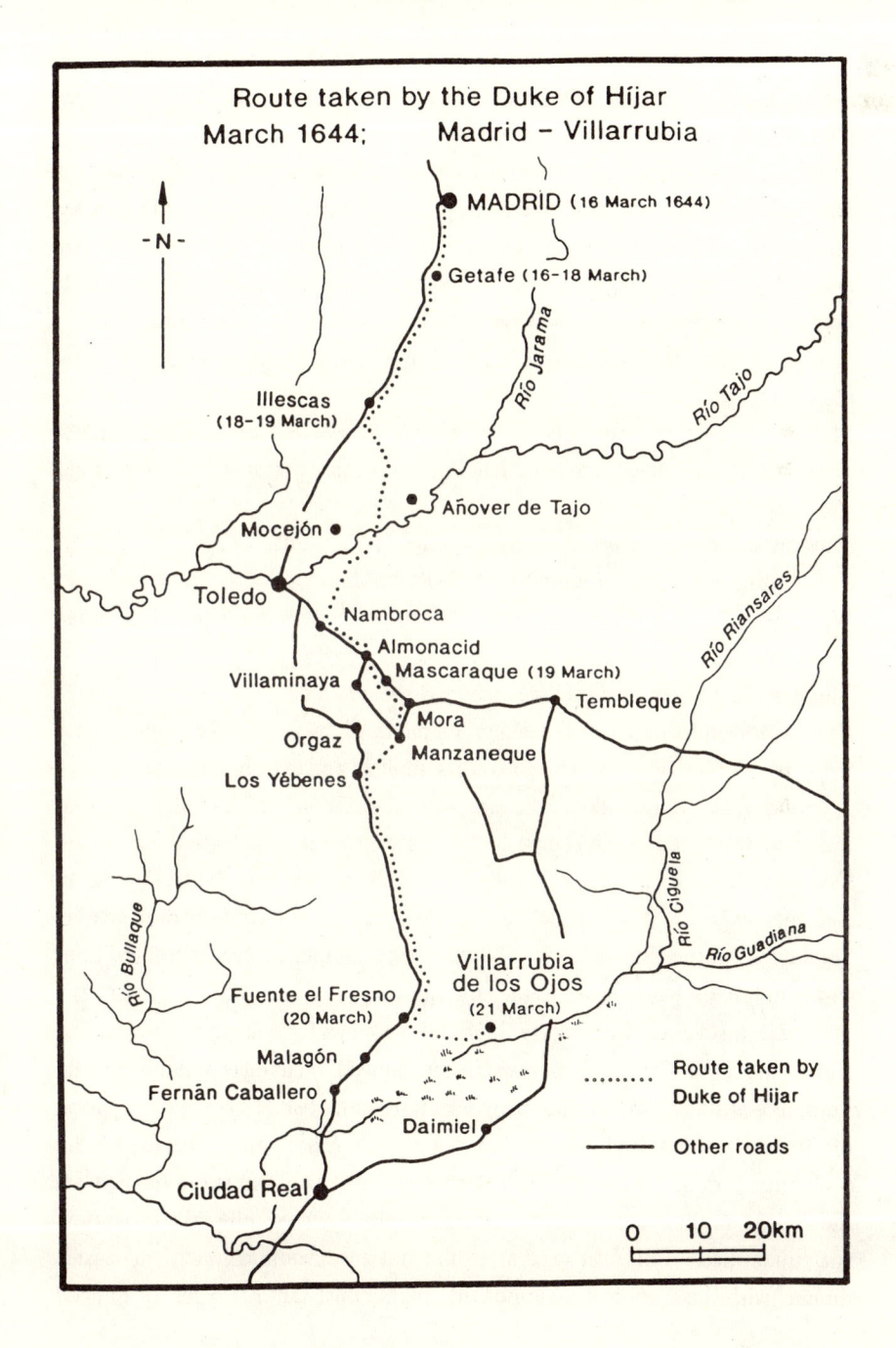

The Road to Villarubia: The Journey into Exile of the Duke of Híjar 133

some of these entries would not be amiss for what they have to tell us of the eating habits and daily life in a Manchegan village in the middle of the seventeenth century.

During the journey to Villarrubia we have noted that the party tasted no meat whatsoever, even though it ought to have been possible for them to have obtained locally some game, such as rabbit and partridge. Their principal diet had consisted almost entirely of cauliflower, eggs (in large quantities) and fish --salmon, sardines, dried cod--, which was mostly of the salted or cured variety, though perhaps the salmon was fresh. For the first week in Villarrubia this regime continued:

Monday 21 March: 6 eggs 'en paguela', 6 poached eggs, French toast (*torrijas*), boiled artichoke leaves (*cardo*), rice pudding with cinnamon, bread, and dessert.

Tuesday 22 March: 8lbs. of lamprey, milk and biscuits,[34] eggs 'en paguela' and fried, fritters (*buñuelos*), lemons, bread.

Wednesday 23 March: mullets (*barbos*), artichoke, eggs 'en paguela', lemons, bread.

Thursday 23 March: invited for lunch by the Capuchins.

Friday 24 March: omelettes and eggs 'en paguela', two eels, bread rolls.

Saturday 25 March: eggs of various sorts, mullets and eels, bread rolls.[35]

Sunday 27 March the Duke ate with the Capuchins and this time he provided the food: 4 chickens, half a lamb, a ham, a kid goat, 1½ dozen 'doughnuts' (*roscas*), a basket of raisins, and an 'arroba' (10-16 litres) of wine. The change in diet is so startling and sudden that it admits of only one answer: Sunday 24 March that year of 1644 was Easter Sunday, when therefore Lent came to an end and with it the self-imposed regime that was rigorously observed in seventeenth-century Spain. As a special privilege granted by the Bull of the Santa Cruzada, Spaniards were allowed to eat eggs and milk during Lent, in addition to the normal fruit, vegetables and fish. Híjar's journey took place during Lent and, as we have seen, his party stuck strictly to the observances right through to Easter Sunday. But once Lent is out of the way, the change in their eating habits is remarkable. Meat of all sorts appears in vast quantities. For example, after the not insubstantial lunch on Easter Sunday with the Capuchins, supper that night consisted of 1½ lbs. of minced roast lamb steeped in lard (*en gigote*),[36] 2 partridges, and a fricassée of turkey (*pavo en pepitoria*). No fruit, no fish, no vegetables, not even the ever-present cauliflower! Still feeling peckish the following morning, the Duke's son had elevenses consisting of a partridge and a piece of steak, followed by lunch of roast kid goat, roast minced veal, chicken,[37] and veal offal (*madrecillas*). Supper was more of the same with further doses of kid goat ('la cinturilla asada y la pierna en gigote'), 2 roast partridges, and sauce.

Lent, then, may have been closely observed, but there is no doubt but that it was adhered to reluctantly if the Duke's orgy of meat that followed it is any guide. Nonetheless, this was not a limited or unidimensional diet. In addition to meat of all sorts --lamb, veal, kid goat, pork, chicken, turkey, partridges, ham--, roasted, stewed, served up in various sauces, they also ate fish, probably caught locally: eels, lampreys, frogs, mullets. There is little mention of vegetables --only 'menestra', cauliflower, artichoke--, but a reasonable variety of fruit appears in the accounts: limes, pomegranates, melon, lemons, oranges, figs. Often these fruits are served 'en azúcar', that is to say in conserves, presumably because they were out of season. The Duke seems to have had something of a sweet tooth: pastry and confectionary (*buñuelos*, *torrijas*, *bolillos*, *roscas*) appear frequently, and once in Villarrubia he liked to eat bread rolls (*panecillos*). Bread naturally enough figures in all of the meals as an accompaniment or as the main course when they ate *migas*. Bread was also the principal food of the Duke's dog. And here one notes with interest that not only the entry 'pan para el perro' almost always appears in the accounts one line above the entry 'pan para el pobre', but that the dog and the pauper received exactly the same amount: 8 maravedises worth of bread each day!

How did the Duke spend his time in his enforced exile in Villarrubia, a village he had only visited three times before, as far as we know, in his life?[38] He appears to have spent many afternoons in the company of a certain Lázaro Hidalgo, who invited the Duke on a number of occasions for *colación*, and on others provided him with articles of food and drink.[39] Thus the wine that the Duke and the Capuchins drank on Easter Sunday was a gift of his. Although not specified, it is possible that they went hunting together. In addition, Híjar must have had meetings with his administrator and agents in

Villarrubia, and with members of the Town Council (most of his designation), but these do not appear in the accounts book. The other powerful group in the locality and whose presence does figure in the *Cuaderno de gastos* was of course the 'Convento de Frailes menores capuchinos descalzos del Seráfico P. San Francisco', who were at that time temporarily lodged in the Hermitage of Nuestra Señora de la Caridad which came under the patronage of Híjar, who had loaned them this temporary home until such a time as they found a more convenient location.[40]

On Saturday 19 March P. Alejandro de Valencia, Provincial of the Order in Castile, laid the first stone of what would be the definitive house of the Capuchin Order in Villarrubia. Villalobos Racionero, in his study of the Duke's exile in Villarrubia, records the inscription on the stone: 'D.O.M. Siendo Sumo Pontífice Vrbano Octauo. Reynando en España Philipo 4º. Patron y Señor de Villarrubia y deste Conuento D. Rodrigo Sarmiento Villandrando de la Cerda. Conde de Salinas y Primer Duque de Yjar. Prouincial desta Prouincia el R.P. Fr. Alexandro de Valencia. Predicador de su Mag^d y Calificador de la Suprema. Se puso esta prima piedra. Dia de S. Joseph. 19 de marzo. Año de 1644'.[41] Villalobos further notes: 'Aun cuando la actitud de don Rodrigo respecto a esta fundación no había estado a la altura de las circunstancias --hacía algún tiempo había movido pleito a los Padres porque, según se dijo entonces, apetecía los bienes que nuestro paisano Pedro Sánchez Conejero legara en 1619 para que se edificase un convento de Frailes Franciscos Descalzos--, la oportunidad de su estancia en Villarrubia determinó al P. Provincial, movido por el Guardián de la comunidad instalada en la citada ermita, Fr. Andrés de Valdemoro, a acometer las obras del nuevo convento, que se puso bajo la advocación del Corpus Christi. Era de esperar que el duque, nombrado patrono por escritura pública en 1642, ayudase ahora a adelantarlas con su presencia y patrimonio. Mas no fue así. Don Rodrigo asistió a aquel acto solemne del día de San José, pero olvidó pronto su compromiso con aquellos hermanos, y el convento hubo de levantarse poco a poco con las limosnas de los villarubieros, principalmente'.[42] Carried away no doubt by his fervour as a 'villarubiero' and by his desire to link the inscription on the stone with the presence of the Duke, Villalobos Racionero committed an unfortunate but understandable

The Road to Villarubia: The Journey into Exile of the Duke of Híjar

error. As we have seen, on Saturday 19 March Híjar had lunch at Illescas before making his way to Mascaraque, and so was nowhere near Villarrubia when the cornerstone of the new convent was symbolically laid. Indeed, his first meeting with the Capuchins did not take place until Thursday 24 March, when he was invited to celebrate Maunday Thursday with them. He returned to the Convent (in its temporary lodging of N.S. de la Caridad) on Easter Sunday. On Tuesday 29 March two Capuchins ate lunch in the Duke's palace, where no effort was spared to satisfy their culinary tastes: a plate of cooked vegetables (*menestra*), roast breast of turkey, 'sopa castellana', half a roast kid goat, roast loin of veal, roast veal chops, a meat loaf (of chickens and lamb), a pot roast of lamb and chicken. All of this was washed down with 'medio azumbre de bino para los frayles'.

Híjar must have spent some of his time in Villarrubia hunting and fishing. There is mention of 3 reales being paid to Domingo de Barrios (one of the Duke's gentlemen) for buying food for the mules in Daimiel, some 16 kilometres to the south. A certain Tomé was paid 12 reales to go to La Benbrilla (Membrilla, near Manzanares?) to get a horse for the Duke. Local disputes and negotiations would also have occupied his time. 12 reales were paid by order of the Duke to a woman who came all the way from Mascaraque to ask for letters of favour for the Mayor of her town. Híjar was also in contact with a certain D. Gaspar de Peñalosa and, we must presume, with his friends in Madrid.[43] In this context, we note that on Wednesday 30 March Juan González, his cook, was sent on an errand to the capital. He was replaced in the kitchen by Miguel Pérez.

As already stated, the *Cuaderno de gastos* which has furnished us with so much detailed information about the journey of the Duke of Híjar into exile in March 1644 ends with the last entry on Thursday 31 March. Almost certainly there would have been other account books for the succeeding months, but none of these has so far come to light. As a document of daily life in Golden-Age Spain this *Cuaderno* is unique: here we have placed before us in profuse and amazing detail the eating habits of a noble family both during and after the period of Lent, the cost of each item of food they ate, the cost of travel and lodging. Other, unexpected details also appear: the cost of washing the table and kitchen linen (5-6 reales a time) and the Duke's clothes (4 reales 4 maravedises); the cost of bringing fresh water from the 'canaleja' (2 reales for each load or 'carga'); the cost of four new pans for the kitchen (2 reales) or of 400 toothpicks (1½ reales).

In short, this *Cuaderno* has furnished us with the sort of picture of life in Golden-Age Spain that is usually missing in most history books, a snapshot of time that brings to life what would otherwise be bare facts and dates. It is offered here in this *Homenaje* to a colleague and a friend whose sudden death left such a large gap, in the certain knowledge that Derek as an historian of Spain would have appreciated and been amused by the richness and diversity of its contents, and as a good 'trencherman' would have certainly relished the culinary delights it reveals.

Que en paz descanse.

The Road to Villarubia: The Journey into Exile of the Duke of Híjar   139

APPENDIX

Quaderno de lo que se gasta en las comidas del duque mi s[eño]r y el marques mi s[eño]r, en la jornada que sus ex[celenci]as acen de madrid a billarubia y de lo que montan las raciones de los criados y comidas de diecisiete mulas y demas gastos echos en la jornada[44]

Don Lesmes de Baldes gentilonbre ocho r[eal]es	008
Don antt[oni]o garces page quatro r[eal]es	004
Domingo de barios quatro r[eal]es	004
P[edr]o Barbero seis r[eal]es	006

Oficiales

Marcos repostero y despensero ocho r[eal]es	008
Ju[a]n gonsales cocinero seis	006
Beltran cochero mayor nuebe r[eal]es	009
Domingo sota cochero seis r[eal]es	006
Ju[a]n cochero de camara seis r[eal]es	006
Domingo sota cochero y lacayo seis r[eal]es	006
fran[cis]co lacayo cinco r[eal]es	005
P[edr]o lacayo cinco r[eal]es	005
Alonso lacayo cinco r[eal]es	005
P[edr]o moço de mulas cinco r[eal]es	005
Marcos moço de mulas cinco r[eal]es	<u>005</u>
	088

Miercoles a 16 de março Cena en getafe

ostras, qriadillas coliflor buebos rellenos, buebos cubiertos de azucar, bolillos de contado que trugo marcos de m[anda]do que le dio el Canonigo de pan para los señores m[edi]o r[ea]l	016
de pan para el perro dos quartos	008
de m[edi]a libra de ygos tres quartos	012
de seis buebos en paguela doce quartos	048
de vn quarteron de aceitunas cinco quartos	020
de vn quartillo de bino m[edi]o r[ea]l	016
de recado a la cocina m[edi]o r[ea]l	016
de vna aroba de carbon tres r[eal]es	<u>102</u>
	238

Miercoles a 16 de março Cena en getafe fue conbidado el Cura

de cinco piensos de cebada a quince quartos cada celemin son quarenta y dos celemines son setenta y dos r[eal]es y doce m[a]r[avedise]s	072-12
de camas quatro r[eal]es	004

140   Trevor J. Dadson

de libra y m[edi]a de Bugias a siete r[eal]es son 10 y 16
    m[a]r[avedise]s   010-16
                                                              086-28

De las raciones deste dia ochenta y ocho r[eal]es   088
                                                              174-28

[Total del día]   0238
                                                              5944
                                                              6182⁴⁵

Juebes a 17 de março de 1644 Comida en getafe

de seis coliflores doce r[eal]es   408
principios de limas   032
de pan comida y cena   036
de ocho buebos en paguela a ocho mrs cada vno   064
de seis buebos estrellados a lo mismo   048
de vna libra de salmon dos r[eal]es   068
sardinas de contado y bolillos y buebos de recado de la   082
    cocina y luces
de vna aroba de carbon tres r[eal]es   102

Colacion

coliflor de contado
bolillos de contado y aceitunas
de m[edi]o pan para migas y de aceite   016
                                                              756⁴⁶

Las raciones conforme la nomina montan   087
de Cebada cinco piensos quarenta y dos celemines y
    m[edi]o a quince quartos cetenta y dos r[eal]es y
    doce mrs   072-12
de pan bino y sal y binagre para las mulas   006
de la limosna de vna missa que oyo el duq[u]e mi s[eño]r   004
de limosna a la cofradia del santissimo sacram[en]to por   016
    m[anda]do del duque mi s[eño]r
diez r[eal]es que m[an]do dar el duq[u]e mi s[eño]r a los
    mosos de caballos del andalucia   010
de camas tres   003
dos r[eal]es que m[an]do dar el marques mi s[eño]r a vna
    ortelana   002
                                                              201⁴⁷

[Total del día]   0756
                                                              6846
                                                              7602⁴⁸

Biernes a 18 de março Comida en getafe

The Road to Villarubia: The Journey into Exile of the Duke of Híjar   141

Principios de limas	042
de pan comida y cena	032
de ocho buebos en paguela a ocho mrs	064
de seis buebos estrellados	048
de vna libra de salmon dos r[eal]es	068
de vna libra de pescado abadego siete quartos	028
de m[edi]o pan para migas tres quartos	012
de aceite y recado de la cocina dos r[eal]es	068

Colacion en yllescas

aceitunas coliflor y bolillos de contado
de pan para colacion q[ue] fueron conbidados quatro
    Religiosos   016
de migas cinco quartos   022
de m[edi]o azumbre de bino ocho quartos   032
de vn limon ocho mrs   008
de carbon quatro quartos   <u>016</u>
    456

Las raciones conforme la nomina montan ochenta y
    ocho r[eal]es   088
de cebada quarenta y dos celemines y dos mas q[ue] se
    comieron los caballos de lemos a quince quartos
    cetenta y cinco r[eal]es y 30 mrs   075-30
Beinte r[eal]es que di al casero donde poso el duq[u]e mi
    s[eño]r por m[anda]do de su ex[celenci]a   020
mas diez r[eal]es de limosnas a la cofadria del santissimo
    de yllescas por m[anda]do del duq[u]e mi s[eño]r   010
de camas quatro r[eal]es   004
de limosnas por m[anda]do del duq[u]e mi s[eño]r   <u>002</u>
    199-30

[Total del día]	0456
	<u>6796</u>
	7252

Sabado a 19 de março Comida en yllescas

Princip[i]os de granadas de contado de azucar dos
    q[uar]tos   008
de pan comida y cena   030
de vna libra de salmon dos r[eal]es   068
de dos libras de sardinas beinte y dos q[uar]tos   088
de vna libra de pescado cecial doce q[uar]tos   048
de medio azumbre de leche cinco q[uar]tos y de
    biscochos doce q[uar]tos y de azucar tres quartos   080
de ocho buebos rellenos dieciseis q[uar]tos y de miel y
    azucar seis q[uar]tos   088
de seis buebos en tortilla doce q[uar]tos   048

142   Trevor J. Dadson

de vna libra de queso diez q[uar]tos   040
de aceite y recados de la cocina dos r[eal]es   068
Bolillos melon y aceitunas de contado

Colacion en mascaraque

coliflor y bolillos de contado
de ygos vna libra m[edi]o r[ea]l   016
de migas ciete q[uar]tos   <u>028</u>
    610
Las raciones conforme la nomina montan ochenta y
    ocho r[eal]es   088
de seis piensos de cebada a dieciseis q[uar]tos el celemin
    nobenta y seis r[eal]es   096
de la cura de la mula pelada   007
de doce erraduras a r[ea]l y quartillo son catorce r[eal]es
    y 20 mrs   014-20
de ocho medidas las cinco de a dos r[eal]es y las tres de a
    r[ea]l y de ocho estanpas de a quarto catorce
    r[eal]es   014
de pasar la barca de tago beinte r[eal]es   020
de una guia de yllescas a la barca seis r[eal]es   006
de vna guia de la barca a mascaraque dieciseis   <u>016</u>
    261-20

[Total del día]   0610
    <u>8860</u>
    9470[49]

Domingo a 20 de março Comida en mascaraque

de seis buebos estrellados nuebe quartos   036
de seis buebos en tortilla nuebe q[uar]tos   036
sardinas de contado
de pan m[edi]o r[ea]l   016
de aceite seis quartos   024
de dos limones quatro quartos   <u>016</u>
    128

Las raciones conforme la nomina montan   088
de cebada cinco piensos a diesiceis quartos el celemin
    montan los quarenta y dos y m[edi]o   080
de la limosna de vna missa quatro r[eal]es   004
de limosna en la yglesia   004
de posada y camas catorce r[eal]es   014
dos r[eal]es en mora a vn portero de buscar vna g[u]ia en
    mora por m[anda]do del duq[u]e mi s[eño]r   002
doce r[eal]es de dos g[u]ias la vna de mora a la benta y la
    otra de la benta a fuente del fresno   <u>012</u>
    204

The Road to Villarubia: The Journey into Exile of the Duke of Híjar   143

[Total del día] 0128
 6936
 7064

21 de março lunes

[*quaderno de lo q[ue] se ba gastando en el P[alac]io del duq[u]e mi s[eño]r y en las rasiones de los criados siguientes*]

Don Lesmes de Baldes quatro r[eal]es	04
Don antt[oni]o garses page dos r[eal]es	02
Domingo de Barios dos r[eal]es	02
P[edr]o Barbero del duq[u]e mi s[eño]r	04

Ofisiales

Marcos repostero y despensero	04
Juan gonsales cosinero tres r[eal]es y m[edi]o	03-17
Beltran cochero de camara quatro r[eal]es y m[edi]o	04-17
Domingo Sota cochero del duq[u]e mi s[eño]r	03-17
Ju[a]n cochero de Camara tres r[eal]es y m[edi]o	03-17
Domingo lacayo tres r[eal]es y quartillo	03-08
fran[cis]co lacayo tres r[eal]es y quartillo	03-08
alonsso lacayo tres r[eal]es y quartillo	03-08
P[edr]o lacayo tres r[eale]es y quartillo	03-08
marcos moso de mulas	03-08
P[edr]o moso de mulas tres r[eal]es y quartillo	03-08
	47-116

Montan las Rasiones 50 r[eal]es y 14 mrs.
Domingo moso de cosina entro con dos r[eal]es de rasion   02⁵⁰

Lunes Comida en Billa Rubia en 21 de março de 1644

de seis buebos en paguela seis quartos	024
cardo g[u]isado de contado de dos buebos dos q[uar]tos	008
de seis buebos g[u]isados seis quartos	024
de vn p[la]to de torigas dos r[eal]es	068
de m[edi]a libra de aros seis q[uar]tos de lec[h]e seis q[uar]tos de azucar y canela ocho quartos	080
pan para la mesa seis q[uar]tos	024
pan para el pero dos q[uar]tos	008
de espesias para la cosina doce q[uar]tos	048
postres de contado	
	284

Colacion de contado q[ue] dio Lazaro ydalgo

Las Rasiones conforme la nomina montan   050-14

doce r[eal]es por m[anda]do del duque mi señor se
dieron a vna muger q[ue] bino de marcaraque a
pedir vnas cartas de fabor para el alcalde 012
de vnas cargas de agua de la canaleja 002
064-14

[Total del día] 0284
2174
2458[51]

Martes Comida en 22 de março

de ocho libras de lanpreguelas dos r[eal]es 068
de seis buebos en paguela seis quartos 024
de seis buebos estrellados seis quartos 024
p[la]to de guñ[u]elos diesiceis q[uar]tos 060
de lec[h]e m[edi]o r[ea]l de biscochos dies q[uar]tos de
    azucar seis quartos 081
de recado para el escabeche dies q[uar]tos 040
de dos limones diesiseis mrs de lunes y martes 016
de recado para la cosina doce quartos 048
de pan para la mesa seis q[uar]tos 024
pan para el perro 008
393

Colacion

de contado de migas doce mrs 012
405

Las Rasiones conforme la nomina 050-14
de la ropa de la cosina y de la reposteria seis r[eal]es 006
de quatro ollas para la cosina dos r[eal]es 002
058-14

[Total del día] 0405
1986
2391

Miercoles en 23 de março Comida

de seis buebos en paguela seis q[uar]tos 024
p[la]to de cardo de contado de dos buebos dos q[uar]tos 008
de recado para enpanar vn barbo 020
de espesias para vn escabeche a vnos barbos que
    presentaron al duq[u]e mi s[eño]r 027
de dos limones para comida y cena 016
de recado para la cosina doce q[uar]tos 048
de pan para las mesas seis q[uar]tos 024
pan para el pero dos q[uar]tos 008

The Road to Villarubia: The Journey into Exile of the Duke of Híjar   145

de quatrosientos palillos doce q[uar]tos   048
                                                                        223

Colacion q[ue] dio Lazaro ydalgo de vn p[la]to de migas   008
                                                                        231
Las Rasiones conforme la nomina montan   050-14
de limosna a dos pobres por m[anda]do del duq[u]e mi
    s[eño]r   001
                                                                        051-14

[Total del día]   0231
                                                                        1748
                                                                        1978

Comida Juebes en 24 de março 1644

fue Conbidado en los Capuchinos

Conlacion, de vn p[la]to picatostes   020

Las Rasiones conforme la nomina   050-14

[Total del día]   0020
                                                                        1714
                                                                        1734

Biernes en 25 de março Comida

de seis buebos en paguela seis q[uar]tos   024
de quatro buebos en tortilla quatro q[uar]tos   016
de dos angilas nuebe r[eal]es   306
quatro panesillos de a m[edi]a libra para comida y cena
    de a media libra de cassa de espinar de arinas
    q[ue] le a dado Lasaro ydalgo
pan para el pero   016
                                                                        362

Colasion dio Lasaro ydalgo

Las Rasiones conforme la nomina   050-14

[Total del día]   0362
                                                                        1714
                                                                        2076

Sabado en 26 de março Comida

Seis buebos en paguela   024
quatro buebos en tortilla   016
Peces y Barbos y angila de contado de recado para
    enpanar la angila   036

cinco panesillos para comida y cena para la mesa
pan para el pero dos q[uar]tos   006
mas medio pan para el pero   016

Colacion de contado q[ue] dio Lasaro ydalgo

                                                                                                               108^{52}

Las Rasiones conforme la nomina   050-14
de la ropa del duq[u]e mi s[eño]r   004-04
de vna carga de agua de la canaleja   002
de vn propio q[ue] enbio Don gaspar de peñalosa al
    duq[u]e mi s[eñ]or por su m[anda]do   010
a vn pobre q[ue] trugo vnas baras para los caballos por
    m[anda]do del duq[u]e mi s[eño]r r[ea]l y m[edi]o   001 17
a Domingo de Barios tres r[eal]es para q[ue] diese de
    comer a las mulas en daymiel   003
de la ropa de la mesa y cosina y reposteria labarla   005
                                                                                                    075-35

Ojo a Ju[a]n de Cardona en quatro beces quatro gallinas y vna perdis por m[anda]do del duq[u]e mi s[eño]r

[Total del día]   0108
                                           2585
                                           2693

Domingo en 27 de março

Comida en Los Capuchinos dicho dia comio el duque mi s[eñ]or en los Capuchinos
Llebaronles por m[anda]do del duq[u]e mi s[eño]r gallinas quatro m[edi]o carnero vn pernil vn cabrito vna aroba de bino q[ue] dio Lasaro ydalgo docena y media de rescas vn cestillo de pasas

Cena

Libra y m[edi]a de carnero en gigote de contado
dos perdices de contado
vna pepitoria de vn pabo de contado
de vna pepitoria de recado diez q[uar]tos   040
pan para el pero dos q[uar]tos   008
                                                                                         048

Las Rasiones conforme la nomina   050-14

[Total del día]   0048
                                         1714
                                         1762

Lunes en 28 de março Comida

almuerso al marques mi s[eñ]or vna perdis y vn pedaso de solomo de contado

Comida

Vn quartillo de cabrito asado de contado
gigote de ternera de contado
vna gallina en chullas de contado
las madresillas de la ternera
dos buebos para el gigote 008

Cena

Vn quartillo de cabrito la sinturilla asada y la pierna en gigote
Vna pepitoria
dos perdices asadas
de recado de la cosina dos r[eal]es 068
pan para la messa cinco panesillos
pan para el pero dos quartos 008
084

Las Rasiones conforme la nomina 050-14

[Total del día] 0084
1714
1798

Martes en 29 de março

Comieron con el duq[u]e mi señor dos religiosos capuchinos
de vna esqudilla de menestra de seis buebos 024
las pechugas de vn pabo asadas
para vna sopa vn panesillo y dos buebos 024
m[edi]o cabrito asado
vn lomo de ternera asado
chullas de ternera asadas
vn pastelon con dos pollos y dos libras de carnero
de los pollos quatro r[eal]es 136
seis buebos para el pastel 024
dos libras de carnero en la olla y vna gallina
de espesias y berduras y azucar quarenta y seis quartos 186
m[edi]o azumbre de bino para los frayles 032

Cena

vn quartillo de cabrito asado
dos perdices asadas
gigote de las piernas del pabo
pan para la mesa siete panesillos de a libra
pan para el pero dos q[uar]tos 008

148   Trevor J. Dadson

pan para el pobre por m[anda]do del duq[u]e mi s[eñ]or   008
                                                                                442

Las Rasiones conforme la nomina   050-14
a tome doce r[eal]es por m[anda]do del duq[u]e mi
    s[eñ]or para ir a buscar vn caballo a la Benbrilla   012
                                                                               062-14
[Total del día]   0442
                                                                               2122
                                                                               2564

Miercoles a 30 de março comida

para almorzar el marq[ue]s mi s[eñ]or vn quartillo de
    abe y vn panesillo
Prinsipio cinco narangas de contado de azucar   008
dos libras de carnero en gigote de pimienta   008
p[la]to de chullas de ternera mechadas de recado   008
vn pedaso de lomo de puerco con sopa dulce de recado
    doce q[uar]tos   048
dos libras de carnero para la olla y m[edi]a gallina de
    espesias   008

Cena

dos perdices asadas de recado   004
m[edi]a gallina en chullas y vn pedaso de ternera de
    recado   008
de ranas y lanpreguelas   062
de recado para quatro enpanadas de ternera   040
pan para comida y cena y almuerso cinco libras de pan
pan para el pero   008
pan para el pobre ocho mrs   008
                                                                                210

Las Raciones conforme la nomina   048-30
a Ju[a]n gonsales cosinero para q[ue] se fuese a m[adri]d
    y diese de comer a la mula del canonigo beinte
    r[eal]es   020
                                                                               068-30

[Total del día]   0210
                                                                                2342
                                                                                2552[53]

Juebes en 31 de março Comida

cinco narangas de asucar   008
dos perdices asadas de pimienta   004
p[la]to de chullas de ternera mechadas de espesia   008
p[la]to de gigote de ternera   008

The Road to Villarubia: The Journey into Exile of the Duke of Híjar   149

Cena

Vna gallina cosida de recado ocho mrs	008
Vn quartillo de cabrito asado y en gigote de recado	008
Vn pernil enpanado de espesias catorce q[uar]tos y m[edi]o	059
Vna libra de lanpreguelas de recado	020
quatro libras de pan a comida y cena y almuerso y merienda	
pan para el pobre dos q[uar]tos	008
pan para el pero dos q[uar]tos	008
	139[54]

NOTES

1. The standard life of the Duke of Híjar is still R. Ezquerra Abadía, *La conspiración del duque de Híjar (1648)* (Madrid: Imprenta M. Borondo, 1934).

2. The last will and testament of Marina Sarmiento de la Cerda is dated Madrid, 28 March 1600 (Archivo Histórico de Protocolos, Madrid: Luis Suárez, *protocolo* 2763, fols 403r-405r). Her extremely frail and trembling signature is that of a person destined not to live long, and it comes as no surprise therefore to discover that she died two days later, Thursday 30 March, *Jueves Santo* (Archivo Histórico Provincial, Zaragoza [AHPZ]. Casa ducal de Híjar. Sala 1ª, *legajo* 381-2). On 7 April she was buried in the family vault in the Monastery of Benebibere, near Carrión de los Condes (AHPZ, Híjar, 4ª-95: 'Entrega del cuerpo de la condesa doña Marina Sarmiento de la Cerda'). The journey of the funeral cortège from Madrid to Benebibere by mule cart and litter seems normally to have taken one week (for example, Diego de Silva y Mendoza died in Madrid on 15 June 1630 and was buried in Benebibere on 23 June [AHPZ, Híjar 4ª-95: 'Entrega del cuerpo del conde don Diego']).

3. L. Cabrera de Córdoba, *Relaciones de las cosas sucedidas en la Corte de España desde 1599 hasta 1614* (Madrid: Imprenta J. Martín Alegría, 1857), p.64, Aviso de 8-4-1600.

4. Doña Antonia de Ulloa, as dowager Countess of Salinas, lived in her palace in the centre of Valladolid. During the years the court resided in Valladolid (1601-06), Diego de Silva y Mendoza was also present there, occupying a 'quinta' on the outskirts of the city (where he entertained the poet Luis de Góngora in 1603) as well as a town house in the centre, in between the palaces of the Duke of Lerma and the Count of Benavente (see Cabrera de Córdoba, p.107, Aviso de 28-7-1601). For much of the time during 1601-05 Salinas took up residence in the Portuguese town of Castelo de Vide (just over the frontier from his *encomienda* of Herrera de Alcántara) in order to ensure that he was properly 'afiliado o matriculado en los libros de los reyes de este reino' and thereby establish his rights to Portuguese nationality and the towns of La Chamusca and Ulme. We are told in different accounts that he had his young son with him (AHPZ, Híjar, 1ª-121-71 and 1ª-284-1,8). Clearly, there was no reason why father and son could not have been in almost constant contact during the formative years of don Rodrigo. Of these early years, the Duke later noted: 'Entre a serbir al Principe y Rey Nuestro S[eñ]or el dia que nacio en Valladolid donde soy vezino ... Bese la mano al Rey N[uest]ro Señor Phelipe 3º llebado por mi Abuela la Condesa de Salinas, Señora de honor, y su hija Doña Madalena Sarmiento Dama de la Reyna N[uest]ra Señora Doña Margarita, y hermana de mi Madre la Condesa de Salinas y Riuadeo por la merced de hazerme primer criado del Principe N[uest]ro Señor y su Menino' (T. J. Dadson, 'Más datos para la biografía de don Diego de Silva y Mendoza, Conde de Salinas', *Criticón*, 34 (1986), 5-26 (p.22)).

5. For this period of his life, see C. Gaillard, *Le Portugal sous Philippe III d'Espagne. L'action de Diego de Silva y Mendoza* (Grenoble: Université, 1982), and Dadson, 'Más datos': 'Fui en su Compañia [*de mi padre*], y assisti a serbir en todo quanto se ofrecio del serbicio del Rey N[uest]ro Señor como fue al reparo de los Castillos de Cascaes, San Juan, San Antonio, Cabeza Seca, La torrebieja, y Belem. Tube la superintendencia de las fundiciones de la artilleria y la de cobrar la que habia perdida fuera y dentro de la barra ... Tube la superintendencia de la fabrica de las Herrerias y Molinos de Berquerena...Assisti al Astillero de las Naos ... Assisti a la fabrica de los hornos de Vizcocho' (p.23).

The Road to Villarrubia: The Journey into Exile of the Duke of Híjar 151

6. See Gaillard, and Dadson, 'Conflicting Views of the Last Spanish Viceroy of Portugal (1617-1621): Diego de Silva y Mendoza, Count of Salinas and Marquis of Alenquer', *Portuguese Studies*, 7 (1991), 28-60, for the unremitting campaign waged against Salinas during the last year or so of his Viceroyalty.

7. The matter of some contraband diamonds and Salinas's claim to one-third of their value dragged on for many years, but the fact remains that in the end no charge for misappropriation of funds was ever brought against him.

8. See Gaillard, pp.362-68.

9. Nonetheless, there is evidence that, at least in the early years of Philip IV's reign, Olivares tried to win Híjar over. In an exchange of letters over the traditional privilege enjoyed by the Counts of Salinas and Ribadeo of eating once with the King on 6 January (*Reyes*) and keeping the King's dress afterwards, Olivares wrote: ' yo me he alegrado mucho de que esto sea por lo qu[e] estimo la persona y casa de bex[a] a quien gu[ar]de Dios como deseo' (British Library, MS Egerton 1133, *Papeles varios de Portugal, Tomo III*, fol. 78r; dated 5 January 1624). Unfortunately, a series of accidents --his own bad health in 1624, for example-- prevented Híjar for some years from enjoying this once-in-a-lifetime privilege.

10. See Dadson, 'La defensa de Aragón en 1625 y el papel desempeñado en su planificación por Diego de Silva y Mendoza, conde de Salinas', *Revista de Historia de Jerónimo Zurita*, 55 (1987), 105-35

11. See J. H. Elliott, *The Count-Duke of Olivares. The Statesman in an Age of Decline* (London and New Haven: University Press, 1986), pp.244-55.

12. See Dadson, '¿Un memorial inédito del conde de Salinas en contra de la política del Conde-Duque de Olivares?', *Hispania. Revista Española de Historia*, 47 (1987), 343-48

13. See P. Arellano Sada, 'Salinas de Añana, a través de los documentos y diplomas conservados en el Archivo Municipal', *Universidad. Revista de Cultura y Vida Universitaria* (Zaragoza), 7 (1930), 481-538

14. AHPZ, Híjar, 2ª-63-14.

15. AHPZ, Híjar, 2ª-63-14. Two years earlier, in 1636, Híjar had sent a *memorial* to the King asking for a moratorium to be placed on his paying interest on the *censos* laid on his estates, 'por la esterilidad de los tiempos, falta de vassallos en sus lugares, y el auer pagado de seis años a esta parte ochenta y ocho mil ducados de los ciento i cinquenta mil que el Marques de Alenquer su padre Virrey i Capitan general del Reino de Portugal quedo deuiendo gastados en su seruicio de V. M[a]g[esta]d y el Duque los pago despues de su muerte'. So bad were the times that the Duke 'no a podido ni puede acudir a la paga de los reditos con la puntualidad que quisiera' (AHPZ, Híjar, 4ª-95).

16. F. Silvela, *Cartas de la venerable Madre Sor María de Agreda y del Señor Don Felipe IV, precedidas de un bosquejo histórico*, 2 vols (Madrid: La Correspondencia de España, 1885-86), I, 414.

17. Matías de Novoa, *Historia de Felipe IV, rey de España*, in *Colección de documentos inéditos para la historia de España*, 69, 77, 80, 86 (Madrid: Imprenta de M. Ginesta, 1876-86), IV, 164.

18. Novoa, IV, 165.

19. Novoa, IV, 165.

20. AHPZ, Híjar, 1ª-81-9, cited by I. Villalobos Racionero, 'Un Grande de España, Amante de las Letras, en Villarrubia de los Ojos de Guadiana (Don Rodrigo de Silva y Sarmiento y la Academia celebrada en la villa de Campo de Criptana el 20 de junio de 1644)'. *Discurso leído el día 18 de junio de 1988, en su recepción pública como Consejero de número* (Instituto de Estudios Manchegos, Ciudad Real), 1-63. Apparently, Híjar wrote numerous *memoriales* to the King in a vain attempt to get his order of exile lifted, the earliest of which is dated 12 March 1644.

21. Villalobos Racionero, p.8.

22. See R. García Cárcel: 'Los viajeros extranjeros viajaron en caballo, aunque algunos como Cuelbis lo hicieron a pie. Este era el modo de viajar de los viajeros autóctonos. Se cubrían así treinta o cuarenta kilómetros diarios. Los viajes de los personajes aristocráticos, por su complejo séquito, eran mucho más lentos' ('La vida en el Siglo de Oro (1)', *Cuadernos. Historia 16*, número 129 (1985), 6).

23. AHPZ, Híjar, 1ª-185-48.

24. The Duchess had died of 'tercianas con sudores sincopales' in the late autumn of 1642, an early victim probably of the plague that swept across Spain in the mid 1640s (*Cartas de algunos PP. de la Compañía de Jesús sobre los sucesos de la monarquía entre los años de 1634 y 1648*, in *Memorial Histórico Español*, 13-19 (Madrid, 1861-65), VII, p. 364). She was buried in Benebibere during the first week of December (see AHPZ, Híjar, 4ª-95, for the 'Relación del viaje a Benebibere en 26 de noviembre de 1642').

25. I have been unable to find out what this term means. It does not appear in Sebastián de Covarrubias, *Tesoro de la Lengua Castellana o Española*, ed. by Martín de Riquer (Barcelona: S.A. Horta, 1943) nor in *Diccionario de Autoridades...Compuesto por la Real Academia Española*, 3 vols (Madrid: Imprenta de Francisco del Hierro, 1726-37). It might conceivably be 'pajuela', meaning 'paja pequeña', but even so its significance as a form of cooking or presenting eggs is not obvious, to me at least.

26. During the sixteenth and seventeenth centuries the average cost of staying at an inn was one *real* (G. Menéndez Pidal, *Los caminos en la historia de España* (Madrid, 1951), p.89; J. Ignacio Tellechea Idígoras, 'Un viaje de Madrid a Valladolid en 1559. Gastos de posada según un codicilo del despensero del Arzobispo Carranza', *Boletín de la Real Academica de la Historia*, 162 (1968), 249-76 (p.254)).

27. See Covarrubias: 'Pescado, *quasi* ciercial, porque está curado al ayre, y el que mejor lo cura es el cierço'.

28. Compare the situation of Seville which only had a 'puente de barcas' until the nineteenth century, whilst there was no other bridge over the Guadalquivir until Córdoba! (García Cárcel, pp.6 and 8).

29. The difference in the cost of guides obviously corresponded to the difference in journey time and distance from Illescas-Tagus and Tagus-Mascaraque.

The Road to Villarrubia: The Journey into Exile of the Duke of Híjar   153

30. See the map on the facing page for the details of the route taken by Híjar.

31. See Carla Rahn Phillips, *Ciudad Real 1500-1750. Growth, Crisis and Readjustment in the Spanish Economy* (Cambridge, Mass.: Harvard Univerity Press, 1979).

32. For the road systems of sixteenth- and seventeenth-century Spain, see Juan de Villuga, *Repertorio de todos los caminos de España* (Madrid, 1546), M. Corchado Soriano, *El camino de Toledo a Córdoba* (Jaén, 1969), N. Salomon, *La vida rural castellana en tiempos de Felipe II* (Barcelona: Ariel, 1982), and Menéndez Pidal, *Los caminos*.

33. The cost of living in Villarrubia averaged between 1700 and 2600 maravedises a day, as opposed to the more than 7000 maravedises spent each day on the journey.

34. This was probably some sort of custard or 'natillas'.

35. 'Colación' each day was mostly *migas* or fried bread (*picatostes*).

36. See Covarrubias: 'Es la carne asada y picada menudo, y particularmente la de la pierna del carnero, por ser más a propósito, a causa de la mucha pulpa que tiene'.

37. In fact, 'vna gallina en chullas'. According to Covarrubias, *chulla* is 'las costillas del carnero cortadas en pieças de dos en dos, que la gente pobre compra, quando no tiene caudal para más. Y también es cosa acomodada para almorçar un bocado'.

38. Villalobos Racionero, p. 18, notes two previous occasions when Híjar had visited Villarrubia: in 1622, accompanying his father on his return in disgrace from Portugal, and in June 1638. He was also there in the summer of 1631, as we discover from a letter he wrote in August to an unnamed addressee ('Vine a Villa Ruuia como os lo dixo Don fer[nan]do de labastida donde he reciuido casi juntas dos cartas v[uest]ras de 23 de Jullio y 9 de Agosto' (AHPZ, Híjar, 1ª-19-1)). He may of course have stayed there at different times when he was younger, but there is no record of this.

39. The name Lázaro Hidalgo does not appear in the list of local dignatories furnished by Villalobos Racionero, but he does mention a Juan Díaz Hidalgo and an Antonio Hidalgo (Governor of the village), which makes me think that the 'ydalgo' of the accounts book is a surname and not a designation of rank.

40. Villalobos Racionero, p.21.

41. Villalobos Racionero, p.52, n.52.

42. Villalobos Racionero, pp.21-22.

43. It is possible that this Gaspar de Peñalosa was related in some way to one of two singular personages whose paths crossed with Híjar during the early 1640s. One was Padre Ambrosio Peñalosa of the Jesuit Order, who became involved with Híjar as a result of the latter's intrigues with the Jesuit priest P. Pedro González Galindo, a thorn in side of the Order for his constant and immoderate attacks on the Count-Duke of Olivares and the depressing political situation. Híjar's involvement with and encouragement of this petty trouble-maker was one of the reasons why the King decided to make an example of him in 1644 ordering his exile. The other was a certain Captain Peñalosa whom Híjar had presented to the King as an expert poisoner who could put an end to the life of the Duke of Braganza, instigator of the

recent Portuguese rebellion. The King, who only showed lukewarm support for the idea, was finally dissuaded by the Royal Confessor Fray Juan de Santo Tomás. Híjar had Peñalosa lodged in his palace in Zaragoza while the negotiations with the King and Confessor took place (Ezquerra Abadía, pp. 119-20). Given this degree of confidence, he seems the mostly likely candidate for the don Gaspar de Peñalosa who sent Híjar a letter, received in Villarrubia on Saturday 26 March 1644.

44. AHPZ, Híjar, 1ª-185-48.

45. In the accounts book, the figures in the right-hand column are expressed in a mixture of reales and maravedises, whilst the daily totals are given in maravedises (1 real = 34 maravedises).

46. This is an error: it should be 856.

47. This is an error: it should be 200.

48. This calculation should come to 7668 maravedises, a difference of 66 maravedises.

49. This is an error: 261-20 reales = 8894 maravedises; the administrator has counted 260 reales instead of 261, a difference of 34 maravedises.

50. In the left margin: 'salio de rasion Ju[a]n gonsales cosinero y entro en su lugar miguel peres'.

51. This is an error: 64 reales plus 14 maravedises come to 2190 maravedises, and not 2174; the difference is 16 maravedises or half a real.

52. There is an error: the total should be 98 maravedises. First of all, the administrator has made a mistake in the cost of the bread for the dog: two cuartos are 8 maravedises and not 6; then, he appears to have seen 16 instead of the 6 that he actually noted down!

53. In the left margin: '[s]alio de rasion Ju[a]n gonsales cosinero entro en su lugar miguel peres cosinero y no se le sento ninguna rasion entro por moso de cosina Domingo con dos r[eal]es de rasion'.

54. The last two or three sheets that probably completed the document are missing.

'SCHEMING IDOLATERS' OR 'TENDER PLANTS': ALTERNATIVE INTERPRETATIONS OF NATIVE RELIGIOUS BELIEFS AND RITES IN SEVENTEENTH-CENTURY PERU

NICHOLAS GRIFFITHS
University of Birmingham

In 1609, the archbishop of Lima, Bartolomé Lobo Guerrero, launched a series of campaigns of extirpation in order to root out Indian 'idolatries', which were understood to 'persist' in the face of Christian evangelization. These campaigns were characterized by a sophisticated repressive apparatus. Special Visitors-General were appointed, with the full powers of the archbishop, to lead investigations into local religious practices, and to conduct idolatry trials against perceived offenders. They were empowered to pass sentence and impose severe punishments, including public whipping, exile and confinement in houses of correction.

Although this first wave of persecution came to an end in the 1620s, the same methods of suppressing Andean religious beliefs and rites were employed in the 1650s and 1660s by Archbishop Pedro de Villagómez. The continuity of principles and methods which characterized these campaigns entitles them to be understood as a distinct movement, 'the Extirpation'.[1]

The Extirpation in Peru formed part of a well-established tradition of forcible repression of native religion in Spanish America. The spiritual conquest of Mexico had begun with the burning at the hands of the inquisitor-archbishop, Juan de Zumárraga, not only of native codices but also of native lords, of whom the most notorious was Don Carlos Ometochtzin of Texcoco, consigned to the flames in 1539. Twenty years later, the Maya regions of the Yucatán had been subjected to the violent idolatry investigations of the Franciscan Provincial Fray Diego de Landa who had tortured and killed numerous Indians in order to elicit confessions of native religious practices. In Peru, the idolatry trials of 1568-71, conducted by Cristóbal de Albornoz, in response to the rise of the native millenarian movement *Taki Onqoy* in 1564-65, confirmed that the response to manifestations of Andean religion was to be a fundamentally repressive and punitive enterprise.

The principal advocates of repression were, in the early seventeenth century, Archbishops Bartolomé Lobo Guerrero (1608-22) and Gonzalo de Campo (1625-26), the Viceroys Juan de Mendoza y Luna, Marquis of Montesclaros (1607-15) and Francisco de Borja, Prince of Esquilache (1615-21), the Jesuit Provincial Pablo José de Arriaga and the secular priest, Francisco de Avila; and, in the mid-seventeenth century, the same Francisco de Avila, the archdeacon of Lima cathedral, Hernando de Avendaño, and the Archbishop Pedro de Villagómez (1641-71). The fundamental principle of the Extirpation was that the Indians, as baptized Christians and full members of the Church, had committed heresy and (more strictly) apostasy by 'returning' to their pagan ways. Thus, for example, in 1609, Francisco de Avila accused the Indians of his *doctrina* (native parish) of apostasy in continuing to celebrate native rites.[2] Similarly, in 1614, the Visitor-General Luis de Mora y Aguilar absolved the inhabitants of the village of Concepción de Chupas of the sins of 'idolatry and apostasy'.[3] This condition was understood to be endemic throughout the entire viceroyalty. Archbishop Lobo Guerrero informed the king in 1611 that 'all the Indians of my archbishopric, and similarly those of the other bishoprics, are today as much infidels and idolaters as when they were first conquered'.[4] The constitutions of the synod of Lima of 1613 made constant references to the Indians as idolaters and apostates.[5] Archbishop Gonzalo de Campo informed the king in 1626 that he had found many parts of his archbishopric contaminated with 'idolatries and heresies', for which reason he recommended that trials of Indians for such offences should be placed under the jurisdiction of the Inquisition. The request was not granted and the Indians remained excluded from the jurisdiction of the Holy Office.[6]

The fundamental principle of the advocates of repression was not religious orthodoxy, accepted by all contemporary theologians and ecclesiastics; on the contrary, this principle was vehemently disputed by powerful and articulate opponents. One of the principal purposes of Arriaga's extirpation manual of 1621, apart from establishing guidelines for proceeding against practitioners of native rites, was to satisfy 'learned and serious people' of the truth of what 'they have doubted and even contradicted on many occasions...that there are idolatries among the Indians, whereas they have said that all are good

'Scheming Idolaters' or 'Tender Plants'   157

Christians'.[7] The issue caused such profound disagreement among the great clerical minds of the era that when Archbishop Gonzalo de Campo first arrived in Lima in 1625, he was so impressed by the strength of passion on all sides that he decided to conduct a personal visit to his archdiocese in order to verify for himself the existence and significance of native religious practices. He wrote:

> I found such a great variety of opinions about this when I arrived in Lima...most of those who told me that there was a great deal of idolatry were theologians, preachers and others with great zeal for saving souls; others told me that it was an invention of the Visitors who under this pretext tried to make money, and that the Indians were victims of a grave injustice when they were thus accused; others said that they believed there was some idolatry but not as much as was claimed...[8]

It is clear that the debate sharply divided ecclesiastical opinion. There was at least a three-way divide on the issue, with two factions opposing the advocates of repression.

The views of those who denied the need for idolatry visitations were significant enough for Archbishop Villagómez to devote the first part of his *Carta pastoral* (1649) to their refutation. The letters included at the back of the work indicate the continuation of a vehement polemic over the existence and significance of native religious practices. The bishop of Cuzco, Juan Alonso Ocón (1643-51), lamented the widespread 'persistence' of idolatry in his diocese and attacked those 'priests and other ecclesiastics' who made cause with 'Behemoth' by denying this ugly truth. The Jesuit Francisco Patiño denounced those who dismissed the existence of idolatry as a wild fantasy or excused it as vestiges inherited from the past. Those priests who failed to perceive or to act against the idolatry under their very noses were themselves guilty of 'interpretative idolatry'.[9]

Thus, the appropriateness of forcible repression as a response to indigenous religion remained a matter of great controversy. The debate derived from disagreement as to the significance of manifestations of native religious rites. Andean religion was perceived by Spanish ecclesiastics according to the dichotomy of 'idolatry' and 'superstition'. The fundamental intellectual premise of the advocates of repression was the assimilation of both of these sins to that of Devil worship; the Indians were apostates and idolaters because, by their beliefs and rites, they had rendered to Satan the worship due to God. The opponents of religious repression, on the other hand, distinguished the more reprehensible sin of idolatry from the lesser one of superstition, concluding that the Indians were guilty only of the latter. This intellectual disagreement was so fundamental that it requires a more detailed examination.

The categories of idolatry and superstition had been clearly distinguished by classical Christian writers. According to Thomas Aquinas, superstition was 'religion carried to excess'. This excess lay, not in giving too much worship to God, but in offering worship to him in some manner which was unfitting or, alternatively, in offering divine worship to something not deserving it. This latter category of superstition could take the form, first, of false observances, which were the expression of the belief that divine powers were found in certain creatures; secondly, of divination, which was the attributing of divine powers to demons; and thirdly, idolatry, or the rendering unto creature of worship due to God alone. Idolatry denoted, then, not only the worship of idols proper, as its etymology (*idolo-latria*) would suggest, but also the worship of any 'creature' or object of creation, which, by definition, could not be divine and hence could not figure as an appropriate recipient of worship.[10]

This classical distinction between idolatry and superstition had largely been lost by the sixteenth century among those writers whose works were to exercise a profound influence upon the fight against native religion in Peru. Instead, the two categories had become closely assimilated. This relative departure from classical positions derived from the Early Modern identification of both idolatry and superstition with Devil worship. For Pedro Ciruelo, the sixteenth-century Spanish authority on superstition and witchcraft, superstition was no longer distinguishable from idolatry since the roots of both offences lay in diabolical intervention. For Aquinas, the sin of idolatry derived principally from the ignorance and vanity of man rather than from the evil machinations of demonic spirits; but, for Ciruelo, diabolical intervention was no longer merely contributory, but became *the* essential cause. Idolatry, the sin against *latria*, was no longer the worship of creature; instead it had become synonymous with Devil worship.[11]

The assimilation of both idolatry and superstition to Devil worship characterized the works of the Jesuit writers who were to provide the ideological basis for the Extirpation. The Jesuit Provincial and missionary in Peru, José de Acosta, followed Ciruelo when he identified idolatry with Devil worship and hence attributed a diabolical origin to native Andean religious practices. The first chapter of the fifth book of his *Historia natural y moral de las Indias* was entitled 'That the cause of idolatry has been the pride and envy of the Devil'; elsewhere he wrote that the honouring of idols was the same as honouring the Devil. The *huacas* (Andean sacred entities) were mere mouthpieces for Satan and their rites and ceremonies were simply a diabolical parody of the true faith.[12]

Although he drew a theoretical distinction between idolatry and superstition, in practice Acosta used the terms almost interchangeably. He frequently assimilated superstition and the worship of *huacas*, referring, for example, to 'the superstitious cult of their idols' or 'all the images and *huacas* and other representations of the superstitions of the Indians' or the widespread 'superstition' of 'different classes of sacrifices and *huacas*'. Considering the association between civilization and religious practices, Acosta interchanged the word 'superstition' for 'idolatry'. He observed that those Indian nations characterized by superior power and organizing capacity had more numerous and more serious classes of 'diabolical superstitions', whereas amongst those who had achieved less progress, 'idolatry' was much rarer. The diligent catequist, he wrote, must fight not only the 'vanity of idols' in general, but must also refute the 'particular gods and *huacas* and other superstitions which are special to their people.' This 'almost infinite variety of superstitions' derived directly from the worship of idols. Thus, superstitions became indistinguishable from idolatry because the former were themselves fragmented derivatives of the latter. It followed that, as residual vestiges of the ebbing tide of idolatrous beliefs, superstitious ceremonies and rites were as sinful as the true idolatrous reverence of creatures, since both arose from the same diabolical origin. Idolatry was the trunk from which grew the branches of superstition, and both were rooted in diabolical inspiration.[13]

The writings of the principal ideologue of religious repression, the Jesuit Provincial Pablo José de Arriaga, were largely derived from Acosta. Although Arriaga's manual only contained a few explicit references to Acosta's *De procuranda* (on pp. 224 and 257), the entire work was founded upon the latter's principles. For example, Arriaga's dictum that the 'traces of idolatry' which remained in Peru had been 'imbibed with the (mother's) milk and inherited from parents to children' echoed Acosta's famous reference to the 'hereditary illness of idolatry' which had been 'contracted in the very mother's breast and suckled by her milk'. Like Acosta, Arriaga distinguished in theory between, on the one hand, true idolatry, the attribution of divinity to creatures expressed in the worship of *huacas* and *mallquis* (mummified corpses, bones or other remains of ancestors), and, on the other, superstition, which included ceremonies, rites and customs. For example, he acknowledged that *zaramamas* (corncobs which emerged joined two together) were not accorded the worship rendered to a *huaca* but were 'superstitiously held as a sacred object'. Even so, like Acosta, the worship of *huacas* was often described indistinguishably as idolatry or superstition. On the one hand, he referred to *huacas* as 'idolatries' (for example, 'their *huacas* and *conopas* and the other instruments of their idolatries'); yet, elsewhere, he grouped *huacas* with superstition ('the *huacas* and other superstitions'). Like Acosta, he believed that Indian superstitions sprang from the trunk of idolatry: 'all are branches and leaves born of the trunk of their gentility and idolatry'.[14]

If Acosta and Arriaga associated Andean religion with Devil worship, not all writers agreed with them. The most famous opponent of the diabolical interpretation of native religion was the Dominican friar, Bartolomé de Las Casas. Las Casas followed Aquinas in attributing to the Devil a complementary role in idolatry. For the Dominican, the true origin of idolatry lay in the perversion of man's natural religiosity. When the guidance of grace and instruction was lacking, the worship due to God could become misdirected by the very strength of mankind's religious appetite, and hence *latria* became idolatry. It was true that Satan was able to take advantage of the misplacement of humanity's religious urge in order to prevent recognition of the true God and to have himself worshipped instead; but the original source of idolatry sprang from man's innate blindness in the absence of the teachings of Christ, and not from the all-pervading power and malevolence of Satan. The intervention of the Devil was limited to the initiation of magical practices among the Indians, which were clearly distinguished as superstitions (the sinful attempt to learn of future contingencies from other than natural or divine sources) and not idolatry.[15]

Like Las Casas, some experts in Andean religious practices were concerned to save the autochthonous religious tradition from obloquy. By sharply differentiating superstition from idolatry, an explicit intention to give worship to creatures in every native rite could be denied. Whereas Arriaga found idolatry in every aspect of daily life, the chronicler Cristóbal de Molina refused to consider that ceremonies linked to the family rites of the cycle of life were idolatrous, but rather defined them simply as expressions of communal solidarity. The native rites of name-giving and the ceremonious cutting of hair were ceremonies performed 'without the slightest trace of idolatry'. Such interpretations were not confined to Peru. In Mexico, the Dominican friar, Diego de Durán, distinguished between true idolatry and superstitious customs. He tolerated the use of floral ornaments on Christian festivals which coincided with those of the deity Tezcatlipoca, finding 'no trace of idolatry in it' since they only expressed 'an ancient custom'. Custom was here distinguished from idolatry by the fact that it was automatic and deprived of all conscious foundation. Since the institutional framework for native religion had collapsed, any survivals, deprived of the fundamental coherence which formerly unified all acts of life, could only be classed as superstition rather than idolatry.[16]

This distinction dominated the debate between the advocates of Extirpation in Peru and their opponents. Among the first to voice their opposition were the mendicant orders. In 1622, the provincial of the Augustinians, Francisco de la Serna, informed the King that 'not even a trace' of idolatry was to be found among the Indians in their *doctrinas*. He pointed out that the investigations of Luis Cornejo, the provincial of the Dominicans, who had been appointed by the archbishop himself to investigate native practices throughout the archdiocese, had concluded that the Indians were not guilty of the worship of idols but rather only of 'abuses and rites' which they observed 'in imitation of their ancestors'. De la Serna was drawing upon arguments familiar to Molina in order to absolve the Indians of the charge of idolatry. In order to settle the matter, the Augustinian provincial declared his intention to conduct visitations to all the villages of the archbishopric of Lima and the bishopric of Trujillo, since he was extremely sceptical of the account given by the Jesuit Arriaga. This open challenge to the ideology of the Extirpation reflected in part the old hostility of the mendicant orders towards the Jesuits; but it also expressed an interpretation of native religious practices fundamentally at odds with that of the advocates of religious repression. The provincial of the Mercedarians clearly shared this alternative interpretation when he informed the king in 1626 that few Indians were idolaters, unless the term was to be extended to their 'false superstitions', in which case there would be few who would not be included. The accusation of idolatry was invalid, not because elements of native religion did not survive, but because Indian rites were only a vestige of the past, a reflex action, a mimicry of their ancestors without the true content of belief.[17]

The Extirpation was attacked not only by the mendicant orders but also by opponents within the religious and political administrations of the archbishopric. In 1622, after the death of Lobo Guerrero but before the arrival of the new archbishop, the *cabildo eclesiástico* (cathedral chapter) of Lima suspended the idolatry visitations, allegedly on the grounds of excesses which had been denounced by the Indians, and began a secret investigation against the Visitors.[18] When Gonzalo de Campo renewed the campaigns in 1625, the *audiencia* (high court) of Lima called into question not only the seriousness of native religious practices but also the methods of procedure of the idolatry campaigns and their apparent excesses. They alleged that the Visitors and the Jesuits were exaggerating the extent of idolatry in order to justify the importance of their own work. If the Indians confessed to idolatry, it was because they were 'simple people' who told the Visitors what they wanted to hear in return for rewards or in order to please them and free themselves from their enquiries. If they did not confess, the Visitors took away their livestock on the pretext that it was destined for sacrifice to the *huacas*. Thus, not only were the charges false, but the investigations subjected the Indians to serious abuses and exactions.[19]

There were many prelates in other dioceses of the viceroyalty who shared reservations about the necessity of campaigns of extirpation. Some even denied the existence of any form of native religious practices. The bishop of Cuzco, Lorenzo Pérez de Grado (1619-27), wrote to the king that he had found his diocese 'clean of idolatries, abuses and ancient rites'. The bishop of Trujillo, Francisco de Cabrera (1616-19), contested the need for campaigns of extirpation in his diocese since not only were the Indians 'as free of these and other similar errors as Burgos and Toledo', but their devotion to Christianity was so strong that he was 'envious of it for the Spaniards'.[20]

But those who denied all trace of ancient belief or custom were few. Most acknowledged that the Indians did indeed preserve vestiges of their former religion, but insisted that these were not to be interpreted as 'idolatry', nor were they to be remedied by trials and severe punishments. The bishop of Arequipa, Pedro de Perea (1619-30), admitted the existence of 'the relics of idolatries and superstitions' among the Indians, but he advanced instruction in Spanish as the most potent antidote. Those who maintained these customs were the unacculturated *hatunrunas*, who lived in villages with little contact with Spaniards; the acculturated *ladinos*, who lived in Spanish towns, were innocent of these practices. Hence, the remedy was greater acculturation, to which end he advocated forbidding the use of the native tongue among the Indians. Instead, they should converse in Spanish, which could be imparted to them by village *fiscales* and *caciques*, especially trained in local seminaries, modelled on the school for Indian chieftains in Lima and replicated in every bishopric. The ultimate goal was the union of both *naciones*, Indians and Spaniards, in one republic. This alternative interpretation of the significance of persisting native customs implicitly denied the foundations upon which the campaigns of extirpation were based. For, despite the fact that the bishop wrote at the height of the trials, he omitted to advance persecution as a suitable remedy. His failure to respond to Viceroy Esquilache's call of the previous year for all prelates to launch idolatry campaigns in their own dioceses must be understood in the context of this alternative interpretation.[21]

Perea was not the only prelate to propose alternative remedies for the 'persistence' of native practices. The constitutions of the diocesan synod for Trujillo, drawn up in 1623 by Bishop Carlos Marcelo Corne (1619-29), denied the existence of 'idolatries' among the Indians and lamented only their 'fraudulent superstitions and abuses'. But, in order to satisfy the demands for further investigations on the part of those who 'claimed' that idolatry was 'universal' throughout the viceroyalty, the bishop appointed, not specialized extirpators of idolatry, but the ordinary ecclesiastical visitors, to make enquiries and find out if any 'heathen rites' were still performed or any 'superstitions, spells or other tricks' practised. If they found evidence of pagan practices, they were to correct the Indians principally through preaching; rigorous punishment would be necessary only for those who were stubbornly rebellious. The term *extirpación* itself was employed only with reference to 'superstitions' and 'magic', not with reference to 'idolatry'.[22]

If Corne and Perea offered tacit and indirect opposition to the techniques of the Extirpation, the bishop of Huamanga, Francisco Verdugo (1621-37), used his authority directly to prevent the extension of its activities to his diocese. In 1621 he suspended the Visitors of idolatry because of the distress they had caused among the Indians, substituting their work with his own personal visits to the Indians in the company of Jesuit missionaries. Like his colleagues in Trujillo and Arequipa, Verdugo was convinced that there were no grounds for accusing the Indians of idolatries. The advocates of extirpation, motivated by private interests and ambitions, rather than by the zeal for souls, had not told the king the truth. They blamed the poor spiritual condition of the Indians upon their innate incapacity and propensity for vice, when in reality it was they themselves who were guilty of failure to instruct the Indians adequately. The Indians were clearly not 'a barbarous people', incapable of understanding the mysteries of the faith. Their instruction had been prevented by the burdens of excessive work upon them, which caused them to flee from the *doctrina* and made it impossible for priests to teach them. After all, if even the Spaniards themselves, despite their indoctrination from a very early age, were sometimes corrupted and went astray from the faith, was it surprising that the Indians, who had been so inadequately instructed, were still infirm in the faith? They were not idolaters, but poor Christians.[23]

The second wave of repression (1649-71) was opposed very articulately by at least one bishop, Francisco de Godoy, the prelate of Huamanga (1652-59). Godoy did not deny the existence of idolatry; indeed, on the contrary, he claimed he had found significant traces of native religious rites. He was even prepared to threaten individual Indians with the traditional punishment for 'apostates of the faith', burning at the stake, in order to terrify them into disclosing their religious practices.[24] But these were to be understood more as 'superstitions' rather than 'idolatries', 'traces' or 'vestiges' of ancient religious practices rather than real apostasy. Such errors were not exclusive to Indians but were shared by blacks, and were to be attributed to the lack of knowledge of the faith consequent upon poor instruction. If the Indians were still practising their old beliefs, it was not because they were inherently wicked, but because the Spaniards had failed in their duty to instruct them adequately. The Indian potential for assimilation of the True Faith was boundless since 'among all nations there has never been any which has received the ceremony of our religion as this one has'. The Indians were the chief attendants at divine worship in Huamanga and received the bishop and his priests with love and devotion. It was this optimism about the Indian character, sharply at variance with the assessment of the advocates of extirpation, which convinced him that, with culture and education, the Indians could become good Christians.[25] Improved preaching would be one principal method. In a letter of 1652, he wrote: 'with ordinary preaching and education, many idolatries which have remained from their ancestors will be eliminated, since there is no means to eliminate them other than by preaching'. The second principal method was the administration of the sacrament of Communion. In subsequent letters of 1656 and 1657, the bishop claimed that 'the principal remedy against their idolatries' was the participation of the Indians in 'the mystery of the Incarnation of the Son of God'. All Indians should be prepared to receive the sacrament 'since whilst they do not take communion, they will not be true Christians'. These two methods were sufficient for the dissemination of true belief among the Indians and for an end to their native practices. Campaigns of extirpation played no part in the bishop's scheme.[26]

For Godoy, the devotion of the Indians to Catholic worship was genuine and confirmed them as true Christians. The survival of native religious practices could not disqualify their devotion. The issue was how to make them better Christians. The interpretation of the advocates of extirpation was, however, irreconcilably opposed. Juan Alonso Ocón, the bishop of Cuzco (1644-51), alleged that, far from being exaggerated, the stranglehold of idolatry in Peru was greater than yet realized, to the extent that Christianity only existed 'in embryo'. The Jesuit Francisco Patiño wrote that, by returning to their heathen ways after hearing the true Faith, the Indians were not only 'damned twice over' by comparison with their former ignorant state, but also by comparison with the Spaniards; for, if Spaniards frequently failed to live a true Christian life, at least they believed in the faith; the Indians, however, were guilty of insincere belief. Thus, if the Spaniards were 'bad Christians', they were still 'good Catholics'; the Indians, on the other hand, were 'Christians in name only' and 'apostates and idolaters' in reality.[27] Whereas, for the opponents of extirpation, the majority of Indians were *passive* idolaters, content to imitate what they saw others do without contemplating the nature of the gestures and the acts performed, for its advocates they were *active* idolaters, guilty not merely of *material* idolatry (through ignorance or confusion) but also of profound, interiorized *formal* idolatry (through pertinacity). For the extirpators and their supporters, 'idolatry' was the effect of a choice rather than the product of deep-rooted habits.[28]

It was the interplay between these two currents of thought which determined two curious characteristics of the seventeenth-century campaigns of idolatry: first, their intermittent occurrence (1609-22, 1625-26 and 1649-71) and, secondly, the infrequency of their extension beyond the confines of the archdiocese of Lima. Both Lobo Guerrero and Villagómez intended to extend the trials to all the dioceses of the viceroyalty, but both only achieved success in part. In 1619 the Viceroy Esquilache ordered visits to be initiated by the bishops of Huamanga, Cuzco, Arequipa, La Paz, La Plata and Santa Cruz de la Sierra.[29] It is clear that there were idolatry trials in Huamanga in the second decade of the seventeenth century, since the letter of Francisco Patiño indicates that Bishop Agustín de Caravajal (1613-18) presided over investigations in his diocese.[30] There were also trials in Arequipa under Villagómez himself (1635-40). The letter of Juan Alonso Ocón, the bishop of Cuzco, refers to idolatry visitations in his diocese in the 1640s: 'I left a judge of idolatry in these provinces, who has been sending me cases of *dogmatizadores* (propagandists of native beliefs)'.[31] Similarly, the bishop of Cuzco, Manuel de Mollinedo (1673-99), gave an account in 1674 of idolatry trials in Pucara in his diocese.[32] But, apart from these examples, there is no evidence that idolatry trials were conducted extensively in the provinces on the scale that they were in the archdiocese.

If most dioceses did not witness a replication of the campaigns of extirpation, it was *not* because the bishops were too self-interested, apathetic or lacking in zeal to lend their support. Instead, as a matter of principle, few agreed with the strategy of campaigns of extirpation. Failing to gain intellectual hegemony, the advocates of repression enjoyed a precarious ascendancy under Archbishops Lobo Guerrero and Villagómez, which was by no means permanently assured; on the contrary, the initiation of a particular campaign of extirpation represented only a temporary victory for its promoters in a long-standing conflict. The crusaders of the Extirpation were not able to take advantage of the authority conferred by orthodoxy, but were forced to present their case and win their battles in every generation. The first campaigns of the seventeenth century were abruptly terminated on the death of their patrons, Archbishops Lobo Guerrero and Campo. The policy of repression remained dormant under their successor, Hernando Arias de Ugarte (1630-38), who was sceptical as to the reality of Indian idolatries. The advocates of repression never won the intellectual argument. Their opponents continued to advocate alternative policies, in the service of a different priority: not to 'extirpate' idolatry, but to make good Christians out of *plantas tiernas* or 'tender plants'. Thus, the dispute which rendered the campaigns of extirpation an object of never-ending controversy remained one between those who believed that they were punishing apostates through a combination of persecution and instruction, and those who believed that by persuasion and patience, they were gradually transforming the Indians from poor Christians into good Christians.

NOTES

1. There were also idolatry trials in the archdiocese of Lima in the eighteenth century, but these fall outside the scope of this article. The movement, 'the Extirpation', with a capital letter, may be distinguished from 'extirpation' in a general sense (just as one may distinguish between 'the Inquisition' and 'inquisition'). This article will use both terms.

2. P. Duviols, *La lutte contre les religions autochtones dans le Pérou colonial: l'extirpation de l'idolâtrie entre 1532 et 1660* (Lima and Paris, 1971), pp.148 and 221.

3. Archivo General de Indias, Sevilla (hereafter AGI), Lima 301, *Manifestación que hicieron todos los indios de un pueblo en razón de ser idólatras ante el visitador de la idolatría*, Concepción de Chupas, 1614.

4. AGI, Lima 301, Letter of Archbishop Bartolomé Lobo Guerrero to the king, 20 April 1611, fol. 2.

5. *Constituciones sinodales del arzobispo Lobo Guerrero*, Lima, 1614, Lib. 1, Tit. 1, Cap. 6, printed in P. Duviols, *Cultura andina y represión: procesos y visitas de idolatrías y hechicerías, Cajatambo, siglo XVII* (Cuzco, 1986), pp.511-14.

6. In 1571 Philip II had formally removed the Indians in the Spanish colonies from the jurisdiction of the Inquisition. The Spanish Crown always refused to subject the neophyte Indians to the rigours and terrors of the Holy Office on the grounds of their 'simplicity and poor understanding' and too recent instruction in the faith. See Duviols, *La lutte*, p.217, and J. T. Medina, *Historia del Tribunal de la Inquisición de Lima: 1569-1820*, 2nd edn, 2 vols (Santiago de Chile, 1956), I, 27-28.

7. P. J. de Arriaga, *La extirpación de la idolatría del Perú*, in *Crónicas peruanas de interés indígena*, ed. by F. Esteve Barba, Biblioteca de Autores Españoles, CCIX (Madrid, 1968), pp.194 and 225.

8. AGI, Lima 302, Letter of Archbishop Gonzalo de Campo to the king, 8 October 1626.

9. Letters of Juan Alonso Ocón, bishop of Cuzco, and of the Jesuit Francisco Patiño, to Archbishop Pedro de Villagómez, 14 October 1648, in Pedro de Villagómez, *Carta pastoral de exhortación e instrucción contra las idolatrías de los indios del arzobispado de Lima*, Colección de libros y documentos referentes a la historia del Perú, ed. by C. A. Romero and H. H. Urteaga, XII (Lima, 1919), pp.273, 277 and 283.

10. St Thomas Aquinas, *Summa theologiae*, edition introduced by T. Gilby O.P., 50 vols (Cambridge, 1968), 2a2ae. 92,1; 92,2; 94,1. Also see P. J. Glenn, *A tour of the Summa* (New York, 1960), p.247, and W. B. Monahan, *The moral theology of St Thomas Aquinas*, 3 vols (London, 1942), III, 9-21. For definitions of superstition and idolatry, also see P. Castañeda Delgado and P. Hernández Aparicio, *La Inquisición de Lima (1570-1635)* (Madrid, 1989), pp.363-64.

11. P. Ciruelo, *Reprobación de las supersticiones y hechicerías* (Madrid, 1538), pp.5-6, 16, 18, 25-26 and 31. Aquinas, *Summa*, 2a2ae, 94,4.

12. J. de Acosta, *Historia natural y moral de las Indias*, 2nd edn, rev. by E. O'Gorman (Mexico,

1962), pp.217, 231, 235, 255 and 278.

13. J. de Acosta, *De procuranda indorum salute*, 2 vols (Madrid: CSIC, Corpus Hispanorum de Pace, 1984-87), II, 255-59 and 269-71.

14. Arriaga, *La extirpación*, pp. 195-96, 198, 205, 215-16, 218 and 244-46. For the reference to the mother's milk, see Acosta, *De procuranda*, II, 255.

15. Fray B. de las Casas, *Apologética historia sumaria*, ed. by E. O'Gorman, 2 vols (Mexico, 1967), I, 381, 387 and 440. Also see D. Brading, *The First America: The Spanish monarchy, Creole patriots and the Liberal state 1492-1867* (Cambridge, 1991), p.192.

16. C. Bernand and S. Gruzinski, *De l'idolâtrie: une archéologie des sciences réligieuses* (Paris, 1988), pp.114-15. C. de Molina, *Relación de las fábulas y ritos de los Incas*, in *Fábulas y mitos de los incas*, ed. by H. Urbano and P. Duviols, Crónicas de América 48 (Madrid, 1989). D. de Durán, *Historia de las Indias de la Nueva España*, ed. by A.M. Garibay, Biblioteca Porrúa, 2 vols (Mexico, 1967), I, 55.

17. AGI, Lima 325, Letter of Francisco de la Serna, provincial of the Augustinians, to the king, 9 May 1622. For discussion of the letter, see Duviols, *Cultura andina*, pp.xlv-xlvi. AGI, Lima 302, Letter of Fray Gaspar de la Torre, provincial of the Mercedarians, to the king, 30 October 1626.

18. AGI, Lima 310, Letter of the *cabildo eclesiástico* of Lima to the king, 8 May 1623. For the secret investigation against the Visitors, see Archivo Arzobispal de Lima (hereafter AAL), Idolatrías 1 (4:7), Información y pesquisa secreta contra los visitadores del pueblo de Santiago de la Nazca, 1623; AAL, Idolatrías 1 (2:6), Información secreta contra los visitadores de la idolatría hecha en la villa de Carrión de Velasco (Province of Chancay), 1622; and AAL, Idolatrías 1 (6:5), Autos hechos en virtud de comisión de Andres García de Zurita contra los visitadores eclesiásticos de la idolatría, Cajatambo (Province of Cajatambo), 1623.

19. AGI, Lima 98, Letter of the *audiencia* of Lima to the king, 30 October 1626.

20. AGI, Lima 305, Letter of Lorenzo Perez de Grado, bishop of Cuzco, to the king, 18 March 1623. AGI, Lima 38, Letter of Francisco de Cabrera, bishop of Trujillo, to the congress of the Company of Jesus, 9 July 1618.

21. AGI, Lima 309, Letter of Pedro de Perea, bishop of Arequipa, to the king, March 1620.

22. AGI, Lima 307, *Constituciones synodales del obispado de Trujillo del Perú*, acción primera, sección 1, cap. 6, fols. 4v and 12. The bishop referred to instructions which he had drawn up to enable the priests to distinguish 'idolatry' from 'superstition' but no trace of these seems to have survived. It is important to observe that the distinction was considered significant by figures of authority at the height of the early Extirpation.

23. AGI, Lima 308, two Letters of Francisco de Verdugo, bishop of Huamanga, to the king, 20 April 1621 and 2 February 1626. The constitutions of the synod of Huamanga of 1629 discussed the need for better quality priests and preaching and made no reference to the elimination of idolatry. AGI, Lima 308, *Constituciones synodales del obispado de Huamanga*, Lib. 1, Tit. 1, Const. 6, 5 August 1629.

24. AGI, Lima 308, Letter of Francisco de Godoy, bishop of Huamanga, to the king, 10 July 1656.

25. AGI, Lima 308, *carta de edicto* issued by Francisco de Godoy, bishop of Huamanga, 15 June 1652.

26. AGI, Lima 308, Letters of Francisco de Godoy, bishop of Huamanga, to the king, 15 July 1652, 10 July 1656 and 18 June 1657.

27. Letters of Juan Alonso Ocón, bishop of Cuzco, to Archbishop Pedro de Villagómez, 14 October 1648 and 14 December 1648, and of the Jesuit Francisco Patiño, to Archbishop Pedro de Villagómez, 14 October 1648, in Villagómez, *Carta pastoral*, pp.275 and 286.

28. See Bernand and Gruzinski, *De l'idolâtrie*, pp.156 and 167-68. Even so, there remained an unresolved contradiction at the heart of the ideology of Extirpation. The assertion that the inclination to idolatry was imbibed with the mothers' milk was an implicit acknowledgement that Indian religious practices were a culturally determined trait rather than a pure act of choice.

29. AGI Lima 38, Letter of Viceroy Esquilache to the king, 23 March 1619. See Duviols, *La lutte*, p.210.

30. Letter of Francisco Patiño to Archbishop Pedro de Villagómez, 14 October 1648, in Villagómez, *Carta pastoral*, p.279.

31. Letter of Juan Alonso Ocón to Archbishop Pedro de Villagómez, 14 October 1648, in Villagómez, *Carta pastoral*, p.274.

32. AGI, Lima 306, *Relación de la visita que hizo Manuel de Mollinedo*, obispo de Cuzco, 20 November 1674.

NINETEENTH CENTURY

CANON AND PREJUDICE

ANA DE BRITO
Instituto Superior de Contabilidade e Administração do Porto

It cannot be said that the concern with the origins of a genre, with its definition and encapsulation in a formula, with the search for perfect and for imperfect examples, is the preserve of the historians of the novel as genre. Countless examples of the preoccupation with the theory and the history of any other genre could be provided, both in literature and in literary criticism, though it is doubtful that the output of such a search equals in political bias the one that is conducted for the genre of the novel. The novel's origin is not lost in the distant past but, to use a biological simile, too many families claim it as their offspring.

Several novels, both past and recent, could be cited as 'self-conscious' fictions, some offering convincing instances of the novelist's awareness of the necessity to discuss questions of principle, and of the impossibility of the task that the novel sets itself, namely to represent 'reality'. But *Northanger Abbey* seems to me to be a particularly interesting meeting-point of a number of arguments proffered by defenders and attackers of the genre, and of genre fiction. I am not arguing for the atemporality of the opinions it conveys, but I believe that the object of these opinions, and the discussion of it represented in this novel may help put into perspective the present-day debate of the issue of fiction and of genre fiction in particular.

One of the objectives of Jane Austen's novel is an apology for the genre, springing partly from a corporate solidarity:

> Let us leave it to the Reviewers to abuse such effusions of fancy at their leisure, and over every novel to talk in threadbare strains of the trash with which the press now groans. Let us not desert one another; we are an injured body.[1]

But this defence appears in a text which can be construed, on the whole, as a defiance of an accepted and widely recognized set of codified devices in novel-writing. As Kenneth L. Moller notes, 'the entire novel is patterned as a sort of antitype to a hypothetical work that is a composite of typical novelist's material'.[2] It is its ambivalence that makes *Northanger Abbey*'s claim that the novel as a genre is respectable all the more forceful.

By drawing attention to the conventions of the genre and subsequently denying herself the benefit of using them, the narrator is according herself the role of a 'biographer' of her characters, not that of a 'contriver'. One of the most evident instances of this procedure occurs towards the end of the novel. The heroine and the actions described in this novel are repeatedly shown deserting the ranks of the genre. Conventions are clearly stated, whole paragraphs and whole pages are written along the lines of the formulae (the gothic novel and the sentimental novel) until the following paragraph or the following page discredits formulaic writing by stating its inadequacy and impossibility:

> A heroine returning, at the close of her career, to her native village, in all the triumph of recovered reputation, and all the dignity of a countess, with a long train of noble relations in their several phaetons, and three waiting-maids in a travelling chaise-and-four behind her, is an event on which the pen of the *contriver* may well delight to dwell; it gives credit to every conclusion, and the author must share in the glory she so liberally bestows. -- But my affair is widely different: I bring back my heroine to her home in solitude and disgrace; and no sweet elation of spirits can lead me into minuteness. But, whatever might be the distress of Catherine's mind, as she thus advanced towards the Parsonage, and whatever the humiliation of her *biographer* in relating it ... (1131, *my emphases*)

This means of vindicating the truthfulness of or authenticating her report, by sacrificing the very conventions that would bring 'delight' and 'glory' to their user is repeatedly employed throughout the novel. It should be noted that this option is presented as no option at all, but as what must be. There is no long train of phaetons to accompany the heroine, but her return is, nevertheless, suitably eventful. It can be argued that this deprecation of conventions operates on the basis of the acceptance of another set of conventional gambits and cannot be taken as a move towards realism. Susan Morgan explains that:

> Having mocked gothic and sentimental conventions throughout the novel, Austen yet resolves the plot by dismissing the heroine

unexpectedly and inexplicably from the abbey and having the hero oppose the angry commands of his father and gallop after her to offer his hand.[3]

Although several different readings of the novel are possible, one may doubt the interest of reading it as two texts, one mocking the conventions of Gothic and sentimental novels and the other going about its business of telling a story in a 'sensible', straightforward way. This approach to the novel seems to be quite frequent. Katrin Ristkok Burlin distinguishes between four types of fiction in the novel: sentimental, Gothic fiction; the satiric, educative fiction of Henry Tilney; the manipulative, egotistical fictions of the Thorpes; and the satiric and realistic fiction of *Northanger Abbey* itself.[4] This implies an appreciation of the novel that is fragmentary and does not take into account the fact that the core of the matter is precisely the diversity of fictions and their different receptions. As Burlin herself points out, some of the situations and most characters are shaped according to formulae, particularly those of the Gothic, sentimental novel. For example: 'Isabella's quick intimacy with Catherine is itself a borrowing from the novel of sensibility'.[5] If we dispensed with these characters and these situations when referring to *Northanger Abbey* itself then we would have very little, if any, text to speak about or, alternatively, we would be forced to interpret parts of it, as Susan Morgan does, as inevitable pitfalls in which a too-critical author is trapped. The temptation to search the text for instances of incongruities and inobservances of the creed is great. But the Gothic and the sentimental formulae are discussed from within, they are part of the story of a supervising narrator sorting out disparate fictions, and we can only speak of *Northanger Abbey* itself if we consider the whole text. When she engages in direct criticism of Gothic fiction, Jane Austen presents us with ironical excerpts that can be read at different levels. This is the case with a paragraph on Ann Radcliffe's works:

> Charming as were all Mrs Radcliffe's works, and charming even as were the works of all her imitators, it was not in them perhaps that human nature, at least in the midland counties of England, was to be looked for. Of the Alps and Pyrenees, with their pine forests and their vices, they might give a faithful delineation; and Italy, Switzerland and the South of France, might be as fruitful in horrors as they were there represented. Catherine dared not doubt beyond her own country, and even

of that, if hard pressed, would have yielded the northern and western extremities. But in the central part of England there was surely some security for the existence even of a wife not beloved, in the laws of the land, and the manners of the age. Murder was not tolerated, servants were not slaves, and neither poison nor sleeping potions to be procured, like rhubarb, from every druggist. Among the Alps and Pyrenees, perhaps, there were no mixed characters. There, such as were not spotless as an angel, might have the disposition of a fiend. But in England it was not so; among the English, she believed, in their hearts and habits, there was a general though unequal mixture of good and bad. (1112)

This is presented as the point of view of the heroine, as a sort of corollary of the lesson she has been taught. She has learned to ascribe little or no relevance, to the information contained in fiction to 'real' life in England. The devices used to describe ironically the naïve confrontation of literature and 'reality' performed by the heroine might lead us to believe that the narrator subscribes to the code proposed in this text. On the other hand, the faithfulness of the description of 'human nature' in Gothic novels is not only not doubted, but ascribed to specific geographic locations. Should this be seen as just an ironic rendering of the heroine's point of view, or is it admissible to read it as positing an authorial distance and estrangement from certain codes of behaviour and their literary translation?

This ambivalence towards genre fiction seems to be a not uncommon literary attitude, since the novel as a modern genre appears to have been undergoing definition and re-definition ever since its appearance. Several instances of this wish to point out and disclaim any connection with genre fiction could be cited. Todorov traces this ambivalence to the Romantic crisis of the early nineteenth-century, but he sees its persistence in the contemporary tendency to reject the separation of genres, verifiable in the agenda of contemporary works of fiction, and in the criticism of people like Maurice Blanchot, for example.[6]

Instead of seeing genre as an operative concept based on structural differences, with which to circumvent the question of literariness, we may use genre in another of its meanings, that of formula fiction. Thriller, fantasy, science-fiction would stand to novels as novels stand to 'literature', in an opposition, that of originality vs derivation, which Said identifies in his essay 'On Originality' and which he sees as subsuming the pair 'creative' text/critical text, but which could very well be used in relation to the pair high literature/genre literature.[7]

That *Northanger Abbey* is, among other things, a novel about the undesirability of genre fiction is unquestionable. In order better to illustrate the formula that is being discussed, one of the devices used is literary borrowing. Peter Rabinowitz, in his essay 'What's Hecuba to Us? The Audience's Experience of Literary Borrowing', inquires into the way the new work uses the audience's knowledge of the original and, as a pre-requisite to the discussion, he distinguishes between an 'authorial' audience and a 'narrative' audience.[8] He classifies both as implied audiences and defines the authorial audience as the hypothetical audience which the author assumes he is addressing, and the narrative audience as the audience addressed by the narrator. It may be assumed that this corresponds, albeit roughly, to the concepts of inscribed reader and narratee of Genette and Prince. Rabinowitz's purpose is not to pursue the debate on the problems posited by reader-response theories in general, but to concentrate on the issue of literary borrowing from the point of view of the audience's experience of it. In *Northanger Abbey*, both the narrative audience and the authorial audience are required to have knowledge of the particular genre (the Gothic romance) that the novel is clearly contriving to show it is unable to emulate successfully. The debate on this inability that goes on in the novel, far from interfering with the creation and maintenance of 'illusion', reinforces it; though there are frequent self-referential moments in the text, it cannot be argued that *Northanger Abbey* fails to establish involvement on the narrative level. As Peter Rabinowitz puts it, 'what reduces involvement on the narrative level is not so much the gap between the audiences as our awareness of it'.[9]

But there is yet another way in which the issue of the criticism of genre fiction as represented in Austen's text could be discussed. Following a proposal of Michael Rifaterre,[10] the coincidence between textual features declaring the fictionality of a story and the assertion of the truth of that story could be seen in such devices as the intrusion of the author or of the narrator, in humorous narratives that act as a representation of the author or of a narrator or that suggest an outsider's viewpoint without fully intruding, or, to give yet another example, in metalanguage glossing narrative language. I would like to give just an instance of how this approach can work: the fact that there is an authorial voice intruding at certain points to re-establish the truthful interpretation of some events implies that the fictional truth is established; by referring to a fictional 'untruth', the real (linguistic, of course) existence of a referent is established and what is questioned is the way it has been referred to. To put it yet in another way, knowing that Catherine was not justified in suspecting a cabinet of containing dreadful secrets reinstates the existence of a cabinet and of a character misled by ungrounded suspicions.[11] In fact, I would go as far as saying that it even posits the possibility of there being such a cabinet elsewhere, in another fiction, that has stepped inadvertently into the terrain of the present fiction. Rifaterre's proposal deals with this issue of the concern with stating the original, non-derivative character of the work of fiction that allows for it to find its place in the house of fiction. The existence of a metafictional text reinforces the truth of the fictional text.

The discussion of the issue of reading and writing fiction is woven into the plot so intricately that it is indissociable from it. Some of the most pivotal moments of the novel centre around the discussion between characters of the above mentioned issues and, as Katrin Ristkok Burlin argues, the central theme of the novel is fiction and many of its characters are 'contrivers' of fictions. She demonstrates that the whole novel enacts a tension between opposite types of fiction promoted by antagonistic characters. This way, characters such as John Thorne and Henry Tilney might be contrasted through the strategies that each employs to fabricate fictions, and through the use they each give their narratives. The recipients of their narratives are, simultaneously, second-level narratees, particularly Catherine, and a first-level narratee, encoded in the text; and the success of the reading involves participating, if only provisionally, in a naïve reading, led by Catherine and, simultaneously, in a more elaborate appropriation of the text mapped out by the narrator with the help of textual 'nods' and 'winks' such as irony and parallelistic devices.

Northanger Abbey does seem to belong, at least sporadically, to the group of the texts that Stanley Fish calls dialectical. In a chapter devoted to Fish's contribution to reader-response theory, Elizabeth Freund explains the concept:

> In this sense the dialectical text is not an end in itself --a transparent message-- but rather the means of inducing and foregrounding the work of interpretation and understanding; the text both sets in motion and throws into relief the consciousness of reading, the laborious business of construing, surmising, articulating, hypothesizing, and hypostatizing an elusive referential meaning.[12]

Confronted with Jane Austen's novel, the readers (this reader, at least) are driven to be acutely aware of their status, due not only to the multiple self-referential moments in the text but also to the request for their active participation in the debate on reading/writing and in the construction of meaning. And the novel is, so to speak, a work in progress, demanding frequent revisions and readjustments.

In the essay already cited, Peter Rabinowitz advocates the necessity of distinguishing between different types of literary borrowing. If we accept the seven types of literary 'recycling' that he offers, it can be said that Austen's novel is 'Criticism' most of the time. Examples of this category cited by Rabinowitz are Woody Allen's film *Play It Again, Sam*, Turgenev's *Hamlet of the Shchigrovo District* and Emma Bovary's relation to romantic fiction. This type of literary borrowing implies that both audiences (the narrative and the authorial) are familiar with the text being assimilated. As is obvious, assimilation does not imply acceptance or agreement; it may, and does in the case of *Madame Bovary* and of *Northanger Abbey*, indicate that the text is being assimilated in order to disclaim more forcefully any affiliation with it. And the fact that it seems somehow more correct to ascribe to Jane Austen or Flaubert the activity of borrowing for ulterior, higher motives, instead of positing intertextual relations tying their text to other texts is an unavoidable trap, I would say, into which we fall when dealing with maternal/paternal figures in the literary canon. It seems wrong to affiliate originating texts. Genre fiction may be the product of a confluence of diverse sources, but Austen appears as one source herself, and anything short of positing this sounds disrespectful and untrue.

The fact that a specific genre (the Gothic novel) is often taken metonymically to refer to novels as a whole remains to be accounted for.

180   Ana de Brito

While appearing to reject its formula, Jane Austen usually refers to it when making the eulogy and the apology for novel writing and reading. It may well be that, in the context of early nineteenth-century literary production, Gothic novels were the most obvious 'trash' to contrast with 'books of information' (1006). Ann Radcliffe's works are mentioned throughout the novel but the background of 'serious' literature against which they are set is less exhaustively defined. We learn that, from fifteen to seventeen, Catherine:

> was in training for a heroine; she read all such works as heroines must read to supply their memories with those quotations which are so serviceable and so soothing in the vicissitudes of their eventful lives. (1006)

The sources from which her heroine picks her quotations are Pope, Gray, Thomson, and especially Shakespeare.

Our attention is drawn to the question of the reading public's and the critics' general disregard of the 'genius, wit and taste' to be found in novels, while they recognize the abilities of 'the nine-hundredth abridger of the History of England, or of the man who collects and publishes in a volume some dozen lines of Milton, Pope and Prior, with a paper from the Spectator, and a chapter from Sterne...' (1019). And a particularly earnest attack is made on *The Spectator* of Addison and Steele (1711-12); Jane Austen's criticism is virulent:

> ... the substance of its papers so often consisting in the statement of improbable circumstances, unnatural characters, and topics of conversation, which no longer concern anyone living; and their language, too, frequently so coarse as to give no very favourable idea of the age that could endure it. (1019)

The stylistic devices used to express disapproval (the negating prefixes, the adverbials of negation, the negative semantic potential of words such as 'coarse' and 'endure') all concur to give a very unfavourable verdict on what polite taste establishes as adequate; the judgement that is passed on an age based on what its public reads is phrased in a typical understatement, but even so, it is formulated as a negative criticism. This seems unexpected; transgression or refusal of polite taste are not what is usually associated with

Jane Austen, particularly if we bear in mind that she admired the prose of *The Spectator* immensely. *The Spectator*, according to Evans and Wall, 'provided a kind of laboratory for fictional point of view, characters and forms which influenced the development of short fiction and the novel during the subsequent century'.[13] Robert D. Mayo notes that *The Spectator* contributed to making fiction acceptable for the readers who rejected it on the basis of principle.[14] Nevertheless, the kinds of fiction *The Spectator* promoted were far removed from 'French novels' and 'scandal novels' and the wish to be dissociated from less morally acceptable fiction made the authors of fiction in the magazine avoid the terms 'novel' and 'romance' and use 'story', 'account', 'history' and related terms instead. The preoccupation with truthfulness that this shows is compared by Evans and Wall to the need that authors such as Defoe and Bunyan had felt to 'rationalize their narratives to a middle-class, puritan audience, wary of idle literature'. It is quite tempting to relate this need to the qualities *Northanger Abbey* seems to claim for itself as narrative and so conclude that the attitude originates in a recurrent condition of writing fiction.

In this novel the representation of reading is closely related to the discussion about writing; still, even if only provisionally, and in order to verify how and to what extent they are interdependent, it seems profitable to disentangle one issue from the other in the discussion of one aspect of reading handled by the novel, namely the distinction of reading publics.

One of the most frequent definitions of reading publics in this novel is based on gender. It is a female heroine who goes through the experience of reading novels, and it is through another female character (Isabella Thorpe) that she becomes acquainted with contemporary Gothic romance. The titles of the books Isabella intends her to read are, on their own, revealing: *Castle of Wolfenbach*, *Clermont*, *Mysterious Warnings*, *Necromancer of the Black Forest*, *Midnight Bell*, *Orphan of the Rhine*, and *Horrid Mysteries*. Catherine had, so far, only read *Sir Charles Grandison*, because 'new books do not fall in our way' (1021), and this novel is a favourite of her household. In order to be appealing, novels have to be 'horrid'. But there seem to be two opposite senses in the word. Gothic novels are 'horrid' and therefore highly entertaining, and Sir Charles Grandison is an 'amazing horrid book' (1021), which can be translated as unreadable. Catherine, nevertheless, thinks it is 'very entertaining'.

But Catherine is halfway through Radcliffe's *The Mysteries of Udolpho* when the discussion about novels takes place between her and Isabella. Reading this type of novel is described as a feminine activity, absorbing, and private:

> ... and if a rainy morning deprived them [Catherine and Isabella] of other enjoyments, they were still resolute in meeting in defiance of wet and dirt, and shut themselves up, to read novels together. (1019)

It is not, however, one that female readers like to admit they enjoy or even engage in. Jane Austen provides us with a list of the most common sentences readers use to disclaim any connection with such reading matter:

> 'I am no novel reader'-- 'I seldom look into novels' -- 'Do not imagine that I often read novels' -- 'It is really very well for a novel' -- Such is the common cant. -- 'And what are you reading, Miss --?' 'Oh! It is only a novel!' replies the young lady; while she lays down her book with affected indifference, or momentary shame. -- 'It is only Cecilia, or Camilla, or Belinda...' (1019)

Samuel Richardson's *Sir Charles Grandison*, 'that amazing horrid book' according to Isabella, was one of the novels Jane Austen most admired, one she was able to quote from extensively and that even inspired her to write a short play; but, as F. T. Blanchard explains, Richardson's reputation in the early 1800s was declining and 'the sheer length of his work began to daunt and to weary an increasing number of readers. He began to seem old-fashioned and, as the Victorian age came nearer, viciously immoral'.[15] This indicates perhaps the nature of the criticism of the prose published in *The Spectator* transcribed above: Austen was voicing a current criticism by ironically giving it her assent.

The issue of the gender-based definition of readers is complicated by there being two male characters who do read novels and by their adoption of very dissimilar attitudes towards novel reading. John Thorpe represents the ambiguous position, one that consists of indicating that he never reads novels, that he has 'better things to do' (1026) and inadvertently betraying that he is in fact an avid reader, though perhaps an inattentive one. Henry Tilney, on the other hand, is willing to confess that he does read novels, and further defines the public of novels by stating that 'they [young men] read *nearly* as many (novels) as women. I myself have read hundreds and hundreds' (1061, *my emphasis*). He dismisses Catherine's belief that 'gentlemen read better books' because novels are not 'clever enough' for them. This paternalistic / patronising attitude, for which Catherine is so grateful that she professes that 'she will never be ashamed of liking Udolpho', can be construed as an indication that the critical tools --and therefore legitimating literature-- were in the hands of the male, while access to the actual reading material comes through a female character. Submission to male authority --in literature or in any other field-- from a character presented as a seventeen year old, not widely read, provincial girl at the beginning of the nineteenth century is hardly worth mentioning; and not all male discourses on literature in the novel are given the same weight and credibility, as I have already indicated. On the other hand, although it would probably be more difficult to prove that women nowadays submit to the literary evaluations of their male acquaintances as readily as Catherine, it is obvious that literary evaluation is, now as then, in the hands of men: Academia is still very much the terrain of male settlements.

It is not surprising that in Jane Austen this gender-based classification of literature should occupy the place of a distinction we might be inclined to think is more common nowadays: a class-based distinction between higher and lower forms of texts. That one of the negative traits of lower forms of literature, such as popular novels, is the influence it may have on their readers is far from discredited nowadays. It is, in fact, one of the reasons given for the crusade against escapist literature by several critics writing on the subject.

Another commentary on the activity of reading found in Jane Austen relates to the bearing of reading novels on 'real' life:

> Catherine sees herself literally and rather crudely as a created character enacting someone else's fiction. She applies literary conventions to her new experience and fails to understand them so long as she lacks that flexible vision which comes through releasing herself from superimposed meanings.[16]

If we subscribed to this view put forward by Susan Morgan, the position would be an obvious one. Yes, this is a novel about the influence of one type of literature on life, and yes, Catherine stands for the need to read sensibly. But then, some textual constraints make it difficult to accept that the design of this novel is to prove that 'misreading' the real is a consequence of reading Gothic fiction. Other characters who do read Gothic fiction (Henry Tilney and his sister) are shown to be quite unaffected by their preferences, even if one of them, Henry, by successfully fictionalizing the abbey, is the indirect author of Catherine's 'misreading' of the place and of its characters. Different approaches to reading generate different reactions. Furthermore, Catherine does not release herself from 'superimposed meanings' when at long last the point that there are dangerously false fictions is driven home to her. She just accepts a new set of superimposed meanings derived from a source she and the readers have learnt to look up to.

Thus, we seem to have reached a reading of this novel which quarrels with the express wish of the authorial voice, which, as Katrin Ristkok Burlin puts it, is to remind the reader that it *is* a novel.

NOTES

1. Jane Austen, *Northanger Abbey*, in *The Complete Novels of Jane Austen* (Harmondsworth: Penguin, 1983), p.1019. All future references will be to this edition.

2. K. Moller, *Jane Austen's Art of Allusion* (Lincoln, Nebraska and London, 1977; first printed 1968), p.17.

3. S. Morgan, *In the Meantime: Character and Perception in Jane Austen's Fiction* (Chicago and London, 1980), p.52.

4. K. R. Burlin, 'The Four Fictions of Northanger Abbey', in *Jane Austen: Bicentenary Essays*, ed. by John Halperin (London, 1975).

5. Burlin, p.96.

6. Tzvetan Todorov, *Genres in Discourse*, trans. by Catherine Porter (Cambridge, 1990).

7. E. Said, 'On Originality', in *The World, The Text, and the Critic* (London, 1991).

8. P. Rabinowitz, 'What's Hecuba to Us? The Audience's Experience of Literary Borrowing', in *The Reader in the Text: Essays on Audience and Interpretation*, ed. by S. Suleiman and I. Crosman (Princeton, 1980).

9. Rabinowitz, p.259.

10. M. Rifaterre, *Fictional Truth* (Baltimore and London, 1990).

11. Todorov states something similar: 'If certain events of a book's universe explicitly account for themselves as imaginary, they thereby contest the imaginary nature of the rest of the book. If a certain apparition is only the fault of an overexcited imagination, then everything around it is real' (*A Structural Approach to a Literary Genre* (1973) quoted in Patricia Waugh, *Metafiction: The Theory and Practice of Self-Conscious Fiction* (London and New York, 1984), p.112).

12. E. Freund, *The Return of the Reader: Reader-Response Criticism* (London, 1987), p.98.

13. James E. Evans and John N. Wall, *A Guide to Prose Fiction in the Tatler and the Spectator* (New York and London, 1977).

14. Quoted in Evans and Wall.

15. Quoted in A. E. Dyson, *The English Novel: Select Bibliographical Guides* (London, 1974), p.60.

16. Morgan, p.61.

PEREDA'S *PEDRO SÁNCHEZ*: THE DICKENS CONNECTION

ANTHONY H. CLARKE
University of Birmingham

The boom in Pereda studies over the past twenty years has not seen significant coverage of the question of influences on, or models for, the major fiction. Montesinos' short and sharp demolition job on Sherman Eoff's championship of the Balzacian connection[1] has provoked scarcely a ripple, while over the last ten years three fine editions of *Peñas arriba* have appeared without their editors noticing that a whole page of the text is lifted bodily from a well-known literary source dating from just a few years earlier. Compared with Galdós studies in this respect, Pereda studies have still a lot of ground to cover. The present contribution,[2] it is hoped, may provide a salutary lesson as to how an influence and model may go undetected for over one hundred years even when similarities and parallels have been firmly established in the critical tradition relating to the two authors concerned. In addition, it attempts to offer a partial explanation for the sudden and surprising novelistic advance represented by *Pedro Sánchez vis à vis* its immediate predecessors in the canon, *El sabor de la tierruca*, *De tal palo, tal astilla* and *Don Gonzalo González de la Gonzalera*.

From the first reviews of *Pedro Sánchez* one of the obligatory points of reference was the picaresque novel, the prime candidate being *Gil Blas de Santillana* because of its unequivocal citation in the text: 'Además, ya no estamos en los tiempos de Gil Blas de Santillana',[3] says Matica at approximately the half-way point of the narrative. J. Ortega Munilla takes up the no doubt deliberate prompt and in so doing makes the first allusion to *David Copperfield* in respect of *Pedro Sánchez*: '¿Qué clase de libro es éste? Una autobiografía, ni cínicamente cómica como la del *Gil Blas de Santillana*, ni sistemáticamente sentimental como el *David Copperfield*, de Dickens'.[4] We need not concern ourselves with the critic's failure to perceive a profounder commentary on humanity in *David Copperfield* than is present in the judgement 'sistemáticamente sentimental', but it is important to register that J. Ortega Munilla's review of *Pedro Sánchez* --the first review proper of the novel, leaving aside brief announcements of its imminent appearance-- is the first and only one to bring together *David Copperfield* and *Pedro Sánchez*, as well as being the first mention of the picaresque link. Both Clarín and Pardo Bázan would later join the critical trend of making much of the latter, but it was not until almost eighty years later that the Dickens connection would be taken up again.

Sherman H. Eoff's approach and contribution to studies on the nineteenth-century novel, with a pioneering comparative and philosophical slant, are well known. In 1961 his *The Modern Spanish Novel*[5] included an essay on Pereda's *Sotileza* and Dickens' *David Copperfield* entitled 'A Fatherly World According to Design'. It represents the first serious attempt to compare their two novelistic worlds and approaches to fiction both from the point of view of a governing principle --divine Providence-- and from that of staple features of the novel form: characterization, descriptive techniques, narrative, imagery and style. Most of its findings were readily accepted by critical opinion at the time, and perhaps the more easily inasmuch as it postulated no direct influence of Dickens on Pereda. The designation of a 'Fatherly World According to Design' ('Un Mundo patriarcal, estable y armónico') passed into critical currency, in Pereda studies at least, because it seemed to encapsulate --as much as any label can-- the dominant critical view of *Sotileza* at the time. It was intended to typify, in addition, the overall characteristics of Pereda's major fiction,[6] just as *David Copperfield* was presented as a representative example of Dickens' novels. Within this somewhat constricted *ab uno disce omnes* approach Eoff makes a brief reference in a note to a similarity he perceives between *David Copperfield* and *Pedro Sánchez*:

> Pereda apparently had little thought of the picaresque kind of narrative when he wrote *Sotileza*. He was sympathetic with picaresque literature, however, especially in a stylistic way, and wrote one novel (*Pedro Sánchez*, 1883) that is quite plainly modeled on the pattern exemplified by *Guzmán de Alfarache*, in which the narrator looks back with melancholy regret on the folly of his youth. *Pedro Sánchez*, incidentally, has one definite mark of similarity with *David Copperfield* apart from the picaresque aspect: the hero finally settles down in happy marriage, after losing his first wife, with the girl who had loved him silently for many years.[7]

Pereda's *Pedro Sánchez*: The Dickens Connection   189

As we shall see directly, Eoff, in focusing on the Carmen/Agnes parallel, fails to notice a host of other similarities between the two novels, one of which is already present --though not given as an important feature common to both novels-- in the above quotation, notably in the reference to the narrator looking back 'with melancholy regret on the folly and mistakes of his youth'. It is impossible to read *David Copperfield* without being aware, both in the act of reading and on reflection, of the extent to which David's record of his own life and encounters is tinged with a gentle irony, taking in both melancholy and regret, in respect of his conduct towards Dora, Micawber, Agnes and even Steerforth, and also in respect of his passage through life itself. This is but one of the many points which the two novels hold in common, some of which would seem to spring from a common source, namely the picaresque.

The commonplaces about the picaresque found liberally scattered through *Pedro Sánchez* reviews and criticism may be due in part to Pereda's heavy-handed hint re *Gil Blas*, but it is also true, as Eoff suggests, that the hero looks back over his youthful failings and inexperience with sad regret. Furthermore, the picaresque connexion is upheld in the strong sense of *escarmiento* at the end of *Pedro Sánchez*, as noted by Pérez Gutiérrez, Gullón and González Herrán, in the first-person narrative, and in the seeking of one's personal fortune amidst the vicissitudes of a new, wider world with its attendant encounters and rich variety of types and experiences.[8]

The picaresque element in *David Copperfield* is almost as much in evidence, though it has not been specifically linked to its Spanish origins in any detailed study, as *Oliver Twist* has, for example.[9] It seems likely that the rich vein of the picaresque in the English novel would account satisfactorily for the more overt touches of this type --the shadow of the Murdstones across David's early life, Creakle's school,[10] the encounters with the endemically hungry waiter at the inn in Yarmouth or with the cutpurse on the Dover Road-- without any need to establish parallels with earlier antecedents in Spain. Echoes of *Tom Jones* and *Roderick Random* abound, and it can scarcely be fortuitous that they are referred to by name in the text, though so too is *Robinson Crusoe*, while *Don Quixote* is predictably all-pervasive. More general picaresque affinities with *Pedro Sánchez* are, of course, the first-person narrative, the ups and downs of the wheel of fortune and the travel element twinned with the idea of the journey through life. Neither David nor Pedro is a *pícaro*, nor are *David Copperfield* or *Pedro Sánchez* picaresque novels, but both Dickens and Pereda are writing with a strong sense of the picaresque tradition in the novel and of their respective debts to it.

Recent criticism on *Pedro Sánchez*[11] has tended to play down the importance of the picaresque in purely novelistic terms, noting instead the extent to which less overt influences and sources may have conditioned Pereda's handling of his first novel with a strong autobiographical element. Pérez Gutiérrez concludes his consideration of the psychoanalytical and mythic-cum-archetypal dimension by embracing in his interpretation elements as disparate as the *Bildungsroman* and Saint Augustine:

> Así, pues, creemos que Pereda acertó a echar mano de dos estructuras literarias que fundió en una sola: la del *Bildungsroman*, o relato del proceso de individuación, y la de la confesión agustiniana o relato autobiográfico del protagonista escarmentado y contrito, a fin de narrar lo que constituye un paradigma, un patrón arquetípico, la transformación del héroe.[12]

This line is skilfully modified and redefined by J. M. González Herrán,[13] who combines Trilling's classic formula for, and redefinition of, an archetypal and dominant structure and pattern in the nineteenth-century novel, as extended and 'matizado' by R. Cardona, with Joseph Campbell's famous *Hero of a Thousand Faces* as modified by J. Villegas,[14] giving a '*Bildungsroman* itinerant' in which the travels and stages ('etapas') of the narrative correspond to the transformations of the hero.

While Saint Augustine and the many-faced hero have not notably exercised scholars in writing on *David Copperfield*, it is evident that this novel shares with *Pedro Sánchez* many of the characteristics of the *Bildungsroman* and of the model described by Trilling. The fact that Trilling singled out *Great Expectations* (along with *Le Rouge et le Noir*, *Le Père Goriot*, *L'Education Sentimentale* and, with slight extension of his definition, *War and Peace* and *The Idiot*) should not blind us to the fact that other Dickens novels meet the conditions almost as well, and *David Copperfield* most notably so. The trajectory in *Pedro Sánchez* is as follows: young man from the provinces / chances of social betterment / journey to the capital / great expectations / the moment(s) of truth / disillusionment / punishment / retribution and moral lesson. In *David Copperfield* the *escarmiento* lacks the sombreness and severity found in *Pedro Sánchez*, but in all other respects the parallel is maintained. The archetypal model adduced by Trilling can be seen to be almost fully adhered to if we add that both protagonists are reasonably well educated but relatively poor; both intelligent but unworldly; both full of wonderment and high hopes, and perhaps most tellingly, both 'have learned something about life from books, although not the truth'.[15] Not surprisingly one critic, D. Fanger, aptly telescopes Trilling's archetype into a skeletal form using the titles of two of the novels which fit his description: *'Great Expectations, Illusions Perdues'*.[16] One may argue of course, that although David loses Dora he gains Agnes, but the period of reflection and recuperation when he travels abroad after Dora's death, as well as the tenor of his observations after his marriage to Agnes, alert us to the fact that the wide-eyed young man travelling with hope and wonderment has given way to a chastened and experienced adult whose quiet happiness is centred on Agnes and his writings.

Thus far, then, the affinities between the two novels under the headings of the picaresque, the *Bildungsroman* and Trilling's model.

Sherman Eoff, as we have seen, drew attention in 1961 to the fact that both protagonists make happy second marriages with the woman who had loved them silently for many years, and that the picaresque element is common to both novels. On Agnes and Carmen there is much more to be said. Both are present in their main role *vis à vis* the protagonist for the greater part of each novel. Both act in such a way that the reader is privy to their love for the protagonist, while the latter remains utterly oblivious of their silent adoration, to the disbelief and disappointment of the common reader. Their social station is different, as is their education, but their novelistic function is the same, that is to say, they provide support, consolation and a firm base for the protagonist in time of crisis, and more importantly, the reader is constantly invited to conclude that Agnes, rather than Dora, and Carmen, rather than Clara, would have been the correct choice for David and Pedro with long-term happiness in view. Choice, based on self-knowledge and self-awareness, is of course a key aspect of each novel, underlined in the retrospective self-communings of the last few chapters. Constraints of space, and not unwillingness to tackle the issue, prevent consideration of the 'what might have been' factor in the two novels; here it is sufficient to note that Agnes and Carmen represent that factor in its most conspicuous and perhaps its simplest form, while elsewhere its use and presence may be covert and more subtle.

The role of Agnes as the never-failing consoler and counsellor, speaking to David at his own intellectual level, cannot be met by Carmen, and yet she is similarly supportive and consoling in her own way. Agnes' solicitude for her father, in his problems with claret and with Uriah, is closely paralleled by Carmen's tender concern for her father, Serafín Balduque. It is, of course, natural enough that they should show such solicitude, but the characteristic is one amongst a number of others, to be viewed in the round, although its significance may be increased by our awareness that the perception that David has of Agnes, and the perception that Pedro has of Carmen --and thus necessarily the perception that the reader has of both-- is dominated by this single key feature of loving concern for the elderly and failing father. Scholars have remarked, inevitably, on the absence of the father figure from the pages of *David Copperfield*, and his unexpected and metamorphosed appearance in the person of Micawber. In *Pedro Sánchez*, by contrast, the mother figure[17] is utterly absent, to the extent that there is not a single mention of her in the text, as compared with the two brief references to David's father in the first chapter. More interestingly, for our purpose, Pedro is aware of his conscience telling him that he has left his father to cope with the problems of old age in the *pueblo* and is confronted by this picture of Carmen constantly caring for Balduque. David never knew his father and only experienced the love of his mother for a few short years, thus the solicitude of Agnes for her father presents him with a picture of feelings *he* has never had the opportunity of expressing. The absence of feelings which are commonplace in normal family relationships is a characteristic shared by both David and Pedro, the former through no fault of his own and the latter by virtue of his life in Madrid and his infrequent visits to the *Montaña*, and in each case that absence of feelings is poignantly highlighted by the contrasting and caring scenes of Agnes and Carmen ministering to the needs of their respective fathers. David views

Agnes as sister rather than as potential wife; Pedro, besotted with Clara, seems to perceive Carmen almost as an asexual being, perhaps a mother figure, since the features which come to dominate his conception of her, after his initial and later references to her eyes and her general neatness and attractiveness, are her matronly and domestic attributes, her cleaning and sewing and preparation of meals rather than her physicality. Carmen in part replaces the mother Pedro has never known, or at least never mentioned, just as the call of 'la Tierra-Madre' in the final pages of the novel will answer to some deep and compulsive psychological need.[18]

Carmen's eyes figure conspicuously in descriptions of her, both on the journey to the capital and in the early part of the Madrid phase. Invariably they express innocence and tenderness, shyness and promise. When David first meets Agnes (chapter XV) her eyes are not mentioned, but her serene and radiant tranquillity is captured in the reference to the 'stained glass window' of David's childhood. From this first symbolical characterization of Agnes will stem the quasi-religious vision of her which recurs frequently and which is sealed by several references to her as his 'guardian angel', twinned with the recurring memory of the stained glass window. No such explicit symbolism attaches to the characterization of Carmen, and yet, even without this, it can be seen that she fulfils the same function for her Pedro, that of the essentially good, pure and faithful woman, the polar opposite, within her sex, of the 'mujer como tentación' or the 'mujer devoradora de hombres' represented by Clara.[19]

In this connection it is necessary to recall that in the typical *Bildungsroman* there is frequently some spiritual or religious crisis within the wider formation of the hero. David's development neglects entirely the spiritual side of things, save for the vision of Agnes' serene radiance elevated to a quasi-mystical dimension by the memory of the stained glass window. David's impressionable mind sacralizes the original moment when he makes the intuitive jump from the outer to the inner persona through the irradiated beauty and calm spiritual strength of the stained glass. The comparison remains with him as a recurring motif for the rest of his life, much as, when he recalls the cottage in Blunderstone, he cannot dissociate his memory of it from the rooks and the wind in the elm trees.

Pereda's novel does portray the protagonist undergoing an explicitly mystical experience, though not in association with Carmen. It conforms far more closely with the conventions of the *Bildungsroman*, even though its repercussions are not seen to an important degree later in the novel. On his visit to Santander with his father Pedro is taken to the cathedral to hear High Mass sung: 'es de saberse que aquella misa, que aquella hora pasada en la catedral, me dejó impresión tan honda, que no han logrado borrarla ni las peripecias más culminantes de mi vida'. The chanting, the majestic music of the organ and the awesome architecture combine to produce in him a state of rapture in which he seems to hear the voice of God and to see Him 'flotando sobre nubes de incienso y de armonías, entre las abiertas bóvedas del templo'.[20] The susceptibility of the protagonist to an experience which is both spiritual and aesthetic comes very close to that of David in his rapturous enshrinement of the Agnes/stained glass motif. Again, while the correspondence of the two experiences would have little force when considered in isolation, it may carry more conviction in a series of similar parallels.

One of the most thought-provoking articles on *Pedro Sánchez*, Pérez Gutiérrez's '¿Por qué *Pedro Sánchez*? (La salida de Pereda hacia dentro)', establishes the significant role in the novel of the 'entonces y hoy' contrast which is set in motion in the first paragraph.[21] Pedro's *entonces* is made up of his *pueblo*, childhood memories, the Valenzuela family, Carmen and her father, the whole Madrid experience, taking in journalism, fiction, the *barricadas*, and so on. Pedro's *hoy* is Pedro alone in his *pueblo* at the end of his life, with Madrid relegated to a very Peredian limbo and all the characters who had impinged on his life during the early years and in Madrid conveniently dead. In the biblical solitariness of this *hoy*,[22] Pedro varies his pursuits of carpentry, fishing and agriculture with writing, setting down his life in the form of a novel, that self-same novel which the reader has in his hands. The *entonces* provides the opportunity for an exercise in nostalgia, whereas the *hoy* gives Pereda a platform from which to criticize, to himself and to subsequent readers, the new-fangled ways. Although the extent to which the novel may be autobiographical has been the subject of some debate,[23] it is generally accepted that a number of aspects closely reflect the author's own life, attitude and experiences. Certainly the *entonces* and the *hoy* encapsulate strands of Pereda's own development, although we cannot say that Pedro is Pereda or that the novel he confesses to having written is in the main Pereda's autobiography in novel form. A closer approximation to the truth about the fusion of fiction and autobiography in *Pedro Sánchez* lies in Pérez Gutiérrez's suggestion that Pedro Sánchez the character reveals another Pereda: '¿no podría ser la otra cara de éste [Pereda], su cara secreta, reprimida? Esa biografía *equivocada* de Pedro Sánchez, ¿no podría encubrir una tentación de Pereda, la de haber sido *otro*?'[24] Thus the novel would consist of the authentic autobiographical elements --the journey from Santander to Madrid, parts of the Bohemian (for Pereda) world of the *posada*, the survey of the mid-century literary scene, the contrast between the *corte* and *aldea*, the *barricadas*-- plus the purely fictional elements, namely the Clara/Carmen opposition, Balduque, the Valenzuelas, Pedro's governorship, the total absence of a mother figure at the beginning and the *escarmiento*, with the annihilation of all Pedro's friends, enemies and loved ones, at the end. The problem with this, of course, lies in determining the extent to which the non-autobiographical elements may, as Pérez Gutiérrez says, 'encubrir una tentación de Pereda, la de haber sido *otro*'. The psychological possibilities and conjectures are almost too dauntingly complicated to contemplate, although the idea is both stimulating and attractive. Certainly the sheer lack of information about Pereda's father[25] may be linked through deep-seated psychological processes with the non-mention of Pedro Sánchez's mother, and the triumphs of Pedro on the Madrid literary scene may well be a projection of Pereda's own ambitions in that respect. Beyond that --for example, tracing Pedro's fateful and fascinated involvement with Clara to a dissatisfaction on the part of Pereda with his own marriage-- one cannot usefully proceed, save to create further fiction.[26]

In many respects *David Copperfield* presents a possible model or source for the foregoing points. The *entonces* and *hoy* motif is strong, coming out in David's nostalgia for the cottage, the rooks' nests, the Peggottys' boat-home and life-style, Traddles and Mr Mell at Salem House, the donkeys on Betsey Trotwood's green, and countless other memories, in contrast with the darkening horizon of maturity and the complications and responsibilities of later life. Ultimately the vantage point from which the novelist within the novel is pictured is one and the same, that is, writing the chronicle of his life with some sort of philosophical detachment and distancing from the events and persons who have filled it. In *Pedro Sánchez*, the revelation of the novelist within the novel is not made until a late stage; in *David Copperfield*, much earlier. Forster had suggested to Dickens that he try his hand at a novel in the first person[27] and *David Copperfield* is his first attempt in this mode, just as *Pedro Sánchez* is Pereda's first.[28] While it is evident that David is Dickens to a far greater extent than Pedro is Pereda, there is in *David Copperfield*, as in *Pedro Sánchez*, a subtle interweaving of the fictional and the autobiographical which provides, inevitably, no clear line of demarcation and perennially exercises and fascinates scholars.

Of the novelist within the novel there is more to say, from a slightly different angle. David has graduated to the dizzy heights of the novel form via his reading, his proficiency in Latin verses, his visits to the theatre, his work on Dr Strong's 'famous Dictionary', his parliamentary notes, his shorthand, and then 'a good many trifling pieces' for magazines.[29] Pedro takes a similar route: his reading, the theatre, Matica's connections, his imitations of Bretón and Zorrilla, his first writings for *El Clarín de la Patria*. The key to David's subsequent success in the novel form is given early on in the reference to his skills as a storyteller at Salem House. Picaresque novels are retold to the sleepless Steerforth from the store of David's childhood reading, with a pointed reference to the Sultana Scheherazade.[30] Pedro's entry to greater literary things comes with the publication of his *Cuento oriental*. Certainly their progress towards literary fame is marked by very similar stages, although a basic difference is seen in the situation from which they write their respective narratives at the end: David happy, fulfilled though mildly chastened; Pedro, disillusioned and severely *escarmentado*. Both write their narratives, however in a serene mood of philosophical detachment and distancing from what has gone before.[31]

The combination of the picaresque heritage, the *Bildungsroman*, Trilling's model and the first-person narrative may go a long way towards explaining a general impression of affinity between the two novels. The parallel we have seen, however, between Agnes and Carmen is not explained by this, and the same may be said of the further parallels between characters which we shall now examine.

Just as Agnes and Carmen are the 'good angels' for David and Pedro, so Rosa Dartle and Clara represent evil or sinister qualities.[32] Rosa's aloofness, her life of futile resentment and self-pity as one-time victim of Steerforth's anger, her dark, brooding presence and aura of sinister power, place her in direct opposition and contrast to Agnes' radiant disposition. Rosa's quintessential image is captured in Steerforth's answer to David's question of 'She is very clever, is she not?': 'Clever! She brings everything to a grindstone ... and sharpens it, as she has sharpened her own face and figure these years past. She has worn herself away by constant sharpening. She is all edge'.[33] Likewise Clara is the polar opposite of Carmen. She is haughty, overbearing, selfish and utterly lacking in warmth and inner happiness. As Rosa's nature and fate are summed up in her sharpness, her 'edge', so Clara's disposition and destiny are expressed and prefigured by references to her singular physique and her sharpness of manner: 'descolorida en extremo, dura de faz y más que medianamente descarnada';[34] 'aquella respuesta seca y prosaica ... infundióme algo como temor, semejante al que produce la soledad de los páramos o la yerta rigidez del invierno'.[35] Then Clara at the end, 'desesperada', living in 'miserable soledad', but defiant to the last: 'en su casa murió impenitente, fría y altanera, como una pagana'.[36]

But the parallel can be carried further. Both Rosa and Clara, as well as being clearly viewed as the antitheses of the 'good angels', are presented, briefly in Rosa's case and at great length in Clara's, as what Pérez Gutiérrez has described, in speaking of Clara, as 'la mujer como tentación'.[37] David's initial encounter with Rosa prompts him to mention that she is 'not agreeable to look at, but with some appearance of good looks'.[38] Her throbbing scar, her wasting 'inner fire', her strange manner and mode of address, cause her to exercise a fascination over David's impressionable mind which is as certain and as overt in the narrative as the different categories of feminine sway held over David by his mother, Peggotty, Agnes and Dora. David is not sexually attracted by Rosa --the narrative does not allow David to be sexually attracted by anyone-- and yet, when David, a year or two after his marriage to Dora, sees Rosa in Littimer's company at Mrs Steerforth's house, he notes: 'The air of wicked grace; of triumph, in which, strange to say, there was yet something feminine and alluring: with which she reclined upon the seat between us, and looked at me, was worthy of a cruel princess in a legend.'[39] Such is the sway of Clara over Pedro. Only on two occasions do we find Pedro succumbing to simpler and more traditional feminine charms as exerted by Clara, when he perceives that she has lost some of her sharp angulosity;[40] in virtually all other descriptions of Clara it is her pallor, her hardness, her statuesqueness, her intrinsic lack of *life* (even her lips are 'yertos') that cause Pedro to comment on the strange 'fascinación ejercida por este conjunto de singularidades plásticas'.[41] Furthermore, Clara in her impenitent imperiousness at the end is strongly reminiscent of Rosa Dartle when the latter, in her final appearance (chapter L) unleashes her full wrath, scorn and inhuman pitilessness on Emily. Pereda criticism has in recent years stressed the link between Clara and certain characters and situations in the stories of Edgar Allan Poe.[42] It is possible, of course, that both Dickens[43] and Pereda were influenced by Poe in the creation of these two harsh, almost demoniacal women, but the close parallel between Rosa Dartle and Clara still stands as one more link in the chain.

If Agnes and Carmen are sisters in their purity and goodness, and Rosa Dartle and Clara sisters in their actual or apparent inhumanity, then Micawber and Serafín Balduque are brothers in comicity, poverty and victimization by the machine of bureaucracy. The similarities are startlingly clear for anyone who takes the trouble to re-acquaint themselves with the texts. The shabby-genteel element is a far stronger part of the characterization of Micawber, as is the sponging and the shamelessness, but all the rest fits neatly into place: a hand-to mouth existence punctuated by moments of glory, comedy of mannerisms and of speech, the habit of reappearing in the hero's life at unexpected moments, their conformity with and then their outbursts against the stolid indifference of the bureaucratic system, and their final, supreme, gestures. The fine irony and affection present in Dickens' portrait of his father is admittedly not a part of the characterization of Balduque, nor is there any indication that the latter had a model in Pereda's own life, but the style of comedy and the whimsical touches of detail are distinctly Dickensian and Micawberish.[44]

An initial feature shared by Micawber's household --wherever and no matter how precariously it be established-- and Balduque's is that both serve as a safe haven, an escape from a harsh and unforgiving outside world, for the protagonists. David and Pedro come to look on the respective households of Micawber and Balduque as an extension of the homes they have left behind. There is a shared irony, too, in that one of the many lessons imparted by the two novels has to do with the fragility of such 'safe' shelters from the rigours of life. As these forces press in on Micawber and Balduque they inveigh more and more against the establishment --symbolized in both novels by red-tape, or *balduque*--[45] until the moment arrives when they crack, momentarily appearing to take leave of their senses. Micawber's love/hate affair with the lot of the humble clerk, civil-servant, reaches crisis point just at the time when he discovers Uriah Heep's dastardly doings in all their enormity. David and others think that Mr Micawber is going mad. The exposure of Uriah then acts as the catalyst which enables Micawber to step free from the shackles of red-tape and desk-slavery, leading to the restoration of his self-respect and the crowning irony of his appointment as judge in Australia. Balduque changes in character, becomes depressed, sees the worst in everything (chapter 23) and becomes as involved in the details of the Revolution as Pedro himself, finally joining Pedro and Matica in the thick of the fighting on the *barricadas*. His words as he avoids Pedro's grasp and exposes himself to enemy fire with an unloaded rifle in his hands are a summation of his *cesantía* and the *balduque* after which he is named. Pedro asks him where he is going: "¡A ganar con mis puños lo que se me debe en justicia! ... ¡A enviar al Gobierno, con una bala, el memorial de mis agravios!' His final cry of '¡Viva la justicia!' echoes one of the main thrusts of his role in the novel; at the same time it reinforces his kinship with Micawber, who had staked all on his personal blow for justice. Micawber is dispatched to Australia, Balduque to a glorious but absurd death; both represent in their lives not only the common man's fight against *balduque* and bureaucracy, but also David's and Pedro's perception of the inherent absurdity of life.

Separated not only by thirty-four years but also by the gulf which sets genius apart from respectable achievement, *David Copperfield* and *Pedro Sánchez* nevertheless betray, as we have seen, a significant and surprising number of similarities. Both acknowledge a debt to the picaresque tradition and refer by name to picaresque novels, with one of these, *Gil Blas de Santillana*, coinciding in both. Two archetypal forms of the European novel, the *Bildungsroman* and the base model suggested by Trilling, seem to join forces and be re-expressed with variations in *David Copperfield* and *Pedro Sánchez*. Both novels are the author's first attempt at a long narrative in the first person, and both are to a greater or lesser extent autobiographical. Certain characters show close affinities: Agnes and Carmen, the two 'good angels'; Rosa Dartle and Clara, the darkly sinister pair, psychoanalytical cases *avant la lettre*; Micawber and Balduque, their mannerisms, their hope that something will turn up, and their struggle against red-tape. There are other character similarities which constraints of space will only allow us to mention briefly: Quica (the *ama de casa* to Balduque and Carmen) is very much in the Peggotty mould; Matica shares a number of key traits with Traddles; the Garcías and the Valenzuelas occupy similar positions to the Murdstones and the Heeps, in that they represent in Pedro's world injustice, corruption, social rivalry, evil.

Thus far the argument, then, in terms of the categories which seem to link the two novels: picaresque, *Bildungsroman*, Trilling's model, first person narrative and characters. The remaining affinities have a certain ragbag unexpectedness. Both protagonists visit the theatre -- perhaps an expected event given Dickens' and Pereda's early interest in the stage, but the circumstances of their visits present a surprising similarity. David goes to the theatre with Steerforth and friend following a highly bibulous 'feast' at his lodgings (chapter XXIV). His drunkenness and rowdiness contrast with the calm presence of Agnes, whom he sees there and who coaxes him to leave quietly. In *Pedro Sánchez* Pedro takes Balduque, Carmen and Quica to the theatre and there sees Clara. What creates a parallel between the two episodes is the simple fact of social embarrassment, of awkwardness, actual, potential or subsequent. David is embarrassed by his behaviour after the event, and has to talk it over with Agnes in order to clear the air. Pedro is placed in an awkward situation in that his being seen with Balduque and Carmen by Clara and company could prejudice his social aspirations. Both authors are underlining a point already broached in their narratives, namely that David and Pedro are walking a delicate tightrope between different social categories and different types of expected behaviour.

Pedro Sánchez has been called a '*Bildungsroman* itinerante',[46] the adjective referring principally, I take it, to the protagonist's journeys and vicissitudes within Spain. *David Copperfield* covers extensive terrain -- Blunderstone, London, Dover, Canterbury, and elsewhere. However, each protagonist undertakes further journeys *after* the process of formation is completed, and in each case as a means of forgetting or coming to terms with personal tragedy. In chapter 58 of *David Copperfield*, following the death of Dora, of Ham and Steerforth, and the departure of Mr Peggotty and Emily for Australia, David leaves England, travels in Italy and Switzerland (and elsewhere in Europe), spending three years away in all, communing with Nature and writing a short story and almost half of his 'third work of fiction'. After his return to England and his marriage to Agnes he completes the narrative which becomes *David Copperfield*. In the final chapter of *Pedro Sánchez*, following the death of Clara, Pedro's marriage to Carmen, then the death of the latter and their child,[47] Pedro too travels in order to forget, to take stock, and to preserve his sanity. Unlike David, when he returns to his *pueblo* he finds further disillusionment awaiting him, but the basic difference between the protagonists at this point --David: invigorated by fresh air and exercise, pursuing more fully his writing, intuiting a new life; Pedro: 'encanecido', preyed on by memories of Clara and the Garcías and taking an unhealthy pleasure in revenge-- should not obscure the fact that the travel section performs in each case the same function. Even Pedro manages to develop new interests --agriculture, carpentry, fishing-- and like David, he writes and completes the novel which is in the reader's hands. Despite Pedro's *taedium vitae*, his travels allow him to achieve some distancing from his tragedy, a sense of perspective, and a fresh start. In David's case his writing and his love for Agnes kindle hope and optimism; in Pedro's case his writing and his hobbies are mere palliatives as he approaches a lonely old age.

Finally we turn to the concept of the reluctant author. In the version of *David Copperfield* which has been reprinted as the standard text the reader learns from an early stage that David is the author --even though he *may* not turn out to be the hero-- and on several occasions subsequently, particularly over the last quarter or so of the novel,[48] David writes about his own position *vis à vis* the fiction he is both inside and outside, without suggesting for a moment that he is reluctant to give this novel to the world at large. However, one of the early full titles of the novel, was: *The Personal History, Adventures, Experiences and Observations of David Copperfield the Younger, of Blunderstone Rookery (which he never meant to be published on any account)*.[49] Although it is evident that the author *did* mean it to be published, there is an interesting parallel here with the 'reluctant author' of the penultimate sentence of *Pedro Sánchez*. After alleging a few lines earlier that he is writing to while away the winter evenings and that it gives him 'cierto placer algo parecido al que siente el avaro al revolver y manosear su tesoro', he states: 'Bien sé que me expongo a que el soplo de algún diablillo enredador esparza, a la hora menos pensada, mis papeles por el mundo'.[50] As with Dickens' title, it patently is *not* Pereda's intention to stand in the way of publication; both statements are tongue-in-cheek disclaimers intended to swell the intimacy/scandal appeal of the narrative, but without the slightest pretence to credibility. It goes without saying that Pereda could hardly be expected to have seen an early parts publication of *David Copperfield* in English, and none of the full titles of the earliest French translations refers to the author's reluctance. On the other hand, the Tauchnitz edition (1850), one of two early English editions published on the Continent, gives the full variant title as quoted above.[51]

In the light of the range of parallels and affinities between the two novels it would seem at least likely that Pereda had a nodding acquaintance with *David Copperfield*. The chance that all the similarities here presented are, quite simply, coincidence seems to me to be remote. Certainly Pereda had the opportunity to read *David Copperfield* while he was in Paris during the first six months of 1865.[52] At that time Dickens and Balzac were *the* authors to read, and it is a commonplace in criticism of the nineteenth-century Spanish novel that most of the major Spanish novelists of the period read their English and Russian fiction in French. Even without the series of similarities shown it would seem probable that Pereda had read the Dickens novel which, from an early stage in its history, came to be seen as one of the most representative, endearing and personal of all his works.[53] Once we take those similarities into account, the probability is considerably increased.

In turn, if we accept the likelihood that Pereda based his *Pedro Sánchez* to some extent on Dickens' *David Copperfield*, then two further points must be made. Firstly, it would be feasible to explain the sudden jump in literary and novelistic quality from the three preceding novels --*Don Gonzalo González de la Gonzalera, De tal palo, tal astilla* and *El sabor de la tierruca*-- to *Pedro Sánchez*[54] by suggesting that the use of certain ideas, situations, characters, narrative formulae from another novel would help Pereda in precisely those areas which he found irksome or difficult, namely plot and character. Invention was never his strong point, and to be handed key characters and key situations on a plate, as it were, would allow him to deploy his own innate skills to greater advantage. The combination of novel and autobiography and the leavening of the picaresque --all within the framework of Trilling's archetype-- permitted a degree of sophistication within his narrative that probably surprised even Pereda himself. Secondly, the conclusion outlined above would necessarily imply a need to rethink, in critical terms, our approach to Pereda's particular art of the novel. No other major novel by Pereda, as far as I am aware, was modelled on another literary source to the degree that I have suggested. If that suggestion is seen to be acceptable, then José María de Pereda --'más bueno que el pan', as Max Aub said of him--[55] may not have gone about the business of novel writing with quite the squeaky-clean integrity that has been thought hitherto.

NOTES

1. *Pereda o la novela idilio*, 2nd edn (Madrid: Castalia, 1969), p.57, n.4.

2. A preliminary and much shorter version of this article was published in *Ínsula*, 547-48 (July-August 1992), under the title 'Así que pasen ciento diez años; el secreto de *Pedro Sánchez*'. Remembering Derek's schoolboyish glee, on many occasions, when the hallowed view of the critical concensus was shattered by some upstart (or even by an established figure such as Derek himself), I felt it appropriate to rework the original article in his memory, incorporating much material which had to be excluded from the earlier format.

3. *Pedro Sánchez*, ed. by J. M. González Herrán (Madrid: Colección Austral, 1990), pp.222-23. All subsequent references to the text will be to this edition, which in most respects displaces Cossío's. The Introduction and many of the notes carry *Pedro Sánchez* criticism to a new, and exciting level.

4. 'Una novela y un drama', *Los Lunes de El Imparcial*, Madrid, 24 December 1883.

5. *The Modern Spanish Novel. Comparative Essays Examining the Philosophical Impact of Science on Fiction* (New York: New York University Press, 1961). Spanish edn., *El pensamiento moderno y la novela española* (Barcelona: Editorial Seix Barral, 1965.)

6. It will become clear, I believe, in these pages that my view rates Eoff's joint assessment of Dickens and Pereda as dated and over-simplified. Quite apart from his signal failure to see other parallels --other than that between Agnes and Carmen-- in *David Copperfield* and *Pedro Sánchez*, he gives no coverage at all to the perception of the inherent absurdity of life which reaches proportions worthy of the Russian novel in Micawber and Balduque. *Sotileza*, of course, is a much more staid and conservative novel than *Pedro Sánchez*, but the subversive power and the vision of the absurd in Micawber are far removed from the notion of 'A Fatherly World According to Design'. F. Pérez Gutiérrez disagrees with Eoff's interpretation for other reasons. See his *El problema religioso en la generación de 1868* (Madrid: Taurus Ediciones, 1975), p.153.

7. Eoff, *The Modern Spanish Novel*, p.41, n.40.

8. F. Pérez Gutiérrez, '¿Por qué *Pedro Sánchez*? (La salida de Pereda hacia dentro)', in *Nueve lecciones sobre Pereda*, ed. by J. M. González Herrán and Benito Madariaga (Santander: Institución Cultural de Cantabria, 1985), pp.115-16, and Introduction to his edition of *Pedro Sánchez* (Santander: Ediciones Tantín, 1992); Germán Gullón, 'El autor como narrador', chapter III of *El narrador en la novela del siglo XIX* (Madrid: Taurus Ediciones, 1976), pp.73 and 83; J. M. González Herrán, *Pedro Sánchez*, Introduction, pp.21-22, p.33 (n.58) and p.34.

9. Sherman Eoff, 'Oliver Twist and the Spanish Picaresque Novel', *Studies in Philosophy*, 59 (1957), 440-47.

10. While some elements of Creakle and his school were culled from *Roderick Random* (see Earle Davis, *The Flint and the Flame. The Artistry of Charles Dickens* (London: Gollancz, 1964), pp.160, 165 and 166) it seems at least probable that, as with Dotheboys Hall in *Nicholas Nickleby*, there was still a lingering memory of his reading of *El buscón*. (See S. Eoff, 'Oliver Twist', as cited above, p.443, and same page, n.10).

11. See particularly the already cited works by Pérez Gutiérrez, '¿Por qué *Pedro Sánchez*? (La salida de Pereda hacia dentro)', p.94, and González Herrán, *Pedro Sánchez*, Introduction, pp.20-23. Germán Gullón ('El autor como narrador', pp.71-73) gives more prominence to the picaresque element, but without convincing this reader that it is anything more than a convenient and conventional peg on which to hang certain aspects and given moments of the novel.

12. Pérez Gutiérrez, '¿Por qué *Pedro Sánchez*?', p.95.

13. *Pedro Sánchez*, pp.23-30.

14. *La estructura mítica del héroe en la novela del siglo XX* (Barcelona: Planeta, 1973). The article by R. Cardona which further elaborated Trilling's base-model is 'A propósito de Turgueniev y Galdós', *Boletín de la Biblioteca de Menéndez Pelayo*, 61 (1985), 201-16.

15. L. Trilling, 'The Princess Casamassima', in *The Liberal Imagination. Essays on Literature and Society* (London: Mercury Books, Heinemann, 1961), p.61.

16. D. Fanger, *Dostoievsky and Romantic Realism* (Chicago: University of Chicago Press, 1967), p.8. Quoted by Cardona, pp.209-10. If we carry the implications of Fanger's telescoped formula through the text of *Pedro Sánchez*, we find, amongst a number of similar references, an overt one (chapter 31, p.424) to *Don Quixote*, perhaps the original of the *Great Expectations* / *Illusions Perdues* concept.

17. This point has been tellingly covered by Pérez Gutiérrez in '¿Por qué *Pedro Sánchez*?' pp.96-97. The total lack of any reference in the text to Pedro's mother must be deliberate, but what this implies has not yet been satisfactorily shown.

16. *Pedro Sánchez*, p.429. See also Pérez Gutiérrez, pp.96-97.

19. Pérez Gutiérrez, pp.99 and 112, and González Herrán, *Pedro Sánchez*, p.32.

20. *Pedro Sánchez*, p.71, and the whole cathedral episode, pp.69-71.

21. Pérez Gutiérrez, p.96. It should be noted that my exposition here of the 'entonces y hoy' dichotomy is based on Pérez Gutiérrez's original concept but follows my own ideas with regard to what constitutes the 'entonces' and the 'hoy'.

22. Pedro shuns company apart from that of the priest. The sentence 'de breves goces y de amargas y muy hondas pesadumbres se compone el caudal de la vida humana' (p.432) has a strongly biblical ring. In addition, the sum of Pedro's punishment and *escarmiento* --nine deaths in all-- recalls some dire Old Testament visitation and Pedro returns to the now 'wilderness' of the *pueblo* and valley which at the beginning of the novel had been described as 'eterno jardín', with obvious connotations of Eden.

23. González Herrán, *Pedro Sánchez*, pp.16-20. He notes that 'Más que las coincidencias importan las discrepancias' (p.17) and goes on to establish the importance and *sentido* of the *lección* of *Pedro Sánchez* as opposed to the 'biografía equivocada' interpretation of Pérez Gutiérrez. In addition to the development and modification I have presented above in schematized form, it should be noted that González Herrán's interpretation differs from Pérez Gutiérrez's in his elucidation of the autobiographical strand: 'la historia de Pedro

Sánchez no sería la que Pereda habría querido vivir sino, al contrario, la que temió haber vivido; la que acaso estuvo a punto de vivir, y, afortunadamente --porque supo tomar la decisión acertada--, no vivió' (González Herrán, *Pedro Sánchez*, pp.17-18).

24. Pérez Gutiérrez, p.117.

25. Benito Madariaga de la Campa's recent *José María de Pereda. Biografía de un novelista* (Santander: Ediciones de Librería Estudio, 1991), brings together more information about the novelist's family than any other source; that the father should be dispatched in fourteen lines is quite simply an indication of the virtual void that exists where for other close members of the family there is sufficient, if not ample, data available.

26. In view of the hazy demarcation between the autobiographical and the 'imagined', the psychoanalytic analysis offered by Pérez Gutiérrez may represent the only way to tease out the deeper implications of *Pedro Sánchez*.

27. *The Life of Charles Dickens* (Oxford: University Press. India paper edition,[n.d.]), p.569.

28. 'Arroz y gallo muerto' (*Escenas montañesas*) and 'Un joven distinguido' (*Tipos trashumantes*) are short first-person narratives prior to *Pedro Sánchez*. (There are several others). *Peñas arriba* (1895) is the only other first-person narrative amongst the major fiction.

29. *David Copperfield*, ed. by Nina Burgis (Oxford: University Press, 1981), p.535. All future references will be to this edition.

30. *David Copperfield*, p.80.

31. It is the function of the European travels of the two protagonists to provide a time lapse and a sense of distancing them from their tragic experiences. In both cases these travels are crucial to the purposed ending.

32. Rosa's story excuses and explains to some extent her conduct and her manner; with Clara there is no vestige of a potential for redemption at any stage, nor any explanation of her cold fury and hatred.

33. *David Copperfield*, p.251.

34. *Pedro Sánchez*, p.85.

35. *Pedro Sánchez*, p.96.

36. *Pedro Sánchez*, p.426.

37. Pérez Gutiérrez, p.99. In the same article (p.112) he refers to her 'belleza medusea' in the context of Mario Praz's essay, 'The Beauty of the Medusa', in *The Romantic Agony*.

38. This is the customary text. The edition by Burgis gives: 'I concluded in my own mind that she was about thirty years of age, and that she wished to be married. She was a little dilapidated --like a house-- with having been so long to let; yet had, as I have said, an appearance of good looks' (pp.249-50).

Pereda's *Pedro Sánchez*: The Dickens Connection   207

39. *David Copperfield*, p.569.

40. *Pedro Sánchez*, pp.203-04, and p.266.

41. *Pedro Sánchez*, p.266. (Within the space of a few lines Pedro stresses her marmoreal quality and her 'grado de morbidez').

42. See particularly the article by Pérez Gutiérrez quoted above (p.113) and the Introduction to his edition of *Pedro Sánchez* (José María de Pereda, *Obras completas*, vol. V (Santander: Ediciones Tantín), in press). See also González Herrán, p.377, n.9 (quoting Cossío's note) and p.431, n.8; Laureano Bonet, 'Sonidos, imágenes, volúmenes: Pereda entre la risa abstracta y la tentación decadentista', *Ínsula*, 547-48 (July-August, 1992), p.19, and my article 'Así que pasen ciento diez años; el secreto de *Pedro Sánchez*', p.21.

43. It is known that Rosa Dartle is in part based on Mrs Hannah Brown, friend and one-time companion to Miss Angela Burdett-Coutts, though the affinity seems to have been to do largely with their shared idiosyncratic way of asking questions. See Marjory Cardwell's article on the original of Rosa Dartle in *The Dickensian*, 56 (1960), 29-33. Nevertheless, Dickens, like Wilkie Collins, was undoubtedly open to Poe's influence, as is shown by *Bleak House* and *The Mystery of Edwin Drood*.

44. See the following descriptions: 'El cual hablaba...pintoresco y entretenido', *Pedro Sánchez*, pp.110-11; his *cesantía* (pp.116-19); his encounters with Pedro and moments of *brujuleo* through Madrid's streets (pp.140-44, p.149), and declarations such as 'Perdone usted por lo poco ... que no es culpa mía, sino de los infames gobiernos que me ponen en tales estrecheces' (p.150), and countless other instances.

45. 'Britannia, that unfortunate female, is always before me, like a trussed fowl: skewered through and through with office-pens, and bound hand and foot with red tape' (*David Copperfield*, p.535). Also the 'Deed', confused by David with certain German 'demoniacal parchments', which delays the clearing up of Micawber's affairs (p.144). There is a fully intended irony in the fact that it is red-tape, in the form of detailed, itemized proof, that allows Micawber to ensnare Heep. In *Pedro Sánchez*, Balduque's name combines the idea of certain pretensions to gentility --again Micawberish-- with the actual meaning: Balduque as Val plus duque, and *balduque* as red-tape. For examples of the latter sense, see *Pedro Sánchez*, pp.116-17, 143-44, 225-27. Carmen's description of her father weighed down by his apprehensions (pp.286-87) corresponds closely to Mrs Micawber's letter to David telling of the uncharacteristic behaviour of her husband (pp.533-34).

46. González Herrán, *Pedro Sánchez*, p.24 and pp.25-26.

47. Several critics in the early reviews commented on the 'clean sweep' of characters. González Herrán quotes Luis Alfonso's reference to the author's 'furia homicida' (p.428, n.5). As I have suggested at note 22 above, this seemingly gratuitous slaughter is consonant with the pronounced Old Testament tone of the final pages.

48. *David Copperfield*, pp.588-89, 673, 699, 723, 741, 748 and 751.

49. Quoted by Philip Collins, *David Copperfield* (Studies in English Literature No. 67) (London: Edward Arnold Ltd., 1977), p.9, and the Burgis edition, pp.xxv and xxvii. Forster quotes from a letter a slightly different suggested title, but with the words 'which he never meant to be published on any account' (p.572).

50. *Pedro Sánchez*, p.432.

51. *Le Neveu de ma Tante, histoire personnelle de David Copperfield* par Charles Dickens, 3 vols (Paris: aux Bureaux de la 'Revue Britannique', 1851). (This is the 3rd edition of this translation; there were further editions in 1859, 1863 and 1971). *Souvenirs de David Copperfield*, 6 vols (Bruxelles: A. Lebègue, 1851). *David Copperfield* roman anglais, 2 vols (Paris: L. Hachette, 1862) (re-issued six times between 1864 and 1876). There were two early English editions published on the continent: *Personal History of David Copperfield*, 2 vols (Paris: Baudry, 1850), and *Personal History of David Copperfield*, 3 vols (Leipzig: B. Tauchnitz, 1850). I am grateful to Dr. R. Hitchcock for transcriptions of title pages.

52. Pereda's biographers have been notoriously vague about his period in Paris, some of them giving the length of his stay as one year. My recent edition of the letters from Pereda to Gumersindo Laverde (*Boletín de la Biblioteca de Menéndez Pelayo*, 67 (1991), 157-270) shows on the evidence of these letters that the period did not exceed six months and that there were certain very specific reasons for the visit. See also the rectification made in B. Madariaga de la Campa, *José María de Pereda. Biografía de un novelista*, pp.131-32.

53. Forster, p.602; Trevor Blount, Introduction to Penguin edition (1966), pp.14-15, and countless similar testimonies in between.

54. In early reviews of *Pedro Sánchez*, Clarín and Pardo Bazán showed their awareness of the difference in literary achievement between this novel and its predecessors. Recent criticism on *Pedro Sánchez* stresses the gap without attempting to explain it.

55. *Discurso de la novela contemporánea* (Mexico: El Colegio de México, 1945; *Jornadas*, 50), p.31.

WOMANPOWER IN GALDÓS'S *VOLUNTAD* (1895)

LISA CONDÉ
University College of Swansea, Wales

For the feminist, the new Isidora of Galdós's play *Voluntad* is one of his more satisfying heroines. This is because there is a considerable amount of what might be termed 'womanpower' at work both in the creation and the realization of the new dramatist's 'mujer nueva'.

The womanpower behind the phenomenon of this prototype can be seen to stem from the woman who inspired and played the role: María Guerrero. Galdós's leading lady was well aware of the strength of the power she wielded over the writer, and reminded him repeatedly of the importance of complying with her wishes. In a letter dated 10 April 1894, conserved in the *Casa-Museo* in Las Palmas, she stressed:

> ¡Yo soy la inspiración! [written in large letters and underlined twice]
> ¡Ole!
> ¿Me molesta V. a mí? ¿Me hace V. rabiar a mí?
> La inspiración no viene.[1]

Galdós, for his part, acknowledged the crucial role played by his leading lady in inspiring the very concept of this play, *Voluntad*: will-power/woman-power. In a letter dated 3 June 1895, in which he invites María to guess the title of the work, he explained:

> El título de ésta es una palabra que expresa la facultad más excelsa de la persona humana, facultad que V. posee en alto grado, y a la cual debe sus recientes victorias, y el puesto eminente que se ha conquistado. (Las Palmas; Caja 2)

Although Menéndez Onrubia insists that *Voluntad* 'es el producto de la errónea interpretación que Galdós hace en su imaginación del carácter y de las actitudes de María Guerrero',[2] the actress was clearly an exceptionally strong, assertive and determined young woman, quite capable of realizing the majority of her ambitions, and in this way highly inspirational to the concept of Galdós's 'mujer nueva'.

The *voluntad* exercised by Galdós's new heroine, Isidora, is a will to power and control, not only over her own actions and destiny, but also over others. She declares her aims: 'Quiero enterarme, disponer, gobernar'.[3] This linking of power with knowledge is an important one for feminists, Cixous concluding that 'with few exceptions, knowledge is constantly caught up in, is entrapped by a will for power'.[4] Power itself, of course, can manifest itself in a variety of ways, and Chris Weedon stresses that 'for feminists, the attempt to understand power in all its forms is of central importance'.[5]

I have adopted the term 'womanpower' for use in this essay in a general sense, rather than with the intention of suggesting that power exercised by women is necessarily essentially different to that exercised by men and/or capable of being pinned down to a specific definition. However, Cixous does distinguish 'woman's powers' as being different:

> I would indeed make a clear distinction when it comes to the kind of power that is the will to supremacy, the thirst for individual and narcissistic satisfaction. That power is always a power over others. It is something that relates back to government, control, and beyond that, to despotism. Whereas if I say 'woman's powers', first it isn't *one* power any longer, it is multiplied, *there is more than one* (therefore it is not a question of centralization -- that destroys the relation with the unique, that levels everything out) and it is a *question of power over oneself*, in other words of a relation not based on mastery but on availability (*disponibilité*).[6]

In Toril Moi's view, with which I concur, this global appeal to 'woman's powers' glosses over the real differences among women, and thus ironically represses the true heterogeneity of women's powers.[7]

In *Voluntad*, Galdós can be seen to disrupt or break down the majority of the traditional binary oppositions attached to male/female roles listed by Cixous, notably those of Activity/Passivity and Head/Emotions, thereby contradicting the patriarchal value system in which each opposition can be analysed as a hierarchy where the 'feminine' side is always seen as the negative, powerless instance.[8] However, the 'womanpower' exercised by Galdós's 'mujer nueva' cannot be totally contained within the definition of 'woman's powers' given by Cixous. For the power assumed by the new heroine of Galdós's contemporary drama and last novels is not just power over herself but also over others, as exercised by María Guerrero, who quite probably prompted this breakthrough in the writer's vision. While female potential is recognized in earlier Galdosian heroines, who assume some control over their destiny within society's limited sphere, they are almost invariably victims. Galdós's 'mujer nueva', on the other hand, disrupts society's patterns in her assumption of total control over self and others, to emerge triumphant.

Although Catherine Jagoe's recent dissertation on gender roles in Galdós takes a totally different approach to my own, she does acknowledge that 'it is tempting to speculate on the personal reasons for the change in orientation on the Woman Question found in his novels'.[9] There is nothing to be gained and much to be lost in my view in ignoring the very obvious connection between this breakthrough and the writer's own experiences with women at this time, particularly bearing in mind these women's practical as well as inspirational roles in his work. While Galdós's lover, Concha-Ruth Morell, failed to realize her ambitions, which failure can be seen to be reflected in *Tristana*, together with her letters, 'literalmente copiadas',[10] the new dramatist was so impressed by the determined and successful María Guerrero that he was prompted to create an equally determined, self-fulfilled and powerful 'mujer nueva' on stage.

Unlike Isidora Rufete of *La desheredada* (1881), who allows her imagination and her emotions to rule her, the Isidora of *Voluntad* is determined to overcome such weaknesses in her quest for control and power. This power is to encompass not only the 'woman's power' described by Cixous as 'power over oneself', but also the other kind: 'power over others'.

The new Isidora first has to struggle against the power of 'romantic love', which had contributed to the downfall of the earlier Isidora and so many like her. This internal struggle is sensitively portrayed by Galdós, and the manuscripts show his own struggle with its expression. It is interesting that Isidora's temptation takes the form of a young man who is a dreamer, an idler and a romantic more akin to the Isidora of *La desheredada* herself. Alejandro is described by Luengo as 'un sonámbulo, con la cabeza llena de fantasmagorías, palabra engañadora, buena figura..., simpático él, eso sí' (CTC, 367). Isidora's infatuation with him, to which she had surrendered prior to the opening of the play, changed her overnight:

> *Nicomedes* ... Y de la noche a la mañana, el amor, el gran disolvente, vino a trastornar todas esas perfecciones y a reducirlas a cero.

Her father laments how 'Aquella hijita tan buena, aquella que parecía la razón misma hecha mujer ... se ciega, enloquece' (CTC, 366).

While Isidora's love for Alejandro does not die, her 'ansia de lo ideal' abates and her 'razón' returns as she seeks her parents' forgiveness and recognizes her lover's unworthiness. Her will, temporarily submerged by her passion, resurfaces to give her the strength to abandon her lover, as she explains, 'Al fin, Dios quiso devolverme la voluntad en toda su fuerza' (CTC, 370). She sees how her emotion had coloured her judgement, as 'todo se me empequeñecía ante la grandeza soñada, ilusoria, de la persona que me llamaba'; then, 'en la realidad, vi todas las cosas de otro modo ... veo muy clarito lo bueno y lo malo que hay en él, y lo juzgo con frialdad'. While far from being evil, Alejandro is 'un soñador incorregible' (CTC, 371).

Isidora faces up to her dishonour, rejecting the traditional solutions of marriage or the convent and instead directing her energy outward to more constructive ends. Although don Isidro would still prefer his daughter to marry Alejandro in order to regain her honour, she declares she is not interested in marrying anyone, but will do all she can to help her father save his business. Insisting on total control over this, she throws herself into the work with great determination.

Nevertheless, the strength of Isidora's *voluntad* is to be sorely tested when her lover returns on the scene, surprising her at her work. As indicated, the manuscripts show a considerable amount of reworking at this point in the Second Act where the heroine struggles to retain her *razón* in the face of her *pasión*. Having recognized and regretted her earlier folly when she had allowed her heart to rule her head and had run away with Alejandro, Isidora is now anxious that the strength of her emotions should never again overcome the strength of her reason and her will. The traditional linking of head/emotions to the male/female hierarchy respectively is reversed here as Alejandro insists that 'estas luchas de la realidad a nada conducen, y que vale más dormir, soñar, entregarse al dulce acaso...', for 'fuera del arte, del amor, de la poesía, nada existe que merezca nuestra atención' (CTC, 388). Yet for Isidora, the real world is one of work, for survival, self-respect and progress, and Alejandro represents the death of her ambitions. This point, together with her struggle against the temptation of romance and her attempt to assume control, were all given greater emphasis in the original manuscripts, prior to the final amendments and deletions made by the director in the *adaptaciones* in the interests of concision. There was also clearly still some concern following criticism of the 'aggressive' and therefore 'unfeminine' behaviour of Victoria, heroine of the earlier play *La loca de la casa* (1893), that Isidora should not appear over-assertive.[11]

In the published version, for example, as Isidora recognizes that giving in to temptation will mean the death of her ambitions and protests: 'Alejandro, me matas...', she then rather weakly pleads 'Déjame, te lo suplico', and the Act closes on a wavering note. Yet Galdós originally intended Isidora's struggle to be stronger and more determined, and her attitude more assertive. The following section was one deleted from this scene, following Isidora's protestation:

Isidora	...Alejandro, me matas. Si me quieres, como dices, déjame vivir.
Alejandro	Vivir ... Trabajar.
Isidora	Sí; esto es la muerte. Déjame. (*Recobrando su energía*) Yo te lo suplico, te lo mando.
Alejandro	¡Despótica!
Isidora	(*Creciéndose hasta llegar a la autoridad altanera y que no admite réplica*). Sí que lo soy. Mando en mi casa; quiero mandar también en tí.
Alejandro	(*Pausa. La contempla fijamente*) Obedezco. (*Dirígese a la puerta y se detiene*)
Isidora	(*Imperiosamente*) ¡Pronto!
Alejandro	Adiós. ¿Hasta cuándo?
Isidora	Hasta nunca.

Alejandro	(*Da algunos pasos hacia ella*) Eso no.
Isidora	Hasta nunca digo. (*Indicándole la puerta con gran decisión y firmeza*)
Alejandro	(*Ya junto a la puerta*) Está bien. Tú mandas.
Isidora	Quiero recobrar mi bendita soledad. (*Vacilación en Alejandro, que al fin se decide a partir, dominado por la voluntad potente de Isidora.*)
Alejandro	Adiós, sí ... adiós.
Isidora	(*Despidiéndole a distancia con un beso volado*) Adiós.

(Las Palmas; Caja 16, Num.4)

From this and other deleted sections of the original manuscripts, it is clear that Galdós wished to stress strongly Isidora's determination to assume power and control both over herself and over others. This determination is still present in the published version and, indeed, still realized, although the force of her struggle is lessened.

From a feminist viewpoint, some fundamental and still unresolved issues are raised here, in addition to that of power, so crucial to sexual politics. The traditional lure of love and romance, and the instilled fear of *soledad*, have long been obstacles to the realization of female autonomy. Here Isidora insists, 'Quiero recobrar mi bendita soledad', just as the heroines of the novels of such recent Spanish women writers as Rosa Montero and Montserrat Roig strive to do; Natalia in Roig's *La hora violeta* admitting 'No sé donde acaba la soledad y donde comienza la autonomía'.[12] The eponymous heroine of Galdós's novel *Tristana* had sought both love and autonomy, wanting to maintain her own household through her own career and thus live independently of her lover. Such an ambition was, of course, both too radical and impractical for nineteenth-century Spain, and thus we find the heroines of Galdós's contemporary drama ultimately demanding autonomy *within* the institution of marriage through a re-working of its traditional terms and roles.

This portrayal of a more enlightened form of marriage may also well have been prompted by María Guerrero, who, engaged to the actor playing the role of Alejandro, Fernando Díaz de Mendoza, was to marry him a couple of weeks after the opening night of *Voluntad*. María pursued her career during her marriage and continued to inspire contemporary dramatists with what Echegaray described as 'su carácter noble, apasionado y arrojadísimo'.[13] The letters conserved in the *Casa-Museo* indicate that María's influence and self-determination persisted, and that she did not assume the traditional role of the passive, submissive wife, the 'angel del hogar'. Her example was to be repeated by a later leading lady for whom Galdós also held the greatest respect, Margarita Xirgu.

Margarita, who was to become a leading actress of the calibre of María Guerrero, was also a highly intelligent, modern and independent-minded young woman whom her interviewer, Magda Donata, concluded 'ha sabido ser una mujer que ve con sus ojos, piensa con su cerebro y juzga con su propio criterio'.[14] Like the *mujer nueva* of Galdós's contemporary plays, Margarita's work was vitally important to her for its own sake, as was her constant striving for perfection and progress. When she married, her husband at first wanted her to give up her career, but she insisted, believing that, in limiting herself to domestic matters, a wife jeopardizes areas of communication with her husband. Furthermore, Margarita is quoted as declaring that 'cuando la mujer sale verdaderamente fuerte, acaso se baste a sí misma más que el hombre'.[15]

Which brings us back to the question of traditional female dependence on the male for love as well as money, together with the emotional fear as well as the social stigma of being alone. Kate Millett in her renowned work, *Sexual Politics*, explains: 'The concept of romantic love affords a means of emotional manipulation which the male is free to exploit, since love is the only circumstance in which the female is (ideologically) pardoned for sexual activity... Romantic love also obscures the realities of female status and the burden of economic dependency'.[16] She quotes the sociologist Hugo Beigel's observation that both the courtly and the romantic versions of love are 'grants' which the male concedes out of his total powers. Both have had the effect of obscuring the patriarchal character of Western culture and in their general tendency to attribute impossible virtues to women, have ended by confining them in a narrow and often remarkably conscripting sphere of behaviour.[17]

It is notable that Isidora assumes power and realizes her ambitions despite being a 'fallen woman', whereas in the case of earlier Galdosian heroines such as the eponymous heroine of *Gloria*, their 'fall' inevitably leads to their doom. This point is vividly illustrated through Galdós's use of the image of 'las alas' throughout his work to denote female potential for independent thought and action.[18] Society repeatedly clips the wings of his heroines, and/or, as in the case of Gloria, they are broken upon their 'fall'. Gloria never recovers, but Isidora is allowed to spread her wings and achieve her potential despite her fall, and society is advised: '¡No le cortéis las alas, y veréis hasta dónde se remonta!' (CTC, 382).

As indicated, disruption occurs in this play in the majority of the binary oppositions listed by Cixous in *La Jeune Née*, which correspond in the patriarchal value system to the underlying opposition Man/Woman, viz: Activity/Passivity; Sun/Moon; Culture/Nature; Day/Night; Father/Mother; Head/Emotions; Intelligible/ Sensitive; Logos/ Pathos.[19] The first of these is the one most obviously disrupted in many of Galdós's contemporary plays, where the heroines are exceptionally active and their male counterparts unexpectedly passive. *Voluntad* is, of course, a prime example of this and thus makes a powerful statement. Cixous concludes that: 'In the end, victory is equated with activity and defeat with passivity; under patriarchy, the male is always the victor'.[20] So is Galdós attempting to subvert such patriarchal norms? As Toril Moi observes, Cixous passionately denounces such an equation of femininity with passivity as leaving no positive space for woman: 'Either woman is passive or she doesn't exist'.[21] Indeed, Moi describes Cixous' whole theoretical project 'as the effort to undo this logocentric ideology: to proclaim woman as the source of life, power and energy and ... to subvert these patriarchal binary schemes where logocentrism colludes with phallocentrism in an effort to oppress and silence women'.[22]

If, under patriarchy, 'the male is always the victor', then this system is clearly being subverted in *Voluntad*. For Isidora assumes total control, and triumphs as victor. Indeed, at the very end of the play, there is an obvious and dramatic reversal of roles as she turns to her partner in the way the traditional male hero might turn to 'the little woman' at his side, to acknowledge her support in his valiant struggles and her share in his glory:

Isidora   Serás mi sostén, mi defensa, mi apoyo en esta lucha formidable, y mi victoria, si la consigo, será también la tuya.
(CTC, 395)

Such a conclusion to the drama really says it all and is, in my view, quite remarkable for its time. Indeed, this 'victory speech' of Isidora's can also be linked to the final set of binary oppositions listed by Cixous as: 'Form, convex, step, advance, seed, progress/matter, concave, ground -- which supports the step, receptacle'.[23] Again conversely, it is Isidora who takes the step, and Alejandro who 'supports the step'.

The remaining binary oppositions listed by Cixous as being linked by patriarchy to Man/Woman can be seen to be at least unsettled in this play, and often linked to the obvious subversion of the Activity/Passivity opposition. Reversal is also found in the opposition Head/Emotions (or Heart, as it has also been translated) which, while very evident in the published version of the play, was clearly meant to be even more forcefully stressed in the original *adaptaciones*, as the heroine shows her determination that her head will prove the stronger. It is Alejandro who is the emotional dreamer, arguably also linking him with the traditionally 'feminine' side of the oppositions Sun/Moon and Day/Night.

The notion of love as a woman's reason for living was hotly denied by the writer Margaret Fuller in 1852 who declared it 'a vulgar error that love, a love, to Woman is her whole existence'.[24] Yet as Gilbert and Gubar point out, she had formerly recognized and analysed not only her imprisonment in romantic plots but the patriarchal structures she knew those plots reflected. In a draft fantasy letter to Beethoven written in 1843 she wrote: 'Is it because, as a woman, I am bound by a physical law, which prevents the soul from manifesting itself? Sometimes the moon seems mockingly to say so, -- to say that I, too, shall not shine, unless I can find a sun. O cold and barren moon; tell a different tale, and give me a son of my own'. The pun on *sun* and *son* is seen as implying that had the writer been a *son* herself she would have no problem and, as in the case of Emily Dickenson, would have no need to enact her ambivalent romance with the 'man of noon'.[25] Our Isidora, in answer to Alejandro's dreaming: 'Sueño con el amor' (CTC, 386) retorts: '¡El amor, valiente tontería!' (CTC, 387). It is she who reflects the 'sun of energy'[26] of which Cixous speaks, as Bonifacio explains: 'iQué actividad! ¡Qué mujer!' (CTC, 377).

The link of Sun/Moon with activity/passivity is also stressed in Mary Coleridge's poem of 1896, 'In Dispraise of the Moon', where the moon acts as a transparent metaphoric substitution for woman, with the sun standing for the male. 'From this point of view', Christine Battersby observes, 'woman lacks her own ego, energy and reason. She reflects male glories in a passive and dead kind of way.' Subversion of this notion is, of course, apparent in *Voluntad* in Isidora's 'victory speech'. Coleridge's poem reads: 'She hath no air, no radiance of her own...' Nor reason, for: 'Light in itself doth not feed the living brain' and 'That light, reflected, but makes darkness plain'.[27] Light and knowledge are constantly sought by Galdosian heroines, as in the case of the eponymous heroine of *Tristana*, who rejects the 'dulces tinieblas' offered by her lover, Horacio, insisting, 'Quiero luz, más luz, siempre más luz' (NIII, 394). Alejandro in *Voluntad* recognizes Isidora's talent and confesses that he needs her 'como el ciego la luz' (CTC, 378).

The Culture/Nature opposition continues to be debated in gender studies, and 'femininity' attributed variously to nature or nurture. Galdós's formerly ambivalent attitude concerning the extent to which it was natural or desirable to improve women's education and opportunities is apparent in an article published in 1892 in which he stressed the need for improvement, 'sin erigir en sistema la pedantería femenina, que daría al traste con las gracias del sexo'.[28] Such ambivalence might also be seen through the protagonist of his earlier novel, *El amigo Manso*, who finds himself torn between the idea of 'la mujer razón' and the appeal of 'la mujer mujer'. Indeed, loss of feminine charm is the traditional male threat to a woman seeking greater knowledge and independence, as clearly illustrated in Horacio's reaction to Tristana's learning.[29] Yet it seems that Galdós suddenly loses his fear of assertive women losing their charm, as evidenced by the heroines of his contemporary drama. In fact, he was criticized in *La loca de la casa* for the assertive, 'unfeminine' nature of his heroine, Victoria, to the point of the charge 'Eso no es mujer'.[30] Hence the director's subsequent attempts to 'feminize' heroines, as evidenced in the following play, *La de San Quintín* where Galdós's direction that the heroine's outfit be 'de un corte un poco varonil' was deleted.[31] Even

Womanpower in Galdós's *Voluntad*   219

in *Voluntad*, where the heroine assumes such complete control, attempts were made to modify her assertive behaviour, as we have already seen.

Some unsettling of the Father/Mother opposition also occurs in this play, as Isidora assumes power from her father. She insists: 'Papá, por Dios, déjame que mangonee, que me meta en todo ... Quiero enterarme, disponer, gobernar', and her mother adds: 'No le pongas trabas' (CTC, 374). Typical male reaction to female authority follows when the agent, Luengo, visits, anxious to conclude negotiations to transfer the business, and is met with Isidora's declaration: '¡Traspasar, rendirnos! ¡Nunca!'. His response: '¿Tú qué sabes, ni qué dispones tú?' (CTC, 376) reveals his immediate incredulity that a woman could have any idea at all of management. Isidora's subsequent assertions are progressively seen as amusing and then presumptuous as he responds '¡Ay, qué gracioso!' and '¡Vaya unas ínfulas que se trae la niña!' Bonifacio admits that at first 'Nos reíamos ... pero pronto, conocimos que la cosa iba de veras' as she is allowed to 'desplegar su actividad ardiente, su energía, su inteligencia' (CTC, 378). Indeed, Isidora soon shows herself to be considerably more effective and ambitious than her father, who admits 'mis aspiraciones son más modestas', to which she responds 'Las mías pican alto' (CTC, 382). Isidora's insistence on exercising her own will, desire and authority here reverses the traditional patriarchal notion as defined by Cixous: 'A will: desire, authority, you examine that, and are led right back -- to the father ... there's no place at all for women in the operation'.[32]

Further disruption is found in this play within the remaining binary oppositions listed by Cixous: Intelligible/Sensitive and Logos/Pathos. In some keeping with Cixous' development of Derrida's concept of *différance* and her notion of 'the other bisexuality,[33] we find that while Isidora is also predominantly on the 'male' side of these oppositions, she is at the same time not without sensitivity or pathos. She does love Alejandro and instinctively wants to be with him, but not at the cost of losing her identity and purpose. Her sensitivity and vulnerability to this love are apparent from such passages as the following:

Isidora   (*Creyendo sentir pasos, se acerca a la puerta del portal*) Paréceme sentir ...

Santos   No, hija. Oyes los latidos de tu corazón, y
              crees que son sus pasos.

Isidora   (*Con la mano en el corazón*) Es verdad...
                                                      (CTC, 393)

Neither is Isidora without imagination and, indeed, it seems she almost has a premonition of Alejandro's sudden appearance as she muses:

Isidora   ... ¡Oh!, no sé qué tengo hoy ... ya me
              equivoqué tres veces. Es la pícara
              imaginación, que se me quiere
              insurreccionar ... (*Oprimiéndose la frente*)
              Imaginación, ten juicio ... no enredes, hija,
              no enredes ...
                                                      (CTC, 385)

Alejandro himself is well aware of the fascination he holds for Isidora, confident that 'este soñador ... tiene y tendrá siempre un lugarcito en el pensamiento de la mujer práctica' (CTC, 386).

Not only does Isidora have to struggle against her lover's power to confuse her judgement and jeopardize her *voluntad*, but she also has to convince him of the importance of her work to her for its own sake and not just as a means to an end. When Alejandro offers her his wealth to save her from her toil, she finally has to spell out: 'Tu apoyo es mi muerte' (CTC, 387). Here Isidora is reminiscent of Tristana who declared 'Libertad honrada es mi tema' (NIII, 380), as she explains:

Isidora   Luchar sola y honradamente es mi orgullo.
              No me prives de esta satisfacción, la más
              noble que puede tener un alma.
                                                      (CTC, 387)

Both of these Galdosian heroines were, of course, simply aspiring to that which men have always assumed as a right: love and/or marriage and some form of career/autonomy. In other words, an identity outside or in addition to the role of daughter, wife, mother: an identity or space of their own. For as 'la Pasionaria', Dolores Ibarruri, was later to stress: 'In the home, the woman was stripped of her social identity ... her own needs were negligible; her own personality was nullified'.[34] Tristana and Isidora's demands, while hardly unreasonable, were indeed progressive ones for a male, middle-class Spanish writer to be promoting in late-nineteenth-century Spain.

The author may be dead, but the circumstances surrounding his conception of 'la mujer nueva' are not without interest. History repeats itself, we are also told, and today's potential 'new man' may well find himself in a similar conflict to that experienced by Galdós one hundred years ago. Through such characters as Máximo Manso in *El amigo Manso* and Horacio in *Tristana*, the conflict between reason and instinct in the male approach towards woman's role in society and the shifting attraction towards the 'mujer razón' and the 'mujer mujer' are explored.

This very conflict in the male between reason and instinct further illustrates the shifting nature of the 'binary oppositions' discussed above. Indeed, the whole question of such oppositions is itself a slippery one, as several critics of Cixous' writings on the subject have already observed. Akiko Tsuchiya, for example, has recently stressed how, despite her insistence on deconstructing such oppositions, Cixous nevertheless at times constructs her own. In particular, Tsuchiya quotes an interview in which Cixous associates 'philosophy' with 'man' and 'poetry' with 'woman', and observes how 'such a distinction, once again, reveals the culturally ingrained binary logic with which Cixous must constantly struggle'.[35]

At the same time, Cixous' insistence that 'we are all bisexual'[36] is not so far removed from the notion Galdós appears to be promoting through much of his contemporary drama that traditional gender roles are potentially fluid and even interchangeable. In feminist re-readings of the traditional 'male canon', it is easy to criticize justifiably the majority of male representations of women. It is not, however, so easy to ignore the differences in the portrayal of the romantic, victimized Rosario in *Doña Perfecta* and that of the 'mujer nueva' epitomized by the new Isidora of *Voluntad*.

In conceding power to his new heroine, Galdós was taking a significant step towards the realization on stage of his concept of 'una sociedad nueva'. In this vision, the essential Krausist ideals of balance, equality and harmony persist and, indeed, still find some echo in current feminist thought.

NOTES

1. Galdós, *Casa-Museo*, Las Palmas; Caja 6, Carpeta 24, Legajo 66. Now published, although this section is incomplete in the publication, by Carmen Menendez Onrubia, in *El dramaturgo y los actores: Epistolario de Benito Pérez Galdós, María Guerrero y Fernando Diaz de Mendoza* (Madrid: C.S.I.C., 1984), p.66. Menéndez Onrubia observes in a footnote: 'No sabe María Guerrero hasta qué punto es verdad lo que dice'. In my view, however, the actress was only too aware of the extent of her power.

2. Onrubia, p.121.

3. B. Pérez Galdós, *Obras Completas*, ed. by F. C. Sainz de Robles (Madrid: Aguilar, 1973): *Cuentos, Teatro y Censo*, p.374. Throughout this study, quotations from Galdós's texts will be taken from this edition, in the following form: *Novelas I, Novelas II, Novelas III,* (NI, II, III) and *Cuentos, Teatro y Censo* (CTC).

4. Hélène Cixous and Catherine Clément, *The Newly Born Woman*, trans. by Betsy Wing (Manchester: University of Manchester Press, 1985), pp.136-60; reprinted in *Feminist Literary Criticism*, ed. by Mary Eagleton (Harlow: Longman, 1991), p.117.

5. Chris Weedon, *Feminist Practice & Poststructuralist Theory* (Oxford: Blackwell, 1988), p.124.

6. Quoted by Toril Moi, *Sexual/Textual Politics: Feminist Literary Theory* (London: Routledge, 1988), pp.124-25.

7. Moi, p.125.

8. Moi, p.104.

9. Catherine Jagoe, 'Ambivalent Angels: Gender Roles and the Ideology of Domesticity in the Novels of Galdós', unpublished dissertation, Girton College, Cambridge, 1988, p.21.

10. As Concha-Ruth herself complained, and as can be verified by comparing the letters conserved in the *Casa-Museo* with those found in *Tristana*. See also A. F. Lambert, 'Galdós and Concha-Ruth Morell', *Anales Galdosianos*, 8 (1973), 34 and Gilbert Smith, 'Galdós, *Tristana*, and letters from Concha-Ruth Morell', *Anales Galdosianos*, 10 (1975), 117.

11. See my work, *Women in the Theatre of Galdós* (New York: Mellen Press, 1990), Chapter VI, for details of contemporary reactions to this earlier play.

12. Montserrat Roig, *La hora violeta* (Barcelona: Plaza y Janes), 1980.

13. Quoted by Menéndez Onrubia, 'Presencia de María Guerrero en la obra dramática de Galdós', *Actas del Tercer Congreso Internacional de Estudios Galdosianos II* (Las Palmas: Ediciones del Excmo. Cabildo Insular de Gran Canaria, 1989), pp.427-34 (p.432).

14. Interview with Margarita Xirgu by Magda Donata, 'Hablando con Margarita Xirgu', *El Imparcial*, 1918 (clipping in album in *Casa-Museo*, Ref. No.318, p.15).

15. 'Hablando con Margarita Xirgu'.

16. Kate Millett, *Sexual Politics* (London: Virago, 1977), p.37.

17. Millett, p.37.

18. See my work, *Stages in the Development of a Feminist Consciousness in Pérez Galdós* (New York: Mellen Press, 1990), Chapters II and VIII.

19. Hélène Cixous, 'Sorties', *La Jeune Née* (Paris: UGE, 1975), p.116. Translation quoted from Moi, p.104.

20. See Moi, p.105.

21. *La Jeune Née*, p.118.

22. Moi, p.105.

23. Full translation of 'Sorties' re-printed in *Modern Criticism and Theory*, ed. by David Lodge (London: Longman, 1988), p.287.

24. Quoted by S. Gilbert and S. Gubar, *The Madwoman in the Attic* (New Haven and London: Yale University Press, 1979), p.605.

25. Gilbert and Grubar, p.606.

26. 'Sorties', from Lodge, p.293.

27. Quoted and commented on by Christine Battersby, *Gender and Genius* (London: The Women's Press, 1989), p.148.

28. B. Pérez Galdós, 'La Enseñanza Superior en España', re-printed in *Arte y Crítica* (Madrid: Renacimiento, 1923), p.245.

29. On learning of her progress, Horacio responds: 'Temo que la *señá* Malvina te contagie de su fealdad seca y hombruna. No te me vuelvas muy filósofa' (NIII, 390).

30. 'Gil Blas de Santillana', 'Comedia, *La loca de la casa'*, *El País*, 17-I-1893.

31. Manuscript conserved in the *Casa-Museo*, Caja 16, Num.1.

32. 'Sorties', from Lodge, p.288.

33. Described as 'multiple, variable and ever-changing'. See Moi, p.109.

34. Quoted by Adrian Shubert, *A Social History of Modern Spain* (London: Unwin Hyman, 1990), p.141.

35. Akiko Tsuchiya, 'Theorizing the Feminine: Esther Tusquets's *El mismo mar de todos los veranos* and Hélène Cixous's *écriture féminine*', *Revista de Estudios Hispánicos*, 26 (1992), 183-99 (p.198).

36. Cixous and Clément, *The Newly Born Woman*, reprinted in *Feminist Literary Criticism*, p.120.

THE NOVELIST INTERPRETS HISTORY: GALDOS'S *LA DE LOS TRISTES DESTINOS*

GEOFFREY RIBBANS
Brown University

The link between history and literature is a subject which Derek Lomax had very much at heart and to which he devoted much of his scholarly activity. Although he did not publish on the subject, he was not uninterested in the variant of the historical novel which Galdós invented and endowed with a name of its own: the *episodio nacional*. It is a subgenre which tackles in a distinctive and original way the specific problems of merging the empirical and the imaginative, the national and the individual.[1] *La de los tristes destinos* (1907), the final volume of the fourth series of *Episodios nacionales* and concerned with a crucial event of nineteenth-century Spanish history, provides a suitable example.

The fourth series is devoted entirely to the reign of Isabella II from October 1847 onwards; the events surrounding her marriage (1846) had been recounted in the last volume of the previous series, *Bodas reales*. In the course of these eleven volumes the reader witnesses the progression of the monarch from being the 'Reina más amada' (II, 1408)[2] to becoming 'la de los tristes destinos'; more than its previous tentative title *Fin de un reinado*,[3] *La de los tristes destinos* implies a measure of inevitability about the outcome: a subject I shall consider shortly.

To open this last *episodio*, which is to culminate in the queen's expulsion, Galdós has chosen to highlight a major event which is particularly apposite: the precipitate, savage execution of sixty-six sergeants from the San Gil barracks accused of participation in the insurrection of 22 June 1866.[4] The rising itself went badly wrong through faulty liaison, with the result that only the San Gil barracks rose up, some of its officers were unintentionally killed and the San Gil soldiers found themselves in armed conflict with those of other barracks. It constitutes the culmination of the previous *episodio* Prim; the two narrations are hinged together, as Jover Zamora has indicated (29, 30),[5] by the twin aspects of the incident, the one focussed essentially on Prim's indefatigable revolutionary efforts, of which it formed a part, the other on the ruthless retribution meted out to the sergeants by the queen's government and the subsequent train of events which led to her expulsion.

The gruesome event had an enduring effect on the young Galdós; he incorporated it in *Angel Guerra* (1890-91) as a poignant memory, significant in the development of his hero's character, and spoke of it in a tone of high pathos in his late *Memorias de un desmemoriado* (1915-16).[6] In the intermediate version unfolded in *La de los tristes destinos* (1907), time and place are laconically indicated from the outset: 'Madrid, 1866 -- Mañana de julio seca y luminosa' (655). The morning is endowed with human qualities specifically related to the victims and their sympathizers. The sun is viewed in terms of pain and violence: 'rayos con movimiento de guadaña', 'rapándose los árboles', 'tejido ... con abrojos', 'espadas llameantes', as it lights up the Cuartel de Artillería (where the prisoners are accommodated) and 'el pelotón desgarrado de plebe' along the Calle de Alcalá up to the Retiro: the route along which the condemned men will be conducted by hansom cabs; the word 'pelotón', typically applied to a firing-squad, anticipates the dire occurrence which is about to take place and identifies the mob with it.

In contrast with the other evocations of the event, a popular scene is grafted on to the historical reality. Among the crowd of curious Madrilenians ('el pueblo de Madrid quería ver...') who turn out to view the spectacle (which Galdós saw unfolding but refused to witness)[7] the most prominent are a couple of rather jaded street-walkers who have appeared as supporters of the revolution in earlier *episodios*, notably *O'Donnell*, twelve years before and at *La noche de San Daniel* disturbances the previous year. They are the Hermosilla sisters, Rafaela and Generosa, known as *las Zorreras*, from their father's occupation as a furrier.[8] For them, however, much more than simple curiosity is involved, since Rafaela is the lover of one of the victims, Simón Paternina. Other figures present are equally survivors of the past: 'una matrona lacia y descaradota', called *Pepa Jumos*, and Erasmo Gamoneda, 'revolucionario y barracadista del 54'. The continuity with past struggles, and particularly with the 1854 Revolution, is thus established; so important is it to Galdós that he unthinkingly resuscitates Gamoneda, whose death in the street battles is recorded in *La revolución de julio* (112; see Jover 61). Both Pepa and the Zorreras participated in *O'Donnell* in the brutal assassination of the police-chief Chico,[9] an act of spontaneous violence which, though by no means undeserved, exemplifies the constant shedding of blood on both sides: what Galdós in *La de los tristes destinos* calls, with grim irony, 'heroica medicina contra las enfermedades de autoridad que por aquellos días y en otros muchos de la historia patria, padecía crónicos achaques y terribles accesos agudo' (655). The Zorreras had in addition other grievances; they had both been sexual victims of the revolutionary philanderer Bartolomé Gracián, killed by Baramendi at the end of *La revolución de julio* (114). Ironically, too, O'Donnell, now the executor of the brutal repression, had been the revolutionary hero of Vicálvaro in the July Revolution.

Pepa and Erasmo endeavour to console Rafaela by evoking on the one hand the tradition of heroic patriotic struggle from the *Dos de Mayo* onwards and on the other both the material comforts --the opulent meal and fine Havana cigars the prisoners enjoyed the previous night-- and their fortitude and dignity. Simón Paternina is singled out for his exemplary comportment. He is at once an enthusiastic partisan of Prim's and a devout Catholic strictly brought up by Carlist parents; by confessing with fervour and integrity he apparently secures for himself, in the minds of his friends, the sure promise of salvation.

In *La de los tristes destinos*, the executions are not directly presented, as they were in *Ángel Guerra*, but the sense of distressful anticipation among the crowd produces varied poignant attitudes and reactions, especially when the fatal volleys are heard. Generosa thinks they should have stayed away, while *Pepa Jumos*, taking a stoical attitude unconsciously reminiscent of Zenon, argues in favour of the cathartic effect of facing adversity: 'Así se templa una y se carga de coraje ... el dolor no es cosa mala' (657). In some Catholic resignation prevails, while others voice angry denunciations, the most vociferous being Rafaela, whose curses are too vehement for the narrator, in his guise as the popular muse of history ('Clio familiar'),[10] to record. Her protests culminate in a pithy '¡Viva Prim! ¡Muera la ...!'; but her companions put their hands over her mouth, leaving unresolved exactly what the missing word, 'la exclamación irreverente' (*puta?*), would have been.

In a significant dialogue between Rafaela and Pepa, the question of the ultimate responsibility for the sentences is raised:

> [C]onfiábamos en que *la Isabel* perdonaría...*[declares Rafaela]* Para perdonar la tenemos... ¡Bien la perdonamos a ella, Cristo! ... A un general sublevado le das cruces, y a un pobre sargento, ¡pum!... Tu justicia me da asco.
> --No hables mal de ella--dijo la Pepa con alarde de sensatez -- que si no perdona es porque no la deja el zancarrón de O'Donnell, o porque la Patrocinio, que es como culebra, se le enrosca en el corazón... (657).

Once more opinions vary. Rafaela has no doubt that the queen is to blame, while Pepa considers her advisors more culpable. From the beginning of the series the question of the queen's instinctive sympathy with the populace has been constantly raised. Now, in the last *episodio*, it is clear that whatever sensitivity towards the people she once had has evaporated completely. The historical evidence seems strong moreover that, against O'Donnell's wishes, the queen herself demanded the harshest of punishments.[11]

The flagrant discrepancy between the treatment of the common people and their social superiors is stressed. The immediate organizers, Pierrad and Hidalgo, managed to escape; Prim himself was not present. The civilian politicians implicated --Castelar, Sagasta, and others-- also got away unscathed; Galdós does not fail to note in the text that both Sagasta and Aguirre escaped with official connivance (677-78); Castelar was similarly allowed to leave the country. As Jover Zamora remarks very justly, 'El escarmiento se hacía, pues, a costa, no sólo de un adversario político e ideológico que había osado recurrir a las armas, sino también de un estrato social jerárquicamente inferior y moralmente ajeno' (34).

As well as being a convinced radical, Rafaela is, like Simón, a sincere if naïve believer, and she devotes half a *duro* --earned in honest work, not in prostitution-- to masses for Simón's soul. She harbours no doubt about the justice of the revolutionary cause as she pictures him, pathetically, informing God of the wickedness of the Conservatives: 'Esta es la historia de España que están haciendo allí *la Isabel* y el Diablo, *la Patrocinio* y O'Donnell, y los malditos moderados...' (659).

These characters are not idealized but shown in everyday gestures, as in the group's first response on hearing the shooting: 'Con estremecimiento y congoja, con ayes y greguería', or in Rafaela's anguished if undignified instinctive movement of revulsion: 'la Zorrera pareció acometida de un violento patatús, resbalándose del inclinado asiento en que apoyaba sus nalgas' (657). Yet a strong compassionate quality subsists. Similarly, popular language, with forms like *dizno*, *naufragios* for *sufragios* and above all the incongruous version of the Passion *consumatomés* (consummatum est), together with frequent anacolutha, add familiarity without destroying the emotion.[12] The effect is tragicomic. The scene is not Romanticized; instead it employs a *costumbrismo* which does not emphasize the picturesque but has a clear ideological and structural purpose.[13]

A final attitude is exemplified by the agent of the secret police, Valentín Malrecado, whose squalid appearance hides his success in keeping in with both sides. 'Hombre avezado a nadar entre dos aguas', as Jover Zamora says (89), Malrecado takes a passive, resigned stance to contemporary politics: 'Hoy les toca morir a éstos, mañana a los otros. Es la Historia de España que va corriendo, corriendo... Es un río de sangre.... Sangre por el Orden, sangre por la Libertad' (658) and he quotes *Confusio*, 'el primer sabio de España',[14] no less, as witness. His cynical opportunism is nonetheless benign, and he supports his friends as and when he can; he has warned Rafaela of the danger Paternina faced (659) and he treats the distraught group, which includes a young mother called Torcuata who suckles her baby throughout the episode, to plentiful drinks, in a sort of wake (Jover calls it a 'velatorio', 89) which has a therapeutic effect. He tells them about the second and third batches of prisoners to be shot and explains his expedient connections in the liberal camp. They all throw at him allegations of favours in cash or kind he has received from many political figures. As *Pepa Jumos* says, 'comes con todos', adding a pragmatic justification for his unheroic if understandable conduct: 'En comer de esta olla y de la otra no hay ningún demerecimiento. Cuando vamos para viejos, traemos a casa todos los rábanos que pasan' (658). Malrecado --the name is significant: a not-too-trustworthy messenger-- resembles the equally appropriately nicknamed *Sebo* (Telesforo del Portillo), who frequents many of the *episodios*. Obliged for simple survival to temporize, they are all things to all men.

Suitably enough, Malrecado provides a link with the fictional story of Pepe

Fajardo, the Marquis of Beramendi, narrator, reflector and manipulator (as well as secret dissident) of the political reality of his time. Malrecado passes messages from two of Beramendi's closest associates, the impoverished aristocrat Guillermo de Aransis and the former Liberal Union organizer Manuel Tarfe; the latter is charged with the mission of seeking a pardon for two recurrent characters of the series, Leoncio Ansúrez and Santiago Ibero, real conspirators who are in imminent danger of being deported in the so-called 'cuerda de Leganés'. Tarfe also receives counsel from another old hand at intrigue, Eufrasia Carrasco. Then, supplied with an indispensable letter from *La madre*, that is, Sor Patrocinio (Beramendi's sister is a nun in the same convent), he puts his petition to the queen. Influence, not merit, is patently the lubricant for success in all political matters. In granting the request, Isabella, now obese, extremely bourgeoise in appearance ('agarbanzada su belleza') and quite disillusioned, has her own agenda: she is concerned to answer the criticism of excessive harshness: 'Eso para que digan que no perdono, que no soy generosa' (662). She also refers to the unhappy marriage of Virginia de Secobio, Leoncio's lover, in terms which apply strikingly to herself: 'Y no hay que culpar a Virginia, sino a sus padres, que la casaron con un hombre afeminado y bobalicón, sin maldita la gracia para el matrimonio'; her 'sonrisa picaresca' indicates that she is thinking of her notoriously impotent consort. By recommending haste in obtaining their release and protesting unnecessarily, in an inconsequential change of subject, that 'Yo quiero mucho a O'Donnell', she forecasts the minister's imminent fall.

This peremptory dismissal, which the hero of Africa can hardly credit, gives rise to his famous exclamation of disgust (unconsciously throwing light once more on the treatment of the lower classes at the time): 'Me han despedido como despedirán ustedes al último de sus criados' (663). In short, O'Donnell is allowed by the *camarilla* to reap the opprobrium of the executions before Narváez is summoned to take over. The conclusion attributed to Adelardo López de Ayala, later author of the famous manifesto of the Revolution 'España con honra': 'Esa señora es imposible' (664; repeated, 677), points directly towards the revolutionary alliance of Progressives, Democrats and dissident Unionists which is soon to bring down the monarchy. In a short conversation with Narváez, Beramendi, as the series' political 'focalizer',[15] finds the tough old warrior weakened and desperate, hounded as he is from right as well as left: 'Yo me encuentro con la revolución enfrente y con la reacción detrás' (689); and he prophesies, rather facilely, that it will be the death of him. In effect, once O'Donnell and Narváez, '[l]os dos puntales de la Monarquía' (732), in Ibero's words, who, for all the monarch's capriciousness, would not countenance an uprising directed against her, are dead,[16] her downfall quickly becomes inevitable. The unscrupulous reactionary González Bravo, appointed in Narváez's place, was foolhardy enough to promote two traditionalist generals (Pavía y Lacy, Marquis of Novaliches, and Concha, Marquis of La Habana) and send into exile, together with Montpensier, the more dominant Unionist generals, including Serrano. The narrator calls it 'un ademán de suicidio' (732).

Beramendi's story continues. As usual, links are forged with the past. His now remote idealization of Lucila Ansúrez, now a mature wife with many children, as the ideal representation of indigenous Spanish values is recalled. His children's birth-dates, like Isabel Cordero's in *Fortunata y Jacinta*, coincide with key historical events: Pepito, with the time of the *ministerio Relámpago* (29 November 1849), Feliciana, with Merino's assassination attempt (1852); a girl, who died in infancy, was born just before Vicálvaro (1854), and finally Agustín (*Tinito*), at the same time as the infante Alfonso (end of 1859); as a consequence the latter becomes the prince's playmate. *Tinito* is thus in a position to appreciate the defective education he is receiving: 'Alfonso no sabe nada. No le enseñan más que religión y armas' (693), a defect admitted by such a stalwart supporter of the dynasty as Novaliches. As a result Beramendi's eager participation in *Confusio*'s ideal recreation of Spanish history takes a curious twist.[17] This degree of ignorance in the heir apparent makes the 'cirugía política' (700) of a revolution necessary so as to provide a spell of exile which will give him outside stimulus and wider perspectives; that done, *Confusio* can cheerfully prognosticate a long, happy and tranquil reign (until 1925!) for Alfonso XII.

The historical reality, by contrast, is shown when Beramendi and his wife visit the queen. She praises inordinately María Ignacia's extremely reactionary late father, provoking in Beramendi a silent rebuke about her grave error in supporting absolutism. He also muses to himself successively about other inherent defects: deficient religious education, ridiculous court etiquette, arbitrary patronage. Her unawareness of why she has lost the allegiance of her subjects and her empty confidence in God's grace provoke a summing up and a farewell in which he creates intertextually the title of the *episodio*:

> No invoques al Dios verdadero mientras vivas prosternada ante el falso. Ese Dios tuyo, ese ídolo fabricado por la superstición y vestido con los trapos de la lisonja, ese comodín de tu espiritualidad grosera, no vendrá en tu ayuda, porque no es Dios ni nada ... Adiós, reina Isabel. Has torcido tu sino ... *Adiós mujer de York, la de los tristes destinos*... Dios salve a tu descendencia, ya que a ti no te salve. (704)[18]

It is an example of the inevitable priority given to historical events within the *episodios*, especially when what is occurring is of particular significance.[19] From the perspective of the fictional story, this is presented in far too explicit a manner; yet it is obviously urgent to give a considered, if fictional and over-simplified, contemporary opinion of the key event taking place and to anticipate the one which is to come: the restoration of the dynasty.

On his release Santiago Ibero is taken by Leoncio into the quintessential Celtiberian family of the Ansúrezs, where he becomes a friend of Lucila's young son Vicente Halconero, who handicapped by his lameness is a bookish counterpart to the activist Santiago.[20] A parting of the ways occurs when Santiago is sought by the police, whereas the less involved Leoncio has no necessity to seek refuge.

Santiago's escape to France, planned by Tarfe and engineered by Malrecado, is effected by the relatively new-fangled means of transport, the railway, lyrically evoked by Galdós as a vehicle of progress. At this juncture the important fictional story of Teresa Villaescusa is resumed,[21] for Santiago encounters her on the train and they arrange to meet eventually in the French Basque Country. 'Extraña cosa' it may be, but as a result of the passionate love she conceives for Santiago, Teresa reforms completely: 'No es la juiciosa que se equivoca, sino la equivocada que rectifica, la fatigada que se sienta y se adormece en la tardía enmienda de sus errores' (706). No conventional dwelling on the shameful nature of her actions here; for Galdós, though not for characters of his making like Clavería and Tarfe, her misdemeanours are 'errores', not 'pecados'. On the political plane, Teresa encourages Ibero to follow his bent in supporting revolutionary activities, with the result that he takes part in the unsuccessful invasion of Aragon (1867) by Moriones in which the impetuous general Manso de Zúñiga is killed. On the personal or fictional plane, she spurs him to overcome his earlier idealistic love for Salomita Galán, who has become a nun at Lourdes. In her honesty and generosity, she offers him the opportunity to give her up, on account of her past life and her age.

Eventually, they go to Paris, where Ibero joins his fictional fellow-conspirators led by Jesús Clavería and Manuel Santa María, as Prim is forging the final revolutionary effort in alliance with the Unionists. He meets Sagasta and assists him in engagingly domestic tasks; a vehement figure called Don José also plays some part (information on his actual identity is deferred: it is a 'proleptic' intervention of Paúl y Angulo, later the chief suspect of Prim's assassination). His father, also Santiago Ibero, intent on separating him from Teresa, plans to come and rescue him just as Armand's father does in Dumas' *La dame aux Camélias* (1848), but this false Romantic image of the fallen woman who sacrifices herself is explicitly rejected: 'Aquí no hay *damas de camelias*, ni Cristo que lo fundó' (735). Instead, Teresa is concealed by her French mentor Ursula Plessis, under whose guidance she learns a useful and satisfying trade --fine embroidery-- an opportunity, as Stephen Miller has indicated, denied women in Spain.[22]

Santiago, for his part, escapes by arranging to be sent on a mission to London, where his personal life and contemporary politics continue to be intertwined. On the journey he meets Clavería. The occasion is used to indicate the growing worries among Prim's supporters about a conspiracy between Montpensier and the Liberal Union; Clavería is at first suspicious that Santiago is bearing letters in its support. When these fears are allayed, he joins Ruiz Zorrilla and Prim; his impetuous nature is shown in the part he chivalrously plays in a tavern brawl for which he is temporarily imprisoned.

Prim's voyage in disguise on the *Zaragoza* and the turning of the treachery of his Italian aide Antoni to his advantage are recounted through Ibero's eyes. On arrival at Cadiz on 18 September Prim answers Topete's reiterated '¡Viva la Reina!' with a '¡Viva la Soberanía Nacional!' '¡Viva la Libertad!' (755), and its enthusiastic reception is recorded:

Oído por la marinería el grito del General, ya no sonaron más los fríos clamores de ordenanza, sino que estalló un '¡Viva Prim!' inmenso, ardoroso, y confundido con el estruendo de la artillería...

At the Customs House, it is recalled how Ferdinand VII was confined by the Liberals in 1823, while the Duke of Angoulême was bombarding the Trocadero; in *Confusio*'s imagination, however, the king was executed there (755); real and imagined history are again confronted. Ibero has an emotional reunion with his old mentor Lagier, who gives him sage advice on the priorities of heroism and peace: '*Nacemos como un libro en blanco ... Reconstruid vuestras personas con actos buenos*' (758): precisely what Santiago, despite conventional male opposition from Clavería and his father, will do, together with Teresa, in the end. The way is not easy, however. Misinformed by another sceptical male, Tarfe, through the intrigues of Teresa's mother, that Teresa has taken to her old ways again with one of the Muñoz family, that is, the rapacious relatives of María Cristina's morganatic husband, the distraught Santiago returns to Madrid. He gives a lively description of the revolution in the streets, before ending up in the Royal Palace, which is saved from looting by a Muñoz, Casimiro, of a very different calibre: a typesetter, who dressed in his most formal clothes has taken charge of the building on behalf of the *Junta revolucionaria*. There, among portraits of monarchs, including Isabella II's, Santiago dreams of Teresa. The parallel between the two women thus continues, to Teresa's advantage. As Peter Bly says, 'The Palace scene has thus established not the similarity but rather the superiority of Teresa to her royal counterpart -- because of her fidelity and sincerity'.[23]

After the defeat of the loyalist forces under the heroic Novaliches at Alcolea, another dawn comes to parallel the bleak, violent scenario of the executions which opened the *episodio*; it has its corresponding 'bandas de curiosos', but this time takes place in the humid North: it is equally marked by death, now alluding metaphorically to the end of Isabella's rule. To salvage something from the situation, Beramendi suggests an immediate abdication in favour of Alfonso, to which Eufrasia adds the idea of seeking Espartero's protection for Alfonso at Logroño, but Carlos Marfori, the queen's latest lover, arrogantly scotches this suggestion as beneath the monarch's dignity.

The departure for exile is described, with a specific reference to executions: 'alguna vaga semejanza tenía con las salidas para el patíbulo. En muchos casos no vale una corona menos que una vida' (777). Beramendi's final meditation emphasizes the bloody record of the reign: 'las 100.000 víctimas inmoladas por Isabel desde su cuna hasta su sepultura. Véase la tragedia de este reinado, toda muertes, toda querellas y disputas violentísimas, desenlazadas con esta vulgar salida por la puerta de Bidasoa' (778); the word 'sepultura', equates her fall with death and burial. A policy which had commenced with deliberate and uncalled-for mass shedding of blood ends with imagery of death and violence, denoting the means by which the monarchy was sustained. Compassion for the individual --'análoga mezcla de compasión e ironía', as Jover Zamora notes (44)-- is likewise not absent, as everyone (Eufrasia, the people of San Sebastián, Teresa) is portrayed as sorry for the queen personally.

What does the 1868 revolution augur for the future? Beramendi comes to the facile and understandable conclusion that the queen herself will not return, and rather obvious hints of the eventual restoration are given. Has the revolution therefore, in Galdós's portrayal, been in vain, as Brian Dendle suggests?[24] Teresa's dissipated mother, *la sutil tramposa*, can after all claim, however incongruously, to be 'la honra de España' (769). As has been pointed out,[25] the two characters who evidently represent the best of Spain, Teresa Villaescusa and Santiago Ibero, who have been tested in difficult circumstances and now newly reunited are conscious of the unorthodoxy of their life, leave Spain along with the exiled queen. Unlike Leoncio, who represents another honest solution (he has a family to support), Ibero refuses the offer from the ever crafty manipulator Tarfe of a job or money, and turns his back on the grossly opportunistic values which link the so-called 'Glorious' Revolution with the Liberal Union:

> Desde aquel momento, el infeliz Ibero, solo, errante, sin calificación ni jerarquía en la gran familia hispana, miró desde la altura de su independencia espiritual la pequeñez enana del prócer, hacendado y unionista. (766)

The *episodio* concludes with a piece of pseudo-dramatic dialogue between the two lovers which offers a sustained oxymoronic contrast between the departing queen and themselves; one fleeing from Freedom, the others seeking Freedom; one suffering from *tristes destinos*, the others pursuing *alegres destinos*:

> IBERO -- Doña Isabel no volverá, ni nosotros tampoco... Ella, destronada, sale huyendo de la Libertad, y hacia la Libertad corremos nosotros. A ella la despiden con lástima; a nosotros nadie nos despide; nos despedimos nosotros mismos diciéndonos: Corred, jóvenes, en persecución de vuestros alegres destinos.

And when they have crossed into France at Hendaye, Ibero takes up the 'España con honra' slogan and inverts it, as, in the last lines of the narration, they seek an unknown European destiny:

> IBERO -- ... Adiós, España con honra. ... Somos la España sin honra y huimos, desaparecemos, pobres gotas perdidas en el torrente europeo. (781)

Individual freedom to develop, as advocated by Lagier, is therefore preferred to the new but very fragile opportunity of overcoming the cynical transactions of the past. It must be remembered that not only was this narrative the conclusion of a series but that Galdós first intended to stop writing further *episodios*.[26] He sought therefore an ending which not only stretched in its implications beyond the actual chronological limits of the narrative to imply indirectly the failure of the Revolution and the inevitability of the Restoration but one which at the same time offered an open-ended if unspecific hope for the future.

The considerable personal sympathy Galdós shows towards Queen Isabella in both the *episodios* and his 1904 articles,[27] which make an attempt to sum up her career, is not to be taken as a complacent or reprehensible exoneration of her conduct.[28] The sympathy arises because Galdós is fully aware of how subject she is to the constraints of historical tradition and circumstance; it is not accidental that the disastrous marriage forced on her is obliquely referred to in her conversation with Tarfe. In many respects, she is, in her virtues and her vices, a representative figure. Despite this degree of understanding, Galdós is nonetheless unequivocal in his assessment of her political legacy. The balance sheet is not a favourable one. As Diane Urey sensibly observes, 'The picture that emerges of her, although not devoid of sympathy, is too replete with irony to be deemed favorable'.[29]

What is important to bear in mind is the steady evolution within the *episodios*: it is a case of gradual emergence or discovery. The queen is presented most favourably at the beginning of her reign, when her spontaneous and popular qualities offer (in novelistic, not in historical, terms) some hope of prevailing. She progressively loses her popularity, however, so that by the late 1860s she no longer commands any respect or esteem; this comes out decisively in the interview with Tarfe. Her fresh sensuality has degenerated into obesity, her naïveté into cynicism, her popular charms into vulgarity and, most evidently, her capricious generosity into cruelty. Her promiscuity has become an international scandal. The free-living Teresa, who leaves Spain at the same time, has shown herself her superior. Isabella herself reveals a complete *desencanto* with political life and on her departure makes a historically authentic statement which demonstrates how out of touch she is with reality: 'Francamente, creí tener más raíces en este país' (777). The apparent fatalism of the ponderous phrase 'la de los tristes destinos' has some justification, for she suffered from infancy from the burden of a stifling, unenlightened environment. But the judgement expressed by Baramendi, 'Torciste tu destino', is equally valid. Isabella II is shown to bear her full share of responsibility for her fate.

NOTES

1. See my forthcoming book *History and Fiction in Galdós's Narratives*, to be published by Oxford University Press, and Hans Hinterhäuser's pioneering study, *Los 'Episodios Nacionales' de Benito Pérez Galdós* (Madrid: Gredos, 1963).

2. All references to Galdós's work are to *Obras completas*, ed. by F. C. Sainz de Robles (Madrid: Aguilar, 1973), II, III and VI; the page references are to vol. III unless otherwise indicated.

3. Consult Rodolfo Cardona, 'Apostillas a los *Episodios Nacionales* de Benito Pérez Galdós de Hans Hinterhäuser', *Anales Galdosianos*, 3 (1968), 119-42 (p.122).

4. '[E]ntre sargentos, cabos y soldados, un antiguo coronel carlista y un paisano' (according to Pirala, *Anales desde 1843 hasta el fallecimiento de Don Alfonso XII*, V, Ch. 37 (Madrid, 1906), II, 95). Modesto Lafuente notes 'muriendo algunos sargentos completamente inocentes, pues estando para cumplir, rehusaron tomar parte en la sublevación' (*Historia general de España*, continuada por Juan Valera, con la colaboración de Andrés Borrego y Antonio Pirala (Barcelona, 1890), XXIII, 303; both apud José María Jover Zamora, 'Benito Pérez Galdós: *La de los tristes destinos* (caps. I y II)', *El comentario de textos, 2. De Galdós a García Márquez*, ed. by Aurora de Albornoz and others, p.98, nn.9, 10.

5. Jover Zamora's study gives a meticulous analysis of the first two chapters of the *episodio*. See also Claire-Nicolle Robin, '*La de los tristes destinos*: un roman historique tardif de Benito Pérez Galdós', *Recherches sur le roman historique en Europe -- XVIII-XIX siècles (I)* (Besançon/Paris: Les Belles Lettres, 1977), pp.211-53.

6. See Jover Zamora, p.36. In addition, in his interview with Olmet and Carrafa in 1912, Galdós declared 'el paso de los coches simones que conducían a los sargentos del cuartel de San Gil al sitio donde fueron fusilados dejaron en mi ánimo vivísimo recuerdo, y han influido considerablemente en mi temperamento literario' (Luis Antón del Olmet and Arturo García Carrafa, *Galdós* (Madrid, 1912), p.30), apud Jover Zamora, p.40.

7. 'Transido de dolor, los vi pasar en compañía de otros amigos. No tuve valor para seguir la fúnebre traílla hasta el lugar de suplicio' (VI, 1431).

8. The name also recalls the colloquial meaning of *zorra* (María Moliner, 3 'prostituta').

9. For an account of this incident see my forthcoming study 'How Galdós and Baroja Treat History: The Murder of Police-Chief Chico in 1854', to appear in *Forum for Modern Language Studies*.

10. The use of an informal narrator reflecting *la historia chica* is characteristic of Galdós throughout his career. The personification of 'Clío familiar' goes a bit further and may anticipate the changes in narrative pattern found in the later *episodios* of the fifth series. For divergent views on narrative viewpoint, consult Diane Urey, *The Novel Histories of Galdós* (Princeton: Princeton UP, 1989), and my forthcoming book *History and Fiction*.

11. Jover Zamora notes that 'determinadas fuentes contemporáneas atribuyen [*a la reina*] un papel importante en la magnitud de la hecatombe' (p.33). Attributed to O'Donnell is the following eloquent phrase: '¿Pues no ve esa señora que si se fusila a todos los soldados

cogidos, va a derramarse tanta sangre que llegará hasta su alcoba y se ahogará en ella?' (Antonio Ballesteros Baretta, *Historia de España y su influencia en la historia universal* (Barcelona: Salvat, 1936), VIII, 75.

12. The Bakhtinian concept of double-voiced dialogue is applicable here. Consult *The Dialogical Imagination. Four Essays*, transl. by A. Lavera and C. Smith (New York: Hill and Wang, 1968), especially 'Discourse in the Novel', pp.324-31.

13. Montesinos calls the first two chapters 'sainetescos y macabros a la vez en alto grado' (*Galdós 3* (Madrid: Castalia, 1972), p.239).

14. See note 22 below.

15. I take the concept of 'focalization' (and, later, that of prolepsis, 73-74) from Gérard Genette, *Narrative Discourse. An Essay on Method*, trans. by J. E. Lewin (Ithaca: Cornell UP, 1972), pp.189-94.

16. In the *episodio*, Ibero reports O'Donnell's death (5. xi. 1867) at Biarritz to Sagasta (728), and Paúl y Angulo announces Narváez's demise (20. iv. 1868, while still in office) to Ibero (732).

17. For a full account of Confusio's ideal history, see my 'La historia como debiera ser': Galdós's speculations on nineteenth-century Spanish history', *Bulletin of Hispanic Studies*, 69 (1982), 267-74.

18. For the reference to *Richard III* and a contemporary political catchphrase, drawn from a speech made in 1865 by the influential traditionalist politician Antonio Aparisi y Guijarro, see William H. Shoemaker, 'Galdós's *La de los tristes destinos* and its Shakespearian Connections', *Modern Language Notes*, 71 (1956), 114-19.

19. For the differences in historical treatment between the *episodios* and the contemporary novels, see my study '¿Historia novelada o novela histórica? Las diversas estrategias contemporáneas en el tratamiento de la historia de las *Novelas contemporáneas* y los *Episodios nacionales*', in *Galdós y la Historia*, ed. by Peter A. Bly (Ottawa: Dovedale, 1988), pp.167-86.

20. Santiago Ibero is single-minded and simplistic enough in his stubborn pursuit of freedom, but hardly deserves Dendle's characterization as 'of disturbed mind', 'either simple-minded or insane', with a 'faulty perception of reality' and 'a psychological need to place a blind faith in a leader or teacher' (*Galdós: The Mature Thought* (Lexington: University Press of Kentucky, 1980), pp.137-38).

21. A paper of mine on Teresa Villaescusa will appear shortly.

22. *El mundo de Galdós* (Santander: Sociedad Menéndez Pelayo, 1983), pp.109-10.

23. 'Galdós, the Madrid Royal Palace and The September 1868 Revolution', *Revista Canadienses de Estudios Hispánicos*, 5 (1980), 1-17 (p.12).

24. Dendle, *Galdós: The Mature Thought*, p.139.

25. For example, Montesinos (3, 149) and Clara E. Lida, 'Galdós y los *Episodios Nacionales*:

una historia del liberalismo español', *Anales Galdosianos*, 13 (1968), 71.

26. When *España sin rey* began to appear as a serial publication in *El Liberal* (16. i. 1908), it was stated that '[a]l publicarse el año pasado *La de los tristes destinos* experimentaron honda pena los admiradores del gran novelista, entendiendo que éste, después de treinta y tantos años, ponía término definitivo al monumento nacional de los episodios'.

27. The result of the two interviews in Paris with the ex-queen in 1902 and published after her death in 1904 (VI, 1190-96).

28. 'La simpatía por Isabel le hace a Galdós cometer la injusticia de ser condescendente con los matones que la sostenían en el trono' (Antonio Regalado García, *Benito Pérez Galdós y la Novela Histórica Española 1868-1912* (Madrid: Ínsula, 1966), p.426). Compare Raymond Carr, 'A new view of Galdós', *Anales Galdosianos*, 3 (1969), 185-90, who, while admitting 'a great deal of "sentimentalismo ñoño" in Galdós's attitude, claims that 'Galdós was surely partly correct in taking the view that she *was*, to a large extent, a victim of circumstances' (P.185).

29. D. Urey, *The Novel Histories of Galdós*, p.109.

MIRROR OF CHANGE:
THE BLACK IN THE NINETEENTH-CENTURY CUBAN NOVEL[1]

SHARON ROMEO-FIVEL-DÉMORET
University of London

In the early years of the nineteenth century, some Creoles began to see a connection between slavery in Cuba and Spanish domination. Not only was the lucrative slave trade dominated by Spanish merchants, but the metropolitan power relied on Creole fears of uprisings among the large and growing Black population to keep the Ever Faithful Isle dependent on the protection of the Spanish military.[2]

It is therefore not coincidental that the first flowering of the Cuban novel should have grown out of an incipient Creole nationalism, and that the circle most supportive of this nascent *cubanismo* should have produced a unique concentration of novels critical of the slave trade and its consequences (and therefore, implicitly, of the colonial establishment), and featuring significant Black characters.[3] Indeed, with virtually all other avenues for expressing Creole grievances closed by a repressive colonial regime, 'los elementos más activos en la protesta contra Tacón y su sistema fueron los jóvenes escritores de la fracasada Academia Cubana de Literatura'.[4]

The portrayal of the Black in the Cuban novel was thus subject to a number of pressures and influences from the outset. Of these, perhaps the most direct, particularly in the first half of the century was the strict censorship governing all discussions in the press, and according to which public meetings would be outlawed, and mention of the inciting words *slavery* and *independence* would be forbidden, as would any public reference to political reform.[5] The delay between the writing and publication of three of the four novels dealt with in the first section of this study testifies to the efficacy of the system.[6] Interestingly, the areas covered by official censorship as summarized above, tacitly admit a close connection between the issues of slavery and abolition, political reform and independence, and literature.

There was also self-censorship. There is contextual evidence of a conscious awareness on the part of novelists that there were limits to the tolerance of their prospective readership.[7] The textual evidence read in the light of the socio-political conjuncture suggests a largely unconscious incapacity on the part of writers to contemplate certain issues, even within the manipulable confines of fiction.

And since the cultured élite were for the most part avid consumers of foreign literature (both in the original language and in translation), literary fashion also played its part in the fictional portrayal of the Black. Romanticism proved to be the most persistent influence, flourishing in Cuba long after it had begun to decline in Europe.[8]

The above factors were of course affected by social and political developments on the island, especially those related to the institution of slavery. And though the precise form and influence of each would fluctuate, they were to affect the fictional portrayal of the Black throughout the century. This evolution may be divided into three parts. The first ends with the so-called *Conspiración de la Escalera* in 1844.[9] The second stretches from *La Escalera* to the 1878 *Pacto de Zanjón* which ended the first war of independence or Ten Years War, and the third extends from 1879 to the end of the century.[10]

All of the novels in this study that fall within the first period were completed between 1838 and 1839; they are the work of Félix Tanco y Bosmoniel, Anselmo Suárez y Romero, Pedro José Morillas, and Gertrudis Gómez de Avellaneda. They trace the first steps in Cuban self-discovery through the novel, evidencing the influence of Romanticism as well as the *costumbrista*'s almost child-like delight in local detail -- a process of self-discovery that begins the fictional exploration of the value and significance of slavery and the place of the Black in Cuba.

All but the last-mentioned of these authors belonged to a circle of young Creoles revolving round, and guided by Domingo del Monte, a leading liberal Creole of their day and doubtless the most influential man of letters of his time. He was a dedicated Cuban nationalist and reformer, decidedly against the slave trade, but no negrophile or abolitionist.[11]

Not surprisingly, these young novelists follow the lead of their mentor. While critical of the dangers to Whites posed by a steadily growing slave population, and of the negative impact of slavery on Blacks and Whites, their

The Black in the Nineteenth-Century Cuban Novel   243

writing shows them to be reluctant to accept the idea of Black slaves as independent beings, outside the control of Whites, with legitimate desires and actions often conflicting with the role assigned them by the White world. Their Blacks are either passive and submissive to White abuse and authority, or menacing and randomly violent, though nonetheless ultimately subject to White control. It is particularly interesting that these novels were written in a decade which saw a number of significant slave uprisings, and at a time when the authorities paid *ranchadores* to hunt runaway slaves.[12]

The exception to this tendency is Gertrudis Gómez de Avellaneda, a woman, who did not belong to Delmonte's close-knit politico-literary *tertulia*. Her Black hero reflects some personal anxiety about 'el peligro negro', as White Cubans ominously referred to their fears of a re-enactment of Santo Domingo's Black revolution on their own soil. Though Sab rails against the immorality of slavery, he reassures his White confidante that the other slaves bear their lot patiently, and that he will not translate his anger at White oppression into violent rebellion.

Avellaneda evidently cannot allow her Sab actually to threaten White society with which she understandably identifies. In this she is rather like her contemporaries, and in fact proves less willing than they to write about the more violent and decadent aspects of Cuban society. However, of the four works of this period, hers is the most radical. Whereas the others tend to focus their criticism on the gross abuses of slavery, she attacks directly the principles underpinning the institution itself. Avellaneda's Black hero reflects much of the independent spirit of his creator, a woman whose intellectual interests challenged contemporary ideas on the proper role of women. The portrayal of Sab is also affected by the fact that his creator was free to publish in Spain, and unlike Delmonte's protegées, was not constrained either by peer pressure or by official censorship.[13]

The 1840s were to mark the beginning of a long silence on controversial Black issues in the aftermath of the Escalera repression. Until censorship began to ease, the available evidence suggests that no novelist dared deal critically with the subject of slavery in Cuba. *El Ranchador*, the work which, of those considered thus far, is most hostile to Blacks and supportive of White dominance, was not published until 1856.

The second period (1845-78) saw the emergence of two novelists featuring principal Black protagonists. Francisco Calcagno and Antonio Zambrana both mark a movement away from Romanticism, towards a rather crude realism in the former, and a precocious quasi *modernismo* in the latter case.[14]

Thanks to the censor, both *Los crímenes de Concha* and *Romualdo: uno de tantos*, were published many years after completion -- the former more than twenty years.[15] Zambrana's novel, written and published in Chile during the Ten Years War, is highly critical of slavery and its most tenacious supporters, Cuba's Spanish-dominated saccharocracy.

Both novelists insist that the institution of slavery must end because it is out-dated and intrinsically unjust, and this in terms that would have been inconceivable for all of the previous generation of novelists, with the exception of Gómez de Avellaneda. But a call for abolition means recognizing Blacks as free agents, whose experiences will have given them a perspective quite different from their erstwhile masters.

Both works reveal varying degrees of ambivalence about Blacks as the equals of Whites. Zambrana suggests at one point that an African world view is a valid and equal alternative to the predominant Eurocentric one. Yet elsewhere he contrasts his African-born hero and near-White heroine as representatives of barbarism and civilization respectively (3 and 135). Furthermore, his novel reveals him to be undecided as to whether Cuba's Black (and in particular, mulatto) women were generally the objects of White male sexual exploitation, or whether White men were victims of irresistible (and therefore slightly sinister) Black feminine charms.

But Zambrana is on the whole more inclined to a sanguine acceptance, and even celebration of Black humanity, dignity and beauty: his handsome slave hero is, in every sense, very self-possessed, proud of his African heritage, unimpressed by alleged White superiority.[16] This respect for things Black may perhaps be partly due to Zambrana's close involvement in the Ten Years War in which many slaves and free Blacks participated, and which saw the prominence of outstanding Black figures like Antonio Maceo.[17]

Also significant is the fact that *El negro Francisco* was written during the author's stay in Chile, the main aim of which was to raise moral and material support for the rebel cause. He thus presents abolition as the main motivation of the Cuban rebels, conveniently glossing over the fact that slavery was a most divisive issue among the revolutionary forces.[18] For as he admits in an *apologia* of their cause published two years before *El negro*: 'una guerra social en nombre de un principio humano, es más respetable que una guerra nacional en nombre de un principio político'.[19]

It is therefore not surprising that, unlike Calcagno, he should wish not only to draw attention to the miserable conditions of Cuba's slaves, but more importantly, that he should create a slave hero and heroine who are recognizably and believably human, yet sympathetic, admirable in every way, and not merely sorry victims. Moreover, their nobility is set against the gross racism and materialism of their owners, who seem to represent the anti-independence, pro-colonialist White slavist interests that so undermined the rebel cause.[20]

Calcagno's novels reveal him to have been a man who saw abolition as an economic and moral imperative, but also as one who contemplates the free Black with a mixture of pity, fear, and even hostility, reflected in the depiction of Blacks in his novels as physically grotesque, inherently barbaric and atavistic except when guided by Whites. He thus represents a point of tension in contemporary Creole society.

On one hand, *de facto* partial abolition brought about through the Ten Years War and its aftermath, combined with the increasingly persuasive economic arguments against slavery, had led an increasing number of slavists to accept --and even desire-- a move to a more modern system based on free labour. On the other hand, centuries of negrophobic propaganda had left many Whites quite incapable of accepting their ex-slaves as equal fellow citizens, and possessed of an almost pathological fear of large numbers of Blacks no longer rigidly controlled by them. More to the point, many feared the labour shortage that would result from Black freedom if this were not managed in such a way as to ensure a continued cheap supply of labour.[21]

Hence Calcagno's production of novels that attack the institution of slavery as well as White cruelty and ingratitude to the creators of their wealth. At the same time he polarizes his Black characters, so that good Blacks are those who suffer uncomplainingly and remain under White tutelage (and therefore available as submissive workers), while bad Blacks are those who do not accept White control: runaways and criminals, or savages who cling to African customs.

The immediate aftermath of the *Pacto de Zanjón* marks the beginning of the third and final period. Though slavery officially ended in 1886, the end of the Ten Years War sealed its inevitable decline. The easing of censorship over the years testifies to the profound change in attitudes over the century regarding the slavery issue: of the three novels relevant to this study published between 1878 and the end of the century, two were published in Cuba, and the third in New York where the author lived as a political exile because of his anti-colonial political activity.[22]

It is noteworthy that of the three novels in this section, only one, Ramón Meza's *Carmela*, is set in contemporary, post-slavery Cuba. At first, the sharp criticism of slave abuse in the work of Villaverde and Morúa Delgado (1882 and 1891 respectively) strikes one as belated or even irrelevant; but it soon becomes apparent that slavery, as such, is not the primary issue in either case.

Villaverde voices a nationalist viewpoint according to which the cruelties inflicted on Black slaves were mainly attributable to the corrupting influence of Spanish colonial rule. More significantly, though his novel is set in the early years of the century, his principal Black protagonists are not slaves, but free. Through their experiences, he analyses the divisive effect on the whole of Cuban society (both Black and White) of the caste system promoted by slave-trading interests as a means of reinforcing both slavery and colonial control. He warns of the explosive potential of the distorsions, frustrations and contradictions created by it, especially among ambitious mulattoes.

Thus the almost-white Cecilia rejects the African aspect of her ancestry, yet is rejected by Whites, and though desired as a mistress, she is not considered by her White lover to be good enough to marry.[23] Her consequent desire for vengeance leads to the tragic dénouement of the novel. José Dolores, the instrument of her revenge, is motivated by anger and frustration at the social and emotional limits imposed on him for no other reason than that he is Black. He is warned by another mulatto friend Uribe that his impatience will lead him to a bad end, and that it would be better to follow his example: 'Haz como el perro con las avispas, enseñar los dientes, para que crean que te ríes' (73).[24] José Dolores insists that he does not mind a violent

The Black in the Nineteenth-Century Cuban Novel   247

end as long as he manages to hurt some of his White oppressors in the process.

Though Villaverde's most famous novel shows him to be attuned to the frustrations of Cuba's mulattoes, his portrayal of the desperate José Dolores and the ambitious but more cunning and almost sinister Uribe suggests a certain fear of their class which he seemed to perceive as a potential threat to White Cubans. Like many of his fellow White liberals, the author of *Cecilia Valdés*, while ideologically hostile (and no doubt sincerely so) to the racially-based caste system into which he was born, betrays an ingrained racial bias against Blacks.

At the same time, the novel as a whole reveals him to be among those who recognized that Cuban society must undergo profound and sustained changes in order to survive in a competitive modern world, and that this required the subversion of old hierarchies and the development of new social and power relationships between Blacks and their ex-masters.

Carmela testifies to many of the tensions and anxieties of the decade in which Meza's novel was written, an 'época de desaliento y pesimismo que fue agravándose en el transcurso de los años subsiguientes [de la Guerra de los Diez Años] hasta el estallido de la guerra de 1895'.[25] In particular, the experiences of his mulatto heroine combine a picture of the demoralization and precarious finances of a section of the established Creole élite with an *exposé* of the persistence and pernicious nature of racism in post-abolition Cuba.

But, like the creations of other writers studied so far, Meza's Black protagonists reflect their creator's 'doble personalidad'.[26] Carmela and her mother are portrayed as the victims of petty racial discrimination, yet, confusingly, it is implied that their downfall may in part be blamed on their pathetic attempts to challenge or circumvent Cuba's rigid caste system. The subversive tendencies of their black servant Tocineta are defused by his portrayal as a semi-comical character whose anger against the system is kept in check by his love for Carmela. Meza seems to be torn between sympathy for the plight of oppressed Blacks (informed by a relatively radical world view), and empathy with his own caste (driven by a cautious conservatism and latent racism).[27]

The mulatto Martín Morúa Delgado is the only Black of all the writers considered in this study. Though appearing five years after the official end of slavery, his novel *Sofía* nonetheless identifies slavery as the central reference point for all issues connected to relations between Blacks and Whites in post-slavery Cuba. He uses the situation of his Black heroine to argue passionately that the problems facing Blacks in post-abolition Cuba are not attributable to the alleged genetic deficiences of Blacks, but to the legacy and warping experience of generations of slavery.

Aimed mainly at liberal White Cubans, his novel *Sofía* warns influential Whites of the dangers of taking Black forgiveness for granted, of ignoring the symptoms of imminent social collapse, persuading themselves that 'mientras el mal se desarrollaba allá abajo, acá arriba no habría motivos de preocupación', refusing to help 'los desheredados de todo por todos' until 'el mal llegaba hasta arriba' (137).

He challenges those who cannot or will not accept that Black Cubans are capable of contributing anything but brute force to Cuban society, insisting that with minimal (but vital) assistance Blacks are capable of catching up with their White compatriots, and that their integration is not a charitable, liberal option, but a *sine qua non* of future White survival and happiness.

Ironically, in his anxiety to arouse pity for the principal victims of slavery and its aftermath, as well as to generate constructive guilt on the part of White decision-makers, Morúa Delgado, like so many of his White predecessors falls into the trap of creating all-powerful masters and a monotonously and unbelievably passive Black heroine. In short, he allows political preoccupations to override aesthetic considerations.

In spite of its brevity, it is no doubt evident from the above discussion that in many ways, the novels considered in this study are not really *about* Blacks, as such; rather, racial issues seem to have provided successive generations of thinking Cubans with an arena in which to discuss the nature of Cuban society, and their hopes and fears concerning its future.

Thus the novelists of the first period present Black characters that reflect, often unintentionally, the principal concerns of a growing number of thinking Cubans for whom a Black population swelled by a flourishing slave trade posed a multiple threat: a cheap and plentiful supply of Black slaves meant costly delays in the modernization of the sugar industry in particular, the progressive brutalization of both Blacks and Whites, and the continued presence of Spanish troops purportedly to protect Cuba's Whites from the threat of a successful Haitian-style Black uprising. Overall, their fictional Blacks provide assurance that oppressed Blacks are either too passive to revolt, or else easily dispatched if they do. The Whites with whom they are contrasted, generally confirm the moral bankruptcy of the colonial system and its supporters, and the superiority of the patriotic Cuban world view.

After a long silence, the second period produces fictional Blacks whose portrayal poses questions many of which are related to the nature and potential influence of a distinct Black culture and perspective, questions regarding the fitness of the survivors of centuries of deliberately dehumanizing practices for what is now seen as an inevitable freedom. Are political and personal autonomy indivisible, or are they the inalienable right of Whites alone?[28] Is there such a thing as a Black Cuban culture, and if there is, does it have anything positive to contribute to a modernizing Cuba? Are the two races so intrinsically antagonistic that they can never function as equals in a post-abolition Cuba? How should Whites respond to the social and economic challenges posed by the final years of slavery?

The last three authors continue the discussion of the causes of, and solutions to, racial conflict and its implications for the present and future peaceful development of Cuban society. The Black creations of the White novelists reveal a lingering inability to accept as full equals the Black slaves and marginals of yesterday. Those of the sole Black novelist reveal a profound understanding of the socio-political, economic and emotional underpinnings of racial conflict, but they suffer from his over-eagerness to contribute both to the advancement of Blacks and Black racial pride, and to the racial integration of Cuban society.

But for all their short-comings, the works of this final group of writers, like those of their predecessors, suggest, overall, a rejection of the ideas of many of their contemporaries who either tried (in print at least) to ignore 'el problema negro', or dreamt of white-washing Cuba (thus solving all its social problems at a stroke), particularly through the enforced 'repatriation' of 'Africans' whether *ladino* or *bozal*.[29] In a century when for the most part, Blacks were practically invisible in Cuban letters,[30] the very existence of works featuring significant Black figures is worthy of note. They constitute a step, however halting and ambivalent, towards the recognition of the pivotal role of Blacks in the process of inventing a unique Cuban identity.

NOTES

1. This study is a revised version of a paper: 'Images du Noir: reflets des peurs et espoirs de la société cubaine du 19ème siècle', presented at *L'Histoire des sociétés coloniales antillaises*, a conference held at the École des Hautes Études en Sciences Sociales, Paris, 18-19 October, 1990.

2. 'Black' and 'White' indicate the official or publicly accepted caste of characters, while 'black' / 'white' refer to their observable colour or phenotype. A 'Creole' is a Cuban-born White.

3. For a very thorough study of the social, political, and economic context of the genesis of the Cuban novel, see Michèle Guicharnaud-Tollis, *L'émergence du Noir dans le roman cubain du XIXe siècle* (Paris: Editions Harmattan, 1991), pp.47-84.

4. Ramiro Guerra y Sánchez, *Manual de historia de Cuba: desde su descubrimiento hasta 1868* (Havana: Instituto Cubano del Libro, 1971) p.360. The 'Academia Cubana de Literatura' was set up by Cuban liberals in 1834 and dissolved in 1838, principally because of the hostility of Miguel Tacón (Captain General of Cuba from 1834 to 1837) and others suspicious that it was a cover for separatist propaganda and activity.

5. Arthur F. Corwin, *Spain and the Abolition of Slavery in Cuba, 1817-1886* (Austin: University of Texas Press, 1967), p.44. See also Raúl Cepero Bonilla, *Azúcar y abolición* (Havana: Instituto Cubano del Libro, 1971), p.29.

6. Anselmo Suárez y Romero, *Francisco* (Havana: Editorial Letras Cubanas 1970; manuscript completed in 1839, but first published in New York: Imprenta Nestor Ponce de León, 1880); Félix Tanco y Bosmoniel, *Petrona y Rosalía* (Havana: Editorial Letras Cubanas, 1980; completed in 1838, rediscovered and first published in *Cuba contemporánea*, 39 (1925); Pedro José Morillas, *El ranchador* in *Noveletas cubanas* ed. by Imeldo lvarez García (Havana: Editorial Arte y Literatura, 1974; completed in 1839 and published in Havana: *La piragua*, 1856); Gertrudis Gómez de Avellaneda, *Sab* (Havana: Instituto Cubano del Libro, 1973; completed in 1839 and published in Madrid: Imprenta Calle del Barco, 1841). As far as possible, references in this study are to more easily available editions.

7. In a letter to Suárez y Romero dated 17 November 1838, his *contertuliano* José Zacarías González del Valle, discusses some of del Monte's critical observations on *Francisco* and passes on a few words of advice. The following is an extract from his closing comments: 'No es, pues [*Francisco*], un escrito incendiario, porque nos falta buena dosis de prudencia y vemos que por desgracia hay que conciliar extremos opuestos: en su ignorancia misma, aunque se quiera no podría circular, sino entre los que alguna parte pueden tener en que vayan neutralizándose algún tanto los efectos de la esclavitud doméstica' (José Zacarías González del Valle, *La vida literaria en Cuba (1836-1840)*, Cuadernos de Cultura: Cuarta Serie, 5 (Havana: Dirección de Cultura, 1938) 91-94 (p.94)).

8. For a discussion of the relationship between socio-political context and Romanticism in Latin America (including Brazil), see Emilio Carilla, *El romanticismo en la América Hispánica* (Madrid: Editorial Gredos, 1958).

9. *La Escalera* saw the execution of Blacks (both slave and free) and the exile of Whites accused of involvement in an alleged plot to overthrow colonial rule with the aid of orchestrated slave uprisings.

10. This study includes only those novels featuring one or more Blacks as significant players, or else as the actual or avowed principal protagonist(s).

11. By abolitionist I mean anyone who desired an immediate or very prompt end to slavery. I do not include those who, while critical of the excesses of the system, or even sometimes hostile to the institution in principle, were nonetheless not in favour of prompt abolition (usually for economic reasons).

12. A *ranchador*, *rancheador*, or *arranchador* was a licensed bounty hunter of slaves. See Manuel Moreno Fraginals, *El ingenio*, 3 vols (Havana: Editorial de Ciencias Sociales, 1978), I, 287-88.

13. It was at the time not uncommon for material to be published without hindrance in Spain, yet banned in Cuba where it was felt that the island's 'special circumstances' (i.e. slavery-based economy) needed to be protected from subversive criticism. Indeed, a shipment of copies of *Sab* was refused entry into Cuba in 1844 (See Edith Kelly, 'La Avellaneda's *Sab* and the Political Situation in Cuba', *The Americas*, 1 (July 1944-April 1945), 303-16. According to two orders imposing the ban (published on pp.350-53 of the above issue of *The Americas*), the novel was unacceptable in Cuba because it contained 'doctrinas contrarias al sistema de esclavitud'. See also Guerra y Sánchez, pp.343-44.

14. Francisco Calcagno, *Los crímenes de Concha*, (completed in 1864, first published in Havana: Elías F. Casona, 1887) and *Romualdo: uno de tantos*, in *Noveletas cubanas*, ed. by Imeldo Álvarez García (Havana: Editorial Arte y Literatura, 1974; completed 1869, first published in Havana: Imprenta del Avisador Comercial, 1881); Antonio Zambrana, *El negro Francisco* (Havana: Letras Cubanas, 1979; first published in Santiago de Chile in 1875). For a discussion of precociously *modernista* aspects of Zambrana's writing, see Salvador Bueno, 'Prólogo' to *El negro Francisco*, pp.7-17 (p.12).

15. As late as 1881 there existed a 'Ley de Imprenta' which 'specifically forbade writers to "defend or expound doctrines contrary to the organization of the family and property", or to excite the animosity of one class against another'; in short, 'the question of slavery remained alive, even after the establishment of the *patronato*' (Rebecca Scott, *Slave Emancipation in Cuba: the Transition to Free Labour, 1860-1899* (Princeton: University Press, 1985), p.136). The *patronato* was conceived as a ten year period of apprenticeship imposed on slaves in place of the payment of indemnity to slave-holders. This period of transition between slavery and freedom, begun in 1880, was eventually ended in 1886.

16. See G.R. Coulthard, *Race and Colour in Caribbean Literature* (London: Oxford University Press, 1962), p.14.

17. Antonio Maceo, a mulatto, participated in the Ten Years War. In the 1890s, Maceo, José Martí and Máximo Gómez were to become 'the outstanding men of the Cuban Independence movement' (Hugh Thomas, *Cuba or the Pursuit of Freedom* (London: Eyre and Spottiswoode, 1971), p.255).

18. See Cepero Bonilla, *Azúcar y abolición*, pp.141-56.

19. Antonio Zambrana, *La república de Cuba* (New York: Imprenta Ponce de León, 1873), p.29.

20. See Cepero Bonilla, pp.179-96.

21. For a discussion of the many measures contemplated and sometimes resorted to by Cuba's *hacendados* to ensure a plentiful and regular supply of labour, particularly as they began to confront the inevitability of abolition, see Moreno Fraginals (I, 287-309).

22. Cirilio Villaverde, *Cecilia Valdés* (Mexico: Editorial Porrúa, 1979; first published in New York: Imprenta El Espejo, 1882); Ramón Meza y Suárez Inclán, *Carmela* (Havana: Editorial de Arte y Literatura, 1978; first published in Havana: La Propaganda Literaria, 1887); Martín Morúa Delgado, *Sofía* (Havana: Instituto Cubano del Libro, 1972; first published in Havana, 1891).

23. For an excellent discussion of this phenomenon of racial and sexual politics which was widespread in nineteenth-century Cuban society, see Reynaldo González, *Contradanzas y latigazos* (Havana: Editorial Letras Cubanas, 1983), pp.124-47.

24. Uribe, a fashionable tailor, is (like most of the characters in the novel) based on a historical figure, a mulatto who was executed during the Escalera repression.

25. Manuel González Freixas, *Sociedad y tipos en las novelas de Ramón Meza y Suárez Inclán* (Miami: Ediciones Universal, 1985), p.35.

26. Ernesto García Alzola, 'Prólogo' to *Novelas Breves: el duelo de mi vecino; Don Aniceto el tendero; Últimas páginas* (Havana: Editorial Arte y Literatura, 1975), p.10.

27. See Dr. Evelio Rodríguez Lendían, *Elogio del Dr. Ramón Meza y Suárez Inclán, individuo de número* (Havana: Imprenta El Siglo XX, 1915), p.44.

28. This is the continuation of a debate begun by Cuban thinkers of an earlier period. See Guerra y Sánchez, pp.390-94.

29. A *ladino* was a Cuban-born Black. Blacks born in Africa were known as *bozales*.

30. See José Antonio Fernández de Castro, 'El aporte negro en las letras de Cuba', *Revista Bimestre Cubana*, 38, 1 (July-August 1936), 46-66, and *El tema negro en las letras de Cuba (1608-1935)* (Havana: Editores Mirador, 1943).

TRISTE FIM DE POLICARPO QUARESMA
AND THE SHADOW OF SPENCERISM

R. J. OAKLEY
University of Birmingham

Lima Barreto's most celebrated novel, *Triste Fim de Policarpo Quaresma*, has a protagonist with a set of ideals and values that are not shared by the vast majority of those around him. Major Policarpo Quaresma lives with his devoted sister Adelaide in a quiet street in the suburbs of Rio de Janeiro. Here he receives a popular composer and guitarist, Ricardo Coração dos Outros, who gives him guitar lessons; and here, too, on returning each day from his office in the Ministry of War, he pursues his patriotic studies. Convinced that Brazil is a country without peer, his historical, geological, geographical and anthropological studies are aimed at confirming his fervent belief. So totally absorbing and manic does his patriotic obsession become that he unconsciously translates an official document into the Brazilian-Amerindian language, Tupi-guarani (he no longer regards Portuguese as sufficiently Brazilian to be the official language of his country) and the document ends up on the desk of the Minister of War himself. Hounded from his job and prematurely retired, Major Quaresma suffers a severe but temporary mental illness. When he recovers, his goddaughter Olga persuades him to retire to the country. There his obsessive patriotism takes the form of an experiment to prove the exceptional fertility of Brazil.

Osman Lins has noted, besides the extreme isolation of Lima Barreto's protagonists, their peculiar passivity.[1] Given the above summary of the early chapters of this novel, this may sound strange. Nevertheless, despite his frenetic activity, Quaresma's fate hangs on the decisions of others. Olga Coleoni is instrumental in sending him to the country. Later, his return to Rio in order to aid Marshal Floriano Peixoto in his campaign to put down the Naval Revolt of 1893 when the pro-monarchist navy turned its guns on the city of Rio de Janeiro, is dictated less by his admiration for the person of the so-called *Marechal de Ferro* than by the succession of reverses he has experienced on the land. He does not exactly enlist as a volunteer in the Iron Marshal's army but finds himself personally invited to do so by the dictator himself. Fearful of irritating Floriano, he accepts. His role in the ensuing civil war is an assumed stance. Quaresma had seen his youthful military ambitions frustrated on health grounds. He made up for it by entering the Ministry of War as a civilian:

> Era onde estava bem. No meio de soldados, de canhões, de veteranos, de papelada inçada de quilos de pólvora, de nomes de fuzis e termos técnicos de artilharia, aspirava diariamente aquele hálito de guerra, de bravura, de vitória, de triunfo, que é bem o hálito da Pátria.[2]

A mild flirtation with the National Guard had earned him the title of major to which he had no right. This form of address had stuck over the years and Quaresma, after initial protests, assented to it. Suddenly, he finds himself transformed into a real major in Floriano's army.

One of the main factors in the fall of the Brazilian monarchy had been the entry into politics of the army. After the Paraguayan War ended in 1870, the army ceased to be a passive political force domesticated by the politicians. Instead, it began to carry its new-found pride and sense of professionalism into the political arena, together with a conscious mission to save the country.[3] This new force in Brazilian politics came to identify itself with a rising urban, middle class in a still massively agricultural society that remained monarchical and anti-militaristic. João Cruz Costa describes the gulf that lay between these two powers:

> A monarquia agrária, impregnada de civilismo, não quis ou não soube captar a nova força, para a qual também não contribuíram os filhos da aristocracia produtora de algodão, açúcar e café.[4]

The army in 1889 represented a force for change not only of regime but also of economic and social structures. The radical young officers from the Military Academy of Rio de Janeiro (acidly described in *Triste Fim* as inflexible practitioners of Comte's Religion of Humanity) were its most vociferous element. To this radical wing of the army the urban middle class allied itself after the military coup of 15 November 1889 which deposed

Triste Fim de Policarpo Quaresma and the Shadow of Spencerism   257

Emperor Pedro II. They did so in order to prevent the ruling Establishment of the old rural oligarchy from closing its ranks and returning to power. It is doubtful if Afonso Henriques de Lima Barreto, future novelist barely into his teens, realized at the time the significance of the struggle going on beneath the anarchy and civil war of the years 1889-95, but his decision to place Policarpo Quaresma's one-man patriotic crusade exactly in the period culminating in Marshal Floriano Peixoto's dictatorship (1892-94) makes manifest his social and political awareness when he came to write *Triste Fim* in 1911. Quaresma's failure to make any significant impact whatsoever on what Lima Barreto evidently realized to be a key question, that of the land and agrarian reform, culminates in the disillusionment regarding Marshal Floriano and the revolutionary power of the *florianista* movement.

Lima Barreto had chosen his historical setting well. The resignation of Marshal Deodoro da Fonseca from the Provisional Government at the end of 1891 after his abortive coup, gave power to his deputy, Floriano Vieira Peixoto, who, when faced with a manifesto signed by a group of generals on 31 March 1892, dismissed and forcibly retired them, assuming dictatorial powers and issuing his own manifesto. In this way he began creating his legend of *Consolidador da República*. Of these generals, Floriano declared:

> Todos eles revelam, porém, um inconveniente espírito de indisciplina, procurando implantar a anarquia no momento crítico da reorganização da Pátria e da consolidação das instituições republicanas...[5]

Lima Barreto will opine causticamente in chapter twelve of his political satire *Os Bruzundangas* (written in 1917 and published posthumously in 1923) concerning the national heroes of Brazil, that the legendary Consolidator of the Republic consolidated nothing. Lima's observations here are revealing as confirmation of the mainsprings of *Triste Fim*. In *Os Bruzundangas* he judges the Iron Marshal to have flouted all the laws of the new regime he purported to champion:

> Entender-se-ia que a havia consolidado se o seu governo fosse fecundo dentro das leis da Bruzundanga. (VII, 105)

Fruitfulness and energy, or lack of them, are the two key structural ideas in *Triste Fim*.[6] Marshal Floriano's dictatorship, like Quaresma's agricultural experiment, is seen as bearing no fruit; neither does his government have that energy to which the major conspicuously exhorts him in the telegram he sends from his country retreat in Curuzu. Instead of the reign of enlightened despotism for which Quaresma had hoped, there emerges a reign of mediocrity and terror; and even this is an unspectacular terror that is 'baço, sem coragem, sangrento, às ocultas, sem grandeza, sem desculpa, sem razão e sem responsabilidades' (II, 192).

The whole of the third and final part of *Triste Fim de Policarpo Quaresma* describing Marshal Floriano's defence of Rio against a disaffected rebel navy is structured around the expectations of various classes -- expectations of which Floriano himself is seen by his supporters as the embodiment. The most intelligent of the *florianistas* saw clearly the crucial nature of the historical moment. Political power throughout these turbulent years right up to the First World War 'estava nas mãos de grupos oligárquicos e as pessoas que estavam no poder preocupavam-se ... com o desenvolvimento econômico num sentido restrito, porém, desejavam que esse desenvolvimento ocorresse sem nenhuma mudança da estrutura social da qual eles eram os privilegiados'.[7] These conservative forces under the Empire were closely allied with foreign, economic imperialism, especially with regard to Brazil as a source of raw, tropical products.[8] The temporary triumph of *florianismo* marked a threat to this alliance and to the continued preponderance of the old rural oligarchy.[9] The end of Floriano's rule in November 1894 and his death in the middle of the following year would mark the end of the possibility of change that inspired that radical exaltation expressed, for example, by Raul Pompéia in his preface to *Festas Nacionais* by Rodrigo Otávio. The author of *O Ateneu* invests Floriano with the mantle of great statesman and messiah fighting against foreign exploiters. The *florianista* movement that for a period of approximately two years ruled in Rio de Janeiro (the mainstay of it were the young positivist officers represented in *Triste Fim* by the sympathetic figure of Lieutenant Fontes) flaunted the form of radical democracy expressed in Pompéia's preface. The positivist wing of the army was an anarchic mixture of tyranny and populist democracy. Lima Barreto's novel condemns it for the same reason as it condemns Floriano the brutish patriot, and, in the final analysis, Policarpo Quaresma himself in his bookish nationalism: for a vagueness of ideals that work towards no precise goal simply because such men are unwilling to lay hold of the wider crisis. The idealism and energy of Lieutenant Fontes contrast grotesquely with Lima Barreto's portrait of Floriano. The exaltation of Raul Pompéia in his essay penned during the seige of Rio by Admiral Custódio de Melo's fleet combines a patriotic fervour with the energy Quaresma shows and Brazil needs. The reality that Raul Pompéia glimpses is submerged in exalted, hyperbolic rhetoric as he recalls the fall of the Empire:

> O dia 15 é um incalculável passo de progresso: sintetisa todos os ímpetos de vitalidade histórica do nosso passado; resume numa só tormenta demolidora todas as dispersas auras de esperança que um dia respirarão os mais diletos filhos desta terra.[10]

In *Triste Fim de Policarpo Quaresma*, Lieutenant Fontes is the personification of the exalted Florianist positivist. He sums up their tragedy -- a tragedy as great as Quaresma's; for like him, the *florianistas* cherish their own brand of sincere, well-meaning utopianism that leads nowhere. The narrator tells us that Fontes was a good man 'e até generoso, mas era positivista e tinha da sua República uma idéia religiosa e transcendente. Fazia repousar nela toda a felicidade humana' (II, 94). His horizons are limited. He merely hates the rebels in Guanabara Bay and sees Floriano as the sword of righteous retribution. As for the *Marechal de Ferro* himself, Lima Barreto uses Floriano to add depth as well as breadth to Quaresma's tragedy through the expectations deposited in the dictator by a series of individuals: the bellicose Fontes; the equally idealistic but mild Quaresma; General Albernaz, racked by financial difficulties and needing a renewal of his commission in order to finance his daughter Lala's dowry; Admiral Caldas who desperately seeks command of a ship; Major Bustamante who seeks promotion to colonel; Genelício, the careerist administrator who aims at promotion in the Civil Service; and finally Olga Coleoni's husband Dr Armando Borges, who has set his sights on a chair in the Faculty of Medicine. Significantly, Lieutenant Fontes, like Quaresma, disappears from view in the closing pages of the novel.

The future belongs to the new, bureaucratic generation: Genelício wins his subdirectorship; Borges will undoubtedly get his chair; and Bustamante, the officer who leads his men from the safety of his office, duly becomes a colonel. Victory over the rebels signifies victory for those who are intent on living off the State. The complexion that Lima Barreto gives to Floriano's triumph over the Naval Revolt in 1894 reflects yet again his belief in the bankruptcy of all utopian philosophies, here represented on one hand by Policarpo Quaresma's naïve patriotism, and on the other, by Florianist positivism. It also betrays Lima Barreto as the assiduous reader of nineteenth-century post-idealist moral and social philosophy -- especially that of Herbert Spencer.

The attraction of Spencer's social and political ideas for Lima Barreto is very evident in *Triste Fim de Policarpo Quaresma*, given the obviously anti-positivist satire that abounds in the novel. Like much of the more sceptical moral and socio-political thought of the mid- and late-nineteenth century, Spencer's writings are a reaction against Comtean positivism. In his *Cours de philosophie positive* (1830-42), Auguste Comte had propounded a highly schematic Science of Society based on eighteenth-century French doctrines of progress. Just as the major branches of science, maths, physics, chemistry, biology and the like have emerged in history, he averred, in a strict order terminating with the science of sociology, so do human civilization and society pass through clearly defined stages. According to Comte's Law of Three Stages, the Religious Stage has given way to the Abstract or Metaphysical Stage by modern times. The Metaphysical Stage in turn will be replaced, finally, by the Positive or Scientific Stage. Seen against a background of such a process and progress, philosophy's true thrust is social: to work towards the reorganization of the moral, religious and political systems obtaining in the so-called civilized world. Improvement of the social organism can and will take place, but only when there is moral development. Revolution and wealth redistribution will not do the trick alone. According to this utopian view, altruism must triumph over egoism. When this happens, the Religion of Humanity shall reign. At the Positive Stage, humanity becomes the Great Being and dispenser of destinies. A similar stance was developed in England by John Stuart Mill in his *System of Logic* (1843).

As a young man, Herbert Spencer, like many of his generation, was attracted to and inspired by the ideas of Comte; but in his vast *Synthetic Philosophy* which he began preparing in the 1850s, Spencer developed an anti-utopian riposte to Comtean positivism. Spencer's *First Principles*, comprising the introductory volumes of *Synthetic Philosophy*, provides the theoretical base for the ensuing survey and analysis of the sciences and human society. In part two of *First Principles*, Spencer conceives the idea of society as an organic whole made up of individuals -- a body 'consolidated' (Spencer's word is 'integration') by the myriad of individuals that comprise it.[11] A period of unstable equilibrium, he warns, will be followed by often violent dissolution.[12] Moreover, the ideal of the greatest amount of freedom possible for the individual is here adumbrated.

The goal of this organic whole, then, is the achieving for the individual of maximum freedom; but on the other hand, in later volumes of *Synthetic Philosophy*, Spencer sees the State as something alien to society, and consequently, existing at the expense of the individual as well. One can see here how Lima Barreto and young radicals like him in Brazil at the end of the nineteenth century, attracted in any case to anarchism, could find comfort in the author of *First Principles* and *The Man Versus the State*. Ideally, Spencer argues, the State should be destroyed, although he knows this will not happen.

Spencer and his disciples had no trust in utopian philosophies. In his *Principles of Sociology*, being volumes six to eight of *Synthetic Philosophy*, Spencer divided society into two types: 'industrial' and 'militant'. In the case of the former, society is subordinate to the individual; and in the case of the latter, the roles are reversed.[13] The chief characteristics of Spencer's industrial society are a greater degree of individual freedom, a diminished respect for government, decrease of patriotism, an increase in the individual's faith in himself or herself, and a marked respect for the individuality of others. The chief characteristics of a militant society, on the other hand, are polar opposites of the above: severe restrictions on individual freedom; subservience to the State; and significantly in the present context, the presence of a fierce patriotism and a marked tendency towards a regimentation of civilian life together with an interpenetration of civilian and military sectors of society.[14] Such a society is born, according to Spencer, in a country that acquires the habit of living on a war footing. Spencer, of course, had in mind Imperial Germany in the closing decades of the nineteenth century and, by the time of the Boer War, the British Empire as well.

Lima Barreto saw the ingredients of such a society in the militarist expansionism and re-arming of Brazil in the first years of the Republic. For *civilistas* like Lima, the process reached its apogee in the democratic assumption of the presidency by Marshal Hermes da Fonseca in the elections of 1910 which would provide the political backdrop to the narrative of his next novel, *Numa e a Ninfa* (1917). His description and interpretation of this phenomenon within the regime that replaced the Empire find beguiling expression in *Triste Fim de Policarpo Quaresma*, which treats precisely of the confirmation of the army's permanent establishment in political life with Marshal Deodoro's coup in November 1889 and Marshal Floriano's subsequent dictatorship. Spencer observes tersely:

> Among the uncivilized there is a marked tendency for the military chief to become also the political.[15]

Pace the ambiguity in the word 'uncivilized', this remark is a truism today and will provoke a wry smile among Hispanists, native as well as foreign, who have meditated upon the course of Ibero-American history since the early nineteenth century. These words were certainly far less of a truism when Spencer wrote them. His analysis of the phenomenon in *Principles of Sociology*, moreover, is detailed and impressive. Furthermore, Floriano's dictatorship in the Brazil of the early 1890s exemplifies Spencer's theory with an uncanny accuracy not lost on Lima Barreto, just as it was not lost on the Brazilian monarchist, writer and diplomat, Joaquim Nabuco, whose *Balmaceda*, written during the Naval Revolt, emphasizes Floriano's disdain for civilian institutions and individuals representing those institutions during his dictatorship:

> Ao lado da tenacidade do soldado há que lembrar a sua impassibilidade, mais extraordinária ainda --a sua inércia, pode-se dizer--, capaz de lançar nos cubículos da Correcção, como nos Pombi e nos Pozzi de uma outra Veneza, os seus ministros da véspera, os seus camaradas de Paraguai, presidentes de província sob quem servira, os seus colegas do Governo Provisório, senadores e deputados que o elegeram ou

Triste Fim de Policarpo Quaresma and the Shadow of Spencerism 263

conspiraram com ele, os seus amigos de todas as épocas, sem que se soubesse a súplica capaz de o mover.[16]

The Paraguayan War and the fall of the Brazilian monarchy were followed by civil war (1891-95). Spencer had described how 'continued militancy is followed by further development of the militant organization'.[17] Of the cadets from the Escola Militar of Rio de Janeiro, the narrator in *Triste Fim* remarks:

> Tinham todos os privilégios e todos os direitos; precediam ministros nas entrevistas com o ditador e abusavam dessa situação de esteio de Sila, para oprimir e vexar a cidade inteira.
> Uns trapos de positivismo se tinham colado naquelas inteligências e uma religiosidade especial brotara-lhes no sentimento, transformando a autoridade, especialmente Floriano e vagamente a República, em artigo de fé, em feitiço, em ídolo mexicano, em cujo altar todas as violências e crimes eram oblatas dignas e oferendas úteis para a sua satisfação e eternidade. (II, 208)

Looking back to Lima Barreto's journal for 1904 we find him already forming a vision of Spencer's interpenetration of the military and civilian hierarchy. In that year, Lima, then a young amanuensis in the Ministry of War, met the current minister at a reception where many officers were present:

> Uma mó de gente em brilhantes e garridos ... uniformes desfiou aos meus olhos ... Os oficiais generais repletos de bordados lembram alguma coisa dos uniformes vistosos de corporações científicas, artísticas e palacianas ... Esses uniformes brilhantes bem demonstram que são de generais de paz; ... Havia cerca de seiscentos oficiais e suponho que quatrocentos houvessem deixado de comparecer; dá um total de mil, que, na proporção média de um para quinze soldados, à vista da variedade de postos, calcular-se-ia oficialidade de uma força de quinze mil. Eis aí como a matemática erra, ou antes, como, para aquém da linha equinocial, variam as coisas mais firmemente assentadas na Europa, porquanto, no Brasil, a proporção de oficiais, entremeando generais, etc., não é de um para quinze, mas sim, de um para dois, que é a da guarnição da cidade do Rio de Janeiro. (XIV, 50)

One can see here in embryo Lima's military satire in *Triste Fim* and his motive for placing such a satire in the chaotic first years of the Old Republic which was to run from 1889 to 1930. Lima's picture of a top-heavy army in which there is one officer to every two men confirms the characteristics of the militant society described by Spencer. This vision of the corridors of power swamped by the uniform is more finely treated in *Triste Fim*. The Iron Marshal's relations with his subordinates are viewed through the naïve and idealistic gaze of Quaresma as he awaits an audience with the dictator. His own lack of comprehension of the scene invests it with a subtle, ironic comedy worthy of the pen of a Stendhal. Floriano's gaze sweeps the room and falls upon Quaresma:

> O major ia aproximar-se, mas logo estacou no lugar em que estava. Uma chusma de oficiais subalternos e cadetes cercou o ditador e a sua atenção convergiu para eles. Não se ouvia o que diziam. Falavam ao ouvido de Floriano, cochichavam, batiam-lhe nas espáduas. O marechal quase não falava: movia com a cabeça ou pronunciava um monossílabo, coisa que Quaresma percebia pela articulação dos lábios. (II, 207)

Such descriptions imply another characteristic also indicated by Spencer: a marked decrease in efficiency in the militant society. In the industrial society the stress of competition breeds efficiency, Spencer tells us, whereas in a militant one, public departments are 'regimented after the militant fashion, all supported by taxes forcibly taken, ... are not immediately dependent for their means of living and growing on those whom they are designed to benefit'.[18] The army itself is a prime example of civil service inefficiency, exemplified, as Spencer noted in 1904, by 'the multiplicity of generals made in satisfaction of base interests, by promotion that is only in small measure determined by merit'.[19] Such inefficiency is exemplified hilariously in *Triste Fim* by Albernaz, the general who never saw a battle, and Caldas, the admiral who never commanded a ship. It is true that neither of these men wins preferment under Floriano, but Bustamante and Quaresma do -- for reasons hardly military. For Spencer, as for Lima Barreto, this peculiar brand of inefficiency, normally associated with underdeveloped countries, has a universal application. In analysing his country at the close of the nineteenth century, Lima is aware of its state of underdevelopment. He also sees it as standing at a social and political crossroads in the Spencerian terms briefly described above. The rise of a militant society produces inefficiency in the Spencerian sense, of many kinds. Policarpo Quaresma is not simply suspended from his job in the Arsenal of the Ministry of War because his document was translated into Tupi-guarani but because that document reached the minister himself without being detected, which consequently exposes the inefficiency of the department in which Quaresma is employed. Later, Quaresma himself, supremely unqualified for war, is incorporated in the army with the rank of major and taught elementary gunnery by his subordinate, Lieutenant Fontes.

Underpinning the foregoing observations on inefficiency in the Spencerian militant society is one of the most important of Spencer's concepts for the reader of Lima Barreto: conflict between the 'system of contract' and the 'system of status'. Militarism creates throughout society what Spencer calls a system of status: a system in which the individual, whatever his occupation, is obsessed with his official position, his 'status', rather than concerned about the actual functions and skills that might justify his status.[20] It is therefore entirely logical that Lima's fictional chronicle of the establishment of a militant form of society in the Brazilian Old Republic should include a substantial satire of a system of status. The incessant applications for preferment made by marginal, military figures in the novel, are eloquent of the obsession with status divorced from merit. Only Bustamente obtains advancement, but his satisfaction in the supremely non-combative role he assumes in the civil war is significant, not to mention his obsession with medals to which he thinks he is entitled as a veteran of the Paraguayan War. Lima Barreto parades before us a series of figures whose official status and carefully cultivated image bear no relation to their real worth. Dr Florêncio, the civil engineer, still exercises his profession but he has lost all the expertise he ever acquired at college, vegetating for years in a sinecure. The up-and-coming young Treasury official Genelício fawns upon his superiors, acquiring a reputation for learning by publishing long articles on accountancy consisting of meaningless statistics and spattered with quotations culled from foreign authors. Finally, there is Dr Armando Borges, supreme example of what Lima Barreto calls in *Triste Fim* and elsewhere the new Brazilian aristocracy: the graduates, the *doutores*. The scroll and ring of the doctor is, together with the military uniform, the other great fetish Lima sees as being worshipped in Brazilian society at the dawn of the republican era. He calls it in the journal of 1904 a 'nobreza universitária' (XIV, 66-67). Lima Barreto was fascinated and disgusted by a fetishism of appearances that he saw all around him in Brazil. The particular fetish varies depending on the function or profession being exercised, but the process is identical; not a process of complete sacrifice and dedication to the exercise of any function, trade or calling, but rather a process of *formação* qualifying a person to status of writer, doctor, soldier, engineer or politician, beside which the bringing to bear of skill and expertise relevant to any particular profession is of secondary importance. Spencer's system of status finds clear expression in this mental and moral climate characterized by lack of integrity, ideals, industry, substance; the absence of what Lima calls in *Os Bruzundangas* 'profundeza de sentimento' (VII, 36).

Lima Barreto found exactly the same idea differently expressed in another of his favourite nineteenth-century thinkers, Carlyle. Carlyle's *Heroes, Hero-Worship and the Heroic in History* is a meditation on the importance of the great man in myth, legend and history. Sincerity in the great man is a total commitment to the activity in which he is engaged -- the complete antithesis of dilettantism:

> Dilettantism, hypothesis, speculation, a kind of amateur-search for Truth, toying and coquetting with Truth: this is the sorest sin. The root of all other imaginable sins. It consists in the heart and soul of the man never having been open to Truth; - 'living in a vain show'. Such a man not only utters and produces falsehoods, but is himself a falsehood.[21]

Charlatanism for Carlyle is profoundly noxious, as it is for Spencer; it undermines the very moral fabric of society. Lack of 'profundeza de sentimento', then, prevents these 'graduates' in a profession from going 'ao âmago das coisas que fingem amar, de decifrá-las pelo amor sincero em que as têm, de querê-las totalmente, de absorvê-las. Só querem a aparência das coisas. Quando ... vão estudar medicina, não é a medicina que eles pretendem exercer, não é curar, não é ser um grande médico, é ser doutor' (VII, 36-37). This phenomenon signifies for Lima Barreto the Spencerian rise of a profoundly inefficient state bureaucracy in which official educational attainment ousts industry, experience and substantial expertise. Lima provides many examples in his more discursive writings. We cite here but one: the case of Brazilian railways which by 1915 would have closed all avenues of promotion for non-qualified personnel in favour of the engineer without experience (XI, 91). Under the Empire, it had been possible for a man to rise to positions of some responsibility on the strength of his experience alone (X, 234-5).

The system of status studied by Lima Barreto in the form of a series of fetishes that he isolates as signifiers of such a system, informs profoundly the structure of *Triste Fim de Policarpo Quaresma*. Armando Borges stands in a central symbolic position in the novel because he marries Olga Coleoni, who is portrayed as the most lucidly intelligent character in the novel. It is Olga who understands in a flash her godfather's motives in sending his telegram offering his services to Marshal Floriano. It is Olga who realizes that the naval insurgents in Guanabara Bay are as much sons of the Republic as anyone else, whose motives can be no more construed as ambitious than those of the *florianista* forces defending the city. She reacts thus to the brutal, unthinking patriotism of her husband (in itself a commentary on the aggressive patriotism against which Spencer warns):

--Mas vocês só falam em patriotismo? E os outros? É monopólio de vocês o patriotismo? fez Olga. (II, 200)

As the narrator is at pains to emphasize throughout the novel, Policarpo Quaresma, too, is a patriot. Quaresma's is the naïve, romantic patriotism of the early, fanciful historians of Brazil: Rocha Pitta and Vicente de Salvador, both of whom figure in the summary of the contents of the major's library. The narrator pits such gentle dreamers against the violent and bloodthirsty patriotism of the positivistic *florianistas* and what he sees as a burgeoning militant society.[22] When, in the final chapter of the novel, she visits Marshal Floriano's headquarters in order to plead for her godfather's life, Olga speaks to one of Floriano's adjutants and is brought face to face with the equally deluding and illusory patriotism that stands between Quaresma and his impossible dream:

--Quem, Quaresma? disse ele. Um traidor! Um bandido! (II, 296)

The intelligent Olga was only pointing out to her appalling husband that the quality of one's patriotism depends on one's point of view. The fact remains that Olga marries Borges. She does so partly because of a deficiency in her education, so the narrator tells us, and partly because she is deceived by her lack of worldly experience into thinking Borges to be an intelligent and honest man with ideals (II, 101-02). The scales fall from her eyes when she sees him sitting by a lighted window at night, surrounded by tomes he never opens, reading cheap novelettes in order to stay awake and enhance his reputation as an industrious man of learning:

> A sala da frente do alto porão tinha sido transformada em biblioteca. As paredes estavam forradas de estantes que gemiam ao peso dos grandes tratados. À noite, ele abria as janelas das venezianas, acendia todos os bicos-de-gás e se punha à mesa, todo de branco com um livro aberto sob os olhos. (II, 197)

The scene echoes strangely that of Quaresma's library at the opening of the novel. Quaresma's library is also book-lined. The comparison is merely on the surface however. The books and shelves in both descriptions are metonymic of a whole world: the world of intelligence, learning, knowledge -- the world of intellectual endeavour; but whereas in Quaresma's library signifieds and signifiers coalesce to form the sign for the presence of substantial learning, in Borges's world the sign is one of yawning emptiness. Borges reads little or nothing of importance; Quaresma voraciously. Borges sits ostentatiously in the window, whereas Quaresma shows his books to no one. Borges's library and his feigned bookish ways are not satirized by his acquaintances because they are consonant with his status as educated, professional man; Quaresma on the other hand is censured for even possessing books:

> --Se não era formado, para quê? Pedantismo! (II, 28)

Moreover, even the educational and intellectual hierarchy in the positivist republic of Brazil appears regimented, policed by a militant sense of status. Genelício will remark concerning Quaresma:

> --Devia até ser prohibido ... a quem não possuisse um título acadêmico ter livros. (II, 78)

Of the alliance between positivistic civilian jacobins and the positivist wing of the army with the coming of the Republic in 1889, José Murilo de Carvalho writes:

> O positivismo, ou certa lectura positivista da República que enfatizava, de um lado, a idéia do progresso pela ciência e, de outro, o conceito da ditadura republicana, contribuía poderosamente para o reforço da postura tecnocrática e autoritária.[23]

In the structure of *Triste Fim de Policarpo Quaresma*, the trajectory of learning and intelligence is a declining one while that of the academic and intellectual façade is a rising one. They meet, sadly, in the person of Olga who loses Quaresma and acquires Borges.

On a broader front, the irruption of the soldier into politics that some fondly believed could spell radical political and social change, offers instead the worst of both worlds: the installation of an essentially militaristic society in Spencerian terms and no radical change whatsoever.

Policarpo Quaresma fights in the Civil War on the *florianista* side and is wounded. The Naval Revolt having failed, the narrative proceeds to the last act in Quaresma's drama on the Ilha das Enxadas where he is sent as prison governor after his recovery in hospital. There, appalled at the brutal and arbitrary nature of the executions of the rebel sailors by the *florianistas*, this final assault on the ideal Brazil he had so single-mindedly and passionately nurtured provokes a heroic gesture of solidarity with the defeated side. There he writes his letter of protest to Floriano, and in doing so, signs his own death warrant. He is sent to join those awaiting the firing squad.

This last phase in the tragi-comic drama of a simple Brazilian patriot is also the final excursion into the Spencerian world-view and takes us full circle to the first and theoretical section of *First Principles* where we learn not only that metaphysical questions are insoluble but also that there must be an inscrutable power behind phenomena that Spencer terms the Unknowable. While in charge of the prison, Quaresma spends hours on the shore, brooding on the brutality and barbarity of the human world. Looking out over the tranquil beauty of Guanabara Bay, it seems to him that Guanabara smiles serenely on his perplexity and sadness. As he tries to make up his mind what to do, each nightfall finds him still gazing out over the bay. Quaresma tries to see into the obscurity before him as though striving to penetrate the mystery of things in an existence absurd in its injustice and cruelty. All this is understood in the final descriptive passages of the novel because it has already been prefigured in the text through the disenchanted, anguished letter describing the campaign in which he has just fought that Quaresma writes to his sister from the hospital where he is convalescing:

> Esta vida é absurda e ilógica; eu já tenho medo de viver, Adelaide. Tenho medo, porque não sabemos para onde vamos, o que faremos amanhã, de que maneira havemos de nos contradizer de sol para sol ...
> O melhor é não agir, Adelaide... (II, 271)

Now, in the dusk, as he strains his eyes, by staring into the darkness over the Bay of Rio, the description of his physical relationship with the phenomena of the natural world of Guanabara carries the burden of his anguish:

> Ficava assim um tempo longo, a ver, e quando se voltava, olhava a cidade que entrava na sombra, aos beijos sangrentos do ocaso.
> A noite chegava e Quaresma continuava a passear na borda do mar, meditando, pensando, sofrendo com aquelas lembranças de ódios, de sangueiras e ferocidade...
> Vinha a noite inteiramente, e o silêncio e a treva envolviam tudo.
> Quaresma ainda ficava horas ao ar livre a pensar, olhando o fundo da baía, onde quase não havia luzes que interrompessem a continuidade do negror noturno.
> Fixava bem os olhos para lá, como se os quisesse habituar a penetrar nas coisas indecifráveis e adivinhar dentro da sombra negra a forma das montanhas, o recorte das ilhas que a noite tinha feito desaparecer. (II, 279-80)

Science and religion, from their opposing, and certainly in the nineteenth century, their warring standpoints, must both accept, Spencer declares, the inscrutability of the universe, and from it deduce the necessity of progress. Critics of Spencer have charged him with doing so but failing to provide at the same time an adequate metaphysic for his evolutionism. Of course, Spencer, like many post-utilitarian thinkers in the nineteenth century, was marked by the post-idealist pessimism fathered by Schopenhauer. So were his readers in the New World. They also understood that Spencer's stance lay somewhere between positivistic optimism and Schopenhaurerian pessimism, just as it lay between utilitarian hedonism and Darwinian evolutionism: human activity, ideally, must militate towards the preservation of the pleasurable life because a constant process of adjustment will lead eventually to the perfect adjustment of society and produce perfect happiness -- of the kind envisaged in the closing pages of *The Principles of Ethics*, for example.[24] The passage, too lengthy to quote here, looks perilously like utopia, but Spencer would have warned that there is no 'quick fix' for the multitudinous ills of Brazil just as he would have reminded his Brazilian readers that in politics human destiny is and always will be a struggle between the individual and the State. Quaresma's anagnorisis logically drives him back into the aprioristic Spencerian Unknowable. Marshal Floriano Peixoto and Major Policarpo Quaresma meet only twice in the course of the narrative. On the first occasion, Quaresma presents the dictator with a report he has written analysing the agrarian problem in Brazil and suggesting some remedies. On the second occasion, he plucks up courage to ask if the Marshal has found time to read it and what he thinks of it. Floriano's reply is desolating:

> --Mas, pensa você, Quaresma, que eu hei de pôr a enxada na mão de cada um desses vadios?! Não havia exército que chegasse... (II, 242)

When Quaresma attempts to persist with his argument Floriano crushes him with a sibylline 'Você, Quaresma, é um visionário' (II, 243).

Between the optimism and impetuous idealism of Quaresma and the nihilistic cynicism of Floriano there is a middle way; and it is left to Quaresma's beloved goddaughter Olga to have a glimpse of what Spencer envisions in his warning:

> While the majority believe that human nature is unchangeable, there are some who believe that it may rapidly be changed. Both beliefs are wrong. Great alterations may be wrought; but only in the course of multitudinous generations...[25]

Ricardo Coração dos Outros and Olga both try valiantly to have Quaresma released from prison. Both fail. Emerging from her unsuccessful attempt to gain an audience with the victorious dictator, Olga looks around her:

> Olhou o céu, os ares, as árvores de Santa Teresa, e se lembrou que, por estas terras, já tinham errado tribos selvagens, das quais um dos chefes se orgulhava de ter no sangue o sangue de dez mil inimigos. Fora há quatro séculos. Olhou de novo o céu, os ares, as árvores de Santa Teresa, as casas, as igrejas; viu os bondes passarem; uma locomotiva apitou; um carro, puxado por uma linda parelha, atravessou-lhe na frente, quando já a entrar do campo ... Tinha havido grandes e inúmeras modificações. Que fora aquele parque? Talvez um charco. Tinha havido grandes modificações nos aspectos, na fisionomia da terra, talvez no clima...Esperemos mais, pensou ela; e seguiu serenamente ao encontro de Ricardo Coração dos Outros'. (II, 297)

Although we know from other writings of Lima Barreto that he read Spencer and subscribed to some of his ideas, there is no way of confirming that Lima had absorbed or even read all those works of Spencer of which mention has been made in the course of this essay. The best that can be done in this area is to note the chief features of the Spencerian analysis of nineteenth-century society and the extent to which the Spencerian vision coincides with the satirical vision offered by Lima Barreto's most realist novel, *Triste Fim de Policarpo Quaresma*. The clear parallels permit us to advance, cautiously, the following claims: that *Triste Fim* is structured in accordance with an attentive reading of Spencer; and that the third and final section of the novel in particular contains a fictionalized restatement of Spencer's evolutionism and of the Spencerian Unknowable. In *Triste Fim de Policarpo Quaresma* Spencer is poetically re-presented and renewed by a Brazilian disciple who was also a convinced and distinguished practitioner of the realist school of prose fiction.

NOTES

1. Osman Lins, *Lima Barreto e o Espaço Romanesco* (São Paulo: Ática, 1976), pp.30-61.

2. *Obras de Lima Barreto*, ed. by F. de Assis Barbosa, Antônio Houaiss, and M. Cavalcanti Proença, 17 vols (São Paulo: Brasiliense, 1956), II, 33. All references to and quotations from Lima Barreto's works are taken from this edition and henceforth indicated in the text by volume and page number.

3. Francisco José de Oliveira Vianna, *O Ocaso de Império*, 2nd edn (São Paulo: Melhoramentos, 1933), pp.131-45.

4. João Cruz Costa, *Pequena História da República* (Rio de Janeiro, 1968), p.12.

5. Cyro Silva, *Floriano Peixoto* (São Paulo, 1963), p.142.

6. See my article 'Triste Fim de Policarpo Quaresma and the New California', *Modern Language Review*, 78 (1983), 838-49. In the same context, see too the following articles: Silviano Santiago, 'Uma ferroada no peito de pé: Dupla leitura de "Triste Fim de Policarpo Quaresma"', in *Presença* (Editora da USP, 1973), pp.163-81, and republished in *Revista Ibero-Americana*, 50 (1984), 31-46; J. C. Kinnear, 'The "Sad End" of Lima Barreto's Policarpo Quaresma', *Bulletin of Hispanic Studies*, 51 (1974), 60-75.

7. Cruz Costa, p.87.

8. Caio Prado Júnior, *História Econômica do Brasil*, 11th edn (São Paulo: Brasiliense, 1971), pp.208-09.

9. Nelson Werneck Sodré, *Formação Histórica do Brasil*, 3rd edn (São Paulo: Brasiliense, 1964), pp.300-05.

10. Raul Pompéia, in Rodrigo Otávio, *Festas Nacionais* (Rio de Janeiro, 1893), p.ix.

11. Herbert Spencer, *First Principles*, 3rd edn, 2 vols (London: Williams and Norgate, 1870), II, 394-96.

12. Spencer, II, 511-13.

13. Spencer, *Principles of Sociology*, 4th edn, 3 vols (London: Williams and Norgate, 1902), II, 568-602.

14. *Sociology*, II, 471-91; 568-602.

15. *Sociology*, II, 577.

16. Joaquim Nabuco, *Balmaceda* (São Paulo, [n.d.]), pp.259-60.

17. *Sociology*, II, 586.

18. Spencer, *The Principles of Ethics*, 2 vols (London: Williams and Norgate, 1893), II, 231.

19. Spencer, *Ethics*, II, 231.

20. *Sociology*, II, 572-602; and *Ethics*, II, 228-36.

21. Thomas Carlyle, *On Heroes, Hero-Worship and the Heroic in History* in *The Works of Thomas Carlyle*, 30 vols (London: Chapman and Hall, 1896-99), V, 73.

22. That such beliefs still held considerable currency in the early 1900s is borne out by the phenomenal success of Afonso Celso's patriotic tract *Porque me ufano de meu país* (1901). His absurd claims for his country are constantly echoed by Policarpo Quaresma. For an excellent study of the relationship between Celso's book and *Triste Fim* see the aforementioned article by J. C. Kinnear. For a broader view of the rhetoric of nationalism in *Triste Fim* and its role in helping to shape the structure of the novel, see Haydée Ribeiro Coelho, 'Retórica do Nacionalismo', *Ensaios de Semiótica. Cadernos de Linguística e Teoria da Literatura*, 6 (Faculdade de Letras da Universidade Federal de Minas Gerais, 1982), 33-47.

23. *Os bestializados: o Rio de Janeiro e a República que não foi* (São Paulo: Companhia das Letras, 1987), p.35.

24. *Ethics*, II, 426-33.

25. *Ethics*, II, 428.

BUSINESS AND POLITICS IN LATE PORFIRIAN MEXICO: THE RECONSTRUCTION OF THE TEHUANTEPEC RAILWAY, 1896-1907*

PAUL GARNER
University College of Swansea, Wales

It is widely recognized that during the regime of President Porfirio Díaz (1876-80, 1884-1911), Mexico experienced a period of profound economic modernization, particularly in comparison with the long years of stagnation and recession during the first fifty years of independence. In the Porfiriato, as this period is known, there was a noticeable expansion of foreign investment and the promotion of agricultural and raw materials exports, the introduction of new energy sources and industrial technology, the extension of financial institutions and the monetization of the economy, and the progressive (although incomplete) integration of a national market through the reduction of internal barriers to trade and through the extension of the railway network.[1]

The construction of an interoceanic railway across the Isthmus of Tehuantepec through the southern states of Oaxaca and Veracruz was an important symbol of this modernization project. Successive nineteenth-century Mexican governments had become enmeshed in a protracted and difficult search for an interoceanic route which would not only extend the domestic transportation network and boost Mexico's export trade, but would also confirm Mexico's future prosperity as an important focus of international commerce. After several unsuccessful and costly ventures, the first Tehuantepec National Railway (*Ferrocarril Nacional de Tehuantepec*) was completed in 1894, but the general defects in construction and the lack of suitable harbour facilities at either the Gulf or the Pacific terminals made the line of little value. The Díaz administration therefore sought to rectify these deficiencies, and in 1898 signed the first of a series of contracts with the British firm of S. Pearson and Sons.

It is my view that the Pearson reconstruction of the Tehuantepec Railway highlights a number of aspects of Mexican political economy in the later Díaz period. Explicit or implicit in many accounts of late-nineteenth-century economic modernization in Mexico (and, indeed, throughout Latin America) is the notion that the process was controlled by a combination of overwhelming external economic forces and powerful foreign interests, to which politicians and government throughout the region were forced (either willingly or unwillingly) to succumb.[2] However, the terms of the Tehuantepec contract, and the fact that it was granted to a British company serve to emphasize the regime's principal concerns in the late 1890s. First, the reassertion of state control and regulation of the Mexican economy, and second, the desire to challenge growing North American control over key economic sectors. In addition, there is evidence to suggest that the business success of Sir Weetman Pearson (later Viscount Cowdray) in Mexico was due principally to the active promotion of his interests by the regime, rather than exclusively to Pearson's entrepreneurial skills, his political influence, or to his financial muscle. Finally, the Tehuantepec contract exemplifies the methods by which business negotiations were conducted in Porfirian Mexico, as seen by the personal relationship between Díaz and Pearson (who became known at the time in the British House of Commons as the Member for Mexico, precisely because of the amount of his time he devoted to the Tehuantepec project). The relationship had developed over a number of years since 1889, the year in which Pearson won his first major engineering contract in Mexico.[3]

Porfirian Railway Policy

One of the best-known statistics of Porfirian Mexico is the phenomenal growth in the railway network during the Porfiriato (from 640 kilometres of track in 1877 to 20,000 by 1910, with an additional 8000 kilometres of commuter and feeder lines employing animal rather than steam traction). The shifts in railway policy from the 1850s to the end of the Porfiriato in 1910 have also been extensively analysed, but a brief summary is appropriate.[4]

The policy from its earliest conception had sought to attract private, initially domestic, capital as the motor force behind railway development. Under the scheme promoted by Vicente Riva Palacios, Minister of Finance during the first Díaz presidency (1876-80), it was to be the individual states within the federation, rather than the federal government itself which were envisaged as the principal contractors, granting concessions and subsidies for local lines which could ultimately be incorporated into a nationwide system. However, the slow rate of progress, the fundamental shortage of domestic capital investment, and the pressure to strengthen US-Mexican commercial and diplomatic ties heralded a shift in policy. A North American railway entrepreneur (W. J. Reverens) wrote to Díaz in 1877 to suggest that the fundamental reason for the failure to expand the railway network in Mexico was the excess of government control and regulation: 'In this country, there is no government intervention in the surveys location, management, rules of freight and of fare ... no free transportation of rails nor maintenance of telegraph wires .... no forfeiture of charter for various minor neglects ... whereas all these have become as traditional in Mexican railway concessions as have been their failure to attract capital'.[5] The message was obviously heeded, because after 1880 the priority became the extension of North American rail lines into Mexico through the extension of federal government concessions and subsidies to initiatives from private (mostly US) capital with little government regulation or control. The result was a system largely financed by, and directed towards the United States, which produced a noticeable shift in Mexico's export traffic to her northern neighbour.

The third stage of railway development occurred towards the end of the 1890s, following the *Ley Sobre Ferrocarriles* of 1899. The purpose of the new law was threefold: first, to integrate the railway system through federal subsidy to new lines which would link the existing network; second, to reduce the levels of government subsidy; and third, progressively to 'mexicanize' the system, to increase the level of state supervision and control, culminating in the formation of a new company in 1907, *Ferrocarriles Nacionales de México*, which gave the government the controlling interest in over two thirds of the railway network.[6]

The consensus view of 'mexicanization' is that it was not a radical shift in policy, but a logical re-organization which maintained the existing priorities of export development. The standard accounts attribute the motivation for mexicanization to a combination of the economic and managerial advantages to the individual railway companies of government control over an increasingly unwieldy and unprofitable network -- control which was more likely to promote reasonable tariffs, efficient service, and improved equipment. It is undoubtedly the case that many US investors were disappointed by the returns on their investment, and thus welcomed 'mexicanization' with open arms.[7]

Few would disagree with John Coatsworth's view that 'mexicanization coincided exactly with the general economic policy orientation of the Porfirian regime, which saw in foreign capital and export markets the key to economic growth and the nation's new-found political stability'.[8] Nevertheless, there can be little doubt that 'mexicanization' was also a response to the growth of nationalist sentiment in late Porfirian Mexico. The particular fear which progressively gripped the Mexican governing class in the last decade of the Porfirian regime was the potential loss of Mexico's political and economic sovereignty to the United States. In the political sphere, the US victory in the war with Spain in 1898, the re-interpretation of the Monroe Doctrine and the interventionist policies pursued in Cuba, Panama, and Haiti confirmed the very real threat posed to Mexican political sovereignty. As Díaz had commented to a North American senator in 1896, 'la doctrina Monroe ni tiene el alcance que lo quieren dar los Estadistas Americanos interpretándola muy libremente, ni puede ser aceptada en términos de decoro por las Repúblicas Hispano-Americanas si no es mediante un pacto que sin lesionar los derechos de las potencias Europeas, prescriba derechos y obligaciones recíprocas dentro del espíritu de ilesa soberanía para todas. Creo que la República Norte Americana no busca ese resultado que la pondría al nivel de todas las que firmaran esa especie de Alianza; pero repito que sólo bajo la forma supra-dicha podríamos los Latino Americanos aceptar lo que nuestra oficiosa protectora nos ofrece tan generosamente'.[9]

In the economic sphere, there was a corresponding fear that the growing tide of North American investment threatened Mexico's economic sovereignty. Diplomatic sources in Mexico confirm the regime's growing preoccupations. The Minister of the British Legation in Mexico City (Reginald Tower) commented in 1908 on the growth of what he called 'self-reliant patriotism or Mexican Nationalism'. He interpreted the economic policy of the Díaz administration as a 'desire to obtain the direction and control of mines and railways, in the expectation that the foreigner will continue to pour his gold into the Republic, notwithstanding the disabilities which will then be imposed upon him'.[10]

Tower correctly interpreted that the overriding sentiment was 'national, but not anti-foreign'. The fundamental Porfirian economic strategy of attracting foreign capital remained intact, but the emphasis was firmly and increasingly placed upon increasing state regulation, and on the attraction of European capital as a counter-balance to US investment. As Díaz recommended in 1889 to his close political ally, the governor of Sonora, Ramón Corral (later Vice-President during Díaz's last term of office), who was seeking advice on sources of capital for his latest enterprise: "[yo] le estimaría a usted que prefiriera el capital europeo, para interpolarlo con el americano, que ya hay mucho en el país'.[11]

The *Ferrocarril Nacional de Tehuantepec*

The circumstances surrounding the development and final completion of the Tehuantepec Railway in 1907 reflect these trends in economic policy, although it is important to emphasize that the trans-isthmus project was always a special case, since from the earliest schemes it was envisaged as an international project rather than a regional or local project. The control of interoceanic communication was inevitably an issue of considerable international and diplomatic interest, given that whichever transport system were ultimately adopted (whether canal, ship railway, or railway) would be primarily intended for interoceanic and not local traffic. Local traffic, without large centres of population and only a small volume of local products to be transported, was always bound to be of secondary importance.[12]

The project had a long history, having been mooted ever since the early colonial period, and the first formal survey had been carried out in 1771. So important was the project to successive Mexican governments after independence that John Coatsworth, who is very critical of the negative impact of nineteenth-century Mexican railway development, ironically sees the Tehuantepec project as the only example of coherent government transport policy: 'To the extent that the government acted on any priorities at all, it devoted its energies to a misguided search for private capitalists, domestic or foreign, willing to complete a line across the Isthmus of Tehuantepec'.[13] As a consequence, more than nine different promoters were involved in the various stages of construction of the railway between 1842 and 1894. The cost in government subsidies was very high.[14]

The most grandiose and ambitious of these concessions was that awarded to a North American engineer, James Eads, in 1881 for the construction of a system which would transport entire ships across the Isthmus on a specially-constructed railway. Apart from the patent absurdity of the scheme, the most noticeable feature of the Eads contract is the extent to which the Mexican government were prepared to waive aspects of Mexican sovereignty and control over the proposed route. Article 27 of the contract, signed by Díaz as Minister of *Fomento* in 1881 after his temporary retirement from the presidency in favour of his *compadre* Manuel González, recognized the rights of any foreign government to protect their investment or their interests, and stated:

> si por causa de la magnitud de la obra ... la compañía recibiere ayuda en dinero o garantías de algún gobierno extranjero, la compañía podrá dar a ese gobierno todas las seguridades de consignación o intervención en los productos del camino, según se obligue con ese gobierno.[15]

Eads died in 1887, and the concession died with him, and thus any potential conflict which might have embarrassed the regime was avoided.[16] However, by the time of the negotiation for the Pearson contract in 1896, there had been a noticeable shift in policy. The priorities were now the assurance of Mexican sovereignty and the avoidance of United States control.

The Pearson Contracts

The long-awaited interoceanic railway was finally completed in 1894, after considerable delays and largely due to the considerable personal interest which Díaz himself had taken in the project.[17] This interest was based not only on the commercial viability and the patriotic symbolism of the scheme, but on a desire to promote the economic development of his native state of

Oaxaca, which had suffered a long period of economic depression in the nineteenth century as a result of the decline in the natural dye (*cochinilla*) trade. He wrote to another of his many *compadres*, the governor of Oaxaca, Gregorio Chávez, in 1890 that 'es grande mi interés en la fácil marcha y pronto término de esta línea que conceptuo fecunda en buenos resultados para el porvenir de nuestro Estado natal'.[18] However, despite the personal intervention of the President, it was clear that the route was still inadequate, and the Díaz administration subsequently sought new tenders for the substantial reconstruction of the line. Various schemes were submitted, but the company which eventually received the contract was that of Sir Wheetman Pearson.[19]

The choice of Wheetman Pearson was made for a number of reasons. In the first place, a close personal and business relationship had built up between the two men since the original negotiations in 1889 for Pearson's first major engineering project in Mexico, the construction of the 37 mile canal and tunnel to drain the central valley of Mexico and thus protect Mexico City from the threat of flooding, which had been a perennial problem since the sixteenth century.[20] There is an abundance of evidence from Pearson's personal and business correspondence of the mutual respect, admiration and genuine affection between the two men (which Pearson is said by his first biographer, J. A. Spender, to have compared to a relationship between father and son). The clearest manifestation of this is in a letter to the manager of his Mexican operation, John Body, in 1913: 'General Díaz was absolutely my hero ... one of the straightest and ablest men I have ever met ... I considered him one of the great men of his age'. So close was the personal relationship that Pearson offered Díaz, after his forced exile from Mexico after the Madero Revolution in 1911, the 1000 acre Pearson estate at Paddockhurst in Sussex 'for life', offering to pay for all expenses, including those of a personal secretary.[21]

Pearson's success was due not only to mutual respect or personal affinity, but also to a combination of business acumen and the careful courtship of powerful interests. Pearson adapted quickly to Porfirian business etiquette. The Díaz family were often guests of the family and regular visitors to the Pearson residences in Mexico City and Veracruz. Pearson boasted that the boards of directors of the various companies he established to run his multiple engineering and business operations in Mexico contained 'the most influential political and financial men in Mexico' (his partners and associates were drawn from the most influential group of presidential advisers during the last decade of the Díaz regime, the *científicos*).[22] He even boasted to the US ambassador in London in 1914 that his firm was considered 'one of the minor departments of state' in Mexico. The firm was careful to pay retainers to prominent politicians, not only to ensure cooperation, but also in appreciation of 'the inadvisability of making enemies of politicians'.[23]

As a result, Pearson was able to develop and consolidate an extensive business and commercial empire in Mexico which involved a tremendous diversity of enterprises. These included the various engineering projects -- the Mexican Canal (1889-98), the Veracruz Harbour Works (1895-1902), the Juile Railway (1896-1900), as well as the Tehuantepec Railway and Port Works themselves (1902-07). His profits from the engineering contracts were invested in his various companies which covered an impressive range of enterprises: in mining (the gold mines of El Oro), public utilities (Pearson's controlled light and power companies in Puebla, Veracruz, Tampico, Orizaba and Córdoba), manufacturing (most notably the jute mills in the state of Veracruz), transportation (the Puebla Tramway, the Aguila Steamship Company), real estate (including extensive urban properties in Mexico City, and the Mexican Estates Company which controlled over 2 million acres of land); and, most important of all, the Mexican El Aguila Company which controlled Pearson's interests in oil. In recognition of his good fortune in his Mexican enterprises, the Cowdray coat of arms included a symbolic representation of a Mexican *peón*.[24]

But there can also be no doubt that Pearson's success was also largely due to the active promotion of his business interests by both Díaz, Finance Minister José Yves Limantour and the *científico* élite. Pearson was awarded government contracts and granted lucrative concessions not only because of his competence and personal contacts, but because government policy favoured European businessmen rather than their North American competitors.

There is also no doubt that Pearson and his business manager in Mexico, John Body, were fully aware of the strategy. 'It is gratifying to know that the

President and Mr. Limantour are now particularly friendly disposed (sic) towards us', Body told Pearson in August 1901, and later that same year he reported that 'Mr. Limantour is more favourably inclined towards us than to the Americans'.[25] In an interview with the *Westminster Gazette*, Pearson declared that 'in Mexico English capitalists meet with exceptional favour by the government. It is true American capital is pouring into the country, but Mexicans are a little afraid of a too-pronounced American invasion'.[26]

As a result, Body was frequently awarded private audiences with Díaz, and his correspondence clearly indicates that he had access to the minutes of cabinet discussions. Inside information even allowed Pearson to be informed of the tenders submitted by rival (usually US contractors) so that he could adjust his bid accordingly.[27] It even appears that Pearson and Body had sufficient influence in government circles to secure the removal of individuals who were obstructing their interests.[28]

Pearson was also attuned to the administration's concerns over the Tehuantepec project. The initial proposal came from Pearson himself in 1896, and amongst the economic arguments put forward (the limited financial risk, the inevitable commercial success) was the unequivocal statement that the Pearson contract would guarantee 'freedom from American control ... [and the] certainty that English trade and English ships would be pre-disposed to use a route controlled by Englishmen'.[29]

There followed a lengthy process of negotiation between Pearson's and the government which culminated in the signing of the first contract in 1898, the conditions of which were subsequently modified in 1899, 1902 and 1904 to include the construction of adequate port facilities at Coatzcoalcos and Salina Cruz. The main provisions stipulated that the Mexican government and Pearson's were to be equal partners, each supplying half the nominal capital investment. Pearson's were to be in charge of not only the reconstruction, which would be carried out at cost price without the normal contractor's premium, but also of the management of the property. The arrangement was described by the Secretary to the British Legation in Mexico City as 'the first instance on record where a national government have taken a private firm into partnership'.[30]

It was envisaged that the partnership would last for 50 years, during the first 36 years of which the Mexican government would receive 65 per cent of the profits, and Pearson's 35 per cent. During the next five years the government's share of the profits was progressively increased until the last five years of the arrangement, when all profits would be disposed in favour of the government.[31] A further clause in the contract specifically prevented Pearson from selling his properties on the Isthmus to North American interests.

The terms of the Tehuantepec contract clearly upset the United States government. In 1902 the Mexican government was formally asked for an explanation as to why 'the United States and its citizens should be so odiously excluded', a complaint which was immediately passed on to John Body by 'one of the members of the cabinet', indicating once again the preferential access to inside information on cabinet discussions enjoyed by Pearson's. The hostility of both Washington and influential business groups in the United States would play a significant role in the demise of the regime in 1910-11.[32]

The engineering works (which Pearson described at the time as 'the greatest of all our undertakings') began in earnest in 1902. The railway line was completed in 1904, but the route did not become fully functional until 1907 because of the long delays in the completion of adequate harbour facilities at Salina Cruz.

There were many obstacles and difficulties which arose during the reconstruction process: given the insalubrious climatic and working conditions, the presence of yellow fever, and the scattered concentration of the local population, the major problem was to obtain (and to retain) both skilled and unskilled labour. The labour problem was partially solved with the importation of over 15,000 contract labourers from China, Japan, Korea, Jamaica and the Bahamas.[33] Frequent and heavy rainfall constantly impeded the work in the rainy season. There were also periodical complaints from Limantour of the prohibitive cost of the project which threatened to 'bring the country to ruin'. In addition, Pearson negotiated a contract with (and bought a large number of shares in) the American Hawaiian Steamship Company which made provision for the annual shipment of between 250,000 to 300,000 tons of Hawaiian sugar from Honolulu to New Orleans, Philadelphia, and New York.

TABLE: *FERROCARRIL NACIONAL DE TEHUANTEPEC*

YEAR	EARNINGS ($)	EXPENSES ($)	FREIGHT LOCAL* (Tons)	INTEROCEANIC (Tons)
1904	1,053,666	1,059,038	34,852	
1905	1,207,749	1,251,086	41,440	
1906	1,276,860	1,387,620	49,475	
1907	3,570,143	2,990,014	70,871	452,571
1908	3,713,122	2,749,602	78,773	574,782 (350,223)
1909	4,863,761	3,279,677	105,476	557,615 (553,275)
1910	6,874,387	3,559,498	140,956	636,474 (434,064)
1911	7,110,487	3,766,424	155,258	825,724 (794,029)
1912	8,387,544	4,295,150	195,929	851,447 (873,495)
1913	(166,082)	(850,827)		
1914	(167,299)	(255,055)		
1915	(128,801)	(8,757)		
1916	n.d.	n.d.		
1917	n.d.	n.d.		
1918	(145,411)	(336)		
1919	(151,977)	(599)		
1920	(153,203)	(511)		
1921	(137,473)	(502)		

* Pearson's figures for local freight (to 1912) exclude Government, Company, Port Works & Transit Traffic. Figures in brackets are from the US Department of Commerce used by Glick.

Sources: Science Museum Archive, Pearson papers, Box 54 (TNR/20); E.B Glick, 'The Tehuantepec Railroad: Mexico's White Elephant', *Pacific Historical Review* (1953), 373-82.

The culmination of the process was the elaborate inauguration of the Tehuantepec Railway in January 1907. This was a well-publicized event, obligingly and extensively covered by the Mexican and international press.[34] Pearson and his wife entertained and provided special trains for over 200 guests, including Díaz, five members of his cabinet (including Limantour), the governor of the Federal District (Mexico City -- who was a business partner of Pearson), the governors of the states of Oaxaca, Estado de México, and Tamaulipas, ambassadors and diplomatic representatives from the USA, Britain, Germany, Spain, Japan, Belgium, Russia, El Salvador, Cuba and Guatemala. President Díaz, in clearly nostalgic mood, reminisced about the dirt road he had inaugurated 48 years ago as *Comandante Militar* of Tehuantepec, and Pearson patted himself and his employees on the back for having succeeded where the previous nine contractors had failed -- an achievement which Pearson apparently regarded as one of the greatest and most difficult of his life.[35]

The guests were apparently most impressed, especially with the banquets -- the reporter from the English language *Mexican Herald* commented on the 'marvel of foresight ... in the fact that the bottled goods lasted to the end'. As a propaganda exercise, it was clearly a success, both for Pearson and for the regime -- the same reporter described the President's 'rugged health and firm, soldierly bearing', and every opportunity was taken to promote the image of a vigorous, progressive, and dynamic regime.[36]

Because the elevated ambitions for the *Ferrocarril Nacional de Tehuantepec* were only shortlived, it is often forgotten that for at least seven years the route was immensely profitable (see Table). Pearson had calculated that the handling of an annual 600,000 tons of freight would signify a healthy profit. The figures indicate that the actual freight carried far exceeded Pearson's own expectations. He wrote to Body in June 1909 that 'the prospects for business are simply realising our wildest hopes'.[37]

Ultimately, however, these hopes were dashed by the combination of the outbreak of the Madero Revolution in 1910, the impact of the First World War, and the competition from the Panama Canal (inaugurated in 1914). Precise attribution for the decline in the fortunes of the Tehuantepec Railway after 1914 is, however, a matter of some debate. For most commentators, the line failed because of the failure to see the potential threat from the Panama Canal. Pearson himself disagreed, and blamed instead the disruption to international trade caused by World War. The disruption caused by the Madero Revolution and subsequent civil war also did not appear to give him undue concern. He wrote to Body in August 1914, making no reference to the seizure of the railway by Carrancista troops in May 1914, but clearly stating: 'with the suspension of European traffic, we have only local and passenger traffic -- we shall be losing money continuously until conditions change'.[38] According to Spender, Pearson believed that with competent management the railway could have survived the competition from the Panama Canal.

Pearson's confident assertions were never tested, since in October 1918 the Carrancista Congress decided unilaterally that it was time for the partnership between Pearson's and the Mexican government in the Tehuantepec project to be terminated. This was no great blow to Pearson, since he received full indemnity according to the terms of the original contract, and by then he had become fully immersed in his most profitable Mexican venture --the oil business--, where once again he had been given vital support by the Díaz administration, without which his venture might well have failed.[39]

In conclusion, it is important to emphasize the symbolic significance of the Tehuantepec railway for the Díaz regime. It represented the triumphant culmination of many years of arduous struggle and sacrifice against innumerable obstacles -- obstacles that were as much psychological and political as geographical or technical. In overcoming them, the regime considered that it had fulfilled important national goals, particularly with regard to the consummation of economic and political sovereignty. Mexico, as the regime saw it, ought now to be considered a modern, progressive, strong and sovereign nation with a positive economic future as the centre of international commerce. The Tehuantepec Railway was therefore a cause for national pride as a representation of profound modernization. As events were shortly to prove, however, this was a cruel illusion. Within a very short period of time, Mexico had descended once again into political anarchy and economic chaos, and the modernization project was put into cold storage for a future generation.

NOTES

* I would like to thank the British Academy and the University College of Swansea for their financial assistance in the research for this article.

1. The literature on the Porfiriato (1876-1911) is rapidly expanding, despite the disproportionate attention afforded the Mexican Revolution (1910-20). The best single source is still the 10 volume *Historia Moderna de México*, ed. by Daniel Cosio Villegas (México: El Colegio de Mexico, 1956-72), especially vols VII and VIII, *Porfiriato: Vida Ecónomica, Primera y Segunda Parte*; a useful summary of the process of economic modernization is Ciro Cardoso (coord.), *México en el Siglo XIX* (Editorial Nueva Imagen, 1980).

2. The dependency orthodoxy of the 1970s has been subjected to rigorous scrutiny. For the respective arguments of the *dependentistas* and the *antidependentistas* (at their most extreme and vitriolic), see the exchanges between D. C. M. Platt and Stanley and Barbara Stein in the *Latin American Research Review*, 1980.

3. For biographical information on Pearson, see J. A. Spender, *Weetman Pearson: First Viscount Cowdray 1856-1927* (London, 1930); Desmond Young, *Member for Mexico: A Biography of Weetman Pearson, First Viscount Cowdray* (London, 1966); R. K. Middlemas, *The Master Builders* (London, 1963).

4. J. Coatsworth, *Growth Against Development: The Economic Impact of Railroads in Porfirian Mexico* (DeKalb, 1981); F. R. Calderón, 'Los Ferrocarriles', in C.Villegas (coord.), *Historia Moderna de Mexico*, VII, 483-634; J. Winberry, 'Development of the Mexican Railroad System', *Geoscience and Man*, 21 (1980), 111-19.

5. Colección Porfirio Díaz (hereafter CPD), Universidad Iberoamericana, Mexico City, Legajo XVII, Caja 9, Documento 4657, W. J. Reverens to Porfirio Díaz 11/5/1877.

6. Winberry, 'Development'.

7. Calderón, 'Ferrocarriles'.

8. Coatsworth, 'Growth Against Development', p.46.

9. CPD: L41:C8:Tomo 18:D 397, P. Díaz to Alfonso Lancaster Jones 31/1/1896.

10. Foreign Office Papers (hereafter FO), Public Record Office (PRO), Kew, Series 371, Volume 480, File 25305, R. Tower to Sir E. Grey 3/7/1908; for confirmation from German and French diplomatic sources, see F. Katz, *La Guerra Secreta en México, Vol I Europa, Estados Unidos y la Revolución Mexicana* (México: Era, 1982), pp.40-46.

11. CPD:L41:C7:T15:D158, Díaz to Ramón Corral 12/3/1889.

12. Miguel Covarrubias, *Mexico South: the Isthmus of Tehuantepec* (New York, 1942), p.164; C. Brasseur, *Viaje por el Istmo de Tehuantepec* (Mexico: Fondo de Cultura Económica, 1981). See prologue by Elisa Ramírez Castaneda (pp.7-20) for details of the diplomatic interests of Britain, France and the United States).

13. Coatsworth, 'Growth', p.44.

14. Estimates range from $20 million (Covarrubias, *Mexico South*) to $38 million (Spender, *Weetman Pearson*).

15. Calderón, 'Ferrocarriles', p.525.

16. Díaz later confessed to the Mexican Minister in Washington (Matías Romero) that 'después de otorgada la concesión al señor Capitán Eads se ha arrepentido el Gobierno de algunas de sus cláusulas, y no se ha empeñado mucho en modificarlas, fundado en las posibilidades de que al fin no se construiría aquella obra' (CPD:L19:C1:D91, Díaz to Romero 19/1/1894).

17. Salvador Malo, the *contratista* for the railway company, thanked the President for his generosity in personally interceding on their behalf to secure the extension of favourable credit terms (Malo to Díaz 2/4/1890 (CPD:L15:C9:D4158)).

18. CPD:L41:C8:T17:D338, Díaz to Chávez 27/6/1890.

19. The government received a proposal from US businessman C. P. Huntingdon, who already had substantial interests in mining and railway companies in Mexico. His bid was rejected on various grounds, one of which was the demand by Huntingdon for the control of steamship traffic from both ports, which Díaz considered 'un monopolio contrario a los preceptos constitucionales'; however, when Pearson later bought up a large number of shares in the Hawaiian Steamship Company, no such objections were raised (or recorded), which suggests that Huntingdon's bid was not rejected entirely on impartial criteria (CPD:L41:C8:T18:D354, Díaz to Huntington 3/8/1895).

20. For correspondence and details of the negotiations over the Mexican Canal, see Science Museum Archive (hereafter SMA), records of S. Pearson and Sons (PEA), Boxes 16 and 17.

21. SMA:PEA:Box A3, Pearson to Body 13/1/1913. Pearson's generosity did have its limitations: had he taken up the offer, the ex-President would have been required to pay for the delivery of milk (Box A3, memo to Lady Cowdray 26/6/1911).

22. The President's son Porfirio Díaz was a director of S. Pearson & Son Sucesores, the company established to carry out the contract work for the Tehuantepec Railway (SMA:PEA:Box A4). For the influence and ideology of Mexico's scientific positivists (*científicos*), see C. Hale, *The Transformation of Liberalism in late Nineteenth-Century Mexico* (Princeton, 1989).

23. SMA:PEA:Box A3, Body to Pearson 2/2/1914. Body was careful to ensure that Finance Minister Limantour received supplies of his favourite Scotch whisky.

24. The Pearson papers contain extensive records of Pearson's Mexican and worldwide business interests. The best summary of his Mexican interests can be found in L. Meyer, *Su Majestad Británica Contra la Revolución Mexicana 1900-1950: El Fin de un Imperio Informal* (México: El Colegio de Mexico, 1991), pp.81-91.

25. SMA:PEA:Box A4, Body to Pearson 17/8/1901 and 27/11/1901.

26. SMA:PEA:Box A9, Westminster Gazette 3/5/1901.

27. SMA:PEA:Box A4 contains details of the negotiations for the Veracruz dry dock contract in 1901, which was awarded to Pearson's rather than their North American rival.

28. FO 371/480/29820, Tower to Grey 14/8/1908 over the dismissal of the Minister of *Fomento* (Development), after a disagreement with Pearson's.

29. SMA:PEA:Box 52/1, Tehuantepec National Railway (TNR).

30. FO/ZHC1/1721: Report of Secretary M. Muller.

31. E. Glick, 'The Tehuantepec Railroad: Mexico's White Elephant', *Pacific Historical Review* (1953), 373-82.

32. SMA:PEA:Box A4, Body to Pearson 3/10/1902. For the growing conflict between Mexico and Washington and the impact this had on the demise of the Díaz regime, see Katz, *Guerra Secreta*, p.40.

33. FO 203/201/173: Consular reports from Salina Cruz from Consul W. Buchanan.

34. Box 53A in the Pearson Archive contains press cuttings and reports from a number of newspapers. There is also a copy of the 'home movie' of the inauguration. The use of the most recent innovations in moving photography is another obvious symbol of the modernization project which the TNR represented. For Díaz's interest in the new medium of cinema and its propaganda possibilities, see Aurelio de los Reyes, *Los Orígenes del Cine en México (1896-1900)* (Mexico, 1983).

35. Spender, *Weetman Pearson*, p.121.

36. SMA:PEA:Box 53A.

37. SMA:PEA:Box A4.

38. SMA:PEA:Box A3.

39. J. Brown, 'Domestic Politics and Foreign Investment: British Development of Mexican Petroleum, 1889-1911', *Business History Review*, 61, 3 (1987), 387-416.

TWENTIETH CENTURY

FORMS OF SPIRITUALITY IN THE EARLY POEMS OF JUAN RAMÓN JIMÉNEZ

DEREK FLITTER
University of Birmingham

The work of Juan Ramón Jiménez, perhaps to a greater degree than that of any other Spanish poet living and working in the twentieth century, is characterized by a single-minded and impassioned striving for personal spiritual fulfilment. Hermetic and self-absorbed, painstakingly revised (or 'revivido', to use Juan Ramón's own preferred term) and ruthlessly edited by the author himself, it is a poetic *oeuvre* remarkable as much for its penetrating self-examination as for its unswerving dedication to, and pursuit of, a definitive yet elusive goal. Jiménez's largely developmental assessment of his own output as a gradually cohering poetic vision, in which superficial adornment was progressively stripped away in favour of a style that was naked and concise, led him to suppress all but a cluster of his early poems from the *Segunda antolojía poética* he compiled with his wife Zenobia Camprubí in 1919. While the poems written before *Arias tristes* of 1903, his first resounding success, are barely represented in the volume, Jiménez opted for the inclusion from his more recent work of thirty-nine poems from *Diario de un poeta reciencasado* (1916), fifty-four from *Eternidades* (1917), and fifty-eight from *Piedra y cielo* (1918). *Arias tristes*, in comparison, is represented by fifteen pieces, while *Jardines lejanos* (1904), yielded just eleven. In choosing to concentrate here upon some of the pieces from Jiménez's earliest collections, it is not my intention to make extravagant claims on their behalf, and thus implicitly to challenge the poet's own assessment of their worth. Rather I wish to consider two principal issues: firstly, the influences under which the young Juan Ramón was working in shaping his early poetry, and, by way of extension, his elaboration of what I would contend were his likely sources; secondly, the extent to which some of the salient themes and patterns of Jiménez's later verse are already present in this early lyric, which itself displays unequivocal signs of Juan Ramón's developing genius.

In 1900, after leaving in the hands of Francisco Villaespesa the final arrangements for the publication of *Ninfeas* and *Almas de violeta*, Juan Ramón returned from Madrid to his native Moguer. Shortly after his return, however, Jiménez's emotional life was thrown into turmoil by the sudden death of his father. The young poet, prey to nervous exhaustion and acute depression, was sent by his family in the spring of 1901 to a sanatorium near Bordeaux. In the following months, he became acquainted with the work of the French Symbolists Verlaine and Mallarmé, and wrote the collection of poems published as *Rimas* in 1902. Jiménez's biographer Graciela Palau de Nemes, referring to the period following the death of his father, comments: 'Buscando explicación y consuelo por la pérdida de su padre, sus pensamientos se volvieron místicos, de un misticismo forzado e inquieto'.[1] It is hardly surprising, then, that the verses of *Rimas* are marked by a delicate and painful sensibility to the poetic trappings of mortality, together with an almost obsessional search for transcendent meaning. A key piece in the collection, and one of the few belonging to it later chosen by Jiménez for inclusion in the *Segunda antolojía poética*, is 'Parque viejo', whose setting is described by Angel González as 'uno de los parques más atractivos y misteriosos de ese gran jardinero que fue JRJ'.[2] Since a full consideration of this poem is essential to my purpose, I now cite it in its entirety:

> Me he asomado por la verja
> del viejo parque desierto:
> todo parece sumido
> en un nostáljico sueño.
>
> Sobre la oscura arboleda,
> en el transparente cielo
> de la tarde, tiembla y brilla
> un diamantino lucero.
>
> Y del fondo de la umbría
> llega acompasado el eco
> de algún agua que suspira
> al darle una gota un beso.
>
> Mis ojos pierdo, soñando,
> en la bruma del sendero;
> una flor que se moría
> ya se ha quedado sin pétalos.

De una rama amarillenta,
al temblar el aire fresco,
una pálida hoja mustia
dando vueltas cae al suelo.

Ramas y hojas se han movido,
un algo turba el misterio;
de lo espeso de la umbría,
como una nube de incienso,

surje una virgen fantástica,
cuyo suavísimo cuerpo
se adivina vagamente
tras blanco y flotante velo;

sus ojos clava en los míos
y entre las brumas huyendo,
se pierde callada y triste
en el fondo del sendero...

Desde el profundo boscaje
llega monótono el eco
de algún agua que suspira
al darle una gota un beso.

Y allá sobre las magnolias,
en el transparente cielo
de la tarde, tiembla y brilla
una lágrima-lucero.

El jardín vuelve a sumirse
en melancólico sueño,
y un ruiseñor, dulcemente
jime en el alto silencio.[3]

Of the poems in *Rimas*, this is one of those most clearly inspired by Verlaine: the melancholy aristocratic garden after dark; the carefully evoked atmosphere of musicality and indefinable yearning; the sense of evanescent visitation. And yet for all that the piece may appear slight and derivative, the subtle use of symbol and the mastery of structure make it so much more than a juvenile imitation. Indeed, for Angel González, 'se perciben sorprendentes aciertos, y originalidad y maestría en la exploración de temas y procedimientos que serán definidores del trabajo futuro de JRJ'.[4] While, in a prologue to the collection as a whole, it was inappropriate for González to enlarge upon this brief but incisive statement in any detail, a closer look at 'Parque viejo' will be seen to elucidate his claim.

Jiménez provides us, in the first stanza, with a potent sense of happening upon a magical domain not subject to the parameters of the world outside, but instead breathing a heightened poetic atmosphere of its own; the poet enters tentatively, aware that he may be trespassing upon its secrets but irresistibly drawn. We therefore find ourselves in the presence --the phrase is not inappropriate, for Nature here is sentient and alive-- of a *paysage choisi*, Verlaine's 'soulscape'.[5]

The tranquil beauty of the garden beneath the stars is rendered by lines that include two key terms in what would be Juan Ramón's imagistic pattern. Firstly, the epithet 'diamantino', a category of value suggestive of the precious quality he feels to be inherent in the scene, and redolent of the *arrobamiento* that increasingly grips the enthralled poet. Secondly, 'transparente', reserved for those fortunate moments when Jiménez felt contemplation of the natural world to yield an accentuated perception of the ultimate meaning that lay beyond it; when the poetic spirit saw not as through a glass darkly, but achieved instead a more direct and intense insight. The third stanza, meanwhile, conveys an organic harmony in which the scene breathes with a musical and emotional life of its own; the sense of vital rhythm and sensual response detected in the sound of moisture dripping from the trees into water is a masterstroke, a sure and deft touch which reveals both the innate sensibility of the young Juan Ramón and his already considerable power to evoke mood.[6]

Towards the middle of the poem, however, and beginning in the fourth stanza, we are made aware of a subtle change of emphasis. In a single long moment of transition, as the poet contemplates first a withered flower and then a dead leaf fluttering to the ground, Juan Ramón provides at once a culmination of the air of suspenseful apprehension incipient in the first lines and a degree of premonition of the transcendent vision that immediately follows. This anthropomorphic natural world studiously recreated in a spirit of almost reverential awe exudes the essential melancholy of beauty that must inevitably fade; in the presence of archetypal images of decay, Jiménez must necessarily confront the anguish of death and mortality. It is entirely appropriate that the first line of the fourth stanza induces the sense of a dream sequence: it enhances the power of visual suggestion in the falling of the emblematic 'pálida hoja mustia';[7] it likewise prepares us for the ephemeral and dreamlike glimpse of the 'virgen fantástica' in the middle of the poem by stressing the deliberate break with the prescriptions of waking reality. The move from contemplation of beauty to a recognition of its transience is a representative and indeed inevitable note in the poems of *Rimas*, produced during a period when Juan Ramón Jiménez was haunted by a morbid obsession with death, afflicted by acute nervous disorder and struggling to come to terms with devastating personal loss. At the same time, however, the further shift --from the contemplation of images of decay to the apprehension of a supernatural presence affording the ability momentarily to transcend that decay--, may be felt to be equally inevitable in the context of what we are already confident is to be more than a mere mood poem.

As leaves and branches appear to part of their own accord, the mysterious vision appears fleetingly out of the trees to fix her eyes upon the awestruck poet before vanishing back into the mist. Her description is not the product of observation but of intuition, of a peremptory emotional certitude that intensifies both the fleeting moment and the consequent numbing loss that informs the final stanzas. The moment itself wavers between the liturgical 'nube de incienso' and, on the other hand, the sensual note struck by the poet's imaging to himself the 'suavísimo cuerpo' that he feels this inexpressibly beautiful vision must possess. To such an extent is the scene marked by a subjective intensity that we are given the adjectives 'callada y triste' in the form of emotional transference, as the poet seems to impose his own resultant mood upon the disappearing figure.[8] The finality of her loss, prompting both the melancholy silence that ends this stanza and the structural reversal of the poem's final lines, would be more brilliantly captured in Jiménez's later revision for the *Segunda antolojía poética*, where 'el fondo del sendero' would be replaced by the telling phrase 'el irse del sendero'; in this 'revivido' form, the vision is made more fully to anticipate the theme of the vocational quest, the unconditional commitment to a poetic task and spiritual goal that would mould the whole of Juan Ramón's later *obra*.

The young Jiménez's growing mastery of poetic structure is seen in the final three stanzas, which act as a mirror image of the first three, leading irrevocably back to the scene encountered at the poem's beginning. A mirror image, however, with crucially changed poetic emphases. The 'acompasado' of the third stanza is exchanged for the 'monótono' of the antepenultimate one, as the poet's apprehension of a harmonious organic nature gives way to profound dissatisfaction; in the wake of transcendent experience, the latent sensuality of the surrounding world is perceived as anodyne, not melodious but striking a single reiterative and ultimately jarring note. Years later, Jiménez would choose further to amend the same stanza, replacing 'suspira' with 'responde' in describing the water's brief rippling: a change that makes more insistent the earlier point, as the magically warm human quality is forsaken in favour of an instinctive reaction that occurs mechanically and is thus devoid of emotional content. The penultimate stanza sees the suggestive possibilities of the night sky similarly changed; the 'diamantino' of the second stanza, that helped to make the atmospheric scene and the poet's experience of it self-sufficient, is replaced by 'lágrima', as the mood becomes one of irretrievable loss and distance. Finally, the 'nostáljico sueño' of the first stanza assumes a definitive note of melancholy in the concluding one, as we are concerned less with pleasurable reverie than with a despairing attempt to recapture in dream something of which the poet has found himself exultantly the owner only to be summarily deprived. The final note is profoundly elegiac as we depart to the sound of the nightingale's lament.

In mentioning later revisions made to this piece, undoubtedly the most telling is the substitution of 'rosa fantástica' for 'virgen fantástica' to describe Jiménez's ideal vision, a change entirely repesentative of the poet's move from the lavish aestheticism of *modernismo* to a more diffuse but surely more potent symbolism. As for Yeats, the rose encapsulates the Ideal towards which Juan Ramón was continually striving.

Dealing briefly with 'Parque viejo', Howard T. Young sees a coincidence of minds between Juan Ramón and Shelley; he successfully likens the piece to Shelley's 'Alastor', commenting on this 'debut of the veiled maiden' in the poetry of Jiménez.[9] He suggests a further linkage, this time with Bécquer: 'The elusive nymph is part of Bécquer's bequest, and she is cousin as well to the maid whose voice chanted a song of love to Alastor's bewildered ears'.[10] While Young refers particularly to the *leyenda* entitled 'Los ojos verdes', I would prefer to view 'El rayo de luna' as bequeathing this legacy. In fact I feel that a close textual comparison leaves little doubt that the latter provided Juan Ramón with a point of departure for 'Parque viejo', although the differing use of imagery and symbol reveals both a deal of originality in Jiménez's version and evidence of what we might term changing strategies in an organic tradition. The excerpt from 'El rayo de luna' upon which I would base my case reads as follows:

> Era de noche; una noche de verano, templada, llena de perfumes y rumores apacibles, y con una luna blanca y serena en mitad de un cielo azul, luminoso y trasparente.
> Manrique, presa su imaginación de un vértigo de poesía, después de atravesar el puente, desde donde contempló un momento la negra silueta de la ciudad, que se destacaba sobre el fondo de algunas nubes blanquecinas y ligeras arrolladas en el horizonte, se internó en las desiertas ruinas de los Templarios.
> La medianoche tocaba a su punto. La luna, que se había ido remontando lentamente, estaba ya en lo más alto del cielo, cuando al entrar en una oscura alameda que conducía desde el derruido claustro a la margen del Duero, Manrique exhaló un grito leve, ahogado, mezcla extraña de sorpresa, de temor y de júbilo.
> En el fondo de la sombría alameda había visto agitarse una cosa blanca que flotó un momento y desapareció en la oscuridad. La orla del traje de una mujer, de una mujer que había cruzado el sendero y se ocultaba entre el follaje, en el mismo instante en que el loco soñador de quimeras o imposibles penetraba en los jardines.[11]

As Juan Ramón was later to do, Bécquer describes the discovery of a *locus amoenus* that provides for a susceptible mind the kind of special ambiance conducive to evanescent visitation. Manrique, known to be of a remote and other-wordly disposition, deludes himself that he has glimpsed the ideal woman of his insistent dreams when what he has really witnessed is no more than a trick of the light, a moonbeam filtering irregularly through the foliage of the trees.

Even a cursory reading of the two pieces conveys an immediate awareness of their similarity. The lexical parallels are themselves numerous: Juan Ramón's setting is of an 'oscura arboleda' beneath a 'transparente cielo', while Bécquer writes of an 'oscura alameda' and a 'cielo azul, luminoso y transparente'; in 'Parque viejo', the figure appears 'de lo espeso de la umbría', while in 'El rayo de luna' Manrique's vision is glimpsed 'En el fondo de la sombría alameda'; Juan Ramón's apparition flees 'entre las sombras' and 'se pierde...en el fondo del sendero', while Bécquer's dream-woman 'desapareció en la oscuridad' as 'se ocultaba entre el follaje'. There are much broader thematic parallels, such as the acknowledged departure from reality and rational perception, which in 'Parque viejo' takes the form of the line 'Mis ojos pierdo, soñando' and in 'El rayo de luna' is revealed in the phrase 'presa su imaginación de un vértigo de poesía'. In both pieces, meanwhile, the moment of discovery, while of almost unbearable emotional intensity, is tinged with uncertainty, reflecting the essentially fragile and ephemeral quality of the experience: Juan Ramón's figure 'se adivina...tras blanco y flotante velo', while Manrique sees only 'una cosa blanca que flotó un momento y desapareció en la oscuridad'.[12] The haziness and lack of definition associated with the most powerful of discoveries is a familiar poetic theme, memorably rendered in the famous lines of Keats, 'Then felt I like a watcher of the skies, / when some new planet swims into his ken'.[13] Closer to the pieces under consideration, however, is Shelley's description of the unnamed poet's dreamy recollection of the 'veilèd maid' in 'Alastor'. Held in rapture by the indefinable beauty of her words, the poet turns towards her, 'And saw by the warm light of their own life / her glowing limbs beneath the sinuous veil / of woven wind'. She is then definitively lost as the poet opens his arms in an attempt to embrace her: 'Now blackness veiled his dizzy eyes, and night / involved and swallowed up the vision; sleep, / like a dark flood suspended in its course, / rolled back its impulse on his vacant brain'.[14]

Any effective linkage of 'El rayo de luna' or 'Parque viejo' with Shelley's poem is impossible, since I have been unable to find any evidence to suggest that the young Bécquer knew the work of the English poet, and Juan Ramón was too loudly enthusiastic upon his later acquaintance with Shelley for us to suspect that the encounter had already occurred by 1901. It is much easier to find circumstantial evidence for Jiménez's debt to Bécquer. The latter's poetry had been one of Juan Ramón's first loves, to the extent that he knew most of the *Rimas* by heart. It was an enduring affection, and during both his short sojourn as a student in Seville, and his later trip to Madrid in 1900 in response to the well-known postcard sent by Villaespesa and signed by Darío,

Bécquer had continued to be required reading for Juan Ramón. The young *modernistas* of Madrid were united in acknowledging Bécquer, or 'el divino Gustavo Adolfo', as their immediate inspiration in preference to the more 'institutional' figure of Núñez de Arce and that of Zorrilla, felt to have outlived his genius.[15] We have in addition the name given by Juan Ramón to his 1902 collection, felt by Graciela Palau de Nemes to be an explicit tribute to the memory of Gustavo Adolfo;[16] Cardwell regards the whole collection as a 'libro que mira explícitamente atrás, hacia Bécquer'.[17]

What I would suggest that Jiménez did in 'Parque viejo' was to use 'El rayo de luna' as a point of departure while adapting the crucial episode contained in it to a Symbolist pattern; Juan Ramón's later revisions of 'Parque viejo' would provide further supporting evidence here. Hence the change from the ruins of the Templar church to the autumnal park as a poetic setting. Ruins were of course a perennial setting for artistic reflection upon transience and mortality, since they emblematized mutability as it affected collective human endeavour; entire cultures and civilizations were as much subject to the ravages of time as individual human lives. This particular *locus amoenus* received fresh literary impetus in the early nineteenth century thanks in part to the compelling tones of the section entitled 'Les ruines' in Chateaubriand's *Le Génie du christianisme* of 1802. Lyrically reworked by Ramón López Soler in the pages of *El Europeo*, it became a consistent feature of Spanish Romanticism, and assumed particular importance for Bécquer, who used the dilapidated Gothic cloister of San Juan de los Reyes in Toledo within just such a pattern on three separate occasions: in the section on the church he wrote for the *Historia de los templos de España* of 1854; in the fourth of the *Cartas literarias a una mujer* of 1860-61; and, to the most marked degree, in the *leyenda* entitled 'Tres fechas' written after 'El rayo de luna' in 1862. The air of mystery and rumours of the arcane surrounding the activities of the Knights Templar therefore made the ruins of their church outside Soria a perfect choice for the evanescent vision experienced by Manrique. For Jiménez, however, writing in 1901 and with the profound impression made by the French Symbolists fresh in his mind, the 'autumnal park overhung with tones of Verlaine'[18] afforded the same possibilities seen by Bécquer in the ruinous cloister of a Gothic church. The potent nostalgia evoked by the timeworn aristocratic gardens is separated from the stimulus to memory exuded by San Juan de los Reyes by a generational poetic divide rather than by a thematic one. Structurally, both the cloister and the gardens within their paling suggest limitation, the circumscription of space, while in each case transcendent experience with points of reference outside the bounds of the human and temporal allows for a crucial but fleeting outlet from those prescribed limits. It is an important motif in late-nineteenth-century poetics generally and in a number of later poems by Juan Ramón Jiménez himself.[19]

I would contend, furthermore, that this climactic extract from 'El rayo de luna' permits a programmatic close reading in terms of poetic symbol and linguistic structures. In the first paragraph, for example, the evocative and sensuous description of natural scenery, as in Jiménez's later poem, establishes a mood, while the three adjectives applied to the sky are all symbolically accessible to the nineteenth-century reader. Firstly, 'azul' was regarded by Victor Hugo as the single word that encapsulated the essence of poetry, in its striving towards the infinite; the colour of sea and sky would later form the title of Rubén Darío's ground-breaking collection of 1888, in this case with the provocative and suggestive addition of suspended stops --that is, *Azul...--*, to reinforce the idea. Secondly, 'luminoso' is an unmistakable period reference to accentuated poetic inspiration, especially used in tandem with the succeeding image of the moon at its height. Thirdly, 'transparente' implies the power of inspiration to render diaphanous that which to the prosaic mind remains opaque. Manrique is thus snatched out of everyday reality into a situation where normality no longer functions: the undermining of rational awareness by the 'vértigo' that overwhelms his imagination stresses this. From the vantage point of this captivating magical scenario, Manrique looks back to the outline of Soria silhouetted against the horizon; it is a two-dimensional and monochrome image lacking colour and depth, lulled to sleep as Manrique forsakes it and plunges into the ruins, perchance to dream.

Thus, while Manrique's story functions uncomplicatedly as a sentimental tale, there is surely more at stake. Bécquer himself hints at the existence within the *leyenda* of more than one level of reading when he states in the first paragraph: 'yo he escrito esta leyenda, que a los que nada vean en su fondo, al menos podrá entretenerles un rato'.[20] At the heart of the tale, however, is

Forms of Spirituality in the Early Poems of Juan Ramón Jiménez   303

more than the self-delusion of the visionary who falls in love with a moonbeam in a ruined church at midnight on the night of a full moon; Bécquer assumes a serious note in assuring us that 'en su fondo hay una verdad, una verdad muy triste'.[21] He describes Manrique's predicament with the enigmatic smile of a profoundly personal imaginative sympathy in *desengaño*. When Manrique in his delirium comes to view wordly glory and pleasure as 'un rayo de luna', Bécquer's reaction is to state that 'lo que había hecho era recuperar el juicio'.[22]

In the figure of Manrique what we surely see is the persistent nineteenth-century theme of the hermetic idealist in search of the spirit of Beauty. Here too Bécquer's tale converges with Shelley's poem. For the degree of narcissism inevitably pertaining to such a quest is illustrated as much by Shelley's poet who 'images to himself the Being whom he loves'[23] as by Manrique's attribution to the ideal woman he has momentarily glimpsed of a series of gradually intensifying features. Expressive and melancholy blue eyes, dark flowing hair, a tall and light figure like that of an angel, a voice like the whispering of wind through trees, all are successively and intuitively created by Manrique. More important, perhaps, is the irresistibly Platonic note that is struck in the lines which follow: 'Y esa mujer, que es hermosa como el más hermoso de mis sueños de adolescente, que piensa como yo pienso, que gusta de lo que yo gusto, que odia lo que yo odio, que es un espíritu hermano de mi espíritu, que es el complemento de mi ser, ¿no se ha de sentir conmovida al encontrarme? ¿No me ha de amar como yo la amaré, como la amo ya, con todas las fuerzas de la vida, con todas las facultades del alma?'[24] Manrique's attempt to flesh out the vision he has just glimpsed sees him recreate his ideal woman in terms of the Aristophanic conception of love as a process of fusion, physical and spiritual, with a predestined 'other half', or 'complemento de mi ser' as he expresses it. The idea constitutes one of the two pieces of philosophical tours de force contained in Plato's *Symposium*; the second, I would argue, was that which would inspire Juan Ramón Jiménez in his poetic reworking of Bécquer's tale.

Surpassing Aristophanes' speech in Plato's schema is the intervention made by Socrates in which he tells of his instruction in the philosophy of love by the priestess Diotima. As Diotima tells Socrates, absolute Beauty is gained by a select few after a rigorous period of initiation and development; from an appreciation of beauty in the physical world, the sensitive soul transcends such lower manifestations and is eventually able to glimpse beauty in its most elevated form. The following question she puts to Socrates seems to me crucial to the understanding of Jiménez's poetics in *Rimas*: 'What may we suppose to be the felicity of the man who sees absolute beauty in its essence, pure and unalloyed, who, instead of a beauty tainted by human flesh and colour and a mass of perishable rubbish, is able to apprehend divine beauty where it exists apart and alone?' There could hardly be a better founding upon which to build the diffuse mysticism of 'Parque viejo': the poetic gaze raised from the latent sensuality of surrounding nature to a spirit of Beauty possessing a metaphysical dimension. It is a dimension even more strongly emphasized in Jiménez's revision of the poem for the *Segunda antolojía*. Here, the line 'se adivina vagamente' would be amended to 'se adivina, eterno y solo', a piece of phrasing that not only recreates the words of the passage cited from the *Symposium* but also stands representatively for the unified wholeness of the enduring One so superior to the variable and changeful Many within the larger Platonic pattern.[25] Amid the swirling dead leaves of the autumnal park, the young Jiménez glimpses a vision that elevates him fleetingly from the realm of the perishable. It perhaps marks the beginning of the search for a personal poetic god that Juan Ramón had claimed to have begun in his youth. In the preface to *Dios deseado y deseante* (1948-49), when quest had become joyful encounter, he could write: 'todo mi avance poético era avance hacia dios, porque estaba creando un mundo del cual había de ser el fin un dios'. During 1901, with the composition of poems for *Rimas*, the incipient quest was acquiring the shape of a yearning aesthetic spirituality with a transcendent Platonic emphasis as the young and hypersensitive Jiménez struggled to come to terms with the apparent finality of death. One of the companion pieces to 'Parque viejo', entitled 'Recuerdos', again irresistibly suggests the pattern found in the *Symposium*.[26] As in 'Parque viejo', the scene is one of a harmoniously pulsing sensual beauty as the poet and his companion walk hand-in-hand along the shore of a lake: 'la tarde estaba hermosa, / el ígneo sol de mayo / sonriendo se moría, / una canción de luces suspirando'. The setting sun is part of a joyfully functioning organic pattern that is self-sufficient and, so long as the question of transcendent meaning is not raised, sufficient to Jiménez himself. Thus the tranquillity of the moment is reflected in the lines 'Estaba mudo el parque, / dormitaban las flores y los pájaros', as nature is lulled to sleep. In revising the poem for the *Segunda antolojía*, Jiménez would opt for an entirely different emphasis, in which surrounding nature reflects back upon the pair their own radiant happiness in rather more extravagant examples of pathetic fallacy: 'Latía el parque, mudo: / se estasiaban las flores y los pájaros'. Although these more lavish lines seem reminiscent of Juan Ramón's earliest output, their purpose is poignantly to intensify the contrast as once more Jiménez's atmospheric scene is not enough; the placid loving calm is broken with a crucial question:

De pronto: Oye -me dijo,
¿por qué el azul espacio,
por qué el cielo purísimo
se mancha al reflejarse
en la inmundicia lóbrega del lago?[27]

The young poet is here painfully reminded that the beauty of the evening scene belongs to the transient and changeful mortal world. He cannot answer the girl's question, but can only tearfully kiss her eyes. The pathos of the moment is again reminiscent of 'Parque viejo', as the poem ends with a nightingale sounding 'un dulce quejido desgarrado'.

In the same section of the *Symposium* from which I quoted earlier we find the possible key to understanding this piece. Diotima continues speaking to Socrates: 'Do you not see that in that region alone where he sees beauty with the faculty capable of seeing it, will he be able to bring forth not mere reflected images of goodness but true goodness, because he will be in contact not with a reflection but with the truth? And having brought forth and nurtured true goodness he will have the privilege of being beloved of God, and becoming, if ever a man can, immortal himself'. The idea is even more famously restated by St Paul in the First Epistle to the Corinthians, where we are described as gazing 'through a glass darkly', a phrase I deliberately used earlier in this essay. Jiménez would seem to perceive that the beauty which the world can offer is but a muddy reflection of that transcendent beauty to which he aspires, the dim reflections in a mirror of St Paul's text. The quest for immortality must necessarily involve the discarding of the transient and perishable; the pattern is one that grows increasingly familiar as we read chronologically through Jiménez's verse. Young sees the issue thus: 'For Juan Ramón, instinctively Platonic at an early stage in his career and consciously so as he grew older, the poet partook of the eternal, the infinite, and the One as he successively reflected (on occasion, perhaps, more clearly than the shadows on the wall of Plato's cave) an ideal form'.[28] While Young is here relating Jiménez's poetic to the conceptual pattern found in the *Republic*, I would suggest that Jiménez's early verse recreates more nearly the set of ideas found in the *Symposium*. It is possible, after all, that Jiménez was already familiar with the basic framework of Platonic ideas on beauty prior to his reading of Shelley's 'A Defence of Poetry' in the Spanish translation published by Leonard Williams in 1904.[29] When Jiménez underlined in his personal copy phrasing such as 'the interpenetration of a diviner nature through our own', used by Shelley to refer to the act of poetic inspiration, and 'the state of mind produced by them is at war with every base desire', affirming the purity of such 'conditions of being', he was applauding the expression of ideas already close to his own heart. The reading of 'A Defence of Poetry', an essay which itself owed so much to Plato (Shelley was, after all, a devoted student and translator of the Greek thinker, as his ebullient translation of the *Symposium* readily testifies), initiated an exceptionally fertile contact between Juan Ramón and his English predecessor, one impressively detailed by Young. One issue less thoroughly explored is Jiménez's poetic debt to 'Adonais', which seems to me to warrant further investigation; given the remarkable coincidence of minds between the two poets, Juan Ramón's increasingly triumphant vision of death as pantheistic fusion may well be culled from Shelley's apprehension of the soul of Keats subsumed into a sentient Nature. Jiménez would surely have appreciated the choice of epitaph for Shelley's grave in the protestant cemetery at Rome: 'Nothing of him that doth fade, but doth suffer a sea-change into something rich and strange'.

Whatever the precise nature of Juan Ramón's debt to the Romantic Platonist, the names of Plato and Shelley were to loom large at each stage of his output. With the composition of *Rimas* in 1901, Jiménez was baring his youthful soul in terms that were intensely spiritual albeit lacking in definition.

Richard Cardwell is surely accurate in his assessment of one of the elements belonging to what he designates the 'nerve centre' of early *modernista* verse in Spain generally and of Jiménez's early work in particular: that of spiritual longing in art. This, he felt, was confused not just with religious sentiment but with aesthetic and even erotic feelings.[30] Of these three, the first two have lain behind much of the present discussion. The third, though more powerfully rendered in terms of sexual disappointment in 'Alastor', is nonetheless indisputably present in 'Parque viejo', as the 'suavísimo cuerpo' of Jiménez's vision is lost to his sight. Cardwell further affirms that by the mid-1890s the 'major call signs' of *modernismo* proper had made their appearance. His summary of these squares closely with the themes I have been considering here: the beguilement of art; the presence of spiritual and intuited essences alongside a recognition of the temporality of existence; the flight into reverie; the lyrical evocation of loss as a device against the terror of death and the pain of physical separation.[31] Yet while the themes adumbrated in *Rimas* are largely generational ones, the same poems testify to Juan Ramón Jiménez's growing stature as a poet, a poet whose innate sense of spirituality and the transcendent would, in years to come, acquire remarkable originality and depth. Out of the early synthesis of sources and influences making up the kind of composite picture seen in *Rimas*, Juan Ramón would go on to develop an entirely individual poetic voice.

To conclude, I think it appropriate, both within the parameters of the present essay and within the broader context of this volume and its inspiration, to cite the following eloquent words of John Henry Newman: 'true life is a hidden life in the heart; and though it cannot exist without deeds, yet these are for the most part secret deeds, secret charities, secret prayers, secret self-denials, secret struggles, secret victories'.[32]

NOTES

1. *Vida y obra de Juan Ramón Jiménez* (Madrid, 1957), pp.75-76.

2. *Rimas*, ed. by Ángel González (Madrid, 1981), 'Prólogo', p.21.

3. *Rimas*, ed. González, pp.69-71.

4. *Rimas*, p.33.

5. Verlaine's celebrated declaration that 'Votre âme est un paysage choisi' was made in *Clair de lune, Fêtes galantes* of 1869.

6. Compare Jiménez's similar evocation of the essential sterility of winter: 'Los jardines se mueren de frío; / en sus largos caminos desiertos / no hay rosales cubiertos de rosas, / no hay sonrisas, suspiros, ni besos': 'Las tardes de enero' (*Rimas*, p.61). Likewise, and more in tune with 'Parque viejo, 'La dulcísima luna ha embriagado el jardín / con sus besos de sueño y de amor. Por las sendas / hay suspiros, sonrisas y canciones... distantes / armonías; hay almas!': 'El palacio viejo' (*Rimas*, p.65).

7. In revising the piece for the *Segunda antolojía poética*, Jiménez would achieve a more careful sense of weighting by a modified punctuation: 'una pálida hoja mustia, / dando vueltas, cae al suelo'. The second stanza would likewise contain a more accomplished balance between semantic meaning and syntactical organization, reading in the 1919 version as follows: 'Y del fondo de la sombra, / llega, acompasado, el eco / de algún agua que suspira, / al darle una gota un beso'. In each case, the revised rhythm metrically rehearses the meaning of the words. In the second stanza, 'acompasado', set alone, is allowed to acquire a sense of musical time, while the *encabalgamiento* after 'el eco', more pointed in the later version, encourages us to pursue that word's resonances into the following verse. In the fourth stanza, meanwhile, the amended punctuation provides a cadence much more appropriate to the fluttering, irregular fall of a leaf to the ground. These examples allow us in turn to acquire a meaningful insight into what Jiménez meant by 'revivir'.

8. A reading of 'Parque viejo' as referring to self-projection via dream might be supported by Jiménez's lines from 'Nocturno': 'y mi alma que se muere de tristeza, / de nostalgia y de recuerdos, / se sumía fatigada / en la bruma de los sueños'; and, later in the same poem, 'y parece que del fondo de las sendas / unos hombres enlutados van saliendo... / Los jardines están llenos de visiones; / hay visiones en mi alma..., siento frío, / estoy solo, tengo sueño...' (*Rimas*, p.72, p.74). Similarly in the poem 'Alborada ideal': '...La sombría alameda / se esfumó entre las gasas de una nube de incienso ,/ y unos ángeles, bellos como vírgenes blancas, / en la nube perdían sus albísimos peplos' (*Rimas*, p.99).

9. See Young's *The Line in the Margin: Juan Ramón Jiménez and His Readings in Blake, Shelley and Yeats* (Madison, 1980), pp.91-99.

10. *The Line in the Margin*, p.97.

11. Gustavo Adolfo Bécquer, *Obras completas* (Madrid: Aguilar, 1969), pp.163-64.

12. This phrase alone, irresistibly reminding us of the *fiat lux* motif that dominates Bécquer's lyrical description of poetic inspiration and composition in the 'Introducción sinfónica', is enough to alert the reader to the possibilities of the sort of programmatic reading I have chosen to make.

13. From the sonnet 'On First Reading Chapman's Homer'.

14. *The Complete Poetical Works of Percy Bysshe Shelley*, ed. by Thomas Hutchinson (Oxford, 1919), p.19.

Forms of Spirituality in the Early Poems of Juan Ramón Jiménez 309

15. Ricardo Gullón felt that, until the appearance on the Spanish literary scene of Juan Ramón Jiménez, Bécquer had represented 'el poniente del romanticismo'; with the work of Jiménez, Bécquer's work had attained the status of 'aurora': see Gullón's *Direcciones del modernismo* (Madrid, 1963), p.28.

16. *Vida y obra*, p.80.

17. 'La belleza interior y la hermosura exterior: Alma y carne en *Azul*...', *Ibero-Amerikanisches Archiv*, 14 (1988), 307-27 (p.322).

18. Young, *The Line in the Margin*, p.97.

19. See for example the poem 'Aún la luna creciente', from the collection *Pureza* (1912). This is a subject to which I hope to dedicate a forthcoming article.

20. *Obras*, p.160.

21. *Obras*, p.160.

22. *Obras*, p.172.

23. Shelley's own words from the preface to 'Alastor': *The Complete Poetical Works*, p.14.

24. *Obras*, p.165.

25. Socrates' conversation with Cebes in the *Phaedo* renders this broader conceptual pattern succinctly:
'Did we not say some time ago that when the soul uses the instrumentality of the body for any enquiry, whether through sight or hearing or any other sense (because using the body implies using the senses), it is drawn away by the body into the realm of the variable, and loses its way and becomes confused and dizzy, as though it were fuddled, through contact with things of a similar nature?'
'Certainly.'
'But when it investigates by itself, it passes into the realm of the pure and everlasting and immortal and changeless; and being of a kindred nature, when it is once independent and free from interference, consorts with it always and strays no longer, but remains, in that realm of the absolute, constant and invariable, through contact with beings of a similar nature' (*Phaedo*, in *The Last Days of Socrates*, transl. by Hugh Tredennick (Harmondsworth, 1969), p.131).

26. See *Rimas*, ed. González, pp.152-53.

27. In revision, Jiménez substituted 'verdina' for the much more extreme 'inmundicia'. The earlier version suggests the trauma of Jiménez's life in the wake of his father's death, as we see evidence of a violent nervous reaction to mortality. The same revulsion for the physical world brought about by morbid obsession can be found in Pío Baroja's *Camino de perfección*, also published in 1902 and a work whose title and theme it is perhaps not inappropriate to adduce in this context.

28. *The Line in the Margin*, p.48.

29. See Young's masterly exploration of the impact of 'A Defence' on Jiménez's poetics in *The Line in the Margin*, pp.41-74.

30. See Cardwell's impressive study *Juan Ramón Jiménez: The Modernist Apprenticeship, 1895-1900* (Berlin, 1977), p.77.

31. *JRJ: The Modernist Apprenticeship*, p.162.

32. *Parochial and Plain Sermons* (London, 1879), V, 243.

'COMO SE FUE EL MAESTRO...'

PATRICIA MCDERMOTT
University of Leeds

Vosotros debéis amar y respetar a vuestros maestros, a cuantos de buena fe se interesan por vuestra formación espiritual. Pero para juzgar si su labor fue más o menos acertada, debéis esperar mucho tiempo, acaso toda la vida, y dejar que el juicio lo formulen vuestros descendientes
Juan de Mairena

¡El pobre señor! ¡Qué bien aquí las palabras! Pobreza señora, con esa señoría cierta que, dándolo todo, de todo se enseñorea, por la rica humildad de su tesoro conocido; que hace señor lo que toca: la estancia austera en que piensa, el paisaje que le da fondo, la cátedra que purifica, el jardín que endulza, la amistad que ennoblece; todo esto que ahora va a ser de nuevo lo que es...
Juan Ramón Jiménez

Al Dios de la distancia y de la ausencia,
del áncora en la mar, la plena mar...
Él nos libra del mundo --omnipresencia--,
nos abre senda para caminar
Antonio Machado

Don Francisco Giner de los Ríos died in Madrid on 18 February 1915 and was buried without ceremony, as he had requested, in the Civil Cemetery between the tombs of his masters Julián Sanz del Río and Fernando de Castro. 'Allí, o dondequiera que mañana reposen sus santas cenizas, el amor de su dilatada familia espiritual no lo dejará solo', wrote one of his disciples Luis de Zulueta in a leading memorial published in *España* on 26 February, which preceded Juan Ramón Jiménez's prose tribute and eye witness account, 'Elegía pura' (quoted above), and Antonio Machado's verse elegy, dated in Baeza on 21 February and addressed simply 'A don Francisco Giner de los Ríos'.[1] A homage in prose bearing the master's name had appeared in *Idea Nueva* in Baeza on 25 February and both elegies were republished in the *Boletín* of the Institución Libre de Enseñanza, the poem in Number 659-660 (February-March) and the prose in Number 664 (July), Machado's only contributions to the magazine of his *alma mater*.[2]

Effectively, the poet's panegyric marked a spiritual pilgrimage back to the origins of conscience and an overt reaffirmation of his allegiance to the spirit and ideal of humanity of Giner and the Institución Libre, as a communicating member of what Zulueta called its *Ecclesia dispersa*.[3] Significantly, when Machado incorporated the verse elegy into his *Páginas escogidas* of 1917, it formed part of the section 'Proverbios y cantares', the testament cast in popular form of his continuing spiritual quest for truth and transcendence, locked in the contradiction of heart and head, intuition and intellect, faith and scepticism, hope and despair.[4] The quest in 'Proverbios y cantares' in this edition is underpinned by two key deaths: the death of his young wife in 1912, the elusive shade of the maternal imago, the lost innocence and wholeness which is the goal of the quest, and with her death the frustration of continuity in the flesh; and the death of his old teacher, the fraternal imago of brotherly love, opposed to the envy of *cainismo*, identifying self in the service of others and offering continuity in the spirit by the transmission of the word and the work from master to disciple through the generations.

When the poet presented a revised and enlarged version of *Campos de Castilla* in his *Poesías completas* later that year, Giner's elegy had been transferred to a final section of 'Elogios', alongside the eulogies of Ortega, Unamuno, Darío, Azorín and Valle-Inclán in Machado's personal pantheon of philosophers and artists as national heroes. This section is a positive finale to the poetic campaign of radical moral rearmament which is the mainspring of the two editions of *Campos de Castilla* (1912 and 1917) and very much in keeping with the national cultural mission of reform through education which the Institución had set itself. It is fitting that the figure who had emerged as leader of the dissenting diaspora, liberal Catholics forced out of the Church in defence of freedom of conscience in 1870 and university professors forced out of their Chairs in 1875 in defence of university autonomy and the freedom to pursue truth and to teach without State or Church interference, should head the section of role models for a future secular society. Most significantly, the elegy is followed by the enigmatic encomium addressed 'Al joven meditador José Ortega y Gasset' (on the occasion of his *Meditación del Escorial*), as architect of a new philosophical edifice, a symbolic Escorial, which would undo the sectarian consequences of the Counter-Reformation in Spain.[5]

'Como se fue el maestro...'   313

Paradoxically, the ideal secular society envisaged by the Utopian *Institucionistas* --a free university and a free church in a free state-- would be a more profoundly spiritual and moral society, working to establish peace and justice, the Kingdom of God on earth. Secularization here, the separation of morality from confessional religion, is a religious, not an irreligious, process. Zulueta describes the pain of Giner's separation from the Established Church:

> ¡Cuánto debió sufrir al tener que abandonar la Iglesia, desgarrándose de la comunidad de su pueblo y de su tradición! Hizo todo lo que pudo para evitarlo. El joven pensador krausista oía misa los domingos y conservaba, como su amigo D. Fernando de Castro, la esperanza en una renovación de la Iglesia española.
> Esa esperanza, como tantas otras en el mundo religioso, se desvaneció después del Concilio Vaticano. Juzgó D. Francisco que no le era lícito, sin hipocresía, continuar llamándose católico. Fuera ya de la Iglesia oficial, su religiosidad se hizo todavía más intensa y más pura.[6]

The apotheosis of Giner as heterodox holy man, in an elegy which is an *aide-mémoire* for a national examination of conscience, brings out the situational irony of the imitator of Christ as the ideal of humanity, living according to a rule of poverty, chastity and obedience to the inner light of conscience, being outside the orthodox communion in late-nineteenth- and early twentieth-century Spain.[7] The implied intertexts in the elegy's frame of reference, Biblical and national, are a stimulus to both a universal and a historical consciousness of the continuity of difference in the *durée* of collective existence.

> Como se fue el maestro,
> la luz de esta mañana
> me dijo: Van tres días
> que mi hermano Francisco no trabaja.
> ¿Murió?...

The definite article establishes both the magisterial role and the Messianic nature of the subject, whose Christ-like identity is reinforced by the reference to the time-span since his active mission has ceased: three days corresponding to Christ's descent into Hell to harrow the souls of the just before His Resurrection on the third day. His Christian name associates him with the cult of St. Francis of Assisi, the cult of simplicity and a return to the purity of the origins of Christianity and that kinship with nature, magnified in the Canticle of the Sun attributed to 'Il Poverello', which was one of the major tenets of Krausism.[8] It is, indeed, the personification of the morning light, symbolizing renewal, that engages the poetic narrative voice in a Franciscan-Socratic dialogue, asking the leading question regarding the death of the individual in a preterite tense whose finality contrasts with the ongoing dynamic of the present tense and the imperative which is the dominant mode of the lyrical grammar of the elegy. The reader is initially left to fill in the solution to the mystery in the gap indicated by the suspension points. The clue that the teaching voice and work is only temporarily suspended is perhaps given in the opening conjunction, an echo of the legendary opening remark of Fray Luis de León in his inaugural lecture on his restoration to his Chair in Salamanca after his acquittal by the Inquisition: 'Como decía ayer...'. If this reading of a very elliptical clue is correct, a parallel is set up between Giner, persecuted by the Neo-Catholic reaction and imprisoned in 1875 in the Castle of Santa Catalina in Cádiz (where the idea of the Institución Libre was born), and Fray Luis, persecuted two centuries earlier for a Humanist interpretation of Scripture which was in conflict with the prevailing Scholastic orthodoxy of the Inquisitors. Such a reading would be in accord with the non-conformist reading of Spanish history as having deviated from its progressive evolution in the course of the sixteenth century and the identification of a dissenting tradition which the non-conformist continues and renews in the present.

    Sólo sabemos
que se nos fue por una senda clara,
diciéndonos: Hacedme
un duelo de labores y esperanzas.
Sed buenos y no más, sed lo que he sido
entre vosotros: alma.
Vivid, la vida sigue,
los muertos mueren y las sombras pasan;
lleva quien deja y vive el que ha vivido.
¡Yunques, sonad; enmudeced campanas!

The change to the plural in the response of the poetic voice evinces collective loss and collective responsibility, a collective knowledge that is both limited and limitless, following the sign of the symbolic path of light which is a clear indication of the way to perfection to be followed in obedience to the master's commands which live on in the living voice of the disciple. Within the dialogue of illumination, the poetic voice now 'throws' the master's voice and his moral imperatives, which are, in turn, reiterations of the 'Commandments of Humanity' transmitted by his master Sanz del Río in his translation of the 'Ideal of Humanity' of his German master Krause.[9] Wearing has shown the closeness of the ideas expressed here --the rejection of useless mourning in favour of positive action in the continuation of the life's work of the deceased by the survivors in a communion of the living and the dead in which the dead are spiritual guides, immortality in memory and the notion that eternal life is determined by the authenticity or inauthenticity of how life is lived-- to key ideas in Sanz's own *Filosofía de la muerte*.[10] They also reveal a substratum of Christian doctrine and the play on *vivir/morir* and *llevar/dejar* recalls the paradoxes of the Gospels and the mystics, but the emphasis here is on the relay of life in the here and now of the collectivity. The concrete symbolization of the final command, contrasting with the more general abstraction of the initial command, conveys the secular forging of the conscience of the race on the anvil of social progress in the silencing of clericalism.

> Y hacia otra luz más pura
> partió el hermano de la luz del alba,
> del sol de los talleres,
> el viejo alegre de la vida santa.

The first part of the elegy establishes the pattern of salvation --death and resurrection--, in the absence which is recalled to living presence in the transmission of the word and work of the master's gospel. The process of transformation (indicated by the initial conjunction) continues in the second part in the narration of his ascension into glory: his translation from time into eternal presence in the Ground of Being which, according to Krausist harmonic philosophy, both transcends and is immanent in Nature. Cobos has pointed to the echo of San Juan de la Cruz in the metaphorical light of the first line.[11] The pattern of light symbolism associates the elegy with the mystical tradition, both national and universal, which represents union with the Godhead as a journey towards the Absolute source of light, the divine

Sun.[12] The light of individual conscience which was a source of illumination in the work of enlightenment in historical time enjoys in death the Beatific Vision of Abel Martín's *Conciencia Integral* or *Gran Pleno*.

> ... Oh, sí, llevad amigos,
> su cuerpo a la montaña,
> a los azules montes
> del ancho Guadarrama.
> Allí hay barrancos hondos
> de pinos verdes donde el viento canta.
> Su corazón repose
> bajo una encina casta,
> en tierra de tomillos, donde juegan
> mariposas doradas...
> Allí, el maestro un día
> soñaba un nuevo florecer de España.

The suspension points mark the mysterious boundary between supernatural and natural vision as the poetic gaze is returned to the acts of the apostles in the land of the living. The command to the militants in the heterodox communion to translate the mortal remains of the man who communed with the divine in nature to a more fitting resting place on the mountain, however, immediately redirects the gaze upwards to a visionary centre, the meeting place of heaven and earth, reinforced by the symbolic colour of the infinite: blue. The general symbolism of the tree as world-axis, the life of the cosmos as generative and regenerative process, immortality, is reinforced by the colour green, symbolizing the renewal of life, of hope springing eternal. The evergreen pine is specifically a symbol of immortality, associated with the vegetation rites of Attis, whilst in Christian tradition, the ilex or evergreen holly oak is the source of the wood of the Cross and the crown of thorns, the tree of self-sacrifice as instrument in the fulfilment of divine mission. But the focus of attention is uplifted away from the suffering of the Passion to the triumph of the Resurrection in the contemplation of the play of golden butterflies, symbolic of the soul and, in their metamorphoses, of resurrection and immortality, and as such in Christian iconography are often placed in the hand of the Christ-child.[13]

In Machado's national symbology in *Campos de Castilla*, the ilex is the emblem of the humility and fortitude of the enduring Castilian spirit ('Las encinas') and the butterfly is the soul of the sierra ('Mariposa de la sierra'). The imagined sacred heart-land of the master, like the poet himself, an Andalusian naturalized in Castile, has a national geographic identity, the Guadarrama, where the Institución had its mountain hut. The repetition of *allí* points to a concrete, and at the same time symbolic, national space where not only is the working of the God of Nature revealed, but also the unfolding of the God of History. The eternal moment in nature is suspended to give way to the indefinite time --'un día'-- of historical vision: the master's dream of the regeneration of Spain which closes the elegy, opening out as a legacy to be fulfilled in the future.

The future mission had already been relayed to the youth of Spain in the jewel-light imagery of the finale of another poem included in the section of 'Elogios', 'Una España joven', which Machado had published on 29 January 1915 in the first issue of *España*. This 'semanario de la vida nacional' was the organ of the *Liga de Educación Política Española*, founded in 1914 by Ortega and a group of familiars of the Institución Libre, including Zulueta.[14] In his founding address in the Teatro de la Comedia on 23 March 1914, *Vieja y nueva política*, Ortega had criticized the 'old' politicians in proposing a 'new' politics which would be the expression of that 'vital' germinating Spain which he opposed to the 'official' Spain in its death throes. In 'Una España joven' Machado had starkly contrasted the sordid prosaic past and the poetic visionary future of Ortega's 'Two Spains', but in his elegy to Giner, true to Giner's harmonic vision, such a contrast is implicit. In his verse elegy the poet filters out all taint of the Manicheism which creeps into the prose obituary in the contrast made between Giner as charismatic teacher of the young, vital Spain and the old style self-publicists and political bosses who are scorned:

> Como todos los grandes andaluces, era D. Francisco la viva antítesis del andaluz de pandereta, del andaluz mueble, jactancioso, hiperbolizante y amigo de lo que brilla y de lo que truena. [...] Yo creo que sólo mueren definitivamente --perdonadme esta fe un tanto herética-- sin salvación posible, los malvados y los farsantes, esos hombres de presa que llamamos caciques, esos repugnantes cucañistas que se dicen políticos, los histriones de todos los escenarios, los fariseos de todos los cultos, y que muchos, cuyas estatuas de bronce enmohece el tiempo, han muerto aquí y, probablemente, allá, aunque sus nombres se conservan escritos en pedestales marmóreos.

In poetry, such satirical invective directed against the 'Other Spain' is reserved to other poems such as 'Del pasado efímero' and 'El mañana efímero' (both written in 1913), and, most importantly, the 'Llanto de las virtudes y coplas por la muerte de Don Guido', in which revolutionary anger is defused by playful mockery.[15] The mock or anti-elegy, as it has so aptly been called, appears to have been composed in conscious ironic counterpoint to the reverential elegy to Giner, a grotesque demythified anti-portrait to be read against the heroic myth of the master.[16] Anti-parallel lives in anti-parallel scripts in which, ironically, the heterodox outsider, condemned by Neo-Catholic reaction as a subversive *texto vivo*, is the 'living text' of an ideal national moral standard by which the archetypal *caballero cristiano* is judged and found null and void, a *texto muerto*.

The process of the intratextual parody --imitation with ironic inversion to establish difference, in which the object of moral satire is negatively marked for destruction and the parodied text is positively construed as ideal moral exemplar-- is mirrored in the intertextual parody of the 'original' elegy in Castilian, the *Coplas de don Jorge Manrique por la muerte de su padre*, Machado's lyrical tabernacle, which Aguirre has called one of the most memorable and consoling Socratic-Christian monuments of the Middle Ages.[17] Here the parody points to the distance between the decadence of the Andalusian Catholic aristocracy in the present and its vitality and stature in the past as personified by the Maestre de Santiago idealized in the poetic testimony of the son. Here, too, the parody unwittingly betrays the conflict between the revolutionary and the conservative impulse as it projects a lost national Golden Age, somewhat different from the historical reality of the Military Orders in the fifteenth century revealed by the 'working hypotheses' of Derek Lomax's research.[18]

Terry, in his Critical Guide to *Campos de Castilla*, suggests, as a possible source for the textual type of Don Guido, Unamuno's essay 'Sobre don Juan Tenorio', in which Machado's other acknowledged modern master contrasts, after Said Armesto, the two national archetypes, Don Quixote and Don Juan.[19] Machado's stereotype also appears to engage in intertextual dialogue with the 'Two Spains' speech of his younger Modernist master Ortega and, on a universal level, with the great ethical books of the Bible such as

Ecclesiasticus, as the poet draws a series of binary oppositions in the negative and positive exemplars of his poetic diptych: 'Evil matched with good, life matched with death, sinner matched with man of piety; so everywhere in God's works thou wilt find pairs matched, one against the other'.[20]

So in the poet's work: sin/piety, folly/wisdom, egoism/altruism, materialism/idealism, body/spirit, corruption/purity, perdition/salvation. The matter, as in Dante's *Divine Comedy*, is eschatological: after death, the judgement: Hell or Heaven. If Giner's elegy is Machado's *Paradiso*, then the 'Llanto' is his *Inferno*. Indeed, the surprisingly non-Spanish name, which is frequently encountered in the *Inferno*, where there is no love but self-interest, recalls in particular the meeting in Circle VIII with Guido da Montefeltro, the Ghibelline leader who had taken the Franciscan habit, condemned for fraud and treachery ('Absolved uncontrite means no absolution'); or earlier in that same circle, Guido Bonati, damned as a sorcerer, whose name is closely followed by a reference to Cain (the man-in-the-moon) and Seville:

> Lo! Guy Bonati; lo! Asdente -- he
> May well wish now that he had stuck to his last,
> But he repents too late;
> [...]
> But come! Cain with his thorn-bush
> strides the sill
> Of the two hemispheres; his lantern now
> Already dips to the wave below Seville[21]

Machado's Don Guido in the Seville of his spoof elegy is trapped in a circle of negative finality, in an endless sense of an ending, underlined by the repetition of *fin* at the beginning and end of the poem and mockingly underscored by the ceaseless tolling of the death knell: '¡Din-dan!'. 'Al fin, una pulmonía / mató a don Guido': the physical cause of death is recorded as on a death certificate ('Poor man sound and strong of body is better off than rich man enfeebled, and racked with disease. Health of the soul, that lies in duty done faithfully, is more worth having than gold or silver; no treasure so rare that it can match bodily strength. Health is best wealth...', *Ecclesiasticus*, 30, 14-16). The categorical fact of death is restated --'Murió don Guido, un señor'-- in the reprise of his life-story, from donjuanesque *señorito* to old *beato*, in the recall of hearsay regarding his horse-play, his wining and whoring and hardheaded restoration of squandered inheritance in single-minded fortune-hunting and marriage of convenience ('Do not follow the counsel of appetite; turn thy back on thy own liking. Pamper those passions of thine, and joy it will bring, but to thy enemies. Love not the carouse, though it be with poor men; they will be vying still one with another in wastefulness. And wouldst thou grow poor with borrowing to pay thy shot, thou with empty coffers? That were to grudge thy own life. / Let him toil as he will, the sot's purse is empty; little things despise, and little by little, thou shalt come to ruin. Wine and women, what a trap for the loyalty of the wise, how hard a test of good sense! He will go from bad to worse, that clings to a harlot's love; waste and worm shall have him for their prize; one gibbet the more, one living soul less. [...] Wilt thou pine away with care for riches, lose thy sleep for thinking of it? These solicitudes breed a madness in the brain...', *Ecclesiasticus*, 18, 30-33, 19, 1-3 and 31, 1-2).

Overt disbelief and the suggestion of sacrilege is expressed in the narrator's incredulous comment on the hypocrisy of the pagan sensualist, '-¡aquel trueno!-', joining a confraternity, donning the habit of the Nazarene and parading in the penitential processions of Maundy Thursday ('Here is one that wears the garb of penitence for wicked ends, his heart full of guile', *Ecclesiasticus*, 19, 23).[22] The fellow is given short shrift and dispatched to eternal death in a patronisingly dismissive apostrophe which uses the familiar form of address to establish the authority and the contempt of the poetic judge in the sustained sarcasm of his one-sided dialogue with the corpse:

> Buen don Guido, ya eres ido
> y para siempre jamás...
> Alguien dirá: ¿Qué dejaste?
> Yo pregunto: ¿Qué llevaste
> al mundo donde hoy estás?
>
> ¿Tú amor a los alamares
> y a las sedas y a los oros,
> y a la sangre de los toros
> y al humo de los altares?
>
> Buen don Guido y equipaje,
> ¡buen viaje!...

The obvious answer to the loaded rhetorical questions is to be found within the authoritative texts established by the multi-textual parody: in the complementary elegy to Giner, in the *Coplas* of Jorge Manrique and in their Scriptural sources, both in the Old Testament ('Love money, and thou shalt be called to account for it; thy quest corruption, of corruption thou shalt have thy fill. Many have given themselves up to the lure of gold, and in its beauty found their ruin; its worship was a snare to catch their feet; alas, poor fools that went searching for it, and themselves were lost!', *Ecclesiasticus*, 31, 5-7) and in the New, particularly, the Sermon on the Mount, the essence of Christianity for the Krausist:

> Do not lay up treasure for yourselves on earth, where there is moth and rust to consume it, where there are thieves to break in and steal it; lay up treasure for yourselves in heaven, where there is no moth or rust to consume it, no thieves to break in and steal. Where your treasure house is, there your heart is too. The eye is the light of the whole body, so that if thy eye is clear, the whole of thy body will be lit up; whereas if thy eye is diseased, the whole of thy body will be in darkness. And if the light which thou hast in thee is itself darkness, what of thy darkness? How deep will that be! A man cannot be the slave of two masters at once; either he will hate the one and love the other, or he will devote himself to the one and despise the other. You must serve God or money; you cannot serve both. (*Matthew*, 6, 19-24).

The poetic gaze focuses on the closed eyes in the dead face, interpreted as signs of that spiritual blindness in life that is carried into eternity: the joined circles that form the mathematical symbol of infinity: in the case of Don Guido, the compound interest on eternal debit, eternal nothing:

> El acá
> y el allá, caballero,
> se ve en tu rostro marchito,
> lo infinito:
> cero, cero.

The focus widens in a mock meditation on the skull (with its implied pun on *calavera*), beneath the waxen skin, whose yellow colour, symbolizing treachery and faithlessness, is linked to that of the candle carried in the Holy Week charade. It travels down the body, laid out for burial in the habit of his lay order (that of the Third Order of St. Francis, whose colour purple symbolizes penitence, but which is also the colour of imperial and sacerdotal power and authority?) and ends with a close-up of the hands crossed over the breast, in a frozen frame that pictorially parodies the secular portraits of noblemen by El Greco.

'¡Oh fin de una aristocracia!': the vital spirit of the old faith is dead and gone from this *cuerpo presente*, which only serves as a *memento mori*, the death mask of 'Black Spain', the dead weight and habit of Establishment traditionalism which Republican Spain wished to jettison. (The gold and the red of blood are the colours not only of the *fiesta nacional*, but also of the flag of the Catholic monarchy). By contrast, the mystical flame of El Greco's religious paintings, the living spirit of what is perceived as a progressive tradition, is projected in purely visionary terms in the figurehead of a Giner de los Ríos transfigured on the mountain like a prophet, in what amounts to a national Sermon on the Mount in elegaic form. Like that of his medieval model Jorge Manrique, Machado's elegy is an *ars vivendi*, a celebration of life that preaches hope and consolation for men of his own persuasion in a time of transition.

> Blessed are those who suffer persecution in the cause of right; the kingdom of heaven is theirs. Blessed are you, when men revile you, and persecute you, and speak all manner of evil against you falsely, because of me. Be glad and light-hearted, for a rich reward awaits you in heaven; so it was they persecuted the prophets who went before you. You are the salt of the earth; if salt loses its taste, what is there left to give taste to it? There is no more to be done with it, but throw it out of doors, for men to tread it under foot. You are the light of the world; a city cannot be hidden if it is built on a mountain-top. A lamp is not lighted to be put under a bushel measure; it is put on the lampstand, to give light to all the people of the house; and your light must shine so brightly before men that they can see your good works, and glorify your father who is in heaven. (*Matthew*, 5, 10-16)

* * *

> But the wise man will be learning the lore of former times; the prophets will be his study. The tradition handed down by famous men will be in his keeping; his to con the niceties of every parable; learn the hidden meaning of every proverb, make himself acquainted with sayings hard to understand. To

great men he will render good service, will be summoned to the prince's own council; will go upon his travels in foreign countries, to learn by experience what the world offers of good and of harm. With dedicated heart, he will keep early vigil at the Lord's gates, the Lord that made him, to win audience for his plea from the most High. His lips will be eloquent in prayer, as he entreats pardon for his sins. At the Lord's sovereign pleasure, he will be filled with a spirit of discernment, so that he pours out showers of wise utterence, giving thanks to the Lord in his prayer. His plans and thoughts guided from above, he will have skill in the divine mysteries; will make known all the traditon of teaching he has received, and take pride in that law which is the Lord's covenant with man. This wisdom of his, extolled on every side, will never fall into oblivion; the memory of him, the renown of him, will be held in honour from age to age. His wise words will become a legend among the nations; where faithful men assemble, his praise will be told. A life that shall leave such fame as one man wins in a thousand; a death not unrewarded. (*Ecclesiasticus*, 39, 1-15)

NOTES

1. *España*, No.5, 6-7, reversed [55-56] in facsimile edition (Vaduz: Topos Verlag, 1982).

2. See J. Campos, 'Antonio Machado y Giner de los Ríos (Comentario a un texto olvidado)', *La Torre*, Año XII, Núms. 45-46 (1964), 59-64, and P. de A. Cobos, *Sobre la muerte en Antonio Machado* (Madrid: Ínsula, 1972), pp.35-45. Both reproduce the prose text and, favouring its prior composition, study the transformation process into poetry. G. Ribbans, who appends the text to his edition of *Campos de Castilla* (Madrid: Ediciones Cátedra, 1989), in a note to the verse elegy, p.235, records that the prose necrology was also published in *El Porvenir Castellano*, 4 March 1915. Subsequent verse quotations in the main text are taken from this edition.

3. *Boletín de la Institución Libre*, Núm. 659-60, p.53, in a two-part article entitled 'Lo que se lleva'/'Lo que se deja' (taken from Machado's elegy). See D. Wearing, *Antonio Machado, the Institución Libre de Enseñanza and Spanish Krausism*, unpublished doctoral dissertation, University of Leeds, 1983, p.73. I am most grateful to my former student for permission to cite this fine piece of research.

4. See O. Macrí, *Poesía y prosa Tomo II: Poesías completas* (Madrid: Espasa-Calpe/Fundación Antonio Machado, 1989), p.923.

5. Article 15 of the Institución's statutes stated: 'La Institución Libre de Enseñanza es completamente ajena a todo espíritu e interés de comunión religiosa, escuela filosófica o partido político; proclama tan sólo el principio de la libertad e inviolabilidad de la ciencia'. Quoted by Wearing, p.287.

6. Zulueta, 'Lo que se lleva'. J. López-Morillas, *El krausismo español* (México-Madrid-Buenos Aires: Fondo de Cultura Económica, 1980), p.158, quotes Giner's article 'Los católicos viejos y el espíritu contemporáneo', in which he distinguishes two tendencies, the sentimental (France and America) and the intellectual (Germany), in an evolving 'cristianismo racional' or 'religión natural', whose common denominator is a belief in the existence and providence of God and the immortality of the soul. López-Morillas places Giner in the sentimental camp.

7. O. Chadwick, *The Secularization of the European Mind in the Nineteenth Century* (Cambridge: Cambridge University Press, 1975), p.156, quotes the historian Edgar Quinet in the 1840s, defending Voltaire, Rousseau and the *Philosophes* as the reformers of a secularized Christianity : 'You seek Christ in the sepulchre of the past; but Christ has left his sepulchre; he has moved on, has changed his place; he is alive, he is incarnate, he descends into the modern world.'

8. Chadwick, pp.255-56, cites a letter from Auguste Comte in 1845 on the meaning of the Catholic cult of saints: 'It keeps the memory of good men and women, offers their lives for our admiration, gives each of us a special patron, the man for whom we have a Christian name in baptism, and solemnly invites us to emulation. It fulfils, he wrote, an instinct in our nature, denies death, and joins the succeeding generations in a single society. Positivism has the task of preserving this continuity in mankind. Its temple is wider than the narrow chapel of Rome, for it will remember all who worked for the progress of humanity.' Chadwick notes the popularity of Saint Francis among secularists at the end of the nineteenth century and Zulueta draws attention to the identification of Giner and his name-saint: 'Así, según el

diverso punto de vista de sus discípulos, a unos les parecía un Sócrates, a otros un San Francisco de Asís.' S. Lipp has subtitled his study *Francisco Giner de los Ríos, A Spanish Socrates* (Waterloo, Ontario: Wilfrid Laurier University Press, 1985).

9. 6º Mandamiento: 'Debes hacer el bien con pura, libre, entera voluntad y por los buenos medios.' 13º Mandamiento: 'Debes hacer el bien, no por la esperanza, ni por el temor, ni por el goce, sino por su propia bondad; entonces sentirás en ti la esperanza firme en Dios y vivirás sin temor ni egoísmo y con santo respeto hacia los decretos divinos.' Quoted, Wearing, op.cit., p.163. Compare Machado's proud boast in his portrait of the artist as an *institucionista* man which heads *Campos de Castilla*: 'y, más que un hombre al uso que sabe su doctrina, / soy, en el buen sentido de la palabra, bueno' ('Retrato').

10. Wearing, pp.93-97, 129-30.

11. Cobos, *Sobre la muerte de Antonio Machado*, p.43. In his note 'Sobre las imágenes en la poesía', *Los complementarios, Obras. Poesía y prosa*, ed. by A. de Albornoz and G. de Torre (Buenos Aires: Losada, 1964), p.709, Machado quotes this image in San Juan as an example of metaphor as expressive response to overwhelmimg emotion: 'En la noche dichosa, / en secreto, que nadie me veía, / ni yo miraba cosa, / sin otra luz ni guía / sino la que en el corazón ardía. / Aquesta me guiaba / más cierto que la luz del mediodía...'. Machado imitates 'el más hondo lírico español' in his use of *silva-romance* in the elegy.

12. Machado ends his prose version with a Teresian echo: 'su alma vendrá a nosotros en el sol matutinal que alumbra los talleres, *las moradas* del pensamiento y del trabajo' (my italics). Earlier in the same, he had stated explicitly: 'Era un místico, pero no contemplativo y extático, sino laborioso y activo. Tenía el alma fundadora de Teresa de Avila y de Iñigo de Loyola; pero él se adueñaba de los espíritus por la libertad y por el amor.' Giner, writing in *La universidad española* on the way the intellectual élite should conduct its mission of enlightenment, recommends that it should act '... no con la condescendencia gratuita del superior gubernamental y benévolo para con el súbdito, inferior y distante de él, sino con la conciencia del hermano para con el hermano, que, sin acepción de personas, reparte como el sol luz y calor a unos y otros, que obra en caridad, que a la vez es rigor de justicia y pone en ello su alma entera.' Quoted, Wearing, p.357.

13. Wearing, p.257, quotes Giner: 'La muerte no es más que un momento del proceso universal orgánico y de su obra de renovación constante.' Zulueta describes Giner's love for nature: 'Amó a la Naturaleza D. Francisco y enseñó a amarla. No es posible explicar a los que no lo han visto lo que era D. Francisco en el campo. Sabía sacar de las cosas naturales todo su divino ideal; poetizaba el paisaje, pero fundiéndose en él y sin tomarlo nunca arbitrariamente como fondo para los propios pensamientos. [...] Ningún pagano amó tanto a la Naturaleza. Para D. Francisco, además, en ella estaba Dios' ('Lo que se lleva').

14. 'Tú, juventud más joven, si de más alta cumbre / la voluntad te llega, irás a tu aventura / despierta y transparente a la divina lumbre, / como el diamante clara, como el diamante pura.' For the founding of the Liga and *España*, see the introduction to the facsimile edition and E. López Campillo, *La Revista de Occidente y la formación de minorías (1923-1936)* (Madrid: Taurus, 1972), pp.44-45. For Machado's association with the Liga, see Wearing, pp.387-88.

15. 'Mas otra España nace, / la España del cincel y de la maza, / con esa eterna juventud que se hace / del pasado macizo de la raza. / Una España implacable y redentora, / España que alborea / con un hacha en la mano vengadora, / España de la rabia y de la idea' ('El mañana efímero'). Zulueta describes Giner's vision of historical development as evolutionary organic

growth: 'Hijo de la Revolución, no creyó jamás en la eficacia de estas bruscas convulsiones sociales. Sostenía que todo pueblo revolucionario era, en el fondo, como el nuestro, rutinario. Sentía el valor y la belleza del desarrollo lento, perenne realización histórica de los principios ideales, cada día más perfecta, siempre imperfecta. No quería romper impíamente la continuidad con el pasado. No hubiera encontrado asiento en el Congreso, porque, en cuanto a los principios, los partidos más radicales le parecían atrasados --¡no piden nada!-- y en cuanto a los procedimientos encontraba exceso, violencia, falta de profundo sentido histórico en los partidos más conservadores.'

16. 'Llanto...' appears for the first time in *Poesías completas* (1917). A. González and A. Rodríguez, 'La elegía como forma poética en Machado', *Papeles de Son Armadans*, Año 22, 87,259 (1977), 23-51, find the evidence for a conscious contrast with Giner's elegy inconclusive. C. Beceiro, 'Un texto de Antonio Machado "Sobre pedagogía"', *La Torre*, 61 (1968), 61-86, speaks of a subconscious contrast.

17. J. M. Aguirre, *Jorge Manrique 'Coplas de amor y de muerte'* (Zaragoza: OLIFANTE. Ediciones de Poesía, 1980), p.9.

18. Popularized in his inaugural lecture on 19 February 1974: 'One can see how marriage and family ties, a desire for private property, growing class-consciousness and the lack of any clear common aim all combined to corrupt the Order and how its history from 1275 to 1493 was one of distintegration and internal feuds' (*Another Sword for St. James*, University of Birmingham, 1974, pp.11-12). For parody, see L. Hutcheon, *Theory of Parody. The teachings of Twentieth-century Art Forms* (New York and London: Methuen, 1985).

19. A. Terry, *Campos de Castilla*, A Critical Guide (London: Grant and Cutler/Tamesis Books Ltd., 1973), p.67. See M. de Unamuno, *Ensayos* (Madrid: Aguilar, 1958), II, 471-78, in which he postulates: 'Si, como el gran poeta portugués Guerra Junqueiro, escribiese yo una *Morte de Don João*, le pondría al que fue seductor de oficio muriendo entre dos frailes, después de haberse confesado y comulgado devotamente y legado su fortuna, no a los hijos de sus desvaríos que pudieran andar por ahí perdidos y sin padre, sino a cualquier convento o para que se digan misas en sufragio de su alma'.

20. 33, 15. *The Holy Bible*, transl. by Knox (London: Burns and Oates/MacMillan and Co. Ltd., 1957), p.614. All quotations are taken from this edition. *Ecclesiasticus*, 40, 11 and *Ecclesiastes*, 1, 7 are the source via Manrique of Machado's river-sea/life-death symbolism.

21. Canto XX, 118-126 and Canto XXVII, 118. *The Comedy of Dante Alighieri The Florentine. Cantica I: Hell (L'Inferno)*, transl. by by D. L. Sayers (Harmondsworth: Penguin Books, 1949), pp.198 and 243 respectively. 'Dante y yo --perdón, señores-- , / trocamos --perdón, Lucía--, / el amor en Teología', 'Proverbios y cantares', xxv, Ribbans, p.219.

22. As in 'La saeta', the commemoration of Holy Week in Seville does not transcend the Passion to Resurrection. F. Cantalapiedra, 'La doble vida de don Guido', in *Antonio Machado, hoy. Actas del Congreso Internacional conmemorativo del cincuentenario de la muerte de Antonio Machado* (Seville: Ediciones Alfar, 1990), IV, 249-60, reads a double ironic meaning in the language of the poem in terms of *germanía*.

DE UNAMUNO, SUBMARINOS Y CONDENAS.
UNOS APUNTES SOBRE DISCREPANCIAS DE UNAMUNO Y SU *LESA MAJESTAD*

DAVID ROBERTSON
University of Stirling

En el capítulo XVIII de su entrañable libro *Vida de don Miguel* Emilio Salcedo nos ofrece una noticia corta acerca de un hecho poco comentado sobre Miguel de Unamuno: su condena a dieciséis años de cárcel en 1920 por injurias al rey Alfonso XIII.[1] Aunque es de sobra conocido que durante su vida de publicista Unamuno tuvo numerosos roces con las autoridades, es curioso, por una parte, que Unamuno recibiera esta condena tan severa y, por otra, que ésta haya sido poco comentada por los que estudian su labor política. En este trabajo nos proponemos ofrecer una breve esclaración de estos hechos, situarlos en su contexto histórico, aportar unos datos nuevos y corregir otros que creemos erróneos.

Salcedo vincula la condena a un artículo titulado 'Ante el diluvio' de 1920, aparecido, según escribe, en Valencia aunque no especifica ni el periódico ni la fecha exacta de publicación. Ahora bien, el único periódico de Valencia en que publicaba Unamuno era *El Mercantil Valenciano* y, por desgracia, la gran mayoría de sus contribuciones a este diario (y a varios otros) aún no han sido recopilados ni re-editados y, por tanto, son desconocidos.[2] Hemos podido comprobar que el artículo citado por Salcedo como el que provocó 'el inmediato proceso' judicial de Unamuno apareció en *El Liberal* de Madrid el 26-9-1920 y al repasar los números de *El Mercantil Valenciano* correspondientes a 1920 nos encontramos con otras pruebas de que la información de Salcedo no corresponde con los hechos. En *El Mercantil Valenciano* de 17-9-1920 aparece en primera página una noticia titulada 'Don Miguel de Unamuno condenado' en que se dan los pormenores del fallo y de ella se saca que, contrario a lo que explica Salcedo, fueron tres las causas que el fiscal de la Audiencia de Valencia levantó contra Unamuno por 'tres supuestos delitos de injuria a Alfonso, contenidos en otros tantos artículos publicados en *El Mercantil Valenciano*'. Citando de la sentencia dictada por la

Audiencia valenciana, la noticia nombra los artículos de Unamuno por los que fue procesado y la sentencia en cada caso.

Estos tres artículos son 'El Archiduque de España' de 27-10-1918, 'Irresponsabilidades' de 17-11-1918 y 'La soledad del rey' de 9-2-1919. Según informa la citada noticia de *El Mercantil Valenciano*, Unamuno quedó absuelto por el último de estos escritos pero por los dos primeros se le condenó a ocho años de prisión mayor y multa de quinientas pesetas por cada uno. A continuación el diario cita las bases fundamentales de ambas condenas y de éstas se hace patente que, de los dos escritos castigados, el que más ofensa dio a las autoridades fue el titulado 'El Archiduque de España' -- es decir, el primero en aparecer-- ya que los considerandos relevantes hacen una extensa relación de los supuestos delitos del autor que nos permitimos copiar aquí, puesto que en ellos se tocan varios temas que trataremos más adelante:

> Que escrito el artículo titulado 'El Archiduque de España', en forma manifestamente despectiva para la augusta persona de S.M. el Rey, a quien irónicamente se le llama archiduque diciendo que es archiduquesa S.M. la Reina doña Cristina, por cuya intervención durante los cuatro años de guerra europea se ha estado jugando a la neutralidad, la cual ha resultado una alcahuetería, que el rey hace dejación de sus funciones de jefe de Estado, permitiendo que su augusta madre sea todavía regente; que ha sido parcial en favor de los imperios centrales con perjuicio de España, induciendo a sus ministros a proceder como si fuera seguro el triunfo de aquéllos; que por la intervención de S.M. doña María Cristina se hizo lo que el procesado llama vergonzoso cachipuche de la incautación de barcos alemanes, que España es un archiducado dependiente de Alemania, y que no hay en la nación voluntad nacional, sino tan sólo voluntad del archiduque, refiriéndose a S.M. el Rey, aparte de otros conceptos e imputaciones que desde luego puede afirmarse que no constituyen una crítica racional y legal de carácter político, sino que realmente traspasan estos límites, y claramente se ve tanto por el sentido general que inspira el artículo como por el de cada uno de los conceptos vertidos en el mismo, que el propósito de su autor ha sido el de menospreciar la augusta persona de S.M. el Rey, y por tanto el de injuriarle, debiendo en su consecuencia estimarse los conceptos mencionados comprendidos en el Artículo 102 del Código penal.[3]

Queda claro, por tanto, que a Unamuno se le procesa y condena por publicar comentarios sobre varios temas de gran conflictividad en la época: la supuesta actuación partidista del rey Alfonso XIII y, notablemente, de su madre, la ex-Regente, María Cristina de Habsburgo-Lorena, en asuntos relacionados con la guerra europea; la neutralidad española en este conflicto y las relaciones entre España y Alemania, y estos comentarios, según las autoridades, constituían un caso de lesa majestad.

Sería conveniente en este punto repasar, aunque brevemente, algunos de los factores que conducen a Unamuno a este enfrentamiento con el más alto poder de su país. Aunque el compromiso intelectual de Unamuno con los asuntos diarios de la dirección de España es constante durante su vida, es a partir de 1914 que se lanza a hacer una labor de publicista beligerante frente al régimen y las figuras que lo encarnan; una actividad que Inman Fox ha calificado de 'casi frenética'.[4] En este proceso hay que tener en cuenta dos factores principales: la amarga polémica ideológica suscitada en España por la guerra que estalla en Europa en agosto de 1914 y la destitución de Unamuno, en ese mismo agosto, y sin explicación o justificación alguna, del Rectorado de la Universidad de Salamanca. La confluencia de este atropello profesional con su radical desacuerdo con la postura oficial de estricta neutralidad adoptado por el régimen frente al conflicto europeo lleva a Unamuno a emprender una nutrida campaña, desde la tribuna y la prensa, no sólo contra los políticos del día sino, a la larga, contra figuras de la familia real.

La relación difícil que tiene Unamuno con Alfonso XIII desde el período 1914-18 en adelante no fue siempre tan mal avenida. Aunque de espíritu medularmente liberal y antimonárquico, Unamuno habla del monarca con cierta simpatía durante los primeros años de su reinado. Comentando un encuentro con el rey durante una visita de éste a Salamanca en 1904, dice 'el mozo me gusta, me parece sencillo y bien intencionado'.[5] No obstante, Unamuno no tardaría en notar otros rasgos del rey que considera poco favorables: por ejemplo, la influencia de su madre, la 'insoportable austríaca', la afición de Alfonso a los asuntos militares y su falta de ideales: 'el muchacho va por muy mal camino; resulta voluntarioso e indisciplinado. Me temo que quiera salir un *petit kaiser*, y ... aquí sería una calamidad nacional. Auguro muy mal de su reinado'.[6]

A pesar de las dudas que alberga acerca de los dotes regios de Alfonso, Unamuno aun no abandona sus esperanzas de que la monarquía pueda servir para encaminar el país hacia una auténtica democracia moderna. En setiembre de 1915, por ejemplo, cuando Unamuno y el Rey coinciden en Guernica, éste extiende una invitación para visitarle en Madrid y que Unamuno no rechaza, aunque cuando pide audiencia en Palacio unos meses más tarde no recibe contestación.[7] Hasta en plena crisis política del turbulento año 1917 y en el contexto del gran mitin de las izquierdas celebrado en mayo de ese año en la Plaza de Toros de Madrid, Unamuno demuestra que todavía mantiene cierta fe en la monarquía aunque sus palabras constituyen una clara advertencia para el trono:

> ... estamos asistiendo a una revolución y los tronos mismos se derrumbarán al cabo al no saber cimentarse en el suelo que está amasado con sangre de esta revolución ... porque si se persiste en la neutralidad a todo trance y costa, muchos que no hemos sido republicanos nunca, que no lo somos hoy todavía, que aún tenemos un pequeño hilo de esperanza de esta monarquía resurgida de la revolución de setiembre y no del despotismo de Fernando VII El Abyecto, tendremos en este caso que hacernos republicanos al cabo.[8]

A juzgar por sus escritos políticos reeditados y no-reeditados que hemos consultado, parece ser que por lo menos hasta mediados de 1917 Unamuno seguía siendo una figura 'recuperable' por el sistema político si éste se reformaba desde arriba. Con sus críticas del aparato político e institucional de la Restauración no trataba de derribar sino de componer, además de reformar el Partido Liberal rescatándolo de la influencia caciquil dominante y convirtiéndolo en un auténtico órgano de opinión pública. Hasta aquí son pocas o al menos indirectas las referencias a figuras de la familia real, limitándose Unamuno a dirigir sus críticas contra los políticos del 'turno' que más despreciaba; el conde de Romanones, Manuel García Prieto y, sobre todo, Eduardo Dato.

No obstante, a partir del verano de 1917 y sobre todo en 1918 cuando la derrota de los Poderes Centrales en el conflicto europeo ya parecía sólo cuestión de tiempo, Unamuno, desengañado sobre la posibilidad de que Alfonso XIII diera una orientación más abierta al régimen y reaccionando contra la sospechada simpatía del rey hacia Alemania, ataca directamente contra el rey y su madre, llevando la batalla política hasta el mismo seno del régimen. En los artículos que escribe para la prensa de aquí en adelante se encuentran, entre los comentarios sobre la situación socio-política española, alusiones constantes al rey en las que Unamuno opina que la monarquía personificada por Alfonso XIII se ha convertido en un obstáculo para la renovación política de España: 'el problema político de España no es tanto de monarquía cuanto de monarca'.[9] Al mismo tiempo, vale la pena notar que ambas la temática y la fecha de publicación de los dos artículos castigados por los tribunales de Valencia coinciden estrechamente con el colapso del régimen del kaiser Freidrich Wilhelm de Alemania en noviembre de 1918. Alfonso XIII, ya hondamente preocupado por la seguridad de su trono desde la caída en Rusia de la dinastía de los Romanov en marzo de 1917, no podía menos que contemplar con creciente desconcierto la desaparición de otra de las grandes coronas y sentir temores por la suya.

La Gran Guerra, de hecho, pone de relieve y subraya los defectos del sistema político español, las fuertes tensiones y el secular atraso de un país en que unos luchaban por la modernización mientras que otros, los más poderosos, querían defender el status quo contra las reivindicaciones de las clases menos privilegiadas. La opción neutralista del Gobierno en 1914 no sólo obedece a la falta de preparación militar de España para una contienda de esta índole y envergadura sino también a una falta de identificación moral-ideológica frente al conflicto, amén del hecho de que la neutralidad proporcionaba a España la oportunidad de obtener pingües beneficios del comercio con los países beligerantes. Era también el caso que la opinión pública se dividió en dos campos bien previsibles --aliadófilos y germanófilos-- sobre esta cuestión, impidiendo, por tanto, cualquier apoyo gubernamental abierto, aunque sólo fuera moral, hacia un bando u otro. Para Unamuno y otros muchos miembros de la élite intelectual aliadófila, la falta de identificación oficial con los Aliados, que para ellos encarnaban valores democráticos y civiles frente a los regímenes autocráticos y militaristas de los Poderes Centrales, constituía una profunda vergüenza nacional. Se recordará que la vecina Portugal, recientemente convertida en república, envió tropas para luchar con los Aliados. La neutralidad española es, para Unamuno, una admisión de debilidad y cobardía moral de parte de la clase política y las figuras de ambos partidos dinásticos a quienes castiga constantemente durante los años de la guerra.

A Unamuno no se le escapa que la victoria de los Aliados en la guerra traería profundos cambios democratizadores no sólo a las naciones beligerantes sino también a España: 'pero si triunfan los ideales expuestos mejor que por nadie por Wilson ... entonces habrá acabado la monarquía española'.[10] Su fe en el triunfo final de los países democráticos explica la envergadura y el vigor de su campaña --cuya verdadera extensión aún se desconoce-- a favor de Inglaterra y Francia durante la guerra. También explica hasta qué punto Unamuno, con el peso de su fama nacional e internacional, resultaba una espina en el costado de las autoridades que temían el efecto de sus palabras, sobre todo en el exterior. Como muestra de la imagen de Unamuno que tenían las autoridades damos la siguiente cita del artículo 'Revoltosos' en el que Unamuno reitera un informe sobre él elaborado por la Dirección de Seguridad en Salamanca que fue presentado en el juicio de Valencia:

> En cumplimento a su comunicación fecha tres del actual en la que ordena se informe sobre la conducta moral observada por don Miguel de Unamuno y Jugo, he de participar a V.S. que en esta jefatura de Policía no constan antecedentes delictivos del señor Unamuno; no obstante, puédesele juzgar como elemento peligroso y perturbador del orden actual según puede precisarse en sus discursos y propaganda.[11]

Pero la cuestión que mejor pone de relieve la problemática del tema de la neutralidad fue la campaña alemana contra la marina mercante de los países que abastecían a sus enemigos, sin excepción de los buques de países neutrales. Durante esta campaña, realizada en gran parte con submarinos, que empieza en febrero de 1915 como reacción al bloqueo de puertos alemanes por la Royal Navy, España, entre otros países, perdió un número elevado de buques y tripulantes a pesar de su declarada neutralidad. Al contrario de las enérgicas protestas del presidente estadounidense Wilson cuando ciudadanos norteamericanos perdían la vida en los ataques alemanes, la reacción española ante esta campaña contra sus buques y la pérdida de tripulantes fue tardía y débil, limitándose en primer lugar a protestas tímidas a

De Unamuno, submarinos y condenas   333

las autoridades alemanas. En *The Times* del 18-9-1916[12] se afirma que las pérdidas de buques españoles --muchos hundidos cerca de las costas peninsulares-- ascendían a cincuenta mil toneladas, pero el Gobierno esperó hasta junio de 1917 para prohibir la entrada en aguas o puertos españoles de submarinos de cualquier nación. La debilidad de la reacción española la atribuía Unamuno a la intervención del Rey y en las decisiones de sus ministros porque aquél, según Unamuno, estaba convencido, junto con otros sectores poderosos de la sociedad española, por ejemplo, los militares, de que la victoria de los Poderes Centrales era inevitable y, además, albergaba esperanzas de que la futura conferencia de paz se celebrase en España.

Finalmente, en 1918, el Gobierno español adopta una postura más enérgica amenazando incautar buques alemanes refugiados en puertos españoles en un quid pro quo por los barcos españoles hundidos y éste será el tema de 'El Archiduque de España'. En este artículo Unamuno cita una noticia de *The Times* que alega que la Reina Madre había intervenido en la decisión que tomó el Consejo de Ministros acerca de la indemnización a cobrar de Alemania para imponer su criterio de que España debía aceptar sólo siete buques alemanes a modo de compensación. El artículo de *The Times* que aquí nos interesa se titula 'German Offer to Spain' y aparece en el número del diario que corresponde al 24-9-1918. En él comenta el Special Correspondent de *The Times* lo siguiente:

> I understand that on the personal intervention of the Queen Mother, whose influence in German circles is, of course, considerable, the Germans have offered to hand over seven of their interned ships and also to respect the Spanish flag at sea, provided it is flown by ships exclusively engaged in Spanish trade.
> This, it will be seen, is a very different thing from the intention, so firmly expressed in the Spanish note. To begin with, making a present of seven ships is quite another matter from having ships seized in proportion to losses suffered. Moreover, the undertaking to respect the Spanish flag is, and must, from its nature, be perfectly insincere. How the number seven is arrived at, moreover, seeing that nearly thirty per cent of the Spanish mercantile marine has already been destroyed by enemy action, it would be hard to discover. The whole proposal is framed in the interests of Germany, who in this case would appear to have enlisted the Queen Mother in the course of negotiations which, however well and patriotically intended on

her part (and no one will accuse her of being urged by any but the highest motives), cannot, in the long run, but be disastrous for Spanish interests.[13]

El artículo de *The Times* insinúa también que la Reina Madre ha impuesto sus criterios sobre los de Alfonso en este asunto.

En 'El Archiduque de España', según se puede ver de la cita que damos a continuación, Unamuno alude al artículo de *The Times* para respaldar la tesis que defiende hace tiempo: que los últimos responsables de la falta de dirección moral del gobierno son el Rey y la Reina Madre que, según él cree, anteponen sus intereses familiares --es decir habsburguianos-- a los de España:

> Y el Times ha acusado a la ex regente --o mejor, a la regente, sin ex todavía-- de haber mediado en el vergonzoso cachipuche de la incautación de esos siete barcos que Alemania nos ha concedido generosamente para que España no se viese en el duro trance de tener que ejercer su derecho contra el imperio de que este nuestro archiducado depende.[14]

A nuestro juicio, es esta alusión a doña María Cristina --hay otra parecida en el artículo 'Irresponsabilidades'-- la que hace caer la ira oficial sobre la cabeza de Unamuno ya que en los artículos escritos para la prensa desde 1917 en adelante abundan los comentarios duros y despectivos sobre el Rey. Son frecuentes los comentarios que aluden, por ejemplo: al parentesco de Alfonso XIII con los Habsburgo de Austria, 'la borbonería actual español es habsburguiana';[15] a los supuestos vínculos secretos entre el rey y el Kaiser, 'procediendo anticonstitucionalmente, en rey absoluto, en emperador habsburguiano, entabló negociaciones directas con el emperador de los emperadores';[16] al hecho de que la monarquía alfonsina favorecía un régimen estancado e ineficaz, ambos paralizados ante la necesidad de renovar el régimen abriéndolo a sectores de la sociedad que reivindicaban sus derechos y ante el temor a que se dieran en España las mismas sacudidas que en Rusia, 'la monarquía no es hoy en España más que una encubridora de las vergüenzas políticas y del mal gobierno';[17] a la teórica 'irresponsabilidad' de Alfonso XIII según la Constitución de 1876 y a lo que para Unamuno eran actos irresponsables del monarca.

Las referencias a doña María Cristina son menos frecuentes y hasta diciembre de 1919 no hemos encontrado otras dignas de mencionarse. En el artículo titulado 'Disolución de crisis' de 15-12-1919, Unamuno hace referencia a la madre del rey: 'en efecto pesa sobre el Poder llamado moderador más presión oculta que las ya famosas Juntas de Defensa'.[18] En 'Un sino trágico' de 28-12-19, Unamuno vuelve a aludir a la Reina Madre y la influencia que ejerce sobre asuntos de Estado: 'la mano oculta', 'alguna persona consejera' y a un supuesto altercado entre María Cristina y el entonces primer ministro Eduardo Dato después del cual parece que éste comentó que 'los mayores de edad deben estar fuera de la tutela materna'.[19]

Cabe preguntarse qué hay detrás de esta constante atención que Unamuno otorga al rey de España. ¿Pura antipatía? No lo creemos, ni creemos que el propósito de Unamuno fuera convertir en bestia negra al rey aunque sus comentarios son duros, llegando a veces hasta el insulto. Creemos que hay que tener en cuenta varios factores: la discutida neutralidad, la destitución, el hecho de que Alfonso XIII era el jefe constitucional de un régimen inepto, débil y mediatizado por intereses particulares que sofocaban cualquier paso hacia la democracia, un régimen sin base popular que en los momentos de crisis --en 1917, por ejemplo, para sofocar el intento de huelga general-- tenía que recurrir a la represión y al Ejército.

También creemos que Unamuno veía en Alfonso el símbolo de un concepto patrimonialista, particular, imperialista de Estado el cual iba totalmente en contra de la idea unamuniana de una nación como una comunidad de individuos libres, independientes y responsables. El significado de este martilleo constante contra Alfonso es que Unamuno quería provocar en el rey una reconsideración del mundo, quería aleccionarle y así redimirle de la tontería. Stephen Roberts ya ha indicado cómo Unamuno entabló una lucha personal contra la tontería durante la dictadura del general Miguel Primo de Rivera y nosotros creemos que esta lucha remonta a los años de la guerra.[20] De hecho, se podría afirmar que durante estos años Unamuno se esforzó por rescatar la monarquía parlamentaria del error y de la tontería puesto que para él, dada la ausencia de conciencia y preparación cívicas, las alternativas --dictadura o república-- no inspiraban optimismo. Sin embargo, Alfonso XIII parece que sólo se salva de la crisis que trae la gran guerra para meterse en otras: el desastre de Annual y la dictadura primorriverista.

Si Unamuno se creía con el deber de combatir las falsedades y la tontería del régimen con las armas de la palabra, la libertad de expresión y la ironía, amén de decir las verdades cuando hacía falta, no se le escapaba que, a pesar de sus faltas, el régimen parlamentario era de civiles, susceptible de mejora y admitía la crítica. Por tanto, era preciso procurar sanearlo por todos los medios a su alcance ya que temía y no sin razón que si el régimen fuera desmoronado por el pretorianismo, podría resultar mucho peor el remedio que la enfermedad: '¿Si al quitar el polvo parlamentario deja allí un rastro de fango? Malo y todo como es el Parlamento, tememos más el baldeo con que lo barran, si lo barren'.[21]

Quedan por aclarar unos puntos más sobre el tema de la condena de Valencia. Pese a que Unamuno era un estorbo evidente para las autoridades está claro que en ningún momento se pensó en hacer efectiva la sentencia. De hecho, al hacerse público el fallo, se dispone al mismo tiempo que se apliquen los efectos de un real decreto de indulto del 12 de octubre de 1919.

Unamuno sostendrá siempre que se le impone esta condena tan severa precisamente para otorgarle luego un perdón: 'había el propósito de indultarme y que el rey apareciese magnánimo, y el de amenazar para posible reincidencia. Y se me condenó *para* que se me indultase'.[22] Desdeñando esta limosna oficial, Unamuno interpone recurso de casación y solicita la revisión de su caso por el Tribunal Supremo, encargando al jurisprudente y político conservador Angel Ossorio y Gallardor los trámites administrativo-legales. Entretanto queda en libertad provisional. Según Salcedo, la vista de recurso que Unamuno impone ante el Tribunal Supremo contra su sentencia se celebra el 8 de enero de 1921, confirmándose el fallo original de Valencia pero que de nuevo no es puesto en vigor.

Si la intención oficial fuera amordazar o amilanar a don Miguel los resultados fueron negativos. Aunque algunos diarios le tienen que rechazar sus artículos por temor a la censura y pérdida de tiradas, Unamuno continúa sus ataques contra las primeras figuras del régimen. En un artículo que escribe en junio de 1921 para una revista argentina confiesa --sospechamos que no sin cierto orgullo-- que tiene 'cinco nuevos procesos encima'.[23]

De aquí en adelante la labor política de Unamuno es mejor conocida y, desde luego, mejor documentada. En gran parte sigue el camino combativo que ya se había marcado en 1914 y que desde entonces se va radicalizando. Su opinión peyorativa de Alfonso XIII sólo se afirma en setiembre de 1923 con la creación de la dictadura militar encabezada por el general Primo de Rivera quien responderá a la negativas de Unamuno de callar sus críticas con la orden de destierro de 1924.

NOTES

1. Emilio Salcedo, *Vida de don Miguel*, 2ª edición (Salamanca: Anaya, 1970), pp.228-29.

2. Existen tres ediciones de artículos de Unamuno recopilados de esta época: *Desde el mirador de la guerra*, ed. de Luis Urrutia (Paris: Centre de Recherches Hispaniques, 1970); *Artículos olvidados sobre España y la primera guerra mundial*, ed. de Christopher Cobb (Londres: Tamesis Books, 1976); *Crónica política española*, ed. de Vicente González Martín (Salamanca: Almar, 1977). Estamos preparando una edición de artículos no recopilados del periódo 1917-21 de periódicos de Bilbao, Madrid y Valencia.

3. 'Don Miguel de Unamuno condenado', *El Mercantil Valencianio*, 17-9-1920, p.1.

4. E. Inman Fox, 'Los intelectuales españoles y la política (1905-1914): el caso de Unamuno', *Volumen-Homenaje a Miguel de Unamuno* (Salamanca: Casa-Museo Unamuno, 1986), p.34.

5. Carta de Unamuno a Pedro Múgica, fechada 28-10-1904, en *Cartas inéditas de Miguel de Unamuno*, ed. de S. Fernández Larrain (Santiago de Chile: Zig-Zag, 1965), p.335.

6. Fernández Larrain, pp.337-38.

7. Salcedo, p.218.

8. Cobb, p.92.

9. 'La gracia de la pantera', *El Liberal* (Madrid), 6-10-1918, p.1. Sin recopilar.

10. 'Cuestión de método', *El Mercantil Valenciano*, 1-3-1918, p.1. Sin recopilar.

11. 'Revoltosos'. *El Liberal* (Madrid), 24-11-1920. p.1. Sin recopilar.

12. *The Times*, 18-9-1916, p.7.

13. *The Times*, 24-9-1918, p.7.

14. 'El archiduque de España', p.1.

15. 'El mitin antihabsburgiano', *La Publicidad* (Barcelona), 22-8-1918, p.1. Sin recopilar.

16. 'La última vileza', *El Mercantil Valenciano*, 28-12-1919, p.1. Sin recopilar.

17. 'La heredada incondicional lealtad', *El Mercantil Valenciano*, 27-1-1918, en Cobb, pp.169-72.

18. 'Disolución de crisis', *El Mercantil Valenciano*, 15-12-1919, p.1. Sin recopilar.

19. 'Un sino trágico', *El Mercantil Valenciano*, 20-10-1918, p.1. Sin recopilar.

20. Stephen Roberts, 'Unamuno contra Primo de Rivera, diez artículos de 1923-1924', *Revista de Ciencias Sociales*, 75 (noviembre 1986), 83-112, y del mismo autor 'Unamuno en el exilio y su lucha contra la tontería', in *Actas del Congreso Internacional Cincuentenario de Unamuno*

(Salamanca: Ediciones Universidad de Salamanca, 1989), pp.591-94.

21. Véase 'Disolución de crisis'.

22. González Martín, p.289.

23. González Martín, p.291.

CONFESSIONAL INCREMENT OR CREDIBILITY GAP? THE RHETORIC OF EXCULPATION IN *LA FAMILIA DE PASCUAL DUARTE*

C. A. LONGHURST
University of Exeter

In a by now classic study of the I-narrator, conceived in part as a rejoinder to Wayne Booth's comments on the subject in the *Rhetoric of Fiction*, David Goldknopf argued that the inherent and most valid reason for the use of such a constricting and awkward form as first-person narration is what he termed the 'confessional increment', namely that 'everything an I-narrator tells us has a certain characterizing significance over and above its data value by virtue of the fact that he is telling it to us'. Contrary to Wayne Booth's argument that narrative person makes little difference, Goldknopf demonstrated that, irrespective of whether the confessional increment carries a major or a minor impact in a given case, 'the character is different from what he would be if the author, or any other narrator, were to give us the same interpretation'.[1] The significance is governed by the fact that a person is revealing, confessing or confiding; but, adds Goldknopf, the situation can be used to produce very different effects. The I-narrator may 'grab us by the sleeve and haul us immediately into the narrative situation. Or he may intervene between us and the narrative situation'.[2] *La familia de Pascual Duarte*, I suggest, shares both of these effects; or rather, as I propose to show, it has one effect superimposed on the other through the author's deft manipulation of his fictional narrator.

'Yo, señor, no soy malo': thus Pascual opens the account of his life. This direct appeal to the reader's understanding and indulgence is followed at once by a claim that each man is the victim of his own fate: some are lucky, some are wretchedly unlucky. Pascual very obviously wants us to accept that he has been the victim of an unkind fate: many times during the course of his account he will insist that his actions were precipitated by an irresistible force and by a preordained set of circumstances which determined his behaviour. Are we to accept Pascual's view of himself as victim? Are we to react to his account in the manner of Father Santiago Lurueña, who is so deeply touched by his reading of the memoir that he sees in Pascual not 'una hiena' but 'un manso cordero'?[3] Or are we to take heed of the transcriber's sceptical comment that 'Pascual se cerró a la banda y no dijo esta boca es mía más que cuando le dio la gana' (159)? It is not of course a matter of taking sides and dubbing Pascual a victim or a monster, although such a simplistic stance has not always been avoided by Cela scholars.[4] It is rather a matter of recognizing narrative devices for what they are and being aware of their rhetorical effects.

There are at bottom only two kinds of ingredients in this story: the facts of Pascual Duarte's life and death, and the particular presentation of those facts in the narrative; and while the facts and their presentation are clearly not the same thing, the latter can certainly affect one's perception of the former. It is the failure to distinguish between the basic data and the way in which the data are used that I believe has led to the naïve *parti pris* approach that has affected many commentators and to the confusing array of motives imputed to the author: moral, political, existentialist, sensationalist, scatological, even humorous.[5] The distinction between the facts and their interpretation is perhaps seen at its simplest in the two letters that, significantly enough, close the book. Pascual's execution and his loss of nerve on the scaffold are unquestionable facts. But whereas the chaplain would have us believe that Pascual exhibited the exemplary behaviour of a repentant man, the civil guard tells us that he behaved like a lunatic and a coward. Just as on this occasion these letters serve to characterize their authors rather better than their subject, so in the last resort it is not just the facts of Pascual's life that serve to characterize him, but beyond them his own narration of those facts. There are of course no unmediated facts in this book, since all information comes from one of several personalized narrators; this is not just an awkward complication, but is the very essence of the novel. The internal tensions created by different narrators has been the subject of an interesting analysis by Robert C. Spires, who points out that Cela's technique creates contradictions in the narrative that undermine the reader's ability to arrive at reliable judgements.[6]

All the same, I would argue that while the narrators may distort the facts and contradict one another, or may even fail to disclose *all* the facts, nevertheless enough remains for us to make that vital distinction between an irreducible minimum of core material and the particular vision imposed on that material by a given narrator, and that perceiving the connection between the two --the facts of the tale and the manner of the teller-- is what makes the reading experience meaningful and rewarding. I would certainly agree with Spires that in this case a moral concept 'is of no consequence in the novel', but not because 'good and evil are eliminated' or because of 'the futility of judging Pascual on the basis of his actions alone';[7] rather because what is paramount is Cela's wilful playing with narrative techniques and devices. This is of course quite different from saying, as Spires says, that we have no basis on which to form an opinion of Pascual's true character. The very way that Pascual narrates gives us an insight into his character, and to suggest, as again does Spires, that we cannot infer anything because it could all be a fabrication of the transcriber is to leave us in a land where fantasy and idle speculation rule unchecked. (Why not, for example, see Pascual, the transcriber and everything else as the fabrication of Don Joaquín Barrera López who after all is the owner of the manuscript?) The fact that the transcriber has an intrusive opinion about Pascual (as does every other narrator including Pascual himself) does not of itself invalidate the facticity of his basic account (or of the priest's or the civil guard's accounts). Pascual Duarte has been convicted of three murders: those of El Estirao, of his own mother and of Don Jesús. The first murder may strike us as being the result of justified anger, since El Estirao had seduced Pascual's wife. But that is not the immediate cause since we read that by then Lola was but a fading memory in Pascual's mind: 'La memoria de Lola, que tan profunda brecha dejara en mi corazón, se iba cerrando y los tiempos pasados iban siendo, poco a poco, olvidados' (127). The immediate cause is El Estirao's triumphant '¿Entonces me quería?' (130) referring to Lola, which touches upon Pascual's weak spot: his obsessive fear of masculine inadequacy.[8] Pascual hates other men's success with women. Nor is the murder an act of self-defence or of bravado. Several times the narration mentions that El Estirao is virtually incapacitated with several broken ribs and therefore defenceless. For this murder Pascual serves only three years of his long prison sentence, a fact which he turns to his advantage by blaming his subsequent misdeeds on the misguided benevolence of the authorities. But it is not difficult to detect in Pascual's declarations an ingratiating posture towards his masters: 'Cumplí excediéndome lo que se me ordenaba, logré enternecer a la justicia, conseguí los buenos informes del director ..., y me soltaron' (133). Three-and-a-half years later he is back in prison, convicted of the murder of his mother. The motive this time is hatred, a hatred nurtured and sustained over a long period, a hatred, too, which is plainly visible throughout the book in Pascual's characterization of his mother. But the hatred for his mother had been compounded by his failure to father a child, for Lola does not become pregnant after the death of their son and Pascual refers to the sexual frustrations of his wife (98-99) and to his own inability to satisfy her (101). The hatred resurfaces during his second marriage and this time reaches its brutal climax; but unlike the previous crime, this one is planned and meditated. It has in common with the previous one that it shows Pascual's inclination to take advantage of the adversary's weak position: El Estirao was incapacitated, his mother is lying in bed. For this second murder Pascual serves thirteen years in prison. Of the circumstances of the third murder we know nothing, or almost nothing. It was committed in 1936, just conceivably under cover of the political upheavals of the beginning of the Civil War, or, as Jorge Urrutia has argued with a good deal of justification, some time before the outbreak of the war.[9] Pascual mentions his victim several times in his account, and it is certainly possible to detect a note of resentment of Don Jesús's privileged position. He writes that he had to eat fish from the river into which the sewers from Don Jesús's house discharge; the mass that Don Manuel says is, according to Pascual, for the benefit of Don Jesús; and in church he is made to sit behind Don Jesús and imitate his movements. That Pascual harbours hostile thoughts is also suggested by his apparently gratuitous comment that 'los habitantes de las ciudades [of whom Don Jesús is the only named example] ni se dan cuenta siquiera de que a dos leguas [...] un hombre del campo se distrae pensando en ellos' (27). We know, too, that Pascual used to go shooting rabbits along the edge of Don Jesús's estate, so we could speculate that Don Jesús surprised him poaching. On this occasion Cela does not allow his narrator to offer us the story behind the facts. Yet through a simple verbal device he allows us a glimpse into his narrator's mind. For the one significant detail about Pascual's third murder is contained in his own dedication of his autobiography to the memory of his victim: 'A la memoria del insigne patricio don Jesús González de la Riva, Conde de Torremejía, quien al irlo a rematar el autor de este escrito, le llamó Pascualillo y sonreía' (19). What strikes one about this dedication is its cynical and unrepentant tone, which is at odds with Pascual's request for forgiveness in the letter to Don Joaquín Barrera López. For in this dedication Pascual is sneering at the weakness of the high and powerful nobleman who under threat of death can only appeal to his assailant with a smile and an ingratiatingly friendly diminutive. And the verb *rematar* underlines the cruel satisfaction of the assailant in finishing off the job, in dealing the *coup de grâce* without mercy, without compunction, with no concession to the victim's appeal.[10] The callousness, not simply of the murderer, but of the narrator, is striking. It is for this third and most brutal murder that Pascual is condemned to death; but I see no evidence that Don Jesús's social status is intended by Cela as the real explanation for the death sentence which is passed on Pascual. Rather the attack on Don Jesús, of whom what we know is that he is a gentle and pious man who loves plants and flowers, seems to be intended as the culmination of a process of envy, hatred and brutality in Pascual.

Cela paints Pascual's sanguinary urges in other ways too, notably in the callous and apparently pointless killing of the dog and the mare. Whether they are psychologically pointless is a different matter. In the case of the bitch, La Chispa, the language in which the description of the incident is couched is so extraordinary and suggestive that it invites interpretation. The bitch looks at Pascual with the cold, accusing eyes of a confessor (his words). But what is she accusing him of? Pascual is slouching on his favourite stone seat: 'un temblor recorrió todo mi cuerpo; parecía como una corriente que forzaba por salirme por los brazos, el pitillo se me había apagado; la escopeta, de un solo caño, se dejaba acariciar, lentamente, entre mis piernas; [...] se veía llegar el momento en que tuviese que entregarme; [...] mis ojos se entornaban' (28). Pascual implies that a sanguinary urge over which he had no control suddenly overcomes him. But the ambiguity of the description and the sexual symbols also suggest an onanist caught in the shameful act. The fact that the assertion of his masculinity is a leitmotif in the story and that at the time of La Chispa's killing Pascual is haunted by the possibility of Lola having another miscarriage lends some credence to this interpretation. An alternative explanation would be that Pascual had killed La Chispa's puppies at birth, which is why he feels accused by the bitch. This would be supported by the parallel language used to refer to La Chispa and to Lola when Pascual proposes an abortion: 'Y ella [La Chispa] me miraba como suplicante' (86), and 'mi mujer puso un gesto como suplicante' (120). The killing of the mare is once again presented as being decreed by fate, personified by 'una lechuza, un pájaro de mal agüero' (81); but Pascual acts in a fit of rage driven by the thought that the mare is responsible for the miscarriage of his wife and therefore for depriving him of the assertion of his manliness through fatherhood. In these two instances we see two forces at work in the presentation of the events, one pulling towards and the other away from the narrator.

Particularly significant in this oblique or double-edged narration of the facts of the story is the way in which two other deaths are presented. One is the death of his wife Lola whom Pascual finds pregnant when he returns from his two-year absence. Inexplicably Pascual gives up the idea of forcing his wife to abort, on which he is so insistent when he first discovers her pregnancy. What he does is to trade the life of the baby for the knowledge of his wife's seducer. Although Pascual simply does not tell us what is going through his mind, the scene of her death is another of those instances in which Cela gives the events an ambiguous presentation:

> Estaba pálida como nunca, desencajada; su cara daba miedo, un miedo horrible de que la desgracia llegara con mi retorno; la cogí la cabeza, la acaricié, la hablé con más cariño que el que usara jamás el esposo más fiel; la mimé contra mi hombro, comprensivo de lo mucho que sufría, como temeroso de verla desfallecer a mi pregunta.
> -¿Quién fue?
> -¡El Estirao!
> -¿El Estirao?
> Lola no contestó.
> Estaba muerta, con la cabeza caída sobre el pecho y el pelo sobre la cara... Quedó un momento en equilibrio sentada donde estaba, para caer al pronto contra el suelo de la cocina, todo de guijarrillos muy pisados... (123)

Has Pascual killed his wife, humiliated by the discovery that his rival El Estirao, who had already seduced his sister and stolen her from him, had now seduced his wife and left her with child? Pascual at any rate holds El Estirao to be responsible for his wife's death: 'salí a buscar al asesino de mi mujer' (125). Furthermore, when El Estirao returns months later, he too assumes that Pascual has killed: '¡Menos matar! ¡Ya vas bien con lo que llevas!' (130). Thus Cela sows the seeds of doubt in our minds while abstaining from giving any kind of confirmation.

But if Lola's death must remain mysterious, the death of the little boy Mario is less so, and here, I believe, there are very good grounds for saying that Cela is inviting us to read between the lines. The first thing that we notice is Pascual's jealousy of his little brother. The scene immediately preceding the discovery of the child's body drowned in the oil vat is particularly revealing. Mario is kicked by Don Rafael and left lying on the ground. Pascual makes much of the outrage that he says he felt, but the plain fact is that he too leaves his brother lying on the ground, whether out of cowardice or out of indifference, and elects to leave the house. It is Rosario who, returning with Pascual two hours later, picks up the child, who is subsequently cradled and comforted by his mother. This scene places Pascual in a very poor light. For despite his protests about his concern for his baby brother he does nothing for him:

> La criatura se quedó tirada todo lo larga que era, y mi madre --le aseguro que me asusté en aquel momento que la vi tan ruin-- no lo cogía y se reía haciéndole el coro al señor Rafael; a mí, bien lo sabe Dios, no me faltaron voluntades para levantarlo, pero preferí no hacerlo... ¡Si el señor Rafael, en el momento, me hubiera llamado blando, por Dios que lo machaco delante de mi madre!
> Me marché hasta las casas para tratar de olvidar; en el camino me encontré a mi hermana [...]
> Cuando volvimos hasta la casa, pasadas dos horas largas del suceso, el señor Rafael se despedía; Mario seguía tirado en el mismo sitio donde lo dejé. (50)

Cela has chosen Pascual's words carefully: notice for example the use of the first-person singular verb in the final sentence of the passage quoted -- not where *they* left him but where *I* left him. Pascual endeavours to say one thing; but the reader is invited to infer something else. Suggestive too is the final scene which we witness before Mario's death, in which the child shows his contentment and gratitude at the loving attention he receives first from his sister and then from his mother: 'el chiquillo se dejaba querer y sonreía' (51). We know that Pascual is pathologically jealous, and the placing of this scene immediately before the description of his death raises the possibility of Pascual disposing of his little brother out of envy, a possibility perhaps reinforced by Pascual's admission that the hatred he developed for his mother dates from the time of Mario's death. The possibility is further strengthened when we come across a reference to a woman and a boy whom he can see from the prison window in front of which he sits writing his memoirs. Although there is no physical resemblance in either case, he is reminded at once of his brother and of his mother: '¡cómo me recordaba a mi hermano Mario!', he says of the child; and then, of the woman, he asks rhetorically: 'Bien distinta era de mi madre y sin embargo, ¿por qué sería que tanto me la recordaba?' (61). His mother had been one of his victims; had his brother been one too? Cela of course can only speak through a narrator who, as we are warned, tells us only what he wants to tell us. But the way Cela makes his character express himself invites speculation, a speculation which in this case turns into near certainty by the inclusion of one single sentence later on in the narrative. Pascual writes: 'El recuerdo de mi pobre Mario me asaltaba; si yo tuviera un hijo con la desgracia de Mario, lo ahogaría para privarle de sufrir' (87). If Pascual is capable of drowning his son, then he was capable of drowning his brother. In his comment Pascual betrays himself: not only is he haunted by the memory of his brother's death but he actually presents himself in the same breath as the agent of death by drowning. Given that Pascual admits to a poor memory, that he may have conveniently forgotten 'cosas incluso interesantes', and that 'otra parte hubo que al intentar contarla sentía tan grandes arcadas en el alma que preferí callármela y ahora olvidarla' (15-16), the possibility is being raised by the author that the character is choosing what to include and what to leave out. The salient events of Pascual's life are the crimes of which he has been convicted; those other events which remain unrecounted could equally be crimes of which he has not been convicted.

We have then a man who has been convicted of three murders, each one more brutal than the last, and who may also have been responsible for two further murders. There is another kind of figurative murder in which Pascual

The Rhetoric of Exculpation in *La familia de Pascual Duarte* 349

frequently indulges in his narration: character assassination. His attacks on his parents --especially his mother-- are so frequent and obvious that they scarcely need comment. It is clear that Pascual still retains the hatred of his parents at the moment of writing, for in his account he makes sure that he lists all their defects and vices, including the mention that his mother developed pustules round her mouth, the implication being that she had contracted venereal disease through prostitution. Pascual spares no attack on his mother and indeed shows no remorse for her murder; on the contrary, his depiction of her is offered in mitigation of his crime. On the other hand Pascual several times claims to feel great affection for his sister Rosario; yet in her case, too, he indulges in malicious insinuation. Let us consider, for example, the following passage:

> No bien se puso buena, y cuando la alegría volvía otra vez a casa de mis padres, que en lo único que estaban acordes era en su preocupación por la hija, volvió a hacer el pirata la muy zorra, a llenarse la talega con los ahorros del pobre y sin más reverencias, y como a la francesa, volvió a levantar el vuelo y a marcharse, esta vez camino de Almendralejo, donde paró en casa de Nieves la Madrileña; cierto es, o por tal lo tengo, que aun al más ruin alguna fibra de bueno siempre le queda, porque Rosario no nos echó del todo en el olvido y alguna vez --por nuestro santo o por las navidades-- nos tiraba con algún chaleco, que aunque nos venía justo y recibido como faja por vientre satisfecho, su mérito tenía porque ella, aunque con más relumbrón por aquello de que había que vestir el oficio, tampoco debía nadar en la abundancia. En Almendralejo hubo de conocer al hombre que había de labrarle la ruina; no la de la honra, que bien arruinada debía andar ya por entonces, sino la del bolsillo, que una vez perdida aquélla, era por la única que tenía que mirar. (40)

Once again the passage tells us as much about the writer as about the person of whom it is written. First it shows the jealousy that Pascual feels because Rosario is the centre of his parents' attention. Then it points out Rosario's selfish and furtive behaviour in disappearing with whatever the family had saved up. The reference to the house of Nieves la Madrileña is simply a sly way of divulging that she went to a brothel. Pascual then pretends to find some good in her by pointing to her generosity; but it is indeed a pretence: the compliment is a backhanded one, if it is a compliment at all, for those presents that Rosario sends back home are merely discarded clothes that do not fit. He then makes a further cynical comment by saying that she could not afford to send anything better because she had to dress the part, by which he means of course dress the part of the prostitute. And as if the two sly references to prostitution were not explicit enough, Pascual includes a third when he says that it was not his sister's honour that was in danger of ruin, for that had been well and truly ruined by then, but her purse. The whole passage is a sustained and malicious attack on his sister based on Pascual's oft-used technique of innuendo and insinuation, and shows particularly well the narrator's cynical and denigratory attacks on other people.[11] This cynicism is noticeable, too, in other gratuitous remarks made by Pascual in the course of his narration. For example, referring to Lola's miscarriage on their return from the honeymoon, he writes:

> Por seguro se lo digo que --aunque después, al enfriarme pensara lo contrario-- en aquel momento no otra cosa me pasó por el magín que la idea de que el aborto de Lola pudiera habérsele ocurrido tenerlo de soltera. ¡Cuánta bilis y cuánto resquemor y veneno me hubiera ahorrado! (85)

Pascual says 'en aquel momento' but of course the idea is going through his head as he writes; we are not dealing here simply with the recollection of an event, but of a thought, an attitude of mind that takes shape in the narrator as he narrates. And as if to underline that this attitude belongs to the present and not to the past, Cela makes his character add the revealing exclamation '¡Cuánta bilis y cuánto resquemor y veneno me hubiera ahorrado!' Pascual intends us to believe that his life has been governed by a fate outside his control. The implication in this particular example is that if Lola had miscarried while unmarried, then the marriage would never have taken place and would not have set in motion the horrible train of events which will lead him to the death cell. There is no recognition of the fact that it is he who is to blame for his wife's miscarriage by leaving her to ride home alone on a mare that had already proved to be nervous and easily frightened, while he himself has a night on the tiles. But there is even more to it than this, for a few pages earlier the narrator has tried to pre-empt any possible attribution of responsibility for the later incident to his own behaviour by insidiously

The Rhetoric of Exculpation in *La familia de Pascual Duarte*   351

claiming that Lola deserves God's punishment. When the newly-weds are entering Mérida their horse is momentarily frightened and knocks down an old woman. The latter is dispatched on her way by Pascual with some monetary compensation and none the worse for the experience. Lola finds the incident amusing:

> Ésta se reía y su risa, créame usted, me hizo mucho daño; no sé si sería un presentimiento, algo así como una corazonada de lo que habría de ocurrirle. No está bien reírse de la desgracia del prójimo, se lo dice un hombre que fue muy desgraciado a lo largo de su vida; Dios castiga sin palo y sin piedra y, ya se sabe, quien a hierro mata... Por otra parte, y aunque no fuera por eso, nunca está de más el ser humanitario. (73)

Here Pascual is not only pontificating in a solemn and self-righteous manner but is doing so with a clear purpose: to shift all the blame for the forthcoming incident on to his wife and present himself as a humanitarian person more concerned for others' misfortunes than is his wife. The narrator's cynical exploitation of the narrative, his attempt to extract a sympathetic response from the reader and to absolve himself from responsibility by displacing the blame on to others is a good illustration of Cela's rhetorical armoury. The author permits his narrator to go some way towards exonerating himself, but he does so in such a way as to allow the reader to grasp the essential cynicism of the character. The narrator's cynicism comes through as well in various gratuitous comments that he interpolates as he narrates past events. Talking of the enmity between his mother and his second wife, he tells us that he realized that the only solution was to go and live somewhere else away from his mother:

> Pude ver que no otro arreglo sino el poner la tierra por en medio podría llegar a tener. La tierra por en medio se dice cuando dos se separan a dos pueblos distantes, pero, bien mirado, también se podría decir cuando entre el terreno en donde uno pisa y el otro duerme hay veinte pies de altura... (149)

The additional comment, which both forecasts and exploits for the purpose of linguistic 'cleverness' the murder of his mother, shows a complete lack of remorse and feeling. 'Poner tierra por en medio' means for Pascual to be separated not by distance but by death, in other words to send someone to his grave. He had been planning for a long time to kill his mother, and many years later, as he narrates the circumstances that led to the crime, he considers what an original interpretation he gave to his decision to 'poner tierra por en medio'. Once again we observe the double effect of Pascual's narration. The author's narrative technique is nothing if not consistent: every defence that Pascual invokes turns into so much evidence against him.[12]

Shifting the blame for his actions on to others or on to an adverse fate is one of the stock devices of Pascual as narrator. He blames his parents for giving him a bad example, his mother for taunting him and provoking him to violence, his sister for giving in to El Estirao, El Estirao for dishonouring his sister, his first wife for having a miscarriage at the wrong time, his mare for causing the miscarriage, his second wife for pressurizing him into disposing of his mother, the prison authorities for letting him out... But in addition Cela allows his narrator to use another and more subtle technique for dissipating personal responsibility: the transition from first-person singular narration to first-person plural or to the impersonal form of the verb. There are many instances of this throughout Pascual's account but it is particularly prevalent when he writes about his longstanding plan to kill his mother. The actual killing takes place some time after his second marriage, but a scene much earlier in the account suggests that he had already come very close to fulfilling his plan many years before:

> Se mata sin pensar, bien probado lo tengo; a veces, sin querer. Se odia, se odia intensamente, ferozmente, y se abre la navaja, y con ella bien abierta se llega, descalzo, hasta la cama donde duerme el enemigo. Es de noche, pero por la ventana entra el claror de la luna; se ve bien. Sobre la cama está echado el muerto, el que va a ser el muerto. Uno lo mira, lo oye respirar; no se mueve, está quieto como si nada fuera a pasar. Como la alcoba es vieja los muebles nos asustan con su crujir que puede despertarlo, que a lo mejor había de precipitar las puñaladas. El enemigo levanta un poco el embozo y se da la vuelta: sigue dormido. Su cuerpo abulta mucho; la ropa engaña. Uno se acerca cautelosamente; lo toca con la mano con cuidado. Está dormido, bien dormido; ni se había de enterar... (102)

Pascual describes the scene, of which the passage quoted is a part, using the impersonal *se* and the pronoun *uno*, and in a few instances the first-person plural. He also uses the present tense rather than the past historic, which has the added effect of attenuating the historicity of the event described --the past historic being the tense of historical narration par excellence-- and reducing it from an action that most definitely took place at a certain time to a general consideration of how a would-be assassin might behave. The combined effect of the impersonal form of the verb plus the use of the present tense is to deflect the attention away from Pascual as agent of the deed and towards him as narrator; away from the precise circumstances that identify him as the would-be murderer --the victim is not identified as his mother but simply identified as the enemy and referred to using a masculine object pronoun-- and towards the act of meditation on the phenomenon of murder in which the reader is almost made into an accomplice. The technique is successful in two wholly opposing ways: for Pascual it is a defence, a smokescreen which helps him disguise the fact that he had come very close to murdering his mother on a previous occasion; for Cela it is a technique that allows him, through his character's own narration, to objectify the coldbloodedness of the narrator in relating his criminal intentions with a complete detachment and lack of emotion, as if it were something that had not involved him personally. On this occasion Pascual, at the very last minute, had not gone through with his plan, preferring flight to La Coruña. But years later the murderous plan was to take shape yet again in Pascual's mind, and once more the genesis of the murder is described by means of a long preamble to the act itself using first-person plural narration, in which the conflict is presented as a contest between *nosotros* and *el enemigo*:

> La idea de la muerte llega siempre con paso de lobo, con andares de culebra [...] Los pensamientos que nos enloquecen con la peor de las locuras, la de la tristeza, siempre llegan poco a poco y como sin sentir, como sin sentir invade la niebla los campos, o la tisis los pechos [...] Hoy no la notamos [...] Pero pasa ese mes y empezamos a sentir amarga la comida [...] nos vamos volviendo huraños, solitarios; en nuestra cabeza se cuecen las ideas, las ideas que han de ocasionar el que nos corten la cabeza donde se cocieron [...] Empezamos a sentir el odio que nos mata; ya no aguantamos el mirar; nos duele la conciencia, pero, ¡no importa!, ¡más vale que duela! Nos escuecen los ojos [...] El enemigo nota nuestro anhelo, pero está confiado [...] La desgracia es alegre, acogedora, y el más tierno sentir gozamos en hacerlo arrastrar sobre la plaza inmensa de

vidrios que va siendo ya nuestra alma. Cuando huimos como las corzas, cuando el oído sobresalta nuestros sueños, estamos ya minados por el mal; ya no hay solución, ya no hay arreglo posible. Empezamos a caer, vertiginosamente ya, para no volvernos a levantar en vida. Quizás para levantarnos un poco a última hora, antes de caer de cabeza hasta el infierno... (151)

In this long interpolation (quoted above only in part) just before the account of the act itself, Pascual makes himself an archetype of Man, or rather he obliterates his own individuality and writes as if it were humanity itself that was planning the murder of an unnamed, impersonal foe. We are thus made into accessories before the fact, we have a share in the responsibility for the crime. Pascual is one of us, or conversely we are at one with him: there is no distinction between him and us, what he does is, according to him, what we ourselves would do. But there is a limit to the extent that Cela is prepared to allow his creature to obfuscate: it is almost as if the author realizes that his narrator is being too successful in disseminating blame. The return to first-person narration makes Pascual's personal involvement chillingly plain: 'me pasé largas horas enteras pensando en lo mismo para envalentonarme, para tomar fuerzas; afilé el cuchillo de monte, con su larga y ancha hoja' (152). Pascual goes on vividly to portray his struggle and determination not, paradoxically, to keep temptation at bay, but, on the contrary, to keep alive and strengthen his murderous resolution: 'Mucho pensé en aquello, pero procuré vencerme y lo conseguí' (153). *Procuré vencerme* means for Pascual overcome his weakness, that is, the possibility that he might lack the resolve to kill. For Pascual it is a matter of resisting, not temptation to kill, but temptation not to kill. It is a complete inversion of normal values.

As well as doing his best to divert blame from himself to others, to an adverse fate, or to humanity itself, Pascual often adopts an ingratiating tone towards his addressee. Who is the *señor* whom Pascual apostrophizes in his narration? Most scholars assume it is the addressee of his letter and friend of Don Jesús, Don Joaquín Barrera López, but this is completely illogical for it would render Pascual's information about Don Jesús redundant and pointless. We must bear in mind that this device is a calque on that found in *El buscón*, where there is no specific personality behind the appellation. If we have to invoke a personality for Pascual's *señor* we would have to consider someone in high authority ('la muy alta persona a quien estas líneas van dirigidas' [34]), which might suggest the presiding judge looking into his case, since it would appear from Pascual's own comments that his case is being reviewed. The narration is peppered with apostrophes to this authority to whom Pascual defers --and by extension to any reader-- and with appeals for understanding: 'Mucha desgracia, como usted habrá podido ver, es la que llevo contada' (59); or 'usted me perdonará, pero no puedo seguir' (61); or 'usted sabrá comprender lo que le digo' (61); or again, 'usted sabe, tan bien como yo' (62). The immediate effect of such apostrophes and appellatives is to persuade the reader that Pascual is talking to a friend, that he is appealing to our good hearts, that he deserves to be listened to and believed. The major overall effect of Pascual's procedure is to pre-empt condemnation on our part, to make us at the very least suspend judgement. Whether we do or we don't should not of course become a moral issue but a matter of identifying and understanding the evidence of the text. And the evidence is negative *to the extent that Cela's technique clearly negates his narrator's affirmations and appeals*. What, for example, are we to make of Pascual's claim to have repented? This claim is made several times, sometimes equivocally (with regret more about the outcome of his misdeeds than about the misdeeds themselves), and sometimes unequivocally: 'Tal vez no me creyera si le dijera que en estos momentos tal tristeza me puebla y tal congoja, que por asegurarle estoy que mi arrepentimiento no menor debe ser que el de un santo' (60). Yet Pascual's protestations of repentance must be taken with a large pinch of salt, given the tone of much of what he narrates. Interestingly, Pascual is aware of this and attempts to forestall the reader's doubts or scepticism:

> No creo que sea pecado contar barbaridades de las que uno está arrepentido. Don Santiago me dijo que lo hiciese si me traía consuelo [...] Hay ocasiones en las que me duele contar punto por punto los detalles, grandes o pequeños, de mi triste vivir, pero, y como para compensar, momentos hay también en que con ello gozo con el más honesto de los gozares, quizá por eso de que al contarlo tan alejado me encuentre de todo lo pasado como si lo contase de oídas y de algún desconocido [...] No quiero exagerar la nota de mi mansedumbre en esta última hora de mi vida, porque en su [*your*] boca se me imagina oír un a la vejez viruelas, que más vale que no sea pronunciado, pero quiero, sin embargo, dejar las cosas en su último punto y

asegurarle qué ejemplo de familias sería mi vivir si hubiera
discurrido todo él por las serenas sendas de hoy. (109)

If Pascual is given leave by his creator to bolster his case by anticipating criticism and incredulity, Cela also makes him contradict himself. Pascual claims to find it painful to relate the details of his life, yet admits that he derives enjoyment from so doing because he feels detached from them; in other words, he has little sense of personal responsibility for his actions. He says he does not wish to overstate the extent of his change because it might provoke the incredulous response of his reader; yet in the same breath he does precisely that, claiming a hypothetical exemplary conduct and denouncing a hypothetical sceptical reaction ('que más vale que no sea pronunciado'). The absence of genuine repentance is made clear in a passage that occurs immediately before the description of the murder of his mother:

> La conciencia no me remordería; no habría motivo. La conciencia sólo remuerde de las injusticias cometidas: de apalear un niño, de derribar una golondrina... Pero de aquellos actos a los que nos conduce el odio, a los que vamos como adormecidos por una idea que nos obsesiona, no tenemos que arrepentirnos jamás, jamás nos remuerde la conciencia. (153)

The important point in this passage is that it simply cannot be taken as a mere indication that at the time of planning the murder Pascual thought his conscience would not trouble him. In writing the passage Cela has quite conspicuously changed the conditional tense of the beginning of the paragraph to the present tense of the end: we never have to regret it, our conscience is never troubled. It is Pascual at the time of writing who is feeling no remorse whatsoever for the murder of his mother, which wholly contradicts his declaration in the covering letter to Don Joaquín Barrera López. Cela goes further in an apparent attempt to invite us to distance ourselves from the narrator and not allow ourselves to be manipulated: he makes use of the transcriber's role to point to another potential contradiction in Pascual's claims. The transcriber informs us that Pascual's claim in his letter to Don Joaquín to have stopped writing ('suspendo definitivamente el seguir escribiendo') is untrue and that Pascual had carefully written out the letter long before he had ceased writing. When he says in that letter 'noto cierto

The Rhetoric of Exculpation in *La familia de Pascual Duarte*   357

descanso después de haber relatado todo lo que pasé' (16), Pascual -- according to the transcriber-- is quite simply telling a calculated lie; he is obviously seeking to create a particular effect upon the reader. The transcriber is countering this and in turn creating the opposite effect. Which brings me to the essential point that I have tried to make in this paper.

Pascual's autobiography is not the confession of a repentant man; it is not a self-purging or an unburdening exercise, not a cathartic or therapeutic activity, not a *descargo de conciencia* as he would have us believe. Much less can it be a denunciation of social conditions or a condemnation of a repressive regime which exacts vengeance on the murderer of a member of the aristocracy; for if it were meant to be this, the constant undermining of Pascual's case would make no sense. Pascual's autobiography is none of these things. Rather it is a rhetorical exercise the nature of which suggests, at the level of the story, one more act of self-assertion by a character who is cowardly and timid and whose whole life has been one continuous attempt to mask his inadequacy by imposing himself and proving his manliness through wanton aggression. At the root of his inadequacy lies his pathological fear of a failing masculinity. This obsession with proving his masculinity through violence and its images comes through time and again in his account, and is connected to the attack on Zacarías, the seduction of Lola with its drawing of blood, the murder of El Estirao and his mother, the possible murders of his wife and brother, and to the killing of the dog and the mare. Deprived by his confinement in prison (as he himself virtually admits [109]) of the possibility of asserting himself through violence, he tries to do so through the written word and through the recollection of his bloody triumphs, which he presents as the result of provocation. But in so doing he also gives himself away, and if we resist his rhetoric, as the author invites us to do, we can see him for the pathetic, pitifully abject and weak man that he is. That of course is the psychological dimension of Pascual's narrative. But the unconscious self-betrayal that his autobiography amounts to and which is Pascual's loss, is Cela's gain. For behind the rhetoric of the character lies of course the rhetoric of the author.

La familia de Pascual Duarte is an exercise in the manipulation of first-person narration. It evinces both of the effects mentioned by David

Goldknopf; a narrative voice trying to pull us in, and another trying to pull us out. It is by and large a skilful exercise, though not a wholly original one. The presence of the Spanish picaresque novel of the Golden Age is too unmistakable to leave us in any doubt about where Cela has learnt his trade. For the authentic *familia* of Pascual Duarte are not the Extremaduran peasants of the early twentieth century or even Spaniards at large in that fateful year of 1936, but Lázaro de Tormes, Pablos de Segovia, and Guzmán de Alfarache. The connection with Cela's own time is there, but it lies in the literary experiment itself. Just as the unthinking attempts of certain political and religious leaders to return Spain ideologically to a distant past were to produce a repressive and anachronistic reality, so Cela's pretension to put this same outlook into practice on the literary front by resurrecting distant literary models was to produce an artistically brilliant but horrifyingly grotesque distortion of those early literary forms. It is little wonder that the censors were nonplussed.

NOTES

1. David Goldknopf, 'The Confessional Increment', in *The Life of the Novel* (Chicago and London, 1972), pp.25-41.

2. Goldknopf, p.41.

3. *La familia de Pascual Duarte* (Barcelona: Ediciones Destino, Colección Destinolibro, 1972), p.161. All subsequent references in parentheses are to this edition.

4. For examples of an all-too-easy descent into a moral condemnation or defense of Pascual (and of the novel), see Jorge Urrutia, *Cela: 'La familia de Pascual Duarte'. Los contextos y el texto* (Madrid, 1982), especially chapters 4 and 5.

5. In his informative and lucid monograph on *La familia de Pascual Duarte*, Jorge Urrutia speaks of 'una confusión evidente entre la historia y el discurso', but does not in the end drive home the distinction, opting instead for what sounds like an existentialist label: 'un intento de expresión coherente de una postura ante la existencia y la realidad' (Urrutia, pp.67 and 126).

6. Robert C. Spires, 'Systematic Doubt: The Moral Art of *La familia de Pascual Duarte*', *Hispanic Review*, 40 (1972), 283-302.

7. Spires, 'Systematic Doubt', pp.301 and 302.

8. Paul Ilie, who has analysed Pascual's *masculinismo*, speaks of 'una básica inseguridad, una semiinconsciente duda en lo auténtico de su varonía... La idea de no ser lo bastante viril es una tortura para Pascual' (*La novelística de Camilo José Cela* (Madrid, 1963), p.52).

9. Basing himself on historical data, Urrutia suggests that Pascual's release from prison could have taken place as a result of Azaña's amnesty of February 1936, and that the method of his execution (garrotte, not firing squad) precludes a political murder (Urrutia, p.66).

10. The idea first put forward by David Feldman ('Camilo José Cela and *La familia de Pascual Duarte*', *Hispania*, 44 (1961), 656-59) and repeated by Alonso Zamora Vicente (*Camilo José Cela. Acercamiento a un escritor* (Madrid, 1962), p.44) that Pascual is not the murderer of Don Jesús but that 'rematar' refers to the mercy killing of an already mortally wounded man has been convincingly quashed by Jorge Urrutia. Pascual's murder of Don Jesús is one of the facts of the fiction.

11. Driven by a sustained if (in my view) misguided desire to exonerate Pascual, Gonzalo Sobejano uses the narrator's characterization of his mother to explain his crime, without a whiff of recognition that Pascual is playing on his reader's sympathies. Sobejano similarly uses Pascual's references to Rosario to show that he is compassionate, without noticing his backhanded approach towards his sister. In what must rank as one of the most naïve readings of the novel, Sobejano's apologia for the character ('víctima principal', 'individuo abandonado', 'víctima de las circunstancias', 'nunca se goza en el sufrimiento ajeno', 'cándida confesión') blinds him to the implications of Pascual's own narrative discourse. Preferring to be guided by a 'realidad injusta' external to the book, he fails to focus on the discursive realities within it ('Reflexiones sobre *La familia de Pascual Duarte*', *Papeles de Son Armadans*, 48 (1968), 19-58).

12. In an early and inexplicably neglected article that remains one of the most alert analyses of the novel, Mary Ann Beck set about refuting many of Pascual's claims and warned that the unwary reader 'cae en la celada que le ha sido tendida por el autor. Equivocadamente se convence de que Pascual ... es víctima y no tiene la culpa de sus atroces actos'. While wholly sharing Beck's sceptical reaction to Pascual's highly coloured narration, I do not see any trap prepared by Cela; merely that which critics intent on seeing an ideological tract instead of a literary experiment create for themselves. The fact that she could write that Cela gives his character 'autonomía completa' and that 'no cabe poner en duda la sinceridad de Pascual' shows that Beck had not fully understood Cela's subtle manipulation of the narrative and the narrator. ('Nuevo encuentro con *La familia de Pascual Duarte*', *Revista Hispánica Moderna*, 30 (1964), 279-98. Reprinted in *Novelistas españoles de postguerra*, El escritor y la crítica (Madrid, 1976), pp.65-88).

'NO PAS EL DOL: EL DESENCÍS'
MOURNING AND EXILE IN JOSEP CARNER'S *ABSÈNCIA*[*]

JOSEP-ANTON FERNÁNDEZ
University of London

By 1920 Josep Carner had become one of Catalonia's most influential intellectuals and 'el príncep dels poetes' of a literature, such as Catalan, in which poetry has an enormous symbolic value. Despite his celebrity, indeed the legend built around him, at the turn of the decade Carner's disappointment with the Lliga Regionalista --the nationalist party he had supported as one of the leaders of the Noucentista movement-- was growing, and as he had failed in his effort to find, as a full-time intellectual, a satisfactory financial position for himself and his family, he decided to sit *oposiciones* and to become a diplomat.[1]

From then on, Carner lived as a foreigner. His personal situation had certainly improved and he was able to maintain a high profile in the cultural scene in Barcelona. In the five years between 1935 and 1940, however, a series of events radically changed his life: in 1935, while a consul in Beirut, both his father and his first wife died; in 1936 the Spanish Civil War started; in 1938 he was expelled from the *corps diplomatique* by General Franco's government; and in 1939 the Spanish democratic regime finally collapsed and World War II started. The Noucentista liberal dream of a civilized Catalonia had vanished: the Catalan language was banned, no books or newspapers were allowed and most of Catalonia's cultural élite were dispersed. If Carner had been an émigré, now he was an exile, first in Belgium, then in Mexico, then back in Belgium. He could never live in Catalonia again, and was only able to return for a short visit a few months before his death in 1970.

Like *Nabí* (1941) and *Llunyania* (1952), *Absència* is mainly the result of Carner's experience of exile and mourning. First published in 1957 as the last section of his colossal *Poesies* (the definitive edition of his collected poems, which involved a massive work of rewriting), a significant number of its forty poems appeared for the first time in this book.[2] In this article I will offer a reading of *Absència* in the light of Sigmund Freud's influential essay,

'Mourning and Melancholia' (1917).[3] My starting point will be Freud's definition of mourning as 'the reaction to the loss of a loved person, or to the loss of some abstraction which has taken the place of one, such as one's country, liberty, an ideal, and so on' (243). I will argue that Josep Carner's poems reveal a political and collective dimension of mourning whereby the work of mourning an abstraction goes far beyond Freud's 'and so on'. I will also argue that the metaphysical tension that had appeared in Carner's earlier poetry (in *El cor quiet*, for example) should also be read as a tension in the related fields of cognition and subjectivity (the field of identity, especially of national identity). Finally, I will suggest that, although *Absència* seems to confirm in many ways Freud's theory, some of these poems appear to challenge certain fundamental aspects of psychoanalysis, such as the centrality of lack and loss for desire and language.

Freud begins 'Mourning and Melancholia' by distinguishing, in a very characteristic yet puzzling move, between mourning (a 'normal affect') and melancholia (a 'pathological condition'), two psychic phenomena produced by 'the same influences' (the loss of a cathected object, that is, an object invested with libidinal energy). Both of them 'involve grave departures from the normal attitude to life', but 'it never occurs to us' to consider mourning as 'a pathological condition' (243).

If the arbitrariness with which both phenomena are granted their normal or pathological status is puzzling --and Freud's own puzzlement was probably at the root of the essay--, it becomes even more so when he compares the effects of mourning and melancholia. 'Profound mourning', he says, 'contains the same loss of interest in the outside world ... the same loss of capacity to adopt any new object of love ... and the same turning away from any activity that is not connected with thoughts of him' (244) that we can find in melancholic subjects. Loss, and death as the ultimate loss, provokes a serious disturbance of the boundaries between inside and outside, and activity becomes incompatible with this absorbing, internalizing and painful process.

'Mourning and Melancholia' is an attempt to theorize the differences between these two phenomena, and its relevance for psychoanalytic theory resides in Freud's elaboration of hypotheses on identification and the formation of the super-ego. However, I would like now to focus briefly on

Freud's definition of mourning, for it seems to rely upon some general aspects of his theory and to have implications that, as I shall argue later, are far-reaching. As we have seen earlier, mourning is 'the reaction to the loss of a loved person, or to the loss of *some abstraction which has taken the place of one*, such as one's country, liberty, an ideal, and so on' (243, *my italics*). This definition is extraordinarily large: it includes not only the ending of relationships and friends leaving for another city, but also exile, emigration, imprisonment, life under a dictatorship and huge political defeats such as, say, the fall of Communism, all of which are equated with the death of a loved person (be it spouse, lover, parent, child, sibling, relative, colleague or friend). Furthermore, if every loss follows one and the same pattern, an object of a more abstract kind that has been lost has been merely *taking the place* of a loved person. That is, every loss is like the loss of a loved person; and presumably the loss of a loved person is nothing but an echo of the Fundamental Loss, the one which takes place in the Oedipal primal scene.

In this essay I will be interested in the specificity of mourning an abstraction, particularly the experience of exile, as it is articulated in Josep Carner's poems, with the help of Freud's essay. Freud, however, does not say anything about exile or imprisonment, experiences which in many cases involve a very extended period of mourning and the need for political activism. Moreover, he considers mourning as incompatible with 'any other activity', although at the same time he defines it as 'work'. Freud describes the work of mourning in the following terms:

> Reality-testing has shown that the loved object no longer exists, and it proceeds to demand that all libido shall be withdrawn from its attachments to that object. This demand arouses understandable opposition -- it is a matter of general observation that people never willingly abandon a libidinal position, not even, indeed, when a substitute is already beckoning to them. This opposition can be so intense that a turning away from reality takes place and a clinging to the object through the medium of a hallucinatory wishful psychosis. *Normally, respect for reality gains the day.* Nevertheless its orders cannot be obeyed at once. They are carried out bit by bit, at great expense of time and cathectic energy, and *in the meantime the existence of the lost object is psychically prolonged.* Each single one of the memories and expectations in which the libido is bound to the object is brought up and hypercathected, and

detachment of the libido is accomplished in respect of it. ... [W]hen the work of mourning is completed the ego becomes free and uninhibited again (244-45, *my italics*)

What Freud does not account for is how the existence of an abstract object --something that exists only in the mind-- can be psychically prolonged. However, for the moment it might be useful to see how Carner deals with the loss of his country. The first poem of *Absència*, 'De lluny estant' (5), is a good example of some of the particularities of exile as a form of mourning:

> Qui veiés, quan l'estiu s'acomiada,
> el camí --la serp blanca i somrient--
> i, al marge d'una cala refiada,
> el pàmpol mort sota d'un pi vivent.
>
> Qui veiés una dansa damunt l'era
> i una serra morada enllà de mi;
> qui topés un aloc de torrentera
> o enmig d'un pedruscall, un romaní.
>
> Més val, però, que a aquests bedolls s'acari
> el meu esment, i a aquest boiram somort.
> En mos camins d'un temps, hom pot trobar-hi
> un àngel trist amb el seu glavi tort.

The title of the poem immediately posits one of the main elements in Carner's mourning: physical distance. The first person singular in which the poem is written and the lack of any direct references to war or exile reveal a private and decontextualized mourning which, as I shall show later, is quite different from that of other poems in the book.

The first two stanzas repeat the same structure: an impossible wish to revisit, or rather to see again a particular kind of landscape is expressed. What the poet is mourning is a Mediterranean landscape, as the 'confident cove' (l. 3), the vine and the pine tree (l. 4) and the rosemary among the rocks (l. 8) clearly indicate. The first line also introduces a temporal reference; the poet wishes to see this familiar landscape at the end of the summer, that is, in the vicinity of autumn: Carner is using here this motif as a correlative for the proximity of death. The use of the cycle of seasons as a pretext for a reflection on death is a recurrent strategy in *Absència*, and many of its poems (for example, 'Si cal que encara et vegi', 'En el davallant', 'Adéus' or 'Tardor sensible') dramatize this theme through the cultural meaning of autumn. This landscape, cheerful as it may seem, contains elements that suggest the coexistence of life and death in nature, such as 'el pàmpol mort sota d'un pi vivent', or the contrast between the festive dance that takes place on the flat surface of a threshing floor (*l'era*) and the elevation of the mountains, shaded with purple (the penitential colour of Lent) which are *beyond* the lyrical subject (*enllà de mi*).

The third stanza acts as a counterpoint to the rest of the poem. As with the other two, it is also introduced by an impersonal verb (*Més val*) and describes a landscape -- the landscape of Northern Europe. This is represented by the *bedolls* (birches) and the *boiram somort* (literally, half-dead fog). The consciousness of the lyrical subject, the poem says, had better *face* ('s'acari el meu esment', ll. 9-10) the reality of the loss of the previous landscape. The symmetrical structure produced by the appearance of the word *camí* (path) in lines 2 and 11 is certainly interesting, for it gives us more information about the nature of the lost object. The land Carner is mourning is not only a landscape, it is also a path. In Carner's poems, the path somehow establishes a link between space and time, thus suggesting movement and change, not a stable and self-identical land -- in 'El riu' (11-12), for example, the Heraclitian river where nothing becomes fixed ('cap signe hi venç ni s'hi detura gaire') is a path which, as in 'De lluny estant', is seen as a snake. In this poem, the link between space and time has been severed, thus establishing a discontinuity in the becomings of the subject: but this also suggests that reality is polydimensional, and that past and present are coexistent. Carner finally introduces here another recurring image in *Absència*: a sad angel with a bent sword that is wandering along Carner's lost paths.

The fact that Carner's paths seem not to have disappeared may suggest, in Freud's words, an opposition to 'willingly abandon a libidinal position', so 'the existence of the object is psychically prolonged'. However, in other poems such as 'Plany al cor de l'hivern' (59) Carner asserts the impossibility of going back, not only in space, but also in time:

Só lluny de tot el que fou part de mi;
¿com tornar enrera en sepultat camí?

Such a form of acceptance of loss (although in this poem Carner insists on clinging to some kind of hope: 'Vull esperar de nou l'inesperat', l. 13) corresponds to a more general attitude towards life and death which is characteristic of poems like 'El riu' and 'Bèlgica'. In 'El riu' (10-11) Carner gives an allegorical voice to a river which, like Heraclitus's river, is in a state of perpetual change and becoming. Carner states here, in two verses with classical ressonances, that life is a flow towards death:

>Sé que és ma vida cada dia empesa
>cap a la mar, on cada riu es fon;

This knowledge (*sé*) implies a revelation that an identity which is self-identical was merely an illusion, but also that the loss of identity should not be the same as indifferentiation:

>Que allí, perduda ja ma fantasia
>d'ésser tot sol i a mi mateix igual,
>pugui un floc de la meva correntia
>caure en ressaca sobre un blanc sorral.
>Potser el frec de la terra em llevaria,
>un plec que fos! del meu oblit final.

Acceptance of loss as an inherent part of life (Freud's 'reality') may be considered to be at the core of a poem like 'Bèlgica' (51-52) where Carner, at the same time that he pays homage to the country where he lived until his death, appears to have accomplished the end of his mourning and accepted his fate of being an exile. These are the first lines of the poem:

>Si fossin el meu fat les terres estrangeres,
>m'agradaria fer-me vell en un país
>on es filtrés la llum, grisa i groga, en somrís,

In the last stanza, as the work of mourning is completed, the 'fear of becoming poor' which according to Freud (252) is characteristic of melancholic subjects seems to have been surpassed, and Carner becomes a part of the landscape again:

>De molt, desert, de molt, dejú,
>viuria enmig dels altres, un poc en cadascú.

De mi dirien nens amb molles a la mà:
-És el senyor de cada dia.

However, the textual history of this poem is relevant here. As we know, Carner subjected his work to a constant process of rewriting and regrouping which culminated with the volume *Poesia* (1957). 'Bèlgica' had previously appeared in Llunyania (1952) and was later included in *Absència*. But it had been first published, in an early untitled version, in Carner's very first book, *Llibre dels poetas*, back in 1904.[4] On the other hand, we also know that in 1919, far before he became an exile, Carner had expressed to Marià Manent his wish to live in Belgium for some years.[5] Significantly, the first line of the poem was added in the 1957 version of the poem, whereas the second and the third are exactly the same as in 1904 and 1952.

This information raises two questions. In the first place, if Carner wanted to leave Catalonia and live in Belgium anyway, does this mean that he had finally attained his Imaginary ideal of society? Secondly, does Carner's constant desire to return to his country suggest an ambivalent relation to Catalonia? I am not using the word 'ambivalent' by chance here. Ambivalence is, according to Freud, one of the distinctive features of melancholia, that is, pathological mourning. In fact, his essay is explicitly a theory of melancholia.

Melancholic subjects, Freud says, show something 'which is lacking in mourning -- an extraordinary diminution in [their] self-regard, an impoverishment of [their] ego on a grand scale. In mourning it is the world that has become poor and empty; in melancholia it is the ego itself' (246). This is caused, he argues, by a regression of the libido into the ego originated by a narcissistic identification with the lost object, to which the melancholic subject had an ambivalent relation, so that 'an object-loss was transformed into an ego-loss'. Freud sums up this conflict in a chilling sentence: 'Thus the shadow of the object fell upon the ego' (249). None of the poems in *Absència*, however, not even 'Dia d'acaballes' (9) or 'A hora foscant' (24), allows us to think that the work of mourning Carner is articulating in his poems corresponds in any way to the pattern of pathological mourning Freud describes in his essay: in them, it is always the world which is diminished, not the ego. This observation, however, does not account for a mourning which, in the case of Carner's, is inexplicably long. Moreover, there seems to be a contradiction in this process, since it appears to be completed and --as 'L'altre enyor' and 'Dedicació' show-- unresolved at the same time.

The question of how a subject overcomes mourning therefore appears. Freud was unable to give a final answer to this problem, but he offers the following 'conjecture':

> Each single one of the memories and situations of expectancy which demonstrate the libido's attachment to the lost object is met by *the verdict of reality that the object no longer exists*; and the ego, confronted as it were with the question whether it shall *share this fate*, is *persuaded by the sum of the narcissistic satisfactions* it derives from being alive to sever its attachment to the object that has been abolished. We may perhaps suppose that this work of severance is so slow and gradual that by the time it has been finished the expenditure of energy necessary for it is also dissipated. (255; *my italics*)

In my opinion, Freud's conjecture becomes highly problematic if one tries to apply it to a case of abstraction-mourning like that of exile. In the first place, it is hardly arguable that an abstraction, in this case a country, 'no longer exists', unless we are talking of genocide or of a total cataclysm. On the other hand, if the abstraction has actually disappeared, Freud's assertion implies that it has disappeared *in its entirety*, leaving no traces at all; it also ignores the political circumstances under which an abstraction disappears: as Benedict Anderson writes, 'nations ... have no clearly identifiable birth, and *their deaths*, if they ever happen, *are never natural*'.[6] Secondly, an exile could have shared the fate of other people from her country, but how could she share the fate of a country that has been lost but that has not totally disappeared? From this point of view it could even be argued that it is the country who has lost the exile, not the other way round. Finally, Freud associates the need for survival to narcissism, which in his developmental model appears to be inherently pathological. As with his views on homosexuality, the deviant is at the core of the normal: the 'normal affect of mourning' comes to an end when the subject compromises with the 'narcissistic satisfactions it derives from being alive'. If, however, as we have seen in Carner's poems, the attachment to the lost object is never completely severed (as poems like 'Lleialtat', 'Dedicació' and 'Cant d'una presència' suggest), does this mean that exile is inherently pathological?

Perhaps at the root of these problems is Freud's own definition of mourning. For Freud, mourning an abstraction is merely the supplement of mourning: an exile's grief for his country is a displacement of that for a loved person. This is clearly consistent with his theoretical model, where lack and loss are crucial notions for the processes whereby subjectivity is constructed, in which Oedipus plays a central role. Since it is hardly defendable, however, that an exile's problems are explained by referring them to the Oedipus complex, it becomes necessary to acknowledge that, as *Absència* shows, exile has a dynamic which is not reducible to a form of mourning of a strictly personal kind, although they are both related and interact with each other. It also becomes necessary to account for the differences existing in diverse kinds of exiles -- to put it roughly, to mourn liberal Catalonia must be quite a different thing from mourning, say, Nazi Germany.

The difference is obviously of a political nature, and 'Sota un cel de cendra' (21-23) provides a good example for my argument. Carner presents here a scene on a foreign mountain where a group of pilgrims implore God's mercy:[7]

> Eren, un dia, sota un cel de cendra,
> pobres romeus en estranger tossal,
> pendís amunt, per codolars, a emprendre
>   que Déu parlés al cimadal.

Although no proper names are included in this poem (as in most of the book), Carner seems to be establishing here a direct link between the Catalans in exile and the diaspora of the Jewish people: an identification, indeed, with all those nations expelled from their own territories or whose rights, like those of Catalonia, had been violently supressed. Problematic as it may appear, this identification is important, because if on the one hand it brings to the text the horrors of the Holocaust or suggests an implausible compulsion to share the fate of the Jews under the Nazi regime, on the other hand it indicates a strong will for survival and the desire to activate a narrative that, precisely through this identification, transforms the *psychic activity* of mourning into the *political energy* necessary to fight oppression, death and humiliation. The presence of the first person plural is a crucial aspect of this poem which is closely related to the transformative act I have just mentioned, and which, I would suggest, opens up the possibility of a collective and political dimension of mourning.

The political importance of mourning has been highlighted by the theoretical production around AIDS. In his reading of Freud's 'Mourning and Melancholia', Douglas Crimp has pointed out how crucial mourning is for gay men in the political struggle against the epidemic.[8] In his article Crimp criticizes Freud for ignoring the collective dimension of mourning: 'Freud can tell us very little', he says, 'about our grieving rituals, our memorial services and candlelight marches ... [A]s against this often shared activity, mourning, for Freud, is a solitary undertaking' (7). However, in the case of gay men, this private activity becomes almost impossible due to the social violence related to the epidemic and to homosexuality: gay men find it impossible to mourn their gay friends *as gay*. In bringing the Holocaust and the AIDS crisis together with the problematic of exile, my intention is not to trivialize the former, but to show how in exile a parallel situation of disempowerment occurs. The pilgrims Carner presents in his poem are the survivors of a defeat, and this has become for them a social stigma (ll.25-26); moreover, the gap between the language of the exiles and that of the country where they are refugees has caused the former to lose its performative power:

> -Oh Tu que ens has creat i que ens governes!,
> ¿com mai tindríem sacerdot ni altar
> si dels estranys bevem en les cisternes
> i un d'una altra parla ens cou el pa?

In these lines the religious and ritual character of mourning is related to its social dimension; but it also brings to the surface some of the particularities of the exile of the Catalans: for them, it is impossible to mourn their nation as a community, because their feeling of foreignness, their lack of adequate institutions and the blurring of boundaries created by the linguistic gap deprives mourning of the conditions that would ensure its effectiveness. In other words, mourning a nation as a community is impossible because the nation is what gives this community a sense of collective identity. Furthermore, this impossibility has its origin in the 'gran malvestat' of line 21, the unprecedented violence inflicted on the Catalan people by the victors of the civil war.

However, as Douglas Crimp suggests, when the survival of a whole community is at stake, this impossibility necessarily becomes a condition of possibilities. 'The violence of silence and omission', he says, '[is] almost as impossible to endure as the violence of unleashed hatred and outright murder. Because this violence also desecrates the memories of our dead, we rise in anger to vindicate them. For many of us, mourning *becomes* militancy' (9). Under some circumstances, what for Freud was impossible (activity) becomes a necessity, a precondition for survival; the work of assessment of the past is transformed into production of energy for a project in the future. From this point of view, mourning becomes work towards something yet to come. This is where hope, the most distinctive feature of exile as a form of mourning, comes on to the scene: not as a way of creating wishful illusions, but as a cognitive weapon:

> Digue'ns que ja no fenyeràs la incúria,
> que a l'esperança donaràs permís,
> que ens llevaràs la més cruel injúria:
> no pas el dol: el desencís.

Carner is here articulating hope in political terms: it is not a matter of facing the 'verdict of reality that the lost object no longer exists', but rather of liberating the possibility of becoming, of imagining the possibility of a return and of asserting the certainty of change. For this reason, the worst (political) affront, he says, is not mourning, but *discouragement*, the giving up of hope. However, Carner's plea for hope is not a moral imperative, but a *strategical* move: as he wrote in 1942, 'una guerra no és mai acabada per una o mil victòries, sinó per la disposició interior del vençut a cessar en la resistència'.[9] Thus, if there is an obvious parallel between Freud's notion of melancholia and Carner's *desencís*, it must be noted that the former is merely clinical, whereas the latter is clearly political. Political, because what is at stake here is the fight against oppression and the imperative of changing those conditions that make return impossible.

In *Absència*, then, we are dealing with a similar kind of mourning to that of AIDS, the Holocaust, or Plaza de Mayo, a mourning that originates from political violence and that is necessarily collective. Considering that Freud wrote his essay during World War I, in the midst of a terrible wave of politically originated violence, it is surprising that he should ignore these aspects of mourning. As with AIDS, and inseparable from the work of mourning, what was at stake in the exile of the Catalans was the survival of a community against the violence exerted on it by an external source; in such a situation hope (the hope of returning and of overturning oppression) becomes a constitutive element of grievance, one that is indispensable for allowing its political dimension to flourish.

In his article, however, Douglas Crimp insists on the need to acknowledge the death-drive, that is, the fact that violence is also self-inflicted. '[O]ur misery', he writes, 'comes from within as well as from without ... it is the result of psychic as well as of social conflict ... By making all violence external, pushing it to the outside and objectifying it in "enemy" institutions and individuals, we deny its psychic articulation, deny that we are effected, as well as affected, by it' (16). As Guillaume Apollinaire said in *Alcools*, hope is a source of violence:

> Comme la vie est lente
> Et comme l'Espérance est violente.[10]

If in a poem like 'Dedicació' (44) Carner proclaims his unbreakable hope, in others, like 'Sobtadament', 'Cor fidel', 'Matí' or 'Lleialtat', this radical determination is in painful interaction with doubt. On the other hand, if 'Sota un cel de cendra' reveals the importance of language in the problematic of an exiled community, I would argue that the linguistic conflict also affects the subjective sphere, for it calls into question and profoundly disturbs the subject's distribution of boundaries between inside and outside, which was previously taken for granted. I would thus suggest that, although Freud's patterns of melancholia do not apply here, in *Absència* a violence against the ego is shown to be exerted from within, and a diminishing of the ego is dramatized.

It has been often noted that Carner's poetry, despite its appearances of superficiality and bonhomie, contains a very important element of conflict which is characteristic, for example, of poems like 'Perdut en mon jardí' or 'Nocturn' in *El cor quiet* (1925). Although not much has been written on

Absència, some critics have pointed out that the same conflict is central to this book. Loreto Busquets and Jaume Pont coincide in considering it as an ontological tension which, as in *El cor quiet*, is resolved in the acceptance of human limits and in the attainment of *assenyament* (wisdom). For example, Jaume Pont writes:

> A despecho de la inevitable vejez y de la muerte, Carner postula la aceptación de los límites del destino humano ... No es extraño que, en la pendiente de su ciclo vital, el poeta decida reconvertir las señales de su agostamiento en lúcida meditación de su destino metafísico ... En *Absència* Carner llega a un punto en que lo único que parece importarle es esa 'unión con la esencia' capaz de justificar su anhelo permanente y universal'.[11]

This reading, however, seems to me unsatisfactory at several levels. Firstly, it ignores the historical contingency of exile, and therefore is unable to account for a tension which takes place elsewhere, in the related fields of cognition and subjectivity. Secondly, I would suggest that it is erroneous to assume that Carner aims to resolve this tension: if he is interested in identity, unity and essence, in *Absència* he also seems to be interested in becoming, difference and substance. Finally, as a consequence of this last remark, such a reading leaves no room for a radical conception of national identity which goes beyond essentialism and that, I will argue, Carner does formulate in some of his poems.

The sonnet 'A trenc de dia' (46) dramatizes some of the issues I have raised:

> Llum fantasmal, arborescents falgueres,
> llot on rodà l'aquàtica avior,
> signes perduts en boires volanderes,
> fites errants del seny i de la por,
>
> negres ocells d'immemorials corberes,
> arbres gements i sense cap saó,
> tels, teranyines, ombres fugisseres
> que encerclar-me voldríeu on no só:
>
> tot fou ordit en la indecisa cova
> en mi nascuda, vista enllà de mi,
> on el dorment avança i no es retroba.

Ja, però, glavi nu, per alt camí,
l'inesperat arcàngel del matí
el cel abranda amb la certesa nova.

As the title itself indicates, the poem represents the moment of daybreak, when perception of external reality is blurred due to the particular quality of light. Being as well the moment of dreams, the perception of internal reality also fades. As a consequence, in this poem the subject loses sight of any certainty. I would suggest that the scene of blurring depicted in the two first stanzas somehow corresponds to the situation of a subject in exile. If, as I have argued above, Carner presents hope as a constitutive element of exile, hope also places the exile in a perpetual state of doubt: not only the possibility of a return is unsure, but also the adequacy of any strategies adopted and indeed the very idea of returning are doubtful. Moreover, exile means the loss of all cultural and personal referents, at the same time that the process of identification with a new country cannot be completed: the practices of everyday life lose their obviousness (in 'A hora foscant' [24], Carner speaks of himself as an 'indecís estranger') and exile results in a form of not-understanding. In addition to the fact that for Catalan intellectuals exile involved losing the possibility of openly being in touch with their own audience, in exile the transparency of language becomes an *impossible* illusion: hence the 'signs lost in unstable mists' of line 3.

The threat that the subject may get trapped in a self-enclosed chaos (1.8) is increased by the overwhelming power of nature and indeed the reminiscence of man's animal kinship (1.2). The presence of the unconscious, together with the menacing suspension of the agencies of consciousness (1.4), offers a serious threat that identity is lost. Other poems, however, show a totally different perspective. In 'Sobtadament' (20) nature, while questioning the subject's identity, remains a benign agency; and in 'Diàleg' (57-58) --where a dialogue between the subject and his own shadow is dramatized-- the subject is presented as always already split, and this is precisely what guarantees certainty against doubt.

The third and fourth stanzas of 'A trenc de dia' shed some light on these contradictions. The threat to identity has been originated *from within* the subject himself: the danger was that of becoming a prisoner of the subject. If the subject is trapped in the world of dreams without being able to 'find' himself (l.11), it is because the boundaries between inside and outside have disappeared (l.10), thus making the whole world become a part of the 'indecisive cave' of line 9; as the adjective 'indecisive' indicates, the effacement of boundaries deeply affects the subject's capacity of agency. Help, however, comes from outside. It is the 'unexpected archangel of the morning' who brings the 'new certainty'. As we know, the figure of the angel raises the issue of communication; if the first poem I commented, 'De lluny estant', was closed with a sad angel wandering along empty paths, now a triumphant angel is the messager not of truth, but of certainty. What certainty can be communicated, though, when language *cannot* be meaningful and every utterance and movement is subjected to the dialectic of hope and doubt? This is, I would claim, the *certainty of change*, which is asserted in the poem 'Dedicació' (44-45):

> El cor oprès,
> per nou espai es torna lliure.
> En món encara no palès,
> res com no puc, m'és tot permès.
> Só del futur que lleva.
> L'esdevenir roda sens treva:
> vull que s'acuiti el seu trepig
> i retre, en ell[,] l'ànima meva
> al que ultrapassi el meu desig. (45)

Carner proclaims here the radical freedom that emanates from becoming: in a situation where everything has been lost, everything is possible because it is yet to become. He also advocates for the acceleration of this endless becoming, and promises to devote himself totally to whatever limits his desire displaces. But, as I said earlier, there is an important element of tension in Carner's poetry, and I would suggest that, far from being something that must be removed or resolved into some kind of essence, this tension acts as the motor of his poetry. Thus, if Carner is interested in becoming, so is he in identity -- more precisely, in national identity.

From the very beginning of his career, Josep Carner was a committed liberal nationalist intellectual. An early supporter of the conservative Lliga Regionalista, in the 1920s he backed the creation of the centre-left nationalist party Acció Catalana; later, in 1936, he supported the Popular Front list and, as Albert Manent reminds us, he was one of the few diplomats to remain faithful to the democratic regime during the civil war. As a cultural activist, together with Eugeni d'Ors he was the main formulator of Noucentisme's political agenda, thus decisively contributing to the establishment of modern Catalan cultural infrastructure. The figure of Carner the Nationalist, however, coexists with that of Carner the Nomad, the deterritorialized diplomat and exile who drifted all over the world. Thus, if Carner the Nationalist was committed to a political project for Catalonia, what kind of national identity could Carner the Nomad conceive? Furthermore, since *Absència* is mainly a book of mourning, do the grievance of Carner the Nationalist for the loss of his political project and the mourning of Carner the Nomad coincide? What is the nature of the object Carner the Nomad is mourning?

If, as Benedict Anderson claims in his book *Imagined Communities*, a nation is 'an imagined political community' (6), mourning a nation presents a double problem. In the first place, the work of mourning being strictly psychic, and the hope of recovering the lost object being a constitutive element of exile, the problem therefore appears here of how to avoid imagining a nation that falls into the realm of the Imaginary -- that is, how to give up a nation that inevitably has changed, without constructing a harmonious and self-enclosed ideal. Secondly, since the process of imagining a nation --of establishing a narrative of national identity-- seems inescapable, there is a further problem, not of inventing a 'truer' nation to be recovered, but of avoiding a Fascist narrative. 'Communities are to be distinguished', Anderson writes, 'not by their falsity/genuineness, but by the *style* in which they are imagined' (6; *my italics*). In other words, since mourning a nation is imagining a community anyway, as I said earlier there *must* be a difference in style between mourning liberal Catalonia and mourning Nazi Germany.

The conception I proposed above of mourning an abstraction as work towards something yet to come appears here once again, and becomes patent in 'L'altre enyor' (25-27), a series of four sonnets in which Carner meets the first problem I formulated. If in the first section he wonders about the possibility of going back to the familiar landscape of his youth, in the second sonnet he states the fact that his country is now different from the one he knew, which is irrecuperable. He is, then, mourning his own past; in the third sonnet, however, he formulates what 'the other yearning' of the title consists of:

> Per l'afalac d'un temps no passo pena.
> És goig no mai hagut el que ara emplena
> de fantasmes i de cants ma solitud:
>
> Mare, encara no nada, el cor t'honora,
> com mai primera, per tot temps senyora,
> amb naus d'afany i torres de virtut.

Carner's 'other mourning' is not that for the country he knew and lost, but that for a joy he has not had yet (*goig no mai hagut*); he is mourning a Mother/land yet to be born (*Mare, encara no nada*). Carner is mourning his land's future becomings, those he cannot see and whose actualization has been upset by political oppression. Furthermore, he is stressing the possibility of becoming rather than of recovering a lost object, and I would suggest that this yearning for something yet to happen corresponds quite well to Gilles Deleuze's notion of 'becoming-minoritatian' and the opposition he establishes between 'model' and 'becoming'. In 'Contrôle et devenir', an interview with Toni Negri collected in *Pourparlers*, Deleuze says:

> Les minorités et les majorités ne se distinguent pas par le nombre. Une minorité peut être plus nombreuse qu'une majorité. Ce qui définit la majorité, c'est un modèle auquel il faut être conforme: par exemple l'Européen moyen adulte mâle habitant des villes ... Tandis qu'une minorité n'a pas de modèle, c'est un devenir, un processus. On peut dire que la majorité, ce n'est personne. Tout le monde, sous un aspect ou un autre, est pris dans un devenir minoritaire qui l'entraînerait dans des voies inconnues s'il se décidait à le suivre. Quand une minorité se crée des modèles, c'est parce qu'elle veut devenir majoritaire, et c'est sans doute inévitable pour sa survie ou son salut (par exemple avoir un État, être reconnue, imposer ses droits). Mais sa puissance vient de ce qu'elle a su créer, et qui passera plus ou moins dans le modèle, sans en dépendre. Le peuple, c'est toujours une minorité créatrice, et qui le reste, même quand elle conquiert une majorité: les deux choses peuvent coexister parce qu'elles ne vivent pas sur le même plan...[12]

Carner, thus, seems to be calling for the becoming-minoritatian of

Catalonia and its constitution as a creative force which operates without a model, present or past, to be followed. It is in 'A la immutable' and 'Cant del fill distant', however, that he appears to be offering a solution to the second problem I mentioned. The sonnet 'A la immutable' (53) presents the opposite pole to the creative force of 'L'altre enyor': the conception of the nation as a destructive force, which is easily identifiable, despite its abstract character, with Nazism or with Franco's Fascist Spain. An 'absolute queen' -- hierarchical and authoritarian-- of its territory (l.1), this entity is founded on destruction (ll.3-4) and is *immutable*, as the title of the poem indicates: it rejects change and 'hates' becoming, desire and thought (ll.5-6). Moreover, its 'God' --its guiding principle-- is that of condemnation and annihilation, and makes it 'rigid' and unproductive (ll.7-8). But, more importantly, in its rise the Fascist empire (l.11) is *imitating* something: it is following a model based on punishment, fear, death and conquest:

¿Què ton adust redreçament imita?
¿Serà patíbul, espantall o fita,
o imperial bastó sobre un barranc?

As opposed to this immutable monster, in 'Cant del fill distant' (31-33) Carner presents another tradition, another genealogy, an alternative concept of nation. In this poem Carner faces the question of whether a return is at all possible, since physical distance has severed the link between the exile and his country, forcing them to engage, each one, in different becomings. Thus, what sense of national identity can be kept in this situation? To this question the loving Mother/land responds:

-Sempre m'han fet plaer --dius amorosa--
les portes lliures, els camins oberts.
Dos fills bessons havia portat a les entranyes,
l'un vora meu, l'altre dispers,
i l'un solcant la gleva i el seu germà les ones,
no mai es deslligaren mon lloc i l'univers,
i tinc, per tant, més que un desig clos entre fites,
i em faig més alta i més igual vora el divers.

Carner is literally saying here that one fundamental part of the Catalan tradition is being away from Catalonia, for she enjoys 'free gates' and 'open paths'. It is important that the word 'path' (*camí*) appears here: as I argued in my reading of 'De lluny estant', Carner's insistence throughout the book on the image of the path suggests a land which is not stable. Carner's Catalonia is a deterritorialized land, a nation which is not self-identical, an entity which is consistent but not self-enclosed, a process. The nation Carner is imagining in his mourning is *a relation to the outside*. What Carner is mourning is not a past or a lost country, but the openness of paths, a relation to his own country as his outside, a flow of endless becomings that has been cut.

It is a striking fact, however, that Carner constantly refers to Catalonia as a Mother. In 'Cant d'una presència' Carner, as well as stating his fidelity to the motherland, speaks in the name of the Mother, and utters the Name of the Mother. Does this suggest an Oedipal nationality, a wish of going back to an undifferentiation with the mother? But in *Absència* it is not Carner who mourns his mother: it is an unborn Mother who mourns her Son, who is lost.[13]

In 'Cant d'una presència' (55-56) Josep Carner states the importance of the language in the survival of his nation:

però mentre soni ma parla en mos llavis
t'estic ran dels braços, encara a tos peus.

I mentre tos cims no s'esfondrin
i al bat de les ones no es negui ton pla,
al cel, a la terra, i a l'àngel, i al monstre
la veu dels qui resten, la pols dels qui manquen ton nom redirà.

In fact, Carner is here making an appeal to one of the main elements of Romantic nationalism: the identification of land with nation, people and language, which constituted a typical discursive strategy to claim legitimacy for an 'eternal' nation that was 'awakening'. On the other hand, the recurrence of the term *cant* or *cançó* (song) in *Absència* suggests another element of Romantic nationalism intimately connected to the one I have just mentioned: the interest in folklore as the genuine expression of the people, safeguard of a national language seen as immanent to the land. Carner himself, in an article written in exile, 'La parla i el cant',[14] makes use of both ideas in his protest against the prohibition of the public use of the Catalan language.

But this also brings to the surface the contradictions of writing in exile, and raises the problem of language and its social function. In the case of Carner and his fellow Catalan exiled writers, the distance between themselves and their audience was absolute: not only because they were writers without an audience, but also because the official policy of the Franco regime had abolished the Catalan audience *as Catalan*, thus threatening the very existence and survival of a cultural industry that had been started with the Renaixença and that was vital for the constitution and maintenance of a Modern culture. Why write, then, when there can be no communication with a non-existent audience? In the same interview I quoted above, Gilles Deleuze suggests that writing is an inherently political act: 'L'artiste ne peut que faire appel à un peuple, il en a besoin au plus profond de son entreprise, il n'a pas à le créer et ne le peut pas. L'art, c'est ce qui résiste: il résiste à la mort, à la servitude, à l'infamie, à la honte' (235). Just as for Deleuze art is not tantamount to communication, for Carner, I would claim, writing in exile was an act of resistance to the death of a people.

In the same article Carner speaks of language as being not communicative but expressive and affective, a combination of gesture, rhythm and modulation: hence the importance of the song, which guarantees the preservation of national identity. For Carner's national self, then, language is central; if it is produced by language --a specific language-- it is also a speaking subject, or rather a producer of signs:[15] it remains a national self insofar as it is able to produce utterances in its own language. However, what is the status of the national speaking self in *Absència*? How is language produced?

Reflection on language and the creative process was a cherished topic for Carner; 'Creació del poema' (60-62) is a rather mysterious example of this aspect of his poetry. The poem tells a miraculous story. It begins with the description of a landscape: an absolute desert 'on jo no era gens' (l.3), where 'I was not'. In this desert, far from everything, in the midst of an absolute solitude and of a total silence (ll.11-14), Carner says, one day a bat (*un muricec*, l.20) attempted to be born: it would be the first being in that desert to delimit space and time with its wings and the beat of its heart (ll.21-22). Ignorant of its origin and of its fate, overwhelmed by the 'dispersion of the void' that his birth has provoked (ll.27-30), and surrounded by 'signs of absence everywhere' (l.32), the bat attempts to 'shake' the desert with the first utterance of its voice (ll.33-34), all against the hostility of the 'silent things' (ll.35-42). A miracle, however, is produced: a passing angel --the most beautiful and cheerful angel, the one without a sword (ll.45-49)-- witnesses the bat's attempt and smiles (l.50). Suddenly, an extraordinary transformation of the landscape takes place: birds migrate longing (*es migraven*) for future songs, 'projects of forest' irrupt, rocks announce the emergence of springs and new hills seem to demand an unknown treading (ll.56-70).

More extraordinary than the appearance of the cheerful angel --who is no longer a messenger, but the agent of transformation-- is the presence in the poem of the bat. Significantly, the Catalan word Carner uses for bat is not the common one, *rata-pinyada*. If the unattentive reader is not aware of this fact, he/she may take the *muricec* for a bird: but, even if it flies too, a *muricec* is not a bird, and Carner's choice is obviously not gratuitous. The *muricec* is a flying mammal, a disturbing and ambiguous animal, a damned creature of the night associated with witchcraft and demonology, and as the word *muricec* indicates, it is blind. But there is yet one more cultural meaning for it: Dracula comes to his victims' rooms transformed into a bat. Deleuze and Guattari write in *Mille plateaux*: 'La pensée est comme le Vampire, elle n'a pas d'image, ni pour constituer modèle, ni pour faire copie'.[16] As we know, vampires do not have an image in the mirror -- and even if they had one, the bat could not see it, for it is blind. Moreover, the bat in the poem, being a damned creature, is radically innocent: it has no origin, or rather its origin is void (ll.23-30).

The concluding lines (71-73) spectacularly bring all these motifs together:

> Em delia fins jo --que m'ignorava.
> Era el començament que començava.
> Era el desert --amb el desig.

The shrieks of the imageless bat, the informed sound-matter that it utters, shake and transform Carner's inner desert, where he is ignored by himself -- he *deletes* himself at the same time as he *desires* (*em delia*). But his desire appears to be immanent to the desert: it has no origin and no justification, it is simply there as a productive force. As with the bat, Carner has no image in the mirror, no model to follow: there is only creation as an absolute beginning brought up by desire. For Carner there is no primal scene in language, and if there is one, it takes place not in the household, but in the desert. In his exile, Carner is not writing in an attempt to fill a loss, but to shake the desert in an act of absolute creation towards unexpected becomings, giving rise to an ever present and productive desire, in complete awareness that silence equals death. Not the silence of a confused poet, not a symbolic death: is it perhaps by chance that 'silence = death' is the slogan of the anti-AIDS activist group ACT UP?[17]

Josep Carner could not return to Catalonia until 1970, for a short visit just before his death. His desire to live his last days in his own country, however, could not be fulfilled for political reasons: as Joan Ferraté reminds us in the introduction to his anthology of Carner's poetry, 'determinats individus "situats en llocs responsables de la cultura catalana", va escriure anys més tard Pere Calders, van interferir en el projecte i el van fer fracassar, amb el pretext que "no trobaven oportú que Carner retornés a Catalunya, perquè a fora tenia el valor d'un símbol i aquesta significació es perdria tan bon punt abandonés el seu exili"' (11). This act of violence against an old man who longed to die in his own country was not exerted by the Fascist regime of Spain, but *from within* the very community he had been mourning for years. Perhaps this fact helps to explain, despite all its tensions and contradictions, the radicality of Carner's poetry and thought. Its will never to give up resistance, its radical tension between identity and becoming, its stress on desire and creativity and, above all, its vision of a nation which is a relation to the outside, were perhaps too threatening for some sectors of a national community which, as history has shown, have later become dominant. Reterritorialized in a foreign country, Carner is still a challenge to Catalan national identity, and his works remain, in Gabriel Ferrater's words, open for us to understand them again and again, 'com una pàtria'.

NOTES

* One day in March 1992 the news arrived that Derek Lomax had died. To me, this news was all the more shocking since I had not seen him or spoken to him for six months, and precisely the next day I had planned to go to Birmingham, where I expected to see him at a moment when I needed his advice. Derek Lomax was and remains for me an example of human kindness, radical tolerance and intellectual rigour. I would like this essay to be my personal homage to his memory and an instrument that helps me to articulate my mourning for him.

1. See Albert Manent, *Josep Carner i el Noucentisme: Vida, obra i llegenda* (Barcelona: Edicions 62, 1969). See also Albert Manent, 'El escritor en el exilio', *Ínsula*, 456-457 (November-December 1984), 26.

2. I am quoting from the following edition: Josep Carner, *Absència* (Barcelona: Edicions 62, 1985). However, I have also used the 1957 edition of Carner's collected poems.

3. Sigmund Freud, 'Mourning and Melancholia' (1917), trans. by Joan Riviere, in *The Standard Edition of the Complete Works* (London: Hogarth Press, 1957), XIV, 243-58.

4. Loreto Busquets, *La poesia d'exili de Josep Carner* (Barcelona: Barcino, 1980), pp.84-85.

5. On the 29th of April 1919 Manent wrote in his diary on a project Carner had told him about of creating a publishing house: 'Un cop organitzada l'Editorial, en Carner se n'aniria a viure uns quants anys a Bélgica, i posaria com a gerent un gran home de negocis: l'Alcàntara' (Marià Manent, *L'aroma d'arç* (Barcelona: Laertes, 1982), p.20). Manent also gives a very interesting account of Josep Carner's first visit to Catalonia since the end of the Civil War, a few months before his death, in 1970.

6. Benedict Anderson, *Imagined Communities* (London and New York: Verso, 1991), p.205. The italics are mine.

7. For the sake of simplicity, and for obvious reasons related to my own competence, I am ignoring the religious element in *Absència*. Certainly, Carner was a Catholic poet, and this is a crucial aspect of his poetry. However, as some poems seem to suggest, and as Loreto Busquets says about the title of Carner's major work, *Nabí*, there could be a direct influence of Spinoza in Josep Carner. If so, it would be of enormous interest to trace the extent of this influence, and to see how much Carner's God owes to Spinoza's God. This kind of study would probably lead to major changes in the way Carner's poetry and thought are perceived.

8. Douglas Crimp, 'Mourning and Militancy', *October*, 51 (1989), 3-18. I am indebted to Eve Kosofsky Sedgwick for all the ideas she shared with the participants in the seminar she ran in the summer of 1992 at the School of Criticism and Theory at Dartmouth College, New Hampshire. At her seminar, centred around the notion of performativity, the topic of mourning was widely discussed, both in its general aspects and with direct reference to the struggle against AIDS, and several theoretical elaborations of the topic were commented, including Crimp's article; she also gave us the opportunity to read some of her unpublished work, for example 'White Glasses', a text which is at the same time a memorial and a reflection on the problematic of identification. It goes without saying that this article owes much to the work that was carried out in her class.

9. 'La inspiració més alta' (1942), in *Prosa d'exili (1939-1962)*, ed. by Albert Manent

(Barcelona: Edicions 62, 1985), p.27.

10. Guillaume Apollinaire, 'Le pont Mirabeau', in *Oeuvres poétiques* (Paris: Gallimard, 1965), p.45.

11. J. Pont, 'Conflicto y tensión en la poesía de Josep Carner', *Ínsula* 456-457 (November-December 1984), 27.

12. G. Deleuze, 'Contrôle et devenir', in *Pourparlers (1972-1990)* (Paris: Minuit, 1990), p.235.

13. 'Só lluny de les teves engires, oh Mare endolada!', 'Cant d'una presència' (p.55). Cf. also 'L'altre enyor', 'Perdurança' (p.43) and the last section of 'Temes de la lírica nàhuatl' (pp.34-36).

14. 'La parla i el cant', in Josep Carner, *Prosa d'exili (1939-1962)*, pp.21-23.

15. See the sonnet 'Unitat' (p.49).

16. Gilles Deleuze and Félix Guattari, *Mille plateaux* (Paris: Minuit, 1980), p.468.

17. See Douglas Crimp and Adam Rolston, *AIDS DemoGraphics* (Seattle: Bay Press, 1990).

LECTURA DE 'LLÀTZER EL RESSUSCITAT', DE CARLES RIBA

ENRIC SULLÀ
Universitat Autònoma de Barcelona

A Derek Lomax, in memoriam,
pels cursos 1978-1979 i 1979-1980,
amb l'Esther

I

Acabat de compondre el 22 de gener de 1955, 'Llàtzer el ressuscitat' és segurament el més reeixit dels tres poemes que componen el llibre de Carles Riba *Esbós de tres oratoris* (1957) perquè 'demostra una fusió gairebé absoluta entre tema i interpretació'.[1] Si bé amplifica el passatge evangèlic amb tradicions apòcrifes, manté un to més homogeni que no 'Els tres reis d'Orient', que deriva cap a les tradicions populars i la moralitat evident, i no força tant la lletra del text evangèlic com 'El fill pròdig', en què la narració original s'amplia i es complica amb motius inventats, a fi de donar lloc a una gran complexitat temàtica.[2] Altrament, de la importància que tenia, ja no el poema sinó el tema per a Riba, en dóna prova una carta a Paulina Crusat (24-I-1955), en la qual reconeix que el poema l'havia arribat a 'punyir [...] com per un impuls vivent de sortir a la llum'.

Com és ben sabut, l'única font de la història de Llàtzer és l'Evangeli de Joan, 11, 1-45 i 12, 1-11. En concret, de Llàtzer, germà de Marta i Maria, només es diu que està malalt i que mor; però l'important és que la seva mort és ocasió d'un miracle de Jesús, obrat no tant per l'amistat amb ell i les seves germanes --que és molt estreta-- com perquè creguin en ell els qui el vegin (Jo 11, 45 i 12, 11). Amb encert, Riba situa l'acció del poema en una època indeterminada però posterior als fets, la qual cosa té com a conseqüència humanitzar el miracle, que llavors esdevé l'objecte de la narració de Llàtzer, ell mateix prova vivent de la veritat del fet meravellós. A més, per tal de concentrar l'atenció del lector en el diàleg entre ells dos, Riba ha prescindit de les germanes de Llàtzer i només fa una menció de Sara l'egípcia (la Negra, segons el poema, v. 269).

L'acció del poema, tanmateix, no transcorre a Israel, a Betània, lloc del miracle obrat per Jesús, sinó a la Camarga, perquè 'segons una tradició molt antiga, recollida per Mistral en el cant XI de *Mireia*, Llàtzer el ressuscitat va fer cap a Provença després de la mort de Crist i fou bisbe de Marsella. Hi fou dut miraculosament en un vaixell desguarnit, a bord del qual els rancuniosos prohoms de Judea l'havien enviat al naufragi juntament amb les tres Maries, la serventa Sara l'egípcia i altres sants deixebles de Jesús'.[3]

El poema no depèn exclusivament de la veu del seu narrador (com a 'Els tres reis d'Orient'), ja que introduiex el diàleg entre Llàtzer i un nàufrag d'origen africà; la funció del narrador, però, no va gaire més enllà d'oferir una mínima localització, indicar els pocs moviments dels personatges i, en algun moment, entrar en la seva consciència. Precisament el nàufrag, un personatge inventat pel poeta amb una clara finalitat dramàtica, és un dels encerts més notables del poema, perquè no solament li permet d'exposar a Riba un punt de vista coherent i plausible sobre la mort i la transcendència, sinó que justifica estructuralment que Llàtzer conti la seva pròpia experiència de mort i resurrecció; narració que Llàtzer efectua en la seva qualitat de testimoni personal, la qual cosa li confereix veracitat i dramatisme i demostra, a més, la força de la seva fe.

Riba precisa que 'Llàtzer i el pobre nàufrag s'entenen en grec, que no és la llengua materna ni de l'un ni de l'altre' (287), recurs mitjançant el qual, 'per un joc subtil, els dos interlocutors, a través de llur coneixença imperfecta d'una llengua comuna, però estranya a tots dos, arriben a crear una atmosfera dins la qual tot llenguatge sembla insuficient per expressar el misteri cristià'.[4] Aquest és un procediment que facilita l'actuació dramàtica de tots dos personatges com a exponents d'actituds oposades davant la transcendència, la cristiana i la humanista atea o, si més no, agnòstica. Altrament, en una carta a Paulina Crusat (24-I-1955), Riba confirma que el vers (l'alexandrí amb cesura, que es combina amb decasíl.labs, octosíl.labs i hexasíl.labs) 'és tractat més dramàticament que no pas líricament i pel seu to he pres com a referència el de Dante (en trobarà algun eco) i, m'he adonat de sobte que així ho feia, el de Racine'.

No és menor la cura a reforçar la versemblança del poema tocant a la localització de la tomba de Llàtzer, però en el difícil equilibri entre la reconstrucció arqueològica i l'actualització simbòlica, cal constatar que Riba ha tendit a potenciar la seva personal interpretació del text evangèlic. De tota manera, demostra el rigor de la documentació la nota manuscrita conservada a l'Arxiu Riba sobre aquesta tomba (sense indicar d'on treia la informació), nota que transcric a continuació (desfent les abreviatures):

> Fixat per la tradició [...] al mateix indret; al flanc Sud Est del Mont de les Oliveres, dalt d'un poble que avui es diu El Azerieh (poble de Llàtzer).
> Canvis en el temps (per consolidar).
> Dins una roca argilosa; a la part pròxima a l'entrada, es conserva la duresa primitiva.
> Damunt s'hi aixeca un oratori; per sostenir-lo a dins, una volta en ogiva.
> Entrada actual, al Nord: 24 esglaons (construïts el 1337). Així, s'arriba en una cambra quadrada d'uns 3 m. de llarg i d'ample. A l'Est, una porta emparedada, que degué ésser la primitiva de la tomba. Per la part Nord d'aquesta cambra, es va a la tomba pròpiament dita. És semblant a la primera. S'hi baixa per 3 esglaons. Destinada a rebre tres cossos, cadascuna [té] el seu banc.
> Tomba igualment venerada per musulmans i cristians.
> El dol durava 7 dies.
> Segons una tradició, les relíquies de Llàtzer [van ser] descobertes en 890 a Xipre.

És evident, com he avançat, que el nàufrag té la finalitat dramàtica de suscitar la narració de Llàtzer, però també té la funció dialèctica de representar una actitud oposada davant la trancendència; el nàufrag, del qual diu Riba que no li desplauria que fos 'un compatriota de Sant Agustí' (287), 'aparece no sólo como la encarnación viviente del hombre de las riberas del Mediterráneo, sino como la más genuina expresión de la mentalidad y el espíritu del viejo humanismo pagano'.[5] Com és dit al poema, Llàtzer ha tingut sempre l'ajuda d'un déu poderós, que l'ha salvat de la mort, mentre que el nàufrag s'ha hagut de salvar amb el propi esforç; si Llàtzer és la prova de la intervenció humana en els destins humans, de la providència, el nàufrag només pot creure en el coratge propi, en l'afany de viure, de salvar-se a si mateix, en un món sense déus. No em sembla excessiu de considerar que el poema presenta la dialèctica (decantada cap als valors que representa Llàtzer) entre els ideals de l'humanisme clàssic i els cristians, l'exaltació de l'humà i de l'esforç de viure en el món s'oposa a la transcendència, a la salvació eterna. Després de *Salvatge cor* (1952), Riba aprofundeix l'experiència de la fe i de la transcendència, i insisteix en el procés de dramatització i objectivació d'aquesta experiència quan als valors cristians els oposa, per tal d'exalçar-los, això sí, els que representa el nàufrag, que, com diu el poema, s'identifica més amb la història d'Ulisses que no amb la de Jesús (vv.15-18); i a penes és necessari de recordar la importància que té per a Riba la figura d'Ulisses (només cal pensar en les *Elegies de Bierville*) per fer comprendre la seriositat d'una tria entre les opcions morals representades al poema.

El poema consisteix bàsicament en un diàleg entre Llàtzer i el nàufrag introduït i pautat pels breus comentaris i les escasses indicacions escèniques d'un narrador extra-heterodiegètic, amb focalització interna en tots dos interlocutors.[6] Convé precisar que és un diàleg relatiu, donat que el nàufrag hi intervé molt menys que no Llàtzer, que es converteix al seu torn en narrador intra-homodiegètic de la seva mort i resurrecció. El diàleg en si constitueix l'acció narrada, i els relats de Llàtzer i del nàufrag, que són una analepsi mixta homodiegètica (perquè empalmen amb el present narratiu), funcionen com una narració metadiegètica que té una funció explicativa (conta com s'han enfrontat a la mort tots dos personatges) i accional (Llàtzer és ell mateix testimoni de la força de la seva fe). L'evocació del miracle i el seu valor com a exemple són, doncs, el veritable centre i ocasió del poema, al qual se supediten les paraules del nàufrag, narrador intra-homodiegètic de la seva experiència de mort, i fins i tot les intervencions del narrador. Ho corrobora la distribució dels 288 versos del poema, perquè és fàcil de constatar que del total correspon un 21% al narrador, un 19% al nàufrag i un 60% a Llàtzer.

El poema consta, així, de tres parts prou diferenciades, precedides de la introducció del narrador, vv. 1-19. En efecte, a la primera part, el nàufrag conta la seva experiència als vv. 20-21, 28-48 i 52-70; el narrador intervé als vv. 70-80 i, al que es pot considerar la segona part, cedeix la paraula a Llàtzer, qui comença a parlar fent una reflexió sobre la mort, vv. 81-103, matisada amb un comentari sobre la vida, vv. 107-14, i enceta després la narració de la seva malaltia, mort i resurrecció, vv. 117-48, 155-206 i 213-68. A la tercera part, que serveix d'epíleg, el nàufrag ofereix la conclusió per a aquells que, com ell, són encara escèptics, vv. 275-81; el narrador --com al principi-- situa l'hora i els personatges, vv. 282-88, i deixa que Llàtzer digui l'última paraula, v. 288. Altrament, l'acció narrada --la trama pròpiament dita-- es redueix a una sola escena: la conversa entre Llàtzer i el nàufrag, que s'esdevé al capvespre prop del mar, i una part de la qual es desenrotlla mentre tornen caminant a la casa de Llàtzer, on arriben ja de nit; les indicacions sobre el pas del temps són bastant precises i no solament tenen la funció de pautar l'acció, sinó que contribueixen a la versemblança de la situació.

II

Els vv. 1-4 els inverteix el narrador a situar el moment, un capvespre, i el lloc, els erms de Provença (la Camarga segons ha advertit Riba a la nota prèvia), amb el mar com a centre d'una complexa metàfora en què refusa la llum (perquè es fa de nit) i el vent (que s'encalma, i propicia així la conversa que seguirà) i tanca en el seu si els corrents salats que són el seu origen. Els vv. 5-10 presenten Llàtzer, que pensa en la mort i contempla la llum del sol ponent. Seguint el seu esguard ('ulls grisos i de mirada llarga', l'única descripció del seu aspecte físic), el narrador introdueix, als vv. 11-15, el seu company, un mariner que ha naufragat fa poc i que ha estat recollit a la platja; de nom estrany, se'l coneix per l'Africà ('el seu *Libys* o *Afer*').[7] Als vv. 15-19 el narrador estableix la relació entre Llàtzer i el nàufrag gràcies a la història de Crist, amb la qual ja fa referència també al tema central del poema: la fe, i, és clar, la falta de fe. Perquè de seguida s'adverteix que el nàufrag africà s'identifica més amb Ulisses que no amb Crist (fet que el poema destaca amb la rima coneixia-reconeixia, vv. 15 i 17). Convé remarcar que si Ulisses com a model de conducta no es pot comparar amb Crist, té, no obstant això, el valor simbòlic --i cultural-- evident de representar l'esforç humà davant les adversitats (a més del que tenia per a Riba personalment, traductor dues vegades, el 1919 i el 1948, de l'*Odissea*).

Les paraules dels vv. 20-21 enceten la part del diàleg corresponent al nàufrag, que com ja ha advertit Riba no s'expressa bé en grec. Després d'una intervenció del narrador, vv. 22-27, en què destaca els ulls dels interlocutors i l'arribada de la nit, continua parlant el nàufrag, vv. 28-48. Amb una certa passió es refereix a la manera diversa com ell i Llàtzer han viscut l'experiència de la mort:

> Esclato si no ho dic:
> tu sempre has tingut un amic
> poderós: no en vaixell... guarnit o no: en xalana
> de pacífic canal
> t'hauria fet passar la mar descomunal,
> per situar-te amb grecs, que són genteta humana (vv.28-33).

Per al nàufrag, Crist és un 'amic poderós' que sempre ha ajudat Llàtzer; com diu la llegenda usada per Riba, aquest va arribar a Provença en un 'vaixell desguarnit' (287), però el nàufrag exagera fins a la hipèrbole quan diu que hauria pogut arribar en una barqueta, gràcies al poder del seu Crist. Ara bé, el nàufrag no s'està de fer ironia sobre els grecs amb qui viu Llàtzer (v. 33, però Llàtzer li replica en un to semblant als vv. 142-43), la llengua dels quals usen tots dos (per a les dificultats amb el grec, vegeu els vv. 23, 70-71, 87, 238 i 274).

Ben diferent a l'extraordinària ajuda que ha tingut Llàtzer, ell ha sobreviscut als perills de la mar (vv. 39-40, que bé podria servir de símbol de la vida i els seus atzars), gràcies al seu propi esforç:

> He tingut voluntat per a poder dir meva
> la força que em venia, fins al cor, de no sé
> quin brut roquer de vida on el món se sosté
> amb el seu mar (vv. 36-39).

Irònicament, el nàufrag, que es qualifica a si mateix d'"ofès i humiliat' (v. 41), s'adreça a Llàtzer com a 'senyor ressuscitat' (v. 40), per retreure-li encara que ell no ha tingut ajuda, sinó que ha estat 'nedant, nedant jo, que sempre m'he salvat' (v. 44). Tot seguit enumera les possibles raons que l'han permès de salvar-se dels tres naufragis que ha patit:

> ¿Per pur afany de viure?
> ¿O per manera extrema d'assaborir-me lliure?
> ¿O per l'horror --jo crec això--
> d'haver vist a la mort la cara? (vv. 45-48).

De les tres raons (que constitueixen una eficaç enumeració paral.lelística d'interrogacions que són alhora disjuncions), la primera corresponent al vitalisme i la segona a un cert existencialisme, el nàufrag prefereix la tercera, ben planera i lògica; totes tres són, al capdavall, aspectes de l'humanisme exempt de transcendència. La tercera és, també, la que encaixa millor amb el context, perquè és una afirmació de la vida davant de la mort, la qual és un dels motius bàsics del poema, ja associat amb Llàtzer des del principi (v. 5).

El nàufrag fa una pausa, durant la qual intervé el narrador (vv. 49-51) per descriure les actituds de tots dos interlocutors i al.ludir a l'hora, i fa el seu últim parlament (vv. 52-70). Com Llàtzer, l'africà parla per experiència pròpia, donat que ha naufragat tres vegades (v. 43), però ara destaca el que va viure a una cova del Cap de Creus (v. 53, un senyal al lector català). El nàufrag explica que va arribar a la cova ('una gran cripta nua, informe, acollidora / sense amor, com d'un rei superb, però avar', vv. 58-59) arrossegat pel corrent, agafat a un tros de la seva nau i ja cansat de l'esforç (vv. 60-63):

> I de sobte vaig veure el Rostre,
> damunt l'obaga humà; però no com el *nostre*,
> no: *com el meu*, exacte, vist talment per mirall,
> però fora de tota edat meva, una mena
> de fetus vell de mi, que m'atreia a una escena
> sense públic ni chors, on pels segles avall
> es peixerà de mi... de mi... (vv. 64-70).

Aquest és, en efecte, el moment crucial de l'experiència del nàufrag i del que la seva actitud ètica representa: en el perill extrem, enfrontat a la mort, veu una imatge de si mateix, fora del temps i de l'espai, que es nodreix d'ell. Aquest motiu es pot relacionar amb un passatge de la XI de les *Elegies de Bierville*, en què, després de la revelació de la presència de déu dins seu, el poeta experimenta una 'més plena / possessió de mi des de la idea d'un déu' (vv. 21-22) o, més significativament, com a resultat de la comunicació mística al poeta li és 'present la meva secreta figura salvada! / com si des d'ara em veiés dintre la llum d'un mirall' (vv. 39-40, i vegeu encara els vv. 47-48). (No em puc estar de fer notar que en les imatges hi ressona un bell passatge de Pau, Co I, 13, 12, a què Riba al.ludeix també a *Salvatge cor*, XIV, 1, v. 13). La diferència entre tots dos contextos és la presència d'un déu: el nàufrag no pot sinó descobrir-se a si mateix, mentre que el poeta a les *Elegies de Bierville* arriba al coneixement de si mateix a través de la fe i de la gràcia, és a dir, de l'acció divina. I és precisament la insistència del nàufrag en la singularitat de la seva experiència la que proporciona un argument important a la resposta de Llàtzer, que matisa la dimensió també singular de la revelació contada a les *Elegies* en atorgar-li un sentit comunitari.

Una intervenció bastant extensa del narrador (vv. 70-80) serveix per traspassar la paraula a Llàtzer, havent emmudit el nàufrag a causa del seu poc domini de la lengua (efecte dramàticament oportú donada la dificultat de l'exposició). De tornada, ja amb llum de lluna (v. 77), Llàtzer s'adreça al nàufrag tractant-lo cristianament de germà (i ho farà de manera sistemàtica als vv. 93, 107, 143, 183, 242, 253, 266 i 288):

> Germà [...] hi ha records sense saber:
> coses que per l'arrel ens han pres tots; n'és una
> el goig i despertar-se'n; i haver volgut per fe;
> i, escolta bé, tornar de la comèdia fosca
> que tu dius que és ser mort, a aquest contínuament
> obrir-se en esperança que jo en dic ser vivent (vv. 81-86).

El narrador introdueix en primer lloc un motiu característic de Riba, els 'records sense saber', als quals ha dedicat l'excel.lent i significativa VI de les *Elegies de Bierville*. Al vers final de l'elegia (v. 42), els amants, que han arribat a un saber veritable en l'acte amorós i en el somni subsegüent a la fatiga eròtica, es desvetllen d'aquest somni platònicament 'recordant; sense saber: recordant' (vegeu també els vv. 28-29 de 'Els tres reis d'Orient'). No pot sorprendre, doncs, que de l'enumeració de records primordials, inscrits al més íntim de cadascú ('sense saber' vol dir independents de la raó), el primer sigui el goig (referit a l'amor); el segon és la fe; i el tercer l'impuls de viure expressat en la magnífica fórmula de 'contínuament / obrir-se en esperança'. Llàtzer considera que el nàufrag ha presentat el perill de mort com una 'comèdia fosca', a la qual ell replica amb un lliurament a la vida basat en l'esperança, no en el temor (vegeu 'Els tres reis d'Orient', v. 27).

> De tota manera, Llàtzer precisa que:
> 'La mort mateixa -- és pel que fou *després*,
> no per memòria o pel que he vist dels altres,
> que et faria un report de com és i del que és,
> on pogués dir no jo, sinó *nosaltres* (vv. 88-91).

No es pot parlar de la mort sinó pel que passa després; en primer lloc, perquè només se'n pot parlar metafòricament --com ho fa el nàufrag-- i, en segon lloc, perquè és el retorn a la vida el que fa possible parlar de la mort (que és absència de vida). Però és la dimensió col.lectiva de l'experiència el que remarca Llàtzer en oposició al nàufrag: aquest ha parlat d'un rostre, 'no com *el nostre*, / no: *com el meu*' (vv. 65-66), mentre que aquell voldria poder dir 'no *jo*, sinó *nosaltres*'. Com observa Terry: 'La inversió dels pronoms sembla indicar que, de les dues experiències de la mort, la de Llàtzer té una validesa universal que l'altra no comparteix'.[8] Dit d'una altra manera, que la mort sigui una qüestió col.lectiva trenca els murs de l'individualisme en què es tanca el nàufrag i prepara el camí a la transcendència cristiana.

Altrament, als vv. 94-103, Llàtzer reprèn el motiu del son (que té una base evangèlica, Jo 11, 11-13) i conta d'una manera sumària com va tornar a la vida: quan es va 'dreçar com per un tust, / com qui dormia i obre els ulls, adust, / entre la nit i una alba plena que ja l'invita' (vv. 95-97, una situació que recorda la del poema 4 del segon llibre d'*Estances*), per bé que amb la incertesa momentània 'd'ignorar el propi nom, / i d'on és que ha tornat, i com' (vv. 98-99). Els vv. 101-03, pel seu costat, recorden els vv. 12-14 i 19-20 de la VI de les *Elegies de Bierville*, per la presència dels motius del camí i de la innocència, a més dels somnis.

Una pausa de Llàtzer, que és aprofitada pel narrador per fer una acotació (vv. 104-06), precedeix una declaració en què s'exposa el nucli temàtic del poema, la reflexió que ha fet del que ha viscut:

> Germà [...] no és cap record que m'acora,
> sinó les comparances al que fou tan senzill;
> dormim i ens despertem en el que ja teníem,
> però viure és fer nostre el que de Déu rebíem,
> perquè Déu és etern prop del nostre perill (vv. 107-11).

Allò que preocupa Llàtzer (el qual usa una expressió que recorda molt els vv. 1-2 de 'Tannkas de les quatre estacions', XVI) no és el record com a tal sinó les implicacions, resoltes amb comparances. Com ja ha dit abans (vv. 82-83), la mort és, efectivament, com un son, del qual es desperta per tornar al que ja es tenia abans (com en l'amor, vegeu *Elegies de Bierville*, VI); però viure és més complicat, perquè (ja hi havia fet al.lusió, vv. 85-86) suposa un esforç constant de fer-se digne del que Déu dóna al creient. En aquest passatge crec que Riba fa referència a un passatge de Sant Pau (Co I, 4, 7): '¿Què tens que no hagis rebut?' (que conté al seu torn un eco de Jo 3, 27). Ara, Déu fa sempre costat al qui creu en ell, com ja havia observat el nàufrag a Llàtzer (vv. 28-33), i el socorre en el perill (que és, de fet, la conclusió de les *Elegies de Bierville* i un dels temes dels sonets de *Salvatge cor*, en particular els XIV, 2, XV, XXII i sobretot XXV, vv. 9-12).

De la mateixa manera que ha intentat explicar --dues vegades-- què és la vida (vv. 85-86 i 110-11), Llàtzer intenta també explicar què és la mort; ho havia provat als vv. 88-89, en què era definida pel que venia després, i hi torna als vv. 112-14:

> 'Però morir, d'ençà que vaig seguir-la,
> sé que és, a tot o res, disposar-se a la Veu,
> un absolut buidar-se per sentir-la...

Fent un hàbil aprofitament en clau al.legòrica de la narració evangèlica i del testimoni del seu protagonista Llàtzer, Riba li fa dir a aquest que la mort és 'buidar-se' de si mateix per poder sentir la veu divina, la crida de salvació: com Llàtzer va ressuscitar quan va sentir la veu de Jesús, així les ànimes dels creients accediran a la salvació i a la vida eterna. Aquesta disposició a sentir la veu, diu Llàtzer, i amb ell Riba, que és 'a tot o res', fórmula on ressona el 'pari' --l'aposta-- de Pascal,[9] un motiu que Riba ja havia utilitzat a *Salvatge cor*, XXVI, v. 5.[10] Subratlla la importància de la veu divina (del Logos, si es vol obrir una porta a la desconstrucció), la interrupció del nàufrag, que ha entrat en la situació narrada i sembla que sent Jesús: 'La veu del teu amic, del teu dolç Galileu...' (v. 115).

Llàtzer comença la crònica de la seva resurrecció partint, no del motiu de la veu, sinó, per metonímia, del mestratge d'esperança de Jesús. Així és, Jesús ensenya l'esperança i exigeix al pur, al creient, que sàpiga esperar, tal com va fer esperar Marta i Maria quan li van fer arribar avís que el seu amic estava molt malalt adduint que la malaltia no era tan greu (Jo 11, 3). Llàtzer evoca 'el llit, vast i vague en la febre, / i el cor perdent-se en la creixent tenebra' (vv. 121-22) i la seva germana Maria somrient dient-li que 'Els missatgers ja són amb Jesús' (v. 126). Pel text evangèlic sabem que, quan Jesús arriba a

Betània, fa quatre dies que Llàtzer és mort (Jo 11, 17); però al poema només consta el testimoni de Llàtzer, que només pot parlar de la mort pel que ell va poder veure, reviscut la crida que el va fer sortir del sepulcre.

Així és, Llàtzer jeu mort a la tomba i sent la veu de Jesús, 'el mot que encara, sí, em comanda' (v. 128), perquè se li ha convertit en una fe, en una forma de vida, i torna de sobte a sentir el seu cos ('em vaig sentir de nou en el meu pes', v. 129). És notable la descripció de la recuperació dels sentits:

> Em retrobava estès damunt del banc
> de la meva tombal alcova;
> ert, fat tot jo, però --¿m'entendràs?-- amb la sang
> voltada pel meu fred dins el cor, talment nova,
> congriada en l'espera de fer un salt renadiu
> cap al que m'era ofert d'un puixant, nou estiu...
>   o jo restaria en el que era
> --ara en prenia esment-- el meu repòs:
> un pur estar embolcat, sense el meu cos
> (oh instrument preciós), ni en oblit ni en llum vera,
> als marges expectants de la Joia Primera (vv. 131-41).

El que diu Llàtzer del 'banc' de la tomba encaixa amb les dades de la nota manuscrita que he transcrit abans (llegades per la tradició, per tant vegeu Jo 11, 38), però després ha d'explicar com torna de la mort, un moment en què, 'ert, fat', se li obren dues possibilitats. L'una és de continuar en un repòs 'sense cos',[11] ni 'oblit' ni 'llum vera'; una situació que contrasta tant amb la resurrecció posterior com amb la resurrecció de la carn per a la vida eterna, que seria la 'Joia Primera' que el mort no té. L'altra opció és de preparar-se a viure, d'esperar 'un salt renadiu' de la sang, abans freda i ara renovada, cap al que se li ofereix d'un 'puixant, nou estiu' (termes ben semblants als de les *Elegies de Bierville*, IV, vv. 13-16), és a dir, una nova vida (literalment i al.legòrica).

L'elecció és clara (cal tenir en compte l'aposta de Pascal), Llàtzer tria la vida, metafòricament 'els [seus] dies', i s'incorpora 'ple de la [seva] ànima' (vegeu *Estances*, II, 21, vv. 8-9), que torna a reprendre el propi cos, la 'sang valenta' (abans freda), que és 'feliç de posseir-se', és a dir, de recuperar la consciència, de torna a ser en suma, i que, a més, és 'violenta', plena d'amorós afany de viure (perquè torna de la mort). Ha ressuscitat, però és encara amortallat i dins de la tomba.

La pausa dels vv. 149-53, que atura dramàticament l'acció, no solament facilita observacions del narrador sobre el pas del temps, sinó que permet recollir unes paraules del nàufrag, que insta Llàtzer a continuar la seva relació en un to de subtil ironia, perceptible tant en la constatació 'sé fets semblants', com en el divertit 'si tant et tempta, magnifica't', excusant Llàtzer de convertir-se en protagonista d'un fet extraordinari (v. 153).

Llàtzer, que callava, fa com si no sentís les paraules del nàufrag (v. 154), i continua explicant (vv. 155-206) l'ordre de Jesús i la seva sortida, dificultosa, de la tomba (Jo 11, 43-44). El primer que diu és que cap goig del món no val el record del que en aquell moment va poder 'veure / fins a tocar salut i paradís' (vv. 158-59); al.legòricament Riba es refereix a la unió mística amb déu, un moment de suprema intensitat després del qual viure es converteix en esperar un altre moment com aquell, o la mort, que serà el camí cap a la definitiva unió en la contemplació (vegeu *Elegies de Bierville*, XI, i, és clar, Jo 11, 25-26). Però, atenint-se a la lletra de l'Evangeli, remarca el narrador:

> És per als fills de Déu, que poden creure,
> que jo testimonio: reconeix-te escoltant (vv. 160-61).

Llàtzer repeteix, als vv. 231-323, aquest mateix motiu, que és fonamental en el tramat temàtic del poema, com a missatge de fe. En efecte, el miracle de què ell és testimoni vivent va destinat als qui creuen (Jo 11, 40 i 45), als qui són capaços de deixar-se convèncer i arribar a creure, entre els quals incita subtilment el nàufrag (el lector?) a incloure's, i, per tant, a reconèixer-se en la història de Jesús (vegeu vv. 15-18). Allò que Riba evita de dir de manera explícita en el poema (l'hipertext) però que ha d'acudir gairebé per força a la memòria d'un lector que conegui l'Evangeli (l'hipotext, en termes de Genette),[12] són les paraules de Jesús fonament del miracle: 'Jo sóc la resurrecció i la vida: qui creu en mi, encara que estigui mort, viurà' (Jo 11, 25).

L'esquemàtica descripció de la tomba segueix la del manuscrit, segons la qual hi ha tres graons de la tomba al vestíbul, obert per ordre de Jesús (Jo 11, 41), en el qual entra la llum. La visió de Jesús causa un gran efecte en Llàtzer:

> No sé si sobre els ulls fou transparent el llenç

o si un plec esbatut em mostrà el que era immens.
Crist era dalt, al mig, creixent en la paraula
dita: aquell 'Surt!' de tot elemental començ:
que crea, que fa nèixer, que és Llum fenent la Faula...
Oh el Mestre ardent, Maria! Marta, el teu Rei a taula! (vv. 167-72).

Jesús és descrit metafòricament com a 'immens', alhora que, en termes de situació, és dalt i fora de la tomba, 'creixent en la paraula', perquè amb ella actua, realitza l'acció dita. I el que diu és 'Surt', (com a Jo 11, 43), ordre que té un sentit literal, ja que fa reviure i sortir Llàtzer, i un de doctrinal, perquè és el de tot 'elemental començ', és paraula que crea i fa nèixer. Si bé és possible que hi hagi una referència al Gènesi, el més lògic és interpretar-la en el context de la resurrecció de la carn i la consecució de la vida eterna, com ho corroboraria que Jesús sigui la 'Llum', la veritat revelada (i la salvació), oposant-se a la 'Faula', els mites i llegendes dels falsos déus (segons *Elegies de Bierville*, VI, v. 35, VIII, v. 28, i 'El fill pròdig', VI, v. 58). El bell quiasme del v. 172 encara contribueix més a l'exaltació de Jesús, 'Mestre' i 'Rei', ara posat en relació a les seves germanes, Maria i Marta (junt amb el v. 123, l'única menció al poema). Que és també la funció dels vv. 173-77, que contenen, a més, una declaració doctrinal inequívoca en formar part Jesús de la trinitat cristiana, perquè brilla 'amb el Pare [...] i amb l'Esperit, en Si un i divers'. El v. 178 enllaça la glorificació de Jesús acabada de fer amb l'afirmació de la conseqüència que la seva intervenció té per a Llàtzer, i els creients. Cridat, Llàtzer surt de la tomba, però també de si mateix (com no és capaç de fer el nàufrag), guiat pel que metafòricament descriu com una 'vivent memòria', un record no sabut que la veu de Jesús posa en acció; una represa del motiu del somni i del record dels vv. 81 i 109-10, sí, però també una al.lusió a la gràcia, que actua en l'individu fins i tot sense que ell mateix ho sàpiga.

I continua Llàtzer la descripció i glorificació de Jesús encetada als vv. 167-77:

Sí, Crist era la vida unint tots els camins,
faç mateixa de la vida, on totes les semblances
es feien fraternals; en aquells trets divins,
jo em veia jo, acceptat en les meves mancances (vv. 179-82).

Si al v. 179 hi ha una al.lusió molt clara a un important passatge Evangèlic, aquell en què Jesús declara: 'Jo sóc el camí i la veritat i la vida: ningú no va al Pare sinó per mi' (Jo 14, 6), al v. 180 es fa també al.lusió a paraules de Jesús quan Llàtzer diu que és Crist 'faç mateixa de la vida' (Jo 11, 25). Basant-se en aquests motius religiosos pot referir-se després al discurs en què el nàufrag ha explicat la seva visió del 'Rostre' (vv. 64-70) per tal de contraposar-li la fe cristiana, en què el rostre no és el seu, sinó que és com el nostre, perquè en ell 'totes les semblances / es feien fraternals'; això no obstant, Llàtzer (i, per extensió, el creient) s'hi pot reconèixer a si mateix, 'jo em veia jo, acceptat en les meves mancances'. A la concepció rasament humana del nàufrag (que potser en última instància es podria relacionar amb els déus indiferents de l'antiguitat), Llàtzer oposa un déu d'amor i de justícia, misericordiós, que accepta cadascú com és (al capdavall, és l'antítesi exposada a la XI de les *Elegies de Bierville*).

Altrament, els vv. 183-84 són prou significatius, perquè Llàtzer hi deixa constància que ha triat (la solució de l'aposta pascaliana) i, reiterant el que ha dit al v. 144, ha volgut 'la vida --joia i foc tot jo, per fe', expressió en què ressona el títol d'un altre llibre de Riba, *Del joc i del foc*, amb els components de vitalitat, passió de viure i inspiració poètica.[13]

Als vv. 185-206 Llàtzer conta la sortida de la tomba, la lluita per pujar, embolicat en la mortalla, els tres graons que menen de la tomba al vestíbul (Jo 11, 44). És un passatge estrictament narratiu, en què es dramatitza l'esforç que ha de fer 'per desfaixar els turmells i compondre el [...] pas' (v. 186), perquè la mortalla l'estreny i li fa mal quan es mou. Lluitant a més contra l'oblit de la mort, aprèn de seguida a caminar i va 'amb gemec cap als tres esglaons':

> I Pujar-los va ser com carregar tres mons
> sobre els meus febles ossos:
> des del primer, un món de somnis morts;
> en el segon, un d'esmes i records;
> i dalt del terç, un d'esperances vanes (vv. 197-201).

La triple enumeració paral.lelística permet de reunir les emocions, els pensaments, rutines i inèrcies que Llàtzer tenia en la seva vida anterior; en ressuscitar, els abandona perquè Jesús li ofereix una vida nova, la de la gràcia (amb un valor general per als creients, si se'n fa una lectura al.legòrica). Surt de la tomba a la fi, 'cap a les sorts humanes', 'seguint Jesús, però fent els [...] passos sol' (v. 206), és a dir, segueix la crida divina, però la responsabilitat de viure, i la manera com ho farà, li correspon exclusivament (la conclusió del motiu de la llibertat dels vv. 144 i 183-84).

Un 'silenci greu' de Llàtzer obre una nova pausa que ocupa els vv. 207-12. El narrador introdueix detalls del lloc i del temps i deixa parlar una altra vegada el nàufrag (que continua realitzant la seva funció dramàtica i dialèctica), que té preguntes a fer i només encerta (com ho requeria el context, val a dir) a demanar per la reacció de la gent que presenciava el miracle. De la resposta de Llàtzer, els vv. 213-41 són destinats a contar les diverses actituds dels testimonis, mentre que els vv. 242-68 són una reflexió sobre els fets esdevinguts que recull i lliga els diversos motius mencionats en altres moments del seu discurs.

Llàtzer diu que hi havia molta gent, 'a munts, / parents i poble' (vv. 213-14), que el va rebre amb un 'crit d'esglai' que va cedir pas 'al silenci i a les converses baixes' (v. 216). Llàtzer recorda alguns trets de l'exterior de la tomba, i --amb una metonímia particularitzadora-- recorda també 'uns noiets que aixecaven cap a mi uns ulls molt vius' (v. 220), una prostituta, 'una doneta / que reia tota sola per sota uns vels llampants' (vv. 221-22) i, sobretot, 'en un rotllo a part, els doctors de la pleta' (vv. 224). Refent el text evangèlic (Jo 11, 46), en què es diu que són alguns dels jueus presents que van a avisar els fariseus (a qui el poema càusticament denomina doctors del ramat, per metonímia), Riba els converteix a ells en testimonis directes del miracle, que es refusen a acceptar perquè ha vulnerat la Llei mosaica en fer-se en dissabte. Jugant amb les rimes, la narració oposa l'ordre d'agafar Llàtzer donada per un dels fariseus, a l'ordre de deixar-lo donada per Jesús, que s'imposa a aquella (una versió més anecdòtica de l'enfrontament que el durà a la creu). Més interessant és que els fariseus se'n van, sense voler acceptar el miracle, incapaços de lliurar-se a l'evidència que posaria en qüestió les seves creences i sobretot els seus privilegis. És el moment oportú per triar un personatge que, dins de l'escena, expressi una opinió representativa i, és clar, favorable. I aquesta és una 'dona del poble', que, eludint de pronunciar-se directament sobre el miracle, ho diu tot mitjançant un encès i doctrinal elogi (vv. 240-41, vegeu Ll 11, 27) adreçat a Maria, 'la mare de Jesús', que Riba ha pres la llibertat de fer present al miracle, i descrita als vv. 236-39 (vegeu 'Els tres reis d'Orient', v. 131).

Precisament la partida dels fariseus ressalta més el que és un tombant decisiu del poema, dramàticament i temàtica:

> I els que havien de creure és llavors que cregueren,
> retrobant Crist en l'acte que així, creient, perferen (vv. 231-32).

El miracle culmina veritablement en la fe dels qui per ell havien de creure; així és, els presents --i els que llegeixen o escolten la narració-- pel miracle descobreixen la fe i l'afirmen, i en aquesta fe alhora es justifica i potencia. Altrament, serveix de comentari a aquests versos una carta a Paulina Crusat (25-II-1955) on, Riba diu que 'un dels punts-clau del Làtzer (quants lectors no se n'adonaran o ho jutjaran heterodox!) és aquell vers on es diu que el miracle en rigor no es perfà sinó en la fe dels qui havien de creure'. L'èmfasi del mateix Riba m'estalvia a mi d'insistir en un moment que també és essencial al text evangèlic (Jo 11, 45) i que resumeix el sentit del miracle, que, en un sentit al.legòric, estimula la fe per la promesa de salvació i de vida eterna.

En la part final del seu discurs (vv. 242-68) Llàtzer procurarà posar en relació la seva experiència amb la del nàufrag, i fer evident a aquest que tenen molt en comú, no solament perquè han viscut la por de la mort i han lluitat contra ella, sinó perquè la gràcia divina és en ells. En primer lloc, Llàtzer introdueix el motiu del cor, com a impuls de vida:

> ¿Què et diré més, germà? Sóc el ressuscitat;
> senyor --només en tant que per la Gràcia
> vaig ser tornat a mi: com tu, que al meu costat,
> per l'indecís camí que ens ha igualat,
> camines, fer de ser salvat
> pel cor i per la seva obscura pertinàcia.
> I tanmateix el cor!... (vv. 242-48).

Llàtzer treu conclusions del seu relat: és, en efecte, el 'ressuscitat', però si ara és viu ho deu a Jesús, a l'acció de la 'Gràcia' divina (amb què l'acció adquireix valor genèric). Com diu Terry de Llàtzer: 'La distància que el separa de l'africà no és insalvable, vist que tothom participa, bé que inconscientment, en la Gràcia divina'.[14] La gràcia també ha salvat el nàufrag, encara que no fos creient; davant de la mort, tots dos han estat iguals, tots dos s'han salvat per l'"obscura pertinàcia' del cor, i és per això que Llàtzer espera que el nàufrag el comprengui.

El cor pren una importància decisiva ara, com a lloc on resideixen no solament les emocions, sinó també originals sabers i la mateixa gràcia divina:

> Tot senyal li és llum, tota moneda or.
> L'enyor, la por, la follia l'habiten;
> però sap més que no sabem sabut;
> i salva donant més que no vèiem rebut:
> són d'ell, germà, els miracles que t'irriten (vv. 249-53).

L'afany de salvar-se del nàufrag i la voluntat de viure (quan ha pogut escollir) de Llàtzer vénen del cor; són d'ell 'els miracles que [...] irriten' el nàufrag, i en ell hi ha un saber 'que no sabem sabut' (un brillant isolexisme) i una força que en surt sense que se sabés que hi era. El cor és el centre de les emocions i les passions ('l'enyor, la por, la follia l'habiten'), però Llàtzer es refereix, en últim terme, a la gràcia, que és el que li costa d'acceptar al nàufrag i a qualsevol no creient.

S'entén mol millor el sentit dels versos de Riba si se'ls posa en relació amb el pensament de Pascal, al qual deu tant en aquesta època. Cal recordar tot seguit el famós passatge: 'Le coeur a ses raisons, que la raison ne connaît point; on le sait en mille choses. Je dis que le coeur aime l'être universel naturellement, et soi-même naturellement selon qu'il s'y adonne; et il se durcit contre l'un ou l'autre à son choix. Vous avez rejeté l'un et conservé l'autre: est-ce par raison que vous vous aimiez?'.[15] Encara es pot matisar més, perquè: 'La conduite de Dieu, qui dispose toutes choses avec douceur, est de mettre la religion dans l'esprit par les raisons, et dans le coeur par la grâce'.[16] Encara és més clar aquest altre passatge: 'C'est le coeur qui sent Dieu et non la raison. Voilà ce que c'est la foi: Dieu sensible au coeur, non à la raison'.[17] Preciso que Pascal no oposa el cor a la raó, sinó que tots dos tenen accés a la veritat cadascun per una via específica. En concret, per a Pascal, el cor és 'le siège des connaissances intimes, immédiates et non démonstrables; ces connaisances sont essentielles soit parce qu'elles constituent le point de départ de toutes les autres, soit parce qu'elles président à la conduite de la vie, soit parce qu'elles découvrent à l'homme ce que lui importe le plus, sa destinée [...] C'est par lui que l'âme se connaît elle-même'.[18]

Que el pensament de Pascal sustentava el de Riba ho demostren encara més, si calia, els dos fulls manuscrits conservats a l'Arxiu Riba que contenen passatges del llibre *Pascal ou le drame de la conscience chrétienne*, de Romano Guardini (la versió francesa del qual és de 1951 i l'original alemanya de 1931). Riba va seleccionar i traduir fragments tan significatius com aquest: 'El cor no és l'expressió d'un contingut emotiu, per oposició a les formes lògiques del pensament; no és el sentiment per oposició a l'intel.lecte; tampoc l'*ànima*, per oposició a l'*esperit*. El *cor* també és esperit: una forma d'aparició de l'esperit. L'acte del cor és un acte fecund per a la coneixença. Certs objectes són donats a la percepció només en l'acte del cor. En aquest cas no hi romanen en una intuïció irracional, ans són accessibles a l'anàlisi lògica i intel.lectual [...] El cor és l'origen de l'amor [...] Aquest amor correspon a la relació entre la idea de fogar dels sentiments i aspiracions de l'home; correspon al moviment que va de la sang a l'esperit, de la presència del cos a l'eternitat espiritual. És ell [l'amor] qui és provat (*éprouvé* [sic]) en el cor'. Potser es podria prendre aquest passatge final com a referència per entendre la preocupació del poema per la resurrecció, perquè, si ja és sabut que l'ànima no mor, el que importa en aquest context és la resurrecció del cos, definitiva i difícil promesa als creients en el Judici Final.

Llàtzer capta la reacció del nàufrag i s'apressa a fer-li palesos els seus propis temors a les conseqüències d'acceptar l'acció de la gràcia: al capdavall, s'és lliure de triar-la o no; l'important és que hi ha elecció perquè l'individu té llibertat per triar:

> Dubtes --i jo mateix sóc temorós
> d'aquesta llibertat, de la qual sóc figura
> contra la mort, i que he de guanyar com si fos
> meu cada instant i simple la natura (vv. 254-57).

Aquesta llibertat és la que ha fet possible que Llàtzer triés entre la vida i la mort; ell mateix i la seva elecció n'han esdevingut 'figura' (en sentit al.legòric), una representació viva i narrativa i doctrinal en suma, que, ben significativament, s'oposa a la mort (que en aquest context podria ser interpretada com la falta de fe). Amb tot, la llibertat s'ha de guanyar, cal fer-se-la pròpia, com si en realitat no fos un do diví i com si no fos tan complexa la natura humana. Quan es té, és la llibertat de viure fent 'nostre el que de Déu rebíem' (v. 110); una llibertat que cal exercir a cada moment, per bé que limitada a apropiar-se del que ha de constituir el destí de cadascú, que, d'altra banda, ja està establert en els designis de la providència.

D'on ve que l'autèntic tema del poema no sigui la mort, sinó la vida, la vida en plenitud de fe i gràcia:

> En cada instant sense morir revisc
> i puix que he vist la Vida, conec millor el meu risc;
> i és per cada acte meu que la Vida em depura,
> i en cada mot tallat a la Seva mesura (vv. 258-61).

Llàtzer usa l'oposició entre mort i vida i els sentits cristians de la vida per configurar el seu discurs. Si reviu a cada instant és per acció de la gràcia, a la qual accedeix per la fe; però sap el risc que corre en viure, que és el risc de perdre la gràcia per obra del pecat, perquè ha conegut Jesús, l'autèntica Vida. Si ha dit abans que 'viure és fer nostre el que de Déu rebíem' (v. 110), ara formula el mateix motiu des de la perspectiva de les vivències (accions i paraules), perquè és mitjançant aquestes que es fa mereixedor del que déu li ha donat (la gràcia, però també un destí en el designi providencial, i la promesa de la transcendència).

A tall de conclusió i per tal de fer veure al nàufrag que l'un i l'altre són més a prop que aquest no es pensa, Llàtzer li fa constar que són iguals davant de déu:

> Però, el que hi ha en el cor de l'home, Crist ho sap,
> com ho sabé quan era germà nostre a la terra:
> sap si temo la mort i el seu estrany arrap,
> jo que en sóc, als teus ulls, la sortosa desferra.
> Com tu la tems, germà... Perquè si diferim
>   en re dos pobres fills del llim,
> és a Déu que ens ha fet, no a nosaltres, que importa (vv. 262-68).

El déu de Llàtzer és un déu compassiu que tindrà misericòrdia del pobre nàufrag i li facilitarà el retorn a casa (v. 288), però abans Llàtzer li ha d'explicar per què. I és ben senzill: Jesús mateix va prendre cos i va viure com a 'germà nostre a la terra' (v. 263); també ell va conèixer les passions del cor i de l'afany de viure, donat que va morir i va ressuscitar. Per la seva pròpia experiència, Jesús sap els temors que habiten els cors dels humans; naturalment sap que tant Llàtzer com el nàufrag temen la mort i estimen la vida. En això no hi ha cap diferència, tots els humans són igual davant déu; però si n'hi havia cap, de diferència, és qüestió de déu i no ha de preocupar els humans. Pot aclarir les implicacions d'aquest passatge el que Riba escriu en una carta a P. Crusat (25-II-1955) a propòsit de la mort de Paul Claudel: '"On vit seul" i no som tanmateix res sense els altres i, res del que cerquem, no ho trobem realment si no pot servir per als qui estimem, coneguts o inconeguts.'

La narració s'acaba quan el narrador (vv. 269-71) conta que Llàtzer i el nàufrag arriben a lloc i els espera Sara la Negra. Al breu intercanvi final, que fa de conclusió del poema, el nàufrag li diu a Llàtzer que el que el mou a evocar aquells fets és l'enyorança de fets extraordinaris (vv. 271-72), però aquest li replica que, si és cert que s'enyora, també hi ha moltes més coses que no sap expressar en el grec en què s'entenen. Un recurs hàbil per aturar-se davant de l'inefable, una vegada Llàtzer ha esgotat els esdeveniments. Arriba llavors el torn del nàufrag de fer palesa la seva reacció a la història, i als comentaris amb què ha estat acompanyada:

> Són coses torbadores
> tot això que m'has dit: per a omplir-se'n els anys,
> referint-hi el que un home ha conegut d'afanys
> i ¿per què no? de goigs... Deixa que hi pensi
> en calma i en silenci,
> quan hauré tornat on vaig néixer. Preveig
> que hi ploraré; però seré a casa... (vv. 275-81).

Les 'coses torbadores' que ha explicat Llàtzer són les veritats de la fe cristiana; una fe que no explica --ni reclama-- només els sofriments, sinó que justifica també els plaers, els goigs, tota la vida en suma; perquè, al capdavall, la fe és una forma de vida. (Aquestra és una reflexió que Riba ha exposat a molts poemes de *Salvatge cor*, darrera d'alguns dels quals ressonen significativament els cants espirituals d'Ausiàs March i Maragall.)[19] Li caldrà temps, doncs, al nàufrag que es reconeix en la història d'Ulisses per examinar la seva vida des de la perspectiva cristiana; com que l'examen el preveu dolorós, espera tenir el consol d'haver tornat a la seva terra natal, i fruir de la seguretat que dóna ser a casa (que es podria llegir, al.legòricament, com un retorn a si mateix, a la veritat íntima, i, potser amb ella, a la fe amagada al cor). Amb tot, crec que és un encert del poema que el diàleg acabi així, amb la declaració del nàufrag que pensarà en tot el que li ha dit Llàtzer, però sense precipitar una conversió que només resultaria versemblant si fos el final d'un procés o la conseqüència d'una evident predisposició (que és, tanmateix, notable); com que no hi ha res d'això, el més lògic és que el nàufrag es limiti a dir que hi pensarà. I això ja és molt, perquè implica que les ensenyances de Llàtzer l'han commogut, però no prejutja la conclusió.[20] Corrobora la meva interpretació la glossa, en carta a P. Crusat (24-I-1955), que Riba ofereix d'aquest passatge quan escriu que 'Llàtzer no és cap missioner celtibèric: indica a l'Africà que, la salvació, la trobarà en el seu cor, i que les diferències entre els homes és si de cas a Déu que importen, no als homes; i hi ha un petit mot, gairebé dit de passada, de l'Africà, que té un valor de clau: tot allò que Llàtzer li diu de la Gràcia, de la vida, de la resurrecció, etc., ell, el míser que ha tingut un viure tan dur, ho compulsarà amb els afanys que ha conegut, però també amb els goigs'. (Una experiència semblada es pot llegir a l'extraordinari sonet 'Hercules OEtæus', *Salvatge cor*, XX.)

La fi del poema arriba després d'una intervenció del narrador, vv. 282-83, que com de costum situa el lloc i el moment, seguida de l'acotació de l'actitud de Llàtzer, a través de la perspectiva del qual és presentat el nàufrag:

>   Llàtzer veié de sobte un home vell
>   en aquell nàufrag sol; i posant-li un palmell
>   suau damunt l'espatlla arrupida, profètic
>   --doctors haurien dit hermètic--
>   va dir: 'Germà, demà tindràs vaixell' (vv. 284-88).

El narrador es permet en aquest passatge una mica d'ironia (i un excel.lent joc de rimes) tocant a la promesa que Llàtzer fa al nàufrag, descrit ara per primera vegada com un home vell i sol, amb l'espatlla arrupida (l'aspecte de qui ha patit viatjant, de qui ha viscut: com Ulisses?): l'endemà disposarà d'un vaixell per tornar a casa. Però, com molts passatges del poema, aquest ha de ser llegit en un pla literal i al.legòric alhora: el nàufrag tornarà a casa i a la fe. I és aquest sentit segon el que suscita l'ús de l'adjectiu hermètic, que s'associa precisament amb 'doctors'. En qualsevol cas, el narrador es limita a citar les paraules de Llàtzer, que, encara en el pla literal, són una mostra evident de generositat i solidaritat, o, per dir-ho en termes cristians, de caritat. Al capdavall, la providència divina també vetlla pel nàufrag i, si aquest sap escoltar el seu cor, hi hauria de trobar la gràcia i, amb ella, la fe. I una raó per viure.

III

En el conjunt de l'*Esbós de tres oratoris*, el 'Llàtzer' destaca, com apuntava tot just començar, per la composició equilibrada i el control notable exercit sobre els diversos temes i motius. Com a les *Elegies de Bierville* i a *Salvatge cor*, Riba comença el llibre amb un to i una temàtica prou musicals i clars que evoluciona cap a una gravetat, solemnitat o passió cada vegada més grans, lligades a una elaboració i complicació de l'experiència que arriba a extrems de notable dificultat; em sembla que, a Riba, els llibres li creixien a les mans (literalment, les elegies i els oratoris s'allarguen), potser perquè se li feien més i més necessaris, més íntims, més seus, perquè s'hi implicava amb una extraordinària intensitat, i amb la necessitat conseqüent de trobar les solucions tècniques i estilístiques adients. Però un procés com aquest no pot sorprendre si es recorda que per a ell la poesia és un 'mètode de pensament i de coneixença; de descoberta de [si] mateix i del món'.[21] S'entendrà encara més el que vull dir si es llegeixen aquestes paraules del 'Pròleg' a l'*Esbós de tres oratoris*: 'Si el poeta és, per definició, aquell que la paraula mena en l'aventura de prendre consciència del seu destí, no hi haurà ningú més estretament compromès pels mots i pels símbols que ells li construeixen'.[22] El compromís de Riba amb les paraules i els símbols dels tres oratoris --i de tota la seva obra-- és certament extrem, tant que pot arribar a afirmar que si cal que el poeta 'cregui perquè ha parlat, aquells que rebran la seva estranya comunicació creuran perquè ell els ha parlat'.[23]

Si es consideren els temes dels tres oratoris es pot dir que 'Els tres reis d'Orient' tracta l'actitud del creient, que mogut per la fe, emprèn el viatge (difícil, ardu i ingrat) cap a la revelació, la transcendència; el guien la gràcia i la innocència amb què els nens reviuen cada any el misteri de l'epifania. 'El fill pròdig', el poema més extens i complex, segueix la figura de qui, refusant la fe que se li revela de bon començ, segueix el seu camí, perquè tria la vida que vol viure, plena de joia primer i de sofriment després, per tornar a la fi a la casa paterna, on l'acollirà la mare i d'on, quan senti la crida íntima, tornarà a sortir. Seria molt senzill parlar del pecador i de les retrobades successives de la gràcia, però prefereixo llegir el poema com la recerca constant de qui vol viure la seva fe arriscant les certeses adquirides a cada instant, descobrint-se i assajant-se a si mateix en cada acte. (L'actitud religiosa de Riba s'inspira, convé recordar-ho, en Sant Agustí i en Pascal.)

Entre aquests dos oratoris, 'Llàtzer el ressuscitat' tracta també de la fe i de la gràcia que l'atorga, i ho fa oposant dues figures representatives, Llàtzer, el creient, i el nàufrag africà, l'agnòstic o no creient. Tots dos s'han acarat a la mort i tots dos n'han escapat; Llàtzer per acció divina, el nàufrag pel propi esforç. La tesi, no obstant, és inequívocament cristiana: és la gràcia, actuant a través del cor, que ha mogut tots dos a salvar-se, a voler viure, i és la caritat que fa que Llàtzer ajudi el nàufrag (i, amb ell, déu). Però hi ha més: la resurrecció de Llàtzer pren un valor més general i, si prefigura d'un costat la del mateix Jesús, de l'altre, esdevé el model de la trajectòria del creient, l'ànima del qual recuperarà el cos i viurà la vida eterna al costat de déu (un subtil aspecte del cristianisme que amb raó va obsessionar Maragall i va preocupar Riba). La resurrecció de Llàtzer --com la de Jesús-- és important perquè convenç els qui en són testimonis, els descobreix la fe; aquesta és la seva justificació: fer creure, realitzar-se plenament en l'acte de fe (vegeu els vv. 231-32 i el passatge de la carta a P. Crusat de 25-II-1955 citat abans). D'aquí que el poema requereixi una interpretació atenta, perquè cal referir-lo constantment al text evangèlic i valorar-ne la fidelitat i les recreacions (sobre material llegendari o producte de la imaginació), amb els pertinents objectius lírics i dramàtics (i els nuclis emotius propis de Riba); però també és lícit de recórrer a una clau al.legòrica i referir-lo sistemàticament al cos doctrinal cristià.

Que hagi proposat sovint una lectura doctrinal del poema m'obliga a plantejar una qüestió delicada, la de l'actitud del lector. Riba és taxatiu en aquest aspecte, perquè, segons paraules que he citat abans, com el poeta ha cregut quan s'ha trobat a si mateix dient les paraules del poema i en elles s'ha reconegut, així el lector creurà perquè el poeta ha parlat i és capaç de copsar en les seves paraules tot el que hi ha de compromís amb la seva veritat. Ho reafirma en un altre lloc: 'Que no s'acosti a un poeta qui no aspiri ell mateix a comprendre els modes de la seva pròpia realitat, i desconfiï de les operacions peculiars de tota gran poesia que insubstituïblement i almenys en part els revelen (no dic expliquen). Qui no se senti amb gust de construir el poema amb el poeta mateix'.[24] Però, arribat en aquest punt, he de dir que no crec que el lector hagi de compartir necessàriament les creences del poeta per comprendre i explicar el poema; ben al contrari, si vol comprendre 'els modes de la seva pròpia realitat', l'esforç de reconstruir imaginativament l'experiència del poeta en els quadres del poema, el treball de 'construir el poema amb el poeta', poden constituir un notable plaer intel.lectual i estètic i un considerable guany moral.

NOTAS

1. Arthur Terry, 'La poesia de Carles Riba', en C. Riba, *Obres completes, I: Poesia*, ed. de E. Sullà (Barcelona: Edicions 62, 1988), pp.5-47 (p.44).

2. Vegeu Lluís Bonet i Armengol, 'L'*Esbós de tres oratoris* de Carles Riba', *Euge*, 9 (1957), 20-35; Jordi Gomis, 'La poesia de Carles Riba', en *Tres poetes i Déu* (Barcelona: Claret, 1979), pp.173-228; Jordi Pinell, 'Tres moments en la poesia de Carles Riba', *Germinabit*, 65 (1959), 35-41, i 'L'esfera del diví en la poesia de Carles Riba', en *Actes del Simposi Carles Riba*, ed. de J. Medina i E. Sullà (Barcelona: Publicacions de l'Abadia de Montserrat i Institut d'Estudis Catalans, 1986), pp.47-59; Enric Sullà, 'Carles Riba', en M. de Riquer, A. Comas i J. Molas, *Història de la literatura catalana* (Barcelona: Ariel, 1985-88), IX, 271-327; A. Terry, 'La poesia de Carles Riba'; Antonio Vilanova, '*Esbós de tres oratoris* de Carles Riba', en A. Rousseaux, *Panorama de la literatura del siglo XX* (Madrid: Guadarrama, 1960), pp.812-22.

3. C. Riba, *Obres completes, I: Poesia*, ed. de E. Sullà (Barcelona: Edicions 62, 1988), p.287. Les següents referències entre parèntesi corresponen a aquesta edició.

4. Terry, p.43.

5. Vilanova, p.812.

6. Uso la terminologia de Gérard Genette, 'Discours du récit', en *Figures III* (París: Seuil, 1972), pp.65-282.

7. Riba, *Obres completes, I: Poesia*, p.287.

8. Terry, pp.43-44.

9. Blaise Pascal, *Pensées*, ed. de Ch.-M. Des Granges (París: Garnier, 1964), pp.134-38 [233].

10. Vegeu també Riba, *Obres completes, III: Crítica/ 2*, ed. de E. Sullà i J. Medina (Barcelona: Edicions 62, 1986), pp.333-39 i 360-66.

11. Per a la metàfora d'aquest com a 'instrument preciós', vegeu *Estances*, II, 20, v. 3, *Elegies de Bierville*, XI, v. 30, *Salvatge cor*, XIV, 2, v. 14, i Riba, *Obres completes, III: Crítica/ 2*, pp.214, 365; vegeu també Paul Valéry, *Oeuvres, I*, ed. de J. Hytier (París: Gallimard, 1957), p.1213.

12. G. Genette, *Palimpsestes. La littérature au second degré* (París: Seuil, 1982), pp.11-12.

13. E. Sullà, 'Les tannkas de Carles Riba', *Llengua & Literatura*, 3 (1988-89 [1990]), 265-336.

14. Terry, p.44.

15. Pascal, *Pensées*, pp.146-47 [277].

16. Pascal, *Pensées*, p.122 [185].

17. Pascal, *Pensées*, p.147 [278].

18. Philippe Sellier, *Pascal et Saint Augustin* (París: Armand Colin, 1970), p.134.

19. Vegeu Jordi Pinell, '«Cor salvatge», dels trobadors a Ausiàs March, d'Ausiàs March a Carles Riba', en *Estudis de llengua i literatura catalanes* (Barcelona: Publicacions de l'Abadia de Montserrat, 1983), VI, 225-59, e també José Luis Aranguren, 'Carles Riba y la poesía religiosa', *Papeles de Son Armadans*, 68 (1961), 137-44.

20. Vegeu, no obstant, Terry, p.44.

21. Riba, *Obres completes, III: Crítica/ 2*, p.253.

22. Riba, *Obres completes, I: Poesia*, p.277.

23. Riba, *Obres completes, I: Poesia*, p.278.

24. Riba, *Obres completes, III: Crítica/ 2*, p.338.

'SALUS ECCLESIAE SUPREMA LEX':
MONARCHISTS, CATHOLICS AND THE FIRST
PORTUGUESE REPUBLIC, 1910-1926*

RICHARD A. H. ROBINSON
University of Birmingham

Portugal during its First Republic provides a classic example of the problems facing the Roman Catholic Church in coming to terms with Republican institutions in Latin Europe. Despite the jurisdictional tensions to which it gave rise, the old alliance of Throne and Altar had generally served the Church well in the fulfilment of its mission. Although there was a tendency for the authority of royal power to increase during the eighteenth century (instanced in Portugal by the suppression of the Jesuits by the royal minister Pombal), it was the French Revolution which inaugurated an age of turmoil. The Civil Constitution of the Clergy of 1790, in its radical attempt to impose the legal supremacy of the State over an international religious institution, occasioned the fall of the Catholic Monarchy in France and had repercussions throughout Latin Europe. Whereas in France the Church thereafter found itself linked to various types of temporal partner until the Law of Separation in 1905, in Portugal and Spain the defeat in the 1830s of the neo-absolutist causes, supported by the clergy, of (respectively) Miguel I and Carlos V at the hands of dynastic liberalism led to ecclesiastical reformation by lay rulers eager to assert state power. The ultramontane ideology and its Iberian equivalents were in retreat before the principle of national sovereignty.

Although practical accommodations were reached between the Papacy and liberal-monarchical regimes before 1878, it was the combination of a new Pope, Leo XIII (1878-1903), and the consolidation of Republican institutions under laicist control in France which prompted a major reappraisal of Vatican strategy, as well as *aggiornamento* on political matters, within the framework of Thomism, proclaimed by the encyclical *Aeterni Patris* (1879), the guiding philosophy of Catholicism. In Portugal, however, this formal adoption of the teachings of St Thomas Aquinas apparently constituted less of an innovation than elsewhere.[1]

Particularly influenced by the consolidation of the Third Republic in France, Leo XIII accepted that the political situation could not be reversed by advocacy of restoration of the Monarchy but believed it possible to correct the errors of the age by working within the established regime. While maintaining the eternal principles that the rights of God took precedence over the rights of man and that there could be no stable social (and, by extension, political) order not in harmony with Divine Law, he sought to match these Catholic conceptions to existing historical circumstances. Provided there was acceptance that all power originated from God, there was no reason why this should not take on republican or representative-democratic form. Democracy and Republicanism could be means to institute an ideal Christian society.

In the social sphere, as his encyclical *Rerum novarum* (1891) signalled, the Catholics' aim should be to encourage the re-emergence of those natural social bodies intermediate between individual and State which would provide a moral and economic corrective to the injustices inherent in the liberal system. In the political sphere the papal grand design, evidenced by advocacy of the realignment (*ralliement*) of French Catholics with the Republic in the 1890s, was to emphasize indifference to forms of government but concern for juridical praxis. The unity of Catholics under ecclesiastical authority was the precondition for promotion of that 'common good' of society lauded by Aquinas and synonymous with the realization of Christian goals.[2]

Leo XIII's hope lay in making legitimate use of liberal and democratic pluralism to draw national societies and their rulers back to eternal Christian truths. '*Instaurare omnia in Christo*' was as much his Thomist slogan as it was more obviously of his successor, St Pius X (1903-14). Both Popes recognized the theoretical autonomy of the political sphere, in which the Church did not as a matter of principle interfere. The emphasis was therefore put on the united religious and social action of the faithful and not on the creation of confessional political parties, useful though such might sometimes circumstantially be for the achievement of Catholic ends. As he made explicit in *Graves de communi* (1901):

> it would be a crime to distort this name of Christian Democracy to politics, for although democracy, both in its philological and philosophical significations, implies popular government, yet in

its present application it is so to be employed that, removing from it all political significance, it is to mean nothing else than a benevolent and Christian movement on behalf of the people.[3]

Certain political problems arose from the French situation which were to recur when these Papal recommendations were applied in the Portuguese context from 1910 (and also in the Spanish from 1931), as they were by the Hierarchy even though the key encyclical, *Au milieu des sollicitudes* (1892), was not in Latin and therefore presumably not intended for universal application. It was not always easy, as the political divisions and polemics demonstrated, to distinguish between vessel and content, between form of government and laws. This difficulty raised related questions. To what extent was it incumbent upon Monarchist Catholics, in the interests of that unity of the faithful which alone could give strength, to sacrifice their legitimate personal preferences as to form of government when the established Republican authorities instituted policies at odds with the Thomist conception of the common good? To what extent had Catholics, as an obligation of conscience, to accept, respect and obey governments which, in the name of national sovereignty, rode roughshod over the inalienable rights of the Church and thus, in Catholic doctrine, violated the boundary between the temporal and the spiritual? At what point did the trampling of the Church's rights justify resistance, even armed resistance, by Catholics to governmental enactments? To what extent had the Hierarchy the right to command the faithful in political matters when these impinged upon faith and morals?

The skeins of theory in practice became tangled and the line between spiritual and temporal indistinct. In Portugal, as in France and Spain, Catholics were divided in their allegiances between supporters of different Monarchist claimants, accidentalists (those who professed indifference to forms of governments) and Republicans. In the French case the Third Republic had been in existence two decades by the time of the *ralliement*, so Portuguese and Spanish polemicists (who characteristically passed over the Portuguese precedent) could ponder the reasons for its failure to prevent anticlerical Republicans separating Church and State by the Law of 1905, a key text for Portuguese and Spanish Republicans.[4]

The End of the Union of Church and State in Portugal

Until the Republic decreed, by the Law of 20 April 1911, the Separation of the State from (as it put it) the Churches, Roman Catholicism was the official religion of Portugal. Since the restoration of independence in 1640 the Monarchy had built up a fair measure of control over the Church in its territories. From 1728 regalism was manifest in the insistence on royal permission (*placet*) for publication of papal pronouncements or decisions. In 1740 the royal right of presentation to bishoprics was recognized. The most serious upheaval in Church-State relations, amounting to schism, followed the victory of the liberal cause under Pedro IV in the civil war in 1834. All the Orders were abolished, as were tithes. Church property was seized by the State and much of it sold. The Nuncio was expelled and appointments of bishops under Pedro's brother Miguel I nullified. Relations between Maria II (Pedro's daughter) and the Holy See were not re-established until 1842. From that time the religious question remained largely dormant until the turn of the century, when the Constitutional Monarchy faced a significant challenge from Republicanism, militantly nationalist and anticlerical on the French model.

Against a background of severe economic difficulties and international humiliation, the liberal-parliamentary system, based on the contrived rotation in power of the Regenerator and Progressist parties by means of elections which the governing faction always won, began to break down in the reign of Carlos I (1889-1908) as these two parties fragmented, but it was not until early 1907 that the King allowed the Liberal-Regenerator João Franco to rule without parliament. The consequence of this experiment was the assassination in Lisbon on 1 February 1908 of Carlos and his eldest son Luís Filipe by Republican extremists. The eighteen-year-old Manuel, Carlos's second son, ascended the throne in his own words 'very young and without the experience or knowledge to be king,'[5] and so was reliant on others' advice. The immediate decision to jettison Franco and try to regain support by appeasing the Republican minority was followed by seven unsuccessful governments in twenty months and an intensification of that political indifference among the armed forces and population at large which observers noted in the opening decade of the century. It was indeed amid such generalized indifference that the Republicans overcame ill-organized Monarchist resistance in October 1910 and Manuel 'the Unfortunate' departed on the royal yacht from Ericeira for exile in Worcestershire.[6]

The religious question had surfaced as an embarrassment for royal governments in 1901 with the 'Calmon incident', when a daughter of the Brazilian Consul in Oporto, a Freemason, was physically prevented by her father and the police from going off to be a nun. This episode and the anti-Jesuit commotion which ensued drew attention to the authorities' *de facto* toleration of the return of some Orders and forced the government to shut some religious houses and promise closer supervision in religious matters. It was however in Manuel II's reign that Republicans made most play with the influence of the Society of Jesus, allegedly exercised through the Queen-Mother. In a belated attempt to disarm Republican criticism the last government of the Monarchy proposed closing some religious houses.[7] Such a policy not only confirmed that the Republicans were setting the political agenda, but it also alienated the King's more militant clerical supporters, who had hoped to free the Church and the Orders from the 'enslavement' of regalist and liberal legislation and thwart the positivist and Masonic-led Republican challenge.

The origins of this militant Catholic movement went back to the 1870s and 1880s, when real efforts began to be made to overcome the division of activists into Legitimists, supporters of the exiled Miguel II who had succeeded his father Miguel I in 1866, and Constitutionalists, who accepted the descendants of Pedro IV but sought to modify clauses in the Royal Charter of 1826 detrimental to the Church. In *Pergrata Nobis* (1886) Leo XIII himself appealed for the 'supreme and most desired union' of Catholics and in 1894 Bastos Pina, Count-Bishop of Coimbra, lamented earlier ecclesiastical backing for Miguelism and sought to apply the doctrine of *ralliement* to the Constitutional Monarchy despite the protests of Legitimists.[8]

The foundation of a Catholic political party (though not so entitled) came only in 1903 when the *Partido Nacionalista* (PN) was launched under the former Regenerator Minister Jacinto Cândido da Silva. Its programme stood for the 'defence of the religious principle' as the prerequisite for orderly and democratic social progress and for 'good harmony between Church and State as the perfect societies they are'. Although a few prominent Catholic laymen disapproved of this political venture, the PN had the effective support of the Catholic social movement, which absorbed much Legitimist energy and consisted of workers' clubs in the north, a youth movement inspired by the *Centro Académico de Democracia Cristã* (CADC, refounded in Coimbra in 1903), as well as other Catholic popular entities. Like the Republicans, the PN won some seats in elections still dominated by the otherwise moribund parties of the regime, amongst whose political agents could often be found parish priests.

The general dynamic of Catholic organization began to falter just as the PN compromised itself with Franco's extra-parliamentary government. Although the party should in principle have gained strength when the Legitimist claimant set aside his claim in 1909 to help Manuel II survive,[9] disputes over whether all Catholics were obliged to vote for the PN threatened unity and on the eve of the Republican revolt leadership passed from the more broadminded Cândido da Silva to the younger Alberto Pinheiro Torres.[10] Governmental management of elections on the basis of a narrow suffrage was generally effective to the end of the Monarchy, but it was the PN and the *Partido Republicano Português* (PRP) who presented rival popular alternative visions (respectively pro-clerical and anticlerical) of the future.

The Republican seizure of power in October 1910 was followed by radical implementation of the easiest part of their programme to carry out to the satisfaction of 'the People', which to them meant essentially their urban, lower-middle-class supporters. Deprived of artificial legal sustenance, the Church would, they believed, wither away. The Provisional Government, with the demagogic Afonso Costa as Minister of Justice and Religious Affairs, immediately enforced Pombal's decrees suppressing the Society of Jesus -- which Costa described as 'an association for robbing and killing'--[11] and the decree of 1834 making all Orders illegal; their property was expropriated. Other decrees in 1910 abolished religious instruction in schools, suppressed holidays on saints' days, forbade the armed forces attending religious ceremonies, legalized divorce and made marriage a purely civil contract.

The reaction of the Bishops to these decrees was to draft a collective pastoral in which they reiterated the doctrine of respect for the constituted power but called upon the faithful to combat by legal means all laws offensive to the Church and religion: 'The respect owed to the constituted power does not mean approval for all the legislative measures promulgated by it'.[12] The government denied this pastoral its *placet*, banning its dissemination, and took action against offending clerics.

Afonso Costa furthermore ignored ecclesiastical suggestions for a separation which could be of mutual benefit to a free Church in a free State, as well as warnings not to follow the French example in all its details and thus incur inevitable papal wrath.[13] Instead, pursuing a hard line which won him the backing of the most militant in the PRP, he decreed the Law of 20 April 1911, whose effect, he assured a gathering of fellow Masons, 'will be so salutary that in two generations Portugal will have completely eliminated Catholicism, which was the major cause of the shameful state into which it fell'.[14]

The Portuguese Law of Separation borrowed heavily from French precedents. Lay welfare bodies with financial responsibility for sustaining worship out of no more than a third of their revenues had to be authorized by the Ministry of Justice, but no minister of religion could be a member of these *cultuais* (as the *corporações e entidades encarregadas do culto* were generally known), nor could he sit on his parish council (*junta de paróquia*). Catholic priests were to register for payment of annual allowances (*pensões*) whose size would be fixed by the State. Offerings and payment of burial fees to the clergy were prohibited. A priest could be exiled from his place of residence or could find his *pensão* suspended or withdrawn if he contravened legislative precepts even by criticizing them. All church property became state-registered property which could either be expropriated or be entrusted to *cultuais*. The State's *placet* remained necessary for publication of papal messages and episcopal pronouncements, while ministers of religion could only correspond officially with the public authorities and not with one another. Graduates of pontifical universities were forbidden to practise as priests in Portugal. Ecclesiastical boundaries could be changed by the State. Preparation for theological studies had to be done in state schools, not in seminaries which had to be inspected by the State. Permission had to be obtained for acts of worship outside daylight hours. Ringing of church bells was strictly controlled and the wearing of vestments or cassocks outside places of worship banned.[15]

By this law, decreed before elections to the Constituent Assembly had been held, the Church in Portugal was thus relieved of its wealth and property, its priests were subjected to the control of possibly unsympathetic lay bodies and its internal life and hierarchical discipline thrown open to meddling by the functionaries of a laicist Republican state run by unbelievers. Collision course with Rome and its Portuguese adherents had been set, not least because the Pope had already condemned the *cultuais* in their earlier French form.

From the Law of Separation to the 'New Republic', 1911-17

The Law of Separation, considered by all Republicans 'the basilar law' of their regime whatever reservations some of them might have about some of its provisions, alienated the Catholic majority of the population. It drove Catholic activists into unforgiving opposition to Afonso Costa and his dominant Democrat faction of the PRP, which was based on the lower-middle class of the capital, was enlivened by anticlerical zealotry and made use of terroristic elements. More moderate Republican leaders, notably António José de Almeida and Brito Camacho, respectively from 1912 chiefs of the Evolutionist and Unionist groups, as well as the formerly Monarchist electoral networks absorbed by the PRP to control the provinces, came to be increasingly embarrassed by its abrasive provisions but were loath to court charges of 'anti-Republicanism' by determinedly opposing the law. The alienation of Catholics and the attempts to take advantage of this state of affairs by Monarchist enthusiasts kept the Republic psychologically on a war footing in its first seven years.

The response of the Portuguese Episcopate to the Law was to issue an angry collective protest against a text exceeding their worst expectations. They did not preach revolt despite this 'gratuitous act of hatred' with which the clergy had been repaid for its deference towards the new regime. The views of the majority had been sacrificed to the demands of an 'audacious but tiny minority [of] anti-religious fanatics [...] All is summed up in four words: injustice, oppression, spoliation, derision'. Although the Bishops admitted the likelihood of a few tares among the wheat, they felt sure the great majority of the clergy would classify themselves as wheat by refusing the *pensões* and preferring obedience to Rome to apostasy.[16]

The collective protest of the Bishops was authoritatively echoed by St Pius X's encyclical *Jandudum in Lusitania* (24 May 1911), which spoke of 'insatiable hatred', 'arbitrary despotism', robbery of the Church in the temporal sphere and enslavement in the spiritual. In Portugal 'open war has been declared on religion' and the worst was to be feared.[17] Clearly resistance to the law and Catholic unity were imperative but the papal condemnation, which fell victim to the governmental *placet*, stopped short of sanctioning rebellion. However as a consequence of their attitude of *non possumus*, by mid-1912 all the Portuguese bishops save one had been banished from their dioceses.[18]

If Catholics *qua* Catholics were not enjoined to take offensive action, Catholics who were also Monarchists might be tempted *qua* Monarchists or patriots to try and overthrow a regime deemed to have brought political and social turbulence in the wake of its violent installation and which had used well-tried methods of manipulation in the election of the Constituent Assembly on 28 May 1911. Rejection of the validity of these elections was a feature of a manifesto issued on 31 May by Captain Henrique Mitchell de Paiva Couceiro, an Anglo-Portuguese soldier who had been Governor-General of Angola, had toyed with the idea of military intervention towards the end of the Monarchy and who had been chief organizer of resistance to the Republicans in October 1910. After calling for a plebiscite on the form of government he left for Galicia to plot the overthrow of the regime with both Manueline and Miguelist Monarchists. His first incursion, with 800 supporters, in October 1911 was ill-coordinated with a conspiracy in Oporto but counted on raising at least the rural population in the north, believed still to be Monarchist and upset by religious policy. In the event he was met by much indifference, even though some priests rallied some villagers near the border. Couceiro's failure was made worse when Manuel, now in Richmond, voiced his disapproval because it had not been a specifically Manueline movement.[19]

Nevertheless the quixotic Couceiro planned a second attempt once he had resolved the dynastic dispute. An agreement that supporters of both Claimants should collaborate against the Republic was reached in the Lord Warden Hotel, Dover, on 30 January 1912, but both Claimants jibbed at signing documents whereby Miguel would have recognized the unmarried Manuel as King and the latter would have recognized Miguel's sons as heirs to the throne.[20] Couceiro's second incursion from Galicia with a thousand loyalists in July 1912 also came to nothing because of superior Republican equipment. The attacks on Chaves and Valença do Minho failed and the popular uprisings and guerrilla movements led by priests in the Terras de Basto in imitation of Miguelist predecessors --most famously by Padre Domingos Pereira of Cabeceiras-- soon collapsed.[21] This second failure to spark a general anti-Republican movement by a mixture of popular uprising in a region of high religious practice and invasion by *émigrés* persuaded many provincial fence-sitters to make their deals with the PRP and Manuel to counsel publicly against armed uprisings.[22]

Apparent lack of enthusiasm nationally for the Monarchy was also doubtless a consideration leading bishops to see the future as a longer-term fight for influence under the Republic as the established form of government. Protests against lay interference in matters ecclesiastical and spiritual were kept up and only a minority of priests --700 according to Afonso Costa, 200 out of 3,600 according to the Vatican-- were tempted by *pensões* into becoming schismatics. In 1912 government sources reported only 87 *cultuais* functioning in the country's 3,800 parishes.[23]

The weapons which the Episcopate intended to use in its struggle and the strategy to be employed were set out in a collective appeal to their flock from Santarém on 10 July 1913. The union of Catholics was necessary to focus their efforts and to encourage the indifferent at a time when there were signs of increased devotion, especially in the capital. Germany, France, Belgium and Italy were cited (as they had been under the Monarchy) as providing organizational examples to follow. Internal divisions among the faithful, including that over the form of government, had to be set aside in the effort to '*instaurare Lusitaniam in Christo*'. The programme of the new *União Católica* (UC) represented an attempt to refound and coordinate under firm episcopal control the lay social entities created in the Monarchy's last years.[24] The moving spirit behind the UC, which was slow to take on much practical reality, was the papal representative in Lisbon, Mgr. Benedetto Masella, a keen advocate of accidentalism.[25] At this stage most Catholic activists seem to have been Manueline Monarchists, at least *in foro interno*, with Miguelist Legitimism confined to the old nobility and nuclei in Braga and Covilhã. Overt Republicans were few but included two priests elected as Evolutionists for northern constituencies.

Given Manuel's official disapproval of violence and the continuing, if varying degrees of repression of both Monarchists and Catholics by the seven Republican governments from September 1911 to January 1915, potential political cleavages were obscured. This changed when, partly as a result of officers wearying of the lack of hierarchical discipline in the armed forces, President Manuel de Arriaga appointed General Pimenta de Castro to lead a government. Supported as a tactical *pis aller* by the minority of Monarchist officers, he allowed non-Republicans freedom to organize and amnestied former incursionists in a gesture of national reconciliation.

This attempted liberalization allowed the emergence of legal Catholic and Monarchist political organizations which just about survived the Democrat-PRP revolution of 14 May 1915. From then until December 1917 the Republic was again dominated by Costa and his followers who, having manufactured their parliamentary majority in the elections of June 1915, clung to power despite increasing alienation of the Unionist Republicans and growing social unrest brought on by food shortages resulting from the dislocation occasioned by the Great War. Despite a worsening financial situation Costa's government acceded to the British request to seize German shipping in the Tagus which inevitably led to Germany declaring war on Portugal (9 March 1916). More controversially a Democrat-supported coalition under the Evolutionist A. J. de Almeida dispatched an expeditionary force to France in early 1917. Then, to add to national divisions, Costa's third government (April-December 1917) reopened clerical wounds by banishing the Bishop of Oporto and the Cardinal-Patriarch of Lisbon from their dioceses for infringements of the Law of Separation and on 29 November banished the Archbishops of Braga and Évora from continental Portugal for protesting against these penalties. All this was in a year when Catholic popular emotions were stirred by apparitions of the Virgin to three small children at Fátima.

Pimenta de Castro's interlude had witnessed the re-emergence of the political face of the Catholic social movement of pre-Republican days. In the opening months of the new regime there had been thoughts of relaunching the PN as an accidentalist force in the service of 'Religion and Country' but the closure by the Republicans in February 1911 of its potential mainstay, the Oporto newspaper *A Palavra*, which had submitted to the Republic 'without fervour; but with sincerity', came as a mortal blow.[26]

At a general meeting of Catholics in Oporto on 11 February 1915 the threads were taken up again and the *Centro Católico Português* (CCP) was founded with the objective of 'organizing Catholics in the political and social fields' so that the laws of the land and its political and social institutions 'may be imbued with Catholic principles'. In the short run the CCP's minimum programme was re-establishment of Portugal's relations with the Holy See, broken off in 1913, and recognition of the liberties of the Church in relation to education, worship and association. In elections it would ally with such 'conservative elements' as would adopt its minimum programme. The moving spirit was Alberto Pinheiro Torres, last leader of the PN, and four of the nine members of its steering committee had been PN candidates in the last elections of the Monarchy. In June 1915, despite some Monarchist hostility, the CCP had the limited success of getting two priests elected out of its dozen candidates in the rural north; the CADC activist (and future dictator) Oliveira Salazar withdrew before polling-day.[27]

A further stimulus to organization, which seemed to urge the faithful to go further down the accidentalist road of acceptance of the Republic, came in the Episcopate's collective instruction of 22 January 1917. In social and political affairs the Bishops:

> imperiously demanded *Catholic Union*, removed from and superior to political differences and secondary to party interests ... It is a most urgent necessity that true Catholics organize legally and be ready to take an active part in public life, not so as to fight institutions, not so as to attain vengeful victory for this or that political ideal, but solely to promote the revindication of the just liberties and legitimate rights of Catholicism.

Catholics must 'unite, organize, in the area of legality'; otherwise they would be Catholics in name only.[28]

The episcopal exhortation prompted the holding in Braga in August 1917 of the First General Congress of the CCP, an attempt to establish it nationally as the political face of the wider UC. Despite the Bishops' patronage and the attendance of many clergy, the CCP's organization, like that of the UC itself, was clearly weak, indeed non-existent in many areas. The former PN leader and editor of the Oporto newspaper *Liberdade*, Pinheiro Torres, was made responsible for the north, the former CADC president and academic Diogo Pacheco de Amorim for the centre and the veteran polemicist and railway expert José Fernando de Sousa, now editor of the Lisbon daily *A Ordem*, for the south.[29]

Episcopal sponsorship for the nascent CCP was something of a problem for Monarchists who claimed also to champion the religious cause, since squaring support for the CCP within Republican legality as recommended by their spiritual leaders with maintenance of overt Monarchism in matters temporal could not under all circumstances prove easy. They could recall that their bishops had stated in December 1910 that:

> the Catholic faith is removed from this political controversy [on the question of form of government] ... Catholics are at complete liberty to debate the problem; they can argue (without offending charity and Christian moderation), they can establish preferences; the Church holds herself aloof from the matter; she does not intervene with her doctrinal authority to proffer judgement.[30]

The dynastic issue remained unresolved and the collaboration recommended by the 'pact of Dover' was made more difficult by the Great War. Manuel had married Auguste Viktoria of Hohenzollern-Sigmaringen in 1913, but he remained in pro-Allied exile in Twickenham. Miguel and his heirs, on the other hand, saw service in the armies of the Central Powers.

King Manuel, who had recorded his disapproval of insurrection before 1914, came out against conspiracy on his behalf for the duration of the war in the interests of national unity and indeed favoured a broad national coalition, though not all his followers heeded his wishes.[31] First under his Lieutenant João de Azevedo Coutinho (September 1913-October 1915), and then under his successor Colonel Aires de Ornelas e Vasconcelos, who was an African campaigner and Minister under João Franco, Manueline Monarchists were grouped in the broadly-titled *Causa Monárquica* (CM). Some remained liberal constitutionalists, others came to hold more illiberal views.

Freedom for Monarchists to organize legally under Pimenta de Castro's rule also drew attention to a new wave of doctrinal Monarchism, propagated by a youthful cluster of Manueline romantics and ex-Republicans inspired by the integral-nationalist school of the *Action Française* of Charles Maurras. These Lusitanian Integralists, who in 1916 organized themselves under the title *Junta Central do Integralismo Lusitano* (JCIL), disseminated a novel creed of 'anti-parliamentary, traditionalist, organic Monarchy'. In this nationalist vision the King would rule with the help of ministerial technocrats as well as reign over an administratively decentralized corporative State with a syndically-managed economy. Arts and sciences would be royally encouraged, while the 'liberty and privileges of the traditional Roman, Apostolic, Catholic religion' would be protected and materially aided by agreement (*concordat*) with the Vatican, with freedom for the Orders specifically advocated.[32] They were political aesthetes who saw their vanguard role as to convert the rest of the élite, especially the rising generation, to their Monarchist future based in a mythified pre-liberal national past, of which Catholicism was an integral part. Once ideological hegemony over currently established ideas, be they Republican or Monarchist, had been achieved, the Monarchy would return by *coup de main*. Always sensitive to charges that their creed was merely a French import, they were not the only Portuguese Monarchists inspired by the *Action Française*.

The King's Lieutenant Aires de Ornelas drew more cautiously from the source and reached different conclusions. For him, Maurras had made the cogent case for Monarchy and the principle of *politique d'abord* could be interpreted in Portugal as putting politics first the better to thwart the Church's enemies. Restoration of the Monarchy, not piecemeal amelioration of the situation, would indeed be preferable for Church and Monarch alike. However, unlike the Integralists, Aires de Ornelas argued that the Royal Charter of 1826 (still essentially the constitutional system in Manuel's reign) had 'brought a return to the national tradition' after the 'despotism' of

Pombal.[33]

By 1917 the ideas of 'the Phantom Captain' Couceiro were also showing the influence of French counter-revolutionary thought. His blueprint for 'national democracy' justified Monarchy and state support for Catholicism with positivistic arguments of 'collective convenience'. Therapeutic Republican scourging would be followed by 'national renewal' and a return to 'good tradition' after a period of constitutional transition had taken the liberal and parliamentary content out of the Portuguese Monarchy.[34]

By the end of 1917, then, the tail of Maurrassian ideas advocated most obviously and effectively by the JCIL, were beginning to wag the still mostly liberal Manueline Monarchist dog. Monarchists and accidentalist Catholics, whose personal preferences as in the cases of the CCP leaders Pinheiro Torres and Fernando de Sousa were known to be Monarchist, were still trying to collaborate within legality in defence of the common cause of religion, but the underlying tensions and contradictions remained unresolved.

From the 'New Republic' to the Military Dictatorship, 1917-26

On 8 December 1917 the Republic of the PRP-Democrats of Afonso Costa was overthrown *manu militari*. The revolution was led by the Unionist Republican Major Sidónio País with the support of a broad spectrum of the discontented ranging from Anarcho-Syndicalist workers through fellow moderate Republicans to more conservative elements and including most army officers and officer cadets. The Revolutionary Committee won power on the Feast Day of the Virgin, Patroness of Portugal. This proved a good omen for Catholics as decrees immediately revoked the banishments of prelates and on 22 February 1918, significant modifications of the Law of Separation were made by the Unionist Minister of Justice and Religious Affairs, Moura Pinto. The failure of the laicist conception of *cultuais* was recognized: the faithful and their priests were now free to create and compose these entities and regulations on expenditure on worship were greatly relaxed -- all of which was second best to the abolition ideally desired by the Church. Restrictions on seminaries were revoked and churches were freely ceded to the *cultuais*. The State's *placet*, carried over from the

Monarchy, was abolished, as were *pensões*, state disciplinary powers over the clergy and the ban on public wearing of cassocks. Despite Catholic regret that Moura Pinto had not gone further and permitted religious instruction in schools and the return of the Orders, diplomatic relations with the Vatican were re-established in July 1918.[35]

Sidónio País's 'New Republic' set out to be more democratic than that of the PRP-Democrats. The President of the Republic and the lower parliamentary chamber were elected by universal male suffrage on 28 April 1918, but the polls were boycotted by the old Republicans because he was making too many concessions to non-Republicans. His own *Partido Nacional Republicano* (PNR) won 108 seats to 37 for the CM and 5 for the CCP. The greater freedom for non-Republicans and the *rapprochement* with the Vatican increased tensions between the CCP and the CM, reflected in bitter wrangles in the election campaign. In the Algarve, for example, the Bishop, Barbosa Leão, accused Aires de Ornelas and the CM of sharp practice which had cheated the CCP candidate, the Miguelist Domingos Pinto Coelho, out of election. In a public polemic the Bishop insisted that religious interests take precedence over secondary political ones and poured scorn on the contention of Aires de Ornelas and the CM organ *Diário Nacional* that religion would be better protected under a restored Monarchy whose regalist practice had been, in the Bishop's view, 'a horror and a disgrace'. He accused the CM of ignoring the Episcopate's instructions and of seeking to confuse Monarchism with Catholicism for their own partisan purposes by falsely claiming a Republic had by definition to be anti-Catholic. While the Bishop admitted that one could be a good Catholic without being a member of the CCP, which was not a political party but part of the episcopally controlled UC, he cast doubt on the devoutness of certain Monarchists.[36] Such polemics were harbingers of greater debates to come.

First, however, came another bout of severe political turbulence. On 14 December 1918 President Sidónio País was assassinated. Amid increasing anarchy opinion, especially in the armed forces, polarized around old-style Republicans and Monarchists. Admiral Canto e Castro, a Monarchist by inclination, was appointed interim President of the Republic. He presided over a brief civil war when Paiva Couceiro, in a surprise move, proclaimed the

Monarchy in Oporto on 19 January 1919. An attempted coup in Lisbon led by Aires de Ornelas and Azevedo Coutinho failed and the Monarchy in the north collapsed after five weeks. Neither Manuel nor most of his followers had favoured Couceiro's ill-prepared adventure, while Catholic activists, including those with Monarchist convictions, feared it could be counterproductive for the newly-won status of the Church. Couceiro had proclaimed the Monarchy as it was on 4 October 1910, with the Constitution then in force, but on 21 January another decree was issued reiterating revocation of the Law of Separation and promising that 'relations between the Catholic Church and the State will be regulated by future agreement between the Government and the Holy See'. This was not enough to dispel fears of regalism and CCP supporters complained of the insurgent Monarchists' arrogance, encapsulated in the slogan, 'Restoration first; God can wait.' They noted too that some Monarchist actions were directed against priests and CCP interests.[37] The failure of Paiva Couceiro's third attempt meant the return of the old Republic but without reversal of the measures concerning Church-State relations, which encouraged Pope Benedict XV (1914-22) in his policy of reconciling Catholicism with Republicanism in Portugal, as elsewhere in Europe.

From February 1919 until its overthrow by the military on 28 May 1926 the parliamentary Republic lurched from crisis to crisis owing to the interplay of post-war dislocation, economic problems, social unrest and military interventions in the political process. Twenty-four governments came and went in seven years but in the four legislative elections held on the restored restricted suffrage the Republican parties always won the great majority of seats. By contrast, in 1919 the CCP won one seat, in 1921 the CM won 4 and the CCP 3, in 1922 the CM won 10 and the CCP 5, and in 1925 the CM won 6 and the CCP 4.

Relations of individual governments with the Vatican varied in degrees of cordiality but all adhered to the *status quo* established in 1918. This return to a degree of normality in Church-State relations was perceived by Monarchists as damaging to their cause. Furthermore, the internal dissension in the Monarchist camp did no service to its credibility. After failing in October 1919 to persuade the childless Manuel to abandon constitutionalism, name an heir, appoint a new Lieutenant and prepare for a rising, the Integralists --in their own words, 'Monarchists because we are nationalists and not out of loyalty to the King'-- broke with Manuel. They transferred their allegiance to the Miguelist cause which, after the abdication of Miguel II in July 1920, was represented by his twelve-year-old son Duarte with, as Regent, his formidable aunt Aldegundes, who had issued a manifesto asking the Portuguese to conquer or die for a 'Monarchy representative of the Municipalities and the Corporations of Intelligence and Labour' which would return to the Church its privileges, liberties and property.[38] In May 1922 the JCIL gave up political activity so that its members could devote themselves to propagating counter-revolutionary doctrine after they and leading Miguelists repudiated the 'pact of Paris' of 17 April, whereby Manuel II undertook to allow a parliament (*Cortes Gerais da Nação*) to name his successor and decide on a constitution in exchange for Duarte getting his followers to obey Manuel as King.[39]

With the Integralists gone and the dynastic question on hold, the ideological issue returned to plague the Manueline camp. In November 1923, two months after General Primo de Rivera overthrew Spanish liberal parliamentarianism, the official organ of the CM, *Correio da Manhã*, carried articles in praise of liberal Monarchy. These prompted by way of reaction the creation within the CM of *Acção Realista Portuguesa* (ARP) for those like the publicist Alfredo Pimenta who advocated 'traditional' (that is, non-liberal) Monarchy but remained loyal to Manuel. Unfortunately a message from Manuel early in 1926, intended to unite his followers by suggesting he would be happy with a traditional Monarchy if, in the event of his restoration, parliament freed him of his oath to the liberal constitution, had the opposite effect. Pimenta and Aires de Ornelas quarrelled over the message's meaning, with the result that ARP broke with the CM.[40]

Although it may be that Monarchist sentiment, of whatever type and depth, was quite widespread in the armed forces by 1926, the political leadership of Monarchism was in complete disarray when the coup of 28 May took place. Since the military movement seemed to promise much that Monarchists wanted short of a change in the form of government, Pimenta was right to call 28 May the 'mortal blow to Monarchist revindications'.[41] Duarte was only eighteen and Manuel, wearying of his quarrelsome following, confided around this time to a British female interlocutor: 'I enjoy the life of an English gentleman and would be reluctant to exchange my present surroundings for the turmoil of statecraft'.[42]

The impetuosity of Paiva Couceiro's attempt at restoration in 1919 and his failure was grist to the mill of ecclesiastics who saw the best course for the Church as working with the Republic. Although the CCP remained an accidentalist organization, a new inflection in favour of the established form of government was to lose it notable activists of a Monarchist persuasion. For other CCP leaders and ecclesiastics, however, the divisions between Monarchists provided evidence of a lost cause from which the faithful must be prized away so as to strengthen the Church's political clout. Although Republicans still considered the modified Law of Separation the Republic's 'basilar law', they seemed increasingly willing to make friendly gestures to the Catholics. For example, in 1922 the new Bishop of Beja, José do Patrocínio Dias, who had won patriotic acclaim for his conduct as a chaplain on the Western Front, was given government protection on entering his diocese to the dismay of local anticlerical zealots.[43] In January 1923 the freethinking President A.J. de Almeida presented the Papal Nuncio, Mgr. Achille Locatelli, a keen proponent of *rapprochement*, with his Cardinal's hat. The Nuncio saw in the President the embodiment of 'the Nation itself', though the President later interpreted the ceremony as reaffirming the supremacy of the civil power in a Catholic nation.[44] Later, parliament approved CCP motions of salutation to Pope Pius XI (1922-39) on the anniversaries of his election and coronation.[45] Whether the Republicans' intentions went beyond dividing the CCP from the Monarchists was unclear.

The CCP's new course was first set at a conference in Lisbon on 22 November 1919 at which a new central committee was elected. Those with known Monarchist convictions, notably Fernando de Sousa and Pinheiro Torres, were replaced by the lawyer and lecturer António Lino Neto as president. Henceforth CCP leaders had to be without party political affiliation so that it could not 'be, or be suspected of being, the instrument of any political party'. Reorganization was thoroughgoing and the purpose of this 'autonomous organization' was defined as to act as a pressure-group and focus for Catholics in politics for 'promoting the Christianization of law, customs and national political life' whilst 'respecting the constituted powers of the State' and 'abstaining from any demonstrations or activity regarding forms of government'.[46]

This stricter accidentalist policy received public support from Benedict XV himself in a letter to the Portuguese Prelates on 18 December 1919 in which he specifically associated Leo XIII's policy of *ralliement* with Portugal by citing *Au milieu des sollicitudes* and exhorting the faithful to unite and obey the civil power in a suprapartisan spirit. The Prelates replied on 4 February 1920, explaining that injustices were still being committed against the Church and Catholics, which could account for local criticism of the CCP's line, but expressing hope for improvement; the day Catholic revindications were satisfied, 'Catholics will not feel themselves to have the right to show themselves enemies of the political institutions which rule them'.[47]

The CCP was thus a weapon to be used by the Vatican in the bargaining process for the realization of more of the Church's aims. Under Lino Neto's leadership the CCP, which he defined as 'neither a party of the Republic, nor a party of the Monarchy: it is an organization *sui generis*',[48] distanced itself further from the Monarchists. More turns of the screw were applied to Catholic activists who were also Monarchists at its Second Congress in April 1922. There defenders of the view to be found in the Catholic-Monarchist daily *A Época*, that loyal advocacy of Monarchy was compatible with the CCP's line, were marginalized. The Congress approved the leadership's conduct since 1919, confirmed Lino Neto as leader and affirmed the need for Catholics to organize, 'sacrificing, not exactly their political opinions, but all partisan political activity, deemed prejudicial for the time being to the defence of religious interests'.[49]

The full case for the CCP's new course was argued most notably by a former CADC luminary and Deputy for Guimarães in 1921-22, Oliveira Salazar. Himself a Monarchist *in foro interno*,[50] he conceded that many prominent Catholics were not in the CCP and had the right, 'which no one has yet contested', to pursue party political objectives. However, although the CCP did not have the monopoly on Catholic activity in politics, with regard to religious affairs it did follow the instructions of Rome, albeit 'without betraying the well-understood interests of our Country'. Catholics certainly had the right in theory to prefer either form of government but in practice had to obey constituted governments 'save in exceptional cases'. They also had to support the Church in the attainment of its rights and therefore had to make a transitory sacrifice of their political opinions to achieve unity in the political sphere to achieve this end. In this context, 'to resolve the political question so as afterwards to resolve the religious question' --the argument of Monarchists -- 'is to subordinate religion to political regime. And the Gospel commands us to concern ourselves firstly with what is important for religion (*Quaerite primum regnum Dei*)'.

Salazar deployed papal encyclicals to support his interpretation, but he still found that 'the duty of obedience [to the constituted power] is not to be confused with adhesion to the regime which His Holiness neither imposes nor even counsels'. Without necessarily adhering to the Republic, Catholics 'truly integrated into the spirit of the Church' must be mindful of the primary need 'to attain the fundamental liberties of the Church within the current regime', which presupposed --a key point-- that the Republic was 'in itself [Salazar's emphasis] not irreconcilable with recognition of the fundamental rights of the Church [nor with the] highest and most vital interests of the nation'. The least Catholics belonging to different political parties could do at election times was unite; otherwise the Catholic cause would suffer certain defeat. The 'provisional and transitory' CCP, neither for nor against a particular form of government, had been approved by Rome 'as a political organism to act by political means' to achieve an immediate religious objective, whatever other objectives its members might have as citizens. He concluded that the Holy See knew best and the CCP's was the correct interpretation of papal instructions until such time as it should pronounce otherwise.[51]

Salazar's interpretation was bluntly challenged by the former CCP luminary Fernando de Sousa in *A Época*: 'To oblige Catholics who are Monarchists --and nearly all of them are-- not to manifest their political convictions *in foro externo* and in the field of legal political activity, when they are convinced that the form of government is not a matter of indifference for the resolution of the national problem, and when they have the incontestable right to fight for what they adjudge most suited to the national interest and traditions, is to demand the impossible'. He argued that neither Pope nor bishops had demanded, as did Lino Neto's CCP, that Catholic Monarchists should inhibit their Monarchism. Although he agreed with Salazar that in general theory Catholicism and Republicanism were compatible, Sousa maintained that Salazar was forgetting that this particular Portuguese Republic was 'genuinely Masonic in origin, is structurally anti-Catholic and professes *laicism*, incompatible with the full freedom of the Church, as its fundamental doctrine'.

Furthermore, Salazar was being unreasonable in wanting the Monarchist majority of Catholics to set aside their convictions since this meant putting the Republic as a form of government first, and this was to put politics before religion. Monarchists organized legally (as they were in the CM) could uphold the Church's cause so, if unity were necessary, why could not the pro-Republican minority yield to the majority in achieving it? Sousa pointed out that in 1921 the Council of the CM had made the CCP's revindications its own. He countered those who pointed to the Constitutional Monarchy's regalism with the observation that Manuel had inherited certain privileges in ecclesiastical matters, but these, like his title *Rei Fidelíssimo*, had been bestowed by the Holy See and could in any case be renegotiated.

Fernando de Sousa also challenged Salazar's remarks on 'adhesivism'. None of the papal encyclicals cited by his adversary had actually counselled 'the sacrifice of political activity in the legal field, which would be equivalent to disguised adhesion to the Republican form, which cannot be imposed on anyone'. Despite Benedict XV's letter of 1919, Sousa denied that the precedent of the *ralliement* was applicable to Portugal, an 'entirely different case'. He complained of the 'hermeneutic evolution' of texts on the part of CCP leaders, culminating in Lino Neto's claim in September 1922 that the Holy See was counselling its sons to 'abstain from demonstrations or actions on forms of government'. This Sousa saw as confusing the sacrifice of Monarchism in the interests of religion with adhesion to the regime, which could only aggravate disunity. In any case Catholics could not be obliged, even by papal instruction, to become Republicans and this, he maintained, was what sacrificing one's Monarchism meant in practice.[52]

Sousa therefore concluded that as a Monarchist and a Catholic he found no contradictions between his political and religious convictions. The programmes of the various Monarchist groups had all now turned their backs on the 'liberal Caesaro-Papism' of the years before 1910. Outside the CCP there could be no objections to Catholic Monarchists advocating their regime's restoration as a solution to the religious problem in opposition to this 'sectarian Republic, political organ of anti-religious and Neo-pagan naturalism which Masonry imposed on the Nation'.[53]

The Bishops themselves countered with another pastoral (29 September 1922) in their proclaimed endeavour to keep the faithful from error. The CCP was described as a sort of 'sacred union' with full episcopal approval and the faithful were told that true Catholics would follow the Pope on matters other than faith and morals where these affected the discipline and governance of the Church. More plainly, the flock was reminded that Leo XIII had proclaimed the Pope's right to choose the means best suited to political circumstances in pursuit of the good of religion. It would be deplorable indiscipline for subjects to judge their mentors. The faithful henceforth had no excuses for shunning the CCP; indeed not to support it would be to disobey the voice of Christ speaking through the Hierarchy. Furthermore, as Leo XIII had also said, docile submission was especially incumbent upon journalists[54] -- a clear reference to critics like Fernando de Sousa of *A Época* who accused the CCP of unwarranted 'adhesivism' to the Republic.

For its part, the Vatican continued to pursue its policy of *rapprochement* with the Republic and on 13 May 1923, sixth anniversary of the apparition of the Virgin at Fátima, the Portuguese Bishops received public support for their collective stance from Pius XI, who expressed his hope for unity among Catholics in matters concerning religion. Fernando de Sousa became the target of a campaign of vilification but kept on justifying his position in memoranda to the Vatican until 1925.[55]

More exchanges started on 14 February 1925 when the Bishops confirmed the daily *Novidades*, official organ of the CCP since December 1923, as the faithful interpreter of episcopal views and specifically reproved *A Época* for propagating orientations 'incompatible with the instructions of the ecclesiastical authorities'. The CCP's adherents had, in the interests of religion, to abstain from manifesting political opinions but since it was not a very strong political force, it could cooperate with Catholics who regrettably refused to join it. This last grudging episcopal admission of pluralism had however to be seen in conjunction with the actions of the Pope, who in early 1925 rewarded Lino Neto with the Grand Cross of the Order of St Gregory the Great, but declined to receive King Manuel when he was in Rome.[56]

Although there could now be no ambiguity as to what were papal desires, Monarchists did not concede intellectual defeat, especially when they saw bishops hostile to their cause using their authority against it. On 15 March 1925 Barbosa Leão, now Bishop of Oporto, issued a pastoral arguing that, even if it was not an obligation of conscience for Catholics to join the CCP, they were not permitted to attack it. Catholic journalists must obey the Hierarchy and *A Época* must be boycotted for it was his episcopal duty to speak out against anybody playing politics who might lead some of his flock into apostasy.[57]

Leite de Faria, Bishop of Braganza and Miranda, was just as forthright in combatting the 'pernicious errors' of *A Época* and its 'web of sophisms'. Catholics must unite in one army, the CCP: 'A Catholic may refuse to become part of the *Centro*; but he will not be able to justify himself with reasons worthy of a devout son of the Church'. *A Época* was 'the newspaper that had done most harm to the Catholic cause in Portugal' and its 'false shepherds' were 'in open and manifest rebellion against ecclesiastical authority'. Religion came before politics and Catholics must obey the constituted power without any reservations while striving to change bad laws. After deprecatory references to the old PN and the Constitutional Monarchy's treatment of the Church, the Bishop declared:

> The Church recognizes and teaches that citizens have the right to profess such political opinions as seem to them most conducive to the common good, as long as they are not in contradiction to justice or religion. But when, in practice --that is, when translated into external activity-- these opinions, though in themselves honourable, prejudice the religious cause, then the Church, as mistress of truth and morality, teaches her sons that they must sacrifice political activity for there to be no reduction in the contribution they can make to the victory of religion.
> This doctrine is the very expression of Christian good sense, and indeed of common sense.[58]

This episcopal conclusion still did not make good sense to Catholics who were Monarchist activists, such as Alfredo Pimenta of ARP, who had abandoned Republicanism in the early years of the regime because of its religious policy, for they saw their potential strength among the Catholic population being drawn away from them. Pimenta viewed episcopal pressure and CCP policy as blurring the line between obedience to the constituted powers and adhesion to the Republic. Monarchists like himself were as keen to win the Church its rights as the CCP and so the Episcopate should leave them full freedom of political activity. Quoting papal texts, he disputed whether Leo XIII's *ralliement*, designed to prevent separation of Church and State under a Republic, was applicable in the Portuguese case, where laicism was an integral and formal part of the Republican regime, which therefore lacked in Thomist terms legitimacy both of origin and of exercise:

> The doctrinal principles of the Constitution of the Republic are formally condemned by the Church, and fall entirely under the sanctions which the Church formulates in its condemnation...
> The Portuguese Republic has as one of its principal ends, as one of its fundamental objectives, war against Catholicism. It had, it has, and it will have. Because its anti-Catholicism is structural, constitutional, organic: it is in its blood, its nerves, its soul and its life -- because it is of Masonic origin, and Masonry is God's enemy...
> Since it is impossible to reconcile the teachings of the Church with the spirit, the soul, the constitutional structure of the Portuguese Republic, Portuguese Catholics cannot cooperate with it, cannot adhere to it, and the *Centro Católico* and the Portuguese Prelates who counsel such cooperation and adhesion, are committing an error with the most grievous consequences.

Pimenta blamed episcopal policy in sponsoring the CCP --which he knew was papally approved if not instigated-- for the disunity of Catholics. He held to the view that God would be restored only with the Monarchy, colourfully noting that 'the Archangel St Michael, when fighting the Devil, did not join, cooperate, respect, obey the fiendish legions. With his sword of fire, he fell upon the Dragon...'[59]

In a further polemical exchange between the Bishop of Braganza and Pimenta the language became more intemperate and each accused the other of misquotation and mistranslation of texts as well as exaggeration. Pimenta argued that the Portuguese Republic was a representation of sedition according to the teachings of St Thomas Aquinas; and the Saint had considered resistance licit in defence of the common good when it faced sedition. 'Catholics cannot defer to a Republic of this nature. *Non expedit!*' By recommending such deference the CCP and their episcopal mentors were helping stabilize an anti-Catholic regime which was only making overtures to Catholics so as to attract them away from the Monarchists. The Bishop was therefore, according to Pimenta, a pro-Republican using religion for anti-Monarchist political ends.[60]

The tone of these polemics between Monarchists and the post-1919 CCP and its mentors in the Hierarchy demonstrated the deepening division between them. The military coup of 28 May 1926 found the CCP leadership engaged in trying to negotiate with Republicans for further revision of legislation on religious matters -- which may in part have been why Lino Neto later replied 'Yes... No... Perhaps' to a journalist inquiring whether the closure of parliament had dealt a mortal blow to Catholic aspirations.[61] Nevertheless it was one of the CCP's luminaries, Salazar, who indirectly benefitted most from the coup, becoming Minister of Finance in 1928 and in 1932 beginning a thirty-six-year premiership.

By then the hegemonic strain in Monarchist ideology had been dealt a severe blow by the Pope's condemnation in December 1926 of Charles Maurras and the school of the *Action Française* for the doctrinal perversion of putting politics before religion. This condemnation of *politique d'abord*, the Portuguese Episcopate formally pointed out, also applied to those with similar ideas outside France.[62]

Ideological and personal divisions and rivalries within the Monarchist camp remained to plague the exiled Manuel,[63] making restoration of the Monarchy a remote possibility both before and after his death in 1932. Restoration of the prestige, but not the wealth, of the Catholic Church did become a reality, however, with the conclusion of the Concordat between Portugal and the Vatican in 1940, when Salazar was the most powerful layman and his student friend and CADC colleague Gonçalves Cerejeira was Cardinal-Patriarch.

In the case of the First Portuguese Republic, as in those of the Third French and Second Spanish Republics, successive Popes used the power of their spiritual authority to pressure the faithful to work within the legality created by Republican institutions to further the Catholic cause, even when such institutions were in hostile hands. Advocates of alternative courses of political action were tarred with the implications of disloyalty and responsibility for divisions inimical to the Church's success, even though the right of the faithful to choose their own politics was still formally recognized. It proved impossible in an imperfect world where there was no necessary harmony between the spiritual and temporal authorities neatly to demarcate what had to be rendered to Caesar and what to God. Consequently, as in earlier centuries, the Holy See asserted its supremacy in grey areas and complicated situations with the argument that the spiritual took precedence over the temporal in the hierarchy of values. In practice, in all three cases, it was a question of *l'Église d'abord*.

NOTES

*I must record my thanks to the Calouste Gulbenkian Foundation for awarding me a *bolsa* in 1973-74, during which time much of the research used in this essay was carried out.

In the text Portuguese names and titles have been spelt in their currently accepted form; in source-notes authors, titles and publishers have been spelt as on the title-page of the work cited.

1. José Maria da Cruz Pontes, 'Martins Capela e o renascimento tomista em Portugal no século XIX', *Revista Portuguesa de Filosofia*, 32 (1976), 63-90 (pp.64-65).

2. For recent discussion of Leonine strategy see Antonio Acerbi, *Chiesa e democrazia da Leone XIII al Vaticano II* (Milan: Vita e Pensiero, 1991), pp.3-83.

3. Official translation in *The Social Teachings of the Church*, ed. by Anne Fremantle (New York: Mentor-Omega, 1963), p.59.

4. Text of 'Loi de 9 décembre 1905 concernant la séparation des Églises de l'État' in Maurice Larkin, *Church and State after the Dreyfus Affair: the Separation Issue in France* (London: Macmillan, 1974), pp.227-41. For a fairly typical Spanish polemical text, see Eugenio Vegas Latapié, *Catolicismo y República: un episodio de la historia de Francia* (Madrid: Gráfica Universal, 1932).

5. Quoted in Miguel de Almeida (Lavradio), 'The Monarchist Movement and the Declaration of 1911', *Seventeenth Annual Report and Review (1990) of the British Historical Society of Portugal* (Lisbon, 1991), 94-117 (p.98).

6. On the fall of the Monarchy see Douglas L. Wheeler, 'The Portuguese revolution of 1910', *Journal of Modern History*, 44 (1972), 172-93, and his *Republican Portugal: A Political History 1910-1926* (Madison: University of Wisconsin Press, 1978), pp.21-61; Russell E. Benton, *The Downfall of a King: Dom Manuel II of Portugal* (Washington, DC: University Press of America, 1977), pp.47-130; Vasco Pulido Valente, *O Poder e o Povo: a revolução de 1910*, 2nd edn (Lisbon: Moraes Editores, 1982), pp.9-121; and for social and economic factors, Manuel Villaverde Cabral, *Portugal na alvorada do século XX: forças sociais, poder político e crescimento económico de 1890 a 1914* (Lisbon: A Regra do Jogo, 1979).

7. Fortunato de Almeida, *História da Igreja em Portugal*, 4 vols (Coimbra: Imprensa Académica, 1910-24) IV-1 (1917), 379-455; and on the Calmon case, *A Palavra*, 12 February-28 April 1901. For a survey of religious matters in the early part of the century, see R.A.H. Robinson, 'The Religious Question and the Catholic Revival in Portugal, 1900-30', *Journal of Contemporary History*, 12 (1977), 345-62.

8. Manuel Braga da Cruz, *As orígens da democracia cristã e o salazarismo* (Lisbon: Editorial Presença/Gabinete de Investigações Sociais, 1980), pp.63-117; and *Carta encyclica do Nosso Santissimo Padre Leão XIII, Papa por Divina Providencia, aos Bispos de Portugal* (Lisbon: Typ. Castro Irmão, 1886).

9. Alfredo Pimenta, *A questão monarchica* (Lisbon: Edição das Juventudes Monarchicas Conservadoras, 1920), p.23n.

10. Braga da Cruz, *Orígens*, pp.121-237 and 399-421; and João Francisco de Almeida Policarpo, *O pensamento social do grupo católico de 'A Palavra' (1872-1913)* (Coimbra: Centro de História de Universidade de Coimbra, 1977-), I.

11. *Diário da Assembleia Nacional Constituinte*, 27 July 1911.

12. *Pastoral colectiva do Episcopado português ao clero e fiéis de Portugal* ([n.p.]: [n.pub.], 1911).

13. [Padre] Santos Farinha, *Egreja livre: conferencia realisada em 12 de Fevereiro de 1911 na Sociedade de Geographia* (Lisbon: Cernadas, 1911), a lecture by a fashionable and influential Lisbon preacher of Miguelist loyalties attended by Costa. Papal rejection of the French Law of Separation and its *associations cultuelles* was contained in St. Pius X's encyclicals of 1906 *Vehementer Nos* and *Gravissimo officii* (Larkin, pp.172-74, 198-200 and 202-03).

14. *O Dia*, 11 May 1911.

15. For a helpfully annotated text see *Lei da Separação: subsídios para o estudo das relações do estado com as igrejas sob o regime republicano*, ed. by Augusto Oliveira (Lisbon: Imprensa Nacional, 1914), pp.40-111.

16. Text in [Cónego] Joaquim Maria Lourenço, *Situação jurídica da Igreja em Portugal*, 2nd edn ([Coimbra]: Coimbra Editora, [1945]), pp.171-77.

17. Text in Rodrigo Costa, *Brado de justiça* ([Manaus (?)]: [n.pub.], 1912), pp.26-36.

18. A. H. de Oliveira Marques, *A 1ª República Portuguesa (para uma visão estrutural)* (Lisbon: Livros Horizonte, [1971(?)]), p.72.

19. On the incursions see Vasco Pulido Valente, 'Retrato do Herói - Paiva Couceiro: de África á Galiza', *Revista K*, no. 11 (August 1991), 89-128; evidence of clerical participation in Manoel Valente, *A contra-revolução monarchica: revelações, critica, um pedaço de historia* (Oporto: Typ. de J. da Silva Mendonça, 1912); for the King's attitude, Miguel de Almeida, pp.100-07, and Rocha Martins, *D. Manuel II (Memorias para a historia do seu reinado*, 2 vols (Lisbon: Sociedade Typographica Editora, [1916(?)]), II, 320-28.

20. Manuel Galvão, *Dom Miguel II e o seu tempo: notas biográficas sôbre o Senhor Dom Miguel de Bragança* (Oporto(?): Edições Gama, 1943), pp.176-206.

21. In addition to Valente, 'Retrato do Herói', see Joaquim Leitão, *Couceiro, o Capitão Phantasma* (Oporto: Typ. da Empresa Litteraria e Typographica, 1914) and the same author's *O ataque a Chaves* (Oporto: Typ. da Empresa Litteraria e Typographica, 1916).

22. Benton, p.152.

23. 'Offício do Episcopado ao Presidente da República' of 15 March 1913, *Echos do Minho*, 27 April 1913 (supplement); Costa's figure in his speech in the *Diário da Câmara dos Deputados*, 10 March 1914; Vatican source quoted in *Echos do Minho*, 24 November 1912; figure on *cultuais* from *Diário de Governo*, quoted by João de Freitas, *A revisão da Lei da Separação do Estado das Egrejas* (Oporto: Imp. Portugueza, 1913), pp.14-15.

24. *Appêllo do Episcopado aos Catholicos Portuguêses* (Guarda: Typ. Empresa Veritas, [1913]).

25. Marcello Caetano, 'Uma página de história', *A Voz*, 29 January 1966.

26. *A Palavra*, 8-13 and 27 October, 12 November, 3 and 16 December 1910 and 3 January 1911; and Policarpo, pp.6-8.

27. *Liberdade*, 25 April and 8-17 June 1915; and *O Imparcial*, 24 June and 1 July 1915.

28. 'Instrucção Pastoral Collectiva do Episcopado Português', *Vida Catholica*, 5 April-20 July 1917.

29. *Liberdade*, 9-14 August 1917; Braga da Cruz, *Orígens*, pp.264-70.

30. Text in *Revista Catholica*, 25 February 1911.

31. *História de Portugal: edição monumental*, vol VII, ed. by Damião Peres (Barcelos: Portucalense Editora, 1935), pp.59-60.

32. 'O que nós queremos', *Nação Portuguesa*, 8 April 1914, reprinted in Leão Ramos Ascensão, *O Integralismo Lusitano* (Oporto(?): Edições Gama, 1943), pp.171-77; on Integralism see also Manuel Braga da Cruz, 'O Integralismo Lusitano nas orígens do salazarismo', in his *Monárquicos e republicanos no Estado Novo* (Lisbon: Dom Quixote, 1986), pp.13-74, and M. V. E. Cardoso, 'The Ideology of Lusitanian Integralism: Saudade, Sebastianism and Ideology in Portuguese Politics, 1914-1933' (unpublished doctoral thesis, University of Manchester, 1983).

33. Ayres d'Ornellas, *As doutrinas políticas de Charles Maurras* (Lisbon: Livraria Portugal, 1914).

34. Henrique de Paiva Couceiro, *A democracia nacional* (Coimbra: França e Arménio, 1917).

35. Alberto Martins de Carvalho, *Alterações á Lei da Separação das Egrejas do Estado* (Coimbra: Typ. Popular, 1918), pp.188-227; Cunha e Costa, *A Egreja Catholica e Sidonio Paes* (Coimbra: Coimbra Editora, 1921); and on the Vatican connection Egas Moniz, *Um ano de política* (Lisbon: Portugal-Brasil, 1919), pp.111-39.

36. Bispo do Algarve, *União Catholica e Centro Catholico Portuguez: attitude da direcção superior do partido monarchico e da parte da sua imprensa na eleição de 28 de Abril* (Lisbon: Typ. do Annuario Commercial, 1918).

37. Arthur Bivar, *Deus adheriu? Pregunta dum monarchico a proposito do despecho da Restauração de Janeiro* (Braga: Livraria Cruz, 1919), pp.20-22 and 82-123; decrees in Campos Lima, *O Reino da Traulitânia: 25 dias de reacção monárquica no Porto* (Oporto: Renascença Portuguesa, 1919), pp.254 and 264-65.

38. Galvão, pp.283-94; *História de Portugal: edição monumental, Suplemento*, ed. by Damião Peres (Barcelos: Portucalense Editora, 1954), pp.230-33.

39. António Cabral, *El-rei D. Duarte II (Rei morto, Rei posto)* (Lisbon: Livraria Popular de

Francisco Franco, 1934), pp.83-87.

40. *História de Portugal, Suplemento*, pp.411-13.

41. Alfredo Pimenta, *O pensamento político do Senhor D. Manuel II através das suas cartas* (Lisbon: José Fernandes Júnior, 1932), p.29.

42. Barbara Cartland, *We Danced All Night* (London: Hutchinson, 1970), p.170. The suggestion in this source that Manuel lost his throne through popular outrage over a steamy affair with one Gaby Deslys is the product of romantic imagination.

43. C. J. Gonçalves Serpa, *D. José do Patrocínio Dias, Bispo soldado, Beja* (Lisbon: União Gráfica, 1959), pp.51, 147-211 and 284-87.

44. António José de Almeida, *Quarenta anos de vida literária e política*, 4 vols (Lisbon: J. Rodgigues, 1933-34), IV, 11-12 and 291-300.

45. *Diário da Câmara dos Deputados*, 12 February 1924 and 8 and 12 February 1926.

46. *A União*, 19 January and 3-28 February 1920 (*A União* was the official weekly of the CCP).

47. Texts of letters in *Centro Católico Português: sua organização, funcionamento, características, e documentos respectivos* (Lisbon: Ottosgráfica, 1928), pp.33-43.

48. *A União*, 26 June 1920.

49. *A União*, 29 May 1922.

50. Author's interview with Manuel Gonçalves Cardinal Cerejeira, Benfica, 5 April 1973 (Cerejeira was Salazar's closest friend and CADC collaborator).

51. Oliveira Salazar, *Centro Católico Português, princípios e organização: tese apresentada ao 2º Congresso do Centro Católico Português* (Coimbra: Tip. de Coimbra Editora, 1922).

52. J. Fernando de Souza (Nemo), *Acção catholica e política nacional. (Estudos críticos de philosophia politica)* (Oporto: Livraria Eduardo Tavares Martins, Suc., [1922]).

53. J. Fernando de Souza (Nemo), *A religião na Monarchia: a solução do problema religioso na restauração monarchica* (Lisbon: Edição das Juventudes Monarchicas, 1923); on Masonry and the dominant United Lusitanian Grand Orient, see Emm. Borges Graïnha, *Histoire de la franc-maçonnerie en Portugal 1733-1912* (Lisbon: A Editora Lda., 1913), especially chapters 13 and 15.

54. Text in *Centro Católico Português*, pp.43-63.

55. Caetano, 'Uma página'; text of letter of Pius XI in *CCP*, pp.63-64.

56. Braga da Cruz, *Orígens*, pp.301-05.

57. *Boletim da Diocese do Porto*, May 1925.

58. Text of pastoral serialized in *Novidades*, 1-14 July 1925.

59. Alfredo Pimenta, *A Republica Portugueza em face da Igreja Catholica e a politica do Centro Catholico* (Lisbon: Acção Realista Portugueza, 1925).

60. Alfredo Pimenta, *A politica do Centro Catholico e a minha resposta ao Senhor Bispo de Bragança e Miranda* (Lisbon: Acção Realista Portugueza, 1925).

61. *A União*, December 1929.

62. Collective Pastoral of 6 April 1927 in *Novidades*, 21 April 1927.

63. See Caetano Beirão and Francisco Quintela, *Quem são os responsáveis pela desorganização da Causa Monárquica? Carta dirigida ao Sr. Dr. Alberto Pinheiro Tôrres* (Lisbon: Tip. da Empresa Nacional de Publicidade, 1931) and Manuel's letter of 19 July 1927 to the Supreme Council of the CM in Cabral, *Duarte*, pp.158-65.

IBERIANISM REVISITED: JOSÉ SARAMAGO'S
A JANGADA DE PEDRA

MIGUEL ALARCÃO
Universidade Nova de Lisboa

Although Saramago's *A Jangada de Pedra*[1] is not by any means his most popular or universally praised novel, the mere existence of an European Community whose shape and implications are a continuous source of reflection and debate at all levels (take the Danish referendum over Maastricht, for instance) would alone justify, in my opinion, a critical examination of the novel's approach to the matter. Moreover, from a strictly literary viewpoint, *A Jangada de Pedra* certainly displays most of the qualities and features identified by some critics as the novelist's 'trade mark': a prodigious, fantastical imagination; an acute awareness of the possibilities, as well as the limitations, of the act of writing and reading; a distinctive use of intertextuality; a striking irony, bitter at times, whereby through characters and narrator Saramago manages to voice his own social and political concerns; an impressive command of the wide range of resources language can offer, such as registers, word-play, set phrases and proverbs. These features, to name but a few, have already been highlighted by such eminent critics as Maria Alzira Seixo,[2] Luís de Sousa Rebelo[3] and, more recently, Teresa Cristina Cerdeira da Silva.[4] However, a comprehensive critical study of José Saramago remains to be written and it may not be too difficult to guess why. Despite the fact that he is now approaching seventy, Saramago's arrival on the literary scene and his standing as one of Portugal's leading novelists at the present time are a comparatively recent phenomenon.[5]

Before we discuss some of the issues raised in/by *A Jangada*, a brief look at its story-line may be helpful. The sudden appearance of a geological split across the Pyrenees, accompanied by an imperceptible quake, causes the Iberian Peninsula to break off and drift away from the rest of Europe, an event perceived on both sides of the mountains as apocalyptic: the End of the World or, at the very least, a first sign of how close to it one may be. Quakes, one will remember, have long been associated with eschatological visions and millenarian beliefs[6] but, having said that, the prospect is further enhanced by the infernal barking of the hitherto silent dogs in Cerbère,[7] the first example of Saramago's handling of classical mythology, as well as historical, biblical and legendary material. Given Cerberus' role as the watchdog of Hades, the unprecedented barking clearly achieves a symbolic, doom-laden intensity, building up suspense.

Once detached from Europe, the gigantic 'stone raft' starts a transatlantic voyage following an unpredictable route that opens up a whole host of possible scenarios, dangers and outcomes until, at the end of the novel, it eventually stops somewhere between Africa and Latin America (the exact place is unclear). This trajectory is complemented at one stage by a rotation which causes the Algarve to become, albeit temporarily, the northernmost province of Portugal. Luckily, by then the foreign holiday-makers on whom so much of the region's seasonal economy depends have long abandoned its ill-fated resorts.

Once on its way, the course taken by this new island is closely watched by people from all sorts of professional backgrounds and walks of life: scientists, engineers, tourists, television and radio reporters and newscasters, the Press and, above all, the politicians, both national and international, whose ethos, decisions and statements the narrator highlights, thereby managing to focus on the contemporary world scene and expose the sometimes dubious threads that help weave the web of international affairs: false solidarity, irresponsibility, self-interest and the like. The only instance of genuine concern over the fate of Iberia is provided by young people all over Europe, as far afield as Finland and the ex-Soviet Union, who organize rallies and dare proclaim their 'Iberian citizenship' by writing it on the walls (162-66). The whole atmosphere is vaguely reminiscent of May 1968 in the streets of Paris which may or may not have been at the back of the author's mind. Nevertheless, their sympathy and solidarity are branded by the politicians as plain anarchism and ascribed by the youths' parents to juvenile idealism.

The separation of Iberia has understandably a stronger and more immediate impact on its populations whose feelings swing from terror to anxiety, from bewilderment to curiosity. Apart from a few sceptical, down-to-earth characters like Roque Lozano (a curious blend of Sancho Panza and

Thomas the Apostle), the narrator singles out and follows the fortunes of two Spaniards and three Portuguese all of whom, at least once, perform actions or witness phenomena that clearly exceed the limits of human capability and understanding and for which, therefore, no rational explanation is to be found.

Whilst standing on a beach in the north of Portugal, Joaquim Sassa throws a stone at the waves only to see it fall much farther than he could have dared to expect. Although a one-off achievement, his unsuspected strength does recall the feats of Heracles or Samson, both mentioned in the novel (178 and 263).

José Anaiço, for no apparent reason, is followed everywhere by a flight of starlings that only vanish for good when Joana Carda, his future lover, enters the stage. His experience may perhaps find a parallel in the Pied Piper of Hamelin, referred to on page 116.

Joana, we are told, has just moved from Coimbra, her marriage having broken up. Her decision to start a new life is ritually translated by the line she draws on the ground with a twig and which proves to be indelible. At the end of the novel, the twig will be left stuck on the grave of Pedro Orce, the elderly chemist from Venta Micena, whose body can sense the slightest quake whereas the most sophisticated equipment fails to do so. Not surprisingly, since he can actually feel the Earth move, references are made to Galileo (139 and 301).

Finally, Maria Guavaira is a young Galician widow who holds a plot of land which she cultivates herself with the help of two labourers, one of whom has his mind set upon marrying her in the near future. Her episode is perhaps the most exquisite and intriguing of them all. The old blue sock she unweaves produces an enormous thread which in turn forms a blue cloud. Joaquim Sassa who, together with the others, had been led to Galicia by the dog who had run off from Cerbère right at the outset, picks up one end of the thread hanging from above only to find Maria Guavaira holding the other end herself. As far as love is concerned, they are thus (quite literally) tied up.

When considering this episode, two likely influences spring immediately to mind. Maria's loneliness as a widow is, to a certain extent, similar to Penelope's, although the latter has allegedly never doubted Ulysses would return from Troy one day. Furthermore, her harassment by a suitor can be compared to that experienced by the faithful Greek woman during Ulysses' twenty years absence. In the *Odyssey*, the first being to recognize and welcome the Greek hero on his return to Ithaca is his dog, Argus; in *A Jangada*, another dog (named Constante or Anjo da Guarda) acts very much as a match-maker, having travelled all the way from Galicia to central Portugal and back.

It seems also possible to compare Maria and Joaquim to Ariadne and Theseus. Ariadne's thread (mentioned at the end of the very first chapter, 18) is credited with having helped Theseus find his way into the Labyrinth of Crete and out again; in *A Jangada*, as I have said, Maria and Joaquim find themselves holding opposite ends of the same thread. In both episodes, therefore, apart from providing some sort of guidance, this thread is clearly meant to lead to a lovers' reunion.

The somewhat magical nature of all these phenomena --and 'magic realism', with its use of fable and myth, has already been identified as a major literary influence on Saramago's career--[8] is undeniable, although each protagonist would agree that a connection between the quake and their feats is far easier to suggest than to prove, not least due to his/her difficulty in ascribing the rational categories of Cause and Effect. Yet, far more important than the shortcomings of human reasoning is the all-pervading sense of magnetism or inevitability that unites in a common quest (and I am using the word deliberately) three men and two women ... to say nothing of the dog.

Incorporating as it does elements of fable, myth and romance, as I have tried to suggest, it is also important to be aware that behind the outward form of a journey across the length and breadth of the former Peninsula, deeper layers of meaning can be discerned in the novel. Eventful and momentous as the journey itself may be, there is also ample scope for mutual and self-discovery as far as feelings and emotions are concerned; in a sense the voyage without matches the voyage within. Love, friendship, jealousy, solitude, commitment, pity, doubt and fear... all these and more are enriching experiences the protagonists will have to go through, work on and learn to live with. Many of their views and debates turn out to be so remarkably profound that indeed there are times when the characters come across as beings enlightened by some sort of Revelation, not unlike that experienced by the Apostles after the Descent of the Holy Spirit.[9] One is bound to ask oneself:

can it all be due to a mere physical change (however radical) in the surface of the Earth? Or is Saramago trying to preach through these Apostles a different Gospel? The question here is that whatever 'message' the reader may choose to read into the novel it cannot be denied that the quake is the fictional pretext for Saramago to examine the present geopolitical situation of Iberia or, in other words, its status and role in a wider European jigsaw. The conclusion is straightforward enough: if Europe is to present and regard herself as a credible and reasonably homogeneous supra-national entity, there are not simply economic imbalances to be lessened and political, military and environmental measures to be agreed upon and implemented: although often overlooked, there is also a cultural diversity that must be not only safeguarded but nurtured as well. Through the narratorial voice, Saramago seems to suggest that this goal cannot be achieved unless long-standing prejudices and stereotypes cease to exist:

> Os europeus, desde os máximos governantes aos cidadãos comuns, depressa se tinham acostumado, suspeita-se que com um inexpresso sentimento de alívio, à falta das terras extremas ocidentais, e se os novos mapas ... ainda causavam à vista um certo desconforto, seria tão somente por motivos de ordem estética... (160-01)
>
> Ainda que não seja lisonjeiro confessá-lo, para certos Europeus, verem-se livres dos incompreensíveis povos ocidentais agora em navegação desmastreada pelo mar oceano, donde nunca deviam ter vindo, foi só por si uma benfeitoria, promessa de dias ainda mais confortáveis, cada qual com seu igual, começamos finalmente a saber o que a Europa é... (162)

If we bear in mind the Communist Party's staunch opposition to Portugal's application for membership to the EEC in the late seventies, and the fact that *A Jangada* came out in 1986 (the year when both Iberian countries were admitted into the EEC), it will no doubt be very tempting to regard the novel as a political allegory or parable. To put it more clearly, the break-up of the geographical union might signify the desirability, in Saramago's view, of reversing a political option seen as potentially harmful or menacing to the national interest. In the novel, as it happens, the separation of Iberia, widely viewed as a catastrophe at first, leads gradually to its self-sufficiency and independence insofar as the eschatological fears and the prospect of chaos give way to a new order and normality. On the other hand, the rest of the Continent (which, as we have seen, manages to come to terms with the situation remarkably well) ends up expressing concern and regret at such a loss through its young people.

In terms of geopolitical options, the physical separation might also be interpreted as the rejection of the 'Land' (Europe) in favour of the 'Sea' (the Atlantic), a dilemma which, incidentally, António José Saraiva has already dismissed as a false one. In an article inspired by a dispute between Spain and Portugal over the fishing industry and maritime sovereignty,[10] Saraiva argues that such an option on Portugal's part would presuppose the existence of a large, updated and well-equipped fleet which is far from being the case, whether one has in mind naval military exercises, commercial navigation or the fishing industry itself.

Likewise, when one looks at the raft's variable course one may perhaps be inclined to interpret it as mirroring the multiple paths that Portuguese foreign policy may have (or has had) to tread. I shall offer here two examples. When the raft is sailing towards North America and collision seems inevitable, is this meant to be a criticism of or warning against economic dependency in view of the substantial loans granted by the IMF in the early days of the post-revolutionary period? Similarly, the raft's subsequent change of direction down the Atlantic would suggest that no foreign policy can afford commitments to our former colonies to slacken or be obliterated, a view which the recent peace negotiations in Angola seem to substantiate by and large.

Tempting as all these hypotheses may be, the fact is we would still be interpreting this novel and its political overtones through Saramago's ideological stance which would predetermine and justify on its own the set-up of a fictional framework. *A Jangada de Pedra* would then be reduced to little more than an imaginative propaganda exercise.

There are obvious dangers here. Firstly, as we know, too ready a link between an author's ideology and the work of art s/he gives birth to may lead us into falling prey to a simplistic determinism that may ultimately curtail, if not deny altogether, the independence and dignity of artistic creation. Secondly, it must be recognized that the Communist Party's official attitude towards the EEC has changed considerably over the years, former opposition having given ground to discrete enthusiasm and ever-watchful participation in the parliamentary sessions in Strasbourg. True, Portugal's membership is now a *fait accompli* and it was certainly regarded by all successive governments since 1976 as an overriding priority; still, I very much doubt the Communist Party would be prepared to turn back the clock to the point of advocating that Portugal should drop out now. Even if that were indeed the case, we have no reason to assume that Saramago would never dare criticize his Party-political guidelines, should he feel inclined to.

There is one last issue we should address here. The old concept of *iberismo* has, perhaps inevitably, been revitalized by the publication of this novel inasmuch as a dystopian Europe is sharply contrasted, as the narrative wears on, to an increasingly utopian Iberia.[11] The apocalyptic prospects impending at the outset clearly wane once the protagonists decide to grant absolute priority to the apparently pointless, endless quest that has somehow singled them out, rather than the other way round. For the five companions, wisdom lies in learning to accept that no human, logical, rational reasons can be advanced to answer their questions. Like the Apostles themselves, once their old jobs and occupations are left behind and their calling is fully accepted, the former Peninsula's harmony, self-reliance and, as we learn in the last few pages, its universal fertility speak louder than words. The simultaneous pregnancy of every woman is presumably due to this second Genesis as though, by becoming encircled by the waters of the Atlantic, this new Iberia, like a child in the maternal womb, is itself waiting to be born. If we pursue this analogy a little further, I would venture to add that the quake functions as the umbilical cord whose severance constitutes the first step towards the birth of a new autonomous being.

To what extent does this new being personify the concept of *iberismo*, very much upheld by and associated with some late nineteenth-century intellectuals?[12] To start with, one has to be aware that the concept itself is not as consistent or easily definable as might be expected, not least because the term was equally applied to two different political models or envisaged scenarios: one on a federal (or confederal) basis, normally associated with republican and socialist thinkers like Teófilo Braga, for instance; the other, subscribed to by Oliveira Martins, founded on an alliance between two sovereign states. Both, however, shared the aim of rescuing Portugal and Spain from their painfully visible decline since the Discoveries, unlike Central and Northern Europe whose nations, with their enterprising economies, scientific achievements and sophisticated technology, now carried the torch of European civilization. Considering the past grandeur of both Iberian countries, the panorama was all the more humiliating and it was hoped that, whatever form it might take, *iberismo* might provide a solution to their common ills, the causes of which had firstly to be scrutinized thoroughly.[13]

For those who may have suspected Saramago was suggesting some form of *rapprochement* with Portugal's age-old 'rival', it may be appropriate to quote Maria Alzira Seixo who, as early as 1987, addressed the matter by noting that 'o iberismo é aqui (*A Jangada*) menos uma concepção socio-política que uma conjunção casual de esforços num mesmo sentido de sobrevivência'.[14] Unequivocal as the reassurance was, the fact is that suspicions about Saramago's hidden meanings, as we shall see, must have lingered on. Besides, I myself believe that *A Jangada* was partly responsible for an upsurge of interest among the intellectuals in such issues as the Iberian identity or the complex relationship between the two neighbour countries. To prove this point, let us mention two authors: Natália Correia[15] and Eduardo Lourenço.[16]

After reviewing the different races and peoples who settled themselves in the Peninsula throughout the ages and their contribution to a common cultural heritage, Natália Correia argues convincingly that Iberian identity is a product of three basic factors: *continentalidade, mediterraneidade* and *atlanticidade*. Equally illuminating are her views on an 'Absolute Spain' versus a 'Spain of the Spains' as the two historical trends that came to be embodied in Castile and Portugal, respectively. The main problem readers may have to face is, however, Natália's poetical outbursts: her extravagant imagery and penchant for sound-effects, when given their head, can at times disrupt one's attention and indeed obscure the very points the author puts across.[17]

For Eduardo Lourenço, the Portuguese image of Europe, based simultaneously on allurement and resentment, has engendered an inferiority complex which has contributed to a hyperconscious (sense of) identity whose symptoms are, among others, nostalgia and messianism. Whether or not Saramago's readers may accuse him of anti-Europeanism, Lourenço is adamant on this matter:

> Seria longo e deslocado ... expor as razões pelas quais a sua [a de Saramago] quevedesca ou swiftiana ficção de uma deriva ibérica que nos afastasse sem fim dessa Europa, olhada assim como lugar de perdição da nossa alma e da nossa identidade, me parece divertida mas falaciosa. Teria de lembrar que essa Europa onde nos dissolveríamos, frágeis capuchinhos do lobo capitalista e multinacional que ela representa, não é culturalmente ninguém, mas o espaço aberto onde durante séculos não desdenhámos de aprender, de ensinar ocasionalmente e de ser vistos, ouvidos e lidos.
> Se alguma vez este alegórico reflexo de pânico diante do nosso futuro como europeus não se justificou é nos dias que correm. A deriva atlântica já a fizemos. É mesmo a essência do nosso específico europeísmo.[18]

Saramago's own views came to be expressed in two newspaper articles and the simple fact that he published them suggests that he either wished or felt compelled to clarify his position to a public that probably received *A Jangada* as an anti-European manifesto (which would be bad enough) or a pro-Spanish one (which would be even worse).

In the first article, Saramago reflects on the traditional image of Spain as Portugal's archetypal enemy whilst hoping for 'uma relação nova que sobrepusesse ao diálogo entre Estados, formal e geoestrategicamente condicionado, um encontro contínuo entre todas as nacionalidades da Península, assente na busca de harmonização de interesses, no privilegiamento das permutas culturais, na intensificação do conhecimento, enfim'.[19] Taking the point a step further, he stresses the desirability of a permanent and close dialogue with all Portuguese- and Spanish-speaking communities throughout the world as the corner-stone of what he terms *transibericidade*. He then concludes, leaving no room for any possible ambiguity or misunderstanding: 'O iberismo está morto? Sim. Poderemos viver sem um iberismo? Não o creio'.

In the second article, 'Europa Sim, Europa Não',[20] Saramago looks further afield, dwelling on the risks of a narcissistic Eurocentrism, as it may lead to an implicit or explicit belief in Europe's innate superiority over other continents, nations or peoples. Inside the EEC itself, Saramago is only too aware that the greater or lesser degree of economic power can easily be made the yardstick by which the cultural standards of its individual country members are evaluated. The article ends with a singular pledge here quoted in its English version:

> *A Jangada de Pedra*, this novel in which I separated the Iberian Peninsula from the rest of Europe is, needless to say, the outcome of a historical grudge. But I hereby testify that I would be prepared to bring my wandering raft back from sea after having learned something during the voyage, if Europe should acknowledge that she is incomplete without the Iberian Peninsula and make a public confession of the errors, injustices and outrages she has committed. For, when all is said and done, if it is expected of me that I should love Europe as if she were my own mother, the least I can ask is that she should love, and indeed respect, all her children as equals.[21]

It seems to me that nothing whatsoever will allow us to speculate on Saramago's *iberismo* if by that we mean (as we often do) the nineteenth-century vision of a federation or alliance. To do so, one would have to turn a blind eye to a substantially different political context (that of today's Europe) where the Community plays an ever more pre-eminent part. Neither do we have any reason to harp on the old clichés and 'impeach' Saramago for his alleged unpatriotism, simply because being anti-Spain does not make one a better (or truer) Portuguese. In Eduardo Lourenço's accurate verdict, 'o anti-espanholismo é a doença infantil do nosso nacionalismo'.[22]

However, in a sense *A Jangada* does present us with an 'Iberianism revisited', if we accept the fact that the EEC, on top of changing our political commitments (after all, Portugal is no longer *orgulhosamente só*), may well have changed the semantics of *iberismo*, both word and concept. If that is indeed the case, then Saramago's Iberianism, far from posing a threat or being a stigma, is a conscience-raiser, one that offers his readers a double challenge. Firstly, it reminds one of the need to preserve Portugal's and Spain's sense of identity in the broader framework of a Europe without frontiers. Secondly, it invites both countries to rethink and, if need be, rewrite their history and their myths, casting aside any destructive ill-feeling or narrow-minded patriotism if

Iberianism Revisited: José Saramago's *A Jangada de Pedra* 453

only because, as António José Saraiva has pointed out, 'Sem Portugal, a Espanha é uma nação mutilada; sem a Espanha, Portugal é um areal estéril',[23] not even the *jardim à beira mar plantado* we all like to claim her to be.

NOTES

1. All page references refer to *A Jangada de Pedra*, 4th edition (Lisbon: Editorial Caminho, 1988).

2. *O Essencial sobre José Saramago* (Lisbon: Imprensa Nacional, 1987).

3. '*A Jangada de Pedra* ou os possíveis da história'. Afterword to José Saramago, *A Jangada de Pedra*, pp.333-49.

4. *José Saramago entre a história e a ficção: Uma saga de portugueses* (Lisbon: Publicações Dom Quixote, 1989). Originally published as a doctoral thesis, it focuses on *Levantado do Chão* (1980), *Memorial do Convento* (1983) and *O Ano da Morte de Ricardo Reis* (1984).

5. His emergence as a fully-fledged novelist can be dated back to 1980 when *Levantado do Chão* was published but there is little doubt that his popularity increased enormously when *Memorial do Convento* came out three years later.

6. 'Ao lado dos mitos diluvianos, outros relatam a destruição da humanidade por cataclismos de proporções cósmicas: tremores de terras, incêndios, desmoronamentos de montanhas, epidemias, etc.' (Mircea Eliade, *Aspectos do Mito* (Lisbon: Edições 70, 1986), p.51). Originally published as *Myth and Reality* (London: Harper and Row, 1963).

7. In an interview published a few years ago, Francisco José Viegas mentions Deodat de Dolomieu's *Voyages aux Îles Lipari* and its reference to the Messina earthquake of 1876 which was allegedly preceded by the howling of the local dogs, an order having been issued to put them down. See Pedro Borges, 'Francisco José Viegas -- o fascínio pelo policial', *Jornal de Letras, Artes e Ideias*, IXth year, 349, 20 March 1989, p.18.

8. In Chris Baldick's words, 'a kind of modern fiction in which fabulous and fantastical events are included in a narrative that otherwise maintains the "reliable" tone of objective realistic report ... The fantastic attributes given to characters in such novels ... are among the means that magic realism adopts in order to encompass the often phantasmagorical political realities of the 20th century' (*The Concise Oxford Dictionary of Literary Terms* (Oxford: Clarendon Press, 1991), p.128).

9. See the discussion of such topics as 'Normality, (pp.125-26), 'Life' and 'Experiences' (p.261), 'Names' and 'Dreams' (p.264), 'God' (pp.269-70) and Pedro Orce's speech on the Great Chain of Being (p.269) at the heart of which, as Luís de Sousa Rebelo has pointed out, the influence of Plotinus is clear ('*A Jangada de Pedra* ou os possíveis da história', p.347).

10. 'Portugal: o Mar ou a Terra?' in *Expresso*, 714, 5 July 1986, p.8.

11. See Manuel Simões, '*A Jangada de Pedra*: utopia ibérica', *Brotéria*, 125 (November 1987), 604-12.

12. Before assessing the views of individual authors who have dealt with the issue of *iberismo* (a larger task than the one I have undertaken in the present study), a general introduction and some references for futher reading can be found in *Dicionário de História de Portugal*, ed. by Joel Serrão, 4 vols (Lisbon: Iniciativas Editoriais, 1963-71), II (1965), 461-63, and A. H. de Oliveira Marques, *História de Portugal*, 5th edn, 2 vols in 1 (Lisbon: Palas Editores, 1975), II,

106-07.

13. Although more of a 'diagnosis' than a 'cure', we should perhaps remember that Antero de Quental's influential lecture at the *Casino Lisbonense*, delivered in 1871, bore the significant title *Causas da Decadência dos Povos Peninsulares*. These causes, according to Antero, were the Catholic Church as it emerged after the Council of Trent (1543), the existence of an overseas empire as an easy source of often misspent revenues, and absolutism, all of which, of course, helped shape Spanish and Portuguese history alike.

14. *O Essencial sobre José Saramago*, p.54.

15. *Somos todos Hispanos* (Lisbon: Edições O Jornal, 1988).

16. *Nós e a Europa ou as duas razões*, 2nd edn (Lisbon: Imprensa Nacional, 1988). This book won the 1988 European Prize for the Essay (Charles Veillon Prize).

17. See Francisco Belard's review 'A Cena Ibérica' in *Expresso-Revista*, 841, 10-16 December 1988, pp.1 and 23.

18. *Nós e a Europa*, p.36.

19. *Jornal de Letras, Artes e Ideias*, VIIth year, 330, 31 October-7 November 1988, p.32,

20. *Jornal de Letras, Artes e Ideias*, VIIIth year, 340, 10-16 January 1989, p.32.

21. 'A Country Adrift', in *The Times Literary Supplement*, 9-15 December 1988.

22. *Nós e a Europa*, p.8.

23. 'Portugal: o Mar ou a Terra?', p.8.

PUBLIC SERVICE BROADCASTING IN THE UNITED KINGDOM AND SPAIN

BARRY JORDAN
University of Nottingham

In the annual MacTaggart lecture, which opened the four-day Edinburgh Television Festival at the end of August 1992, Michael Grade, chief executive of Channel Four, ended the eerie public silence which has long shrouded the United Kingdom's most important cultural institution. In a quite unprecedented and extraordinarily vitriolic attack, he accused the BBC Board of Governors of operating a 'pseudo Leninist' management style (a reference to their secretive, highly interventionist policy), which was stifling talent and diversity, undermining staff morale and putting the organization on a course of 'terminal decline'. He then alluded to Sir Michael Checkland's rather effusive decription of the BBC as 'a billion pound business', regarding this as a wholly unacceptable expression of support for commercialism over other concerns. He also admonished the Corporation's new plans for 'distinctive programming' and its commitment to occupying the 'higher ground' as an 'elitist', 'Alice in Wonderland' policy, which represented an abdication of its public service responsibilities. Such scathing remarks were greeted by some media wags as an expression of sour grapes in that Grade was not considered for the job of Director General which the then deputy director, John Birt, would take up early in 1993. Marmaduke Hussey, Chairman of the BBC Board of Govenors dismissed Grade's remarks as 'total rubbish' and 'wild accusations that don't stand up'.[1] However, Grade's critique nonetheless brought to the surface a number of issues which another BBC Board Member, Lord Gordon Lennox, was quick to acknowledge. Gordon Lennox admitted that some members of the Board were rather unhappy about its secretiveness (especially in its appointments), its lack of accountability and its unusual eagerness to involve itself in managerial decision taking. What was needed was a whiff of glasnost, a re-democratization of the Board and a return to its main function, that of defending the public interest rather than the interests of the accountants or the government of the day. Morever, Gordon Lennox was careful to stress that another of the BBC's primary obligations in its programming was to cater for 'all classes ... and all interests' and not merely for an élite. Such elitism, he remarked had thwarted the operation of public service broadcasting in the USA, a model which the Corporation was coincidentally monitoring very closely. In the absence of broad, universal programming for all, he argues, how could the BBC defend the principle of a compulsory, universal licence fee?[2]

That the ex-director of programmes for the BBC should raise the issue of editorial control should not surprise us, given the battering which the Corporation took during the Thatcher years and its apparent readiness to acquiesce to political pressure. That Grade should touch upon fundamental matters of the BBC's identity and purpose and accuse it of reneging on its public service mission is perhaps rather more suprising, given its perceived public image as the mother and model of all public service television broadcasters. For Grade, staunch defender of 'broad television programming' and 'producer independence', the Board's obsession with costs, commercialism and management discipline is increasingly thwarting notions of public service and consumer choice, and, as we bump along the floor of the recessive 90s, perhaps marks the beginning of the end of public service broadcasting in the United Kingdom as we know it. In view of the BBC's recent deal with BSkyB over football transmissions and other arrangements with commercial operators in the pipeline, Marmaduke Hussey's words may be prescient: 'The new world which we have to think about is going to be composed of many different television channels and radio channels. We have to define the arguments for a BBC that is funded by a universal and compulsory license fee'.[3] One of the virtues of Grade's remarks is that they have forced on to the agenda a range of issues concerning the nature and direction not only of the BBC but also of other national television services over that next decade or so. In particular, they have put a spotlight on the concept of public service television in the United Kingdom and encouraged debate over the definitions and parameters of what constitutes a public television service. In this essay, and taking the case of the BBC as a point of reference, I would like to examine some of these issues in relation to the situation as it has developed in Spain since the beginning of television broadcasting in the 1950s.[4] My interest lies in determining the extent to which, under a pluralist, democratic and increasingly de-regulated Spanish system, based predominantly on advertising, the definition of the public interest has become more a matter for the conglomerates and advertisers than the official regulators and audience pressure groups. Before examining the Spanish experience in more detail however, I should like to explore the notion of public service, bearing in mind the example of the United Kingdom.

Public Service and Broadcasting: Some Diverging Views

What does the word 'public' mean in the context of broadcasting? If broadcasting is defensible as a public service then it can only be as a service to the public. Of course, different constituencies differ in their approach to this question, giving rise to considerable confusion. For example, the broadcasters themselves see the defence of the public interest as a major priority but this is invariably deflected in terms of their own immediate interests, that is, in relation to the defence of their jobs, their particular franchises or the justification of the licence fee. The politicians pay lip service to the notion of the public good, but often regard the operations of the television services in terms of a conspiracy directed against them and thus against the public service that they see themselves as representing; as a result, the media have to be made 'responsible' in their output and 'disciplined' in their treatments.[5] The relation between politics and broadcasting thus becomes one of manipulations and pressures, overt and covert, especially in regard to news and electoral coverage. As for the academic constituency (such as Hall and Williams, for example),[6] the media have been seen by and large as a loose but nonetheless linked network of manipulators; audiences are routinely misled, conned or hoodwinked, given only a partial and highly selective view of a more complex reality. The role of education and indeed academic analysis is therefore to inculcate a set of critical reading habits and an awareness of how these manipulations take place. As for audience pressure groups, such as the Broadcasting Standards Council in the United Kingdom or Mrs Whitehouse's Viewers and Listeners Association, their particular interests tend to focus on the defence of certain notions of morality, especially in regard to the televising of pornography and use of bad language. All in all, when invoking the concept of public service, certain dominant and very powerful institutional views on the role of broadcasting seem to emphasize notions of social control, cultural standardization and ideological misrepresentation.

Public Life of Broadcasting

Here, in the light of the above remarks, I would like to take up a view developed by Paddy Scannell that broadcasting might be regarded not simply as the terrain on which powerful and antagonistic sectional interests struggle for ideological or political dominance but in terms of a form of public good.[7] That is, a form of cultural life or representation which plays a crucial role in maintaining the basic plurality of late capitalist society. Scannell derives his definition of public good from some of the writings of Jürgen Habermas; in particular his notion of a historically-evolved 'bourgeois public sphere' which, in its operation since the Enlightenment, has contributed to the democratization of everyday life. Though clearly limited in its cultural and class parameters, Habermas's concept is useful in focusing on a set of cultural practices and modes of lived experience which form a public arena, a space in which a certain economic and political body expresses itself and exercises its relative dominance.[8] In a similar manner, so Scannell argues, we might regard the output of national broadcasting (in this case, the BBC) as another public sphere with its own parameters, purposes, rules and effects and whose main obligation is to function as a public service. In this connection, the notion of public service can be viewed in relation to the nature and 'mix' of programme output. The latter, the organized output of television production, can be seen as a kind of public life, a public sphere which arises through the televisual creation of 'real world' events and public occasions, such as the Coronation, the 1966 World Cup, the toppling of the Berlin Wall; that is, outside events made available by television to the public. This public life also exists in terms of the many forms of output produced by and within organizations; or example, a chat show, a game show or a political interview. The interplay between these forms of output (outside broadcasts, internally produced shows) may be seen as constituting the public life of broadcasting. Of course, such a public life, a televisual culture, would be pointless without regard to the audience, a general public on whose behalf this public life is routinely accessed and produced.

Public Service Broadcasting

Clearly, in any definition of public service broadcasting, one of the fundamental prerequisites must be the provision of a series of *mixed* programming on national channels *available to all*. The television authorities must see it as part of their basic commitment to the notion of public service to make programmes available to anyone with a receiving apparatus anywhere in the country. Such an investment is also a sign of commitment to the notion of a national audience, whose interests are placed above strictly commercial criteria. Obviously, where commercial criteria are dominant, broadcasters will provide a service only to the most profitable markets, usually densely populated urban areas that can deliver large audiences to the advertisers without too much difficulty. Likewise, the markets for cable will be sought and developed in the more affluent areas; the poorer areas and remoter regions will be ignored. So, one marker of public service is the universal distribution of television services. The other fundamental prerequisite is the supply of mixed programme services to a nationwide audience. Here, I refer to a wide mix of programmes delivered on a single channel, such as news, current affairs, chat shows, game shows, quizzes, soaps, sitcoms, police series, major drama, documentaries (involving social issues, history, science, wildlife), as well as religious programmes, children's programmes, ballet and sport. As mentioned above, broadcasting brings into being a televisual culture in common to whole populations. Of course, economic and political pressures threaten to fragment television services into multi-channel options (cable, satellite) owned by entrepreneurs and conglomerates. Such services tend to rely on low-cost repeats of popular Anglo-American series, feature film or generic programming (that is, where all the material broadcast by a particular channel is of the same kind). This is the type of programming we find in American cable services, such as the subscription film service Home Box Office, as well as MTV and CNN News. Generic programming has the effect of fragmenting the general public into particular tastes and markets, which advertisers are increasingly keen to target. In so doing, it threatens the idea of equality of access for all to entertainment, information and culture in a common public domain. The proponents of these more recent forms of television output will argue that their product helps to enhance rather than limit consumer choice and that in the future consumers will choose what they want and pay for what they get; they will not require a Board of Governors to monitor their choices for them. Of course, consumers are by no means all equal in their purchasing power. Moreover, the growing privatization of information, culture and entertainment may lead to the creation of a two-tier society of those who, precisely because of their differential purchasing power, are rich and poor in such resources. This seems to undercut the basic democratic principle which underlies the notion of public service broadcasting. The latter clearly depends on a public right of access for all to a wide and varied range of common information, entertainment and cultural services carried on nationwide channels. This should be seen as an important right of citizenship in a democracy. It is a means whereby common knowledges and pleasures in a shared public life can be maintained and recycled as a social good and in principle would seem to be worth defending.

Television in Spain

If the debate in the United Kingdom over the future of public service broadcasting has only just begun in earnest, in Spain it has long formed part of the complex background against which television operations are conducted. Of course, one of the key terms in the United Kingdom scenario is absent from the Spanish debate; that is the issue of the licence fee, which does not apply and is not used as a means of financing public television. In this sense, because it does not pay a licence fee, the Spanish viewing public does not have a direct contractual obligation with the national supplier of television output, an obligation which would obviously inform the nature and mix of the programming. The public interest and the concept of public service are thus defined in the absence of a universal and compulsory fee linking programme policy and output to the consumer. Indeed, since all television services in

Spain are funded predominantly by advertising revenue, the notion of public service is more problematic and the defence of the public interest tends to be left to the government of the day, to its committees and to a much smaller extent to audience pressure groups, as we shall see. And unlike broadcasting services in the United Kingdom, whose political outlook and varying allegiances are officially neutral but in practice more subtly expressed, Spanish television services, largely because of the legacy of Francoism, remain highly politicized. In the case of the national broadcaster, for example, *Televisión Española* (TVE) is rarely out of the media spotlight and its operations, the role of its managers and the behaviour of its political masters are constantly under scrutiny. In July 1992, for example, Pilar Miró, ex-Director General of TVE, was finally cleared of the charge of restocking her wardrobe through the unlawful appropriation and misuse of public funds.[9] At the same time, Javier Arenas, media spokesman of *Partido Popular* (PP), accused the present Director General of TVE (José García Candau) of engaging in more than 30 instances of 'irregularidades financieras', mainly in the contracting out of programme production to independent producers.[10] Such accusations form part of a long-running campaign by PP to discredit not only Candau but also TVE's *Consejo de Administración* and, moreover, to embarrass the governing party. Corruption, malpractice, alleged embezzlement, theft, political control and bias, are hardly news when it comes to the operation and management of Spanish television. In this sense, little seems to have changed in TVE's internal functioning since the dictatorship. At the same time, during the transition and after, successive governments have been unwilling to sacrifice the considerable advantages of political patronage they inherited from the dictatorship over appointments in the television industry. They have therefore maintained a significant degree of political influence over the medium, often under the guise of defending the public interest. Not surprisingly, current opposition parties such as PP also invoke the public interest in their campaigns to discredit the management of TVE and the probity of the governing party. As Equipo Reseña quite correctly point out: 'Estamos en el vicio impertérrito de que la televisión monopolística del Estado tiene que ser la televisión monopolística del partido en el poder'.[11] In other ways of course, things have changed quite fundamentally and although the two main national television channels remain the effective fiefdom of the party in power, Spain has become a diverse, competitive, multi-channel and indeed multi-media broadcasting arena. If anything, these developments have complicated rather than simplified the terms of the debate, alluded to above, concerning the relationship between television as public service/public good and the pressures of commercial imperatives. The following notes are an attempt to show how Spanish television has dealt with this issue and to suggest how it might fare in the future.

Television and Dictatorship

There is hardly any need to point out that, under the watchful gaze of General Franco and those ministers, such as Arias Salgado, who supervised their operations, the media in post-Civil War Spain were without exception controlled by the state by means of laws, regulatory measures and frequently through the state ownership of outlets, such as newspapers and radio stations. Indeed, in order to supervise the flow of information into and out of the country, laws passed in 1938 and 1939 defined the press and radio as national institutions subject to state control.[12] Such blanket interventionism did not exclude the entry of private interests into the media arena. But if private companies wished to establish press or radio outlets, they had to undergo the arduous process of applying for administrative licences, a bureaucratic exercise inevitably facilitated by the workings of *enchufe* and bribery. The development of television in Spain would thus take place against this background of total governmental control. When the first official television broadcasts began in Spain, on 28 October 1956, the service was established as a public state monopoly dependent on the government and funded by the state from its *Presupuesto General*. Spanish television thus emerged as a tool of government, a product of Francoist *dirigismo* and indeed its original sin, as Bustamante points out, is to have been subject to implacable political intervention.[13] What is perhaps less well known, as Macía reminds us, is that right from its inception and unlike most other European services, Spanish television followed the American example by accepting advertising and from approximately March 1958 began earning revenue from those primitive *rótulos* or *cartones* used in its incipient *spots publicitarios*.[14] Thus, while in the rest of Europe we find the rise of national television services conceived to a greater or lesser extent in terms of a public service, the system which emerges in Spain already responds to commercial as well as international pressure, but always in harmony with the political interests of the Francoist state. Absent from the Spanish experience, at least under the dictatorship, would be any attempt to help foster an educated, well-informed and demanding viewing public. Indeed, the regime required the exact opposite from its population and this repressive, xenophobic and paternalistic legacy would inevitably permeate the attempts, after the fall of the dictatorship, to challenge the power of the central state and indeed to disengage broadcasting from the apparatuses of state control. It may be worth recalling that there was an attempt in the late 1950s to raise revenue by means of the introduction of a licence fee or 'canon', then priced at 500 pesetas. However, through a mixture of public resistance and administrative apathy and incompetence, the collection of the fee was never fully implemented or developed into a workable system and it was thus left to wither away a decade later.[15] To sum up, television in Spain developed historically almost in tandem with television advertising, with commercial considerations as well as political ones forming an integral part of the agenda of successive Ministers of Information and Directors of Television. Politically controlled, centralist, lacking legitimacy and public confidence during the dictatorship, how would TVE purge itself of its Francoist heritage and construct a de-politicized, public service profile appropriate to a modern, pluralist, democratic society?

Television after Franco

As Philip Deacon has clearly shown,[16] the Constitution of 1978 provided the main reference points for the post-dictatorship debate over the nature of television services in Spain. In Article 20, the Constitution guaranteed freedom of expression for all, the freedom of the press, radio and television and the dissemination of ideas, in and out of the country, without censorship. It also recognized and protected the rights of the different linguistic communities in the country and foresaw their eventual access to the media.

At the same time, however, Article 38 also recognized and saw fit to protect the exercise of free enterprise, an obligation which would have far-reaching consequences in the broadcasting sphere. And finally, in Article 128, Clause 2, under the rubric of public sector activities, the Constitution proceeded to define broadcasting as an essential public service requiring governmental regulation if not support. It is the apparent contradiction in the Constitution between the acceptance of free enterprise and the freedom of expression on the one hand and the designation of national broadcasting as an essential public service on the other which has led to severe legal confusion ever since and numerous appeals to the Constitutional Tribunal, especially from interested parties in the television business who want to establish their own channels. Indeed, constitutional guarantees on the defence of private enterprise and the freedom of expression would seem to remove any obstacles to interested groups wishing to enter the media arena.

Perhaps the most important move in the regulation of the media in Spain came in 1980, when the *Estatuto de la Radio y la Televsión* became law and provided a new structure for existing television and radio services. The Statute reasserted the right of government to control the media through various committees. However, the new law said nothing regarding the rights of private enterprise and the eventual introduction in Spain of commercial television.[17] Under the terms of the 1980 Television Statute, *Radio Televisión Española* (RTVE) was established as a public corporation in order to provide television and radio services to the country through *Televisión Española* and *Radio Nacional de España* (RNE). RTVE was thus given the monopoly over the two terrestrial television channels, TVE1 and TVE2. RNE had one AM network and four FM networks, one of which broadcasts different programmes in the regions. Both TVE and RNE, the two branches of the national corporation, would be governed by an Administrative Council comprising 12 members of parliament, chosen proportionally according to relative party strengths. The role of the Administrative Council would be to respond to and finally approve plans regarding the general principles and policies to which all broadcasting should broadly adhere. Separate advisory councils for television and radio were also established. The Advisory Council would have the opportunity to present opinions and reports to the

Administrative Council regarding programming policies. Ultimate responsibility for the service rested, however, with a Director General, who appointed the chief executives of the television and radio services. The post of Director General, needless to say, was a political appointment made by the party in power; of course, if and when parliament was dissolved, the incumbent would cease to hold office. As regards policies for the regions, in each of the autonomous communities, there would be a regional advisory council of RTVE which would advise and report to the regional RTVE executive on matters of broadcasting policy and practice. However, even during their relatively short existence, it is widely believed that neither the national nor the regional advisory councils exert much influence on the management of television and radio services, although there was the arguably exceptional case of a recent Advisory Council Report being highly critical of certain aspects of television output in the province of Navarre.[18] The 1980 Television Statute, which gave birth to RTVE, also foresaw the need to allow the autonomous communities to express their regional identities through the establishment of their own regional television services. To this effect, in December 1983 and under a socialist government, a law was passed which provided the legal basis for the establishment of the so-called 'tercer canal' in the various regions.[19] What is perhaps surprising is that the new law on the third channel was pre-empted by almost a year in the Basque Country, where *Eusqual Telebista* was set up in January 1983. Soon after, Catalonia developed its own third channel, TV3 (January 1984) and then Galicia, TVG (July 1985). Since then other third channels have come into being: Andalusia (*Canal Sur*), Valencia (*Canal 9*), Madrid (*TeleMadrid*); moreover, both the Basque Country and Catalonia have created their own fourth channels, without any clear legal basis, it seems, and other regions are in the process of negotiating their own third channels. Let it be remembered that these third channels (fourth in two cases) are dependent on the authority of the parliaments of the autonomous communities and thus, not unlike the national channels, subject to political pressures.

In 1988, after a long period of debate and numerous opposition amendments over the terms to be imposed on private television,[20] the Spanish Parliament finally passed a law allowing the goverment to grant licences to three private television channels. Their remit would be national although part of the terms of the licence would require them to provide a parallel service in terms of regional programming. Virtually all opposition parties argued that the limitation on only three commercial channels be rescinded and that the television arena should show a far greater degree of competition and deregulation. The government refused to consider any change in this regard, already conscious perhaps of the potential pressure on advertising revenue three new operators would bring. Ownership of the companies had to be predominantly Spanish; moreover, an emphasis was placed on domestic output, that is, 15 percent of output was supposed to be produced 'in house' and at least 40 percent drawn from Spanish or European Community production. Such apparently stringent targets were to be attained over a three year period. Initially, the PSOE bill also included the provision of a supervisory body for the new commercial stations but this was later dropped, a move which perhaps belied the government's full commitment to the defence of standards and public service. The licences were awarded in 1990, intitially for a ten-year term, to *Tele 5* (a Berlusconi-backed station) and to *Antena 3* (both dependent on advertising) and *Canal Plus* (a subscription service or pay-television channel). These commercial channels, like their national cousins, would be obliged to observe the same fundamental principles as outlined in Clause 4 of the 1980 Statute. So, in broad terms, at present Spain has two public channels, three private ones as well as regional channels dependent on the governments of the Autonomous Communities. Save for the subscription-based Canal Plus, all channels depend financially on advertising revenue. It is also useful to recall that since 1990, TVE no longer figures, at least officially, in the General State Budget; in the regions, however, as previously mentioned, television financing derives from a mixture of commercial advertising and subsidies from the Autonomous Community budgets.

Public Service versus Private Enterprise

As we have seen, the designation of national television as an essential public service was enshrined in the Constitution, despite the fact that the same

Constitution also acknowledged and defended the principle of private enterprise and thus the freedom of private television operators to enter the market. Moreover, as Deacon has shown, during the period of debate and negotiation over the introduction of commercial television in Spain (1978-88), the PSOE as well as the PCE consistently rejected demands for the establishment of a *Comisión Nacional* for television, preferring Parliament to to be the controlling body.[21] During the 1980s, the PSOE government maintained its position, anxious to ensure its own political control over the media rather than establish structures which would keep 'big government' at arm's length from the broadcasting services. Not surprisingly, the main opposition parties and pressure groups have claimed that the government has effectively 'nationalized' the main national services and monopolized what should be a basic human right. In the ensuing struggle over the regulation of existing television services and the introduction of commerical television, the concept of public service has unfortunately become identified with the political interests of the governing party; and the PSOE government shows no sign of relinquishing control in favour of a new regulatory body. To a considerable extent, this 'top down' management style also affects the operations of the *canales autonómicos*, in the sense that regional channels (whatever the political complexion of the regional government) are subordinate to RTVE in Madrid and cannot act independently when Madrid demands priority in transmission.[22] Notwithstanding such political influence, there are numerous legal norms and official guidelines governing the operations and output of all broadcasting services, which spell out in some detail the obligations of the broadcasters towards the public and the public interest. It is worth considering these in a little more detail.

According to the Preamble to the 1980 Television Statute, television and radio services are regarded as crucial public services on two main grounds: firstly, they are seen as essential vehicles for the provision of information, participation of citizens, formation of public opinion, access to and advancement of the educational system as well of the language and culture of Spain's regions and communities; secondly, they are viewed as essential means for protecting the rights and freedoms of minorities as well as women. Such ideas endorse civic values, national and regional identities and the protection of minorities. Taking into account the context in which these norms were drafted (1977-80), they were no doubt inspired by desirable political objectives whose role was crucial in the drive to consolidate democracy in Spain. Article 4 of the Statute presents a series of recommendations which apply rather more specifically to programming content and general policy. It proposes the following principles: information should be true, objective and impartial; information should also be distinguished from opinion, and where necessary the identity of the opinion holder should be revealed; respect for social, cultural, political and linguistic pluralism; respect for privacy, reputation and the good name of the individual; protection of children and young people; respect for the principles of freedom and equality outlined in Article 14 of the Constitution. Underlying these principles, there is clearly a desire to break with the past, to separate the operation of the media from the state and make them more responsive to the needs of the individual, the regional communities and the various minorities and thereby enhance their democratic and pluralist outlook. However, if the UCD government of the day took it upon itself to uphold and guarantee the democratic functioning of the media, it still retained considerable power in making key appointments, a power which tended to bring into question such democratic principles and does so to this day.

Once the 1980 Statute had been ratified and this had been made law, let us not forget by a UCD government, the RTVE Administrative Council produced a further series of Principles and Guidelines for the operation of television and radio services.[23] Published in 1981, these guidelines fell into two main categories, those 'basic' ones which applied to all programming, and those which applied to more specific areas of broadcasting. Paramount among the general guidelines were the democratic and civic values underlying the Constitution of 1978 and the active promotion and protection of those values by the media. Also important was the need to foster support for national unity and solidarity among all Spanish citizens while respecting the linguistic, cultural and political rights of regional communities. The media were also encouraged to promote dialogue and debate as a means of settling disputes, to encourage a respect for the authority of public institutions, to explain to the public the problems of the national economy (in order to avoid the association between democracy and economic instability -- a serious problem in the early 1980s) and to show that the media reflect life as well as promote the participation and cultural enrichment of the citizenry. Once again we find the broadcasting services involved in what only can be seen as a pseudo-political role, that of disseminating and thereby helping to consolidate the underlying principles of the Constitution and thus its pluralist, nationalist, democratic ethos. With regard to the regions, the statements of principle which have informed the establishment of the autonomous television services largely repeat the above guidelines. Most include articles which refer specifically to the protection and promotion of regional languages and cultures and thus to the goal of reinforcing regional identities as far as possible. Of course, the introduction of the 'tercer canal' in the regions has by no means been a straightforward process, with central government anxious to avoid political manipulation of services in the 'normalización' of the language as well as too much competition over advertising revenue.

Other rules and guidelines developed in order to ensure standards and protect the public have been produced with regard to advertising.[24] Up until 1988, advertising was regulated by the *Ley General de Publicidad* (LGP), first promulgated under Franco in 1964 and designed largely to protect the regime's institutions, its notions of good taste and standards of good conduct. The LGP was modified in 1988 and in 1990 it was accompanied by a series of norms on Advertising produced by TVE's Administrative Council. The 1990 norms are therefore the main guidelines which regulate most media advertising in Spain. Apart from condemning the use of advertising to incite or otherwise promote bad behaviour, disorder and violence and protecting standards of good taste, especially in regard to language, these recent norms have focused specifically on the promotion of alcohol and have imposed a series of restrictions on presenting alcohol in terms of personal, physical and particularly, sexual success. In this connection, there exists little or no legislation or formal guidelines regarding the portrayal of sex and violence on the small screen. Such guidelines that do exist have to be found in legislation passed in 1977 and 1982 in relation to film. Here, the main provisions have to do with controls on the exhibition of films whose main subject is sex or violence; these carry an X rating and can only be exhibited in special auditoriums with specific numbers of seats and with advertising confined to the inside of the premises. Guidelines for the regulation of pornographic material in relation to young people rely on Article 20.4 of the Constitution which recognizes the need to defend public morality against the corrupting effects of material which undermines 'the basic principles of collective sexual morality'.[25] The fact that there is no specific rule book on the broadcasting of pornographic material on television has allowed both the national and the commercial channels, aware of the need to capture audiences and increase market share, to broadcast material of a type which borders on the pornographic. Well-known recent examples are TVE's scheduling of films from the Emmanuelle series at times of the day when young children would still be watching; Canal Plus also decided to broadcast films which had already been shown in X-rated theatres and would normally be confined to such places. Such activities have certainly given rise to criticism and have tarnished the image of the broadcasters; yet, so far there appear to be few effective controls over these developments.

As we have seen, Spanish broadcasting is not short on legislation and sets of norms to provide a framework within which broadcasting activities ought to take place. However, many of these norms and guidelines exist at the level of general principles and have not been elaborated into more specific commitments and policies. Indeed, so far the Spanish system has not been able to bring forward an effective method of regulation of programme output; nor has it managed to re-define the notion of public service in relation to the more complex multi-channel and multi-media situation. Machinery to police the system and to speak up for the public interest is either too politicized or simply unavailable. Of course, in principle, the Administrative Council of RTVE has considerable authority and wide-ranging powers to oversee the operations of the national channels. However, because of its composition and the fact that its members are mainly chosen from the political parties, its activities tend to focus on the politics of broadcasting rather than on the maintenance of programming standards. And as previously mentioned, the Advisory Councils linked to State and regional televison, that is, the lower level regulatory bodies, have signally failed to step into the breach and make an impact on standards. The introduction of commercial television in Spain should have been a golden opportunity to take a serious look at programme standards and introduce some form of regulatory machinery which would oversee the commercial channels and take the other existing channels into account. Sadly, the government missed the opportunity and apart from guidelines on ownership, advertising and defence of home-produced programmes, the law failed to pujt in place a credible supervisory body for the new commercial sector. Obviously, the commercial channels are bound by the principles of the 1980 Statute; moreover, the 1988 Law does indeed stipulate that violation of the norms on advertising and programming will result in sanctions being imposed by the government to regulate the amount of advertising and programme quality. Here, as in other areas, there has been no effective regulation or action. Where the government seems reluctant to get involved, Spanish people themselves are beginning to develop their own organizations and pressure groups in order to monitor and improve programme quality and standards. Indeed, a National Federation of Viewers' Associations has recently emerged as an umbrella organization whose aim is to press government and the commercial operators to be more accountable on specific programming issues.[26] The demands of the Federation include: exclusion programmes dealing with sex and violence from prime-time scheduling; the exercise of more control over the use of obscene language; the need to avoid promoting certain stereotypical images as desirable role models; the non-exploitation of women as advertising stereotypes and sex objects. Other bodies are beginning to throw their weight behind this viewers movement, including the Catholic Church, with a view to putting pressure on the advertisers and their sponsors.

Conclusion

Earlier in this study, I tried to define the notion of public service in terms of a kind of public life produced or created by television output. The latter, following my definition, was based on the principles of universal distribution of output and a wide and varied range of information, entertainment and cultural services carried by national channels. It was my contention that such public output constituted a public good and that this should be defended as a right in a pluralist democracy. As we have seen, owing to the recent upheavals in United Kingdom broadcasting, the definition of this right as well as its defence have become the object of an increasingly acrimonious and polarized public debate. Indeed, as recent events have shown and in the wake of Michael Grade's acerbic criticisms, the BBC management team has come under even greater pressure to spell out its position and outline its vision of the Corporation's future, especially in view of the recent comments made by its former Director General.[27] In a quite unprecedented and astonishing attack on the Corporation, delivered at a Royal Television Society Symposium lecture on the future of the BBC, Sir Michael Checkland began by telling an audience of media professionals that his boss, the sixty-nine year old Chairman of the Board of Governors, Marmaduke Hussey, was simply far too old to be leading the Corporation into the next century. And quite apart from being too old, he was far too remote from the daily realities of broadcasting consumers, as were the majority of the members of the Board of Governors. Checkland also referred to the 'lunatic decision' which had bound him to his successor as Director General, John Birt, for twenty-one months, a handover period which was nothing less than a 'futile transition'. In a lecture which portrayed Corporation at war with itself, Checkland also alluded to other instances of managerial bungling, the likelihood of swingeing financial cuts and the collapse of morale among the staff. Underlying Checkland's outburst was the very real fear that under the stewardship of incoming John Birt, the BBC would be inclined to follow the American model of public service broadcasting. That is, because of increasing financial pressures and difficulties over justifying the receipt of a universal licence fee, it would be forced to deliver a much slimmed-down service, one which would aim to occupy the 'higher ground' of news, current affairs and rather more selective cultural activities. (This is precisely the sort of definition of programming that Michael Grade had earlier criticized as being too narrow and elitist and an abdication of the BBC's public service role. At the same time, it is also the definition which seems consistent with government proposals in the recent Green Paper). In the same lecture, Checkland made a strenuous plea for a clear and unequivocal separation of powers between the management of the Corporation and the Board of Governors, whose role is now the subject of a forthcoming internal review. At last, within the BBC, it seems that the walls of

Public Service Broadcasting in the United Kingdom and Spain   475

silence over internal policy have come crashing down to reveal much bitter and corrosive in-fighting, particularly over the nature and future direction of the service. However damaging this may be in the short term, the gloves are clearly off. This will no doubt provide a context in which matters of policy and the degree of the Corporation's commitment to providing a publically-funded service can be debated in a much more open, serious and realistic manner.

If the notion of public service broadcasting in the United Kingdom is now in the melting pot, afte weeks of muttered curses and public denunciations, in Spain the situation is perhaps rather less fluid. Indeed, by comparison with the startlingly frank pronouncements of Sir Michael Checkland, the approach of his Spanish counterpart, Jordi García Candau, has been positively Anglo-Saxon in its reserve and secretiveness. As mentioned earlier, this has much to do with the fact that, at present, García Candau is under investigation for certain financial irregularities in the way TVE negotiates its programme contracts, documentation on which matter the Director General is still resolutely refusing to hand over to the investigating parliamentary committee.[28]

Leaving these local, legal difficulties aside and returing to the question of RTVE's programming duties and commitments to the Spanish citizenry, there is no doubt that, to some extent, the experience and practice of Spanish television seems to fulfil the definition of public service outlined above. The national channels do indeed broadcast nationwide and attempt to provide a broad and varied service of informational, entertainment and cultural programming. Moreover, they have played an important role in the consolidation of Spanish democracy and at least juridically are enjoined to guarantee the promotion of civic and pluralist values. However, on the negative side, no solution has yet been found to de-politicize the national channels by separating the running of the service from government control and establishing an independent broadcasting authority. Clearly, television is simply too important politically to be given its independence. Nor has there been established any really effective system of regulation. This has meant that programme standards and quality have been at best variable and at worst appalling. Indeed, given the lack of regulatory influences, programme planners from both the private and public services have turned increasingly to sex and violence as a way of delivering audiences to the advertisers. This reminds us of the the central fact that all television services in Spain rely heavily on advertising revenue and, on the whole, commercial criteria tend to prevail over notions of programme quality and public service. In this regard, the existing regulatory machinery (RTVE's Administrative Council and the Advisory Councils) is generally viewed as exercising a political role but having little or no influence on programme standards. This situation has become so grave that voluntary associations, until recently fairly quiescent, are now beginning to challenge the programmers and broadcasters and, in time, will no doubt force politicians and television managers to modify and improve their services and policies. Such countervailing pressure is to be welcomed and it may even have an impact on the advertising industry as viewers' associations campaign against advertisers who sponsor unwholesome programmes. In the final analysis, what is required is a complete re-think by goverment of its attitude towards public service broadcasting and how best to ensure the creation of a non-politicized, independent, universally-available broadcasting system which protects quality and standards. If the notion of 'essential public service' is to mean something more than the vested interests of the party in power, then the government might begin by putting into practice those norms and guidelines already contained in the current plethora of existing broadcasting legislation.

NOTES

1. *The Sunday Times*, 30 August 1992, pp.1 and 4.

2. See *The Independent*, 29 August 1992, p.2, *The Sunday Times*, 30 August 1992, p.4, *The Independent*, 31 August 1992, pp.2, 14 and 16 and *The Independent*, 18 September 1992, p. 6. which documents the resignation of the BBC's Head of Natural History, a 'creative person' who did not like 'being told what to do by accountants'.

3. *The Sunday Times*, 30 August 1992, p.4.

4. As well as *El País*, I have used the following sources for my account of Spanish television: Manuel Vázquez Montalbán, *El libro gris de televisión española* (Madrid: Editorial 00, 1973); Pedro Macía, *Televisión hora cero* (Madrid: Ediciones y Reproducciones Internacionales, SA, 1981); Justino Sinova, *La gran mentira* (Barcelona: Editorial Planeta, 1983); Miguel de Aguilera, *El telediario; un proceso informativo* (Barcelona: Editorial Mitre, 1985); John Hooper, *The Spaniards. A Portrait of the New Spain* (London: Penguin Books, 1986), pp.130-43; Enrique Bustamante and Ramón Zallo (coordinadores), *Las industrias culturales en España. Grupos multimedia y transnacionales* (Madrid: Akal Comunicación, Akal, 1988), pp.109-62; Philip Deacon, 'The Issue of Commercial Television in Spain' (unpublished paper delivered at A.C.I.S. Conference, Bristol Polytechnic, September 1988, 14pp); Equipo Reseña, *Doce años de cultura española (1976-1987)* (Madrid: Ediciones Encuentro, 1989), pp.215-38; Esteban López-Escobar, 'Vulnerable Values in Spanish Multichannel Television', in *Television and the Public Interest. Vulnerable Values in West European Broadcasting*, ed. by Jay G. Blumler (London: Sage Publications, 1992), pp.161-72; Rosario de Mateo and Joan M. Corbella, 'Spain', in *The Media in Western Europe. The Euro Media Handbook*, Euro Media Research Group, ed. by Berut Stubbe Ostergard (London: Sage Publications, 1992), pp.192-206.

5. Heritage Secretary Peter Brooke (successor to the ill-fated but much admired David Mellor, who was regarded by the media professionals as very much an ally) published a Green Paper on Broadcasting in late November 1992 (delayed from September) which spelt out in some detail the Conservative Government's position on the role and future of the Corporation. Some of the main points of the document (60,000 copies of which were produced and distributed at the taxpayers' expense) had already been leaked to the press, particularly the decision to retain the licence fee as the only practicable basis for financing public broadcasting. However, the government saw fit to end the BBC's unique position as monopoly recipient of the licence fee and showed itself anxious to open up the public broadcasting field to other providers. Also, in order to collect the licence fee and regulate public services, the Green Paper suggested the creation of a Public Service Broadcasting Council. Such a Council would require 'service-provision contracts' from public service providers; under this scheme the BBC Board of Governors would be required to fulfil a re-negotiated remit. Moreover, the Corporation was anticipating being asked to reduce its operations to a set of 'core activities' in both television and radio, thus rationalizing its two television channels and its network of local radio stations. Such changes were to form part of a series of 'efficiency reforms' (such as large staff reductions, greater use of independent producers), successful completion of which would be a prerequisite for the renewal of the BBC's charter in 1996. It would have been up to Sir Michael Checkland, the BBC's outgoing Director General, to present the Corporation's response to the Green Paper. Checkland was to have remained at his post until his official retirement date of 28 February 1993. However, in a rather unexpected move, he announced his decision to leave by Christmas 1992, thus

handing over the reins of power to John Birt earlier than planned. It was Birt's responsibility and indeed one of his first major tasks as new Director General to reply to the Green Paper, a process he initiated (amidst a major public scandal over his personal tax affairs (see *The Sunday Times*, 14 March 1993, Main Section, p.9)) by producing and distributing 25,000 copies of the BBC's mission statement 'Extending Choice' to interested parties. The Corporation's response was followed up by well over 5,000 submissions from other organizations and individuals with an interest in the future of the BBC. This consultation process, which has formally come to an end and is threatening to overwhelm the authorities (given the massive amount of paper generated) will probably take a year or more to complete, and will be followed, some time in 1994, by a White Paper outlining the government's final proposals. (See *The Sunday Times*, 8 November 1992, Main Section, p.6; *The Independent*, 11 November 1992, p.4; *The Guardian*, 19 April 1993, Media Section, pp.13-14). As the Minister pointed out recently, the maintenance of the 'status quo' at the BBC was simply not an option. Countering such official rhetoric, it was precisely the managerial status quo of the BBC (including the 'port and cigars' appointment of John Birt) that the Shadow Heritage Secretary, Ann Clwyd, severely criticized, arguing that the Corporation's Board of Governors, seen as unrepresentative and unfairly appointed, should cease playing 'an increasingly active and possibly improper role in internal management' and give way to an independent Board of Trustees. Clearly, the Labour Party is concerned that after one of the most extensive and far-reaching national debates ever held concerning the future of a key national institution, nothing will change and it will still be 'business as usual' (see *The Independent*, 1 May 1993, p.3).

6. See Stuart Hall and others, *Culture, Media, Language* (London: Hutchinson, 1980); Raymond Williams, *Culture* (Glasgow: Fontana, 1981.)

7. Paddy Scannell, 'Public Service Broadcasting and Modern Public Life', in *Culture and Power; A Media, Culture and Society Reader*, ed. by Paddy Scannell, Philip Schlesinger and Colin Sparks (London: Sage Publications, 1992), pp.317-48.

8. Jürgen Habermas, *Communication and the Evolution of Society* (London: Heinemann, 1979). See also, 'Modernity: An Incomplete Project', in *The Anti-Aesthetic*, ed. by Hal Foster (Port Townsend: Washington Bay Press, 1983), pp.3-15.

9. See *El País*, 7 July 1992, p.12 which reminded us that Miró's trial and acquittal in regard of the embezzlement of 8.5 million pesetas and the possibility of a 14-year prison sentence had been 'Un asunto lamentable resuelto con sentido común'.

10. See *El País*, 25 May 1992, p.88 in which Arenas accused Candau of 'Un auténtico despilfarro y descontrol del gasto'. See also *El País*, 2 June 1992, p.64; 9 June 1992, p.62; 17 June 1992, p.65, and 24 June 1992, p.59.

11. Equipo Reseña, *Doce años de cultura española*, p.222.

12. R. de Mateo and J. Corbella, 'Spain', p.193.

13. Bustamante and others, *Las industrias culturales en España*, p.121.

14. Macía, *Televisión hora cero*, p.88.

15. Bustamante, p.123.

Public Service Broadcasting in the United Kingdom and Spain 479

16. Deacon, 'The issue of Commercial Television in Spain', p.2.

17. As Deacon reminds us, this omission partly explains the attempt by *Antena 3*, in December 1980, to set up a nationwide private television service and when that failed, to take legal action against the government via the Constitutional Tribunal, which was also unsuccessful. Even in 1988, when commercial television was finally introduced in Spain, it would still be subject to considerable political control (Deacon p.3).

18. López-Escobar, 'Vulnerable Values in Spanish Multichannel Television', pp.162-63.

19. At the time, as Deacon has shown, the PSOE government argued that an expansion in the numbers of broadcasting outlets would probably increase the pressure of competition for a limited amount of advertising revenue. With more stations seeking a slice of the advertising revenue cake, the assumption was that less money would be devoted to programme production and thus programme quality would decline as cheaper foreign imports replaced home-produced programmes. This assumption has not been altogether borne out since television advertising expanded in the 1980s at the expense of advertising in other media, such as the press (Deacon, p.5).

20. Deacon, pp.6-8.

21. Deacon, p.4.

22. Deacon, p.5.

23. López-Escobar, pp.165-66.

24. López-Escobar, pp.166-68.

25. López-Escobar, p.167.

26. López-Escobar, pp.170-71.

27. See *The Guardian*, 21 October 1992, pp.1 and 18.

28. See *El País*, 6 October 1992, p.56, in which García Candau cleverly exploited the notion of business confidentiality in order to deny Javier Arena, spokesman of *Partido Popular* and member of the Administrative Council, access to RTVE documents, arguing: 'no resulta legalmente exigible acceder a la petición interesada, toda vez que RTVE y sus sociedades tienen carácter de sociedad anónima'.

ASPECTS OF THE NEO-PICARESQUE IN TWENTIETH-CENTURY GERMAN LITERATURE

WILFRIED VAN DER WILL
University of Birmingham

There was a spate of picaresque novels in Germany in the period that followed World War II. They were written by authors who were clearly familiar with the genre. At first sight, however, the most recent generation of *pícaros* lacks certain features one might consider *de rigueur* for the type. For example, they are not constantly in search of food, nor do they have to pit their wits and a good deal of cunning and calculated malice against their fellows and masters in order to obtain the necessary daily sustenance. If, as some interpreters have held, the *pícaro* is essentially associated with poverty and an irreversibly lowly social position,[1] then the question to what extent these novels can legitimately be labelled 'picaresque' demands an answer. Talk of the neo-picaresque would require heavy qualification if a state of destitution were considered integral to the *pícaro*'s life. It is for this reason that we must first turn to the *pícaro*'s historical origins in order to determine what distinctions between the traditional and the contemporary form of the picaresque have to be made.

The text of the *Lazarillo de Tormes*, quite apart from its overt moral charge which is packaged in allegorizing pointers and teaching tracts, evidently carried hidden within it a literary model of great fertility. It might initially have seemed that the picaresque figure could not be imagined without its distinct Spanish background. This was therefore sometimes retained when the picaresque style was adopted in other literatures, as in Alain René Le Sage's *Gil Blas of Santillana* (1735). But French, Dutch, English and German adaptations and re-inventions in the seventeenth and eighteenth centuries soon revealed that the *pícaro* was perfectly capable of life in the other native milieux of Western Europe. Even Spanish authors of the late sixteenth and early seventeenth centuries did not feel constrained by the original picaresque figure. There was a gap of forty-five years or so before the *Lazarillo* was recognized both as a literary type and a mode of narration that might spawn others of its kind. The significant historic interval could account for the fact that the model never became dogmatically prescriptive so that even in the early process of creative exploitation the *pícaro* was immediately subjected to more or less incisive transformations. While this origin of the *pícaro* as a malleable figure might explain its further literary sojourn, its transnational modulations and its national mutations in the two hundred years or so after its first appearance, it is in fact the origin of the *pícaro* that calls for explanation.

The hypothesis that we would advance, without here attempting to prove it in more than outline, is the following: the genesis of this literary type and its subsequent realizations is bound up with the transformation of late medieval to early modern society. In other words, in these novels there is reflected a distinct socio-political macrocontext which is characteristic of much of sixteenth-, seventeenth- and eighteenth-century Western Europe and through which the preconditions for a picaresque intertextuality are established. The times are such that the general acceptance of religious faith and widely held assumptions about the god-given fixity of social position are not yet shaken. However, conceptual, economic and social forces such as the decentring of the earth, the global expansion of trade, and the growth of the merchant class are beginning to threaten the medieval ethos. The new mode of narration is able to absorb, both consciously and subconsciously, observations of ideological fissures, capture the new uncertainties and provide portayals of the disjunctures between moral posture and immoral reality of the high and the low. In order to make its point, this type of novel does not strain for balanced social realism, but rather concentrates on aspects of moral imperfection which are projected in drastic, satirical or grotesque magnification.

In his brilliant essay, 'On Re-Reading the Lazarillo de Tormes',[2] the late Derek Lomax suggested that the novel depicted a background of moral dissatisfaction engendered by a society which was experiencing increased wealth and demanded heightened standards of religious commitment. This thesis decoupled the *pícaro* from an essential association with economic decline and general social poverty. Rather, Derek's essay leads one to infer that the historical moment of the nascence of the picaresque can be characterized as a situation of rapidly growing merchant capital in the ports and the centres of inland trade. Wealth was created on an appreciable scale in sixteenth-century Spain through manufacture (particularly cloth and shipbuilding), trade (particularly wool) and the expansion of agriculture. The economic boom under Charles V favoured the merchant and manufacturing classes. The new wealth brought with it possibilities of swift upward and downward social mobility and it attracted beggars from inside and outside Spanish society. The wheel of fortune appeared to be turning faster. Suddenly inflicted poverty, particularly amongst members of the traditional social orders, sharpened the experience of individual uncertainty. The basic constitution of the life-world began to change in the transition of late medieval to early modern Spain and this change persisted throughout the downturn that the economy suffered around 1600. The early picaresque novel therefore reflects not just the more or less static, 'institutionalized' social marginality which we must assume existed throughout the Middle Ages,[3] but the urban and country milieux of a clergy, a clerisy, an artisanat and a lesser aristocracy that were all particularly threatened by the new developments. These undermined the powerful image, preached throughout the Middle Ages, of a society as a well-ordered hierarchy in which everyone had a fixed place.[4] The image was of the three orders or of an organic body politic in which the higher and the lesser organs lived in symbiosis and hence in fundamental harmony. While these images were of the stuff that ideologies are made of, they had an inherent persuasiveness which contributed to social stability, however precarious in reality this may have been. However, the appearance of the picaresque genre reflected social changes and signalled a changing structure of sensibility which was less prepared to accept as true the image of the hierarchically ordered society. These narrative accounts showed, from a conservative or reformist point of view, that there were dissonances which plainly upset the idea of social harmony.

The picaresque narrative was therefore anchored in the social experience of the harsh realities of a period of transition. But this type of narrative was not programmatically anti-traditional. It by no means set out to challenge the values of feudal society fundamentally. Rather, it expressed concern over the degree to which these values were flouted by various representatives within the feudal hierarchy. The early Spanish picaresque novels did not directly attack the image of the well-wrought social structure in which all human beings shared community on the basis of their acknowledged inequality. Instead, the authors provided fictional autobiographies which exposed the social and moral degeneracy not merely of the individual protagonist but of a wide range of representatives from various niches of a social fabric that was clearly cracking. The picaresque novel, first created when Spanish society was in economic upswing, reflected not poverty but the hypocritical blight that befell the accepted value system, and it registered distortions to which the individual characters were subjected when they tried to worm their way out of social marginality back into the recognized society of orders. This type of novel offered itself as a narrative device for dealing with large amounts of action centred on one figure illustrating the instability of social position and a threatened decay of the feudal-Christian code of values. We can only speculate as to why it took over forty years before the *Lazarillo* found a successor (*Guzmán de Alfarache*). The fact that it had been put on the index by the Inquisition will certainly not have acted as any kind of stimulant for would-be imitators. But after the first novel had finally been recognized as a matrix pregnant with other possible realizations, the picaresque mode became firmly established as one of the archetypes of narration. It was incorporated in the techniques which could be drawn upon by authors of the seventeenth and eighteenth centuries to assist the narrative imagination and to deal with social changes and shifts in perception from medieval to early modern society. This hypothesis also serves to explain why the picaresque narrative made the rounds in Western-European societies. It established a literary pattern which could be recognized even when some of its constituent parts were varied. It ought perhaps to be conceived as a literary cluster growing out of late medieval and early modern perception, capable of being remodelled by individual authors and absorbed in different national traditions.

These general considerations are so far not designed to shed any distinguishing light on the neo-picaresque. On the contrary, we have suggested a limited time span, from the sixteenth to the eighteenth centuries, for the evolution of the picaresque, defined by criteria of socio-economic history. Our hypothesis would lose all plausibility if it was not specifically formulated to apply to a particular period. Indeed, F. W. Chandler[5] and many of the subsequent studies of narrated roguery talk of the erosion of vital features of picaresque fiction quite soon after it had been established in Spain. In particular, Scarron's *Roman Comique* dispenses with the master-servant relationship, and in Grimmelshausen's *Simplicius Simplicissimus* the stress appears to be on a succession of adventures rather than on the fate of an opportunist thief. Chandler held that the original picaresque form had been exhausted by the middle of the eighteenth century at the latest. This leaves us with three choices with regard to twentieth-century picaresque novels. We must either modify our hypothesis to encompass these modern varieties, or furnish a fresh hypothesis for the re-appearance of picaresque figures and modes of narration, or we must altogether abandon the notion that there is such a thing as the neo-picaresque.

It is very difficult to do the latter when one looks at the evidence. The drole figure, the opportunist genius of survival in difficult circumstances, even the calculating little thief eager to make his point, are all present in twentieth-century literature. One of the most famous is Jaroslav Hasek's *The Good Soldier Schweik* (1926). This figure is introduced as one 'who, having left the army many years before, when a military medical board had declared him to be chronically feeble-minded, earned a livelihood by the sale of dogs -- repulsive mongrel monstrosities for whom he forged pedigrees'. These opening remarks immediately point to a low-class person who has to use all his wit and cunning to find a marginally profitable existence. However, for all Schweik's similarities with the traditional *pícaro*, the novel also makes plain that this renaissance of the picaresque is governed by a single, overriding motivation, namely to show the difficulties not just of the physical survival of the individual but more especially of preserving his individuality and human dignity. The neo-picaresque signals a shift beyond the marginal figure's search for an integrated life within established society at whatever cost to his moral and social dignity. Instead, authors choose the picaresque mode of narration to explore the safeguarding of moral integrity against the corrupting influences of bureaucracy and ideology. Jaroslav Hasek's *Schweik* has become a classic example of this narrative project.

Schweik was fathered by an author who hated the repression of the Czechs within the Austro-Hungarian Empire. The satirical arrows of his humour are directed not against the frailty of human nature but against the 'organizational support structures of human existence, the conventions and institutions governing intersubjective relations'.[6] Such conventions and institutions ossify, become superseded by the dynamics of real life and then act as atavistic obstacles to it, unless they are abolished or altered and brought in line with present needs. Institutions which have become detached from real life reduce men to mere tools of an incomprehensible authority that demands the carrying out of obscure commands. Observations of this kind may have been particularly acute in a multi-national state which was held together by the power of a bureaucracy and a military that had forged these nations into a mock-symbiosis, just as it held together in artificial fusion vestiges of feudal-absolutism and the expanding presence of modern capitalism. *The Good Soldier Schweik* is neo-picaresque in its fierce anarchism and calculating satire of authority, but the social background which it describes is not that far removed from *Lazarillo* or *Guzmán*. Schweik still has to go through the humiliating experience of being a servile underling, practically a piece of property, whose masters may sometimes sell him or lose him at cards to other masters.[7] The limited intelligence of the protagonist, the master-servant relationship, the near-feudal aspects of life in Austria-Hungary, the old-fashioned Catholicism of the social milieu, the changing environment and the different superiors with whom Schweik has to accommodate himself, all retain features of the traditional picaresque novel. However, Schweik is not faced with a straight choice between integrity and physical survival, but between making a cunning stand against complicity with superiors and being robbed of his individuality and dignity by their humiliating idiocy. In Schweik's eyes superiors are merely the character masks of ideological and political power.

While for Lazarillo everyone is a potential enemy who must be outwitted to ensure survival, Schweik's enemies are quite specifically army officers, civil servants, and members of the Austro-Hungarian aristocracy. Brecht's adaptation of the Schweik-figure in his play *Schweyk im Zweiten Weltkrieg* (1943; Schweyk in the Second World War) stresses the fact that times have changed to make it too difficult even for the most cunning survivor to succeed. The totalitarian control of society leaves no space for the little man's satirical teases of the representatives of power or their lethally heroic ideology. Schweyk is acutely aware of the cleavage between 'the ordinary people' and 'the great men'. It is the latter's chief design to get the lesser folk into the history books merely as a dumb mass capable of attracting honour only as a pliable tool to augment the glory of the 'great men'. Schweyk's comment is this: 'The little man shits on great times, he wants to go to the pub a little and he wants his goulash for the night'.[8] Paradoxically, kowtowing to power is the only way of prolonging life: 'In such times you do have to knuckle under. It's a matter of practice'.[9] A sentence like this shows the miserable philosophy of the cornered picaroon. It seems to indicate a reversion to the traditional picaresque choice. But even knuckling under does not help. At the end of the play Schweyk disappears in a snowstorm near Stalingrad, having been recruited by Hitler's army. The lesson is clear: under totalitarian conditions mere cunning cannot protect the individual from perishing.

In stark contrast to Schweyk's sombre demise Thomas Mann's *Bekenntnisse des Hochstaplers Felix Krull* (1910/1953; Confessions of Felix Krull, Confidence Man) shows a figure of sunny disposition within materially privileged surroundings. The protagonist's cunning is displayed within a social context where it is not sheer physical survival that has to be secured. Rather, Felix Krull is shown as a sophisticated manipulator of his own identity to enable him to advance to a higher class. As a confidence trickster he is able to overcome the limitations of his background (bankrupt bohemian bourgeoisie) by enacting the manners of a young nobleman. His language is modelled on the smooth parlance of the aristocracy. As is indicated by his first name, Felix is privileged by good fortune and manages to be master of his own dispositions, even though he has to work his way up from positions of lowly service (liftboy, waiter) before he can pass himself off as a count. When he steals it is only because the opportunity is exceedingly tempting or because rich ladies want to be stolen from by him. His main occupation is to steal himself into the hearts of other people by artful deception; he is a 'Herzensdieb' (thief of hearts) in a metaphorical sense.

It is not possible to rank this novel as picaresque unless it is conceded that a modern metamorphosis of the genre has taken place. Traditional picaresque features are certainly in evidence (journeying, stealing), but they have undergone profound transformation and been put in a new context. In the Spanish picaresque novel the cheekiness with which the protagonist insists on reference to himself as the first and foremost person constitutes an ironic counterpoint to the insignificance of his social standing. To reach the same effect, Thomas Mann inflates Krull's ego by allowing him to evoke Saint Augustine's and Rousseau's confessions even in the title, quite apart from having the narrator indulge in continual self-praise of his inborn talents. Felix steals, like many of his petty-thieving ancestors, but he does not do so out of sheer hunger. Stealing is part of the artistic opportunism with which Felix exploits and explores the possibilities of his own protean character in an effort to go beyond the limitations of individuality and reach out into an existence of Dionysian joy, of 'pan-eroticism', as Thomas Mann puts it.[10] The first-person narrator wishes to give an account of his life and in so doing he acts as a 'chronicler and analyst of décadence' (Th. Mann, *Betrachtungen eines Unpolitischen*), revealing society's moral corruption to legitimate the protagonist's actions. Social grace and love of beauty are projected as extra-ethical categories. A Nietzschean 'only-art-can-justify-life' is at work here and the *pícaro* has become a narcissistic aesthete, one who lives in the high noon of his histrionic self-manipulation. Consequently, Krull's perspective as first-person narrator can throw ironical and satirical spotlights on aspects of social reality (as when he deceives the army doctors to avoid military service) but that reality remains substantially limited to remnants of feudal aristocracy and a leisured bourgeoisie before World War I. The theme of bourgeois decadence and its reproduction by a mimetic *pícaro* ultimately encapsulates the novel in a bygone age.

It is clear that Thomas Mann's novel is a conscious modulation of the picaresque matrix: 'The narrative, presented in the form of memoires, belongs to the type and tradition of the novel of adventure whose German archetype is *Simplicius Simplicissimus*'.[11] Apart from this 'archetype' Mann is credited with having known *Gil Blas*, but might not have read the Spanish examples of the genre. He was, however, a comprehensive *poeta doctus* and cannot have written in ignorance of the narrative possibilities afforded by the picaresque style. His main source for the novel, the Romanian Georges Manolescu's *Ein Fürst der Diebe. Memoiren* and his *Gescheitert. Aus dem Seelenleben eines Verbrechers* (A Prince of Thieves. Memoirs; Failed. Inside the Psychology of a Criminal; both published in Berlin in 1905) furnished

Mann with an example of the modern rogue which clearly became very influential for the elaboration of the Krull story.[12]

Similarly, other German authors played with the picaresque genre after 1945 and refashioned it to suit their own narrative purposes. Rudolf Krämer-Badoni did so in his novel *In der großen Drift* (1948; The Great Drift). Albert Vigoleis Thelen's first novel, *Die Insel des zweiten Gesichts. Aus den angewandten Erinnerungen des Vigoleis* (1953; The Island of the Second Vision. From Vigoleis's Applied Memoirs), owed much of its stylistic artistry to familiarity with the picaresque tradition. The author had strong connections with Mediterranean culture. He had lived in Mallorca in the early 1930s, partly as a guide and partly as Count Kessler's secretary. The book is a mixture of the author's authentic autobiography and the narrator's fictional one. Author and narrator are close, but not quite interchangeable. Tantalisingly the author's imprimatur states right at the beginning: 'All characters of this book live or have lived. But here they figure only in the redoubled consciousness of their personality, including the author...' The narrative itself is an exercise in reflection on contemporary experience: emigration from Germany to Holland, thence to Mallorca and further to France and Portugal, always with German and Spanish Fascism as the political backdrop. Apart from the protagonist's roving life there are other traditional picaresque features. Vigoleis is concious of 'not being of memorable birth'.[13] In other words, the worm's eye view of world affairs is assured. The near-bankruptcy of the financial arrangements supporting the narrator's life furnish reminiscences of picaresque poverty. But, true to the neo-picaresque pattern, the story is about physical suvival only in the sense that the protagonist and his friends have to give the slip to their Fascist persecutors, be they Nazi or Falangist. Vigoleis has left-radical and anarchist leanings. His wit is not entirely sufficient to guarantee him his life, reaffirming the element within the neo-picaresque formula that the subversive intellectuality of the rogue may afford him some protection against being corrupted by the ruling ideology, while the threat to his life remains. Vigoleis is saved by the arrival of a British destroyer offering to take political refugees from Mallorca.

The most important and best known German novel in the neo-picaresque mode is, of course, *Die Blechtrommel* (1959; The Tin Drum) by Günter Grass.

The author himself has been somewhat ambiguous in acknowledging this literary heritage. In an interview in 1970 Grass appeared to dismiss it in one sentence only to end up acknowledging it in the next: 'It is certain that neat little labels like "the new picaresque novel" are not at all helpful. The book [...] stands in an ironic and detached relationship to the German *Bildungsroman*. It is strongly connected with that European novel tradition which stems from the picaresque novel with all its refracted derivations'.[14] Grass then goes on to reel off an impressive, though not exhaustive, list of authors in whose tradition he would consider it legitimate to set *The Tin Drum*, such as Rabelais, Fischart, his sixteenth-century German counterpart, Grimmelshausen, Sterne, Goethe, Jean Paul, Joyce, Dos Passos and Döblin. It is clear that Grass's chief interest is to prevent his novel from being seen in an all too narrowly defined literary tradition. This is a legitimate concern, but it cannot absolve literary historians from establishing vital connections with a historically established mode of narration, while giving due recognition to the originally modern aspects of the author's work. Grass's own argument, far from denying this, supports the notion that the picaresque narrative has become an asset within the literary heritage which can be inter-culturally appropriated and modified under specific epochal circumstances to absorb other aspects of the narrative tradition and to serve contemporary authorial intentions.

Yet many literary historians have argued that the protagonist of *The Tin Drum*, Oskar Matzerath, cannot be classified as a modern *pícaro*. Foremost among them is Hans Mayer, who holds that Grass's hero can neither be seen as a 'successor of *Gil Blas of Santillana* nor of the Goethean Wilhelm Meister'.[15] Surprisingly, Oskar is interpreted by Mayer as entirely separate from society, a character without development and not involved in social conflict. Instead, Oskar is seen as an artistic construct, 'pure consciousness almost non-corporeal',[16] in order to facilitate 'the satirical novel of a modern representative of the Enlightenment'. In other words, Oskar's dwarfishness and his idiosyncratic behaviour are narrative devices to unmask 'the underside of a family, a town, a petit-bourgeois stratum'.[17] If this were true, then *The Tin Drum* might at best be understood as a very limited panorama of life in Danzig and Düsseldorf from the 1920s to the 1950s, whose distortions and absurdities would have to be attributed solely to a grotesque dwarfish observer.

In stark contrast to the above, John Reddick considers this kind of satirical reflection on society as quintessentially picaresque. He identifies Oskar's detached, unemotionally cold perspective, his super-cleverness as the 'brainbox Oskar' and equates this persona with 'picaresqueness'.[18] While in substance this argument is akin to Mayer's, it leads to quite a different and arguably more correct literary-historical location of the novel. Yet there are aspects of Reddick's interpretation which must be challenged. For neither does Reddick see any need to distinguish the traditional from the modern *pícaro*, nor does he define Oskar's 'picaresqueness' any further then 'an ostentatious mask' of the narrator to support his role as an outsider. In Reddick's view the *pícaro* dupes society, avoids social involvement and maintains a position of invulnerability and intellectual aloofness. This is, however, only one side of Oskar, according to Reddick. Far from striking any agreement with Mayer, he perceives another set of characteristics in Oskar which motivate this figure to become involved and emotionally entangled. Hence Reddick's suggestion that Oskar also exhibits a 'tears persona', which is radically different from the position of picaresque detachment. One scene in which this 'unpicaresque emotional involvement' is said to reveal itself is when at his mother's funeral he wishes to be buried with her.

There can be no doubt that Reddick's is the more comprehensive of the two interpretations. But it, too, remains unconvincing because of its rigid division between Oskar's alleged picaresque observer status and his tragic existentialist involvement in the narrated story. Such conceptual rigidities breed inevitable contradictions. For example, why should Oskar's intervention at a Nazi rally, when he spreads confusion in the Party orchestra with his subversive drumming, be the deed of a detached 'watcher, not a doer',[19] and hence be typically picaresque, while his desire to find solace in merging with the earth and his mother's rotting bones[20] or in creeping under his grandmother's skirts,[21] 'close to my poor mama's beginnings',[22] just after the funeral, be non-picaresque? Images of the *pícaro* wishing to merge with mother and seeking to return to the womb can easily be recognized as stemming from a desire to shrink back from the alienation and harshness of the world with which he is faced and to strive back to a realm of innocence and oblivion. Proceeding by a mostly precarious birth from this realm, the *pícaro* soon becomes resentful of being irrevocably separated from it. For example, just after Christian Reuter's Schelmuffsky has decided to leave his mother's womb, four months prematurely, he exclaims 'O damn! how desolate is this world!'[23] He then goes on to say: 'I was fully intent on returning to the cavity again, but, the devil be damned, I couldn't find my way back from whence I came'.[24]

It is evident that the conditions of modernism under which the neo-picaresque appears are quite different from the late medieval and early modern times of the traditional picaresque story. However, it should also have become clear why it might be attractive for contemporary authors to seize on the picaresque and modify it to suit their distinctly modern purposes. Rather than interpret the traditional picaresque novel as a satirical onslaught and a subversive revolutionary critique of society it was suggested initially that we should understand it as a description of human fortune on the margins of established society and a lament on the deteriorating morals of a changing society of orders. Marginality is portrayed in the traditional picaresque novel neither as a privileged space nor a desirable life style. On the contrary, the fictional autobiography is often employed as an instrument of the fictive narrator to give an account of the miseries of his life in order to justify his present position. In contrast to this, the neo-picaresque revival of the genre varies this narrative pattern by putting a new accent on marginality as a position of relative safety from incorporation and seduction by ideology. It acts as a guard against being swept away by mass hysteria or becoming trapped by a burgeoning state bureaucracy. However, marginality does not provide an ultimate safe haven from these scourges of modernism. The desire of the modern *pícaro* to be an ordinary and accepted citizen, able to live without his individuality, integrity, dignity and humanity being threatened, ultimately remains a utopian hope or a paradisiacal dream. The lures of conformity are in any case too subtle and the realities of modern life too all-pervasive to make him (or her) immune from the guilt of sharing in them.

Yet the modern picaresque narrative allows protagonists to be shown as indefatigable subversives within the typical adversities of mass society. In a world of ideological mass-manipulation and material seduction the modern *pícaro* can be stylized as a figure of ideological nonconformism, of the virtue of poverty amongst the seductions of affluence and as a secular saint who defends his integrity by insisting on a strict abstinence from the corrupting influences of material affluence or spiritual incorporation by mass ideologies, be they denominational or party-political. All these possibilities of the picaresque (and more) are rehearsed in a variety of novels which I referred to at the beginning.[25] They are mostly of post-*Tin Drum* (that is, post-1959) vintage, although some were conceived earlier, and there is evidence that they have learnt not only from the picaresque tradition but also from each other, which is sometimes acknowledged by barely concealed references. For example, in *Casanova oder der kleine Herr in Krieg und Frieden* (1966; Casanova or the Little Man in War and Peacetime) by Gerhard Zwerenz there is a literary invective against a 'small kid with dark hair, a remarkable moustache and an explosively protruding Adam's apple'. This is easily recognizable as a reference to a creature concocted of Oskar Matzerath in *The Tin Drum*, Joachim Mahlke, the hero of Grass's novella *Katz und Maus* (1961; Cat and Mouse) and the appearance of Günter Grass himself. The invective is an ironical vote of thanks to an acknowledged master.

Zwerenz's protagonist, Michel Casanova, is characterized in the novel as 'the type of man who is absolutely unadjusted' to the social system. He swears never to allow himself to become trapped by it and to 'spit on its catechisms and its one-way streets'. His idea of freedom is to follow his phallic desires and to fight convention and prudery. His idea of paradise is to live in happy promiscuity and this is illustrated in the novel by the story of the Casanovites. Another author, Paul Pörtner, uses the protagonist, Tobias Immergrün, in his eponymous novel (1962; Tobias Evergreen) as a kind of marionette demonstrating the degree to which the individual has become an object 'turned inside out, ironed into shape, massaged, cut to size, turned on its head, straightened out, made to stand upright and to walk forward' by modern advertizing, the military, and his work situation. Martin Beheim-Schwarzbach's *Die diebischen Freuden des Herrn von Bißwange* (1964; Herr von Bißwange's Thieving Joys) turns the traditional feature of the *pícaro* as a frequent thief into a practice of ideology-critique and anti-bureaucratic strategy. The hero steals neither out of physical need nor because he is a random kleptomaniac, but because he wants to confuse those in authority. He targets government offices to take away important rubber stamps. A member of parliament has the manuscript of his speech temporarily taken so that it can be amended by the subversive hero. A tenor finds his signed photographs stolen. The aristocratic *pícaro* projects an extreme degree of self-control and asceticism. His acquisitions are a protest against the immorality of contemporary acquisitiveness, the corruptions of the state administration and the personality cult of the media. The novel originally bore the title *Der Unheilige* (the Unholy One). This was clearly not meant to indicate a figure beholden to the devil but one who cultivated an idiosyncratic integrity outside canonical sainthood. Here again, the vital neo-picaresque features are in evidence, in that a consciously anti-ideological commitment is coupled with outsiderness so that the protagonist can keep at a mental distance from the 'outer-directed' crowd.[26] The neo-picaresque anti-hero is thus an ingenious literary development: recognizable as a derivation from the traditional picaresque hero it enables contemporary authors, especially perhaps in Germany, to deal with the modernist ravages of extreme alienation in general and the castigation of the Fascist past in particular.

Grass's Oskar Matzerath, however, is a figure who least easily fits into this clear-cut definition of the ideologically disengaged protester occupying a position of social marginality. Grass's picaresque protagonist is socially involved and he thus shows that the extensions of the neo-picaresque embrace greater complexity. To be sure, the traditional picaresque mode of narration is most succinctly defined in *The Tin Drum* by its narrative perspective from below and by its employment of fictional autobiography, with the *pícaro* as a narrative centre of an ensemble of episodes seen through his obviously limited consciousness. The narrative can be seen to be governed by the narrator's interest to take stock of his life or to attempt to justify, obscure or distort his past actions. As fictive author the *pícaro* is at all times so overtly in control of the narrative that the reader is left wondering at every turn to what extent the narrated figure might not be a deliberately false projection. However, beyond these traditionally picaresque determinations of the narrative the real fascination of the central figure is generated by its calculated ambiguity as both detached observer of German society from the late 1920s to the early 1950s and as a conformist participant of Germany's Nazification. Grass's real genius is to exploit to the full a paradox that can be traced back to the very earliest picaresque novel. It matters little that Grass probably did not know it at the time of writing *The Tin Drum*, for the pattern occurs in later picaresque novels also. There is, on one hand, the narrating Lázaro's desire to be part of established society and, on the other, the portrayal of his younger self, Lazarillo, as a roguish existence buffeted about by cruel social circumstance. Yet there is a vital difference between the traditional and the modern depiction of the *pícaro*. The progression from the immature Lazarillo to the mature Lázaro is one of relentless dehumanization without much of a struggle against it by the protagonist. In the neo-picaresque novel that struggle, though predetermined in its outcome to go against the integrity of the individual, is the central theme. Oskar's deformation as a hunchback after 1945 physically visualizes the deformations he and his generation have suffered as a result of involvement with Fascism and war.

In order, briefly, to illustrate Oskar's role as observer and protesting critic I refer to the section, mentioned earlier, where he gives an account of his destructive drumming, ranged mainly against the 'brownshirts' at Nazi rallies, but also against other political and ideological colours and conventicles:

> For several years, until November '38, to be exact, my drum and I spent a good bit of our time huddling under rostrums, observing successful and not so successful demonstrations, breaking up rallies, driving orators to distraction, transforming marches and hymns into waltzes and foxtrots.[...]it was not only demonstrations of a brown hue that I attacked with my drumming. Oskar huddled under the rostrum for Reds and Blacks, for Boy Scouts and Spinach Shirts, for Jehovah's Witnesses, the Kyffhäuser Bund, the Vegetarians and the Young Polish Fresh Air Movement. Whatever they might have to sing, trumpet, or proclaim, my drum knew better.[27]

Against this comprehensive scepticism in regard of all ideologies we have to hold Oskar's complicity. Grass himself suggested, that the figure is to be understood as a 'mouthpiece' of a petit-bourgeoisie seduced by Fascism.[28] He actively contributes to the entertainment of the German troops on the Western Front. One of his abnormalities is to be endowed with a voice that can shatter glass. Invaluable assets of French culture and art perish under his destructive attacks, which are clearly analogous to the brutal destruction wrought on France as a result of Nazi aggressiveness:

> My number was conceived along historical lines. I started off with glassware from the reign of Louis XIV, and continued, like history itself, with the reign of Louis XV. With revolutionary fervour I attacked the crockery of the unfortunate Louis XVI and his headless and heedless Marie Antoinette. Finally, after a sprinkling of Louis-Philippe, I carried my battle to the vitreous fantasies of the Third Republic.[29]

Just as the traditional *pícaro* embraced the duality of roving rogue and settled family man, so the modern *pícaro* embraces that of ideological critic and accomplice of the status quo.

I hope to have shown that the interpretation of Oskar Matzerath as a modern *pícaro* has the advantage of neither having to foreshorten nor to inflate the meaning of the many symbolical, allegorical, ironic and satirical images used in the text. It also does not lead to a loss of interpretative representation of narrative complexity. The value of recognizing the picaresque style and the picaresque figure as a hermeneutic reference becomes evident when one compares it with other interpretative procedures. For example, portraying Oskar as the archetypical petit bourgeois[30] means losing sight of his deviance in the role of the dwarfish cretin, which allows him to gain a protesting distance to the small-shopkeeper milieu of his family and to ideological movements in and around Danzig. Portraying him as some kind of chthonic god[31] entails the failure to see his embeddedness in a specific historical environment and that in fact he never achieves communion with the life-forces in his mother's and grand-mother's womb. His critical intellectuality makes him singularly unfit to be passed off as a Dionysian dwarf come to enrapture society by the rhythms of his drum. Oskar is a marginal man, severed from the soil, the integration with family, the world of the adults, religious faith and all integrated and integrating relationships with other human beings. As a figure suspended between different nations and political ideologies he has but one desire, namely to maintain his sollipsistic separateness for fear of too much involvement. This is true both of the narrated Oskar and Oskar the narrator who in his mental asylum wishes to have the dividing bars of his bed raised against visitors, his minder, Bruno, and the 'guilt-laden life' of the general public. But it is precisely in his attempt at forging for himself a narcissistic value system, in contradistinction to the values of the social environment, that he becomes enmeshed by guilt and conformism, tying him back to his petit-bourgeois provenance. By clinging to his role as a cretinous three-year old he has to live in constant fear of a master race intent on liquidating its imbecile off-spring. He thus causes his mother untold grief, ultimately driving her to depression and death. By the same strategy, screaming for his drum, he is instrumental in his Polish father, Jan Bronski, becoming trapped in the Danzig post office where he is rounded up and killed by the Nazi Home Guard. In his instinctive conformism he knows that at the time of the Nazi ascendancy it is best for him to deny any possibility of being in any way affiliated with Poland. Similarly, he rids himself of his German Nazi father only when the Russians invade and when it is opportune to deny any associations with Nazism. There is considerable reluctance on the part of the authorial Oskar to own up to his involvement in guilt. True, he mentions his participation in a number of incriminating acts, but then tries to fool the reader by making them look like accidents or chance happenings. These narrative ruses ultimately fail to convince the reader because from the beginning Oskar is gifted with a super-alert awareness, fully conscious of what he is doing at all times. His cretinousness is a mask behind which he attempts to hide both his guilt and his critical faculties. Oskar's social disengagement, like that of the small-shopkeeper stratum from which he originates, is at all times overlaid with a tacit political and ideological complicity with Fascism.

Against this background of factual social reference which underlies the text of *The Tin Drum* the narrative perspective of provincial self-centredness seems designed to obscure all connection with the wider historical context. The fictional autobiography is presented as a story of an individual, a family, and an entire class seemingly oblivious to the history by which they are all engulfed. Superficially they appear enclosed in a world moved and motivated only by its own indigenous forces. Within this world Oskar is projected as a trivial genius and a genius of triviality, manically preoccupied with stereotypical notions of the half-educated mind. Just as after the end of the war he is used as a motif in modelling groups in Düsseldorf to illustrate one element in a more or less contradictory pair such as 'The Beauty and the Beast', 'Madonna and Child' he harbours an ideology of primitive dualism, of drives and intellect (*Trieb und Geist*), Rasputin and Goethe, man and woman, good and evil. These polarities determine Oskar's view of history as a game of self-cancelling forces, absurd in their circularity. History is an endless show of destruction and reconstruction, as Oskar demonstrates in a survey of the history of Poland.[32] His own narrative game is to play with historical, philosophical and mythological notions and to build up a trivial network of cross references between world history and his own little world. Jan Bronski's death in the post office is paralleled with Hitler's war against Poland, the conquering of Maria with the German armies' occupation of France, Oskar's coming to a halt in Lina Greff's ample body with the German army getting stuck in the Russian mud, Oskar's murder of Matzerath with the defeat of the Third Reich.[33] By their very idiosyncrasy the equations between Oskar's little world and certain military and political events are calculated to render absurd and hide the individual's fateful encapsulation in a specific context of historical involvement. The trivialization of historical dialectics, the secularization of myth and religion are part and parcel of the mentality of the petit bourgeois class which, clinging to its myopic constraints, vehemently denies all responsibility for the course of politics. Oskar shows the hybrid nature of the modern *pícaro*, who is both the accomplice and the enemy of all tendencies which diminish individual accountability. Like the modern writer, he is both the beneficiary of contemporary society and its subversive critic.

NOTES

1. Compare Michael Nerlich, *Kunst, Politik, und Schelmerei. Die Rückkehr des Künstlers und des Intellektuellen in die Gesellschaft des zwanzigsten Jahrhunderts dargestellt an Werken von Charles de Coster, Romain Rolland, André Gide, Heinrich Mann und Thomas Mann* (Frankfurt a.M/Bonn, 1969), pp.21-22.

2. Derek Lomax, 'On Re-Reading the Lazarillo de Tormes', in *Studia Iberica: Festschrift für Hans Flasche* (Berne/Munich, 1973), pp.371-81.

3. Bronislaw Geremek, *The Margins of Society in Late Medieval Paris*, transl. by Jean Birrel (Cambridge and Paris, 1987).

4. George Duby, *The Three Orders. Feudal Society Imagined*, transl. by A. Goldhammer (Chicago/London, 1980) (French original 1978).

5. F. W. Chandler, *The Literature of Roguery* (New York, 1907).

6. Gustav Janouch, *Jaroslav Hasek: Der Vater des braven Soldaten Schweik* (Berne, 1966), p.105.

7. Jaroslav Hasek, *The Good Soldier Schweik* (Harmondsworth, 1965), p.158.

8. Bertold Brecht, *Schweyk im Zweiten Weltkrieg*, in *Gesammelte Werke 5* (Frankfurt a.M., 1967), p.1927.

9. Brecht, *Schweyk*, p.1938.

10. Compare Thomas Mann, 'Einführung in ein Kapitel der *Bekenntnisse des Hochstaplers Felix Krull*', in *Gesammelte Werke in Einzelbänden, Rede und Antwort* (Frankfurt a.M., 1984), p.311.

11. Mann, p.310.

12. Compare Hans Wysling, 'Archivalisches Gewühle. Zur Entstehungsgeschichte der *Bekenntnisse des Hochstaplers Felix Krull*' in *Thomas Mann Studien I* (Berne and Munich, 1967), pp.234-57, and Klaus Hermsdorff, 'Bekenntnisse des Hochstaplers Felix Krull. Der Memoiren erster Teil', in *Das erzählerische Werk Thomas Manns. Entstehungsgeschichte, Quellen, Wirkung* (Berlin and Weimar, 1976), pp.396-430.

13. Albert Vigoleis Thelen, *Die Insel des zweiten Gesichts. Aus den angewandten Erinnerungen des Vigoleis* (Munich, 1990), p.8.

14. Heinz Ludwig Arnold, 'Gespräche mit Günter Grass', in *Text + Kritik, 1/1a: Günter Grass*, 5th edn (Munich, 1978), p.6.

15. Hans Mayer, *Das Geschehen und das Schweigen: Aspekte der Literatur* (Frankfurt a.M., 1969), p.38.

16. Mayer, p.41.

17. Mayer, p.43.

18. John Reddick, *The 'Danzig Trilogy' of Günter Grass: A Study of 'The Tin Drum', 'Cat and Mouse' and 'Dog Years'* (London, 1975), p.62.

19. Reddick, p.61.

20. Günter Grass, *The Tin Drum*, transl. by R. Manheim (London, 1989), p.160.

21. Reddick, p.60.

22. Grass, *The Tin Drum*, p.163.

23. Christian Reuter, *Schelmuffskys wahrhaftige curiöse und sehr gefährliche Reisebeschreibung zu Wasser und Lande*, ed. by I. M. Barth (Stuttgart, 1979), p.12.

24. Reuter, p.12.

25. See Wilfried van der Will, *Pikaro heute: Metamorphosen des Schelms bei Thomas Mann, Döblin, Brecht, Grass* (Stuttgart, 1967), where more of these contemporary picaresque novels are discussed.

26. Compare David Riesman, *The Lonely Crowd: A Study of the Changing American Character* (New Haven and London, 1950).

27. Grass, *The Tin Drum*, pp.119-20.

28. Günter Grass, quoted by Brode (see footnote 30), p.31; compare also 'dieses geduckte Verhalten des Kleinbürgers, des Opportunisten' of which Grass speaks in connection with *The Tin Drum* in the interview with Arnold, *Gespräche mit Günter Grass*, p.5.

29. Grass, *The Tin Drum*, p.323.

30. Compare Hanspeter Brode, *Die Zeitgeschichte im erzählerischen Werk von Günter Grass* (Berne, 1977).

31. Compare Edward Diller, *A Mythic Journey. Günter Grass's 'Tin Drum'* (Lexington, Kentucky, 1974).

32. Grass, *The Tin Drum*, p.388.

33. Compare Brode, p.31 ff.

UN EJEMPLO DE LA PRESENCIA INGLESA EN BUENOS AIRES: LA CONSTRUCCIÓN DEL TÚNEL DE CARGAS

MARTÍN BLAS ORDUNA
Universidad de Buenos Aires

A Derek, que hubiera venido a Buenos Aires

El ingeniero William Lowe Brown nació en Wigan, Lancashire, Inglaterra. Estudió en Liverpool y se recibió como Maestro de Ingeniería y Doctor de Ingeniería en la Universidad de esa ciudad. Durante los primeros años de su profesión se introdujo en la temática ferroviaria y en la construcción de túneles, haciendo su práctica en 1897 y 1898 como ayudante de la construcción del subterráneo del ferrocarril Central de Londres.

Después de desarrollar esta tarea en la capital inglesa, viajó a Egipto para participar entre 1899 y 1904 como Ayudante constructor Ingeniero del Assuen Dam y Asyut Barrage. Antes de llegar a la Argentina, estuvo hasta fines de 1909 en New York, donde ocupó el cargo de Ingeniero Residente de los túneles del ferrocarril de Pennsylvania, bajo el río Hudson.

Durante la primera guerra mundial William Lowe Brown volvió a Gran Bretaña y llegó a ser teniente coronel, participando en el Cuerpo de Ingenieros de Redes. Quizás uno de sus trabajos más importantes lo realizó en Argentina, adonde viajó para dirigir las obras de los túneles subterráneos del Ferrocarril Oeste de Buenos Aires.

Estos túneles son dos, uno para trenes de pasajeros y otro para trenes de cargas. Este último se destaca por sus particulares condiciones frente al túnel de pasajeros, que es mucho más corto y consiste simplemente en el descenso derivado de la línea principal --a metros de la estación terminal de pasajeros del ferrocarril-- que lleva a una estación de transferencia subterránea donde se hace conexión directa con el tren metropolitano (subte).[1]

El túnel para trenes de carga desciende por un acceso diferente al anterior y tiene la característica de atravesar subterráneamente todo el centro de la capital, no sólo por debajo de una avenida sino a la vez de otro túnel por el cual circula la Línea A de 'subtes', la misma a la cual se accedía a través de la estación de transferencia antes mencionada. A esta condición del túnel de correr bajo un sector de la ciudad de alta densidad edilicia, se agrega su considerable antigüedad, teniendo en cuenta el tipo de construcción de que se trata y el contexto en que era construido.

En los primeros años del Siglo XX, la ciudad de Buenos Aires, que ya era capital federal de Argentina, experimentaba un rápido crecimiento: su población, de 663.854 habitantes en 1895, había pasado a 1.242.278 en 1909, y a 1.560.163 en 1914. El desarrollo de Buenos Aires como metrópoli se veía acrecentado por su tradicional función de puerto,[2] que servía a las necesidades del país agro-exportador. Precisamente, la mayor cantidad de granos de exportación provenía de la región pampeana, área servida por la red del Ferrocarril Oeste (F.C.O.), empresa a la cual llegaba el ingeniero Lowe Brown a finales de la primera, década del este siglo.

Este ferrocarril es el más antiguo de Argentina (1856),[3] y se extendía hacia el Oeste, cruzando las provincias de Buenos Aires, Córdoba y San Luis hasta Mendoza -- estado provincial limítrofe con Chile. La mayor parte de la red estaba sobre la pampa húmeda, de donde los trenes de carga transportaban los cereales al puerto de Buenos Aires. El trayecto del 'campo' al 'puerto' se podía realizar sobre las vías del F.C.O. hasta su estación terminal en Buenos Aires (estación 'Once'), distante aproximadamente a cuatro kilómetros de los diques de embarque; motivo por el cual, los vagones con este destino debían ser desviados y utilizar las vías de otros ferrocarriles con la consiguiente pérdida de tiempo y gasto para la empresa. Sobre el particular, se expresaba el mismo ingeniero Lowe Brown: 'si el ferrocarril hubiera dispuesto de un acceso propio al puerto, por lo menos 325.000 toneladas de cereales al año hubieran podido despacharse directamente, representando en total un aumento en las entradas de 36.500 libras; y si a esto se agregan las entradas debidas a tráfico de importación el aumento sería de unas 40.000 libras'.[4]

Considerando la situación planteada, la empresa planeó hacer una conexión directa con el puerto, pensando como única solución la vinculación a través de un tren subterráneo,[5] que se aprovecharía no solo para la

La construcción del túnel de cargas 503

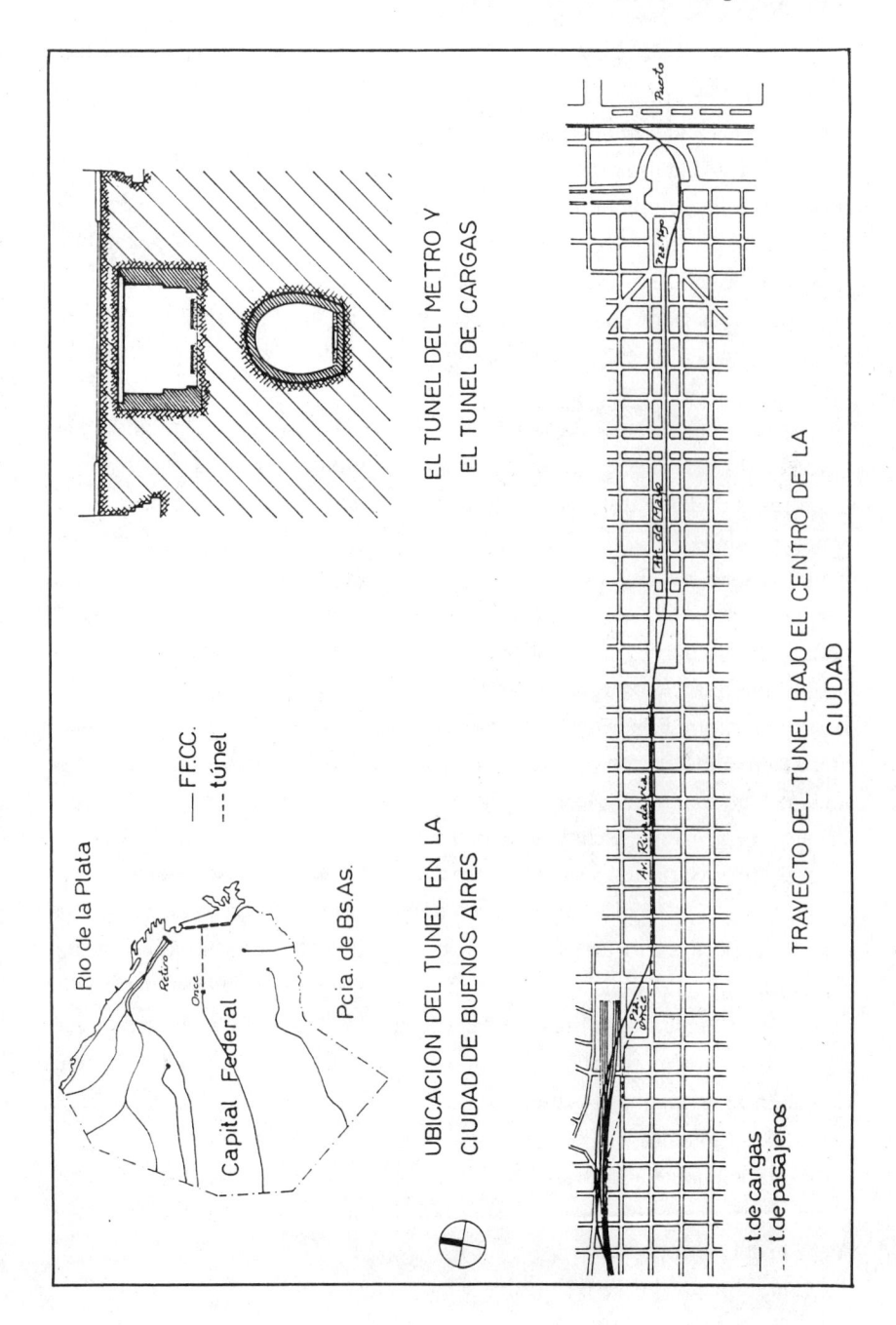

circulación de trenes de carga sino también de pasajeros, es decir, los mismos trenes provenientes del interior del país tendrían posibilidad de alcanzar el centro, de la ciudad subterráneamente.[6]

Mr. David Simpson, otro ingeniero británico elaboró el anteproyecto en 1906. Se había graduado en la Universidad de Edimburgo y arribado a la Argentina en 1887, incorporándose al plantel del Ferrocarril Trasandino. Luego de trabajar en Cuba, había vuelto a Buenos Aires en 1896 realizando diversas tareas para el F.C.O., entre las cuales, una de las últimas fue el anteproyecto del túnel, ya que al año siguiente (1907) volvió a radicarse en Londres.

Además del trabajo efectuado por David Simpson, la Compañía del Ferrocarril solicitó al Congreso de la Nación la autorización legal para la obra. Mientras el Poder Legislativo resolvía a lo largo de tres años esta concesión, la Municipalidad de la ciudad otorgaba otra para la primera línea del metropolitano de Buenos Aires, parte de cuyo trayecto coincidía con el propuesto por el F.C.O.: ambos proponían la circulación prácticamente en línea recta por debajo de las así llamadas Avenidas de Mayo y Rivadavia.

La superposición surgida provocó la modificación del primer proyecto, un nuevo estudio, y la iniciación de conversaciones entre las dos empresas, las que finalmente llegaron a un acuerdo que consistía en la construcción de dos túneles bajo las avenidas; uno para el metropolitano (Línea A) y otro por debajo del primero, exclusivamente para trenes de cargas, con lo cual la empresa ferroviaria cedía su aspiración a controlar el tráfico de pasajeros.

La resolución técnica de este caso atípico para la época pudo llevarse a cabo gracias al suelo arcilloso de la ciudad, que permitió la construcción temporalmente independiente de los túneles, siempre que mediase entre ellos una diferencia de altura mínima de dos metros. Sin embargo, hubo dos lugares del trayecto en los que no pudo guardarse la distancia mínima, ya que de haberse respetado, se hubiese descendido en profundidad, aumentando la longitud del túnel bajo el nivel del agua subterránea, además de hacerse más crítica la pendiente a lo largo del acceso Oeste del túnel. En estos dos casos fue necesario hacer en primera instancia la construcción del túnel de cargas y luego la del metropolitano.

Con respecto al acceso Este del túnel, es decir la salida al puerto, hubo de considerarse, por la proximidad al Río de la Plata, la calidad del suelo compuesto de tierras de relleno de variada calidad. Para hacer factible la materialización de la boca del túnel fue necesario levantar el nivel del terreno, removiendo más de cuatro hectáreas, y construir un muro de retención sobre la playa del puerto a través del cual se abrió el acceso al túnel.

Así quedaban unidos dos puntos de la ciudad a través de una obra de gran envergadura que hoy, perdida entre la historia del esplendor del ferrocarril y las profundidades de la tierra, pasa inadvertida para muchos habitantes de Buenos Aires que sin saberlo, transitan varios metros más arriba por la actualmente llamada 'city porteña'.

Efectivamente, en dicha palabra ('city') que denomina el centro histórico de la ciudad o microcentro, y que en verdad suena casi como metáfora sin una mayor relevancia semántica --aunque sí económica y política--, se condensa la realidad de una Buenos Aires que vivió desde sus primeros pasos como metrópoli una relación económica, social y cultural muy estrecha con Inglaterra. Es así como, aunque en la actualidad no existen los hombres que la construyeron, existe y se mantiene aquello que ellos en un pasado han hecho, proyectado y levantado como testimonio histórico que hace perdurar una presencia.

Bastaría profundizar en la obra de Lowe Brown, para poder agregar que el acceso al túnel desde el puerto está a escasos metros de lo que fue uno de los más grandes edificios públicos levantados en el Siglo XIX, la así llamada Aduana Nueva (1855-94),[7] la cual fue construida por el ingeniero también inglés, Edward Taylor. No sólo otras obras suyas como el Club del Progreso en el ámbito del microcentro, sino además las de otros británicos dieron su impronta a la ciudad. Podría mencionarse la obra de Eustace Lauriston Conder, autor de una de las más grandes estaciones terminales de ferrocarril, la de 'Retiro',[8] de amplias dimensiones espaciales semejantes a las de sus similares europeas, como la londinense Victoria Station. En general, los contactos con Inglaterra se extendían aún más, si se considera que la mayoría de los materiales utilizados en las construcciones venían de ese país y de las propias fábricas que proveían a las empresas de ferrocarriles.

Otra personalidad que sobresale entre los arquitectos británicos que edificaron en Buenos Aires es la de Sydney G. Follett, quien trasladándose a

Argentina para colaborar con el mismo Lauriston Conder, dio nombre al estudio que hasta hoy, luego de cien años, sigue construyendo destacados edificios bajo la dirección de Ricardo Follett. Este estudio realizó más de 600 obras, entre las que se destacan el edificio de Gath y Chaves, el Banco de Londres y América del Sud, The Royal Bank of Canada, y una de sus últimas obras, la embajada de Canadá (1991).

También en lo referido al puerto, la presencia inglesa fue desde un principio más que categórica: el ingeniero portuario John Hawkshaw elaboró en Londres, junto a sus colaboradores, los planos para el proyecto de puerto impulsado desde Buenos Aires por Eduardo Madero, que constituye actualmente el sector de puerto que lleva su nombre y al cual arriban las vías del túnel de cargas. Los planos de Hawkshaw fueron materializados por los constructores Thomas Walker y Cía., y proveyeron la maquinaria hidráulica Armstrong, Mitchell y Cía.

En los viajes realizados a Londres por Madero, además de haberse podido conseguir los servicios de Hawkshaw, se había logrado el financiamiento de la Baring Brothers, la cual se comprometía a colocar el préstamo en la Bolsa de la capital británica. Las obras de este puerto se desarrollaron a lo largo de diez años, habiéndose comenzado en 1887.

Como puede apreciarse en definitiva, no sólo el túnel de cargas y quienes tuvieron que ver con su construcción --que, a modo de ejemplo fueron considerados en estas páginas-- ni tampoco únicamente construcciones que pudieran estar vinculadas al ferrocarril y al puerto, sino incontables obras arquitectónicas recibieron en Buenos Aires la influencia inglesa (ya fuese por las personas que las edificaban o por el estilo al que respondían), la cual se extendió incluso socioculturalmente a diversos sectores porteños.

Baste entonces el breve estudio sobre el túnel de cargas, que todavía sigue cumpliendo su función, enterrado en una capital del Cono Sur del continente americano, sobre cuya estructura de hormigón rodeada de tierra, se extiende otra similar por la que circulan miles de personas por día en los vagones del metropolitano, y transitan sobre ambas peatones al ritmo de las grandes ciudades del mundo como París o New York a una velocidad de 1,50 metros por segundo,[9] para descubrir aquellas vinculaciones --que simbólicamente se hallan en algunos casos bajo tierra, latentes, inadvertidas-- entre dos pueblos, y que por sobre intereses particulares constituyen una muestra de la cooperación existente entre los hombres más allá de los límites de sus propios países.

NOTAS

1. Nombre dado por los porteños al metropolitano, abreviación de tren subterráneo.

2. La ciudad fue fundada en 1536 por Pedro de Mendoza con el nombre de Puerto de Nuestra Señora Santa María del Buen Ayre.

3. La mayor parte de la red del F.C.O. pertenece actualmente a la línea Domingo Faustino Sarmiento de Ferrocarriles Argentinos.

4. W. Lowe Brown, 'Los túneles del Ferrocarril Oeste bajo la ciudad de Buenos Aires', *Boletín Sudamericano de Ferrocarriles*, año IV, 8 (1919), 10.

5. El trayecto entre la estación Once y el puerto corresponde a la parte más céntrica de la ciudad.

6. La palabra 'centro' no responde en Buenos Aires a su centro geográfico, sino al administrativo, próximo al Río de la Plata y aledaño a la histórica Plaza de Mayo, sobre cuyos bordes se levantan el antiguo Cabildo, la Catedral, la Casa Rosada (de Gobierno) y el Banco de la Nación, entre otros.

7. La construcción de la Aduana Nueva comenzó en 1855 y fue demolida en 1894, luego de haber cumplido sus funciones, durante casi cuarenta años.

8. Frente a la estación se levanta, sobre la antiguamente, llamada Plaza Británica, la Torre de los Ingleses, con 76 metros de altura, donada a la Argentina por los residentes británicos durante el Centenario de la Revolución de Mayo, en 1910.

9. P. H. Randle, *Espacios y Escalas Urbanas* (Buenos Aires: OIKOS, 1989), p.VIII.

BORGES TRANSLUZ CHESTERTON

WALTER CARLOS COSTA
Universidade Federal de Santa Catarina

A tradução esteve, desde sua infância bilingüe, intimamente ligada à prática textual de Jorge Luis Borges. É, quase folcloricamente, famosa sua tradução do conto 'The Happy Prince', de Oscar Wilde, publicada aos oito anos de idade no jornal *La Nación*, em Buenos Aires. Essa tradução anunciaria, emblematicamente, o futuro escritor. Apesar de sua obra de tradutor não ser muito volumosa, compreende todos os gêneros que ele próprio praticou (ficção, ensaio, poesia) e apenas grandes autores, como Faulkner, Virginia Woolf, Whitman e Kafka. Não menos importantes, porém, são as milhares de citações explícitas e implícitas de autores estrangeiros que desconcertam ou divertem os críticos em busca de intertexto nos escritos de Borges. Por último, há os trabalhos de tradução incluídos nas inúmeras antologias que Borges organizou, em geral em colaboração. A este último conjunto pertence o pequeno texto que passo a analisar a seguir, publicado pela primeira vez na *Antología de la literatura fantástica*.[1] O original inglês, publicado originalmente em *The Man who knew too much*, é reproduzido de *The Book of Fantasy*.[2] Como se trata de um texto curto, vale a pena reproduzi-lo antes da análise:

The Tower of Babel

'the story about that hole in the ground, that goes down nobody knows where, has always fascinated me rather. It's Mahomedan in form now; but I shouldn't wonder if the tale is a long way older than Mahomet. It's about somebody they call the Sultan Aladin: not our friend of the lamp, of course, but rather like him in having to do with genii or giants or something of that sort. They say he commanded the giants to build him a sort of pagoda rising higher and higher above all the stars. The Utmost for the Highest, as the people said when they built the Tower of Babel. But the builders of the Tower of Babel were quite modest and domestic people, like mice, compared with old Aladdin. They only wanted a tower that would reach heaven, a mere trifle. He wanted a tower that would pass heaven, and rise above it, and go on rising for ever and ever. And Allah cast him down to earth with a thunderbolt, which sank into the earth, boring a hole, deeper and deeper, till it made a well that was without a bottom as the tower was to have been without a top. And down that inverted tower of darkness the soul of the proud Sultan is falling for ever and ever.'

La Pagoda de Babel

-Ese cuento del agujero en el suelo, que baja quién sabe hasta dónde, siempre me ha fascinado. Ahora es una leyenda musulmana; pero no me asombraría que fuera anterior a Mahoma. Trata del sultán Aladino; no el de la lámpara, por supuesto, pero también relacionado con genios o con gigantes. Dicen que ordenó a los gigantes que le erigieran una especie de pagoda, que subiera y subiera hasta sobrepasar las estrellas. Algo como la Torre de Babel. Pero los arquitectos de la Torre de Babel eran gente doméstica y modesta, como ratones, comparada con Aladino. Sólo querían una torre que llegara al cielo. Aladino quería una torre que rebasara el cielo, y se elevara encima y siguiera elevándose para siempre. Y Dios la fulminó, y la hundió en la tierra, abriendo interminablemente un agujero, hasta que hizo un pozo sin fondo, como era la torre sin techo. Y por esa invertida torre de la oscuridad, el alma del soberbio Sultán se desmorona para siempre.

O texto acima é um extrato, mas um extrato com um sentido completo em si mesmo. É uma pequena história embutida em uma história maior. Vale lembrar que Borges se esmerou em desenvolver, ao longo dos anos, um senso agudo para detectar, em obras e autores heteróclitos, *morceaux de bravure* assim, blocos narrativos autônomos exemplarmente resolvidos.

Borges expressou em muitíssimas oportunidades sua admiração por Chesterton, de quem teria tomado alguns de seus procedimentos. Esta admiração especial pelos textos do inventor do Padre Brown, expressa reiteradamente em prefácios, ensaios e contos, aparece sintetizada na seguinte passagem:

Chesterton es uno de los primeros escritores de nuestro tiempo y ello no sólo por su venturosa invención, por su imaginación visual y por la felicidad pueril o divina que traslucen todas sus páginas, sino por sus virtudes retóricas, por sus puros méritos de destreza. Quienes hayan hojeado la obra de Chesterton, no precisarán mi demostración; quienes la ignoren, pueden recorrer los títulos siguientes y percibir su buena economía verbal: 'El asesino moderado', 'El oráculo del perro', 'La ensalada del coronel Clay', 'La fulminación del libro', 'La venganza de la estatua', 'El dios de los gongs', 'El hombre con dos barbas', 'El hombre que fue Jueves', 'El jardín del humo'. En aquella *Degeneración* que tan buenos servicios prestó como antología de los escritores que denigraba, el doctor Max Nordau pondera los títulos de los simbolistas franceses: *Quand les violons son partis*, **Les palais nomades**, **Les illuminations**. De acuerdo, pero son poco o nada incitantes. Pocas personas juzgan necesario o agradable el conocimiento de *Les palais nomades*; muchas, el del *Oráculo del perro*. Claro que en el estímulo peculiar de los nombres de Chesterton obra nuestra conciencia de que esos nombres no han sido invocados en vano. Sabemos que en los *Palais nomades* no hay palacios nómadas; sabemos que *The Oracle of the dog* no carecerá de un perro y de un oráculo, o de un perro concreto y oracular. Así también, el *Espejo de magistrados* que se divulgó en Inglaterra hacia 1560, no era otra cosa que un espejo alegórico; el *Espejo del magistrado* de Chesterton, nombra un espejo real... Lo anterior no quiere insinuar que algunos títulos más o menos paródicos den la medida del estilo de Chesterton. Quiere decir que ese estilo es omnipresente.[3]

O fato de Borges considerar Chesterton um mestre da fabulação e do estilo --duas áreas em que ele próprio é largamente considerado como um mestre-- torna particularmente interessante a análise de tradução de 'The tower of Babel'.

Um primeiro aspecto que chama a atenção quando se compara o texto-fonte e o texto-alvo é o enxugamento que o primeiro sofre no último, como podemos ver na seguinte tabela:

The Tower of Babel		La Pagoda de Babel	
Total de palavras	223	Total de palavras	172
Palavras diferentes	120	Palavras diferentes	103
Taxa de repetição	1.85	Taxa de repetição	1.66

O texto inglês contém 41 palavras *a mais* que o texto espanhol. Nas traduções 'normais' ocorre, com frequência, o contrário, o texto traduzido para o espanhol tendendo a ser mais prolixo que o original inglês. A que se deve, então, este comportamento borgiano, quando se sabe que, em geral, os textos traduzidos explicitam o que é apenas sugerido ou simplesmente ambíguo nos textos-fonte?

Um exame mais detido dos dois textos leva a uma constatação evidente: Borges privilegia, de forma sistemática, o 'princípio da escolha aberta' em detrimento do 'princípio idiomático'.[4] Em outras palavras, buscando sempre a *palavra justa*, Borges reduz drasticamente o peso das expressões idiomáticas, como se pode ver na lista a seguir:

rather	[omitido]
a long way	[omitido]
they call	[omitido]
our friend	el
rather like him	también
in having to do with	relacionado
or something of that sort	[omitido]
quite modest	[omitido] modesto
old Aladin	[omitido] Aladino
a mere trifle	[omitido]
deeper and deeper	interminablemente

Percebe-se claramente que o procedimento favorito de Borges para apresentar um texto espanhol mais seco é a omissão pura e simples das expressões idiomáticas. Apesar de seu elogio à 'economia verbal' de Chesterton, Borges procede a uma verdadeira operação cirúrgica no intuito de cortar o pronunciado coloquialismo do texto inglês. Como resultado temos uma mudança radical de registro do narrador: de um contador de histórias que mistura alegremente ítens cultos e populares passa-se a um narrador culto e aforístico. Os leitores familiarizados com a obra de Borges não terão dificuldade em identificar esses elementos como constituindo, precisamente, certos traços típicos do autor de *Ficciones*. A relação com o leitor muda também: enquanto o texto chestertoniano pede um leitor mais participativo, ou menos distanciado, o texto borgiano parece exigir um leitor cúmplice e contido, decifrador de alusões, completador de elipses.

O descarnamento operado por Borges se vale não somente da eliminação de expressões idiomáticas; eliminam-se também sequências tidas como inessenciais ou, talvez, deselegantes, como a seguinte:

The Utmost for the Highest, as the people said when they built the Tower of Babel.

Algo como la Torre de Babel.

Do mesmo modo, a forma verbal complexa *was to have been* (cujos equivalentes mais próximos em espanhol seriam *tendría que haber sido* ou *hubiera sido*) se reduz a um direto *era*:

> till it made a well that was without a bottom as the tower *was to have been* without a top.

> hasta que hizo un pozo sin fondo, como *era* la torre sin techo.

O efeito da transformação é, novamente, uma mudança no plano interpessoal do texto, o leitor sendo convidado a preencher a lacuna aspectual. No texto-fonte, ao contrário, tudo se acha bem claro, com um narrador preocupado em transmitir uma mensagem inequívoca.

O emagrecimento radical que sofre o texto chestertoniano não se limita, porém, ao que poderia ser caracterizado como a obsessão do estilo lapidar em Borges.

Por outro lado, Borges não só se mostra um escritor autônomo enquanto tradutor, ele exibe também alguns dos traços, comuns à maioria dos tradutores, que têm sido apontados inúmeras vezes por teóricos e críticos de tradução. Assim, em:

> It's *Mahomedan in form* now; but I shouldn't wonder if the tale is a long way older than Mahomet.

> Ahora *es* una leyenda *musulmana*, pero no me asombraría que fuera anterior a Mahoma.

a lenda em questão é referida, no texto-fonte, como sendo *maometana* apenas *na forma*. Borges 'esquece' o importante detalhe *in form*, além de normalizar *Mahomedan* (que remete imediatamente à figura do profeta) em *musulmana*. Enquanto a primeira decisão aponta para um 'cochilo' de Borges, a segunda parece motivada pelo cuidado em evitar a repetição *Mahomedan/Mahomet*.

No próximo exemplo há duas mudanças típicas das traduções de Borges que, sem cerimônia, toma liberdades de criador em relação ao texto de Chesterton:

And *Allah* cast *him* down to earth with a thunderbolt, which sank into the earth

Y *Dios la* [torre] fulminó, y *la* hundió en la tierra

Allah é traduzido como *Dios*, uma escolha que sugere o caráter cristão do leitor ideal de Borges. Já a passagem de *cast him down to earth with a thunderbolt* para *la* [torre] *fulminó* representa um distanciamento do sentido original: em vez do sultão ser diretamente fulminado é a torre que o é. Em inglês o ato de Allah parece muito mais brutal, já que é o próprio idealizador da torre que é atingido.

A alteração do aspecto ideacional do texto-fonte que se depreende do exemplo acima não altera o fato de que em termos de representação o texto de Borges segue bem de perto o de Chesterton. Parece existir uma empatia de base entre tradutor e traduzido. Esta empatia revela-se, de maneira mais evidente, na reprodução de aliterações, que, segundo nota Uspênski, constitui um dos traços distintivos da escrita chestertoniana.[5] Um caso representativo desta atenção a uma marca do estilo de Chesterton por parte de Borges (cujas obras, aliás, não podem ser acusadas de musicalidade), é o grupo nominal *soberbio sultán*, cuja aliteração (inexistente em inglês) parece compensar uma outra aliteração do texto-fonte não reproduzida em espanhol.

Se Borges submete, como vimos, o texto de Chesterton a uma severa dieta, pode-se dizer que junto com as gorduras também desaparece algum tecido substancial. As virtudes, que acredito inegáveis, da concisão borgiana têm o seu contraponto negativo na destruição de alguns paralelismos como *it's* ... *it's* e o jogo de contrastes entre os pronomes *they* e *he*. Borges lança mão das possibilidades do sistema espanhol para eludir essas repetições. No entanto, penso que tanto os paralelismos de compatibilidade como os de contraste desempenham uma função importante a nível macrotextual, inclusive para ajudar a definir o estatuto do narrador.

Finalmente, é curioso observar que o título, que não foge do padrão chestertoniano, é original da tradução, sendo dado por Borges a um fragmento de *The man who knew too much*. A organizadora da coletânea em inglês traduziu o título do espanhol, mas preferiu, de forma pouco chestertoniana ou borgiana, escolher o previsível e seguro *The Tower of Babel*.

Esta, como outras traduções de Borges forma, como que uma continuação de sua obra e seus admiradores e estudiosos podem distinguir nela o que na obra própria parece mais opaco.

Também os anglófonos que frequentam Chesterton, para quem os textos deste são aparentemente unívocos, a aceitar ou rejeitar, ganhariam conhecendo esta e outras versões de Borges. Nela há uma variante de Chesterton, que o autor não explorou, com os mesmos elementos básicos de seu mundo imaginário *mais* a alquimia verbal borgiana. A experiência com outra textualização explícita da mesma mensagem pode ter a saudável consequência de convidar o leitor a considerar outras variantes possíveis e, assim, enriquecer sua leitura. Em vez de lamentarmos a evidente infidelidade estilística de Borges, devemos agradecer a sua existência e estudar os seus segredos.

NOTAS

1. Jorge Luis Borges, Silvina Ocampo, e Adolfo Bioy Casares, *Antología de la literatura fantástica* (Buenos Aires: Sudamericana, 1940).

2. Jorge Luis Borges, Silvina Ocampo, e Adolfo Bioy Casares, *The Book of Fantasy*, introduced by Ursula K. Le Guin (London: Black Swan, 1990).

3. Borges, *The Book of Fantasy*, pp. 120-21.

4. Estes conceitos são desenvolvidos por J. Sinclair, *Corpus Concordance Collocation* (Oxford: Clarendon Press, 1991), pp.109-10.

5. B.A. Uspênski, *A Semiótica em Chesterton*, tradução de Aurora Fornoni Bernardini, in Bóris Schnaiderman, *Semiótica Russa* (São Paulo: Perspectiva, 1979), p.162.

FAMILY HISTORY AND SOCIAL CHANGE IN
TWO SHORT STORIES OF JULIO RAMÓN RIBEYRO

JAMES HIGGINS
University of Liverpool

In the development of modern Peruvian narrative a major contribution was made by the generation of the 50s, whose leading figures were Enrique Congrains Martín, Oswaldo Reynoso, Eleodoro Vargas Vicuña, Carlos Eduardo Zavaleta and Julio Ramón Ribeyro. While the fiction of the preceding decades had been predominantly regionalist, the young writers of this new generation turned their gaze towards the city to record the impact of the modernization of coastal Peru which was taking place at that time. However, the significance of their work goes beyond the thematic. In fact, an important rural narrative was also produced and, irrespective of the subject-matter of their fiction, the writers of the 50s were concerned, above all, to bring a new professionalism to literary activity and to renovate narrative expression. In international terms it could hardly be claimed that they were great innovators, but in the national context they laid the foundations of a modern narrative tradition. Less provincial in outlook than their predecessors, they were familiar with the great literature of the twentieth century --Zavaleta, for example published articles on Faulkner-- and they sought to renovate and update Peruvian narrative by incorporating the technical advances of mainstream Western fiction. Their work, in effect, was a kind of literary equivalent of the modernization that was currently taking place in the socio-economic sphere. In that sense the generation of the 50s prepared the ground from which was to spring the new narrative of Mario Vargas Llosa, José María Arguedas (in his second phase) and Alfredo Bryce Echenique.

Recognized as the outstanding writer of this generation, Julio Ramón Ribeyro (b. 1929) is a true man of letters whose work includes philosophical meditations (*Prosas apátridas*, 1975; *Prosas apátridas aumentadas*, 1978) and literary criticism (*La caza sutil*, 1976), as well as eight plays, the most important of which are *Vida y pasión de Santiago el pajarero* (1960) and

Atusparia (1981). He has also published three novels --*Crónica de San Gabriel* (1960), *Los geniecillos dominicales* (1965) and *Cambio de guardia* (1976)--, but this is a genre which he has never fully mastered and he is very much a minor novelist. As a short-story writer, on the other hand, he has to be accounted a major figure. As Miguel Gutiérrez has pointed out, 'no sólo es el más grande maestro del cuento y la narración corta del Perú, sino uno de los mayores de la lengua española del siglo XX y su nombre con toda justicia debe figurar al lado de Borges, Rulfo, Cortázar, Onetti y García Márquez'.[1]

While many of the sixty-four stories contained in the three volumes of *La palabra del mudo* are concerned with universal themes, one of the most interesting aspects of Ribeyro's work is the image which it offers of his own society.[2] Ribeyro is a writer with an acute awareness of historical change and the Peru depicted in his short stories is a society in the process of transformation. A native Limeñan, he witnessed at first hand the dramatic growth of the Peruvian capital in the 40s and 50s as a result of the increasing industrial development of the coast and the accompanying massive influx of migrants from the provinces, and in common with the fiction of other writers of the generation of the 50s, many of his stories register the so-called process of modernization which transformed Lima from a small city of 330,000 inhabitants in the 1930s into a sprawling metropolis of 3.5 million by 1975. Furthermore, the history of his own family gave him direct personal experience of social change. In the nineteenth and early twenthieth centuries the Ribeyros were a prominent upper-middle-class family who could boast among their members two Presidents of the Supreme Court, a Rector of San Marcos University and a Vice-President of the Republic, but his somewhat unworldly father was an unsuccessful man of modest means who never rose above a mediocre position with a legal firm, and his long illness and early death in 1945 left the family in difficult economic circumstances. That experience is also recorded in Ribeyro's fiction, in stories where the decline of his own family is depicted as symptomatic of the decline of the less competitive and adaptable sectors of the traditional élite. Hence, in contrast to the work of most of his fellow writers of the 50s, Ribeyro's fiction puts the modernization of the 40s and 50s in wider perspective, as the culmination of a much longer process which brought about the transition from a traditional pre-capitalist society to one embarked on capitalist development.

Thus, 'El ropero, los viejos y la muerte' (1972) and 'El polvo del saber' (1974) both narrate episodes of Ribeyro family history, episodes which mirror the decline of the family and, by extension, of the élite to which it belonged. However, these stories do not merely register social change by showing the displacement of a traditional élite by new social forces, but, by opposing the values embodied in the respective classes, call into question the direction in which Peruvian society is moving. Both stories have very simple plots whose significance, however, is expanded by means of symbolism and patterns of parallels and oppositions which suggest levels of meaning beyond the literal.

'El ropero, los viejos y la muerte' recounts an incident which occurred shortly before the death of the author's father: Señor Ribeyro was entertaining an old friend, Alberto Rikets, and while the children were playing football in the street, the latter's son, Albertito, accidentally kicked the ball through an open window and smashed the mirror of an old wardrobe in Señor Ribeyro's bedroom.[3] The plot is minimal, but, as we shall see, it is densely charged with meaning.

A family heirloom handed down from generation to generation, the magnificent old wardrobe is a symbol both of the Ribeyros' former greatness and of their present decline. It is the last vestige of a once substantial patrimony which has been whittled down over the years and which is further reduced after the father's death, when his children each inherit a drawer, the vestige of a vestige. Moreover, when Señor Ribeyro gazes into the mirror where his forbears once contemplated themselves, a contrast is established between his mediocrity and the eminence of those illustrious men who were leading figures in the public life of the nation:

> Se miraba entonces en él [el espejo], pero más que mirarse miraba a los que en él se habían mirado. Decía entonces: «Allí se miraba don Juan Antonio Ribeyro y Estada y se anudaba su corbatín de lazo antes de ir al Consejo de Ministros», o «Allí se miró don Ramón Ribeyro y Alvarez del Villar, para ir después a dictar su cátedra a la Universidad de San Marcos», o «Cuántas veces vi mirarse allí a mi padre, don Julio Ribeyro y Benites, cuando se preparaba para ir al Congreso a pronunciar un discurso». Sus antepasados estaban cautivos, allí, al fondo del espejo. Él los veía y veía su propia imagen superpuesta a la de ellos, en ese espacio irreal, como si de nuevo, juntos, habitaran

por algún milagro el mismo tiempo. Mi padre penetraba por el
espejo al mundo de los muertos, pero también hacía que sus
abuelos accedieran por él al mundo de los vivos. (32)

However, as the passage quoted indicates, the contrast is counterbalanced by an equivalence. The wardrobe represents a tradition linking past and present and the two interact in the mirror as Señor Ribeyro sees his own image merge with that of his forbears. It is no accident that the wardrobe is so positioned that he is able to see himself in the mirror when he sits up in bed. The mirror, in fact, occupies a central place in his life, for in it he finds a sense of identity deriving from an awareness of being part of a tradition which still carries prestige in spite of the family's economic decline.

As in many of Ribeyro's stories, a trivial incident here assumes a significance that in realistic terms is disproportionate to the event itself. The momentous implications of the smashing of the mirror are highlighted by the fact that the kick responsible for it is presented as a prodigious feat never likely to be repeated:

Albertito, con un golpe maestro, que nunca ni él ni nadie
repetiría así pasaran el resto de su vida ensayándolo, había
logrado hacerle describir a la pelota una trayectoria insensata
que, a pesar de muros, árboles y rejas, había alcanzado al
espejo del ropero en pleno corazón. (36)

Señor Ribeyro's reaction also seems to go beyond the bounds of normality. Not only is he upset, as one would expect, but the heart goes out of him and, never again mentioning his forbears, he turns his thoughts to death. The shattering of the mirror, in fact, shatters him psychologically by severing his links with the past and destroying his sense of identity. With its mirror broken, the wardrobe becomes an inert, lifeless object, symbol of a tradition that is now dead, and the empty space marking the spot where he formerly felt himself in touch with his forbears represents the void that now stares him in the face:

Al perder el espejo el mueble había perdido su vida. Donde
estaba antes el cristal sólo quedaba un rectángulo de madera
oscura, un espacio sombrío que no reflejaba nada y que no
decía nada. (37)

The complete emptiness which has taken possession of his life is emphasized by the final lines of the story, where, cut off from his forbears in this world, he prepares to join them in the great vacuum of eternity which, as an atheist, is all he believes awaits him beyond the grave:

> [...] sabía que pronto había de morirse y que ya no necesitaba del espejo para reunirse con sus abuelos, no en otra vida, porque él era un descreído, sino en ese mundo que ya lo subyugaba, como antes los libros y las flores: el de la nada. (37)

It is significant that the incident occurs during a meeting between the Ribeyro and Rikets families which turns out to be a disaster for the former and that the damage is done --inadvertently-- by the son of the latter. For various elements in the narrative suggest that the kick which shatters the mirror symbolizes a process of socio-economic change which saw the less competitive sectors of the old élite superseded by a new, more dynamic entrepreneurial class. Thus, a series of antithetical parallelisms establishes a contrast between the heads of the two families. As a member of a once powerful family, Señor Ribeyro retains a certain inherited prestige, whereas Rikets' name suggests that he comes from more recent and humbler immigrant stock. But without a tradition behind him, Rikets looks forward to the future, as is implied by his building of a house in Chaclacayo, whereas the extent to which Señor Ribeyro's life is dominated by the past is indicated by the size of the wardrobe, which takes up almost half his bedroom, and his habit of gazing into the mirror is symptomatic of a backward-looking attitude. And as a descendant of illustrious politicians, lawyers and academics, Señor Ribeyro is a shadow of former glories, a man who has only with great difficulty managed to purchase the house in Miraflores and has only recently acquired a decent set of dinner dishes to entertain guests, whereas Rikets has risen from modest beginnings to be a prosperous businessman able to build himself a sumptuous summer residence in Chaclacayo. The two men are also quite different in temperament. Rikets is practical, industrious, ambitious. By contrast, Señor Ribeyro's habit of reading the newspaper in bed suggests that he is indolent, and an introspective, contemplative nature is pointed to by his love of books and gardening and by his cutting himself off from social contacts. These differences in temperament are reproduced in their offspring.

The imaginative Ribeyro children regard Albertito as too dull and stupid to share in their favourite diversions and capable of playing only mechanical games that require little inventiveness, but when it comes to football he demonstrates an unexpected vigour and ability. Thus it is intimated that the Ribeyros, while possessing attractive qualities, are too unworldly and impractical to compete with the unimaginative but more industrious and practical Riketses of this world.

Significantly Señor Ribeyro and Rikets are initially presented as resembling each other in age, educational background and physical appearance (33), for this initial identification puts the two men on an equal standing and implies that they started out in life on equal terms only for the former to be left behind by the latter. And the game of football which their children play in the street can be read as a metaphor of the competition between the two families in the real world. Initially, the Ribeyro children enjoy a sense of superiority, but when Albertito's turn comes to shoot it is he who takes the initiative. His first shot is saved only with difficulty, the second scores a goal and the third, the one that smashes the mirror, signals symbolically 'defeat' for the Ribeyro family and 'victory' for the emergent Riketses.

However, the parallel between the declining Ribeyros and the emergent Riketses is a double-edged one which questions the nature of success. It is not just that the impractical Ribeyros come across as more attractive human beings than the unimaginative Riketses. They also possess a spiritual life which the others lack. Symbol of that spiritual life is the old wardrobe, which for the Ribeyro children is not just a piece of furniture but 'a house within the house', a fantasy world which they enter to play all sorts of imaginative games. And Señor Ribeyro, a contemplative more interested in his own inner life than in worldly success or material possessions, may be regarded as a success in his own terms. For he is a man whose reading has prompted him to ponder the meaning of life and who has found meaning and contentment by literally and metaphorically cultivating his garden:

> Desde hacía años mi padre había descubierto las delicias de la jardinería y la profunda verdad que había en la forma de un girasol o en la eclosión de una rosa. Por eso sus días libres, lejos de pasarlos como antes en fatigosas lecturas que lo hacían

meditar sobre el sentido de nuestra existencia, los ocupaba en tareas simples como regar, podar, injertar o sacar malayerba, pero en las que ponía una verdadera pasión intelectual. Su amor a los libros había derivado hacia las plantas y las flores. Todo el jardín era obra suya y como un personaje volteriano había llegado a la conclusion de que en cultivarlo residía la felicidad. (34)

However, just as Albertito in a sense imposes the game of football on the children by finding the ball forgotten beneath the bed and by his ineptitude for games of the imagination, so in a wider sense the Ribeyros are obliged to participate in a game imposed by others, a game for which they are not temperamentally cut out and in which they are foregone losers. The success of the Riketses, therefore, implies not only the triumph of one class over another but the triumph of one set of values over another, the seemingly inevitable triumph of a soulless materialism that no less inevitably raises questions about the quality of life in a society dominated by the Riketses and their kind.

'El polvo de saber' again recounts a story of family decline through the history of an heirloom, this time the narrator's great-grandfather's magnificent library of ten thousand volumes, a symbol of the family's status as members of the nation's social and cultural élite. Inherited by great-uncle Ramón, the library was to have been passed on to the narrator's father, Ramón's favourite nephew and his surrogate son. However, the latter was fated never to come into his inheritance, for Ramón died intestate and his widow, nursing a grudge against his family, refused to honour his wishes. With the father a family tradition of social eminence is now broken, for his loss of his inheritance reflects the loss of the social position which his family had traditionally enjoyed. Excluded from Ramón's house and from the library where he spent the happiest years of his life, he is effectively cast out of the privileged world of his forbears. From now on his role is to contemplate the house from the street, to look in enviously from the outside on a world to which he no longer belongs, and the railings and shuttered windows of the now uninhabited house symbolize the gulf between the downfallen condition of the present generation and the glories of a lost past:

Mi padre pasaba entonces a menudo delante de esa casa,
miraba su verja, sus ventanas cerradas e imaginaba las
estanterías donde continuaban alineados los libros que nunca
terminó de leer. (50)

After the death of the father and of Ramón's widow, the former's descendants are further cut off from the heritage of the past, for his son never even manages to set foot in the house, which he sees only from the outside, and the library passes into the hands of the widow's heirs. As in 'El ropero, los viejos y la muerte', there takes place an inversion of positions which reflects changes in the socio-economic structure. While the continuing decline of the once-élite family is implied in the irretrievable loss of the library and of the privileged status associated with it, the emergence of other sectors to occupy their former position is suggested by the fact that it passes into the possession of persons who have no traditional claim to it and who, moreover, are identified with agricultural and commercial activity:

Su casa de la calle Washington y todo lo que contenía fue
heredado por sus parientes y de este modo la biblioteca se alejó
aun más de mis manos. El destino de estos libros, en verdad, era
derivar cada vez más, por el mecanismo de las transmisiones
hereditarias, hacia personas cada vez menos vinculadas a ellos,
chacareros del sur o anónimos bonarenses que fabricaban tal
vez productos en los que entraba el tocino y la rapiña. (51)

An inexorable process of social change in the direction of a relatively more egalitarian and democratic society is indicated in the latter part of the story when great-uncle Ramón's magnificent mansion, symbol of the exclusive and privileged world of the élite, is converted into a boarding-house for students, and when the narrator is at last able to enter it, it is in the company of one of the students of humble provincial background who now occupy it and with whom he now mingles. There he sees the decline of his family's past splendours mirrored in the furnishings, which not only have suffered a deterioration but have also been 'democratized', stripped of the patrician character they had in former times and reduced to just another collection of old furniture:

No me fue difícil reconocer sofas, consolas, cuadros, alfombras,
que hasta entonces sólo había visto en los álbumes de fotos de

familia. Pero todos aquellos objetos que en las fotografías parecían llevar una vida serena y armoniosa habían sufrido una degradación, como si los hubieran despojado de sus insignias, y no eran ahora otra cosa que un montón de muebles viejos, destituidos, vejados por usuarios que no se preocupaban de interrogarse por su origen y que ignoraban muchas veces su función. (52)

And the completeness of that decline is highlighted at the end when he discovers that the library, dumped in store-rooms and left to rot, has been reduced to a pile of dust, and the one book which he manages to retrieve intact is but a sorry relic of a glorious past now gone forever and of a once-flourishing class that is now extinct:

Apenas abrí la puerta recibí en plena cara una ruma de papel mohoso. En el piso de cemento quedaron desparramados encuadernaciones y hojas apolilladas ... La codiciada biblioteca no era más que un montón de basura. Cada incunable había sido roído, corroído por el abandono, el tiempo, la incuria, la ingratitud, el desuso ... A duras penas logré desenterrar un libro en francés, milagrosamente intacto, que conservé, como se conserva el hueso de un magnífico animal prediluviano. (53-54)

The disintegration of the library, in effect, symbolizes the disintegration of the social ascendancy of the family and of the élite to which it belonged.

The library, of course, symbolizes more than status, for it clearly has the habitual connotations of knowledge, wisdom, culture. Its holdings constitute the sum of what a cultured man of the late nineteenth century was expected to know (50), and for the narrator it is 'la clave de la sabiduría' (49), the key of wisdom that unlocks life's secrets and gives access to an enriched existence. In fact, it is that life-enhancing knowledge rather than material possession of the books which he and his father long to acquire. Invited to choose which of his uncle's possessions he wishes to be bequeathed, the father unhesitatingly plumps for the library, and his son inherits 'esa codicia y esa esperanza' (50). And their obsessive habit of stopping to stare in at the mansion where the library is housed is an indication of how much that knowledge means to them.

It is significant that it was in his grandfather's library rather than at university that the father received his intellectual formation (50), for on one level it represents a culture that is the exclusive property of an élite, accessible only to a privileged few. Insofar as culture signifies power, the library may be seen as a symbol of the know-how which enabled the élite to achieve social ascendancy, and, beyond that, of the confident certainty of a class at home in an ordered world securely under its control. That know-how and the certainty that accompanies it are what the father and his son fail to inherit. The decline of the family begins with the former, whose knowledge is incomplete since he has had opportunity to read only part of the library's contents, and it continues with the latter, who has no access to the library and must make do with a knowledge that is public property, available at a university increasingly open to upwardly-mobile sectors of the middle and lower-middle classes. The disintegrating library, therefore, would seem to symbolize the eroded self-confidence of a class in face of a changing, uncertain world it has lost the know-how to master. There is, furthermore, an ironic twist in the story's ending. For, seeing the knowledge that he and his father had so eagerly sought now reduced to dust, the narrator realizes that the wisdom which served his forbears so well in the past is obsolete and useless in the changed world of the present:

> Allí no quedaba nada, sino el polvo del saber ... El resto naufragó, como la vida, como quienes abrigan la quimera de que nuestros objetos, los más queridos, nos sobrevivirán. Un sombrero de Napoleón, en un museo, ese sombrero guardado en una urna, está más muerto que su propio dueño. (53-54)

And that revelation throws a retrospective light on the family's decline, for it implies that the father, formed in the nineteenth-century tradition represented by the library, and the son, whose preoccupation with the family heritage contrasts strongly with the ambition and practical outlook of his student friend, have been living in the past and never learned to adapt to changing times and have thus helped precipitate the decline of their family's fortunes.

However, as in 'El ropero, los viejos y la muerte', the declining family embody certain values which reflect critically on the nature of the new society which has come into being and on the emergent sectors who have superseded them. For, on another level, the library, more than just a source of practical wisdom, is a 'fuente de luz y placer' (54), a source of intellectual enlightenment and pleasure, and ultimately, therefore, it stands as a symbol of the world of the spirit. Sharing a common love of books, the great-grandfather, great-uncle Ramón, the father and the narrator constitute a tradition of learning, of culture, of cultivation of the spirit. The passage of the library from their hands into the hands of Ramón's widow, an avaricious old woman with no interest in culture, and for whom it is merely a possession, and subsequently into the hands of her heirs, farmers and manufacturers with no cultural tradition or inclination, seems to mark the emergence of a materialistically-minded society that has no regard for things of the soul:

> Me parecía un crimen que esos libros que un antepasado mío había tan amorosamente adquirido, coleccionado, ordenado, leído, acariciado, gozado, fueran ahora patrimonio de una vieja, avara que no tenía interés por la cultura ni vínculos con nuestra familia. (50)

This is confirmed by the fact that the inhabitants of the boarding-house have no appreciation of the antique furnishings around them and that the narrator's student friend, an ambitious provincial, appears to have no interest in books other than in those which serve the practical purpose of helping him to pass his exams. All of this prepares us for the climax of the story, where the horrifying philistinism of the modern age is exposed by the revelation of the fate that has befallen the library, abandoned to rot as a heap of useless old rubbish. The criminal neglect which allows the library to deteriorate into a pile of dust is, in effect, a damning indictment of the narrow materialism of the new social order, which, in displacing the old élite, has also jettisoned its respect for culture and its concern for the life of the spirit:

> Cada incunable había sido roído, corroído por el abandono, el tiempo, la incuria, la ingratitud, el desuso. Los ojos que interpretaron esos signos hacía años además que estaban enterrados, nadie tomó el relevo y en consecuencia lo que fue en una época fuente de luz y de placer era ahora excremento, caducidad. (53-54)

Some left-wing critics have accused Ribeyro of being a reactionary whose 'negatividad extrema' is tantamount to 'una toma de posición por quienes ... dominan [el mundo], un tomar partido en contra de quienes tratan de transformarlo'.[4] Such criticism is unfair, for if stories like those analysed betray an understandable nostalgia for a lost past, Ribeyro is too lucid to want to stop the march of history. A close reading of his fiction makes it clear that he conceives change as both inevitable and desirable, and if he opposes past to present it is because, in common with many of his compatriots, he questions the type of change that has been imposed on Peru in recent decades.

NOTES

1. Miguel Gutiérrez, *La generación del 50: un mundo dividido* (Lima: Labrusa, 1988), p.138.

2. See Julio Ramón Ribeyro, *La palabra del mudo*, 3 vols (Lima: Milla Batres, 1973 [I, II] and 1977 [III]). A further seven stories are to be found in *Sólo para fumadores* (Lima: El Barranco, 1987). References in this essay are to the anthology *La juventud en la otra ribera* (Barcelona: Argos Vergara, 1983).

3. My interpretation of this story owes much to the excellent reading of James P. Chambers in his doctoral thesis, 'Doubt and Uncertainty in the Short Stories of Julio Ramón Ribeyro: A Study of Characterization, Narrative Technique and Story Structure in *La palabra del mudo*', Oxford, 1984, pp.112-16.

4. Alejandro Losada, *Creación y praxis. La producción literaria como praxis social en Hispanoamérica y el Perú* (Lima: Universidad Nacional Mayor de San Marcos, 1976), pp.92-93.

URUGUAY: THE BURDEN OF THE PAST

HENRY FINCH
University of Liverpool

Uruguay is famously the country of the middle way, the country in which nothing happens; but in apparent contradiction, it is also the country of perpetual crisis. It is a disconcerting experience for the periodic visitor to Uruguay to listen to discussion of 'the crisis', only to realize that the country had apparently entered a new crisis since the previous visit without the earlier experience reaching a resolution. Uruguay's is a crisis which has never gone critical, but has instead changed its character in a process of continuous transformation: a kind of chronic crisis, in fact. It is perhaps worth noting that Uruguayans often appear to be highly ambivalent about the enduring nature of the country's problems. On the one hand there is self-criticism of the country's seeming inability to identify and implement solutions; on the other, there is a kind of perverse pride in its capacity to find ways of coming to terms with the unacceptable. The truth of the matter is perhaps that for most of this century the country has regarded itself as prosperous, and has ordered its affairs on that assumption, whereas only in brief and exceptional periods of time has it been able to sustain satisfactory rates of economic growth. When talk of crisis first became current, in the 1960s, it did so essentially in response to the ending of post-war industrial growth in the second half of the 1950s. The secular economic stagnation which has characterized Uruguay since then lies at the centre of its problems; but it would be quite wrong to suppose that the social and political edifice had previously rested on a secure economic base. This essay examines two features of Uruguay's twentieth-century experience which continue to cast a long shadow: the low level of investment in productive capacity; and the party system which impedes the formulation and implementation of coherent policy initiatives.

Prosperity and Stagnation: the Non-Investing Economy

In spite of the long stagnation, Uruguay still has one of the highest levels of per capita income in Latin America,[1] and this pre-eminent position had probably been attained at least by 1900. Uruguay was a spectacular beneficiary of the creation of an international economy in the nineteenth century. Average incomes in Uruguay are relatively high, and have been for over a century, essentially because the per capita endowment of land producing exportable commodities (and services) is high. But neither the exploitation of the land, nor the distribution of its benefits to the economy as a whole, has proceeded in a straightforward manner.

The primary requirement for the development of the livestock (or arable) industry was the introduction of technologies developed abroad. In the industrialization of livestock, new technologies created new export products (meat extract, frozen and chilled meat). In the production of the livestock itself, the result of technical improvement was a surge in output during the period in which the new technique was extended to the industry as a whole. The most obvious examples concern the introduction of pedigree sheep from the 1860s, and Hereford cattle from about the beginning of this century. But whether the form of technology incorporation was that of pedigree livestock, or wire fencing, or (most obviously) the *frigorífico*, the requirement on Uruguayan producers was to react to the availability of the new technology, rather than to modify or adapt it to local conditions. The pattern of production was thus broadly speaking imitative of practice elsewhere. That might have been entirely satisfactory had the livestock industry possessed an open frontier allowing it to expand indefinitely using land on an extensive basis; or if the technology of pasture improvement employed in other countries had been appropriate to the climatic, geological and cultural conditions of Uruguay. But since neither of these conditions was true, the livestock sector has been capable of very limited growth since the 1920s.

The unwillingness or inability of livestock producers to improve their pastures and increase the nutritional capacity (and thus the livestock population) of their land has preoccupied policy makers (and latterly aid donors) for a large part of this century. It is not an issue to be explored here, except to point out the limits which it continues to place on both traditional exports and raw material supply to certain non-traditional export industries (for example, leather goods and textiles). What is relevant here is that the problem has implications for the nature of the relationship between the landowning class and the state. For the development and adaptation of technology in the basic sector of the economy, competitive in structure and owned by nationals, is precisely an area in which one might expect to find the resources of the state deployed. But in the Uruguayan case, what is remarkable is the very limited attention paid to problems of pasture development and animal husbandry. The neglect was not accidental. When the state did begin to interest itself in the problem of technology incorporation and adaptation, during the two presidencies of José Batlle y Ordóñez (1903-07, 1911-15), the thrust of its activities was directed towards the diversification of the economy. Arable agriculture (in particular), dairying, fishing, mineral exploration, and manufacturing, were the sectors benefiting from state-funded research activities. The livestock sector, prosperous, dominated by *latifundistas*, and still growing, was to be the source rather than the beneficiary of state expenditure.

The extraordinary phenomenon of *batllismo*, which so sharply divides the nineteenth- from the twentieth-century histories of Uruguay, may be judged to rest on two features of the economic, social and political structures of the country.[2] First, in spite of the crucial position of the livestock export sector in the economy, the rural economy has only been able to support directly a small and diminishing proportion of the national labour force. Second, the entrenched early position of Montevideo based on its commercial and financial interests, and the leading role of European immigrants in the process of capitalist modernization of the livestock sector in the final third of the nineteenth century, together determined that the newly-dominant landowning class had little direct representation in the Uruguayan state. These structural features of the Uruguayan system have remained essentially true down to the present.[3] In a schematic way they help to explain why and how the development of Uruguay in this century has been so overwhelmingly urban. Irrespective of the particular ideological input of Batlle y Ordóñez himself, it is clear that the social stability of the country, and its capacity to retain population in the face of the superior attractions of Argentina, rested on the need to redistribute in favour of the urban economy part of the economic surplus generated in the livestock sector.

Estimates of long-run income growth for the period before 1945 should perhaps be regarded still as provisional, but the general picture is clearly one of slow growth. For example, in the 'golden age' of 1900-13, with the incorporation of the fresh meat trades and only limited protection for manufacturing, the volume of commodity exports grew at an annual rate of only 2.5% (zero growth per capita). Though in value terms they doubled, in Argentina in the same period the value of exports trebled.[4] For 1913-28 the average annual growth of GDP per capita is estimated at 0.7 per cent, and for 1928-43 per capita GDP contracted by 1.3 per cent annually.[5]

The growth record for the decade after 1945 shows a rather different but not necessarily more reassuring picture. Industrial production expanded at the annual average rate of 6.1 per cent, total GDP at 4.8 per cent, and GDP per capita at 3.4 per cent.[6] These rates probably represent the best performance by the Uruguayan economy in any ten-year period this century, but its limitations are clear. First, in comparison with economic performance for Latin America as a whole during 1945-55, the rate of GDP growth in Uruguay is rather below the regional average (though its low rate of population growth makes Uruguay's performance look considerably better in per capita terms).[7] Second, investment rates in Uruguay were probably at an historically high level, but they have lagged well behind those for the region as a whole in subsequent periods and may well have done so before 1955 (Table 1). Indeed, net investment in Uruguay must have been remarkably low in some years. Third, although the origins of manufacturing for the domestic market go back to the beginning of the century, the rapid growth phase of import-substituting industrialization (ISI) --that is, the post-war decade-- was extremely brief in duration. Moreover, the industrial structure which resulted from the interventionist devices of multiple exchange rates and trade and exchange controls was high-cost and inefficient, with very limited diversification away from the production of consumer goods for domestic demand. Although prices to the rural producers of exportable production did not decline in real terms during this period (and indeed rose sharply during the Korean War boom), nonethless up to 1953 they were rising less rapidly than world prices.[8] The rural export sector was thus required to subsidize the

TABLE 1

Ratio of Gross Fixed Investment to GDP,
Uruguay and Latin America (%)

	Uruguay	Latin America	
A			
1955-9	16.0	16.9	
1960-4	14.6	16.1	
1965-9	11.9	17.8	
1970-4	9.9	20.3	
1975-9	14.6	22.4	
1980-4	13.7	19.6	
1985-9	8.2	16.2	
B			(ranking, 24 countries)
1960-9	10.4	18.8	23
1970-9	12.5	22.9	24
1980-7	12.2	18.0	21

Sources:

A Banco Central del Uruguay; UN ECLA *Economic Survey of Latin America*

B Inter-American Development Bank, *Economic and Social Progress in Latin America: 1988 Report* (Washington, 1988), table III.1, p.30

expansion of manufacturing industry through the transfer of some part of its potential earnings. It would be wrong of course to jump to the conclusion that this interference in the internal terms of trade by itself explains the post-war stagnation of the rural sector. In part, the expansion of domestic incomes provided an alternative outlet for exportable production; but more fundamentally, output growth continued to be constrained by the use of primitive animal husbandry techniques on unimproved pastures.[9]

Unless some remarkable breakthrough occurs in the technology of pasture improvement, Uruguay is very unlikely to move on from the extensive pattern of land use in livestock production. The World Bank has devoted considerable effort since 1960 to the promotion through the *Plan Agropecuario* of pasture improvement amongst rural producers, but the very limited results achieved suggest that there is little scope for further gains. Indeed, Lovell Jarvis has suggested that on certain assumptions perhaps as little as 13 per cent of pasture area in Uruguay is capable of being profitably improved, compared with a maximum level of improvement of just 10 per cent of pasture area, achieved in 1973-75.[10] As significant as this remarkably low ceiling, perhaps, is the lack of sustained commitment to investment in improvements: by 1974 investment was already declining in response to the dictatorship's policy of controlled prices to the livestock sector, and the liberalization of 1978 failed to stimulate an equivalent amount of new investment. In 1990 the area under permanent pasture was 60 per cent (100,000 hectares) less than in 1975.[11] Fundamental though the livestock sector is to Uruguay's export performance, both traditional and non-traditional, future growth is very unlikely to be based on increases to the animal-carrying capacity of the pastures.

This study does not comment on the nature and sustainability of the economic growth achieved since 1985, although it is clear that in addition to its apparent basis in favourable external trends some important changes in the economy are occurring.[12] What does need to be emphasized is that the long economic stagnation since 1955 (punctuated by brief intervals of growth, most significantly in the mid-1970s) should not be contrasted with some previous and mythical golden age, or seen as an interruption in the growth path of a previously dynamic economic system. Rather, the stagnation marks the end of extensive (and slow) growth in the livestock economy, and the exhaustion of the (briefly-viable) domestic-market based option. The duration of the stagnation has revealed the slow response of the economic system in overcoming the limitations of both strategies. Accustomed to managing its affairs on the basis of relatively low rates of investment but high disposable incomes, Uruguay found itself ill-prepared for the adjustments --or more probably radical changes-- which are now required for economic success.

The Problem of the Political Parties

The forum in which one expects those changes to be proposed, discussed, modified and prepared for implementation is the political system. At the risk of expressing naïve views about the functions of political institutions, we might propose that political parties have a central role to play in the democratic process, articulating interests and constructing alliances, while competing for control of the executive arm of government and ultimately of the apparatus of the state. Successful parties are those which secure sufficient material and popular support to enable them to organize effectively enough to win power in elections. Successful party systems are those which give expression to interests and opinion on a competitive basis, such that the framework of democratic institutions is perceived as both representative of conflicting views and equitable in its treatment of them, and therefore preferable for reasons of long-term stability to an authoritarian exercise of government. On such criteria, how well does the Uruguayan political system perform?

That it has at least two successful parties is indisputable, but the efficacy of the party system is more debatable. Indeed, it is suggested in this section that although the two major parties, *Blanco* (*Nacional*) and *Colorado*, occupy a central position in the political system, the functions they perform within it have traditionally had little to do with the organized expression of interests and opinion. Although the majority faction within each party controls the process of preparing a statement of party principles, in neither party is that faction in a position to impose a 'party line' on other groups. Rather, they are free to organize, make and dissolve alliances, establish networks of support, and present their own lists of candidates at elections. What makes such fragmentation possible is the electoral system of the double simultaneous vote (DSV), a device for holding primary elections at the same time as general elections. By this means each party can field multiple presidential candidates and strengthen rather than weaken its total vote, victory going to the most-voted faction candidate of the most-voted party.

To a limited extent one can discern among the factions of a single party a gradation from left to right which is perhaps the most common organizing principle of parties in other representative political systems, particularly in Europe, and which is hard to detect between the two parties themselves. Thus it is easier to say that the *batllista* alliance (*Batllismo Unido*, itself composed of two major sub-factions) of the *Colorado* party is to the right of the *Corriente Batllista Independiente*, or to the left of the *Unión Colorada y Batllista*, than it is to say that the average member of the *Colorado* party stands to the left or right of his/her opposite number in the *Partido Nacional*. In the past the *Colorados* have been regarded as urban, generally more reformist, of greater appeal to immigrants and the working class, whereas the *Blancos* have a stronger rural and conservative base. During the 1970s and 1980s, however, it was the *Blancos* who appeared more radical, with the *Colorados* finding more support in the interior as they lost ground in Montevideo to the left-wing *Frente Amplio* coalition.

The reasons for the self-identification of individuals with the *Colorado* or *Blanco* parties is hard to understand, except as competing routes to power and influence. In that sense the *Colorado* party exists because there is a *Blanco* party, the *Blancos* because there are *Colorados*. The observable shift in the centres of gravity of the parties, is largely a consequence of the changing relative strengths of the factions composing the parties. Within factions there is a much greater degree of internal consistency on policy issues, yet it would be an error to suppose that a constant policy orientation is itself the adhesive which holds the faction together. Rather, it is the identity of the faction leader which defines the faction's policy stance and is the real basis of each faction's popular standing. That is why the personal qualities of faction leaders, and their close relationship (frequently of family) with party leaders of the past, is the principal public expression of a faction's identity. The *lemas* of the factions generally consist either of an anodyne slogan wholly inoffensive on

Uruguay: The Burden of the Past 539

left-right or any other criteria (for example, *libertad y cambio, renovación y victoria, unidad y reforma, por la patria, idea y acción*)[13] or reference to party leaders whose period of eminence is so remote as to empty their names of all but symbolic significance, notably José Batlle y Ordóñez and Luis Alberto de Herrera. Only the rare use of 'popular' in a *lema* betrays a slight leftward leaning. In short, party factions present themselves and invite support on the basis of what their leaders 'stand for', rather than what policies they wish to implement.

The politics of personality rather than programme is to be observed not only in the organization of the party system, but also in the substance of the electoral choice itself. Elections in Uruguay are rarely conducted with explicit reference to issues of economic and social policy, for example. Proposals for constitutional change, on the other hand, in which the political élite has an immediate and profound interest, are typically elaborated with enormous care and, as in 1966, overshadow the election of president and congress. Indeed, the election of President Gestido that year exemplifies particularly well a general rule about the electoral process in Uruguay, that voters choose an administration rather than a government.[14] A further instance of this distinction arose in very unusual circumstances, in the *concertación* process in 1984. When the military withdrew from power in the final months of that year, leaving great confusion and unsettled issues over a wide range of economic, social and political matters, the two parties met with the *Frente Amplio* coalition, trade unions, employers' associations and other social groups in an attempt to agree on the policies that would be implemented from March 1985 onward. Indeed, it was intended that the *Concertación Nacional Programática* (CONAPRO) should be completed *before* the elections were held in November 1984, so that the electoral choice would be unencumbered by any major policy issue. The parties had therefore on the one hand to give at least formal support to the CONAPRO proposals, but on the other to differentiate themselves in front of the electorate. Of course, the aim was in part to save democracy from itself, to avoid the opening of divisions which might be exploited by the armed forces and enemies of democracy on the extreme right. But in spite of the exceptional circumstances this was very much the sort of election that the parties were accustomed to contest, in which what was at stake was each candidate's fitness to govern rather than a defined policy stance.

There are a number of reasons which help to explain the lack of policy content in Uruguayan politics. One has to do with the presidential system of government, in which the executive arm is more clearly separated from the legislative process than in parliamentary systems, and in which legislation is not originated primarily by those whose constitutional function is to implement it. Another, more specific to Uruguay and derived from the voting system, has to do with the weak position in which the president is placed under the 1967 constitution (even though intended by its authors to provide stronger government than that of the collegiate executive, the *Consejo Nacional de Gobierno*, since 1952). Because primaries are not normally separated from the presidential election itself, and because there is no second-round voting, the successful presidential candidate receives a personal vote which is invariably a minority of the total poll (21 per cent for Lacalle in 1989, 31 per cent for Sanguinetti in 1984, 23 per cent for Bordaberry in 1971, 21 per cent for Gestido in 1966), and can therefore claim no personal mandate. He (no woman has yet stood for the presidency) may even, as in 1966, fail to win a majority of the votes in his own party; or, as in 1971, receive fewer votes than a candidate of another party. In addition, the emergence of a third grouping as a major electoral force has reduced the victorious party's vote to 41 per cent in 1971 and 1984, and to 37 per cent in 1989; the president is thus denied a congressional party majority, and has to construct cross-party agreements based on proposed government programmes or the inclusion of members of other parties as ministers in the government. It is not surprising, therefore, that whereas political parties in many other political systems have the function of securing agreement between different tendencies within the party on a common programme *before* elections, in Uruguay it is the reverse. First the elections must be won, on the basis of multiple party lists and a voting system which is so secret (as the joke goes) that even the voters do not know who they are voting for, and only after the elections is there a coalescence of party factions into a governing alliance.

The central institutions within the political system of Uruguay are the two traditional parties, *Blanco* and *Colorado*. They have succeeded in establishing their identity as the legitimate and exclusive national expression of democracy, much as parliament in the United Kingdom or the constitution of the United States are regarded. Within the political culture of Uruguay, parties of ideology are seen as alien, not representative of the authentic political tradition of the nation.[15] They unite only those who are able to agree on their policy orientation, whereas the traditional parties bring together Uruguayans who may have widely contrasting views of the direction the country should take, but who submerge such differences in their shared party heritage. The idiosyncratic electoral legislation protecting the position of the traditional parties thus finds its justification in the preservation of a system which ensures the expression of national rather than merely sectional or class interests.[16]

'Traditional' is the label conventionally applied, but it would be more accurate to describe the parties as anachronistic: not in reference to the date of their foundation, but rather to their original and continuing nature and its inappropriateness at the end of the twentieth century. It is important to bear in mind that the parties emerged early in the nineteenth century, at a time when neither the concept of nationhood nor the machinery and functions of a centralized state had any effective meaning in Uruguay. The parties, and the allegiances which hold them together, pre-date (except in a purely formal sense) the nation. In practical terms party organization in the nineteenth century consisted of networks of personal loyalties within the hierarchies of *caudillo* landowners. Central to the party division lay the violent antagonism in the River Plate region between liberal unitarians and federalists, a conflict accentuated in Uruguay by the intervention of allies of both forces from neighbouring countries. Following the *Guerra Grande* (1838-51), intervals of uneasy peace (punctuated by outbreaks of fierce civil war) were achieved through the negotiation of party pacts, leading by the 1870s to more formal agreements on territorial areas of dominance. However, this early expression of *coparticipación*, in which the executive arm of government was divided between the parties on the basis of the political control and administration of departments, was inconsistent with the strengthening demands of a capitalist landowning class (having little affiliation to either party) for a centralized state authority to put an end to territorial feuding and the damage to property which invariably resulted. Moreover, these same forces of modernization now endowed central government with the resources (British capital) and technology (railway, telegraph, armament) to curb the power of the regional *caudillos*. The debilitated political élite of Montevideo was displaced by the military for a crucial decade after 1876, and the last significant armed uprising by *Blanco* revolutionaries was crushed by government forces in 1904.

With the benefit of hindsight, the defeat of Saravia at Masoller in 1904 is seen to have marked the final supremacy of civil politics over *caudillismo*, and the end of territorial *coparticipación*. That was not necessarily the contemporary view, however, and the need to seek an accommodation with the minority party did not disappear. Quite apart from whatever legitimacy the *Blanco* party could claim as a national institution, the continuing threat of further uprisings in the north by *Blanco* radicals made it urgent to grant concessions to the *Directorio* of the *Blanco* party in Montevideo, to ensure its supremacy and thus the peace of the nation.[17] That is why DSV was introduced, in the *Ley de Lemas* of 1910. Batlle y Ordóñez, on his return from Europe in 1911, continued to urge the necessity of *gobierno de partido* (that is, a public administration composed of loyal supporters of the ruling *Colorado* party), but the *Blanco* party was successful in securing the retention of *coparticipación*. Now the doctrine was redefined, particularly after the compromise between the parties which enabled the first collegiate constitution to be adopted in 1919, to mean that both parties would share the right to nominate to public posts. Although in the new era of enlarged political participation and free elections the majority party would hold the reins of government, the minority party was not to be deprived of its share of the spoils of power.

Thus was put in place the structure within which the *Colorado* and *Blanco* parties have developed their parasitical relationship with the apparatus of the state. It did not happen immediately, nor was such a development necessarily anticipated. Batlle y Ordóñez had his own reasons for seeking an expansion of the public sector, and *empleomanía* in the 1920s, though certainly present, did not assume excessive proportions. But from the *pacto del chinchulín* of 1931,[18] via the growth of the bureaucracy under the Terra regime and the introduction of 3+2 appointments in the public sector under the second collegiate constitution of 1952, to the uninhibited clientelism of the years of stagnation and crisis after the mid-1950s, the parties have progressively appropriated the resources of the state for their own sustenance. The result is a state apparatus and public sector whose contemporary characteristics are not merely size, but also grotesque financial --but more importantly, functional-- inefficiency. 'El Estado, que a principios de siglo asumió la función de diversificar la economía mientras protegía a los social y económicamente débiles, se ha corrompido hasta convertirse en una presencia arbitraria e indiferente que domina las vidas de todos, sirve a los intereses privados de pocos y no satisface el interés colectivo de nadie'.[19]

Conclusion

The aim of this essay has been to suggest that some important aspects of Uruguay's self-image are composed of myth, while others, not mythical, have negative rather than positive value. Uruguay's former (and, for some, continuing) prosperity cannot be doubted, but it was based in the past on fortuitous natural circumstance rather than the accumulation of reproducible capital. In earlier periods the country lived well and honourably by the process of passive adaptation rather than active change, and that has contributed to a society which is conservative, resigned, and disposed to seek solutions from the state which for various reasons the state is now unable to provide. Problems of inflexibility and unwillingness to innovate are compounded by an ageing population, the product of low population growth and large-scale emigration.

Politically, the external view of Uruguay (pre-1973) as one of the most democratic nations of Latin America appears to be shared internally: democratization saw the political system simply restored, rather than reconstructed, almost as if the events of 1973-85 had never happened. But it would be a great error to suppose that the collapse of democratic institutions and the military coup in 1973 were due simply to the external intervention of Tupamaro guerrillas and of elements within the armed forces, with the political parties caught up in the tragedy like innocent bystanders. It is suggested in this essay that the entrenched position of the traditional parties, protected by DSV, obstructs the representational function of the political system and impedes the practice of effective government.[20] In addition, the traditional and still dominant political skills of establishing agreement or consensus, of finding 'the middle way' by negotiation and transaction, were developed in an earlier age of more assured prosperity. Both the first period of *batllismo*, during which income was generated in the rural sector while population concentrated in the city, and the *neo-batllista* years of industrial production for the domestic market, primarily required the political system to devise and deploy mechanisms of income redistribution and political incorporation. For all the rhetoric of utopia and uniqueness, it is the politics of populism that has been Uruguay's speciality.

Until 1973, and (less certainly) since 1985, the country has continued to conduct its political life as if little had changed. But in the post-populist age consensus on policy is more difficult to find when there is no longer patronage to distribute, and when there are hard decisions to be taken. The counterpart of consensus then apparently becomes the notion of 'governability', by which the opposition concedes to the administration on issues of interest or principle in order to sustain the framework of government.[21] Yet as Carlos Quijano pointed out long ago, disagreement on policy is normal: 'Toda política, es obvio, tiene su reverso. Toda opción es excluyente. Puesto que gobernar es optar, gobernar es crearse adversarios o enemigos'.[22] It is hard to see democratic virtue in the suppression of dissent, even when self-imposed; rather, virtue lies in achieving an institutional framework and set of political values within which policy disagreements can be registered and sustained without endangering the stability of the system.[23] If Uruguay is not to fall into the abyss again, the democracy of consensus must eventually be replaced by the democracy of disagreement. For that to occur, losers in the political game must be persuaded firstly that the policies they are asked to accept (but with which they disagree) are just; and secondly that the structures of the game allow alternative options to be developed and considered. The danger suggested in this essay is that the failure of the institutional system to fulfil the second condition will undermine the willingness of the Uruguayan people to accept the first.

Uruguay: The Burden of the Past   545

NOTES

1. Uruguay's per capita income of US$2989 in 1988 was exceeded in Latin America only by four small Caribbean economies and Venezuela: Inter-American Development Bank, *Economic and Social Progress in Latin America*: 1989 Report (Washington, 1989), p.463.

2. The relationship of the ideology of Batlle y Ordóñez to the contemporary *Colorado* party, or to the *batllista* faction itself, is a matter of dispute. The historian sees little connection, other than the political advantage which is perceived to follow from the use of the name. However, Batllismo is cited as a doctrine, which 'constituye el núcleo inspirador del Partido Colorado' in the 'Programa de Principios' of the party, in *Por un Uruguay Para Todos* (Montevideo: Publicación Diario *El Día*, 1984), p.32.

3. Landowners have achieved more direct representation for brief exceptional periods beginning in 1916, 1933, 1958, and perhaps 1968.

4. M. H. J. Finch, *A Political Economy of Uruguay Since 1870* (London: Macmillan, 1981), pp.124-26.

5. Luis Bértola, *The Manufacturing Industry of Uruguay, 1913-1961* (Göteborg-Stockholm: Institute of Latin American Studies of Stockholm University, 1990), table IV.2, p.121.

6. Finch, *Uruguay*, tables 8.1 and 6.10, pp.223, 172.

7. United Nations, *The Economic Development of Latin America in the Post-War Period* (New York, 1964) table 6, p.6.

8. Finch, *Uruguay*, table 4.5, p.113.

9. In the face of diminishing meat exports post-war, export volume up to the mid-1950s was largely sustained by the changing balance of the animal population in favour of sheep, by the changing functional composition of the flocks, and by further substitution of higher-yielding, wool-bearing breeds (Corriedale and Ideal).

10. Lovell S. Jarvis, 'Predicting the Diffusion of Improved Pastures in Uruguay', *American Journal of Agricultural Economics*, 63, 3 (August 1981).

11. Celia Barbato de Silva, *Política Económica y Tecnología* (Montevideo: Ediciones de la Banda Oriental, 1981), table 12, p.60; *Búsqueda*, 617 (12 December 1991).

12. A significant structural shift is the marked increase in the export coefficient during and after the neo-liberal period:

TABLE 2: *Ratio of Exports to GDP (%)*:

1955-59	9.8
1960-64	13.1
1965-69	15.6
1970-74	12.7
1975-79	17.6
1980-84	18.51
1985-88	24.9

Source: Banco Central del Uruguay (BCU), *Boletín Estadístico*; BCU, *Producto e Ingreso Nacionales*.

13. These random examples are put in lower-case letters to emphasize their lack of substantive content.

14. Perhaps the example is too apt, since Gestido was explicitly regarded as an 'honest administrator' following his period as president of the railway system AFE. Sudden changes in political direction ('U-turns') are not rare in democratic politics, but Gestido had barely served six months before the interventionist economic team was ousted to make way for the IMF.

15. 'El Batllismo no es un artículo importado, ni un catecismo dogmático, ni una especulación doctrinaria despegada de nuestra realidad. Es el fruto maduro de la evolución de un Partido que, salvo breves interrupciones, gobernó al país durante noventa años ... Así como el Partido Colorado es intransferiblemente uruguayo, en muchos aspectos el Uruguay de hoy sigue siendo indesmentiblemente colorado' ('Programa de Principios' of the *Colorado* party, *Por un Uruguay Para Todos*, p.32).

16. On the other hand the traditional parties are a unifying force to the extent that they blur the difference in the political cultures of Montevideo and the Interior. This difference is revealed, for example, in the concentration of support for the *Frente Amplio* in Montevideo; and by the results of the April 1989 referendum on the amnesty law, in which 67% of Interior voters approved the law compared with 43% in Montevideo.

17. Milton I. Vanger, *The Model Country: José Batlle y Ordoñez of Uruguay, 1907-1915* (Hanover, N.H. and London: University Press of New England for Brandeis University Press, 1980), pp.71-72.

18. The pact extended *coparticipación* to the public corporations as the price of an inter-party pact to permit the creation of ANCAP. It signalled the definitive abandonment by the *batllista* Colorados of *gobierno de partido*.

19. Henry Finch, 'Paradojas de un Estado Peculiar', *Brecha*, 30 September 1988, p.7.

20. But it must also be conceded that the parties do constitute a bulwark against the political extremes to which other countries are periodically drawn, and against elected tyrannies.

21. It was to assure the governability of the country that Wilson Ferreira Aldunate, principal critic of the dictatorship from exile, imprisoned on his return to Uruguay in 1984, and excluded from the elections that year, persuaded his *Por La Patria* faction of the *Blanco* party to support the amnesty law of December 1986.

22. *Marcha*, 1336 (30 December 1966).

23. Daniel L. Levine suggests that one lesson is the need 'to restructure our understanding of just what political legitimacy entails. This means thinking about legitimacy less in terms of substantive programmatic consensus and more as a set of operative rules which make conflict, change and conciliation posssible without institutional collapse' ('The Transition to Democracy: Are There Lessons from Venezuela?', *Bulletin of Latin American Research*, 4, 2 (1985), 61).

THE DECEPTIVE SIMPLICITY OF MARIO BENEDETTI: NARRATIVE TECHNIQUE IN 'EL PRESUPUESTO'

P. A. ODBER DE BAUBETA
University of Birmingham

Readers of Benedetti are not unfamiliar with the concept of the 'grey man',[1] 'el hombrecito entre chaplinesco y kafkiano que verá siempre postergados sus sueños', who lives and works against 'el fondo gris de la vida funcionarial'.[2] Mercedes Rein suggests that, like his characters, 'la escritura de Benedetti es opaca, grisácea, despojada de efectos intensos'.[3] Precisely how Benedetti achieves this quality of 'greyness' has yet to be established. However, a close examination of one of Benedetti's best known short stories, 'El presupuesto', may reveal some of the ways in which he paints the little grey man, notably through his handling of deixis, irony, repetition and other rhetorical devices.

The first-person focalization of this story is clearly marked in its opening sentence, 'en nuestra oficina';[4] the narrator participates in the events he recounts. One question to be borne in mind is whether there exists any distance or conflict between the narrating self and the experiencing self, and whether the narrator ever voices implicit or explicit moral judgements about the behaviours and attitudes he is describing. Because of the preponderance of first-person plural verb forms and possessive adjectives that are accumulated in the first paragraph, it becomes clear that while the narrative's point of view may be entrenched in the person of one character, we are effectively being told about the lives or experiences of a collectivity rather than those of an individual: 'la mayoría de nosotros', 'nuestros escritorios'. Within the office, Christian names or surnames are never used: characters are identified by their position within the office hierarchy -- el Jefe, el Auxiliar Primero, el Auxiliar Segundo, el Oficial Primero, el Oficial Segundo, las dactilógrafas, el portero. This use of antonomasia contributes significantly to the construction of 'grey' characters, and the greyness is further increased by the anonymity of the narrator who reveals neither his name nor his rank.

As regards the handling of time within the story, this tends to be a linear representation of temporality, free from analepses or prolepses, and marked at various stages by a series of deictics whose function is to indicate chronological progression. Whether or not this is parallelled by an intellectual progression, a growth in awareness on the part of the collectivity, remains to be seen.

The predominant tense in the first paragraph is the imperfect indicative: the narrator is setting the scene, describing a way of life that may or may not be disrupted by the events to be narrated in the story. This notion of a continuum is crucial to Benedetti's theory of the short story, according to which 'el cuento es siempre un corte transversal efectuado en la realidad'.[5] To depict the 'reality' of his setting and plot the narrator opts for the imperfect indicative. However, because his perception of this reality is critical, we may anticipate the use of certain strategies to undermine his narrative, principally a recourse to irony. Ironic touches are present throughout the narration, achieved through the careful selection of adjectives, and the juxtaposing of the trivial with the momentous. For instance, the Jefe's habitual reminiscences are reduced to 'su vieja emoción y las quinientas noventa y ocho palabras de costumbre' (9). The oxymoron, 'vieja emoción', conveys a certain amount of pathos, as does the reference to the concrete number of words that constitute the Jefe's account of what was apparently the most important moment in his life, 'el lejano y magnífico día' (9) when he was told there would be a new budget for his office. At the same time, by juxtaposing 'lejano' with 'magnífico', the narrator detracts from the importance of the event, creating instead an effect of bathos, setting up an opposition between the Jefe's vision and that of the reader.

In the second paragraph, there is a shift to the present tense, the timeless or gnomic present, used to express 'eternal' truths:

Un nuevo presupuesto es la ambición máxima de una oficina pública. (9)

At first sight, this may seem a perfectly normal utterance, not in the least untoward. But then the reader begins to reconsider, and possibly even challenge it. First of all, Benedetti is using personification -- a public office cannot have ambitions, only the people who staff that office. Secondly, there is also a psychological metonymy: the office and the staff are

Narrative Technique in 'El presupuesto' 549

indistinguishable, they are defined by the office, they only have an existence thanks to the office, financially, socially and emotionally.

The narrator then reverts to first-person plural imperfect verb forms, in order to continue his description of office life. The community to which he belongs is described as a 'pequeña isla administrativa' (9), and the office staff are compared to Robinson Crusoe on his desert island, the collectivity equated with a fictitious individual. The combination of an adjective and noun that are not normally paired together produces another thought-provoking oxymoron, 'desesperada resignación' (9).

The impression that we have already gained of the office staff functioning as a group, a cohesive unit, is now reinforced by the narrator's description of the ways they make their life tolerable, through a kind of 'cooperativismo harto elemental' (10). Each one contributes to the office food and drink supply, everyone reads the newspaper, paid for by the Jefe who earns a little bit more (the typists and the doorman are exempt because they earn less), and everyone goes to see different films so that they can all be up to date on the latest movies. They play games that cost nothing -- chess and draughts. There is not only a division of labour, but of expenses and social responsibility too. This is all narrated in a very matter-of-fact way: there are no superfluous adjectives or adverbs to convey emotion or intensity, and the workaday narrative style reflects both the dreariness of their lives and the lengths to which they must go in order to get by in a dull, indifferent world. Likewise, the description of their actual work suggests that they are doing nothing of any moment or urgency.

The paragraph on Security instantly recalls Liano's comments on the 'pequeña burguesía ciega, encerrada entre las cuatro paredes de su apatía, inseguridad, aburrimiento y falta de una verdadera conciencia de clase'.[6] The Jefe emphasizes that as civil servants at least they have job security. This allows the narrator/author the opportunity to make an ironic observation on the government, stressing the fact that the senators hardly ever meet. The reverse side of the job security question is that they are also sure never to get a pay rise. Hence they are trapped, badly paid but better off than if they had no job at all. What we see here is the aptly named *homo burocraticus* at his most resigned,[7] as the narrator describes the office staff's collective acceptance of their lot, 'conformes con nuestro pequeño destino' (11). Again, Benedetti uses an unusual pairing of adjective and noun to make his point. In a literary context, destiny is usually given the 'epic' treatment, qualified by an impressive adjective of size or grandeur; it is not reduced and trivialized down to 'pequeño'. But that is all that the narrator and his fellow office workers have to look forward to, the stability that comes from working and living in a 'callejón sin salida'.[8] The ability to place a (low) monetary value on their lives --'nuestras vidas de setenta pesos' (11)-- reveals that there is an awareness on the part of the narrator about the limitations of their existence. He is fully conscious of the prevailing attitude among the staff, an unquestioning acceptance that verges on passivity. We should note the recurrence of certain abstract nouns and their related adjectives: 'conformes', 'conformidad', 'desesperada resignación', 'resignación'. On one level Benedetti is describing a routine, a linear reality, in concrete terms and with a preponderance of finite verbs in the indicative mood. On another level, through the insertion of abstract nouns and pre-nominal qualifying adjectives with a certain subjective charge, he also succeeds in depicting the psychological and emotional response to that reality on the part of his narrator and the characters presented through his narrator's vision. There may even be a suggestion that through their willingness to conform, the office staff are to some extent responsible for their uncomfortable situation.

With the news of the possible pay rise --the new budget-- comes the introduction of the element that disrupts the continuum, the element that will effect some change in the characters' lives, 'como si nos hubiesen sacudido a bofetadas toda la conformidad y toda la resignación' (11). Finally, something has happened to disrupt the ordinariness and routine of their lives, and the reaction to it is marked in linguistic terms by a shift from the first-person plural to the first-person singular: 'en mi caso particular' (11). It is as though the impact of the news on the narrator causes him to feel less like a member of the collectivity and more like an indvidual: 'mi caso', 'se me ocurrió', 'yo no había sabido', 'quería comprar', 'extraje', 'no sé', 'mis deseos', 'mi nombre inscripto', 'en mí' (11). This is a radical change of focus. The anonymous 'funcionario' is no longer speaking for the collectivity, but voicing his own wishes and preferences, aspirations and longings of which he may not even have been aware while he was functioning as a member of the group. Now he talks about the 'sótano de mis deseos' (11) and a desire that is 'enraizado en mí'. All traces of individuality were submerged in the collectivity, now they are beginning to emerge, not just in the narrator but in the others. They all have hidden dreams. The pathos --or irony-- lies in the fact that theirs are lacklustre, almost paltry dreams about possessing banal material objects which are not in the least exciting or dramatic. The narrator's heart is set on a fountain pen, and his colleagues too, divulge the information about what they want to acquire.

The phrase, 'ese enorme futuro que apareja toda posibilidad' (11), contrasts with the 'pequeño destino' mentioned above. It is also extremely ironic, given the size of the pay rise they can expect, a fact of which the reader is reminded by the insertion of the almost parenthetical 'por mínima que sea' (11); the adjective 'mínima' somehow cancels out 'enorme', and perhaps foreshadows the disappointment which the office staff will later experience when they return to reality.

The next paragraph is particularly interesting from a structural point of view. It consists of three sentences, each beginning with the same phrase: 'Vi y oí además' (11-12). This is an example of the rhetorical figure of anaphora, deployed to underline descriptive and emotional effects, especially common in public oratory. In the first sentence, the verbs are in the imperfect, in the next two, the tense is simple past, and this shift indicates that the protagonists have progressed from a vague covetousness to making definite plans about how they will spend their additional income. The narrator is also emphasizing the fact that they now have individual plans and desires; where in the past they used to share everything, they now talk about themselves and their plans, though without really listening to each other.

The floodgates open. The 'excepcional tarde de bizcochos' (12) is just the beginning, the 'paso primero'. First of all they indulge in unwonted extravagance, buying cakes, then they go out and buy the object each of them most longed for, 'mi lapicera, el sobretodo del Oficial Segundo, la cartera de la Primera Dactilógrafa, la bicicleta del Auxiliar Primero' (12). There is no description of how happy or satisfied they feel. Instead, the passage of time is marked by one of a series of deictic indicators, 'Al mes y medio' (12), followed by a fine example of Benedettti's terse, compressed style: 'todos estábamos empeñados y en angustia' (12). Within one short paragraph, we move from the optimistic 'paso primero' through a month and a half which represents not only financial loss, but the destruction of their hopes.

The narrator now reverts to the first-person plural, because they are once again a group, bound together this time by their debts and disenchantment, their longing for good news, and their subsequent relief when the Jefe de Contaduría dies. The narrator is not blind to the group's essential selfishness: 'Nos pusimos egoísticamente alegres' (12). Their suffering is having a dehumanizing effect on them, making them more callous, less compassionate, somehow immune to the suffering of others.

Next, there is a break in the narrative, a new section which marks a new phase in the lives of the protagonists. It is by no means inaccurate to describe the office staff as the protagonists of the story. They are just as central to the action of the story as the anonymous narrator who is telling their story. Once again, the passage of time is marked:

> A los cuatro meses de la muerte de don Eugenio nombraron otro jefe de Contaduría. (12)

Significantly, the dead man is now given a name, an identity that extends beyond his role in the Civil Service hierarchy. In death he has acquired a personality that he did not have in life. The message being conveyed to the reader is that the office, the Civil Service, somehow depersonalizes and dehumanizes those who operate within it. They have no names, they rejoice when someone dies, and they become subsumed into a greater (grey) mass.

The next point that emerges from the narrative is the order of priorities in the office:

> Esa tarde suspendimos la partida de ajedrez, el mate y el trámite administrativo. (12)

They carry out their work, but only after a fashion. They are not particularly efficient or hard-working. Moreover, they become so nervous that they have to leave the office in order to unwind by looking in shop windows. This is one of the few references to the urban landscape that we find in this story. We assume that the action unfolds in the capital, but there is remarkably little to suggest the workings of a big city. This is presumably in order to emphasize their isolation and the fact that they are cut off from life and the wider society.

Throughout this section, the narration is in the first-person plural, with corresponding verb forms and possessive adjectives: 'nuestro panorama'. The office staff are characterized by a childlike naïveté, a willingness to believe that the budget will be approved and that their situation will eventually be resolved. In this respect, they seem to exhibit many of the characteristics of Gabriel García Márquez's colonel, in *El coronel no tiene quien le escriba*. However, they do demonstrate a dawning awareness that the situation will not be resolved:

Allí comenzó la etapa crítica del desaliento. (13)

Once more, the passage of time is marked for the reader by a deictic phrase, 'a los ocho meses de la noticia primera' (13). We are not merely told that eight months have elapsed. During those eight months a series of things has gone wrong. For the last two months the narrator's pen has not been working, and he has not even finished paying for it -- 'mi lapicera adquirida a pagar en diez cuotas' (13). Where before we were given a list of all the items that the office staff rushed out and bought, we are now presented with a sad and pathetic catalogue of disasters: the pen no longer works, the Auxiliar Primero has broken a rib through riding his bicycle, the Auxiliar Segundo has had to sell his books, the Oficial Primero's watch loses time, the Jefe's shoes are already worn through, the Oficial Segundo's overcoat looks ridiculous because the lapels are worn and will not lie flat. Here the the author goes into some detail because there is a particular point to be made: that their dreams, their limited ambitions, have come to nothing. These goods provide a measure of the pettiness of the staff's desires and aspirations. Furthermore, most of the items cannot be shared, suggesting selfishness, and they also enhance the status of the owner, implying vanity.

The workings of the government machine, 'la telaraña burocrática',[9] are extremely slow and ponderous, almost Kafka-esque. There are no clear channels of communication, information is unclear, based on rumour, and half-truths, and no one seems able to influence the course of events, which appear to have a momentum of their own. The narrator offers a further, ironic, insight into how business is conducted in their office: all the paperwork is treated in the same way, whether it is labelled 'muy urgente', 'trámite preferencial' or 'estrictamente reservado' (13). We are never told exactly what kinds of papers they are processing, and it does not really matter. What is important is that they do not function very efficiently. There may even be an underlying suggestion that they do not deserve a pay rise.

The linear progression of the narrative is further indicated by an adverbial phrase accompanied by a simple past: 'Una vez supimos' (13). This is immediately contrasted with 'Otra vez supimos' (14), a phrase which is repeated --a further instance of anaphora-- to reinforce the effect of monotony, and to underline the fact that there are conflicting versions of the truth, or at least conflicting hypotheses and rumours.

The remaining paragraphs are narrated in the imperfect tense, with a conscious inclination towards the durative aspect. In other words, this is an enduring situation. The matter of their budget is due to be discussed on the following Friday. However, the expression 'a los catorce viernes' informs us that their hopes have not been fulfilled, even after fourteen weeks of waiting. Their life is marked off in Saturdays, when they discover that the budget has not been discussed on the previous Friday. Again there are reminiscences of *El coronel no tiene quien le escriba*, where the colonel goes to the dock every Friday to see if the mail launch has brought his long-awaited letter. As with the colonel, their wait has taken over their lives, it occupies all their thoughts and consumes all their emotional energies. Nothing else matters. Here we see how the intensity and concentration of the short story can be used to good effect.

Benedetti's reliance on repetition as a stylistic device is further seen in the following sentences, where he repeats both structure and words 'Y no pasaba nada. Y no pasaba nunca nada de nada', in order to convey the growing disillusionment of the narrator and his colleagues.

In the third section of the short story, there is another shift, a reversion to the first-person singular narrative focalization:

> Yo estaba ya demasiado empeñado para permanecer impasible. (14)

This is perhaps one of the 'asomos de santa cólera' experienced by *homo burocraticus*,[10] though Oviedo takes the pessimistic view that such outbursts are to no avail, limited to mere words, never culminating in any decisive action. There is in fact a suggestion that the narrator's initiative is prompted by petulance:

> La lapicera me había estropeado el ritmo económico y desde entonces no había podido recuperar mi equilibrio. Por eso fue que se me ocurrió que podíamos visitar al Ministro. (14)

It might be suggested that no one obliged the office staff to rush out and indulge themselves, therefore the predicament in which they now find themselves is of their own making. Arguably, the protagonists of this story do not really inspire (or deserve) the reader's sympathy.

The next paragraphs are narrated in the simple past tense, in the plural. The office staff are once again acting as a unit, practising what they will say to the Minister. The childlike qualities of the characters are quite apparent, although this is an extremely serious matter. Like children, they are manifestly not in control of their lives and future. Although they decide when they are ready to see the Minister, and arrange an interview, there is more than a little irony in the narrator's description of what it in fact *means* to see the Minister: a wait of two and a half hours, then an interview with the Secretary because the Minister is not available.

Here we find another instance of Benedetti's oblique style. Instead of a direct statement to the effect that the Jefe, the leader of the group, was very nervous, we find the throw-away line:

> Sólo llegamos a presencia del Secretario, quien tomó notó de las palabras del Jefe -- muy inferiores al peor de los ensayos, en los que nadie tartamudeaba. (15)

This exemplifies one of the classic techniques of the short story, the representation of characters through their actions, not lengthy descriptions. The reader can deduce from this brief comment that whereas in the rehearsals the Jefe was forceful, lucid, able to get his point across, at 'the moment of truth' he stutters and stammers, is hesitant, apologetic, and easily dismissed.

We are reminded of the naïveté of the characters when we are told that the Secretary conveyed to them the Minister's personal response and he was not even in the building. The narrator states 'Nos pareció un poco extraño' (15), but he admits that they are more comfortable believing their own optimistic explanation, that the Secretary had consulted the Minister by telephone:

Pero en realidad nos convenía más confiar un poco. (15)

The final paragraph begins with another time reference, 'Al otro día' (15). The reader, like the characters, knows perfectly well what will happen. Once again they are fobbed off, once again they are disappointed.

Critics and writers alike frequently discuss the 'effect' of a short story. We find this literary preoccupation expressed by Edgar Allan Poe in his 1842 review of Hawthorne's *Twice-Told Tales*, by Horacio Quiroga in a letter to José María Delgado dated 8 June, 1917,[11] and by their admirer, Benedetti himself:

el cuento y la nouvelle tienen en común su empleo del efecto...
el efecto del cuento es la sorpresa, el asombro, la revelación.[12]

The scene in which a story is set may frequently contribute decisively to the overall effect of a short story, thus setting should not be underestimated as a vital element of narrative technique. As is appropriate for brief narrative, where economy is viewed as desirable, if not essential, descriptions of setting in 'El presupuesto' have been pared down to the absolute minimum. This is perhaps because readers are expected to fill in the gaps for themselves, drawing on their own experience, and perhaps because, as Rutherford maintains, setting 'serves as a reinforcement for the text's themes: themes that are combined into the setting, which thus acquires symbolic values'.[13] Benedetti's landscape is as nebulous and grey as the characters who inhabit it. It has even been described as a 'no-paisaje'.[14] The city is never named, there are no street names, no allusions to squares, avenues, public transport or descriptions of buildings. The only clues are the references to the cinema, the shop windows, the Auxiliar Primero's bicycle, the Ministry, and the Minister's car.

In some prose narrative, there may be a conflict between the setting and the characters. Here there is no conflict: on the contrary, the setting appears to have taken over their lives, to have consumed them, draining them of energy and spontaneity, of their ability to fight back. In a sense, the characters *are* their setting, a part of the administrative island which is their office. If the office is a 'no-paisaje', they are non-characters, anonymous, grey, with no life outside their place of work and no satisfaction or fulfilment in it. If we push our interpretation to the limits, the office becomes a metaphor for an entire city, country, or even continent.

Benedetti does not of course invent the figure of the clerk, who has a distinguished literary ancestry in his own right. For the nineteenth-century Russian Natural School, 'the choice of a government clerk as hero was almost a formula of the age'.[15] In fact, we might draw a number of parallels between Gogol's *The Overcoat* (1842) and 'El presupuesto'. The tragic outcome in Gogol's narrative is not matched in the Uruguayan story, but there are a number of correspondences: Akaky Akakievich Bashmachkin's existence is described as 'the uneventful life of a man quite content with his four hundred roubles a year',[16] while Benedetti's narrator states 'en realidad, la vida que pasábamos allí no era mala' (10); the Oficial Segundo's 'sobretodo' inevitably recalls Bashmachkin's overcoat, and Benedetti's clerks' change of attitude and behaviour is strongly reminiscent of that experienced by Gogol's downtrodden official: 'He livened up and like a man who has set himself a goal, became more determined' (86).

Following Gogol, Fyodor Dostoevsky also depicts ineffectual clerks who are defined by their place in the office hierarchy and whose humdrum lives are dominated by the need to make every rouble count. Dostoevsky's most notable creation is Makar Alexievitch Dievushkin in the short novel *Poor Folk* (1846), whose worldly goods after thirty years in public service amount to a pair of torn shoes, ragged clothing ('More than once I have asked for an increase of salary')[17] and a bundle of love-letters. Nor should we overlook Titular Officer Golyadkin in *The Double* (1846), *Gospodin Proxarchin* (1846), or Marmeladov in *Crime and Punishment* (1866).

Benedetti's narrative also has elements in common with another short story, Maupassant's 'La parure' ('The Diamond Necklace'), which portrays members of the same social group, the lower reaches of the bureaucrocacy. Again the protagonists must spend their lives struggling to survive: Monsieur and Madame Loisel must pay off the debt they have incurred; their lives become increasingly circumscribed, the husband doing extra work as copyist for five *sous* a page, the wife haggling with the shopkeepers of the *quartier*.[18] Perhaps it is also worth remembering Maupassant's 'Les joyaux' (translated as 'The Jewels' or 'The False Gems'), in which the protagonist, Monsieur Lantin, is a 'senior clerk at the Ministry of the Interior with a salary of three thousand five hundred francs a year'.[19] The twist in Maupassant's tale lies in the fact that while the clerk's dreams of domestic bliss come to nothing, he receives more than adequate material recompense for his emotional suffering.

Also part of the 'tradición funcionarial' is the *Historia de un pequeño funcionario*, published in Montevideo in 1928 by the Argentine-born Manuel de Castro, one of 'los primeros en intentar captar el espíritu gris e insensible de la creciente vida burocrática del país'.[20] In this depiction of the Montevidean middle class, 'Castro logra dar, con estilo sencillo fluido el sofocado universo de ambiciones menores y lóbrega mezquindad de un grupo social condenado en sí mismo, revelando las influencias de la novelística rusa del siglo XIX'.[21]

Finally, even closer to 'El presupuesto' in time if not in authorial intention, we find another work from the River Plate region, Marco Denevi's three-act play *Los expedientes*, described by Agustín de la Saz as 'la sátira del hombre de la clase media en su despacho'.[22] Premièred in 1957 by the Comedia Nacional Argentina in Buenos Aires and published in the same year by the Editorial Talía, *Los expedientes* satirizes 'lo absurdo de la burocracia, deteniéndose principalmente en la burocracia de la oficina gubernamental argentina'.[23]

'El presupuesto' shares a major motif found in all these works: the thwarting of desires and dreams. Unlike the Russian or French characters, however, Benedetti's protagonists are depicted only in their working environment and in relation to one another. Nevertheless, Gogol, Dostoevsky, Maupassant, de Castro, Denevi and Benedetti have one principal feature in common: all of them use the petty functionary, wife or lover for the same purpose, to make penetrating observations about human nature and society. By selecting a first-person narrative focalization, Benedetti is able to make a series of comments, explicit or implicit, about an inward-looking, claustrophobic society whose ineffectual citizens are caught up in and alienated by a ponderously inefficient system, and he does so from the point of view of those at the bottom of the social pyramid. Moreover, given the fact that the world of the office is not anchored to any particular geographical reality, these observations need not be limited to Uruguayan society but may have a more general application, as Benedetti himself has pointed out:

> Cada pueblo del Interior, cada oficina de la Capital, cada uno de nuestros intensos y efímeros entusiasmos, puede ser un formidable tema de cuento. Aun ese Montevideo que vive encerrado en sí mismo, de espaldas al resto del país y al resto del continente, es también un tema de cuento; claro que un cuento un poco sórdido, mera variante local del tema universal del egoísmo.[24]

As a result of his carefully honed narrative technique, Benedetti's 'El presupuesto' is a deceptively simple piece of writing. His language has been described as 'aparentemente antipoético, sin brillos espectaculares, acaso vinculable a la tradición del sencillismo'.[25] The salient point here is his *apparent* simplicity. Benedetti is a master of understatement; critics have already drawn attention to the fact that frequently it is what Benedetti does not say that matters most. What he chooses to say is expressed very competently, with notable skill in his handling of tense and aspect. As Rodríguez Monegal has observed, 'Como el tiempo es la sustancia de sus cuentos, y como Benedetti (a pesar de su facilidad, a pesar de su fluidez) es un técnico impecable, la medida del cuento es aquélla en la que está más cómodo'.[26] Benedetti marries form and content by using certain stylistic devices, among which repetition predominates, to render the banal nature of his clerks' existence, as threadbare as their clothing, constructed on habit, and dominated by an *idée fixe*, the new budget. Of particular interest are the varying degrees of narrative distance created through deixis and shifts in focalization. Through his first-person narrative we are shown a 'before' and an 'after', neither of which offers any hope of a satisfactory outcome to the protagonists. A contrastive technique is used throughout the story to show the negative effects on the protagonists of the news of the pay rise, which brings to the fore their petty selfishness and greed, but never prompts them to take any effective action to resolve the situation. Despite his apparent detachment and ironic vision, the narrator chooses to ally himself with the group, expressing only an implicit criticism of their collective behaviour: to go any further would be to call into question the validity of their entire way of life, a question that he is not ready to pose, let alone answer.

NOTES

1. Hugo Alfaro, *Mario Benedetti (detrás de un vidrio claro)* (Montevideo: Ediciones Trilce, 1986), p.22.

2. Ángel Rama, 'La situación del uruguayo medio', in *Mario Benedetti, Variaciones Críticas* (Montevideo: Libros del Astillero, 1973), pp.74-82 (p.74).

3. Mercedes Rein, 'Mario Benedetti', in *Diccionario de Literatura Uruguaya. A-K* (Montevideo: Arca-Credisol, 1987), pp.84-89 (p.85).

4. Mario Benedetti, 'El presupuesto', *Montevideanos* (Montevideo: Editorial Alfa, 1972). All subsequent references in parentheses are to this edition.

5. Benedetti, *Sobre artes y oficios*, cited by Jorge Ruffinelli in 'El cuento como afirmación y búsqueda', in *Mario Benedetti, Variaciones Críticas* (Montevideo: Libros del Astillero, 1973), pp.108-23 (p.115).

6. Dante Liano, 'Album de familia: la pequeña burguesía en la narrativa de Mario Benedetti', *Studi di Letterature Ispano-Americana*, 13-14 (1983), 210-12 (p.212).

7. José Miguel Oviedo, 'Un dominio colonizado por la poesía', in *Mario Benedetti, Variaciones Crítica* (Montevideo: Libros del Astillero, 1973), pp.147-58 (p.149).

8. Oviedo, p.148.

9. Alfaro, p.23.

10. Oviedo, p.149.

11. Horacio Quiroga, *Cartas inéditas. Volumen II* (Montevideo: Instituto Nacional de Investigaciones y Archivos Literarios, 1959), p.62.

12. Benedetti, *Sobre artes y oficios*, cited in Rufinelli, p.113.

13. John Rutherford, 'Story, Character, Setting and Narrative Mode in Galdos's *El amigo Manso*', in *Style and Structure. Essays in the New Stylistics*, ed. by Roger Fowler (Oxford: Basil Blackwell, 1975), pp.177-212 (p.185).

14. Oviedo, p.149.

15. J. Coulson in the Introduction to Fyodor Dostoevsky, *Notes from the Underground/The Double*, transl. by Jessie Coulson (Harmondsworth: Penguin, 1972), p.8.

16. Nikolai Gogol, *The Overcoat*, published in *Diary of a Madman and Other Stories*, transl. by Ronald Wilks (Harmondsworth: Penguin, 1972), p.77.

17. Fyodor Dostoevsky, *Poor Folk. The Gambler*, transl. by C. J. Hogarth (London: Dent (Everyman's Library), 1969), p.53.

18. Guy de Maupassant, 'The Diamond Necklace', in *The Complete Short Stories of Guy de*

Maupassant (London: Blue Ribbon Books, [n.d]), pp.28-33.

19. Guy de Maupassant, 'The Jewels', in *Selected Short Stories*, transl. with an introduction by Roger Colet (Harmondsworth: Penguin, 1971), pp.157-65 (p.157).

20. John E. Englekirk and Margaret M. Ramos, *La narrativa uruguaya. Estudio crítico-bibliográfico* (Berkeley and Los Angeles: University of California Press, 1967), p.90.

21. Sylvia Lago, 'Manuel de Castro', in *Dicionario de Literatura Uruguaya. A-K* (Montevideo: Arca-Credisol, 1987), pp.146-48 (p.147).

22. Agustín del Saz, *Teatro social hispanoamericano* (Barcelona: Editorial Labor, 1967), p.145.

23. Ivonne Revel Grove, *La realidad calidoscópica de la obra de Marco Denevi* (México: Costa-Amic, 1974), p.17.

24. Mario Benedetti, 'La literatura uruguaya cambia de voz', in *Literatura uruguaya siglo XX* (Montevideo: Arca, 1988), p.31.

25. Rein, 'Mario Benedetti', p.85.

26. Emir Rodríguez Monegal, *Literatura uruguaya del medio siglo* (Montevideo: Editorial Alfa, 1966), p.218.

BETWEEN HISTORY AND LITERATURE:
A DIALOGUE BY JUAN JOSÉ ARREOLA

MAURICE BIRIOTTI DEL BURGO
University of Birmingham

Three years ago I began a dialogue with Derek Lomax about the nature of historical inquiry in which I was cast in the role of the young doubter and he in the role of the established authority whose discipline was being challenged. The conversations which made up this (tragically foreshortened) dialogue were always very long and very entertaining, but by the end of them I had the uncomfortable feeling that I no longer knew who was subverting whose position. This article and its tentative conclusion are offered as a homage to the complexity of Derek Lomax's thought, even --or perhaps especially-- when it was at its most devastatingly simple.

The article is based on a dialogue by Juan José Arreola which reminds me of my conversations with Derek Lomax. I begin by contextualising the dialogue, go on to offer a reading whose main premise is that it is a literary attack on historical practices, and finally raise questions about the validity of such a reading, concluding that the dialogue does not in fact refute the validity of historical method, but reinforces it.

History in Mexico

Under the dictatorship of Porfirio Díaz at the end of the nineteenth century, intellectual life was held in the grip of positivism. European notions of scientific rationalism dominated all the cultural fields; the writing of history was no exception.[1] A rigid belief in the possibility of a supremely factual narrative, scientifically proven by meticulous attention to detail, and in a complex technological discourse gave history a privileged position over other forms of narrative literature in its veridical rigour and its potential for inscribing into the fabric of Mexican life the teleological rationale behind the stability of strong government: Progress.

The Revolution of 1910 brought many changes on the level of cultural activity as much as socio-political structure. As an antidote to the quest for objectivity, always dominated by European discourses, which characterized the nineteenth century, intellectuals of the years immediately after the Revolution rallied around the watchword of an extraordinary cultural productivity: 'el Espíritu'. The *Ateneo de la Juventud* of the 1920s and *Los Contemporáneos* of the 1930s privileged less technocratic, less scientific forms of discourse. Under these conditions, the novel, the short story, the lyric poem and the prose poem flourished.[2] 'Literature', so little considered by the technocrats of the Porfiriato, returned with a vengeance. At least in part, the tremendous surge in Latin American literary production that has been such a notable phenomenon of twentieth-century culture, is due to this post-revolutionary renaissance of interest in the literary work, in its 'spirituality', and in its non-veridical narrative.

But the Revolution also demanded a new History: a reappraisal of the past which stigmatized the years of liberalism and of dictatorship, and which both rehabilitated Mexico's indigenous legacy into the structure of its narrative, and inscribed the events of the revolutionary period into the fabric of a new national consciousness.[3] Successive administrations vied --and continue to vie-- for the right to appropriate the narrative. As Florescano puts it, 'L'usage infatigable que les gouvernements contemporains [du Méxique] ont fait du passé en général et du passé révolutionaire en particulier est sans aucun doute l'un des cas les plus notoires de l'utilisation du passé pour légitimer le pouvoir'.[4] Politically overdetermined, the struggle for historical legitimacy which raged between the various factions working in the 1930s, 40s, 50s and 60s became ever more acute. Their guarantee was precisely, and ironically, the kind of quest for objectivity favoured by the positivists, this time bolstered by the professionalized and institutionalized models of academia which were developing in Europe and North America, and which have become so familiar in the structures and specialisms of the modern University. Historical studies which took as their premise the scientific reconstruction of the past in all its most factual details burgeoned.

As the Revolution became Institution, the writing of history, as a scientific endeavour, turned to the academicism of the University. This academicism was characterized by certain key features, not unique to Mexican historiography, but always specifically determined by the post-revolutionary context in which they are located, and with which they are charged.[5]

In the first place, there is a belief in the legitimating power of the Institution, its name, (the University of ...), its titles (Professor, PhD etc.) and its various practices. Secondly, there is a belief in the recuperability of historical information, in History as a re-enactment of the past, a reification of memory, in which, above all, the past is knowable. Thirdly, historical academicism endows the reliable historical source with supreme authority; a process by which a text from the past becomes not so much narrative, as documentary evidence. Fourthly, this sort of History clarifies and tabulates the information gleaned in ways that will make sense of *what really happened*: in this way, History orders the past, creating a complex taxonomy whose rigorous ability to account for 'information' becomes its own guarantee of veracity. Fifthly, there is a belief in the passage of time in some sequential fashion, whatever the overriding metaphor for this movement might be (a straight line towards Progress or Decadence, a circle of repetition, a spiral of repetition and change, a chain of cause and effect). And finally, there is an insistence on the transparency of History's own rhetoric, on the irrelevance of its various linguistic strategies and ruses, on its own language acting simply as a vehicle for the *Truth*.

In a Mexico which seemed to move (and continues to move) inexorably towards increasingly technocratic models of capitalist 'prosperity' predicated on the 'success' of the North American experience, the writing of History increasingly resembled the discourses of science in its attention to the minutiae of specialist knowledge rather than the narrative processes of Literature.

De Balística as Socratic dialogue

For some, true to the cultural possibilities offered by the *Ateneo* and *Los Contemporáneos*, the onslaught of Progress, its technologies and its institutional cosmopolitanism represented a betrayal of the spirituality of the cultural tradition invoked by such masters of post-revolutionary reconstruction as Alfonso Reyes, and José Vasconcelos. In 1952, Juan José Arreola, a self-professed auto-didact, distanced from the institutional legitimacy of the University, published his most famous collection of short stories, *Confabulario*. In its prologue, he articulates his allegiance with those who use language for spiritual rather than technocratic purposes: 'Amo el lenguaje por sobre de todas las cosas y venero a los que mediante la palabra han manifestado el espíritu desde Isaías a Franz Kafka'.[6]

De Balística,[7] a profoundly ironic dialogue about History, articulates, as I shall argue, a savage critique of historical academicism, and constitutes a brilliant attack on the authority of History as Institution, privileging instead the 'spirituality' of literary narrative and poetic genre. In it, a young scholar, a PhD student who has to present his thesis in Minnesota on Roman catapults, has come to Spain to meet one of the leading authorities on the subject. Confused by many aspects of his field of study, he asks the master for help in understanding its complexities. The master can give him assurances only that all the anecdotal evidence suggests in fact that no catapult was ever fired. The student is dismayed as the Authority gives him no evidence to help him except a questionable rock which he claims was a missile (despite his suggestion that catapults were never fired) and a series of 'tips' on how to get through his next conference paper in the USA. The student feels confused, and starts to have grave doubts about his subject matter.

Historical methodology comes under heavy fire in this dialogue: its very form as dialogue suggests a challenge to the monolithic structures of historical inquiry (the monograph, the doctoral thesis, the seamless conference paper). In its trajectory of question and answer, assertion and refutation, and in its reduction to aporia of the unsuspecting student --reminiscent of Socratic dialogue-- it breaks down the key assumptions and characteristics which are typical of historical academicism.

In the first place the dialogue satirizes the institutionalisation of historical narrative. It is hardly surprising that the student comes from the United States. He legitimates his presence by reference to his supervisor -- 'el profesor Burns', and he mentions continually the onerous task that lies before him of completing his doctoral thesis, particularly when he despairs of his interlocutor's cutting and categorical rejection of all he has learnt. The satire of the repeated pleas to return to the 'serious' legitimacy of the institutional frame scarcely needs elaboration:

> No olvide usted, por favor, que a mi regreso debo presentar una tesis doctoral de doscientas cuartillas sobre balística romana, y redactar algunas conferencias. (91)

Nor, indeed, does the mordant attack on academia's mechanical reduction of language:

> Piense usted [... e]n las dos mil palabras de cada conferencia en Minnesota. (91)

As Professor Burns' reputation is undermined by the onslaught of the master's dismissive refutations, the student's legitimating frame is brutally undercut: in its absence, his protestations founder and have no basis.

But the rapier is not reserved for the institution alone; the student has come convinced of the possibility of knowing some incontrovertible fact about Roman ballistics. His supervisor has tried to re-enact Roman practices in a performative gesture in which History is literally reified:

> Ante un público numeroso, el profesor Burns prometió volarse la barda del estadio de Minnesota, y le falló el jonrón <=home-run>. Es la quinta vez que le hacen quedar mal sus catapultas, y se halla bastante decaído. Espera que yo le lleve algunos datos que lo pongan en el buen camino... (90)

The master replies that this is scarcely surprising, as no one since the Renaissance has ever managed to make a catapult work.

The student's desire for reification continues unabated as he demands a coin 'como recuerdo' (94) which turns out to be unavailable, and in any case to have an erratum on it (95). It is doubtful whether the object will provide the kind of proof required of it by the student. The master's final gesture, the one intended to stem the flow of protestations from the student is precisely to present him with the sort of evidence he requires, but once again the status of the object is far from straightforward:

(En este momento, el arqueólogo vio en el suelo una piedra que le pareció muy apropiada para poner punto final a su enseñanza...) (99)

On producing this object as the answer to the student's problems, he adds:

Yo mismo le obsequiaré una documentación en regla para que las autoridades le permitan sacarla de España. (99)

In this way doubt is cast on the very process by which objects gain a legitimate and privileged status, by which they are identified as the factual element from which the edifice of History is constructed.

In addition, the master undermines his interlocutor's belief in the authority of the historical source. When the student complains that his supervisor's explanation of the sources has left him baffled the master seems delighted:

-Cíteme usted, por favor, algunas autoridades antiguas sobre el tema. El profesor Burns ha llenado mi mente de confusión con sus relatos, llenos de repeticiones y de salidas por la tangente.
-Permítame felicitar desde aquí al profesor por su gran fidelidad. Veo que no ha hecho otra cosa sino transmitir a usted la visión caótica que de la balística antigua nos dan hombres como Marcelino, Arriano [...](91)

In the vision of historical knowledge posited by this dialogue the historical source resembles more closely Literature ('relatos', 'visión caótica') than Science: all attempts to read them as Science indeed end, as we have seen, in Professor Burns' unfortunate failure to build a machine that works.

The student's desire for 'algo positivo' (95) is no doubt reminiscent of the positivist dream of absolute objectivity. It converts itself into a desire for a system of classification and tabulation; taxonomy as the basis for ordering the past.

The master proves impervious to the desire to classify into rigidly defined and determined categories:

-Y usted y su famoso profesor de Minnesota ¿pueden decirme acaso cuál es la diferencia que hay entre una balista y una catapulta? ¿Y entre una fundíbula una doríbula y una palíntona? (92)

Instead of the neat and scholarly process of definition the student requires, the master offers nothing more than a little elementary etymology (95-96), and presents a historical vision, once again, of chaos rather than order.

Perhaps most striking of all the dismissals is the master's challenge to the logic of historical time, in which temporal moments are clearly distinguished and in which the sequential (and therefore non-reversible) nature of events is posited as a *sine qua non* of academic exposition. When the student challenges the master on the nature of the rock which he produces as a missile, the master's 'proof' short-circuits the normal process of historical inquiry:

> Tan seguro estoy de que lo es [a missile], que si usted, en vez de venir ahora, anticipa unos dos mil años su viaje a Numancia, esta piedra, disparada por uno de los antillanos de Escipión, le habría aplastado la cabeza. (99-100)

Far from providing the truth sought by the student, this answer produces in him a sense of the impossibility of his task, a confusion which forecloses his desire to inscribe memory as History, and creates instead, a desire for the erasure of memory:

> Se pasó la mano por la frente, como queriendo borrar, de una vez por todas, el fantasma de la balística romana. (100)

The notion of time contained in the master's response, alogical, confusing, bizarre, lays to rest once and for all the desire to 'do' History.

Finally, the master provides the student with a mode of rhetoric entirely alien to academic practices, proceeding in his assertions by means of anecdote rather than the rigorous processes of historical exposition. Lapsing regularly into the overtly poetic (for example, 'Adolfo Schulten que se pasó la vida escarbando en los escombros de Numancia' (95)), he suggests that his interlocutor do the same in order to survive the ordeal of his conference papers in Minnesota:

> Sea pintoresco [...] Sea poético [...] Sea imponente [...] Sea pertinaz. (97-98)

Pointing up the very path of the historical process which usually remains transparent, the master demonstrates History's linguistic constrictions, and its status not as Science but as Rhetoric, as simply another manifestation of the process of producing narrative: History, in short, as Text.

All that the master does put forward as a theory of Roman ballistics, moreover, is an insistence on metaphor, precisely that feature of discourse in which definition is at its most literary, and equivalence at its least scientific. He suggests that:

> La balista era un arma psicológica, una idea de fuerza, una metáfora aplastante. (99)

and that:

> Todo el Imperio Romano no era más que eso, una enorme máquina de guerra complicada y estorbosa, llena de palancas antagónicas, que se quitaban fuerza unas a otras. (97)

The master's position, in other words, moves away from the rhetoric of reification and towards the poetics of metaphor. The war machine itself, nomadic, chaotic, non-functioning, impractical, improbable, stands as a metaphor for the kind of History the master represents -- an antidote to the dry academicism of the institutional seekers of objectivity.[8]

The dialogue itself is framed within two paragraphs which declare its allegiance to High Literature, to the prose poem and to the almost obsessive attention to prose rhythm and to style which characterizes Arreola's literary output. 'Esas que allá se ven', which appears at the start of the dialogue, 'vagas cicatrices entre los campos de labor, son las ruinas del campamento de Nobílior'(89), was later to be repeated as part of a collection of prose poems in *Bestiario* (1958).

The dialogue ends with the immensity of the poetic moment, so radically opposed to the relentless passage of historical time:

> Y maestro y discípulo se quedaron inmóviles, eternizados por un instantáneo recogimiento, como dos bloques erráticos bajo el sol grisáceo. (100)

Between History and Literature   571

The spirit returns one final time to claim its revenge over the dry academicism of the University: History has been undermined, the student reduced to confusion, and the poetic moment triumphs.

De Balístca as 'Relajo'

That is the end of my reading, but it is not the end of my argument. There are a number of problems in the formulation which I have articulated which do not, I think, invalidate its explanation of the dialogue, but demonstrate how, in the process of reading key contradictions begin to appear.

In the first place, the reading suggests that the dialogue works like a Socratic dialogue refuting one by one the key assumptions of contemporary historiography, and that the master, like Socrates, undermines the values inherent in the notion of History, just as if he were laying bare the foundations of Virtue or Beauty, leaving his unsuspecting victim in a state of abject aporia. The comparison is useful as far as it goes, but it ignores one fundamental fact: the master proceeds in his assault on authority not, like Socrates, through an ironic disavowal of all knowledge, but precisely *because* of his knowledge and the authority it bestows. It is because he is 'una autoridad universal', a 'norte seguro' (89) and, as he himself asserts, probably the most knowledgeable expert on the subject that we believe him. His attack on historical knowledge is predicated on the historical knowledge he holds; his attack on authority, upon the authority which that knowledge confers: the reverse of the Socratic procedure.

Secondly, to read this dialogue as an attack on contemporary historiography is to confer upon it the status of an argument, to read what it posits and what it refutes as if it were engaging with academicism at the level of the academic work. In other words, to read this literary work as an attack on the serious work of academic exposition is to read it precisely also as a serious work of academic exposition; the process of reading it is predicated on the very assumption it refutes.

Finally, the reading locates the dialogue within a context. It argues that it is only in the context of the increasing power of scientific approaches to writing History that this attack --with its PhD student from Minnesota, its invocation of 'positive' facts and its explicit clash between order and chaos--can be understood. Furthermore, it argues that the dialogue leaves us with the triumph of metaphorical language over the discourse of scientific rationalism: a notion reminiscent of the heyday of the *Ateneo de la Juventud* and of *Los Contemporáneos*. But this is a formulation *within* History, which indeed cannot be articulated without a set of historical givens. In other words, this attack on historical time remains rooted in, precisely, historical time.

As this dialogue tears apart the foundations of contemporary historiography, it also shatters its own legitimacy. Perhaps, rather than the Socratic dialogue which it recalls at first sight, it resembles more closely the Mexican practice of 'relajo' in which the satirical denunciation of value extends to the value of the person engaging in the 'relajo', indeed to that of the 'relajo' itself.[9] Perhaps, indeed, the best metaphor for the story's logic is not simply the war machine, but that image of the war machine in one of the master's anecdotes, which destroys itself:

> Se estropeó por completo [...] y el brazo poderoso que debía lanzar la descomunal pedrada quedó en tierra exánime, desgajado, soltando el canto de su puño (94)

The problems which I have outlined in this section do not negate the reading which I made of the story. They are simply inherent to it. They arise out of the principle which I offer as my tentative conclusion: that to try to escape the authority of History is always to reinscribe it. Scientific historicism with all its absurdities and contradictions remains the central means by which we understand the past and the passage of time. Just as much as History with its need for language and rhetoric to create its narrative effect can be said to be a part of Literature, Literature always exists and is defined within and against History. In trying to undermine the practice of History, this dialogue reinforces it: its authority, its rigour, its persuasiveness as an explanatory model. History, it might be said, has the last laugh. Derek Lomax, I hope, would have smiled.

NOTES

1. See L. Zea, *El Positivismo en México* (México: FCE, 1943), for a survey of positivism and its influence.

2. See Carlos Monsiváis, 'Notas sobre la Cultura Mexicana en el Siglo XX', in *Historia General de México*, Vol II (México: Colegio de México, 1976).

3. As Florescano puts it, 'Le passé préhispanique fut un des domains les plus fouillés par le Rachat Nationale' in 'Le Pouvoir et la lutte pour le pouvoir dans l'historiographie moderne et contemporaine' in *Champs de Pouvoir et Savoir au Méxique* (Paris: GRAL, Editions des CNRS, 1982), p.174; and 'A l'opposé, le passé colonial est devenu la bête noire de l'histoire du Méxique', p.175.

4. Florescano, p.178. For the importance of history in the educational process in Mexico, see also M. Robles, *Educación y Sociedad en la Historia de México*, (México: Siglo XXI), especially Chapter XI, pp.191-204. See also D. Cosío Villegas, *Nueva Historiografía Política de México Moderno* (México: FCE, 1965).

5. The following enumeration of features is, in part, based on the reflexions of Enrique Krauze in 'Historia ¿Para Qué?' in E. Krauze, *Caras de la Historia* (México: Joaquín Mortíz, 1983). It also owes a great deal to the work of Pierre Bourdieu in *Distinction: A Social Critique of the Judgement of Taste*, transl. by R. Nice (London: Routledge, 1984); Michel de Certeau, especially 'History: Science and Fiction' in *Social Science as Moral Enquiry*, ed. by R. Bellah and others (New York: Columbia University Press, 1983), pp.125-152; and Dominick La Capra in *Soundings in Critical Theory* (Ithaca: Cornell University, 1982).

6. Juan José Arreola, 'De Memoria y olvido', in *Confabulario* (México: Joaquín Mortíz, 1988; first published 1952), p.10.

7. Juan José Arreola, 'De Balística' (México, Joaquín Mortíz, 1988), pp.89-100. All subsequent references in parentheses are to this edition.

8. For a description of War Machines as a metaphor for the nomadic and chaotic organisation of intellectual strategies, see G. Deleuze, and F. Guattari, *A Thousand Plateaus: Capitalism and Schizophrenia*, transl. by B. Massumi (London, 1988).

9. The word here is used in the brilliant and witty definition elaborated by Portilla in a seminal article. For a description of this process and how it differs from familiar European practices of articulating irony, see J. Portilla, *Fenomenología del Relato* (México: FCE, 1984), p.25: 'El relajo puede definirse, en resumen como la suspensión de la seriedad frente a un valor propuesto a un grupo de personas. Esta suspensión es realizada por un sujeto que trata de comprometer a otros en ella, mediante actos reiterados con los que expresa su propio rechazo de la conducta requerida por el valor', and p.26: 'El relajo es así, inexorablemente una autonegación', p.26.